CUSTER

CUSTER
FAVOR THE BOLD

A
Soldier's
Story

By D.A. Kinsley

Originally published in two volumes as
FAVOR THE BOLD: Custer, the Civil War Years and
FAVOR THE BOLD: Custer, the Indian Fighter

Published in 1988 by

Promontory Press, a division of LDAP, Inc.
166 Fifth Avenue
New York, NY 10010

By arrangement with Henry Holt & Co.

Library of Congress Catalog Card Number: 88-60851
ISBN: 0-88394-074-4

Printed in the United States of America

★

To Dan and Eve Kinsley;
to the benefactor of Kinsley, Kansas;
and to the Sioux Nation,
whose blood the author shares:
Pêhîhonskâ Ktêpî!

★

★ CONTENTS ★

Part I

The Civil War Years

Introduction

Part II
Custer the Indian Fighter
Introduction

CONTENTS

★ PART I ★

PART 1

Custer's Last Stand is one of the most dramatic and romantic tragedies in American history. It has inspired more fabulous paintings than any other military event since the dawn of civilization. And the epic hero, a legend even in his own time, still lives enshrined by all the mystery and glamour that immortalize a man transcended into myth. Every effort to debunk the man and explode the myth has failed.

There are at least two (and sometimes three) copies extant of Custer's letters: one being his original, the second a copy made by him, the third a copy made by his wife or another. Each is different so far as length and content are concerned. The selections chosen for this biography derive from the two or three copies. Aside from private collections, semi-private and public repositories for Custer manuscripts include the Custer Battlefield National Monument, the United States Military Academy, the National Archives, the Library of Congress, Yale University Library, Detroit Public Library, Lincoln Memorial University, the Monroe County Historical Society, and the New York Historical Society.

Manuscripts, books, monographs, periodicals, and newspapers by the hundreds have been consulted over the past twelve years. A selected bibliography of important books will be found at the end of this volume. With the exception of letters, hitherto unpublished manuscript material is indicated by a footnote.

Since Civil War events are so controversial, some explanation must be made for the narratives found in this biography. They encompass the best of each account, to form a representative whole, in the interest of clarity, lest we lose our subject in a maze of events. Dialogue is not an arbitrary invention of the author, but is directly quoted from sources or carefully constructed from paraphrases.

D. A. KINSLEY

OHIO:
THE ASPIRANT

A FORLORN lover, sixteen years of age, gripped a quill between the first and second fingers of his big bony hand and scratched a letter to one of the most influential men in Congress:

Hopedale, Ohio
May 27th, 1856

To the Hon. John A. Bingham
Sir:

Wishing to learn something in relation to the matter of appointment of Cadets to the West Point Military Academy, I have taken the liberty of addressing you on the subject. . . .

I am desirous of going to West Point, and I think my age and tastes would be in accordance with its requirements. . . . I am now in attendance at the McNeely Normal School in Hopedale, and could obtain from the Principal, if necessary, testimonials of moral character. I would also say that I have the consent of my parents in the course which I have in view. Wishing to hear from you as soon as convenient,

I remain,
Yours Respectfully,
G. A. Custer

George Armstrong was the fateful child born to Emanuel Henry and Maria Ward Kirkpatrick Custer on Thursday, December 5, 1839, in the farmhouse at New Rumley, Harrison County, Ohio. Since two infants had died before him, his charmed life set a precedent. Three more sons and a daughter enlivened the Custer homestead in the years to follow.

Emanuel Custer was a man of the soil, and also a blacksmith, "the best in miles around." And it soon became apparent that, in the forge of their love, he and Maria had hammered out a son who showed all the earmarks of a soldier. When clouds of conflict gathered over the Rio Grande in '45, Jacksonian Democrats (of whom Emanuel was the most blatantly diehard in a Whig stronghold) proclaimed "Our voice is for war!" Little "Autie," waving a penny flag, echoed "My voice is for war!" till his freckled angel face was a devilish red, halo'd by golden curls. Bedecked in a bantam velvet uniform with big brass buttons, and shouldering a toy musket, he would strut behind his tall, bearded father during weekly militia drill. Veterans of the New Rumley Invincibles laughingly admired the Custer boy as "a born soldier." He could spout and carry out the manual of arms like clockwork.

Autie was an impulsive, precocious little imp who never ceased to amaze his father. Emanuel later wrote: "When Autie was about 4 years old he had to have a tooth drawn, and he was very much afraid of blood. When I took him to the Doctor to have the tooth pulled it was in the night & I told him if it bled well it would get well right away, and he must be a good soldier. When we got to the Doctor he took his seat, and the pulling began. The forceps slipped off, and Doc had to make a second trial. He pulled it out, and Autie never even scrunched. Going home, I led him by the arm. He jumped & skipped, and said, 'Pop, you & me can whip all the Whigs in Ohio!' I thought that was saying a good deal, but I didn't contradict him!"

Autie shot up lank and wiry. As a farmboy, he worked the land from the time he could walk, driving into his bones that unrelenting energy and initiative which would characterize his manhood. His father set a bold example of industry and independence, a cynical sense of humor and plain-spoken practicality, and the boy idolized him. Here was a man who romped with his son, who talked with him and treated him as an equal, holding a loose rein in one hand and an admonitory whip in the other.

Armstrong was quick to learn, but lacked scholarly patience.

2

His breathless exuberance allowed little time for study. The strongest wrestler, the fastest runner, the best rider—the all-around roughneck and practical joker—could barely settle his restless imagination. He was like a high-spirited colt, ever champing at the bit. None could tame him, nor would they ever. He was charmingly wild.

A good speller, Armstrong led the class in spelling bees, during which he was in academic glory. On one occasion, a truant rival stood outside the schoolhouse window, making faces and ornery gestures at him. Patience lost, Armstrong lunged to the window and smashed his fist through the glass, fetching his tormentor a bloody nose.

At the age of ten, Autie went to live with his newlywed half sister, Lydia-Ann Reed, in Monroe, Michigan's second oldest settlement. There he worked and played on the farm for a couple of years; and there he first saw pert, dark-eyed Libbie Bacon, only child of the awe-inspiring Judge Daniel Stanton Bacon, Monroe's "first citizen." Swinging on the front gate as Autie came gangling down Monroe Street, her cherub face dimpled with a devilish smile, she said, "Hi, you Custer boy!" and ran into the house before he could pull her pigtails for making him blush. If anyone had then suggested Autie would one day marry that girl, he'd have been damned sorry for it.

Adolescence transformed George Armstrong Custer into an aspiring romantic. He cultivated *savoir-faire* to beguile the girls, and even attempted to intellectualize his vaulting ambition. This subtle transformation put him at the head of his class, a teacher's pet whom none dared challenge; and his first paying job, when he reached sixteen, the age of graduation, was that of substitute principal and teacher in a one-room schoolhouse. There he debated and disputed with his students, damning Whigs as "radical nigger-philes" and denouncing "Black Republicans" as antislavery fanatics. A Southern sympathizer, young Mr. Custer blamed all the hullabaloo over the Negro on Northern capitalists, abolitionists, religionists, and other meddlesome, greedy "scoundrels." Indeed, it was "blackleg politicians" who were making all the trouble. If

3

war came, he would certainly not fight for the do-gooders, the cant-
ing hypocrites, and the spoilsmongers.

Harvest-time found him home in New Rumley, presenting a
month's wages (twenty-five dollars) to his parents. Later, before
glory had rewarded his humble origin, he wrote: "You & Mother
instilled into my mind correct principles of industry, honesty, self-
reliance; . . . and I feel thankful for such noble parents."

Armstrong's first affair occurred while he was teaching part
time and studying literature at McNeely Normal School in Hopedale. Mary ("Mollie") Holland was the teenage daughter of an
affluent farmer who trusted that the outspoken young Democrat
would make a promising son-in-law. Mollie encouraged Autie to
be a professor or a lawyer, never a soldier, and her exciting interest
in him led to a passionate understanding. "You occupy the first
place in my affections, and the only place as far as love is concerned," he penned to his sweetheart. "If any power which I
possess or control can aid in or in any way hasten our marriage,
it shall be exerted for that object. But I will talk with you about
it when I see you next at the trundle-bed."

That trundle bed in the Holland homestead was a nightly
rendezvous, where dreams of the future were revealed with bated
breath. He ended his sweet note: "Farewell, my only Love, until
we meet again—From your true & faithful Lover, Bachelor Boy."
He enclosed a poem, the sentiments of an unfledged Don Quixote:

> *To Mary*
> I've seen and kiss'd that crimson lip
>   With honied smiles o'erflowing,
> Enchanted watch'd the opening rose
>   Upon thy soft cheek glowing.
>
> Dear Mary, thy eyes may prove less blue,
>   Thy beauty fade to-morrow;
> But Oh, my heart can ne'er forget
>   Thy parting look of sorrow.

These words were indeed an ominous portent of permanent
separation. When next they met at the trundle bed, Mr. Holland

caught them *in flagrante delicto*. The Whig-Presbyterian Capulet banished the Democrat-Methodist Romeo from his domain. A tearful Juliet pleaded with her father that they were in love, and wished to wed. But Mr. Holland could not conceive of such passionate impetuosity on the part of two teenagers, so he forbade them ever to see each other again.

Armstrong was not willing to give up without a fight, but Mary suddenly grew cold and indifferent. She did not answer his painfully ardent letters, nor did she care to see him on the sly. The situation was hopeless, and it soured him on the female sex; "a fickle lot," he complained, salving his soul with cynicism. He did not wish to remain in those parts another day, and that was why he wrote to Representative Bingham—to escape and forget.

Even before he met Mary, Armstrong had contemplated the United States Military Academy for its educational prospects; but adventure and glamour were also tugging on his boyish heartstrings. Could he better realize and fulfill himself, satisfy eloquent aspirations, in a classroom or on the paradeground? Mollie never had wanted him to be a soldier. Soldiers could never settle down, and their wives could never be happy, for soldiers are apt to be killed in battle or (at best) continually separated from their loved ones; besides, a soldier's pay and prestige would not be that of a lawyer or professor. Well, West Point cadets could not marry—so he would be a soldier, just for spite. He would not stagnate into a pedagogue. Mere learning now seemed a stumbling block, West Point a steppingstone to greatness. He would damned soon show Mr. Holland that he was worthy of Mary's affection. He would make a name for himself that no man could ignore.

The obstacles to his admission were few, but they were formidable. He challenged them with the dauntless spirit of youthful resolution. His father's reputation as a conservative Democrat was notorious, and Congressman Bingham was a liberal Republican, but this was just the kind of dare that Armstrong loved to take. Emanuel was agin' it; said there was no use trying, that *he* had no influence and couldn't help him. "Then I'll try for myself," Autie answered. "I'll trust to my own efforts, and I won't give up till I get an appointment."

5

"Pop" Custer patted his plucky son on the shoulder and gave his blessings, although Mother had misgivings about such a drastic decision. She knew full well that West Point was designed to make soldiers, not scholars, and she fancied that her boy had purely intellectual ideals.

"I had not been long in Congress when I received a letter, a real boy's letter, that captivated me." Thus reminisced Representative John A. Bingham of Ohio. "Written in a boyish hand, but firmly, legibly, it told me that the writer—a 'Democrat boy,' that I might be under no misapprehension—wanted to be a soldier, wanted to go to West Point, and asked what steps he should take regarding it. Struck by its originality, its honesty, I replied at once."

Bingham responded that an aspirant had already been appointed to the Academy from Custer's Congressional District for the first semester of '56, and that another youth was eager for appointment to the second term; but that if Custer would send Bingham the required personal particulars, he would do his best to secure an application as soon as possible. Fired with enthusiasm, Armstrong scrawled:

> McNeely Normal School
> June 11th, 1856
>
> Hon. John A. Bingham
> Dear Sir,
> . . . I feel myself compelled to write again to express my sincere thanks for your prompt attention, explicit information as to qualifications, &c. I will also add that in all the points specified I would come under the requirements set forth in your communication, being about 17 years of age, above the medium height, and of remarkably strong constitution & vigorous frame. If that young man from Jeff. County of whom you spoke does not push the matter, or if you hear of any other vacancy, I should be glad to hear from you.
>
> Yours with great respect,
> G. A. Custer

Armstrong would not be seventeen for nearly six months; but he would spend that time in studying at McNeely, teaching grammar school, and working on his parents' farm. During the summer, Mr. Bingham returned to Ohio; and young Mr. Custer hastened to pay him a visit. The Congressman was impressed with the frank face and modest determination of the farmboy, and Armstrong returned home happy in the assurance that he would get his heart's desire.

"Mother is opposed to it," he wrote to Lydia-Ann in Monroe, "but Pop . . . favors it very much."

Mother Custer soon reconciled herself to the sad fact that her boy Autie wanted to be a soldier, not a scholar. "He's lost his girl," she told her husband. "He hasn't said anything, but I've sensed it all along. That's why he wants to go to West Point."

Emanuel smiled. "It's the best of all cures."

February, 1857: Flushed with excitement and anticipation, the curly-headed "Buckeye" ripped open the official envelope (House of Representatives stationery!) addressed to George A. Custer, Esq. Mr. Bingham invited him to strike out for West Point, there to be registered and examined as a cadet candidate. His appointment was signed by none other than the Secretary of War, Jefferson Davis, himself a graduate of the Point.

That evening, the Custer household was a scene of chaotic merriment.

★ 2 ★

WEST POINT:
CUSTER'S LUCK

CADET Lieutenant George Armstrong Custer, Officer of the Guard at the United States Military Academy, began his tour of duty at the usual hour on the morning of June 29, 1861. Stalking the wet grassy streets of the city of tents at the summer encampment, he mulled over his precarious position in life.

Five days ago, by the skin of his teeth, Custer had passed his final exam as a West Point cadet. Only thirty-four "graylegs" graduated; and of these, thirty-three were rated above him. "A damned nice thing," the Duke of Wellington would have said. "The nearest-run thing you ever saw in your life!"

The resignation and departure of Southern cadets had deprived the Point of a few individuals who, had they remained those two months after the bombardment of Fort Sumter, would probably have contested with Custer the dubious honor of bringing up the rear of the class. The daredevilish Ohio boy's studied ignorance of discipline and authority nearly landed him on the "foundation list," which announced dismissals for misconduct and/or academic failure. But Custer had been dead set on making the grade, not getting himself kicked out just for the hell of it.

"I would not leave this place for any amount of money," he wrote his folks, "because I would rather have a good education & no money than have a fortune & be ignorant."

The United States Military Academy at West Point was then described as "one of the most absolute despotisms on earth." "My

8

career as a cadet," Custer remarked years later, "had but little to recommend it to the study of those who came after me, unless as an example to be carefully avoided."

The grilling entrance exams had separated the men from the boys, and Armstrong had been somewhat surprised to find himself a man. However, his shock of golden curls doomed him to the pet name of "Fanny" among the "plutes" or upperclassmen. "Hey, Fanny! Did you ever get your tail wet?" Unappreciative, Fanny sheared his golden fleece; but since a "baldie" was not the regulation haircut in those days, Mister Custer was obliged to wear a blond wig for several weeks. And thus the demerits began to add up.

Cadet George A. Custer was first on the demerit list of his platoon leader, Lieutenant William B. Hazen. His chronic disobedience monopolized the "skin-book," which chronicled cadet demerits. Page after page cited Mister Custer: late for parade, talking on parade, face unshaven, hair unkempt, equipment dirty, uniform disordered, shoes unpolished, slackness in drill, minor insubordination (such as failure to salute a superior and "not casting eyes to the front after being ordered to do so at parade"), sitting down on sentry duty, A.W.O.L. after hours, "room grossly out of order" (in the field, "tent out of order"), "tobacco-smoke in Qrs.," gambling in quarters, late for class, inattention in class, neglect of studies, slovenliness, and so on, *ad infinitum.*

In pranks and practical jokes, Cadet Custer was without equal.

"Sir, how would you say 'Class dismissed' in Spanish?" he asked the unsuspecting Spanish professor. When the answer came, Squad Leader Custer led his group out of the room.

It was his brazen delight to declare, before professor and class, that his lesson was unprepared—perhaps "due to the fact, sir, that I swam the Hudson last night to win a bet and get in on a banquet at the James' home." Or perhaps he had spent the night at Havens' Tavern, off limits, swigging rum flips and caterwauling:

> "Come, fellows, fill your glasses
>   and stand up in a row:
> For sentimental drinking,

9

we're going for to go;
In the army there's sobriety—
promotion's very slow;
So we'll cheer our hearts with choruses
at Benny Havens', Oh!"

One of Mister Custer's superiors prided himself on a flock of prize hens whose buff cock, "Mr. Chanticleer," kept the cadets awake with his infernal crowing. One night the nuisance was plucked from his perch and doomed to a stewpan in the tower room of the 8th Division, Old North Barracks. A trail of yellow feathers across the Barracks Area betrayed the culprit. An indulgent Lieutenant Hazen guarded the dark secret; but Cadet Custer was cited for "bread, butter, potatoes, plates, knives & forks in Qrs." Again, "room grossly out of order, bed down & floor not swept" (of feathers). Seven demerits. Excuse? Loss of weight due to outrageous mess-hall rations. Hazen nodded grimly. "Shrapnel" (beans), "creamed foreskins" (chipped beef), and "tar-water" (coffee) were Point specials—morning, noon, and evening.

By the time Fanny earned the dubious honor of hazer, he had been redubbed "Cinnamon," thanks to the spicy hair oil that slicked his red-gold locks. Now the fun was only beginning. "Animules" (wide-eyed newcomers) were saddled with such fatigue duty as clearing out "abandoned" rooms—which were still being occupied by officers. The Code forbade plebes revealing who directed them to do these dire deeds, so they bore the demerit brunts alone. Other unfortunates were dragged out of bed in the dead of night, ordered to knock on officers' doors in their underwear, and meekly to inquire the direction of the nearest privy.

"West Point has had many a character to deal with," wrote fellow classmate and Buckeye, Morris Schaff; but it may be a question whether it ever had a cadet so exuberant, one who cared so little for its serious attempts to elevate and burnish, or one on whom its tactical officers kept their eyes so constantly and unsympathetically searching as upon Custer. And yet how we all loved him, and to what a height he rose!"

Schaff was the runt of the class; and when a big Southern bully

10

threatened to flatten him for defending Senator ("Bluff Ben") Wade of Ohio, Custer slapped the little fellow on the shoulder and said, "If he lays a hand on you, Morry, I'll maul the earth with him." Following up, the Southerner earned himself a black eye.

Armstrong was reputed to be the second strongest cadet in his class. The first was his best friend, Thomas Lafayette ("Texas Tom") Rosser, a gentle and genial giant, dangerous when provoked. And a formidable drinker. During practice marches, when Custer and Rosser brought up the rear of the column, two horses would invariably be found outside a tavern by the passing rear guard. "Hey, you two!" someone would warn. "Hurry up before Hazen catches you!" They did. In winter, their saddlebags were loaded with snowballs to heave willy-nilly as they rode along.

Some declared Custer the best horseman and athlete at the Point. He excelled in mounted drill, performing a jump on "Old Wellington" that rivaled the record-breaking hurdle made by U. S. Grant on "Old York" in an earlier year. However, he nearly flunked Cavalry Tactics, proving that he understood the obstacle course better than the maneuver manual.

His old love for adventure literature found a new outlet in Cooper's *Leatherstocking Tales,* which inspired an essay entitled "The Red Man," an expression of Armstrong's youthful admiration for the free and noble savage.

Custer's feverish ambition lacked direction, discipline, purpose. The absolutism of the Academy was a challenge to his inordinate sense of independence and self-determination. He wanted recognition, but on his own terms. When he got it, adversely, he laughed it off. Seemingly happy-go-lucky and devil-may-care, startlingly restless and fitful, the blue-eyed goldilocks was in fact moody, unhappy, intensely dissatisfied with himself. He endeavored to hide his true feelings with unpredictable prankishness, thus winning the affection of his fellows, but he could not fool his superiors. He impressed them as an *enfant terrible,* bidding for disapproval and punishment, then acceptance and indulgence. He would not be disciplined, but demanded respect. He was contradictory, enigmatic, but so puckishly charming that he was tolerated and in-

11

dulged when he should have been dismissed as an undesirable. Perhaps there was something in him worth saving, worth appealing to, after all. Hazen, foremost in forbearance, hoped to draw it out —by alternately punishing and pampering him, tightening and easing the rein, hoping for a favorable reaction. But for all his noble effort, he was only teased and tricked.

Custer prided himself on amassing demerits just under the limit (100 per semester) for expulsion, 97 being his closest shave; though once, thanks to his own miscounting, he accumulated 129— but was secretly saved by his unproclaimed patron, that "freak" (cadet staff officer) who signed W.B.H. in the conduct book. Hazen, harboring a hidden admiration for the winsome rebel, reduced his number of demerits to within the limit, thus saving Cinnamon from the foundation list.

When not involved in personal affairs, Cadet Custer was arguing politics and getting into minor scraps over the seething relationship between North and South. Still a Democrat, he disfavored Lincoln's election; said it would mean war, as Honest Abe was the precious tool of every crusading tyrant and radical do-gooder in the "Abolitionist conspiracy." "These Black Republicans will either deprive a portion of our fellow citizens of their just rights or produce a dissolution of the Union," he declared. "It's no wonder Southrons are determined not to submit to such aggression." But Armstrong's views were no longer entirely pro-Southern, for he saw fanatics and opportunists in that cause as well. Like it or not, Abraham Lincoln was elected President of the United States by majority rule—the democratic process—and when he was hung in effigy (from an elm outside the Barracks) by Southern cadets, Custer climbed up and cut him down. This kind of demonstration just wasn't the American way, he thought—talk of shooting men out of office, of hanging "niggerlovers," of dividing the nation by violence. It was dangerous bitter-endism.

Would Custer, in the event of war, fight for the North? The question troubled him. It was one of possibly dying to save the Union or to save slavery. Wild talk of "invaded rights" and "future independence" echoed in his unsettled mind, aggravated by the ardent drawl of "hot-blooded Southrons."

Secession came, and chums parted. Those from the South—imitating the treasonous action of their Senators and Congressmen, and influenced by the insurgent appeals of family and friends at home—tendered their resignations from the Academy and hastened to take command of volunteer forces mobilizing in the Confederacy. There was no bitterness in parting; rather the sadness that friends must now, by principle, be foes. The strange contrast of feeling was later noted by Custer: "Those leaving for the South were impatient, enthusiastic, and hopeful. Their comrades from the North, whom they were leaving behind, were reserved almost to sullenness—were grave almost to stoicism."

On April 10, 1861, Armstrong penned to Lydia-Ann: "In case of war, I shall serve my country according to the oath I took here. . . . I feel confident we will be at war within less than a week." Three days later, as expected, news reached West Point that the gathering clouds had burst over Fort Sumter. The United States was at war with itself.

The prospect was at first fascinating. But raw reality had a fiendish way of making things ugly and frightening, and this Custer would soon learn by unpleasant experience.

May 31, '61. Three weeks till graduation. "We study incessantly," Armstrong informs his favorite sister. "I & others only average about 4 hrs' sleep in the 24. I work until 1 at night, and get up at 5. I lost 5 lbs. already! All my classmates are becoming pale & thin. We do not complain. On the contrary, everyone is anxious & willing. At least 20% will probably 'flunk out,' but I have no intention of being among the number. . . . It is my great expectation to fight for my country, and to die for it if need be. The thought has often occurred to me that I might be killed in this war; and if so, so be it."

Monday, June 24. The most astounding event since the bombardment of Fort Sumter was the graduation of George Armstrong Custer from the United States Military Academy. The conspicuous wag made a solemn bow to the Superintendent when handed his diploma. The class cheered.

After a month of anxiety and cramming, Mister Custer had

13

passed the final exams. He graduated fifth from the bottom of the class in Cavalry Tactics, third from the bottom in Strategy & Grand Tactics, and at the foot of the class in General Merit. He was No. 34 in a class of thirty-four. "Well, somebody had to be last; and I earned the dubious distinction!" But the last was destined to become the first, for none of the other thirty-three cadets of the Class of '61 rivaled the name and fame of Fanny, the misfit-rantipole who would emerge as *beau sabreur* of the Union Army.

Lieutenant Custer was "Recommended for Dragoons, Mounted Rifles, or Cavalry." Well, if nothing else, the lad could ride and wield a saber. The Commandant underscored Cavalry.

Saturday, June 29. The summer sun had nearly vanished below the wooded hills, flushing the Academy Plain with an eerie glow, when Lieutenant Custer made his evening rounds. Approaching the guard tent, he was attracted by a disturbance. He rushed around the tent to find two plebes swapping bare-fisted blows inside a pressing circle of rooters and agitators.

"Stand back, you animals!" he said, thrusting his way through the mob of cadets. "Let's have a fair fight!"

These words no sooner left his lips than someone muttered, "Hey, here comes Hazen!" The two combatants and their over-zealous spectators beat a hasty retreat to their tents.

Making an about-face, Custer strode stiffly and swiftly to the guard tent. He was about to duck inside when the razor-sharp voice of First Lieutenant William B. Hazen, Officer of the Day, stopped him in his tracks.

"*Mister* Custer!"

Custer snapped a salute.

Hazen halted and froze. "*Mister* Custer, aren't you the Officer of the Guard?"

"Yes, Mister Hazen."

"Then why didn't you suppress that riot?"

Custer scowled. "What riot?"

Hazen sniffed. His face tightened. "Mister Custer, you're under arrest." He then turned to Lieutenant Wesley Merritt, standing with

14

arms folded in an attitude of utmost gravity. "Mister Merritt, see that Mister Custer has accommodations in the guard tent while I report this incident to Colonel Reynolds."

Merritt nodded. When Hazen was out of sight, he said, "Well, Custer, you've certainly got yourself flummoxed at a most inopportune time! Rumor has it we're pulling out tomorrow. There's a big fight brewing in Virginia. The Rebs are reported a day's march from Washington, and we're going to hit them before they can cross the Potomac."

"Don't worry—don't worry," Custer blurted. "I'll be there."

Merritt smiled, shrugged. "Well, who knows? Before this is over we may all end up under generals' epaulets!"

"Or under six feet of ground."

On the following morning, Custer was ordered to report at the tent of the Commandant.

Lieutenant Colonel John F. Reynolds, a lean and sun-bronzed hero of the Mexican War, glanced up from his field table as the subaltern entered and saluted.

Custer stood at stiff attention for what seemed an eternity, staring blankly at the rear of the tent while Reynolds patiently examined Custer's record. Perspiration beaded on Custer's brow. At last "Old Pop" Reynolds leered at him. Lanky but well-knit, Custer was every inch a potential *cavalier*. His handsomely fair, lavishly freckled face was accented by a long sharp nose, flashing blue eyes, and a shock of golden-red curls pomaded with cinnamon-scented hair oil. Custer's brass-studded, blue-gray uniform perfectly fit his statuesque frame; and Reynolds noticed that he wore his class ring on the little finger of his hefty right hand. Engraved inside the band was *Per Angusta ad Augusta* (Through Trials to Triumphs).

"Well, Mister Custer, what do you have to say for yourself?" Colonel Reynolds flicked his hand for Custer to stand at ease.

Lieutenant Custer let the air out of his chest, snuffed sharply, and said with spirit, "If you please, sir, I was selected to be the last O.G. of our graduating class."

Reynolds arched a brow. "Do you know why you were accorded such an honor, Mister Custer?"

15

"Yes, sir," Custer answered, grim-faced. "Because I was the worst student in the class, and therefore apt to make the best soldier."

Reynolds gazed at Custer's dossier. "You've made quite a record for yourself, I daresay. Ninety-seven demerits in the last six months: only three short of dismissal. Low marks in academic subjects: little interest shown. Graduated at the foot of the class." He shook his head. "Not much to recommend you."

Custer lowered his eyes. His lips twitched.

Reynolds glanced at the eye-opening skin-book. W.B.H. had cited Cadet Custer, from June 6 to 29, for 52 demerits in excess of the 97 which had crowned the last semester ending June 6. . . .

"*June 13th.*—Late at parade. . . . *June 19th.*—Not shaved at Gd. Mtg.; no buttons on collar at Gd. Mtg. . . . *June 25th.*—Tent out of police at Ev'g Insp. . . . *June 26th.*—Tent out of order, a.m."

And *now*, 5 demerits for: "*June 29th.*—Officer of the Gd.— Gross neglect of duty not suppressing a quarrel in the immediate vicinity of Gd. Tent, he being present, 8 & 9 p.m."

Reynolds said in reference to this final offense, "And what was *your* duty in this instance, Mister Custer: you being Officer of the Guard?"

"My duty as Officer of the Guard was plain and simple. I should have arrested the two combatants and sent 'em to the guard tent for violating the peace and regulations of the Academy."

"Indeed! And why didn't you do just that?"

"Well, sir, the instincts of a sportsman prevailed over the obligations of an Officer of the Guard."

"Very well, Mister Custer." Reynolds summoned Hazen to return Custer to the guard tent. "Court-martial proceedings will be held pending orders from Washington."

At midday, long-expected special orders arrived by telegraph from Washington. Each member of the class of '61 was directed to leave West Point at once and report to the Adjutant General of the United States Army for assignment to active duty. Each member, that is, but one. George Armstrong Custer's name did not appear on the list. He was ordered detained, under arrest, to await

16

approval of the Commandant's application for a court-martial "to sit on his case."

Lieutenant Custer cracked a halfhearted smile as he watched his thirty-three buddies file past the "doghouse tent." He stood at the entranceway, grabbing the hand of each as they marched by.

"So long, Custer." "Good luck, Cinnamon." "See you at the front." "What's the last word?"

"Promotions or a coffin!" he replied.

Within a few hours, the Commandant's application received official approval at the War Department; and a military tribunal was assembled immediately to review formal charges and determine the degree of Cadet Custer's punishment.

Lieutenant Stephen Vincent Benét, who became the grandfather of celebrated poets, acting as Judge Advocate and seated midway at the long tribune table, arraigned the prisoner with the long face and looks black enough to be worthy of a trial for high treason.

Although, as Custer later noted, "the trial was brief, scarcely occupying more time than did the primary difficulty," the miscreant suffered over two weeks of agonizing detention pending a unanimous decision. As telegrams flashed back and forth from West Point to Washington, and while the Superintendent (Colonel Richard L. Delafield) and the Commandant (Colonel Reynolds) put their heads together with Lieutenant Hazen and members of the court-martial, an unhappy cadet stood in fear of missing that big battle and a possible promotion. All who could leave the Academy had done so. It was his lot to be last again, and perhaps late. He now began to see himself as a damn fool who had pressed his proverbial luck too far; and if he were the least bit fortunate, he could not expect less than six months' suspension.

Monday morning, July 15. Lieutenant Custer, standing "in a brace" (at rigid attention) before the court, barely listened as Benét read the indictment: " '. . . That he, the said Cadet Custer, did fail to suppress a riot or disturbance near the guard tent, and did fail to separate said combatants; but, on the contrary, did cry out in a loud tone of voice, "Stand back, boys; let's have a fair fight," or words to that effect.' How say you? Are you guilty or not guilty?"

17

"Guilty!" Custer answered.

A few moments later, after much scribbling and whispering at the seats of justice, Lieutenant Benét read the verdict to an anxious accused: " 'It is the decision of this court to reprimand Cadet Custer for conduct unbecoming an officer and a gentleman. The court is thus lenient in the sentence, owing to the peculiar situation of Cadet Custer represented in his defense, and in consideration of his general good conduct as testified to by Lieutenant Hazen, his immediate commander.' Case dismissed. The prisoner is released from custody."

The "peculiar situation" of Cadet Custer was that he had an influential benefactor in Washington, Congressman Bingham, who secured his release by pulling the necessary strings at the War Department. Lieutenant Hazen had no desire to torture the hotspur with further detention—and so testified as to his "general good conduct," thus belying the records. A special order, signed by the Adjutant General of the Army, directed Lieutenant Custer to report to Washington at once. "This order," he later wrote, "practically rendered the action and proceeding of the court-martial nugatory."

Hopping aboard the first down-river steamer (July 18), and whistling with exuberant anticipation as he watched the Point fade from view, Mister Custer stopped off in New York just long enough to buy a lieutenant's outfit and have his picture taken at Brady's studio for sister Lydia.

Saturday morning, July 20, found him hopping lightheartedly off the train in the Capital. Though one trial had ended, another was just beginning. Equal to the first, Armstrong fancied himself fit for the second.

18

★ 3 ★

WASHINGTON: OLD FUSS-AND-FEATHERS

A FRECKLE-FACED youth, wearing a rumpled lieutenant's uniform and toting a big carpetbag, swaggered into the War Department building on the sultry afternoon of July 20, 1861.

The cobblestone streets of the Capital were swarming with people. George Armstrong Custer scowled through the glaring heat at hundreds of government officials in swallowtails and toppers, crinolined ladies with soft-tinted parasols, yelping kids and barking dogs, overloaded carriages racing and rattling down Pennsylvania Avenue toward the Potomac. It was Saturday, and the whole city stampeded on a weekend outing—to watch the coming big battle in Virginia.

Lieutenant Custer entered the Adjutant General's office, dropped his bag on a chair, and asked a sweating orderly to whom he should report.

"Give me your papers and take a seat," the orderly replied, giving Custer's golden locks a lowering look.

The Adjutant General's office was mobbed and buzzing with military personnel. Seated with his bag on his lap, Custer sensed a tingle of excitement and anticipation. He saw dozens of anxious-looking orderlies flitting from room to room with stacks of enormous envelopes in their arms. Cabinet officials darted to and fro, causing the top brass to jump up from their desks. It was easy to see that the U.S. Government was surging into war.

At 2 P.M., Lieutenant Custer was startled out of his growing impatience and bewilderment.

"Mister Custer?" a voice cracked. Custer lurched to his feet. It was the lowering orderly-lieutenant. He jerked his thumb. "Follow me."

Custer strutted after him. In a few seconds he was clicking his dusty heels and saluting Adjutant General Lorenzo Thomas, a stately, white-haired brigadier in gold-braided blue.

"So you're Custer, eh?" the A.G. said with a smile. He glanced at Lieutenant Custer's order of instructions, signed by Colonel Reynolds, then eyed the shavetail appreciatively. Custer was quite a striking figure, he thought. "Perhaps you'd like to be presented to General Scott, Mister Custer. He may have some special service for you."

Custer was flabbergasted. Lieutenant General Winfield Scott, lionhearted veteran of the War of 1812 and the Mexican War, was General-in-Chief of the United States Army. Cadet Custer had often seen the towering form of this venerable warrior during his summer visits to West Point. Of all the high-and-mighty officers in "this man's army," General Scott was the most unapproachable. He was like something sacred, and even those who called him "Old Fuss-and-Feathers" feared and respected him.

Custer blushed, answering the Adjutant General's incredible offer in the affirmative.

"Please to follow me," Thomas said, rising from his desk.

Trembling with excitement, Lieutenant Custer strode close behind General Thomas into the next room of Army Headquarters. There he beheld the majestic person of Winfield Scott, who was seated at a table piled and spread with maps and documents. With him in heated discussion were several members of Congress, Mr. Bingham among them. Holding up a huge map of Eastern Virginia, General Scott was showing the Senators the respective positions of the Union and Confederate forces southwest of Washington. Custer was now certain that a pitched battle was in the making.

For a tense moment he stared at the old chief and was charmed by his deep, grinding voice. Scott's forbidding face was accented by angry eyes, grim mouth, a craggy nose, and bushy white side whiskers. His gold-braided dark-blue tunic was unbuttoned; and

20

though seventy-five years found him swollen with dropsy, plagued by gout and vertigo, he was still the "Fire-eater of Chippewa."

Scott leered at Thomas, suddenly stopped talking and laid down the map. "Yes?" he grated, shifting his massive form in the heavy black chair.

"General, this is Lieutenant Custer of the 2nd Cavalry. He's just reported from West Point, and I didn't know but you might have some special orders to give him."

General Scott gave Lieutenant Custer the once-over, then offered his brawny hand. Custer grinned.

"Well, my young friend," the General said, easing back in the chair and locking fingers over his paunch, "I'm glad to welcome you to the service at this critical time. Our country has need of the strong arms of all her loyal sons in this emergency." He then cocked an eye at Thomas. "To what outfit has Mister Custer been assigned?"

The A.G. replied, "To Company G, 2nd Cavalry, now under Major Palmer with General McDowell out at Centerville."

The General nodded, pursing thin lips and twiddling his thumbs. He fixed his shadowy eyes on Custer. "We've had the assistance of quite a number of you young men from the Academy, drilling volunteers and so forth. Now, what can I do for you? Would you prefer being ordered to report to General Mansfield to aid in this work, or is your desire for something more active?"

Custer fumbled for words. "Well, if you please, sir, it's my earnest desire to join my regiment at once with General McDowell." He lowered his eyes, nervously fingering his kepi. "I'm anxious to see active service."

"A very commendable resolution, young man!" Scott turned to General Thomas. "Make out Lieutenant Custer's orders, directing him to proceed to his outfit at once." He again fixed his eyes on Custer. "Have you been able to provide yourself with a mount for the field?"

"No, sir—not yet. But I shall set about doing so at once."

The General knit his brow. "I fear you have a difficult task before you; because if rumor's correct, every serviceable horse in

21

the city has been bought, borrowed, or stolen by citizens who have gone or are going as spectators to witness the battle. I only hope Gen'l Beauregard may capture some of 'em and teach the damned fools a lesson. However, what I desire to say to you is, go and provide yourself with a horse if possible and call here at seven o'clock this evening. I desire to send some dispatches to General McDowell at Centerville, and you can be the bearer of them. You're not afraid of a night ride, are you?"

"No, sir!"

"Good! I trust you to perform a very important service. If I'm to believe Mr. Bingham here, you're just the man I need."

Custer flipped his cap back on his head and saluted briskly.

What a fluke! he thought, leaving the War Department. He wondered what those other poor devils, his thirty-three fellow classmates, were doing at this time. Drilling raw recruits? Sweating out office duty? He chuckled. Custer's Luck!

"A horse! A horse! my kingdom for a horse!"

These words occurred to Lieutenant Custer in his wearisome quest for a mount. He footslogged all over Washington, looking in at every livery stable he could find. They were cleaned out. There wasn't a horse to be had in the whole Capital City! The stablekeepers told him, "Sorry, soldier. You're too late. All our horses have been let."

Custer's heart was in his shoes as he ambled along Pennsylvania Avenue. His shadow was lengthening, and a searing sun stared him straight in the face. He grimaced, yanking the visor of his kepi down over his eyes. He felt sick, not knowing what to do.

Should I steal a horse? He glanced sideways, feeling a twinge of conscience. No, that would never do.

Lieutenant Custer had abandoned all hope of enjoying his big moment, shivering to think how he must face General Scott as a failure, when suddenly he spotted a familiar form in the crowd and waved.

Spindle-shanked Lieutenant Alexander C. M. Pennington looked over in surprise, reining his horse in at the curb.

22

"Hulloo, Alex," Custer said, shaking his hand heartily. "What are you doing here?"

"I'm attached to Captain Griffin's battery out at Centerville with General McDowell. We're all primed for the big engagement with Beauregard tomorrow. The Cap'n sent me up here to fetch a remount he left when we pulled out a couple of weeks ago. And d'you know who that horse might be?"

"Not Old Wellington!"

Pennington nodded: the very ripsnorter on which Armstrong made the highest jump since Cadet U. S. Grant broke the hurdle record on Old York.

"Well, I'm damned! Where is he now?"

"The Cap'n has him quartered in the Treasury Building!" Under emergency conditions, the cellar of the Treasury Department then served as an officers' remount stable.

"Alex, I need your help. Let me ride Old Wellington out to Centerville."

"Of course! Ready to move?"

"Not till seven."

"Seven! It's twenty-five miles out to Centerville, and my orders are to report before dawn."

"All right—all right! But I've *got* to have a horse. General Scott assigned me to special duty this afternoon. That means I'm under government orders to get important dispatches down to General McDowell. He said to report at seven—with a horse. All I need do is pick up the dispatches, and we'll be off directly. See here, you're not the only one who's got to get to Centerville before daylight!"

"Well, why the devil didn't you tell me straight off you were under special orders from General Scott!"

Custer grinned, gripping an old hazer's hand.

Lieutenant Custer snapped shut his pocket watch. It was 7 P.M. Striding into the Adjutant General's office, he reported as ordered.

Lorenzo Thomas handed him a packet of dispatches. "I presume you've found a horse?"

23

Custer beamed, tucking the packet into his tunic.

Thomas extended his hand. "Good luck, Mister Custer."

Armstrong rushed out of G.H.Q., whistling absently. Alex Pennington was waiting for him outside the War Department building. Custer jumped on Old Wellington and away they rode, clattering over the cobblestones and into the ruddy haze. How good to straddle that old horse, who pranced and snorted with the delight of recognition!

Cantering across Long Bridge, which spanned the purling Potomac, Custer and Pennington jogged down Fairfax Courthouse Road toward Centerville. The hours flew on eagle's wings as they stirred the warm, night-veiled stillness with chatter, laughter, and . . .

> "We'll hang Jeff Davis on a sour-apple tree
> As we go marching on!"

★ 4 ★

BULL RUN:
THE BOY HERO

$\mathbf{A}$T approximately 2:30 on the fateful Sunday morning of July 21, 1861, Lieutenants George Armstrong Custer and Alexander C. M. Pennington trotted into the Union Army bivouac outside Centerville, Virginia.

The eerie glow of campfires flickered in the pitch-darkness of the surrounding countryside. Custer saw hundreds of blue-clad troops lying along the roadway, their haversacks under their heads, snatching a few winks of sleep before bugles sounded "Assembly." Others, sitting or standing in small groups, smoked and chatted to while away the remaining hours. Officers trudged up and down the highway, their tunics unbuttoned and slouch hats in their hands. Nodding noncoms, leaning precariously on their bayoneted muskets, stood alone in the high meadow grass. A few old campaigners, perched on fence rails, puffed away on their pipes or cigars and longed for the break of day.

Despite the hum of voices and the crackle of fires, a tense ominous hush had settled over the encampment. Custer shared in the anxiety that foreboded a decisive battle. Indeed, the imminent encounter would either arrest the rebellion and crush the Confederacy or make it a living, formidable power in the land. Custer, for one, had no illusions. This would be war to the death.

"There's General Headquarters," Pennington said, pointing to a white canvas marquee. It was the largest tent in a circle floodlighted by a blazing bonfire. "You may leave Old Wellington with the General's striker, compliments of Captain Griffin."

Custer nodded, expressing thanks and gripping his friend's

25

hand. Then, gently heeling Old Wellington, he picked his way among the scatter of snoring soldiers and trotted into the open area lit by glimmering fires.

The clopping of shod hoofs on hard ground brought a bare-headed officer out of the nearest tent. Custer drew rein and saluted as the man approached, having noticed that a gold oak leaf decorated each shoulder strap on his blue service coat.

"Whom do you wish to see?" the smooth-shaven gentleman asked, returning the young six-footer's salute with a casual gesture.

"General McDowell," Custer replied, adding proudly, "I'm Lieutenant Custer, bearer of dispatches from General Scott."

The gray-haired officer nodded, holding out his hand. "I'll relieve you of them."

Custer thrust his fingers into his tunic, clutched the packet of documents, then hesitated. He wanted to deliver the dispatches in person.

The officer, still holding out his hand, offered a thin smile. "It's all right, Lieutenant," he said quietly. "I'm Major Wadsworth of General McDowell's staff."

Without choice, Custer pulled the packet out of his jacket and handed it to the Major.

Major James S. Wadsworth entered the G.H.Q. tent with General Scott's dispatches. Through its half-open flaps, Lieutenant Custer saw him hand the packet to a big-bodied officer sporting a trim imperial and wearing a gilt-buttoned frock coat.

Leaving the tent again, Wadsworth walked up to Custer and said, "What's the latest news from Washington?"

Custer shrugged. "Everybody there is looking to the Army for news!"

"Well, I guess they won't have to wait much longer. The entire Army is moving to attack the enemy today."

Custer snorted. "Last I saw, sir, the whole damn city was turned out to see the show!"

"What time did you leave?"

"A little after seven, sir."

"Well, I daresay you must be pretty tuckered out! Come down

off that horse and have some breakfast. It might be the last bite you get for the next twelve hours."

Custer was dog-hungry and dog-tired, but he sat bolt upright in the saddle and said, "Thank you, sir, but hunger and fatigue are nuisances a soldier shouldn't acknowledge."

Wadsworth patted Old Wellington's neck. "Well, at least have some compassion for this poor animal."

Custer nodded, swung out of the saddle, handed the halter to Wadsworth.

While the Major amused himself with the gastronomic welfare of Old Wellington, the Lieutenant stretched his cramped legs and ran into a former classmate (and honor student), Lieutenant Henry W. Kingsbury.

"Well," Custer said, "in what condition do I find you?"

"Aide-de-camp to General McDowell."

"It pays to know the right people!"

Kingsbury said, "You look grubstruck."

Custer smelled the remains of breakfast and nodded.

Kingsbury called over to the campfire, where several "bean-jockeys" were cleaning up the mess equipment. A few moments later, Custer was squatting on the ground in the flickery light, sipping a cup of black coffee, munching an army beefsteak and "januwine" Virginia corn pone, his first and most memorable breakfast in the field. It would be his last bite to eat for over thirty hours.

Making quick work of his morning meal, and too excited to sleep, Custer jumped up and strode over to Major Wadsworth, who was rebridling Old Wellington.

"Sir, could you direct me to Major Palmer's cavalry?"

"Certainly, Lieutenant. You'll find them a few hundred yards up the road."

Custer saluted and started to walk away.

"If you're a cavalryman," Wadsworth suggested, "won't you need a horse?"

Custer stopped short. The thought never occurred to him!

Wadsworth smiled, handing Custer the halter. "Take Old Wellington, compliments of General McDowell."

"Much obliged, sir!" Custer lurched into the saddle. "And return my thanks to General McDowell!" Tipping his cap, he dashed off into the darkness.

The Centerville Pike was inundated with infantry. Turning off into the fields along the road, Lieutenant Custer followed the whitewashed rail fence until he came upon a mounted column. It was still so pitch-black that he could barely see a hand in front of his face, but the jingle of riding gear and the snorting of horses assured him he was in the right place.

"Beg pardon." He addressed the wraithy forms. "What cavalry is this?"

"Major Palmer's."

"Can you tell me where Company G, 2nd Cavalry, is?"

"At the head of the column."

Urging Old Wellington up to the head of the column, Custer reined in and said, "Is the commanding officer of Company G, 2nd Cavalry, present?"

"Here he is," somebody answered.

One of the mounted figures spurred up alongside him. Custer saluted. "Sir, I'm Lieutenant Custer. In accordance with orders from the War Department, I report for duty with my company."

"Glad to meet you, Mister Custer," the company commander said with facetious formality, offering his hand. "We've been expecting you, as we saw in the list of assignments of the graduating class from West Point that you had been marked down to us." Muffled laughter intimated that Custer's Luck was a standing joke. "I am Lieutenant Drummond. Allow me to introduce you to some of your brother officers." Thomas Drummond swung his horse toward the small group of men behind him. "Gentlemen, permit me to introduce to you Lieutenant Custer, who has just reported for duty with his company."

Custer gallantly doffed his kepi and nodded to each of them, although he could see but little more than the dim outlines of horses and riders in the inky darkness. All the better, for their grimaces of suppressed laughter would not have been appreciated. In accordance with the chivalrous code, they acknowledged his courtesies by bowing and uncapping also.

"Having just arrived," Drummond said, "I don't suppose you're familiar with the enemy's position and our plan of action."

Custer answered that he was not, so Drummond explained that they were deployed in four divisions: Tyler's, Hunter's, Heintzelman's, and Miles's. General Tyler's command would pull a feint by threatening the heavily manned Confederate left at the stone bridge crossing Bull Run creek, while Generals Hunter (with the cavalry) and Heintzelman moved up to Sudley's Ford and crossed over to attack and turn this huge flank kept occupied by Tyler on the Federal side of the creek. Meantime, General Miles would keep the Rebels amused by cannonading their center and engaging their right at Blackburn's Ford. "In this way, we'll run Beauregard clean into the sea!"

The first flush of pearl-gray light found the world at peace. A sepulchral stillness overspread the crisp, dewy air.

With head held high and cap cocked rakishly on his curls, Lieutenant George Armstrong Custer sat his horse like a seasoned trooper. With furrowed brow he gazed into the bright southern sky, darting a glance now and then at his pocket watch. He listened, waited silently.

6:15 A.M. Custer snapped shut his watch. Old Wellington pricked up his ears and snorted. The battle began as three deep-echoing roars, about three miles south of Centerville. A few seconds later a continuous thunder erupted, and the milky iridescence of the horizon was veiled with a murky shroud.

Lieutenant Thomas Drummond lowered his telescope and smiled. "A fine Sunday morning, gentlemen." He nodded in the direction of the rumbling cannonade. "That's General Miles, hitting Beauregard's center."

"Then we should be moving out pretty soon," Custer muttered nervously.

"Here comes the Major now!" said Second Lieutenant Leicester Walker, Custer's fellow platoon leader, Company G.

Major Innes N. Palmer, sporitng a fiery Vandyke, pulled up in front of the column. He flicked his gloved hand at Lieutenant

29

Drummond. His voice was shrill in the warm, gentle breeze: "Attention! By fours: column forward, walk *march!*"

Drummond repeated, "By fours: troop forward, walk *ho!* Guide left!"

Custer echoed, with a slight tremor, "By fours: platoon forward, walk *ho!* Guide left!" Though he had nearly flunked Cavalry Tactics at the Point, Armstrong (master of practice, not theory) knew all the commands in *Gilham's Manual.*

Major Palmer swept off his campaign hat and waved the 2nd U.S. Cavalry on. "A hot and cloudless day ahead, Mister Custer," he said, reining in alongside the freckled youth.

Custer eyed the sky. Not even a single puff of vapory fleece flecked the pale-blue, saffron-fringed heavens.

"Ready for your baptism of fire?"

Custer revealed a weak grin. His lips trembled. "As ready as I'll ever be, sir."

"Scared?"

"I don't rightly know, sir. Are you?"

Palmer burst out laughing. He abruptly dropped out of line to watch his regiment march by.

The seven companies of cavalry spearheading Brigadier General David Hunter's 2nd Division ribboned slowly down Centerville Pike, clattered over the suspension bridge spanning Cub Run, then veered off to the right on Sudley Road about a quarter-mile below the creek.

Snaking along the dusty byway, they were soon swallowed by an immense forest. For two long and unlively miles, Lieutenant Custer listened to a humdrum of twittering birds, the rattle of equipment, and a resonant booming that rolled ever louder over the hills and treetops from along Bull Run.

For a moment he wondered what effect this flank movement and surprise attack—technically called *coup de main*—would have upon an enemy whose force of arms and firmness of spirit were a matter of pure conjecture. Would the Rebs break and run? Or would they stand and die in the last ditch? Custer shuddered to think of what lay ahead.

The 2nd U.S. Cavalry wheeled out of the woods at approximately 9:30. The swelling sun radiated a hot, hazy glow. Custer could feel its infant beams glaring across his shoulders. Dewy cobwebs and misty blankets of morning gems sparkled in the lush green fields.

Major Palmer waved his hand toward Sudley Springs. "Form companies! Right oblique, trot *march!*"

The regiment swung off the road about a hundred yards from Sudley's Ford, jogged across the wet grassland, and came to a halt at the springs.

"Dismount!" the Major intoned. "Sergeants will supervise the watering of horses by platoons."

For a stirring half-hour, Lieutenant Custer stood by his mount and watched an unbroken stream of gay-jacketed doughboys swashing across the shallow ford and surging up the wooded hillside. Musket barrels and bayonets flared in the radiant sunlight. Between each scrambling infantry regiment Custer saw batteries of horse artillery furrowing the slick embankment, barreling over Bull Run, rolling up the opposite slope out of sight.

This wild scene was made even more violent by an earth-shaking, thunderous drumfire. Custer shivered with excitement, and his sweaty palms tingled. The woods and hills for miles around echoed and re-echoed with the hollow roar of cannon and musketry.

At ten o'clock, Lieutenant Custer saw Major Wadsworth galloping down the gently sloping meadow to where he and the 2nd Cavalry were awaiting orders to advance. Wadsworth drew rein beside Major Palmer, and Custer heard him say breathlessly, "General McDowell desires you to move across the creek and up the ridge at once, there to support Griffin's battery."

Palmer nodded and touched his hat. He reined his horse around. "Mister Drummond," he cried, "lead out with your company! By column of fours, at the gallop! Bugler, sound 'Boots and Saddles!' "

Custer lurched into the saddle and hustled Old Wellington into line alongside Lieutenant Drummond. He set his teeth. This was it!

Drummond turned in the saddle and waved his arm toward Sudley's Ford. His voice was sharp above the din: "Gallop *ho!* Guide left!"

31

Company G splashed across the creek and rode hell-for-leather up the hill. When they reached the crest, Lieutenant Custer saw rawboned Captain Charles Griffin galloping his guns into position along the tree-dotted ridge.

The view presented to Custer's eyes was spectacular. The densely wooded countryside was cut up by a brilliant patchwork of green fields and clearings, ribbonlike roads and snaky streams, fringed by a wavy line of purplescent ridges. Wispy strands of bluish smoke marked the spots echoing a crackle of fusillade, and towering white puffs tumbled over the pastures from belching field-pieces on either side of Bull Run. At the foot of the hill, clouds of dust and gun smoke hovered in the sticky stagnant air. When these wavering mists shredded and wafted into the trees during momentary lulls, Custer could see far-reaching thickets of glittering bayonets. Hunter and Heintzelman were launching their flank attack; while on the Centerville side of Bull Run, Tyler and Miles poured a raking fire all along the Rebel lines.

Observing Griffin's artillery being wheeled into a strategic position, the disquieted Confederates ranged their guns and opened up on the ridge with a barrage of round shot and shrapnel. Recalling the old code that it was unsoldierly to duck, Lieutenant Custer held his head erect and gritted his teeth.

Until now, the battle had been much like tactical maneuvers at the Military Academy. They were the days of disciplined frolic, when serious injury resulted from tumbling off an artillery caisson or vaulting from a mount that stopped short before a hurdle. On this day, for the first time in his life, death stared him full in the face. The death of shattered, bloated, blackened corpses. The death of protruding tongues and twisted limbs and eyes lolling out of their sockets. The death of stench and shrieking, cold-blooded murder.

Armstrong turned to fellow shavetail Leicester Walker: "They say you never hear the one that hits you!"

Walker answered with a nervous, sickly chuckle. Licking dry lips with a dry tongue, he eyed the stormy sky and checked his fidgety mount.

Custer was fascinated by the sharp, vicious hiss of solid shot as

32

it tore through the air overhead. The tune of flying cannon balls was indeed a familiar one—a haunting melody of artillery exercises at West Point—but he listened with anxious interest now that the direction of the projectiles was toward instead of away from him. They seemed to sing a disturbingly different song when let loose in battle!

At that moment, Custer saw General Hunter's adjutant come at a slashing pace up the ridgeway from the right flank of the Federal forces. He pulled up in front of Major Palmer, saluted, panted, "Sir, a battalion of enemy cavalry is moving to the attack of this battery." He turned his head and pointed to the far side of Stony Ridge. "The horse were seen amassing behind a stone house on the Warrenton Pike. They're now heading up Sudley Road toward the right of our line. General Hunter directs you to advance at once to the base of the hill and repel the enemy's assault."

Palmer touched his hat, swung his horse around. "Attention! Form platoons! Prepare to advance!" His voice was solemn and severe. "Please to understand, gentlemen, that it is our duty to protect these guns. On reaching the foot of the hill, we shall doubtless be ordered to charge the enemy. May none of my boys give his country cause to be ashamed of him." He waved his hat. "At the trot: column forward, *ho!*"

"Platoon forward, *ho!* Guide right!" Lieutenant Custer shook off his jitters and took account of himself. Until now, he had never ridden at anything more menacing than a three-foot hurdle, or slashed at aught more aggressive than a "leatherhead" stuffed with tanbark. But what lay ahead didn't leave him in much more of a sweat than what lay behind. Custer knew only too well that he was riding in front of a seasoned outfit of "bridle-wise" troopers, all of whom would have an eagle eye on their new officer to see how he stood up under fire.

Company G (1st Platoon, Second Lieutenant G. A. Custer, in the lead) picked its way down the rocky slope. Custer heard the cannon booming several hundred yards ahead. Along the ridge above him, Captain Griffin opened up a plunging fire on the Rebel position. The whole hillside quaked with deafening shocks. Rolling musketry sounded like thousands of firecrackers, while twanging

33

Minie balls and shrieking shells ripped the trees to skeletons. An acrid haze of livid smoke burned Custer's watery eyes, and the stifling reek of gunpowder made his nostrils tingle. In a fever of excitement, he wanted to shout at the top of his voice.

Trotting out of the timber that skirted the foot of Stony Ridge, Palmer's cavalry deployed by company in the open fields parallel to Warrenton Pike. There they waited, their steeds bobbing and blowing spiritedly, watching for the signal to advance. The enemy horse, also deployed in column of companies, had halted on the far side of the pike, apparently waiting for final orders to attack.

Les Walker, sitting in front of his own platoon several yards from Custer, glanced over and said in a grave voice, "Custer, what weapon are you going to use in the charge?"

Well aware that the old troopers behind him were looking and listening, Custer blurted "The saber!" He whipped out his sleek new blade and flashed it over his head with a sardonic grin. (In practice drill at the Point, the commands were "Draw saber! . . . Present saber!")

Walker, one of those political appointees, reckoned that's the way they did things at West Point. So he smiled and unsheathed his saber, resting its pommel on his hip and its blade against his right shoulder as he had seen Custer do with a cavalier flourish. ("Carry saber!")

Lieutenant Custer sensed a vibrant thrill of anticipation. From his imaginative boyhood he had always pictured the dashing dragoon in a wind-blast cavalry charge, waving curved steel over his plumed head and cleaving the skulls of all who dared to stem the tide of his death-defying onslaught. This was the image conjured by Lever's *Charles O'Malley of the 14th Light Dragoons,* a dog-eared adventure novel that little Autie used to hide behind his big geography book in that one-room schoolhouse back at Monroe, Michigan.

"The saber is a beautiful weapon," Custer said aloud to Walker, who was all ears. "It has only one drawback. In order to be effective, it has to be used at close quarters. So close that if you don't unhorse your opponent, he'll most likely cut you down for it." Custer suddenly thrust the blade back in its scabbard. ("Return

34

saber!") "So much for the saber." Without uttering a word, he unsnapped his holster and yanked out his Colt revolver. ("Draw pistol!")

Walker no sooner observed Custer's switch of weapons than he did likewise, sheathing his sword and drawing his pistol.

"Now as for the revolver," Custer said, hefting it in his hand, "it has one advantage over the saber. You don't have to get up alongside your opponent to polish him off. You can choose your own time and distance. Sure, you might miss your aim. But you've got six chambers to empty; and if one, two, or three miss, there are still three shots left to fire at close quarters." Custer shoved the Colt back in its black leather case. ("Return pistol!") "On second thought," he added, cutting his eyes at Walker, "it's pretty damned hard taking anything like accurate aim in all the rush and confusion of a charge. That would be just a waste of bullets. Then you'd be slapdash in the midst of your enemies, and slashing right and left at each other, in which case a saber would be of much greater value and service than an empty revolver." So Custer pulled out his sword again and flicked it against his shoulder.

Walker was prompted by this sudden switch. As if in pantomime, and appearing rather befuddled, he followed Custer's example, holstering his pistol and unscabbarding his sword.

These waggish changes of mind and weapons were soon checked by a burst of yelling and cheering all along the reserve lines of Hunter's division. Custer looked up, saw that the Confederate cavalry had suddenly disappeared; saw Major Wadsworth loping over the smoke-shrouded meadow, waving his slouch hat and shouting, "We've whipped 'em on all points! We've taken all their batteries! They're running fast as they can, and we're after 'em!"

Lieutenant Custer snatched off his cap and fetched a wild yell. He then fished out his pocket watch. It was three in the afternoon! The scythe of Time had done a quick thrashing of those five fiery hours across Bull Run.

(Wadsworth rode over to Major Palmer, and Custer heard him say hoarsely, "The enemy left has been forced back from Bull Run. We're in complete possession of Warrenton Pike leading from the stone bridge.) Thanks to the artillery, Beauregard's front lines are being broken and routed. Even the right and center are giving way in disorder. It's reported he's calling up his last reserves to restore some confidence and order. General McDowell is pressing us to follow up the retreat before enemy reinforcements can arrive to check our advance." He gasped for breath, mopping his streaky brow. "General Hunter has been rendered *hors de combat*. General Heintzelman therefore directs you to remain in support of Griffin's battery, which has now been ordered to move up to the front. Carry on, Major!"

Custer glanced behind him, spotted the horse artillery rumbling up Sudley Road in a whirlwind of dust. Smoke-smudged gunners, hunched together on the ammunition wagons, whistled and waved and they swept by.

"Guide center!" Palmer barked. "Column, forward at the gallop!"

Company G bolted after the battery. Guidons rippled in the smoldering breeze. Bounding over fence-lined fields littered with hundreds of dead and wounded, the 2nd Cavalry cut across Warrenton Pike and Young's Creek, then dashed up a tree-skirted vantage point on which Griffin was unlimbering his eleven 10-pounders.

When Company G breasted the ridge, Lieutenant Custer sighted Alex Pennington relaying orders to Captain Griffin. Leaving his platoon to Lieutenant Walker, he darted ahead and called out to the departing officer.

Pennington reined his horse around.

Custer plucked off his cap, wiped his grimy-wet face on a gold-braided sleeve. "We've got 'em on the run!" he said, grinning like a minstrel. The two subalterns shook hands heartily.

"The Rebs are giving way everywhere," Pennington replied, beaming. "The day is ours, Fanny!"

They laughed and chatted for a few moments, gazing out over the battlefield. Mile-long waves of gaily clad infantry flooded the countryside, turning back the scattered gray-brown tide.

Bugle blasts, a roar of voices echoed faintly from a thick belt of dark-green timberland girding the base of the ridge. Custer and Pennington shifted their eyes in the distracting direction. Suddenly

36

they spied several thousand troops surging out of the woods. Muskets gleamed, bayonets twinkled in the glare of the sun.

"Who the devil are they?" Custer said, squinting.

Pennington stared openmouthed. "God knows; some of our reserves."

"Our reserves hell! *Look!*" Custer pointed to the Confederate Stars and Bars flapping above the glittery forest of spikes.

While two lieutenants gaped in disbelief, the huge column poured out in skirmishing order across the plain and halted within three hundred yards behind the right flank of the Union Army. Like lightning, men of the first Confederate battleline leveled their muskets and fired a murderous volley into the backs of Heintzelman's advancing brigades.

"*Look!*" Custer said, grabbing Pennington's arm and pointing into the gap below them. "They're bringing up guns. And look— *cavalry!*"

"Oh my God, we're outflanked for sure!" Pennington jerked on his reins. With a frightened look on his face, he clapped spurs to his horse and disappeared down the wooded hillside.

Custer swung around and charged back to his own outfit, which was now spilling down the rapid slope close behind Griffin's battery.

A thunderous sheet of billowy smoke ripped from the heavy Confederate field artillery now in position along Warrenton Pike. Shot and shell hissed and screamed high over the heads of the Confederate firing lines, bursting in deadly white puffs among the Union rank and file.

Through wavering swells of dust and smoke, Lieutenant Custer saw at a glance that General Heintzelman's whole division was crumbling under a raking cross fire. "We're flanked! We're flanked!" raged from one end of the right wing to the other.

Rebel "redlegs," bouncing over the bumpy ground on their clanking caissons, returned a vocal salvo: "Push ahaid, boys!" "Pitch into them damn Yankees!" "Drive 'em into the Potomac!"

Reaching the foot of the ridge, Custer noticed for the first time that Captain Griffin's mounted artillerymen had abandoned their guns on the heights, but were dragging their unlimbered ammunition

37

wagons after them. What disorder! It was every man for himself, and devil take the hindmost.

Custer urged Old Wellington alongside Lieutenant Drummond, who seemed uncommonly cool. "Where do we go from here?" he shouted.

"The Major says head for Heintzelman!"

"If this is a retreat, sir, we'd do well to cover it!"

Both he and his senior officer knew how a massive rush of enemy cavalry could cut fleeing infantrymen to pieces. Leading Company G, they rode at full gallop over smoke-drifted fields and into the ramble-scramble Federal lines.

Custer saw hundreds of panic-stricken recruits throw down their rifles and run blindly toward Bull Run. Regimental officers darted to and fro, beating deserters over the head and shoulders with scabbards and the flats of swords, rasping and snarling, "Come back, you arrant cowards! Pick up those weapons! Back into line! You goddamn' poltroons, stand and fight!" Others, at the same instant, were shoving their way in a wild-eyed daze through shattered ranks of cursing diehards, sputtering and bawling, "Turn back! Turn back! We're whipped! We're whipped!"

Custer grabbed one of these political appointees by the arm. "What d'you mean, 'Turn back'? Why aren't we fighting?"

"We're whipped, that's why!" the youth gasped, fear etched on his pimply face. "We're all in retreat. You're all to go back."

"Who says we're whipped? Who ordered a retreat?"

"General McDowell!"

Custer released his grip on the youth's arm. "You're lucky I don't shoot you," he growled, then raced through the mad chaos toward Bull Run.

Custer and the 2nd U.S. Cavalry were again separated for a short while. Plunging headlong into the retreating masses, he caught sight of a covered wagon—the 3rd Division H.Q. van—rolling along Warrenton Pike in a storm of dust. Guarding it was Company G.

Cutting across the swarming field, bowling men over as he went, Custer charged onto the pike and up to the wagon. "Make way there!" the driver was shouting. He gagged and coughed in the powdery fog. "Make way for the General!" In front of the wagon,

Major Palmer and several troopers were swinging their hats and bellowing, "Clear the way!"

Through open flaps at the rear, Custer saw grizzled old Brigadier General Samuel P. Heintzelman sitting with a bloody handkerchief wrapped around his head. There was no doubt about it now. The Union Army was officially on the run!

Howling, clawing hordes mobbed the stone bridge spanning Bull Run. Through choking heat and dust, Lieutenant Custer noticed hundreds of others scrambling down the steep banks and stumbling across the creek. Wagons and guns, jammed on the bridge, were heaved into the water by the crush of frantic soldiers. Rearing, whinnying artillery horses and kicking, braying transport mules were cut loose from their traces and mounted by two or three men together. Ambulance drivers lashed their straining teams, grinding at a funeral pace over the bridge, their vehicles packed with unwounded troops and dozens of runaways hanging on the sides and back.

Custer was so disgusted he felt like crying. His own fear, conquered, turned to hatred against those less self-reliant and adventurous, less reckless and strong-willed, than himself.

He jogged over the stone bridge behind the Headquarters wagon. On Centerville Pike he urged Old Wellington up alongside Major Palmer, whose dust-begrimed face was twisted with a black look.

"Beg pardon, sir, but why are we retreating?"

"Why? I'll tell you why! Because we're licked—busted—that's why!"

Custer thought better of saying another word to his snarling superior.

The road from Bull Run to Cub Run was strewn with castoff weapons and equipment. Muskets, forage caps, crossbelts, jackets, cartridge boxes, haversacks, band instruments, State and regimental colors—even the Stars and Stripes—were thrown down and left to be trampled in the dust.

Custer glanced at his watch. Half-past four. He looked ahead. Ominous black thunderclouds were piling up on the blue-and-purple ridges around Centerville. Flashes of lightning winked white-hot at the garish sun. Armstrong heaved a sigh. Come what may, a good heavy downpour would settle this accursed dust.

39

When the terror-driven swarms surrounding General Heintzelman's wagon pushed within a hundred yards of Cub Run, they found themselves running into a cul-de-sac. The young lieutenant now kept his snappy blue eyes peeled for trouble.

The approach to the suspension bridge was clogged with broken-down, overturned carriages. Suddenly, from a hill five hundred yards to the right, he saw three white spurts of smoke and heard the same number of sharp reverberations. Three well-placed howitzer shells plowed up the macadamized causeway in front of the bridge, scattering a deadly swirl of shrapnel, gravel, wood splinters, and wheel spokes. As if frozen by an electric shock, the clamorous mass of fugitives quivered to a breathless standstill.

Custer later wrote: "One who has never witnessed the conduct of large numbers of men, when seized by a panic such as that was, cannot realize how utterly senseless & without apparent reason men will act. And yet the same men may have exhibited great gallantry & intelligence but a moment before."

Lieutenant Custer glanced around. No one seemed to know what to do! Bolt into the woods? Tumble for cover behind the steep embankment? *Boom!* Wheezing canister shot blasted the roadway, smashing one of the barriers in a gust of grit and splintered boards.

Custer chanced his luck. Recalling Napoleon's *coup de maître* on the bombarded viaduct at Lodi, he galloped up to the bridge and jumped off his horse. A capsized ambulance and a smashed buggy blocked access to the span. Custer laid hold of a wheel, gave a forceful yank, lugged the hospital wagon out of the way.

Shrieking shells burst several yards from his body, showering him with dirt and crumble. The wavering throng of petrified soldiers watched in openmouthed wonder as Custer gripped a buggy wheel and dragged the vehicle aside. The passageway across Cub Run was now clear.

"Who is that boy, Major?" grizzle-bearded, crinkle-faced Sam Heintzelman called out to Palmer as they crossed the bridge. "Is he one of your people?"

"I should say so, sir! That's Lieutenant Custer of Company G."

While Heintzelman's troops streamed in disorder across Cub

Run bridge, Lieutenant Custer (under Palmer's orders) led his platoon up the creek to flush out Confederate sharpshooters who were harassing the retreat from a wooded rise. Scattering the snipers with his approach, Custer and his orderly horsemen forded at a spot where the steep banks had collapsed, then galloped off toward Centerville.

His first battle seemed like a tragicomic nightmare—an unreal, unsatisfying experience—and it stunned his consciousness. He was one of the last to leave the field, but foremost to leave with honor. All at once, fate was thrusting him to the fore with reckless design.

ARLINGTON HEIGHTS: FIGHTING PHIL

THE rain fell in torrents, drumming with a hollow roll on ankle-deep mud. A murky shroud clouded the morning glow with evening gloom. It was July 22, 1861.

Slouched in the saddle, Lieutenant Custer walked his weary horse into the Union Army encampment at Arlington Heights. Not having slept since the night of July 19, he had been running on nervous energy for well over thirty hours.

Too worn out to care about food, Custer didn't wait for his outfit to be assigned its bivouac. Soaked to the skin, he slipped down from Old Wellington, grounded the reins, flopped full length under a tree. A second later he was sound asleep, his forage cap pushed over his face.

Custer slept around the clock, in a driving rain that raged intermittently for nearly forty hours.

Tuesday, July 23. At daybreak, he lurched out of the arms of Morpheus. Someone was shaking him.

Custer shoved his cap back on his head, suddenly remembering where he was. He cracked a sleepy smile and picked himself up. He was caked with mud from head to toe.

"Looks like a fine day ahead," Lieutenant Drummond said. "You're wanted at Headquarters. I think Major Palmer has a surprise for you. That was some show you made the other day. Old Heintzelman was pleased as Punch. Your name was cited in Washington 'for bravery above and beyond the call of duty.' What that will mean for you is anybody's guess."

"Well, I'll damn soon find out!" Custer said, making tracks toward the regimental Headquarters tent. He ducked through the entranceway, snapped to attention with a stiff salute. "Lieutenant Custer reporting as ordered, sir."

Major Innes Palmer looked up from his field table. "At ease, Mister Custer." Without expression, he handed Armstrong a piece of paper. "This is an order from General Kearny. He's our new brigadier. Upon my recommendation, and that of General Heintzelman, General Kearny has selected you to serve on his staff."

Custer smiled timidly, glancing at the special order.

Major Palmer sniffed, sorting out his papers. "Not much of an appointment," he said dryly. "The General asked for a junior officer who could best be spared." He cocked an eye at Custer.

Lieutenant Custer blushed with embarrassment.

Palmer broke into a frowning smile. "Mister Custer, let it be said that you look like anything *but* an officer, much less a recent graduate of West Point. I suggest you clean yourself up before reporting to the General. If I know Kearny, he should take you by the seat of your dirty pants and dump you into the nearest watering trough."

Custer saluted, turned sharply on his heel and strutted out of the tent, his sights set on a bright new horizon.

Custer admired Brigadier General Philip Kearny as one of the most romantic figures of the age. He was the richest man in the U.S. Army. His father, a founder of the New York Stock Exchange, had left him over a million; but he forsook it all for a life of adventure—to become the "Dashing Dragoon," the "Beau Sabreur of America," Kearny *le Magnifique*. This old soldier of fortune, an honored graduate of Columbia College, began his stormy career as an Indian fighter on the Midwestern frontier. Kearny, whose left arm was blown off during the Mexican War, also served as military attaché with the French Army in Italy and Algeria, twice winning the Légion d'honneur. "To him," said Emperor Louis Napoleon, "the smell of gunpowder and the whine of bullets were as perfume and music." Winfield Scott paid him the greatest tribute: "Soldiers will follow such a man to the very gates of Hell." He was now "big gun" of the 1st New Jersey Volunteer Brigade, to which the 2nd U.S. Cavalry had been assigned by the new General-in-Chief, George B. McClellan.

Custer tingled with apprehension and excitement as he stood face to face with the far-famed brigadier—the "Achilles of the American Army," the "Human Thunderbolt," the "One-Armed Demon of Battle"—"Fighting Phil" Kearny. A rawboned "bantam" with ramroddy frame, the "shavetail general" was quick as lightning. His eyes burned through Custer, and a sinister smile hollowed his soldierly face. It was the face of an eagle: fierce, scarred, fashioned by devils. Custer glanced at the empty sleeve pinned across his breast. Kearny sported a flowing white Vandyke, which accented his classic Roman nose. Oriental style, his saber stuck out from his sash like a cockspur. Phil Kearny not only looked gamecocky, but his voice even had the guttural cluck which characterizes that gallant bird. Custer was magnetized.

The General's headquarters were located in the bishop's house of the Alexandria Theological Seminary; and Kearny, an avowed agnostic, greeted Custer with a cynical remark concerning the incongruity of such a place and his own beliefs. Custer, the first staff officer detailed to Kearny, was awkwardly amused.

"You made quite a name for yourself, boy," General Kearny rasped, glaring at him with ghoulish appreciation.

Lieutenant Custer shrugged modestly, fumbling his kepi and at odds with himself to keep from blushing or stammering. "Well, sir, it was my first battle; and I tried hard to do my best."

Kearny nodded sharply. "What did you think of your first big fight?"

"Well, sir, I little imagined when I rode out of Washington with General Scott's dispatches that the following night would find me riding back again with a defeated and demoralized army."

Moments later Kearny said: "I need lads like you. Lads with grit, and pure cussedness. I asked Heintzelman for a Pointer I could trust, and he straightway recommended Custer. How would you like to be my personal aide?"

"Well, that would be quite an honor, sir!"

Kearny nodded. "Do what you're told and you might even make

adjutant general. As of now, boy, you're hereby commissioned First Lieutenant, U.S. Volunteers."

"Sir, I shall do my best to deserve that distinction."

"I'm sure you will. Just remember, boy: Fortune favors the bold. We're sore in need of *real* soldiers, not pompous pencil-pushers. We can thank our inferior superiors, our fatuous moss-backs, for the abortion at Bull Run. I hold a tight rein in my teeth, and I mean to make the 1st New Jersey the best brigade in the Army. Will you help me?" *Would he!* "Now listen carefully, Mister Custer. You're going to supervise the 'physical torture' of four raw regiments of Jersey recruits. I want you to lick 'em into shape. I want 'em hard as nails. Drill 'em like hell. Drill 'em till they drop! Shoot a few if you have to. But make 'em know what discipline is."

Custer nodded gravely.

"I don't give a goddamn what you do, so long as you make 'em into soldiers. Understand?"

"I understand perfectly, sir."

"How perfectly?"

"As perfectly, sir, as I won't hesitate to shoot a *few* in order to make soldiers of 'em all."

Kearny gave a shout of laughter. "You'll do!")

In the course of their interview, Kearny revealed himself to Custer with pointed remarks: "I love war. It brings me an indescribable pleasure, like that of having a woman." And he was never done damning "bureaucrats and rear-echelon popinjays who always hamstring a fighting-man." Indeed, it was the delight of "that one-armed devil" to teach Lieutenant Custer how to kill; and his motto seemed to be:

> Let us fight for fun of fighting,
> Without thought of ever righting
> Human Wrong.

Kearny was brutally realistic—a practical, even philosophical, butcher—and his ruthless honesty appealed to the ambitious youth seeking an idol with whom to identify and to emulate. Fortune could not have placed him in better hands.

First Lieutenant George Armstrong Custer, special aide to Brigadier General Philip Kearny, licked the volunteer brigade into shape—and without shooting anyone. He helped make them worthy of their name: "Kearny's Tiger-Fighters." For this achievement Custer was breveted Adjutant, New Jersey Volunteers.

In midsummer of '61, special orders arrived at Camp Arlington from the War Department. Under the new reorganization plan, Regular Army officers were unauthorized to serve under Volunteer brass.

Custer bade General Kearny a fond farewell. Fighting Phil had made a lasting impression on his fair-haired boy.

Lieutenant Custer was kicked upstairs to the 5th U.S. Cavalry and appointed aide-de-camp to Brigadier General George Stoneman.

The Grand Army of the Potomac settled down in its entrenched camp at Arlington Heights, and spent the fall and winter months recruiting and training for a spring campaign.

Custer and his classmates spent their weekends carousing in luxurious Washington, whose palatial saloons and bawdyhouses were the delight of West Point sophisticates. The guzzling of cobblers, smashes, juleps, flips, and slings, and the company of wanton wenches seemed to ease the burden of tension imposed by discipline and daily grind. But dissipation bred satiety and Armstrong was soon sick of it all. Sybaritic splendor repelled him and he longed for the simple gaiety of Midwestern America. Granted "sick leave," Custer headed home in October of '61.

Visiting Lydia-Ann and Cousin David in Monroe, the "boy hero" was besieged by "hussies" with amorous proposals. He thus became the great scandal of such stiff-necked Presbyterians as the Bacons, who regarded those "ill-bred" Methodists as little better than heretics. And the inevitable climax came when George Armstrong, wassailing with some of his old cronies, swilled himself sick on "rotten" applejack and went reeling and retching,

46

staggering and groaning down Monroe Street, past the Bacon domain, where the staid Judge observed—but hardly recognized—him.

A quaint tradition enshrines this episode. It is the moral fable of a penitent prodigal "taking the pledge" on bended knees before his compassionately reproachful sister, bent on saving him from the deadly clutches of Demon Rum—as apocryphal as the notion that the agnostic-fatalist "got religion" after his marriage to a devout Presbyterian. But "swearing off—take the pledge" yarns were characteristic of the temperance-conscious nineteenth century, with its faddish evangelism and its anti-booze crusades.

The truth is, Armstrong had so sickened himself that (after a judicious scolding from Lydia-Ann for making a public spectacle of himself) he settled with his own conscience never to touch ardent spirits again, a vow he honored for the rest of his life. Custer thus became an abstainer on principle—perhaps the worst kind.

Disenchanted with his unsophisticated surroundings, Lieutenant Custer gladly headed east in early February of '62. His leave was up, and gone were the days of simple youth. After five years of cosmopolitan experience, the old scenes seemed strangely new and unfamiliar. Little of his identity did he find there, and the lost was scarcely worth finding.

The Northern press was screaming "On to Richmond!" and the Northern soldier was in sore need of a place in the sun.

Arrived at the Capital, where he and his buddies sparked the painted women, Autie lettered his sister: "All the ladies invited us in. In some houses they were in bed, but all got up. Everywhere we were offered fashionable wine & liquors, but *nowhere did I touch a drop.*" Lydia-Ann smiled when she read this. Autie was trying so hard to be a *chevalier sans peur et sans reproche.*

On Sunday, March 9, 1862, Major General George B. McClellan—"Little Mac" to the Boys in Blue, "Tardy George" to the world—reckoned the psychological moment was at hand to obey President Lincoln's long-ignored Special War Order No. 1 of January 27, directing him to advance on Richmond.

47

On that gusty day of reckoning, Lieutenant Custer, riding proudly beside General Stoneman, marched at the head of a cavalry and horse-artillery brigade second to none in his eyes. He had put them through a complete course of sprouts. They fairly smarted with *esprit de corps*.

All quiet along the Potomac? "Scarcely a 10 minutes' interval during the day that the Rebels & our men do not fire at each other," he wrote home. "At night, when it is too dark to shoot or be shot at, both come out of hiding-places & holler at each other, calling names & bragging what they intend to do. . . . But we will soon decide the question. The great battle will probably come off before this reaches you. Gen'l McClellan is here to lead us, so we are certain of victory."

By the end of the month, Custer hoped to see General Joe Johnston whipped clean out of his boots, Richmond taken by storm, and the Confederacy crushed. "I have more confidence in Gen'l McClellan than in any man living. I would forsake everything & follow him to the ends of the earth. I would lay down my life for him. Every Officer & Private worships him. I would fight anyone who said a word against him. . . . The greatest expedition ever fitted out is going south under the greatest & best of men. We are not certain whither we are bound, but are confident this will be Richmond. We expect a battle on the way, and we are confident of victory. With McClellan to lead us, we know no such word as 'fail'."

⋆ 6 ⋆

CATLETT STATION: CHARGE!

MONDAY morning, March 10, 1862. Golden gleams dappled a mackerel sky, brightening the drab and dreary brown of vapor-laced hills. To a rhythmic rub-a-dub of snare drums, the Grand Army of the Potomac tramp-tramp-tramped southward along soggy Warrenton Pike. A mild winter was giving way to an early spring thaw. Things were looking up, and Custer bet his boots on a successful comeback. General Joe Johnston, well posted on McClellan's dreadnought advance, had long since abandoned his superior positions at Bull Run and Manassas Junction. It was Mac's plan to keep him running all the way to Richmond, where he'd be "caught like a rat in a trap."

The 5th U.S. Cavalry, Major Charles J. Whiting in command, spearheaded the Army of the Potomac. Ten miles southwest of Manassas, the advance guard was approaching Warrenton Junction. The scouts were riding in, and the entire column came to a sudden halt.

Lieutenant Custer sat cooling his heels with the headquarters company. He watched, lost in thought, as his horse enjoyed a quiet nibble on yellow patches of wild grass fringing the railway embankment of the Orange & Alexandria Line.

"I wonder what's up," full-bearded Major Whiting muttered, glancing back toward the main column.

"Could be they've spotted Johnston's position," Custer responded, also staring as if in a daze. "I hope we drive him across the Rappahannock!"

A few minutes later, General Stoneman's adjutant (Colonel

49

William N. Grier) galloped up to the vanguard and addressed
Major Whiting: "Our scouts report seeing enemy pickets in considerable force on a hill about a mile ahead, just beyond Catlett
Station, this side of Cedar Run. General Stoneman directs you to
push skirmishers forward at once and drive the enemy outpost
back across the creek, then hold your ground till we arrive in
support."

The very second Grier whipped away, Custer touched Whiting's
arm and spoke out: "If you please, sir, may I have the honor of
driving in those pickets?"

The Major said, "How many men do you want?"

"As many as you see fit to give me, sir. Twenty or more," he
added without hesitation.

"Take fifty. Lead out your company, Lieutenant, and drive in
those pickets."

Custer smiled and saluted with a snap. He wheeled his horse
around and his voice swelled with buoyant emotion: "Headquarters
Company! By fours! Guide right! Forward at the trot!" He then
reined rightabout-face, waved his kepi, repeated the command in
a high voice: "Forward *ho!*"

A half-mile down the pike, Custer and his troop jogged past
Catlett Station. Suddenly the young lieutenant stopped short and
held up his hand. "Company, *halt!*" He reached into his kit and
pulled out a spyglass. Aye, there they were, about five hundred
yards away. He could see them clearly. A long gray-brown line of
mounted bushwhackers, with shotguns and carbines perched against
their hips, stood watching and waiting atop the tree-dotted hillock
almost directly ahead.

Custer shoved the spyglass back in his kit and signaled his men
with a flick of the arm. "Column, right wheel—*ho!*" Fifty blue-
bloused troopers followed their lieutenant off the highway and into
the open fields. A few moments later, Custer swung his horse
around. "Left into line!" Like clockwork, the column of fours
turned and fanned out in single rank across the squashy meadow.
He raised his hand. "Company, *halt! Right dress!*" Custer reined
about-face. He then motioned the advance. "At a walk: troop forward, *ho!* Guide left!"

The long blue line ambled slowly onward. Within four hundred yards of the ridge, Lieutenant Custer turned in the saddle and said, "Hold the pace! Dress to the guidon!" He unsnapped his holster. "All right, boys, let's show 'em we mean business. Draw pistols!" Custer pulled out his Colt, and fifty cavalrymen obeyed at once. "Raise pistols! At the command, fire a volley into the air! *Fire!*" The sharp blast of fifty-one revolvers rang on the crisp, still atmosphere.

Custer scanned the ridge. The Rebel vedettes were still there, watching and waiting. His icy-blue eyes flared with anger: I'll damn soon show 'em!

"Return pistols!" Custer thrust his revolver back in its holster and clutched the grip of his blade. "Draw sabers!" he said, drawing his sword. There was a raspy clatter of cold steel behind him. "Trot *ho!*"

Lieutenant Custer inspected his company, from one end of the line to the other. Their performance was perfect. His lips quivered, so he tightened them against his teeth. His tone was sharp: "We're going to take that hill, and we're going to drive those people back where they came from. Gallop *ho!*"

Custer flashed the saber over his head. "*Charge!*" he shrilled, springing forward at full gallop. Brandishing their blades with one wild yell, fifty troopers dashed after him.

The horsemen on the ridge poured down a volley. Slugs zipped and whined, spattering like hailstones right and left, as Custer and his command charged up the slope.

The Confederate pickets did not linger to challenge their attackers. Custer crowned the hill to see them galloping across the wooden bridge over Cedar Run.

Fifty Federal troopers whooped and whistled, lifting their caps and waving their sabers. "They laugh that win," and Lieutenant Custer did his fair share of crowing.

That evening, General Stoneman and Colonel Grier sat by Custer's campfire. The dark-bearded brigadier was pleased with the manner in which his aide had performed a routine piece of duty.

"In my opinion, General," Lieutenant Custer said, dunking his

51

hardtack in a cup of cool tea, "the Rebs respect cold steel more than they do hot lead. We'd do well to remember that when it comes to winning battles."

Stoneman nipped off the end of his cigar, struck a match on the heel of his boot. "Then you think we'd have won at Bull Run if McDowell had flanked Beauregard with horse instead of foot?"

"To be sure! Cavalry is the eyes of an army, and without it a general is blind to pitfalls and crippled by surprises. If we had been kept in advance at Bull Run, skirmishing and scouting on the right, Johnston could not have surprised us as he did with that decisive flank attack. We mustn't fool ourselves that artillery alone will decide this conflict, as General Scott supposes."

Stoneman nodded, puffing thoughtfully on his cigar.

Custer added, "I mean to prove that one brigade of horse is worth all the foot and guns in the field. If we had been given an even chance at Bull Run, instead of an empty promise, we should be in Richmond by now."

Nervous excitement kept Lieutenant Custer awake till 2 A.M., when he finally settled to sleep. An hour later, General Stoneman roused him with a shake of the arm. "Custer, I should like to send you on a scouting party across Cedar Run. How do you feel?"

"Fit as a fiddle!" he said, jumping to his feet.

"Good. Then you can proceed directly."

"Mind if I draw some rations to take along? No telling how long I'll be."

"Take the enemy's measure and I shall personally cook your breakfast for you."

"Fair enough, General!" He glanced at his watch. "I'll be back in three hours sharp."

Colonel Grier stirred, addressing the Brigadier in a dragging tone of voice: "Oh, he can eat and sleep as much as anyone when he has the chance. But he can do without either when necessary!"

"Gladly!" Custer said. "I haven't had my clothes off for a week. I haven't even had time to wash and shave. But that suits me fine. When this lieutenant's uniform wears out, I'll exchange it for a captain's. As for shaving"—he lightly rubbed the blond stubble fringing his upper lip—"I've a mind to grow a splendid mustache!"

A week later, Lieutenant Custer was handed a copy of the Richmond *Examiner*. He cackled at Confederate exaggeration, writing to his family: "They say I had 500 men when we routed the pickets. I had 50. They acknowledge having 300—the number I reported to Gen'l Stoneman. They say they killed 40 & took 100 prisoners. The truth is, they shot 3 & took no prisoners. At this rate of Brag, we are confident of victory!"

★ 7 ★

WILLIAMSBURG:
HANCOCK THE SUPERB

Gᴇɴᴇʀᴀʟ Joe Johnston was still on the run, but it was merely a waiting game for Little Mac until he set his back against the wall in armed defiance.

The showdown finally came on Monday, May 5, 1862. When Johnston withdrew his forces south of the Rappahannock, entrenching the Richmond Peninsula or Northern Neck, McClellan shifted his Army of the Potomac to Fortress Monroe and began his 100,000-man drive up the Neck toward the Confederate capital. The Blue and the Gray spilled blood at historic Williamsburg.

Kearny referred to his chief as "The Virginia Creeper." He wrote: "We advance, not as fierce invaders, but like timid trespassers."

It is a moot point whether Mac overestimated the enemy's strength or wished to engineer a tactical victory both bloodless and decisive. As Lincoln's private secretary, John M. Hay, informed historian John G. Nicolay: "The Little Napoleon sits trembling before the handful of men at Yorktown, afraid either to fight or run. Stanton [Secretary of War] feels devilish about it. He would like to remove him, if he thought it would do."

McClellan wired Lincoln, "All is being done that human labor can accomplish," then lettered his wife: "If they will simply let me alone, I feel sure of success."

It is easy to understand why the starry-eyed Armstrong Custer adored the General-in-Chief, though in character as soldiers they were different as chalk from cheese. McClellan was a lover of pomp and circumstance, of playing a gentleman's war game, of intellectualizing "the business of barbarians." Hence Kearny, who viewed war as "the devil's own fun," saw McClellan as "an impostor."

The romantic and chivalrous in Custer insisted that bloodshed and brutality, for a worthy cause, could somehow be glamorized and glorified for the sake of acceptance; otherwise, men at war must lose their minds. Little Mac's unrelenting honesty and individuality, his magnetic love for the common soldier, were great attractions. Hate his methods, but admire the man! Of course, it was McClellan who would give Custer his first big break. That was reason enough for a Captain's undying devotion to his General. As Custer later admitted: "McClellan is damned near the only man I ever loved."

Warwick Court-house, Va.
April 20th, '62

My darling Sister,

Our Army is encamped in front of the Rebels. We are getting ready for the expected battle. . . . We had quite a little skirmish the other day, and got pretty badly whipped. . . . I was in the woods with our sharpshooters. Everyone got behind a tree & blazed away as hard as he could. But the Rebs made their bullets fly so thick it was all we could do to look out for ourselves. It was nearly an hour before we could get up. I got awful tired of my hiding-place. Finally we were re-inforced, and soon the Rebels were playing our game of hide-and-seek. . . .

Day before yesterday we buried our dead (slain in the skirmish) in the clothes they wore when killed, each wrapped in his blanket. No coffins. It seeemed hard, but it could not be helped. Some were quite young & boyish; and looking at their faces, I could not but think of my own younger brothers. One, shot thro' the heart, had been married the day before he left Vermont. Just as his comrades were about to consign his body to the earth, I thought of his wife, and not wishing to put my hands in his pockets, cut them open with my knife, and found knife, porte-monnaie [wallet] & ring. I then cut off a lock of his hair & gave them to a friend of his from the same town, who promised to send them to his wife. As he lay there, I thought of that poem— "Let me kiss him for his mother"—and wished his mother were there to smooth his hair. . . .

55

The expected engagement will come off any day now. It is hard to tell how many troops McClellan has here now, but I think about 130,000.

Give my love to David, the family & friends, and write *soon*. Good-bye, my darling Sister. Good-bye, all of you.

Armstrong

On April 30, Joe Johnston had been in communication with Robert E. Lee, Jeff Davis' chief military adviser: "We are engaged in a species of warfare at which we can never win. It is plain that Gen'l McClellan will . . . depend for success upon artillery & engineering. We can compete with him in neither."

May 4. McClellan telegraphed Secretary of War Edwin M. Stanton: "Yorktown is in our possession. No time shall be lost. I shall push the enemy to the wall."

May 5, '62. It was a dank, chilly day. Murky mists hung over the James and York rivers, burying the colonial town of Williamsburg in a drift of storm clouds. A drizzling rain sprayed Lieutenant Custer's frowning face as he rode shivering behind "Old Baldy," Brigadier General William F. Smith.

By now, every high-ranking officer in McClellan's command was soliciting Mister Custer's services; and Custer, like a fickle but foxy mistress, gave them each a fling.

For the past few days, the high-spirited lieutenant had launched into aerial reconnaissance and topography for Chief of Intelligence, General Smith. "It is a kind of danger that few persons have schooled themselves against," Custer wrote home, "and still fewer possess a liking for." In a balloon a thousand feet in the air—with field glasses, compass, notebook, and pencil—Mister Custer contemplated "the magnificent scenery" that "is being made the theatre of operations of armies larger and more formidable than have ever confronted each other on this continent before." He noted, pointedly enough, that the balloon was fastened to the earth "like a wild and untamable animal, about one mile from the nearest point of the enemy's line." When sudden gusts insisted on blowing his observation post toward the Confederate lines, where hillbilly sharpshooters took long-range cracks at potting the "damn-Yankee" spy,

56

Mister Custer (having conquered a fear of height) insisted on four guide ropes instead of two. A Shakespearean thought struck him: "O for a horse with wings!"

"I made ascensions almost daily, principally to ascertain if any change in the enemy's position was observable," Custer said. He was first to spot Johnston's evacuation of Yorktown at 2 A.M. of the fourth, thus confirming rumors with his eyewitness report.

When he wasn't volunteering and being selected for special (detached) service, Lieutenant Custer was invariably asked to lead every important scouting party out of the Union lines. In less than a month this boy hero had broken all exploit records. He seemed to work wonders, and only the envious considered him a show-off. Being so much in demand, he thus became the Army of the Potomac's honorary mascot. Custer's Luck was proverbial.

Skiff Creek separated the Federal brigades of General Smith from Confederate General Longstreet's division. Old Baldy turned to his new aide and pointed up the muddy turnpike. "Mister Custer," he croaked, "I want you to take a run up to that bridge and see if it's clear for passage."

Custer snapped a salute. Reining his horse out of line, he sploshed through the eerie fog, far ahead of the column.

A few abandoned villas and tumble-down shacks lined the roadside, but none gave him any indication of being haunted by snipers. The Rebs seemed rather cocksure in their own neck o' the woods.

Custer checked his mount to a jog trot as he got within sight of the wooden bridge spanning Skiff Creek. The dull slipslop of hoofs soon roused a sharp response: "Halt! Who goes thar?"

A prickly chill raced through Custer's nervous system. He checked his mount and slipped out of the saddle. Unsnapping his holster with trembling fingers, he drew and cocked his revolver. He then heard the ominous clicking of percussion locks. Two wraithy forms emerged from the mist.

Before they could level their muskets, Custer shot the sentinels point-blank. He watched their bodies fall to the plank roadway, then stalked forward with caution.

Phantoms flitted through the smog in front of him, and voices echoed, "Fall back! Fall back!" When the spectral shapes disappeared, Lieutenant Custer saw red and yellow flickers glowing in the smoky haze. The crackle and sputter of flames told him the bridge was on fire.

Ground-reining his horse, he rushed to the center of the roadway. With his bare hands, he snatched up the flaring torches and firebrands and flung them into the water, then stamped out a scatter of sparks.

Custer hopped on his horse and splattered back to the waiting column. He tipped his hat to General Smith: "The bridge is now clear for passage, sir."

Old Baldy nodded. "We heard firing ahead. Did you run into any trouble?"

"Yes, sir. Enemy pickets setting the bridge on fire. I shot two and the rest skedaddled. There's no more fire, and the bridge is safe for travel."

The brigadier laughed in his beard. "Very good, Mister Custer. I'll send skirmishers across at once."

Two dead Rebels, a charred roadway, and burned hands demonstrated Mister Custer's report. Old Baldy dashed off a dispatch to Little Mac, citing his *aide extraordinaire* for valor in the face of the enemy.

After crossing the creek, Smith's division slogged straight ahead into the woods and halted to await further orders from the corps commander, General Sumner. Meanwhile, Hancock's brigade (detached "on a scout") sloshed off to the right into a swamp. "If the enemy are found in great force," Smith instructed Hancock, "report at once, hold your ground, and I will support you. If no word reaches you in due course, withdraw, as I will be engaged elsewhere and unable to support you."

Lieutenant Custer, with Old Baldy's permission, guided Brigadier General Winfield Scott Hancock to the projected turning of "Old Pete" Longstreet's left flank. It was midday, and the distant thunder of rolling gunfire warned of a stormy afternoon in the making.

An hour later, Hancock's brigade was brought to a sudden standstill in the tree-girt marshland. Without using his field glasses, Lieutenant Custer at once recognized Fort Magruder. Only yesterday this aeronautic spotter had sketched a rough plan of Confederate left-wing fortifications along the York River, so he knew every emplacement and rifle pit under Longstreet's command.

General Hancock, who was the image of Louis Napoleon with his aristocratic imperial and prominent nose, lowered his telescope and said in liquid tones, "Mister Custer, inasmuch as you have thoroughly surveyed the enemy position, I invite your honest judgment of my order of battle." Custer nodded expectantly. The blue-blooded brigadier pointed to a ridge of rising ground overlooking the fort. "I shall place the artillery in battery on the crest of that hill, directly in front of the enemy's advanced works, and clear them out by short-range bombardment." He then directed Custer's attention to a chain of embankments that girdled the bristling fringe of outworks. "When the forward entrenchments are cleared, I shall send a skirmish line and two regiments in column assault across the dam and into the works. Does that appear feasible to you, Mister Custer?"

Custer grinned. "May I help lead the way, sir?"

Hancock regarded him with lustrously solemn eyes. "You certainly may, Lieutenant. What need I say more?"

Mister Custer presented quite an eccentric sight as he trotted out in front of the skirmishers. A moth-eaten slouch hat was jauntily cocked on his golden-red curls, now coiling down the back of his neck. His shabby cavalry jacket, stripped of brass buttons and shoulder straps, flew open in the misty breeze; and his mud-splashed top boots were gaping at the seams.

"Who's that young guy?" one of the doughboys muttered, affixing his bayonet. ("Guy" then bore the connotation of a grotesquely dressed fellow.)

"Looks like an unpressed gentleman of the press," another drawled.

"Well, if he is," a third cracked with a flash of tobacco juice, "he'll get his fool self blowed chock-full o' holes!"

Major Charles H. Larrabee (5th Wisconsin), who was detailed to lead the skirmishers, chuckled as he shook Lieutenant Custer's hand. "The men seem to take you for some bohemian war correspondent, out on a lark."

59

The conspicuous subaltern blushed. "After all, you can't expect men not to judge by appearances! Shall we advance?"

In several booming minutes, Hancock's howitzer battery swept out the foremost earthworks with a plunging fire. The heavy fog had lifted; and Custer watched dozens of Rebel riflemen scrambling over the parapets, up the glacis, into the redoubt ditches.

Snare drums rattled, regimental colors were unfurled, bugles blared the assault. Lieutenant Custer waved his "shocking-bad" hat and let out a lusty yell. With a roaring sea of bluecoats behind him, he charged across the embankment and swung from his saddle in a rifle pit fifty yards beyond a narrow string of dams. Hancock's brigade now occupied the outworks of Fort Magruder. It was 1 P.M.

Rolled into position behind the embankment, Union fieldpieces peppered the jagged line of redoubts with grape and canister. Confederate smoothbores returned a ricochet fire, sending showers of round shot buffeting down the glacis and swishing smack into the gabioned bulwark.

The Brigadier General and his staff, including a foot-loose and fancy-free A.D.C., crouched on their knees in a mucky lunette. Two dispatch riders had been sent to General Smith—then to the corps chief, Brigadier General Edwin V. ("Old Bull") Sumner— begging for reinforcements. General Hancock snapped shut his gold pocket watch. "Gentlemen," he said between deafening crashes, "it's now two o'clock." His rueful eyes settled on each of them in turn. "We'll wait till four. If no reinforcements arrive by then, we shall have to withdraw."

"But, General," Custer exclaimed, "we've got that fort in the palm of our hand. Indeed, Longstreet is far stronger than we are. But that's not why he won't come out and drive us off. Fearing we may lure him into a trap, he's too prudent to admit that attack is the best defense. So let's take a dare. One mass attack will clean the whole lot of 'em out in short order."

Hancock nodded irritably. "Mister Custer, my orders are to wait on General Smith."

There was nothing more Custer could say. Orders were orders, and had to be obeyed. Or did they always? Exceptions often prove the rule. Many a battle was won by justifiable disobedience, making authority a matter of individual judgment. But this was dangerous thinking. A subordinate's duty was to serve his superior without question. Custer let it go at that—for the time being.

Laughing and joking and swearing like a trooper, this reckless young officer darted through the trenches in a droning hail of musket balls. "Stand fast, boys!" he repeated, patting a few shoulders. "We'll beat 'em! Give 'em another volley now!" Within an hour, every boy in blue recognized "Curlylocks" Custer as a "stout fellow."

4 P.M. General Hancock scanned the thinly treed swampland with his telescope. "Oh, for God's sake," he grumbled, "where's Baldy?" Two more aides had been dispatched to division and corps headquarters, soliciting support. "One brigade is all I ask." Still no reply. Hancock swore under his breath. "Baldy must be in one hell of a fix, or Old Bull doesn't seem to realize that this brigade holds a position which could well turn the trick." (The fact was, Smith had ordered up the whole division to Hancock's support, but was stopped by Sumner, who ordered Hancock to withdraw and Smith to hold his ground. Baldy, in a towering rage, ignored part of the order by not communicating with Hancock, who was left on his own hook.)

Hancock gazed at the lowering sky. Inky billows blotched a mizzly sea of gray. "I'll wait a half-hour longer. If Smith doesn't reach us by that time, I guess we'll *have* to retire." He swore into his patrician tuft.

Lieutenant Custer blurted out, "But *why*, General? Here we are, left in the lurch—not a favorable word from anyone. I say they don't care a damn for us. Instead of fighting the enemy, they fight among themselves. Well, sir, if ignoring some senseless order means deciding a victory and perhaps winning this war, then let's be insubordinate with flying colors!"

Hancock knit his brow. Before he could respond, one of his aides said, "General, look! There's a big movement in the enemy position."

Hancock lurched to the rampart and raised his field glasses. "God Almighty," he said, "they're pulling in reinforcements." He swore aloud. All his thoroughbred dignity vanished from sight and sound.

"General," said Major Larrabee, "what are we going to do?"

"Abandon our position," Hancock replied.

"And be whipped on the run, sir?" Custer said hotly. "Take another look. Those Rebs are massing to sortie." On impulse, he grabbed Hancock's arm. "General, we've got no choice! It's either attack or be attacked!" Custer glared in earnest. "Just give the word, sir, and I'll lead us over the top."

Hancock's scowl faded to a smile. "Gentlemen," he said, casting a winking glance at his anxious staff, "it's too late to withdraw. As Mister Custer has so appropriately reminded us, attack is the best defense. Gentlemen, we move to the attack!"

Armstrong was beside himself with joy.

"Fix bayonets!" The sharp barking of sergeants was soon throttled by a harsh clatter of cold steel.

At that moment, Custer heard a bloodcurdling howl swell from the Confederate ranks. He looked up, saw a wave of gray-coated shock troops spilling out of the redoubts.

Lieutenant Custer jumped on his horse and bolted onto the parapet in full view of the onrushing enemy. "Keep steady, boys!" he said, prancing along the breastworks. "Keep steady!"

General Hancock mounted his charger and trotted through the entrenchments to the center of his battleline. "Aim low, men! *Aim low.* Don't be in a hurry to fire till they come nearer. You must hold this ground, or I'm ruined!" The raging tide of Confederates flooded the glacis a hundred yards ahead. Hancock doffed his campaign hat. "Gentlemen," he roared, "we have the honor of saving an army. A volley, then charge bayonets!"

The order surged like an electric current along the bristling front. *Crash!* Hundreds of muskets spewed. Lieutenant Custer swept off his weathered "sloucher" and waved it flauntingly. "All right, boys," he cried, "give 'em the cold steel! Charge, boys, *charge!*"

With a whoop and a hurrah, a steel-thicketed torrent of Federals gushed over the earthworks and up the glacis. In that explosive second, Custer recalled what Phil Kearny once said to him: "My boy, on every occasion I can make men follow me to hell!"

Twenty yards before collision. Custer saw the solid gray line waver, swerve, fall to pieces. The impact of Hancock's counter-assault was staggering. Two brigades of Confederates broke and ran.

Custer hollered himself hoarse. Whipping his steed on with that frazzled hat, he plowed harum-scarum into the retreating masses. A large battle flag, the Southern Cross, suddenly caught his eye. Veering to the left, Custer made a left-hand grab and yanked the folded banner out of the color sergeant's grasp. In the next minute, singlehanded, he rounded up six prisoners: a captain, a standard-bearer, and four privates.

Hancock's brigade decided the day by outflanking Johnston's Army of Northern Virginia, causing it to retreat up the peninsula, and so ended the Battle of Williamsburg. Little Mac wired Washington: "Hancock was superb to-day." Thus, thanks in part to Custer, originated the sobriquet of "Hancock the Superb."

Lieutenant G. A. Custer was again cited for gallantry above and beyond the call of duty. General Hancock's particular mention of Custer's enterprise in his official report (". . . Lieutenant Custer, Fifth Regular Cavalry, volunteering and leading the way on horse-back") certainly attracted the attention of a G.I.C. in need of special aides. McClellan would keep Custer in mind.

Swoshing through the muggy gloom, and shouldering a splendid trophy, Custer herded his prisoners to division headquarters for interrogation. He not only captured the most enemy soldiers of any Yank on his own so far, but also seized the first Confederate flag since the outburst of civil war.

The freckled subaltern presented his prize souvenir to the adventurer-grandson of King Louis Philippe, debonair Prince Robert Philippe Louis Eugène Ferdinand d'Orléans, duc de Chartres. He in turn, being one of the General's aides, delivered the captive colors into George B. McClellan's hands; and Little Mac, according to military custom, sent the token of initial victory up to President Abraham Lincoln at the White House. Pride, pomp, and circumstance of glorious war!

63

⋆ 8 ⋆

CHICKAHOMINY: LITTLE MAC

T̲HE sun oozed light across a cloudless sky on the morning of May 6, 1862. Standing alone in one of the redoubts of Fort Magruder, Lieutenant Custer glimpsed at rose-warm rays flushing up to the zenith like the brilliant arcs made by showery bombs. It was a sight for sore eyes.

Rambling over the combat area, Custer peered at the fruits of victory. Thousands of dead bodies lay bunched and scattered in the mud. Was this the "glory" of war? Death or Glory! The spectacle of slaughter seemed less terrible to him the more he contemplated it. Its agonizing ugliness soon aired a peculiar fascination. The nauseous stench of bloated carcasses, the sickening-sweet aroma of congealed blood, the striking poses of split-second death—a myriad rigid, rotting specimens of humanity—were unreal to the happy-go-lucky youth from Ohio. And that Phil Kearny was a funny old devil. "My boy," he had said, "you'll make a lovely corpse." In four months, at Chantilly, Kearny himself was to become the victim of an enemy bullet.

Lieutenant Custer stalked into a barn honeycombed by shot and shell. No one had to tell him it was the field hospital. The inebriant stink of putrefied flesh and gore made his head swim. He gazed at crowded rows of wounded troops sprawling around the inside walls: a hellhole of bawling, bleeding, rattling, writhing, gangrenous, groaning Federals and Confederates. Negroes, serving as stretcher-bearers and sawbones' assistants, scampered to and fro. Three huge and heavy wooden tables stood in the center of the barn. A team of surgeons leaned over them, probing and hacking

64

away. Custer saw their bare arms and linen aprons smeared and speckled with blood. Crimson puddles splotched the dirt floor at their feet. Piercing shrieks and rasps of torture made him tremble.

Above the pandemonium, Custer caught snatches of a grisly ditty being sung by a drunken sergeant with a bloody stump:

> "Saw my leg off,
> Saw my leg off,
> Saw my leg off—
> *Short!*"

In a corner by the door, a waist-high pile of amputated limbs was attracting swarms of flies and other vermin.

Suddenly he spotted a familiar face. It was that of John W. Lea, one of his roommates at the Point. Lea was looking also. "Cinnamon!" he cried, bobbing up on his elbow.

Custer beamed. "Gimlet!" He hurried over and knelt down next to his old Mississippi buddy. Their hands clasped. Lea burst into tears and threw his arms around Custer's neck.

Custer, his lips quivering and throat swollen with emotion, hugged Lea till he checked his sobbing with a decisive sniff. "Say, what the devil happened to your leg?"

"You-all damnyankees half blew it off, that's what!" Lea answered. "No bulletholes, I see. You always were a lucky cuss. Say, how far have you been boosted?"

"First lieutenant."

"Shuckins, man, I'm a Cap'n now! You're just in the wrong army, that's all!"

"When's the last time you ate?"

"I reckon I haven't had me a bite in twenty hours!"

"Then let me get you something. And from the looks of those holes, you'll also need some new socks. I've got an extra pair I'll bring you."

"Thanks, Cinnamon—but don't trouble over me."

"No trouble at all." Custer slipped a hand into his coat pocket and pulled out his leather poke. "Here's a couple of bucks to see you through."

Lea broke down again. "Bless you—bless you, man. I swear, if ever I learn you've been taken prisoner, I'll surely see to it you're treated just as kind as I am."

Lea then insisted on writing in Custer's notebook: "*Wmsburg, 5-6-62.—If ever Lt. Custer, U.S.A., should be taken prisoner, I want him treated as well as he has treated me.—J. W. Lea, Capt., C.S.A.*"

According to Artillery Captain Charles S. Wainwright, Lea had reason to be grateful: "The Rebel wounded in our hands, and our prisoners generally, express much surprise at receiving such kind treatment. They had been told by their leaders that they would all be murdered."

The two friendly foes talked of old times, asking each other dozens of questions about former classmates, then shook hands in solemn adieu.

As Custer was leaving the barn, he ran into the duc de Chartres. "Your brother?" the sporty young prince murmured sympathetically.

"No," Custer replied, "just an old friend. Why? Does that surprise you?"

"*Mais non!* In times like these, friends are more faithful than brothers."

General Joe Johnston and his outmatched Army of Northern Virginia withdrew up the Richmond Peninsula to the "Queen City of the South," there to recruit for a comeback. Tardy George McClellan followed in cold pursuit, lumbering along at a snail's pace through nearly three weeks and forty miles of slashing rain and slushy roads. Little Mac was plagued by neuralgia and malaria, mementos of the Mexican War, and Kearny still declared, "McClellan is incapacity personified."

On a bright and sunny Thursday, May 22, 1862, Lieutenant Custer and a vanguard scouting party of the Grand Army of the Potomac watered their horses in the cloudy shallows of a bog-bound river.

Gray-bearded Brigadier General John G. Barnard, Chief of Engineers, mopped his face with a sweat-soaked handkerchief. "The Chickahominy," he sighed.

"Looks like an infernal swamp to me," Custer said dryly. He ran his eyes over a weird setting of moss-festooned, creeper-entangled timber, of gnarled roots and snarled underbrush: a prehistoric bottom land of reek and slime. The deep-black Chickahominy slugged and swirled along, sometimes lost in this strangling morass. Custer cocked his ears. Above the purl of water and the twitter of birds, the shrill whistle of a locomotive echoed in a whisper out of the southwest. Custer grinned. "Richmond!"

Barnard nodded. "Five miles. We've got them by the short hairs now."

"Aye," Custer said, absorbed in thought, "if we can get across this swamp! All the bridges are broken down or burned. Those lively devils left 'em with the bare piles sticking up, but God knows how long it would take to build new roadways."

"If that was our only problem," Barnard responded, "I should lay new bridges. With enough lumber, we could have them down in a day or so. The real trouble is, we've got to stick close to the railroad—keep it covered—so we can draw supplies from the coast." The chief engineer eyed the dark, rustling flow. He then glimed at Custer. "General McClellan wishes he knew how deep it is."

Custer darted a glance at Barnard. "Well, I'll damn soon show him!"

Custer pitched out of the saddle. Drawing his revolver, he sploshed recklessly through mucky shoals and out into the shadowy stream. The thick sticky ooze of the riverbed sucked his booted feet, and an icy undercurrent lashed his legs, but soon he turned around mid-tide and shouted, "Here's how deep it is, General!"

Barnard waved in acknowledgment, chuckling to see Custer standing in the middle of the river with his six-shooter held above his head and the water eddying around his armpits.

Suddenly it struck the old brigadier's mind. Lieutenant Custer was a perfect target for enemy pickets lurking in bushes and trees along the other bank! Did that young fool realize it, or was he blindly showing off in his notorious fashion? Custer's Luck? Poppycock!

Barnard motioned for Custer to come back. Custer, pretending not to see his signal, swished about face and waded all the way across. The General half laughed, half swore into his silvery beard. He licked dry lips, unconsciously fidgeted with slackened reins. Sooner or later that "precious fool" would get his curly head blown off.

Mister Custer scrambled up the spongy bank and slipped into a swampy thicket. He vanished from sight.

General Barnard watched and waited for what seemed an eternity. He strained his ears, expecting any second to hear the vibrant crack of a pistol or musket. At long last his tight nerves were loosened. Lieutenant Custer crept out of the brush, grinning broadly, and waved "all's well" with his shiny Colt. Barnard drew a deep breath, beckoned with his own revolver.

Fortune favors the bold! Every day this daredevil was proving himself an exception to the rule that "the better part of valour is discretion." And, as Phil Kearny so aptly quoted, "Valor displayed by a handsome body is all the more pleasing."

The chief of U.S. Army Engineers mopped his brow with pleasureful appreciation as he witnessed a dripping-wet, mud-slopped cavalry lieutenant drag himself out of the miry river.

"It's fordable," Custer grunted sheepishly, vaulting with a squish into the saddle.

"So I noticed," Barnard retorted, expressing grim-faced approval of the stunt. "We'll return to General Headquarters."

Well! Custer thought. I'm in for it now!

The two officers jogged side by side for several minutes of tense silence before General Barnard finally spoke: "Enjoy your explorations?"

"Yes, sir," Lieutenant Custer answered courteously. "For your information, sir, I got a good look at the enemy outpost stationed on the far side of the river. I was hiding only a few yards from one of their sentries: a lazy good-for-nothing fellow, I daresay!"

"Indeed! And what did you find out?"

"Well, General, after making a careful reconnaissance of the whole enemy position, I found their main picket post is so situated in a bend of the river that it might easily be cut off and captured by a surprise attack from a point either higher up or lower down." Custer added shamefaced: "That's what took me so damned long. I had to get this settled in my mind."

Barnard squinted at Custer. "The General will be anxious to hear this."

Army Headquarters had been established at the Widow Gaines's house, about a mile from the Chickahominy. As Lieutenant Custer and General Barnard were trotting toward the white picket fence surrounding the elegant homestead, Major General George B. McClellan and his staff came striding out the front door and off the colonnaded porch.

Custer at once recognized the G.I.C., with his dark-blue campaign cap dashingly atilt on close-cut reddish-brown hair and his unbuttoned service coat revealing a slightly bowlegged but well-knit body. Little Mac, with his thick drooping mustache and quick-step swagger, was a man to be reckoned with. His fiercely scowling expression and deep-set, anxious eyes—accented by those "melancholy" mustachios—were the outward aspects that most attracted Custer to McClellan. It was the pained look of emotional hunger Custer often felt severely inside, but that his devil-may-care nature never dared to unmask.

The jaunty General and his colorful gathering of personal staff officers mounted their steeds for a routine tour of inspection. Brigadier Barnard paced up alongside McClellan, astride his jet-black "Dan Webster," but Lieutenant Custer fell in behind the cavalcade. He was put to the blush, not because of his daredevilry, but because he looked shockingly unsoldierly. Soaked to the skin and smudged with mire, his yellow hair dangling in corkscrews over his ears, Mister Custer clashed flagrantly with the swanky gentlemen prancing in front of him.

Presently, the duc de Chartres, resplendent in his blue-and-gold hussar uniform, trotted back and reined in beside the crestfallen subaltern. "General McClellan wishes to see you at once," he said, winking.

Custer gaped. "You're jesting!"

"General McClellan wishes to see the officer who went down to the river with General Barnard. Pardon, but are you not that officer?"

Custer reddened, nodded.

"Then please to follow me." The swashbuckling prince cocked an eye at the sloppy lieutenant as they rode to the head of the entourage. "Ah, you went to the river!" He smiled. *"Cela saute aux yeux!"* (That goes without saying!)

General Barnard hemmed solemnly as the two riders pulled up. "General McClellan, may I present Lieutenant Custer?"

"Mister Custer," the frowning General chirped, thrusting out his hand. "Pleased to meet you."

Custer saluted briskly, clasped McClellan's small hand in his own hefty grip. "It's an honor, sir," he quavered, his freckled face a heated pink. He tightened his lips and forced a sophisticated coolness.

Little Mac sized him up in a second. A peacock masquerading as a mudlark! Custer's dark-blue tunic was worn to a ragged purple, his white ducks ripped and bedrabbled, but a starchy bearing and a strikingly intellectual countenance beneath a cocked flop hat betrayed the cavalier.

McClellan dispelled Custer's self-consciousness with a warm smile, a few inviting words: "Ride along with me, Lieutenant."

By all means! Custer was anticipating.

As they jogged forward, the General said in regardful tones: "General Barnard reports your having accomplished an act of daring on the banks of the Chickahominy. Tell me all about this crossing of the river and what you saw on the other side."

Little Mac's rousingly casual manner set Custer at ease. He wasted no words in telling the General all about the Confederate outpost and how easily it might be captured, considering it was situated in a hook of the Chickahominy and considering he had proven the river passable by wading across it with ease. McClellan nodded.

"You know, Mister Custer, you're just the young man I've been looking for. How would you like to come on my staff?"

70

Armstrong was flabbergasted. "Did I hear you correctly, General?"

"You did," McClellan snapped. "How say you? Will you accept?"

"*Yes, sir!*" Custer said, beaming. "Thank you, sir!"

The General jerked his head. "Oh, don't thank me. You did something for me, and I'm doing something for you."

That evening, as the two aides were "taking the air" outside G.H.Q., the duc de Chartres said to Lieutenant Custer, "Tell me, how did you feel when the General spoke to you?"

Warmth of emotion welled in Custer's throat, and his eyes filled with tears. "I felt I could have died for him."

McClellan later expressed his own feeling for that "slim, long-haired boy, carelessly dressed." He said, "In those days, Custer was simply a reckless, gallant boy undeterred by fatigue, unconscious of fear; but his head was always clear in danger, and he always brought me clear and intelligible reports of what he saw under the heaviest fire. I became much attached to him."

"General, may I have the privilege of taking some troops over to capture that picket post on the other side of the river?"

Lieutenant Custer stood with head erect, hat in hands, before the General-in-Chief of the Grand Army of the Potomac.

Major General George B. McClellan nodded. "Very well, Curly! [He was first so to nickname Custer.] I'll detail two companies of horse and one of foot for detached service. They will report to you this evening, and you can make the attack at dawn tomorrow." He thrust out his hand with a frowning smile. "Good luck, Mister Custer."

Custer saluted and squeezed the General's hand. "If you please, sir, 'Luck' is my guiding star."

Little Mac tossed his head. "You underrate yourself! Nothing venture, nothing win. One eye on heaven and one on the main chance. That's not luck. That's destiny!"

In the damp, cold, pitch-dark predawn hours of Friday, May 23, 1862, Lieutenant Custer waded midstream for nearly a mile up and down the Chickahominy. Although the bed was boggy as ever, he found the river fordable from one point of the bend to the other. Hopefully, heavy rain would hold off long enough for the whole army to cross.

In the gray light of a breathless daybreak, Custer inspected his detachment. A squadron of the 2nd U.S. Cavalry and Company A, 4th Michigan Infantry, were in skirmishing order and ready to move. Still sopping-wet from his aquatic scout, he was steeped in anxious thought as he walked his horse along the swampy banks.

Suddenly he heard: "Say, ain't that Armstrong Custer?"

"Damned if it ain't!" another answered. "Yo, Autie!"

Struck with surprise, Custer shot a glance at the line of thirty blue-jacketed troops. Instantly he was hailed with faint whistles and muffled welcomes: "Hullo there, Aut!" "Why, it's Armstrong! How-do, Autie!" "Give us your fist, Armstrong!" "Howdy, Custer!"

Custer grinned. There stood thirty of his old school chums, the very bunch of "roughnecks" who had chosen him as their leader—because he could lick every one of them. The whole company had been mustered in from hometown Monroe!

Custer rode slowly down the line, leaning over and quickly grabbing all the outstretched hands, chuckling and blushing in his unforgettably familiar way. He then paused and reined his horse around, sidling to the center of the ranks.

"Well, boys, I'm glad to see you—and you don't know how glad!" Custer swept off his campaign hat as the soldiers began to wave their caps. "But I tell you I'm very busy now—too busy to talk, except to say this: All Monroe boys, follow me! Stick to me, and I'll stick to you!" He waved his hat and nudged his horse. "Come on, Monroe!"

"Let's go, Monroe!" a sergeant said, succeeded by, "That's us, Armstrong!" and "You bet we'll follow!" and "Give 'em hell, Autie!"

Custer charged into slimy shallows, furrowed the Chickahominy, bolted up a slithery bank. Thirty "Wolverines" came dashing after him. The cavalry forded close behind.

While Captain Drummond and his squadron stood in reserve

along the banks, Lieutenant Custer and his Michiganders stalked through several hundred yards of soggy bottom land underbrush. Not a picket on the prowl. What harebrained cocksureness!

Custer's sharp nose soon whiffed the smoldering smell of campfires. A short distance ahead, in a natural clearing, he spotted the enemy outpost, still "doing a Rip Van Winkle," as it had been the day before. There seemed to be no fear of any sudden move or surprise attack from "Old Slowcoach" McClellan, for whom Confederates held a humorous contempt.

Custer dismounted and motioned his detail to halt in skirmish line at the edge of the thicket. Company A leveled bayoneted rifles, every eye cocked for the deadly signal. Their leader, his hand poised in the air, gave the bivouac a cursory look. No more than a hundred "Butternuts," over half of them asleep, the others just "lollygaggin' about."

Custer felt a thrill of anticipation. He lowered his arm. "Fire!"

A vibrant eruption of flash and smoke burst from the brush, spattering a hailstorm of bullets among the tents and camp circles. Cries of alarm were instantly followed by a mad scramble of half-naked, unarmed men.

Custer leaped on his horse and waved his hat. "Go get 'em, Wolverines!" He sprang forward. "Give 'em hell!"

Before three-quarters of the pickets could unstack their muskets, the skirmishers outflanked and stampeded them into the swamp.

"Drive 'em down to the river!" Custer said, brandishing a Confederate battle flag, the second color captured by the Army of the Potomac's honorary mascot.

Over fifty Rebels were rounded up and herded across the Chickahominy. That was the abrupt end of newly appointed General Robert E. Lee's northeast outpost. Lieutenant Custer reported to General McClellan flushed with victorious pride.

McClellan hoped that this minor offensive action would temporarily silence the saber-rattling, radical politicians and journalists who were bellowing "On to Richmond!" "Take Richmond!" and accusing him of arrant cowardice. In the official reports, Custer's exploit was therefore elaborated as a major four-hour engagement (directed by Colonel D. A. Woodbury of the 4th Michigan) in

73

which Lieutenant Custer, being only one of four guides, distinguished himself valiantly. According to McClellan's O.R. to Stanton, the Confederates (losing over a hundred killed and captured!) were driven farther south of the Chickahominy and one of their railroad depots seized. An excellent example of history being "a set of lies agreed upon"! But under the critical circumstances, the lie was innocuously convenient. It silenced the carpers and criticasters—for a short while.

"I thanked him [Custer] for his gallantry," McClellan later wrote, "and asked what I could do for him. He replied very modestly that he had nothing to ask, and evidently did not suppose that he had done anything to deserve extraordinary reward."

A fortnight later, Custer, his heart pounding, ripped open an official envelope and read the following special order:

> War Department, Washington
> June 5th, 1862
>
> Captain George A. Custer
> Additional Aide-de-Camp
> Sir:
>
> You are hereby informed that the President of the United States has appointed you Additional Aide-de-Camp on the staff of Major-General George B. McClellan with the rank of Captain in the service of the United States, to rank as such from the fifth day of June, 1862. . . .
>
> Should you accept, you will at once report in person, for orders, to Major-General George B. McClellan, U.S. Volunteers. This appointment to continue in force during the pleasure of the President of the United States.
>
> Edwin M. Stanton
> Secretary of War

9

WHITE OAK SWAMP:
EXCALIBUR

"**I** THINK the time is near," Lincoln wired McClellan on May 25, "when you must either attack Richmond or give up the job."

Reluctant to launch an all-out offensive against Richmond, despite the prodding of President Lincoln and the carping of the Northern press, McClellan entrenched along both sides of the Chickahominy and continued to feel out Lee's strength by baiting him on into the open. Mr. Lincoln telegraphed, tongue in cheek: "If, at any time, you feel able to take the offensive, you are not restrained from doing so."

Lee rose to McClellan's bait, but with eyes wide open. He sent "Stonewall" Jackson three miles above the point where Custer had attacked the picket post; and on June 26, at Mechanicsville, the bloody Seven Days' Battles began with a Confederate flank movement that ended in a standoff for both armies.

Captain George Armstrong Custer was in the saddle day and night: scouting, carrying orders, bringing up reserve brigades that saved many a desperate hour. Running on nervous energy, through steaming heat and muggy blackness, he slackened his frantic pace only long enough to swallow coffee and hardtack. "I was in the saddle 4 consecutive nights & as many days," he wrote home. "I generally had but one meal—breakfast (coffee & hard bread). We are now strongly posted on the banks of the James."

Weakened by heavy casualties and want of reinforcements, with his York River Railway supply line cut off by Confederate forces, General McClellan was driven to shift his base of operations from

75

the Chickahominy southward to the James River. This change of base was dubbed "Mac's Grand Skedaddle," which prompted him to contact Secretary Stanton: "I have seen too many dead & wounded comrades to feel otherwise than that the Government has not sustained this army. If you do not do so now, the game is lost. If I save this army now, I tell you plainly I owe no thanks to you or to any other persons in Washington. You have done your best to sacrifice this army."

Not Stanton, but the President himself, replied, "Save your army at all events. Will send reinforcements as fast as we can. Neither you nor the Govt. is to blame."

On the Fourth of July, at Harrison's Landing (on the James), the "Young Napoleon" held a grand review to boost the low morale of his "beloved boys." Mounted behind him, Captain Custer thrilled to the chief's stirring eloquence: "Your achievements of the last ten days have illustrated the valor and endurance of the American soldier. . . . Your conduct ranks you among the celebrated armies of history. No one will now question that each of you may always say with pride, 'I belonged to the Army of the Potomac.' "

With such bombast and spread eagle to inspire an illusory sense of achievement, no wonder the Boys in Blue loved Little Mac! But to such perceptive cynics as Phil Kearny, he would always be "Gen'l Bunkum."

"I shall watch over you as a parent over his children," he added, evoking great emotion. "It shall be my care, as it has ever been, to gain success with the least possible loss; but I know that, if it is necessary, you will willingly follow me to our graves for our righteous cause."

"Our George" made the dirty business of war seem less dirty, more glamorous and rewarding; more an appeal to civilized manhood, not primitive animalism. In other words, McClellan intellectualized "the business of barbarians," restored sanity to "an epidemic insanity," humanity to an inhuman "feast of vultures." Custer could admire and appreciate this—though he, like many others, failed to understand or explain it.

Custer was dazzled by bravado. This war was a great game to

76

him now, and the General-in-Chief was giving him a virtual free hand to play as he damn well pleased. Who could ask for more? Tactics and strategy to him were mere words, without practical meaning. Action was all he understood; and so long as Captain Custer was actively engaged, the whole army could vegetate! And so long as General McClellan was agreeably indulgent, whatever his "faults," he was Armstrong's idol: "the man I love like a father." The "slim, long-haired boy" still needed discipline—and plenty of it—but Little Mac was not the Dutch uncle to dish it out. Curly will tame himself, he mused. Experience will make him a man. Was this a vain expectation?

On the morning of May 31, before the disastrous Battle of Seven Pines (Fair Oaks), a Confederate special courier from the personal staff of General Joe Johnston was captured by General Silas Casey's pickets. He was Lieutenant James B. Washington, son of Colonel Lewis W. Washington, the Harpers Ferry commandant held prisoner by rabid abolitionist John Brown during his abortive raid.

"Jim!" Custer cried when the youth in gray was escorted to G.H.Q. for interrogation. "Jim, you old son of a gun!"

Custer and Washington (a native of Virginia) had been pals at the Point. The fact that most of Custer's best friends were South-erners, hence official enemies, was a standing joke in the Union Army. Confederate greats such as Fitzhugh Lee, John Pelham, Steve Ramseur, Tom Rosser, and P. M. B. Young—all school chums of Custer—expressed at one time or another the thought that Fanny was obviously in the wrong army; that he treated Southern cronies better than his own troops; and that they couldn't understand why he decided to defend the Union cause, except for the sake of his home State. Custer's flamboyant chivalry belonged to the Old South, to such enfabled cavaliers as Jeb Stuart and "Ranger" Mosby, to such glorious blunders as The Charge of the Light Brigade.

Washington had sprouted a blond mustache, while Custer had cultivated "splendid Dundrearies," curly golden side whiskers and mustache befitting his new rank and position, so they joked in the tradition of a hirsute age. The two friendly foes posed a striking contrast, and camp photographer Mathew B. Brady took a picture of them together. With the kindly McClellan's permission, Custer cared for Washington during his detention and saw to it that he was exchanged without delay. To men like Custer and McClellan, this was a gentleman's war; and the age of chivalry had not passed into sophistry.

"I'll never forget your kindness," Jim said at parting. "If ever you're in the Shenandoah, do pay us a call. Yank or no Yank, you'll always be welcome at the Washington house."

During the engagement at Malvern Hill (July 1, 1862), Captains Armstrong Custer and Nicholas Bowen of the "Topogs" (Topographical Engineers) distinguished themselves by dashing along the Confederate lines Indian style: leaning forward, half out of the saddle. Each collected $10 from blustery Brigadier General Thomas F. Meagher of the Irish Brigade, who had dared them to defy death "like two Toms o' Bedlam."

"*Yo,* Johnny!" Custer shouted to Rebel vedettes. "Let's have a wild-goose chase!"

"Catch those damn-fool Yankees!" snarled Major General D. H. Hill. "How dare 'em mock the Army of Northern Virginia!"

A cross-country race resulted, with Custer and Bowen outstripping and finally losing their pursuers. On the way back, however, they fell upon these same "Johnnies" resting their horses in the shade of a few trees. The two Yanks nodded suggestively at each other, spurred forward howling like banshees, and stampeded the untethered mounts. The half-dozen vedettes jumped to their feet, firing lead and profanity at their assailants—but to no avail. On July 17, 1862, G. A. Custer (Brevet Captain, U. S. Volunteers) was promoted to 1st Lieutenant, U. S. Regulars. Unfortunately, that double status did not draw double pay—but entitled one to be called "Captain" instead of "Mister."

Thursday, August 7, 1862, found Captain Custer on a punitive expedition against a marauding regiment of Jeb Stuart's hit-and-run Black Horse Raiders, which had been harassing McClellan's communications for the past month. Riding several hundred yards ahead of the flying column, he spotted a Confederate cavalry encampment on the hazy fringe of White Oak Swamp, about ten miles north of the James. It was 11 A.M.

Custer raced down the dusty road and gag-checked his horse alongside Colonel William W. Averell, commander of the three hundred troopers (5th Cavalry) and four light guns. "Half-mile ahead, Colonel," he exclaimed, snatching off his broad-brimmed hat and wiping a streaky-wet face across his sleeve. He grinned boyishly. "We've caught 'em napping, sir. Shall we give 'em a rude awakening?"

Round-faced Averell scratched his thin imperial, then turned in the saddle. "Bugler, sound the 'Charge'!"

Captain Custer reined his horse around as the scrawny lad lifted bugle to lips and blasted that soul-stirring signal. Away they sprinted, whooping and hollering.

Custer saw the startled raiders break up their camp and scatter in all directions as three hundred Feds came charging down upon them. Riding into and after the swirls of runaways at a breakneck pace, the young captain drew his revolver and started popping them off their saddles.

Finding themselves trapped on three sides, and leery of retreating into the stagnant swampland, over half of the Rebel horsemen threw up their hands in despair. They had lost at their own game. Captain Custer and several others bounded away in pursuit of the few who dared to make a cross-country race of it.

Plunging into the brush, Custer heard a youthful voice crackle: "Captain! Captain!"

He pulled up short, scowling. "What's the matter?"

The scrawny buglerboy bolted into view. "Two secesh are after me!" he gasped, looking as if he had seen a ghost.

Custer darted forward, discovered a pair of Rebel officers skulking on horseback through the bushes. Casting a glance at the frightened youth, he cocked his Colt and said sharply, "There's a pistol in your hand. Use it! You take the left one; I'll take the right."

79

As soon as the Confederates saw and heard the Union officer, both swung about and clapped spurs to their steeds, each heading for a different direction.

Custer dashed after one of them, out of the shrubland and across the savanna. The spongy terrain prevented either rider from making any headway. Custer raised his pistol to fire, when suddenly he spied a rail fence looming at him.

The Rebel officer gathered his horse for a leap and cleared the fence in style.

Custer saw him look back just as he reached the fence. "Take 'er boy!" Custer cried, and his mount hurdled over as handsomely as Old Wellington had in the jump fests at West Point. Gaining ground within ten yards of his man, Custer again leveled his revolver and shouted, "Surrender or I'll shoot!"

The Confederate turned a deaf ear to his threat. Custer took a haphazard shot at the man, hoping to throw a scare into him. "If you don't stop, I'll blow your damned head off!"

Still no response. The Rebel only flogged his horse all the harder.

Custer took deliberate aim and fired. The gray-clad officer swayed for a second, then reeled from his saddle and bounced to the ground.

Catching the dead man's mount, Custer grabbed the halter and slapped leather to overtake the other Rebel officer, who was galloping fifty yards away.

"Stop or I'll shoot!" he called; but the man paid him no mind. Swearing between clenched teeth, Custer fired a couple of rounds at him. This brought the Confederate to an abrupt standstill. His horse reared and tumbled, but he sprang from the saddle.

Custer loped over to him. Flushed with anger, he pointed his revolver and said, "Surrender at once or I'll kill you!"

The Confederate stood fingering a Sharps rifle, settling his mind whether to back down or face up to his challenger.

At last he handed over his gun with a sneer. Custer motioned his prisoner to "get a move on."

Several minutes later, Captain Custer and Lieutenant Richard Byrnes captured another Rebel raider who had leaped from his mount and made a break for the swamp. At that moment Colonel Averell ordered a bugler to sound the "Rally," and so ended another mission.

The singlehanded seizure of two Confederate officers never occupied Custer's thoughts so much as the spoils of war: a beautiful bay charger, a silver-studded black morocco saddle, a richly engraved double-barreled shotgun, and a splendid toledo with its long straight blade Spanish-inscribed: *No me tires sin razón, no me envaines sin honra* (Draw me not without reason, sheathe me not without honor))

Custer kept the saddle, the sword, and the thoroughbred bay— whom he dubbed "Roanoke"—but sent the shotgun home to his kid brother, "Bos" (Boston).

Writing to the Reeds, Armstrong described his cross-country chase as "the most exciting sport I ever engaged in."

10

WILLIAMSBURG: FOR SOUTHRON RIGHTS, HURRAH!

C ONVINCED that the Peninsular Campaign was a complete failure, and that any further attempts to take Richmond would be fruitless, President Lincoln ordered General McClellan to abandon operations and withdraw to Williamsburg. Mac was thereby unofficially relieved of his supreme authority on the eastern front; and Major General John Pope ("Old Blowhard"), with the army of reinforcements promised McClellan, left Washington to take Richmond in a manner that suited "Honest Abe & the political hacks."

The slighted—indeed, disgraced—G.I.C. had penned to his wife in July: "Their game seems to be to withhold reinforcements & then to relieve me for not advancing, well knowing that I have not the means to do so." Now, ordered to abandon the James River base, McClellan scrawled angrily: "They are committing a fatal error in withdrawing me from here, and the future will show it." It did—at the Second Bull Run fiasco, thanks to General Pope.

McClellan wrote home in late August: "Every day convinces me more & more that it is the intention of Halleck [Commander-in-Chief] & the Govt. to drive me off." Major General Henry W. ("Old Wooden-Head") Halleck was no friend of the President or of the Secretary of War, but was angling for power on his own hook. Lincoln called him "a moral coward—little more than a first-rate clerk," and Stanton considered him as "probably the greatest scoundrel & most bare-faced villain in America—totally destitute of principle."

When Halleck found it convenient so to Barnumize, he said,

"McClellan is the ablest military man in the world." But Mac had no pretensions: "Of all men whom I have encountered in high position, Halleck is the most hopelessly stupid. He is a *bien mauvais sujet* [out-and-out good-for-nothing]." McClellan also knew of Stanton's scheme "to get rid of McClellan," and commented: "I think that he [Stanton] is the most unmitigated scoundrel I ever knew, heard, or read of. I think that . . . had he lived in the time of the Saviour, Judas Iscariot would have remained a respected member of the fraternity of the Apostles, and that the magnificent treachery & rascality of E. M. Stanton would have caused Judas to raise his arms in holy horror & unaffected wonder."

Navy Secretary Gideon Welles branded Stanton as "mad . . . and determined to destroy McClellan," because Mac's generals were "mere tools & parasites who will not fight." Kearny wrote that such "has-been" veterans as Heintzelman and Sumner were "stupid, weak old fools," and adding: "It is too horrible to see this Army saddled with imbeciles."

A young admirer, bright-eyed and golden-haired, stood gallantly by his defamed patron, adoring him all the more when he remarked dryly, "Those hounds in Washington are after me again. I'm afraid I'm a little cross to them: that I don't quite appreciate their sincerity and good feeling. *Timeo Danaos et dona ferentes* [I fear the Greeks, even when bringing gifts]. When I see such insane folly, I feel that the final salvation of the country demands the utmost prudence on my part, and that I must not run the slightest risk of disaster. Every poor fellow that's killed or wounded haunts me. If anything happened to this army, our cause would be lost." Surely a man so outspoken, so openhearted, must be right!

As soon as the Army of the Potomac was again encamped in and around quaint colonial Williamsburg, Captain Custer scouted up his old Academy buddy, Captain John W. Lea. A silver-haired Negro preacher showed him the way to a cottage where "Marse John" was staying with friends.

Custer slapped the dust from his dark-blue uniform with the brim of his black slouch hat, slipped the kind old gentleman a greenback, and swaggered up the garden walk to greet his nearest and dearest enemy: "Well, I'll be hanged, Gimlet! You're hopping about most splendidly! Still on parole, eh?"

Lea nodded. "I see you're a Cap'n now. Man, you're surely gettin' as jim-dandy as we-uns!" He grabbed Custer's arm. "Cinnamon, come in an' meet the folks. 'Pon my word, they're the finest people ever lived."

Custer followed Lea into the house, where he was honored with gracious hospitality—even though the entire family were "strong secesh."

After a few hours pleasantly spent in conversation, Captain Custer bade the nice folks adieu and rode back to camp—but not until he had promised to return and spend the night at their house. This was perhaps the easiest promise he ever made. There were two flirty young belles in that country-style cottage.

Given leave by General McClellan, Captain Custer washed, shaved, shifted into a fresh uniform, sprinkled his golden fleece with cinnamon scent, and paraded back to his place of welcome.

After being stuffed full of "Southron fried chicken & fixin's," Custer was invited into the parlor, where he listened to "some very fine music—secesh." While the lady of the house was banging out "Maryland, My Maryland!" on the piano, Lea leaned over and whispered in Custer's ear, "Well, now, what do you think of our two little fillies?"

Custer cast a furtive glance at them. "Very beautiful, to say the least!"

The girls, who were seated on a lavender-plush sofa across the room, fluttered their fans and smiled.

Lea's eyes glimmered with pride. "Well, I reckon you should know I'm having the weddin' bells tuned for the elder of the two: she there on the right. We'll be gettin' churched this coming week, I expect."

Custer shrugged sportively. " 'Hanging and wiving goes by destiny.' " He tapped Lea's arm. "But let me congratulate you on the wisdom of your choice and wish you every imaginable success."

"Glory be man! You must come to the weddin'."

"Well, I'd sure like to, Gimlet; but I could only get a twenty-four-hour pass. We're moving out the day after tomorrow."

"Then we'll hold the weddin' tomorrow evening. You shall have the honor of standin' up with Cousin Maggie, t'other young lady there."

At nine o'clock the following evening, Captain Custer and Captain Lea took their proper places in the parlor. "Old Gimlet" seemed "perfectly happy & resigned to his fate." The Episcopal minister stood in staid composure, his eyes downcast on the open service book in his hands.

Suddenly the proud mother of the bride struck up the wedding march on the parlor grand, and two lovely young ladies sashayed into the room. Custer had never seen such gorgeous creatures as these. Both were arrayed in pure-white satin gowns, with modest wreaths of golden daffodil buds on their heads.

The bride approached her groom, who was decked out in a swanky gray uniform trimmed with gold lace. Captain Custer wore his social full-dress outfit of dark Union blue, garnished with gilt buttons and gold-braid shoulder straps. The best man tingled all over as he offered his arm to the maid of honor, who received it in an amorously aggressive manner that took him by surprise. These "respectable" Southern belles were some hot stuff!

Captain Lea uttered the traditional responses in a deep, liquid voice; but his "darlin' sweetheart" became mortifyingly tongue-tied after the first breathless "I do." Custer imagined the poor girl was excited and confused.

As soon as the ceremony was over, Captain Custer kissed the bride and shook hands with the groom, wishing them all possible happiness in his fetchingly bashful fashion. He then ventured to say, "Beg pardon, Mrs. Lea, but being your husband's boon companion, I deem it my duty to ask you why you failed to answer that question about 'love, honor, and obey.' "

"Well, I declare, Captain Custer!" she answered coquettishly. "Love and honor him I surely do, but I neglected to respond purposely so as to be free from any obligation of obeying. Does that answer your question, sir?"

Put to the blush, Custer was at a loss for words. Lea spoke up to save him from embarrassing silence: "She and her dear mama came one day in their buggy to carry vittles to the wounded of both armies. We-uns took a shine to each other right from the start; so she had me hauled out of that wretched barn, took good care of me in this heavenly home, and surely taught me how to obey a woman. Now I'm in harness, full willing and happy. I reckon that's what comes of love, honor, *and* obey!"

The bridesmaid had no sooner hugged and kissed the bride than she slumped down on the sofa and burst into tears. The two gallant captains rushed to her side.

"Why, Cousin Maggie," Lea exclaimed, holding forth a hand-kerchief, "what are you cryin' for? There's nothin' to cry about. Oh, I know"—he grinned, glancing at his buddy—"you're cryin' because you aren't married! Well, here's the minister and here is Cap'n Custer, who I know would be surely glad to carry off such a pretty bride from the Southron Confederacy."

Custer blanched.

Cousin Maggie dried her eyes, sniffing with a toss of the head: "Captain Lea, you are just as mean as you can be."

Supper was then announced. Mrs. Lea took her husband's arm, while Captain Custer had the pleasure of escorting Cousin Maggie into the dining room.

"Miss," he said waggishly, "I can't see how so strong a Seces-sionist like yourself could consent to take the arm of a Yankee officer."

She looked up at him with a slight nudge. "You ought to be in *our* army, sir."

"And what would you give me if I left the Northern army and joined the Southern?"

Maggie stopped short. "You aren't in earnest, are you?"

Custer laughed nervously, and said nothing.

After supper, all the folks returned to the parlor for some Victorian entertainment. Cousin Maggie swayed over to the piano, beckoned Captain Custer to sit by her side, and began to play. Everyone—even the "Yankee"—rattled the windows in chorus:

"Ole Missus married Will the Weaver;
  William was a gay deceiver:
    Look away, look away, look away, Dixieland!
  But when he put his arm around 'er,
  He smiled as fierce as a forty-pounder:
    Look away, look away, look away, Dixieland!"

Captain Custer flipped over the sheets of music, singing himself red in the face, while Cousin Maggie kept pounding the keys:

"Hurrah! hurrah! For Southron Rights, hurrah!
  Hurrah for the Bonnie Blue Flag that bears a single star!"

Cards followed songs—euchre and brag, the North against the South—and though Custer was quite a sharp, Lea seemed to have all the luck. "Lucky at cards, unlucky at love!" the loser cracked.

Captain Custer stayed till midnight, then bade one and all a fond farewell. Cinnamon and Gimlet had embraced as brothers, shouted "Auld Lang Syne," flung their empty champagne glasses into the fireplace. Now it was time that both went back to war.

Returning to camp, Armstrong was surprised to learn that General McClellan had suddenly shifted his headquarters to Yorktown. Word had it that Mac was headed for Washington, there to ask the President why he had been shelved. Till his return, no big move was anticipated. Well, Custer thought, no sense in staying here! So he rode back to Williamsburg, and a warm welcome, there to pursue his flirtation with Cousin Maggie for several exciting days. But when the unblushing belle proposed immediate marriage ("so demonstrating that your intentions are strictly honorable, Armstrong, and that you do not trifle with my affections"), the bold cavalier was frightened off.

★ 11 ★

ANTIETAM:
FATHER ABRAHAM

O<small>N</small> August 30, 1862, Lee and and Jackson dealt Pope a crushing defeat at Bull Run. Old Blowhard, who had blustered he would take Richmond as McClellan never could, now limped back to Washington with all the wind knocked out of him. "The cry 'Little Mac' grows louder every day," Major Wainwright noted, "not only from his own old army but from all the other troops."

Mr. Lincoln had no choice but to give Little Mac a second chance which the old stand-by, swallowing his pride, accepted for the sake of saving the Union. He wrote: "Now that they are in trouble, they seem to want the 'Quaker,' the 'procrastinator,' the 'coward' & the 'traitor.' *Bien!*" But did "they" want him as much as the President did? Apparently not. War Secretary Stanton and Treasury Secretary Salmon P. Chase blamed the Bull Run disaster on "the intrigues and insubordination of McClellan's pets," adding that they would rather lose the Capital than keep Old Slowcoach: a characteristic expression of their "radical irresponsibility." General Halleck said little or nothing, not wishing to aggravate either faction, but John Hay agreed that "McClellan acts as chief alarmist and marplot of the Army." Lincoln, however, would take his chances.

In the first week of September, "Uncle Bob" Lee and his Butternut Boys forded the Potomac and invaded Maryland. Ultimate objective: Washington. Without a minute to spare, Little Mac pushed his Grand Army of the Potomac northward by forced marches, heading off the Confederates about ten miles southeast of Sharpsburg on Sunday, September 14.

"My general idea is to cut the enemy in two & beat him in detail," he wired Lincoln. The President replied, "God bless you, and all with you. Destroy the Rebel Army, if possible."

Custer was now temporarily assigned as aide-de-camp to Brigadier General Alfred Pleasonton, newly appointed chief of the 2nd (Cavalry) Division, 5th Corps. Custer found Pleasonton to be a "lone wolf" of untamed temperament. Savagely handsome, and sporting a shaggy auburn beard, he stalked with a vengeance in sleek jack boots, a riding whip snapping by his side. This "hide-tickler" was Pleasonton's emblem of authority. Custer never saw him without it. It was looped to his wrist, and he flicked it as a wild bull flicks his tail. His soubriquet was "Old Whiplash."

Forcing the gaps at South Mountain and Elk Ridge, McClellan drove Lee back to his entrenchments around Sharpsburg. There "Marse Robert" deployed his divisions for five miles along Antietam Creek, from one elbow of the Potomac to another. Little Mac forged ahead and challenged him face to face.

Wednesday, September 17, 1862. Captain Custer gazed at a lurid sky, the deathbed of a gory day. Sulphurous clouds of smoke, tinged a hot coppery hue by the rays of a setting run, draped the shell-raked woods and dragged across body-strewn fields exuding the damp moldy stench of blood. Bullets hummed close overhead, splintering the orchards; and spent shot hurtled through the high zigzag fences, plowing up cultivated land with a rasping whir that made his flesh creep. The distant muttering of musketry and the thundery echo of artillery had become so monotonous as to be no longer noticed.

General McClellan, puffing coolly on a cigar, kept an eye glued to his telescope. Mounted beside him, Captain Custer was also watching the battle through his field glasses. On the far side of Antietam Creek, fitful masses of bluecoats were slowly, agonizingly driving shattered gray lines before them.

"By God," the General said, "this is a magnificent fight! It will cover all our errors and misfortunes forever. Now, thank God,

I don't care a twopenny damn for those who have criticized my
leadership."

Custer lowered his glasses. "General," he said earnestly, "the
Rebs are giving way on all fronts. Their center is reported extremely weak and vulnerable. Let's throw all the reserves [Porter's
5th Corps] in at once, cutting 'em clean in half, and we'll end this
war tomorrow." (Custer admittedly wanted McClellan to give
Pleasonton and the cavalry a chance to demonstrate their brute
force.)

Handsome, trim-bearded Major General Fitz-John Porter,
mounted on the other side of McClellan, snapped in response,
"What precedent is this: a staff officer giving unsolicited advice to
his commanding general? Learn your place, sir!"

Brusque, bushy-whiskered Brigadier General George Sykes, one
of Porter's divisional chiefs, blurted in Curly's defense, "General,
I favor Captain Custer's suggestion. If we can cut through the heart
of Lee's army, we can't but bust him up *in toto*. I beg you'll permit
me to advance my division."

Giving McClellan no chance to reply, Porter said angrily, "What
nonsense is this? Before you permit such an imprudent move, just
remember, General, that I command the last hope of this army in
the event of a reversal."

Mac hesitated, perceptibly disturbed, then said: "Custer, I want
you to ride forward to Pleasonton. Tell him to advance a couple
of squadrons in support of Burnside. I want that entire unit to
hold its ground at all hazards. We'll roll Longstreet right up into
Sharpsburg, and that should finish the Confederate Army."

Custer saluted, but without his usual snap. He was disappointed,
confused. What made Mac so cautious, so calculating? Boldness
was certainly not his strategy. He made haste slowly, making assurance doubly sure. Was this the best way, the winning way? Custer
was troubled, doubt-ridden.

He heeled his horse and galloped down Sharpsburg Pike, across
the bronze-colored creek. The fields on either side of him, scythed
flat by shot and shell, were heaped and scattered with the dead
and the dying. He hadn't time to look, but he heard the shrieking
and the moaning and the wailing. The reek of mangled, bloody,

gangrenous humanity was enough to make him sick. Ambulances and stretcher-bearers were everywhere.

Captain Custer drew rein on high ground beyond Boonsboro Bridge, a narrow stone viaduct spanning the sluggish Antietam, where General Pleasonton was reconnoitering with a cavalry patrol.

"Sir, General McClellan desires you to advance a couple of squadrons to the support of General Burnside. He is to lose no ground, at any cost."

"What the damn-hell . . .!" Pleasonton rapped, snapping his whip. "What damn-foolish orders are they? Instead of supporting Burnside, we damned well ought to be striking Lee's center with every last man of us. I'm satisfied that reports of enemy disintegration are accurate. Smash through the center, and Bob Lee can be licked in detail."

"That's what I tried to tell the General," Custer rattled excitedly, "and Sykes agreed with me; but Porter wouldn't hear of it: said that nothing but the reserves could save this army in the event of a reversal, and so Mac daresn't spare 'em."

"Rubbish! Porter talks like a man with a paper gut." Regaining his composure, after "goddamning" McClellan for his "damn-foolish prudence that's costing this army a great victory," Pleasonton instructed Custer to carry out the G.I.C.'s orders.

Moments later, Captains Custer and Elon J. Farnsworth dashed across the creek, up the winding road, over the tree-crowned rise toward Sharpsburg with a detachment of the 8th Illinois Cavalry.

After reporting to General Burnside, who would hold his ground "at all hazards," Custer and Farnsworth bivouacked on the turnpike—in the midst of a horrifying pandemonium. The fields on either side crawled and smelled and cried with death. Sleep was impossible in this arena of the most fearful slaughter that Custer had ever seen. It was difficult to look upon whole companies cut down like so much grain, forced through the threshers of hell. He could not turn his face from death; it was everywhere and blatant, mocking the fanciful glamour and glory of storybook battles, of chivalrous wars. If a man's nature was melancholic, he went mad or learned to live with what he hated. But if his nature was *couleur de rose,* he gazed with unseeing eyes at spectacles that

91

challenged the illusive grandeur of brain-spattering terror. And this was the very malignity of Glory: its ensorceling illusiveness.

Daybreak, September 18. What Custer did was without precedent. Taking one company of the 8th Illinois, he penetrated the Confederate lines at their weakest point. Over a mile westward he swept—past the outskirts of Sharpsburg, past outlying and inlying pickets—through the center to the rear to Lee's position.

"I'm off on a scout," he told Farnsworth—but what he meant was "a raid." He had to satisfy himself that Federal troops could cut through the enemy's heart. The obsession had kept him awake half the night.

Custer's hit-and-run tactics left the battle-weary Confederates stunned, dumbstruck. He swiped at outposts, charging across Hagerstown Pike and along the flanks of D. H. Hill's division, then whirled back again—flushed and exultant.

"I've done it!" he panted, jumping from his lathery horse.

"Done what?" Farnsworth said.

"Rode through the whole Rebel Army!"

Farnsworth scowled, his mustachios twitched. He grinned. "Shall I report that to Pleasonton?"

"If the battle renews—*yes*. If not, it's all the same!"

The battle did not renew. Both sides, having lost thousands, were sick and tired of fighting. So nothing was said of "Custer's Raid!"

Without warning, the hottest and bloodiest battle of the year had ended in another standoff for both armies. Three thousand Rebel reinforcements under A. P. Hill had come storming across the Potomac at the crucial moment, in late afternoon of September 17. They smashed headlong into A. E. Burnside's left wing, hurling him back over the Antietam. Two days later, General Lee slipped away into his stamping grounds of Old Dominion. Little Mac, who "always saw double when he looked Rebelward," was reluctant to give chase. It sufficiently satisfied him that "the general result [of Antietam] was in our favor; that is to say, we gained a great deal of ground & held it." However, "I ought to treat Burnside

92

very severely. . . . He is . . . not fit to command more than a regiment."

"The action of the Army against the Rebels has not been quite what I should have liked," Mr. Lincoln told his Cabinet. "But they have been driven out of Maryland, and Pennsylvania is no longer in danger of invasion."

"My dearest Sister," Armstrong wrote from Sharpsburg on September 21. "You are perhaps in doubt whether I am still among the living or numbered with the dead. These few lines will show you that I belong to the former. . . . I intend to make myself as troublesome as possible, hoping for a furlough—and I would not be surprised if I still have an engagement in Williamsburg. [Thoughts of Cousin Maggie haunted him.] Kiss all the girls for me, and tell them I am sorry I cannot be there to perform that duty myself."

Sick of battle, the spectacle of agony and death, Custer again yearned for the simple pleasures of home. "'Tis beauty calls, and glory leads the way."

On Thursday, October 2, 1862, the President of the United States made an appearance in camp to review the troops and confer with their chiefs. This final and most fateful two-day meeting of Abraham Lincoln and George B. McClellan was vividly fixed in Custer's memory for the rest of his life.

Friday was a bright, brisk Indian-summer day. Before the "council of war" began, Lincoln and McClellan, surrounded by a cluster of staff officers, gathered outside the white General Headquarters marquee to pose for photographer Alex Gardner.

The two great men faced each other—a strange and seriocomic contrast—and for a moment Custer sensed a feeling of mutual admiration radiating between them. The President stood with his left hand resting on the back of a camp chair, a warm smile wrinkling his hollow cheeks. A gangling sulphite sporting tarbrush Galways, he was neatly dressed in black frock coat and stovepipe hat. A majestic rustic, Custer thought. Mr. Lincoln towered head high above them all.

The dapper General assumed his usual jaunty stance, clad in a blue service frock and campaign cap, his drooping mustache and bantam goatee accenting bony cheeks and habitual scowl. Heavy military boots helped give him stature.

After the still shot was taken, the principal subjects entered the G.H.Q. tent for a conference. President Lincoln began by saying in his appealingly firm but modest manner, "General McClellan, I'm hoping you will shake off this bad case of the slows. It's contagious and enervating all around. Why, your army seems to dwindle like a shovelful of fleas tossed from one place to another!"

McClellan flushed hotly. "But Mr. President, I am sore in need of fresh troops and supplies. My cavalry is broken down, and——"

"Will you pardon me for asking what the horses of your army have done that fatigues them so much?"

The General looked away without answering.

Mr. Lincoln smiled. "Ours was a qualified victory. Though Lee gained an advantage late in the day, still and all his forces were pretty badly whipped. General, you should have went after him the next day and finished the job you so ably started."

McClellan nodded grudgingly, perhaps only half listening to what his supreme commander was saying.

"You are now nearer to Richmond than the enemy is. Why can't you reach there before him—unless you admit he's more than your equal on a march? At least try to beat him to Richmond. I say *try*. If we never try, we shall never succeed. Now if Lee makes a stand, moving neither north nor south, I would fight him on the idea that if we can't beat him when he bears the wastage of coming to us, we never can when we bear the wastage of going to him. But as we must beat him somewhere or fail finally, we can do it easier—if at all—when he's near to us than when he's far away. If we cannot beat the enemy where he now is, we never can."

Mr. Lincoln stood up straight, lifting his hat from the map-littered field table. He eyed Little Mac, beaming warmheartedly. McClellan looked up with furrowed brow at the President, who broke the moment of tense silence: "It's all easy if our troops march as well as the enemy. It's unmanly to say they can't do it. What I have said, General, is in no sense an order. All I ask is that you beware of overcaution as well as rashness, but with energy and vigilance go forward and give us victories." He added emphatically, "I regard you as the only general in the service capable of organiz- ing and commanding a large army, and I shall stand by you against all comers. I wish you to continue your preparations for a new campaign, and to move when ready."

McClellan eyed him narrowly. "Am I to have a free hand at last, Mr. President?"

Lincoln frowned. "General, you have saved the country. You must remain in command and carry us through to the end."

"But that will be impossible, Mr. President, should certain in- fluences at Washington be too strong for you. I won't be allowed the required time for preparation."

"General, I pledge myself to stand between you and harm."

Grinning and glaring respectively, Lincoln and McClellan shook hands. That was the end of the conference.

When the Chief Executive had left Camp Sharpsburg, General McClellan laid bare his mind to a sympathetic Captain Custer: "No matter what they say, our victory here was complete. I don't know nor care how he feels about it, but I feel some little pride in having defeated Lee and saved the North. What need I pursue and annihi- late an already beaten and demoralized army? Is there no sanity or humanity left in us? Well, I feel I have done all that can be asked in saving the country. If I continue in its service, I at least have the right to demand a guarantee that I won't be interfered with. I know I cannot have that assurance so long as Stanton re- mains Secretary of War and Halleck his flunky. It's no lie they poison Lincoln's mind against me."

"What does it matter, General?" Custer said with mixed emo- tion. "Let 'em say and do what they damned well please. Feather- bed generals, blackleg politicians: what do they know? In any event, sir, the whole army is a hundred percent behind you. You know that, General. You know we'd fight our way to hell for you. So you mustn't worry, sir. Just pay 'em no mind."

"Curly, my conscience is clear. I have no need to worry. But I think they're all pretty well scared in Washington—and probably with good reason. So I'm confident the disposition to be made of me will depend entirely upon the state of their nerves. If they don't feel safe up there, I shall no doubt be shelved to a subordinate command. If they're at all reassured, you'll see them get rid of me altogether. But it's all the same to me. I'll be only too happy to get back to a quiet life again. I'm sick and tired of the troubles I've had: of being a target for the abuse and slander of all the rascals in the country."

"But they wouldn't dare get rid of you! This army would sooner disobey Washington than lose their General."

"You flatter me, Curly. But don't be foolish. These politicians will stop at nothing to fight this war *their* way, instead of leaving it to those who stake their lives to do the dirty work. Mr. Lincoln fancies himself a first-rate strategist, and God help him who thinks otherwise. I shall say nothing of Stanton and Halleck."

"Idiots, the lot of 'em!"

That night, in a heat of anger, Custer wrote:

My darling Sister,
We have fought the greatest battle [Antietam] ever fought on this continent & were victorious. Gen'l McClellan, after quietly submitting to the dastardly attacks of his enemies, has put it beyond the power of the most lying to injure him. But what is remarkable, his enemies are all to be found among those who from lack of patriotism or from cowardice (and in some cases from both causes combined) have remained at home instead of coming forward & fighting for their country. The *N.Y. Tribune* is among the most prominent of the vile sheets that have assailed Gen'l McClellan. His enemies dwindle down in importance until they reach such insignificant & lying personages as the editor of the *Monroe Republican*. I do not remember his name, but I think he could devote the columns of his paper to a more worthy purpose than defaming & basely slandering those of his fellow-countrymen who have gone forth to battle in defence of their country while he, like the mean cowardly liar he is, remains at home. If I could meet him, I would horsewhip him. . . .

Your loving Brother,
Armstrong

★ 12 ★

CAMP WARRENTON: THREE TIMES AROUND AND OUT

O<small>N</small> October 6, 1862, McClellan received an executive order "to cross the Potomac and give battle to the enemy." The Federal chief still made a play for time, alleging lack of supplies.

On October 10, acting under General Lee's orders, Jeb Stuart made a spectacular cavalry raid into south-central Pennsylvania, burned out the Union depot at Chambersburg, then rushed back to Virginia with his booty. This was the second time "Beauty" rode around Mac's army.

The President immediately wrote to his General that these Confederate *coups de main* and their own *laissez faire* reminded him of a game called "Three Times Around and Out." McClellan replied to this pungent hint that "an ounce of discretion is worth a pound of wit." In private conversation, however, Father Abraham considered Little Mac's conduct "shocking and atrocious." Stanton and Hay accused him of "mutinous imbecility," and Treasury Secretary Salmon P. Chase declared, "McClellan is an imbecile, a coward, and a traitor—and ought to be shot!"

Major Wainwright scratched in his journal: "It is said that what little cavalry we have is so badly off for horses that they can do nothing. But with the exception of the few regulars & two or three other regts., I fear our cavalry is an awful botch."

Having given up with Stanton, McClellan wired Halleck on October 12: "It is absolutely necessary that some energetic means be taken to supply the cavalry of this army with remount horses. Our cavalry has been constantly occupied in scouting & recon-

97

noissances; and this severe labor has worked down the horses & rendered many of them unserviceable, so that at this time no more than one-half of our cavalry are fit for active service in the field. Custer could testify to this critical truth! With its "eyes" half blind, the Army dared not move. Pleasonton's horse were no match for Stuart's; and without mounted protection, infantry was between the hammer and the anvil.

Mac noted on the twenty-fifth: "If any instance can be found where over-worked cavalry has performed more labor than mine since the Battle of Antietam, I am not conscious of it."

With the long-awaited arrival of a thousand remounts, General McClellan finally moved his army across the Potomac and into Virginia on October 26. But for ten days he failed to go after the enemy. Meantime, still holding the initiative, Robert E. Lee stole a march on his slow-moving opponent by throwing himself in between Richmond and the Yankees.

Camp Warrenton. Friday, November 7, 1862. 11 P.M.

A flaky torrent was falling as Custer held open a G.H.Q. tent flap for two high-ranking officers. One of the gentlemen who entered he recognized as Major General Ambrose E. Burnside, chubby-faced and bald-headed, whose bushy Dundrearies were about to make a name for him.

"General McClellan," Burnside said after a warm but noticeably self-conscious salutation, "I'm pleased to present to you General Buckingham, Mr. Stanton's Adjutant General."

"General Buckingham," McClellan said, thrusting out his hand, "welcome to Camp Warrenton."

"Thank you, General," bald-headed, white-bearded Brigadier General Catherinus P. Buckingham said stiffly, shaking hands in a halting manner.

McClellan scowled. "What can I do for you gentlemen?"

Burnside, hands clasped nervously behind his back, gazed in discomposure at the stack of captured battle flags in a corner of the marquee. Buckingham seemed less embarrassed, although he cleared his throat several times. He then pulled an envelope out of his overcoat and handed it to McClellan.

There was a strained stillness as Little Mac ripped open the envelope and glanced at its contents. Buckingham narrowly watched him, waiting for a reaction.

Without the slightest expression of feeling in his voice or on his face, Little Mac read the curt document aloud.

"Executive Mansion, Washington
November 5th, 1862
"By direction of the President, it is ordered that Major-General McClellan be relieved from the command of the Army of the Potomac, and that Major-General Burnside take command of that army.

A. Lincoln"

Custer was stunned. His blanched face reddened with rage as he glared from Burnside to Buckingham to McClellan. He need not have been so surprised or angry. McClellan wasn't. A watched pot is long in boiling, but it boils just the same.

Little Mac dropped the executive order on his field table. "General Burnside," he said evenly, "the army is yours. With General Buckingham's leave, I shall remain here a day or two in order to give you all the information in my power."

Burnside and Buckingham left the tent.

"Well, who in hell do they think they are?" Custer raved, his freckled face red as fire. "I'd damn soon show 'em if I were you, sir!"

Custer wanted satisfaction. No one, not even the President, could sack *his* patron-General! And what villainous folly, turning over an entire army to one "not fit to command more than a regiment"!

Making tracks from one staff officer's tent to another, Captain Custer spread the word. Within ten minutes, every man of General Headquarters had crowded into Custer's tent. Half of them were hot with redeye whiskey, so Curly had a fighting-mad following.

Face flushed with passion, bright-blue eyes ablaze, golden-red ringlets tossed back behind his ears, Custer whipped out his mag-

99

nificent toledo. Clasping the grip and the tip between his fingers, he flexed the blade above his head.

"The motto on this is my own," he cried. "Draw me not without reason, sheathe me not without honor." The aides cheered, brandishing their whiskey bottles and forage caps. "I say let's make the General our President! We'll run those arrant polecats out of Washington, and then come back and whip the pants off 'Old Spades' Lee!"

"Three cheers for Little Mac!" one hothead responded, slapping his holster. "We'll march on Washington, make him our Chief, and lick the Rebs to boot!"

"Mac for President!" the others roared. "Down with the dictators!" "Let's toss that Goddamn Baboon [Lincoln] into the Potomac!" "Lynch Stanton! Tar and feather Halleck!"

In the midst of all this whistling and whooping and wild talk, a dissenting voice suddenly arose: "The whole lot of you: for God's sake, dry up! Enough of this spread-eagle and bunkum! Here's my poke. Fifty bucks says not a damned one of you will march on Washington as long as Uncle Abe's greenback mill keeps grinding. Now put up or shut up!"

"Dry up yourself, Martin!" another growled. "If Mac goes, I go. Damned if I'll serve the Baboon and his Jackass government. I'd as soon resign and go home."

"Hah! Here's fifty bucks says you'll never resign, much less bite the hand that feeds you."

"Take your money and go to hell!" Custer lashed, shaking his sword. "I say let's get the General, round up the army, and march on Washington. All those in favor, follow me!"

Two-thirds of the staff cheered lustily. Out of the tent they rushed, hot on the heels of their leader. Unmindful of the cold and snow, Custer trembled with excitement.

As they approached the G.H.Q. marquee, Captain Custer raised his hand for absolute silence. It came when General McClellan stepped out of his tent. A tense hush fell over the inflamed junior officers. As Custer cried, "Lead us to Washington, General; we will follow you there," the others nodded, grim-faced.

Little Mac stared for a moment at his youthful and lusty staff. He stood a lonely man in the silent white shower, his head bare and overcoat unbuttoned. Custer was anxious to speak, but McClellan commanded the scene.

"I am surprised and grieved to hear such sentiments from my own boys: from you who have served with the Army of the Potomac. You do not feel one bit more bitterly towards those people than I do. I fear they have done all that cowardice and folly can do to ruin our poor country, and the blind people seem not to see it. It makes my blood boil when I think of it. But I owe a great duty to you noble set of men, and that is the only feeling that restrains me. Let me remind you that we are soldiers—alike with the private in the ranks—bound to obey the government we have sworn to serve, whatever its orders might be. Just think for a minute. Imagine the terrible consequences of such a course as you are bent on pursuing, in the very midst of a rebellion that threatens the life of our nation. Think how it would result in cutthroat anarchy; how every army and State would feel free to operate in bloodthirsty lawlessness; how then, indeed, secession must triumph. I would cheerfully take the dictatorship, and agree to lay down my life when the country is saved, but I fear that my day of usefulness to the nation is past—at least under this administration. I willingly accept everything God has brought upon me. Perhaps I have really brought it all on myself. I do not know. While striving conscientiously to do my best, it may well be that I have made great mistakes my vanity does not permit me to see. I guess when you see so much self-blindness around you, you can't very well arrogate to yourself greater clearness of vision and self-examination. But when all is said and done, I am content. My conscience is clear. Besides, I've had enough of earthly honors and place. I believe I can give up the life of a soldier and retire to privacy once more: a better man than when I gave up my home, and left my wife and child, with wild ideas of serving and saving the Union. I feel I have paid all that I owe her. That is why I say to you, boys, it will not do to parade the tattered remnants of my departed honors to the gaze of the world. I trust you will accede

101

to my wishes. Consider them the last instructions of your old chief. Gentlemen, please to remember that we are here to serve the interests of no one man. We are here to serve our country. Well, boys, thank you for listening and—goodnight."

All quiet along the Potomac.

On Monday morning, November 10, General McClellan and his personal staff rode into the lines at Camp Warrenton, where the Grand Army of the Potomac was entrenched for the winter. His farewell address caused gray-haired veterans to weep. One eye-witness (Colonel Francis A. Walker) tells us: ". . . when the chief had passed out of sight, the romance of war was over for the Army of the Potomac."

"Such a sight I shall never see again," said Charles S. Wain-wright, in describing the event. "Not a word was spoken, no noisy demonstration of regret at losing him, but there was hardly a dry eye in the ranks. Very many of the men wept like children, while others could be seen gazing after him in mute grief—one may al-most say despair—as a mourner looks down into the grave of a dearly loved friend. The General himself was quite overwhelmed, as well he might be, to see such affection and devotion testified towards him. Napoleon's farewell at Fontainbleau may have been more impressive—doubtless it was, for the French are great at scenic effect. But I could not have supposed there would be such a display of feeling from Americans."

Tears in his eyes, Captain Custer rode away from the grand review with his fellow officers.

"Go home to Monroe," the General told him that afternoon. "I'm leaving for Trenton directly. Home again, thank God! Don't worry about me anymore. You've got your own career to consider. You're still on solid ground, Curly. I have seen to it you shall hold command of Company M, 5th Cavalry: your old outfit. Your appointment to my staff, you recall, was only to last 'during the pleasure of the President.' Now that he's displeased, we Volun-teers are on 'waiting orders.' You've earned a leave of absence. Take it and go home. And when you return, stand by General Burnside as you've stood by me; and all will be well."

To Custer, it looked as if his much-flaunted luck had finally run out. All his achievements were no account, all his chances shot. He had taken the bull by the horns only to get butted.

The boy hero went home.

★ 13 ★

MONROE:
LIBBIE

A RAW, scolding wind from Lake Erie whipped Captain Custer's overcoat and whistled about his ears as he walked down the snow-swept Main Street of Monroe, Michigan.

People stopped and stared, attracted by the ringlets and the rakish strut.

"Who's *that?*"

"*That?* Why, Armstrong Custer!"

"*Custer?* Well, I'll be————! He's bea-u-ti-ful!"

Curly swung past the barbershop.

"Haircut! haircut!.Hey, Armstrong! When are you going to get a haircut?"

He kept moving, without an answer, eyes straight ahead.

He almost hated to be home! A second after he stepped off the train he felt he wanted to jump back on again. Why hadn't General McClellan invited him to Trenton? Why did he have to suffer alone? What was there here for him? Just the same old faces and a few gawking new ones. Oh, well! The folks (who had recently moved to Monroe from New Rumley, Ohio) would be mighty glad to see him, and he had promised them all a visit several letters ago. Things weren't half as bad as they seemed. Dame Fortune wouldn't dare desert him. She was just being fickle for a while, that's all!

Thursday, November 27, 1862—Thanksgiving Day—found Captain Custer drifting into an open-house party at Boyd's Sem-

104

inary for Girls. All eyes were instantly upon him. He cut quite a gay figure when he swept off his kepi and swanked about the room in a blue-denim blouse topped with a red-and-white checkered neckerchief, his white ducks tucked into black Wellingtons, sporting cinnamon-scented tresses accented by a reddish-yellow mustache and bantam tuft. With his Spanish sword swinging from his belt, and a holstered revolver on his right hip, he looked like one of the Three Musketeers brought up to date.

A few moments later, as he stood gulping punch and "laughing it up" with a circle of admirers, someone tapped him on the shoulder and said, "Captain Custer, may I introduce to you Miss Bacon?"

Custer veered around and set eyes on "the prettiest girl in Monroe."

Elizabeth Clift Bacon, the curvaceous twenty-year-old daughter of Judge Daniel Stanton Bacon, was wearing a fawn-colored lace-fronted hoopskirt that exposed her lovely white neck and shoulders to advantage. Her delicate features were enriched by rosy cheeks and the most luscious lips he had ever seen. Her luxuriant chestnut-brown hair, combed back and knotted in a waterfall of "follow-me-lads," revealed fashionable 'spit curls ("beau-catchers" or "kiss-me-quicks") on either side of her forehead. Her eyes were the dancing gray-blue of Lake Erie. Armstrong was entranced.

The fair charmer offered her hand with a subtle smile. "Captain Custer," she murmured, in the sweetest voice he had ever heard.

"Miss Bacon," Custer quavered, blushed, clicking his heels and taking her soft slim fingers. He bowed, gallantly kissed her hand, saying, "An honor, Miss Bacon. Indeed an honor!"

"Thank you, Captain." She nodded, beaming. "You may call me Libbie if you like."

Custer's face assumed its natural color. "Libbie," he blurted, knitting his brow. "That's it: Libbie Bacon!" His bold, handsome face glowed. "I've met you before. Yes, and you spoke to me first."

Libbie frowned playfully at this perky young spark. "Oh, you must be mistaken, sir."

"Oh, no I'm not," he answered at once, his bright eyes full of fun. "It was—let me see—seven, eight, nine years ago. You were

105

swinging on a gate, and I came by, and you said to me, 'Hi, you Custer boy!' Then you ran off into the house before I could pull your pigtails."

The impulsive gallant had ungallantly routed a lady's frail dignity. "Oh, you're joshing me, Captain," she countered, remembering the incident with amusement.

This Captain Custer was a very impudent young man—but she liked him. His nervous energy and excitable manner of speaking, in spurts and gushes, were at first irritating and then appealing. He was aggressively sincere, gregarious with a vengeance. His unrestraint was overpowering, annoying to men but amusing to women. He radiated extroversion to a degree that laid bare the abysmal depths of his loneliness, betrayed his craving to love and be loved. There was something enchantingly strange and passionate and untamed about him that, despite all womanly reason, struck Libbie's emotions almost at once.

It was an embarrassing moment, so Libbie changed the subject. "Well, Captain"—she smiled subtly—"I believe your promotion has been very rapid." Her deftness at handling boyish men was disarming, and Armstrong found himself at a desirable disadvantage.

"Well, Miss," he faltered, "I believe I've been very lucky."

"My heart could have told her of a promotion far more rapid in *her* power only to bestow," the smitten swain later confessed. "How I watched her every motion, and in that throng of youth & beauty she reigned supreme. I knew it was love, and I felt it was glory."

When Libbie Bacon left, Custer went home to dream.

The following day, Libbie was whisking up the walk of the local seamstress to have a coat altered, when suddenly she spotted Armstrong gangling down the street. Her heart fluttered. Reaching the door, she rang the bell and turned her head. There he was, standing at the white picket gate, looking at her.

She waved. "Hi, you Custer boy!"

On Sunday morning, from her pew in the Monroe Presbyterian Church, Libbie saw Captain Custer in the amen corner. Oh, but he looked such unholy things at her! And she made eyes back at him.

106

For the first time in their adult lives, both Autie and Libbie were wondrously in love.

Monday, December 1, 1862. Captain Custer came prancing down Monroe Street, swung through the Bacons' front gate, went whistling up to the door. He knocked and debonairly snatched off his cap.

The lord and master of the house appeared: a square-jawed, portly gentleman with grizzled mutton chops and a stony stare. Yes, here stood Judge of Probate (retired), President of the Monroe Bank, Director of the first Michigan railroad, schoolteacher, lawyer, one of Monroe's earliest settlers and territorial legislators: a self-made man and model American pioneer whose only daughter was not merely the loveliest creature in town, but "a thoroughly educated young lady," who had been the valedictorian (*summa cum laude*) of her class. "*Ah,* Captain Custer!" he rumbled. "What can I do for you?"

"Your Honor," Custer ventured unblinkingly, "I——"

Judge Bacon hemmed. "I expect you've come to see my daughter, eh?" Before Custer could even answer, the scowling giant forged on. "Libbie, like her Aunt Harriet, has many suitors—many of the mustached, gilt-striped, brass-button kind—more interesting to her than to me. My wife and I have a great deal of anxiety about her, but I expect this is true of all parents of fanciful girls. You're welcome to come in, Captain. I'll see if my daughter is disposed to bear you company."

Custer nodded, struggling not to blush or stammer. "Thank you, sir," he said, and stepped into the Daniel Stanton Bacon domain.

The Judge stalked through the anteroom into the parlor. "Follow me, Captain, and take a seat. My wife and daughter both are so fond of society that this house at times is almost like a tavern." His deep-echoing voice thundered up the staircase: "Oh, Libbie! *Libbie!*"

Custer heard the patter of feminine feet in the hallway above and a sweet-ringing voice: "Yes, Pa?"

"Captain Custer pays you a call!"

"Oh! Tell him to wait, Pa. I won't be but a minute."

"He's waiting. Oh, wifey! *Wifey!*"

"Land sakes, Daniel Bacon, what's the matter?"

"One of those mustached, gilt-striped, brass-button critters will get our Libbie yet!" The Judge lumbered out of the room.

Alone for a minute, Armstrong gazed at two large oil paintings that embellished the parlor walls. One was of physic-faced General Winfield Scott seated on a white charger, the other of sour-looking General Sam Houston with his right hand thrust *à la Napoléon* in a black frock coat. They added something to the lofty atmosphere. The hammering-out of crude America: something a rugged blacksmith's son could appreciate with homespun pride. Armstrong had inherited the iron hands of his father, and there was still a raw frontier to forge.

The young romantic was roused from his daydreaming when Libbie Bacon came skipping down the stairs, her winter coat slung over her arm.

"Hi, Autie." She beamed, brisk as a lakeland breeze. "Or should I address you as Captain?"

Custer lurched to his feet, bowed and kissed her extended hand. "If you're Libbie, I'm Autie!"

"So be it, Autie!"

"Well, you're sure a frisky one today! I thought you might like to go for a sleigh ride along the lake."

"Just the two of us?"

"Of course!"

"I'm an only child," she later told him, "but I wasn't spoiled. Ma died when I was twelve. Pa remarried, but it wasn't the same. How shamelessly I traded on this. What an excuse I made of it for not doing anything I didn't want to do. And what excuses were made for me on that score!"

"Your father doesn't like me, does he?" Armstrong would ask.

"Oh, pay no mind to that. Pa doesn't like any of my sparkers, especially those in uniform. He says all you soldiers are addicted to Demon Rum."

"Ha! Your father should know the Custers better than that. We're not a drinking family, even though we *are* Methodists."

"Tell that to a hidebound Presbyterian! Oh, but I mustn't talk that way. I'm such a creature of guilt, steeped in sin."

"To be sure! I don't think the Judge would approve of this sleigh ride. We're having too much fun!"

"Oh, he's not as bad as all that. Pa just has his old-school ways, that's all. He told me I may laugh and play to my heart's content, and promenade in good weather, but I mustn't ride on fast horses— and *no* boat rides—and have as little to do with fast young men as is consistent with propriety."

"Nothing about sleigh rides, though."

"You know, Autie, sometimes I worry about Pa. Why, I'm even unpatriotic enough to feel glad he's too old; because he certainly would have gone to fight for the Union."

"And made a fierce general!"

"I suppose you'll be a general someday."

"If I'm lucky."

"Luck isn't everything, Autie. When you have an aim in life, you've got to go after it. It doesn't just come to you."

"You don't have to tell me that! The army is a good teacher in that respect. Pardon my asking, but do *you* have a particular aim in life?"

"Well, now, I'm glad you asked that question; because I can't understand how any girl can go through life without an Aim. It's not *all* a man's world, you know."

"Well, I won't be one to argue that! So you have an aim then."

"Yes."

"What's that?"

"*You.*"

For the next couple of weeks, with one eye on her suspecting father and the other on her beau, Libbie Bacon laughingly informed all her taletelling female friends: "It never fails. Whenever I put my nose out of doors, I have the escort of one of General McClellan's staff: Captain Custer. . . . Oh, no, I don't care for him *except* as an escort."

But George Armstrong Custer didn't beg the question. He made it

109

known to one and all that he was going to marry Elizabeth Clift Bacon, come hell or high water. "I was not ignorant of her father's proclivities, of the well-nigh insurmountable obstacles," he admitted. Yet he dared to fish in troubled waters. To him, Judge Bacon was just another challenge to be met and mastered. And when Miss Bacon's legion of sparkers withdrew in favor of the fearless Captain Custer, Libbie found herself buffeting the waves of paternal protest.

"I don't want that hellion in my house," the Judge boomed. "I forbid you to invite him here or have anything more to do with him. No daughter of mine is going to be the scandalous talk of the town."

Libbie was almost in tears. "Oh, Pa, how can you say such things? I told Mother of my relationship with Captain Custer, and she wants me to enjoy myself as much as I can."

"*Hem!* Never you mind what Mother says. I forbid you chasing after that man like some lovesick calf."

"Well, Pa, it just so happens I like him very much; and besides, it's pleasant always to have an escort to depend on." Tears welled in her eyes and trickled down her burning cheeks. "But I'm sorry I've been with him so much, and you'll never see me in the street with him again—and never here at the house except to say goodbye. I'll tell him never to meet me, and he has the sense to understand."

"Well, then, you promise never to see him again?"

"No, Pa. I won't promise *never* to see him again. But I won't cause you any more trouble, just be sure of that."

"Now listen here, young lady——!"

"Oh, Pa, you've never been a girl. You can't tell how hard a trial this is for me. I never had a trial that made me feel so badly. I love Armstrong Custer—yes, I *love* him—and the Monroe people will please mind their own business and let me alone. If the whole world oh'd and ah'd, it would not hurt me as much as your displeasure. So don't blame Captain Custer. He has many fine traits, and Monroe will yet be proud of him. Oh, Pa, it would make me so happy knowing you place your entire confidence in me. But I suppose that's too much to hope for."

Libbie turned and ran upstairs. Judge Bacon heaved a sigh and stomped out to get some air.

Armstrong's amorous aspirations by no means overshadowed his glory-hunting ambition. They were a vehicle, a goad. They made ambition worth while and meaningful. Learning that Governor Austin Blair contemplated the formation of a new volunteer cavalry regiment, the 7th Michigan, Captain Custer made a bid for colonelcy. When Blair ignored his application, Custer was reminded of the fact that only political appointees were commissioned to command volunteer outfits. How to become a political appointee? With the endorsement of Congressman John A. Bingham, Armstrong approached Judge Isaac P. Christiancy, influential member of the Michigan Supreme Court and father of the State's Republican party. Charmed by the bold yet modest youth, Christiancy spoke to the Governor. Blair shook his head. "Custer is using you to his own advantage, just as he used Bingham. His people are rabid Democrats. He himself is a McClellan man; McClellan's fair-haired boy, I should say. Sorry, Your Honor, but I cannot place myself in such a compromising position, whatever his qualifications. No, I have nothing for him."

"I'm sorry, my boy, but Governor Blair says he has nothing for you." The Judge had tried!

Custer nodded glumly, thanking him for his efforts. Damnation! He had failed ingloriously in his attempt to impress and persuade a second judge, as influential as the first, who had flatly refused to patronize him in any way. The Custers were "quite ordinary people"—ultraconservative Democrats and backwoods Methodists, by God!—with whom cosmopolitan and progressive (Republican-Presbyterian) folk did not associate.

In the third week of December, 1862, staggering news reached Monroe of a Union fiasco at Fredericksburg. Reacting radically to McClellan's conservatism, Burnside as much as ordered the Army of the Potomac to commit suicide. On December 13, "Old Ace of Spades" Lee dealt this "bungling boozer" a disastrous defeat. "We

111

have hard times," Judge Bacon lamented, "and the worst is yet to come."

Mr. Lincoln again lowered the axe, this time on Old Burnie's head. "Having got rid of McClellan does not seem to satisfy them [Stanton and Halleck]," Major Wainwright noted. "They would have every man killed off that ever served under him." After Governor Blair's refusal of an appointment, because he was a "McClellan man," Custer was of like opinion: that the Radicals were out to "get" the Reactionaries.

January 26, 1863, found Major General Joseph Hooker in full command. Captain Custer vaguely remembered "Fighting Joe": tall, athletic, clean-shaven.

"My plans are perfect," the new G.I.C. gasconaded. "May God have mercy on General Lee, for I'll have none!" But Hooker had acquired his nickname by accident, not incident. (A careless typesetter, instead of headlining FIGHTING—JOE HOOKER, omitted the em dash and thus perpetrated a paradox)

"I am asked on all sides here if he [Hooker] drinks," Wainwright scratched in his journal. "Indeed, I should say that his failing was more in the way of women than whiskey." Joe was a "genial toper" to his admirers, but to such critics as historians (then Captain) Charles Francis Adams he was "little better than a drunken West Point military adventurer" whose headquarters were "a combination of bar-room and brothel, . . . a place to which no self-respecting man liked to go, and no decent woman could go." The temperate McClellan was being replaced with dissipaters, whose incompetence was beyond the control of political hacks and warmongering opportunists. Custer acknowledged the notoriety of Fighting Joe as a brandy-faced lecher, whence the term "hooker," a large drink and a luring doxy. Alas, the Grand Army of the Potomac had lost all its grandeur in a popping of corks and squealing of wenches. General Headquarters was general disorder.

Custer, who looked not upon the wine when it is red, wanted no part of this cockeyed crew. Besides, he was waging his own private war on the homefront, with an indefinite leave to win or lose. Love was now the challenge. Let glory wait till spring, and a new General-in-Chief—perhaps, hopefully, Little Mac.

112

Army morale hit an all-time low when the War Department's General Orders No. 1 for 1863 contained the President's Emancipation Proclamation. Custer, like a good Democrat, agreed that it was "issued to please the Radicals" and "to estrange the whole population of the Southern States, to turn into Rebels those who have heretofore been Union men, and to still further embitter the feelings of all." He wrote to McClellan: "Where, but in Radical circles, do we hear Slavery mentioned as an issue? The Union— it is the *Union* we are fighting for! Those Black Republicans & fanatic Abolitionists ought to be horse-whipped, beginning with Sen. Wade & ending with Mr. Greeley." Indeed, Custer held Sherman's view that the war was not caused by slavery, but "was all the result of the machinations of unscrupulous politicians scheming for power, working upon a restless people who were suffering from an overdose of democracy."

Autie and Libbie continued to see each other on the sly until the end of January, when Captain Custer received an unexpected invitation from General McClellan to appear at his just-acquired New York mansion.

Custer was at cross-purposes. He certainly wanted to see McClellan again—for that might be to his professional advantage— but he feared leaving his sweetheart in the midst of their romantic crisis. And yet, until he had proven himself worthy of her, a longer stay in Monroe *did* seem hopeless. As he had always known, there was no glory to be won at home. Here he was running in circles, slashing at shadows.

When Judge Bacon learned that General Joe Hooker had been appointed big gun of the Army of the Potomac, a diehard pro-Lincoln Republican was suddenly—miraculously—transformed into a bitter-end pro-McClellan Democrat.

"Scandalous," he bellowed. "Scandalous, I say. Two drunkards in a row. Well, this is the last straw. Burnside was a blunderhead, and just you wait and see: that Hooker will sow the wind and reap the whirlwind. McClellan never drank and never lost a battle. If he erred, he did not err through strong drink."

113

"Nor did his right-hand man, Captain Custer," Libbie interjected pertly.

"How's that, young lady?"

"You know perfectly well, Pa, that Armstrong Custer never touches the Demon Rum."

"No, I mean about his being McClellan's right-hand man."

"Why, I thought you already knew that, Pa!"

The Judge shook his head. "I knew the lad was on McClellan's staff, but never that he was the General's special aide."

Libbie thrilled. "Oh, Pa, he's the General's best friend! He's his closest confidant. Why, of all his personal staff, McClellan invited Autie to come to New York and help him write his official report for the President."

The Judge leered. "And who told you that, young lady?"

Libbie blushed.

"Never mind. McClellan is the only sober man left to save the Union. And any friend of the General's is a friend of mine. When is Captain Custer leaving for New York?"

Libbie's heart fluttered. "Tomorrow morning."

"Good. Then we can have him to dinner this evening and give him a hero's send-off at the station in the morning. It's about time one of Monroe's leading citizens honored one of her most worthy sons."

Custer blushed at a glorious send-off, complete with three-piece band. Libbie blew him a dozen kisses; and away he chugged in a drift of steam, waving his cap from the rear platform of the caboose.

★ 14 ★

BRANDY STATION:
OLD WHIPLASH

C APTAIN George Armstrong Custer, "awaiting orders," enjoyed a two-month stay in the Big City with Major General and Mrs. George B. McClellan. Armstrong agreed with Major Wainwright that "New York seems to be more wild with gaiety than ever. Money is worth nothing a bushel, and 'shoddy' reigns supreme." Indeed, the city still flaunted its gay sophisticated identity, apparently indifferent that a great civil war was raging. Custer found this apathetic self-indulgence stupid and disgusting—nay, outrageously unpatriotic—and took a decided dislike to the fool's paradise of speculators, profiteers, and Copperheads. The country-bred conservative was naturally shy of the cynical liberality of the city, sick of "idleness, dissipation & theatre-going."

With Custer's able assistance, McClellan quickly composed his voluminous *Report on the Organization of the Army of the Potomac, and Its Campaigns in Virginia & Maryland*. It was a prosaic, unadorned reflection of the author's perfectionistic precision. Wainwright adjudged it the work of "a man confident in the purity of his intentions & the perfect honesty of all his actions," without "the least attempt to shift responsibility on the shoulders of his subordinates. Thro' the whole report runs a care & consideration for his men, an actual love for his army, which is most beautiful. No wonder we all loved him if there is any truth in the old proverb that 'love begets love.' " Thus the secret of McClellan's success—and failure.

115

On April 16, 1863, a special order arrived in New York from Washington. Brevet Captain G. A. Custer, relieved of "nominal staff duty," was to report for active duty with his regiment.

Sallying forth from winter quarters along the Rappahannock, General Hooker and the Army of the Potomac were launching their first offensive against General Lee and the Army of Northern Virginia in the foredoomed spring campaign of '63. Reorganization and reinforcement of the old G.A.P. included the formation (in February of '63) of a three-division Cavalry Corps commanded by one of Custer's old patrons, Major General George Stoneman. Wainwright esteemed it as "probably the largest body of cavalry ever seen on this continent—there being 11,000, it is said"— without knowing that J. E. B. Stuart was now nearly as strong.

Little Mac bade Curly Godspeed and sped the parting guest on his way south.

The day he rode into Camp Falmouth, Captain Custer was summoned to the headquarters tent of the 1st Cavalry Division. There he was greeted by whip-cracking Brigadier General Alfred Pleasonton.

"Curly," he snapped, flicking his hide-tickler, "I want you as my special aide. I'll make no bones about it: you're a man after my own heart. Pure rambunction. Well, will you accept?"

"Indeed I will, sir!" Custer answered at once, grinning broadly. So they shook on it.

Hallelujah! He was back in the staff-officer's saddle again, now special aide to Hooker's soon-to-be Chief of Cavalry. Things *militaire* were looking up once more.

A few moments later, the red-faced G.I.C. came reeling into Pleasonton's tent. "Al," he blared, "we've got to set 'em up for the kill: cut Lee's communications and supply lines. By God, if Stoneman doesn't do it, I'll sack him and take command of the cavalry myself! Who ever saw a dead cavalryman? Why, I've yet to see one! 'Let your watchword be *fight, fight, fight,*' I told him; 'and let all your orders be *Fight!*' And what does he report? Can't fight—can't even *move*—because the river's in flood. God damn it!" Hooker lurched out of the tent, grumbling, "Who ever heard

116

of a dead cavalryman? I'll offer a hundred-bucks reward for a dead cavalryman!"

"What does he mean by that?" Custer said with a sneer.

Pleasonton snorted. "That the cavalry wasn't worth powder to blow it to hell till he ordered its reorganization and expansion. Well and good. But its value hasn't increased with the appointment of Stoneman: a first-rate brigadier, a second-rate division commander, and a third-rate corps commander."

On April 13, Hooker had sent Stoneman with the 2nd (Gregg's) and 3rd (Averell's) Divisions up to the Rappahannock on a flank movement to chop off Lee's rear and so "set him up for the kill," a massive assault left and center. However, thanks to heavy rains, the river swelled to such a size that Stoneman dared not cross— and so was stranded on the north bank, at Rappahannock Station, where Lee could watch him and smile. Mother Nature had checkmated Fighting Joe's brilliant move, but she could not check his ardor.

When sober, Hooker penned to the President: "We have the finest army on the planet. The enemy must either ingloriously fly or come out from behind his defences & give us battle on our own ground, where certain destruction awaits him."

When drunk, the General telegraphed: "I will either win a victory or go to Hell."

Lincoln wired back: "Carry plenty of water along."

"God Almighty cannot deliver Lee from my hands!" Hooker concluded.

Fighting Joe was whistling down the wind. On Sunday, May 3, 1863, the Grand Army of the Potomac suffered a slaughterous stampede at Chancellorsville. Horace Greeley, one of the sharptoothed old journalists whom Custer wanted to horsewhip, poured out vials of inky wrath: "My God, it is horrible—*horrible!* And to think of it: 130,000 magnificent soldiers so cut to pieces by 60,000 half-starved ragamuffins." Crusty old James Gordon Bennett of the *Herald,* who deemed competitor Greeley "a fit subject for the gallows," was inclined to agree—and demanded the reinstatement of McClellan, "the only man who can save the Union."

Old Whiplash Pleasonton saved the shattered Federal infantry from further disaster by heading off Stonewall Jackson's massive flank movement at Hazel Grove, about a mile from Chancellorsville.

Commandeering abandoned artillery, Pleasonton accosted Colonel Pennock Huey of the 8th Pennsylvania Cavalry: "Sir, you must charge into those woods with your regiment and hold the Rebels until I can get some of these guns into position. You must do it at whatever cost."

Huey nodded grimly, saluted. "I will!"

The 8th Pennsylvania (about five hundred troopers) was nearly wiped out in the delaying counterassault, launched at dusk. "But," writes Captain Willard Glazier, "the precious sacrifice was not in vain. The Rebel advance was greatly checked, as when a trembling lamb is thrown into the jaws of a pursuing pack of ravenous wolves."

Captain Custer was mounted beside General Pleasonton when he dealt the knockout blow that enabled Hooker to withdraw across the Rappahannock in safety. It was, indeed, "a moment of trembling suspense." Twenty thousand Confederates burst from the woods, six deep in line along a quarter-mile front two hundred yards ahead, rending the air with their wild yell. Pleasonton barked "Fire!" and cracked his whip. Custer saw four deployed batteries of horse artillery, twenty-two fieldpieces double-charged with grape and canister, erupt a thundrously withering ricochet fire that swept the "Sword of the Confederacy" off the field.

Bloody but unbowed, the 1st Cavalry Division retired close on the heels of Fighting Joe Hooker.

"Some of the papers are very severe on Hooker," Colonel Wainwright remarks, "and insist upon it that he was drunk."

"The whole Army are speaking against him & asking for McClellan," Custer wrote home; and General Hancock assured his wife that "Hooker's day is over." But not before he had sacked General Stoneman and appointed General Pleasonton as C.O. of the Cavalry Corps. According to Hooker, Stoneman was greatly responsible for the fiasco, having taken Gregg's and Averell's divisions on a futile raid ("wild-goose chase") or diversionary movement toward Richmond, leaving only Pleasonton to support all the infantry. Yet these were Stoneman's orders, since he could not cross the Rappahannock, and his ill luck was that he didn't get back in time to keep his commission. Hooker did what Mc-Clellan and Burnside never would: blamed everybody else for his own blunders. Any scapegoat was good enough for Fighting Joe, so long as that scapegoat had little or no influence in Washington. However, the only consideration that saved Hooker for a second chance was the advantageously tragic death of Stonewall Jackson, Lee's "right arm." A quirk of circumstance!

On May 6, Custer penned home in jubilation that he was now aide-de-camp to a corps commander, one who praised Hooker for replacing "that third-rater" (Stoneman) with "a man [Pleasonton] who knows his business & does it." Rivalry was ruthless, animosity crucial, and the young captain soon learned that "the weak" fall by the wayside when there's a war to be won. A waverer he would never be!

Beaten and crippled, the Boys in Blue were in for a month of convalescence. Captain Custer hung up his hat with General Pleasonton in a big Sibley tent at base camp, Aquia Creek Landing, which McClellan once described as "a wretched place, utterly unfit for the landing & supplying of a large body of troops." But Fighting Joe wasn't too particular. Not in his condition!

"Everyone should live in a tent," Custer said one evening. "During the summer months at least. There would be less sickness, more enjoyment of health."

Pleasonton grunted. "Remind me to send to Baltimore tomorrow. We're getting low on supplies."

Custer turned up the lantern and went on with his letter to Libbie: "You need have no anxiety about my food. I live with the Gen'l. He sends almost daily to Baltimore for fresh fruit & vegetables. . . . The Gen'l has a negro cook. Her husband waits on table. We call her 'Aunt Hannah. . . .' So you see, we don't go hungry when not moving or fighting. . . . P.S.—The whole Army are still very bitter on Hooker, speaking against him & asking for McClellan, *the only man I ever loved.*"

119

Three weeks later, Autie excitedly informed Libbie of a secret mission he had accomplished for Generals Hooker and Pleasonton on May 21-24. (It was a daring and dangerous venture that took him deep into enemy territory, there to intercept and seize a civilian caravan bound from Richmond to Urbanna, then up the Rappahannock to Lee's army at Fredericksburg, with official mail and extra pay for Confederate troops) Won't the Judge sit up and take notice now! he thought. Certainly Hooker and Pleasonton did! They had deemed the enterprise virtually impossible; but as Custer had declared himself game to challenge the impossible, they determined to put him to the test—with the aid of seventy-five crack troopers. He passed with flying colors, openly declaring, "I'll be a general before this is over!" He seemed dead sure of it, for it was his destiny. "Gen'l Hooker sent for me & complimented me very highly on the success of my expedition, and the manner in which I had executed his orders. He said it could not have been better done, and that he would have something more for me to do."

President Lincoln contacted General Hooker: "What next? . . . Keep the enemy at bay & out of other mischief, by menaces & occasional Cavalry raids, if practicable."

June 6, 1863. Sober for a change, Hooker put his finger on the regional map sprawled across Pleasonton's field table. Custer and other staff officers stood around watching and listening.

"Al," the G.I.C. said, "our scouts report that Lee is moving up the east side of the Blue Ridge Mountains towards Harpers Ferry. We can only suspect by this that he's planning another full-scale invasion of Maryland and Pennsylvania. We've got to stop him before he crosses the Potomac. Jeb Stuart is covering his right with ten thousand horse. Knock out Stuart and you paralyze Lee. He can't advance without mounted protection and support, nor can he be guided with any degree of certainty. Knock him out, I say, and that should hold 'em long enough for us to muster the necessary strength to resume the offensive by taking Richmond right under their noses." Hooker tapped a spot on the map with the tip of his finger. "Stuart will be stopping at Brandy Station for a grand review. That's the time and place to hit him. If you can't cut him to

pieces, at least shake him up—put him on the run, harass him—
anything to stop Lee dead in his tracks. You have at least a thirty-
mile march. Take your entire corps and leave tomorrow. And bear
in mind, Al: the element of surprise is essential to our success."

The word spread. Wainwright noted in his diary: "Something is
certainly in the wind. . . . The Cavalry, I hear, are to make a grand
reconnoissance or demonstration towards Culpepper."

Custer was atingle with anticipation. At last, after two agonizingly ill-fought years, someone was acknowledging the active
rather than the passive usefulness of cavalry. Ever since Bull Run,
Custer had been convinced that cavalry (not artillery, as General
Scott had predicted) would decide the war for either side as the
eyes and arms of a military body. Now that the Confederates were
wielding it with deadly effect, it was high time the Federals beat
them at their own game.

June 8. Late that night, by lantern light, Autie penned what
might have been his last note to Libbie: "I will wake the Gen'l at
2 A.M., and at 4 we cross the Rappahannock to strike at Brandy
Station & Culpepper. I am in excellent health & spirits—am feeling
fit as a fiddle—and never felt better in my life, but the chance of
my being killed to-morrow is just as great as ever before. In case
anything happens to me, burn all my letters."

Ghostly darkness ere daybreak, Tuesday, June 9, 1863. Before
the sun's dry-hot rays could slowly dissolve a soupy fog that
blinded the valley, the U.S. Cavalry Corps split into two tactical
units and splattered over the Rappahannock at Beverly and Kelly's
fords, above and below the washed-out Orange & Alexandria Railroad bridge, toward Brandy Station and Culpeper Courthouse.

Custer rode with Pleasonton and the right wing, crossing at
Beverly Ford, north of the bridge. The welcome departure of
heavy spring rains made the river passable at both fords. Morning
mist, and the grinding water wheel of a nearby abandoned mill,
veiled the fording columns and drowned their noise. No enemy
pickets or vedettes were encountered on the north bank, but chal-
lenges greeted them in the southern shallows: "Halt! Who goes
thar?" Captain Custer, leading a skirmish line of the 8th New York

Cavalry, fired his revolver in the air and shrilled, "Drive 'em in, boys!" Men shouted, horses bolted; spray flew, weapons barked. Gray-clad sentinels were scattered helter-skelter, rounded up by skirmishers in blue. The column cantered on, unopposed.

A couple of miles southwestward, down the spongy dirt road, they sighted their objective. Captain Custer adjusted his spyglass. General Pleasonton unsheathed a terrestrial telescope. They scanned the panorama.

Through sparkling haze, Custer gazed at blue-green fields and rolling purple hillocks. Stone walls laced the meadows. Narrow belts of tall trees and brush fringed the heights, along the skirt of which were encamped what appeared to be two divisions of Butter-nut cavalry.

Pleasonton clapped shut his telescope, pointed with his quirt. "D'you see those guns?"

Custer nodded, observing two unlimbered batteries of horse ar-tillery. What the General then said seemed unthinkable.

"Take the 1st Brigade, 1st Division. Form column of squadrons and charge for those guns. Don't stop till they're yours. Under-stood?"

Custer gaped, then nodded.

A corps commander ordering his special aide, a mere captain, to lead a brigade! Unheard-of, incredible! Perhaps. But Pleasonton was no ordinary general, no common man. He was still testing the boy hero, saddling him with greater, more decisive responsibility; trying his nerve, his spirit; grooming him for high and independent command. He had faith in this young hotspur, realizing that Custer wanted only to demonstrate his superiority in action. Pleasonton gave him that critical chance, flouting all the rules of rank. How often had Curly begged for endorsement of his appointment as colonel of the newly raised 7th Michigan, or of some other volun-teer outfit, and how often had Pleasonton unsuccessfully acceded, knowing the lad was equal to the task! But Custer had been branded a "McClellan man," and was therefore under a cloud. Well, Pleasonton wanted to win this war; so he would help Custer find his place in the sun, despite all precedence and opposition.

Old Whiplash flicked his quirt at a thousand enemy campfires.

122

"Hold the rest of this unit in reserve. While you charge for the guns, I'll take the 2nd Division and drive the Rebs through the woods. Immediately you've got those guns, report to me and guard 'em with your life. Understood?"

Custer nodded, nervously tucking his spyglass away in his kit.

Pleasonton tapped his whip. "Good. Now deploy your brigade and charge immediately."

Custer saluted, snapped assent, reined his horse around, and dashed down the column to call up the 8th New York, the 8th Illinois, and the 3rd Indiana Cavalry. Every nerve in his body was strung for action. He was still in a daze, half-conscious of the significance of the moment; aware only of "necessity's sharp pinch," that he must take those guns and hold them at all hazards.

General Pleasonton spurred off to the left, leaving Custer alone: alone with an awesome, albeit welcome, responsibility. The left wing had crossed Kelly's Ford without opposition, and was now deploying for battle under cover of meadow mist. A spectral glow shrouded the valley, causing many to shudder; and the sepulchral stillness was chilling, causing horses to champ and fuss. The sun was up, burning off the haze, and the moment of glory was nigh.

When fifteen hundred troopers of the 1st Brigade, 1st Division, stood ready in extended order across the valley, Captain Custer sidled front and center. He saluted Colonel Benjamin F. ("Grimes") Davis, 8th New York, brevet brigadier of the outfit and a gallant Mississippian. Davis liked Custer and understood Pleasonton's intentions, so there was no dispute over the captain's nominal authority. Besides, the ungrudging colonel had already won his spurs during the fall campaign of '62.

"Buglers, sound the 'Advance'!" Custer said, sweeping off his slouch hat and flashing Spanish steel. He swung his mount about and rose to the trot. "Come on, boys! Give 'em the saber! Charge!"

The 1st Cavalry Brigade thundered at full gallop over the plain, bugles blasting and voices roaring. Dazzling ribbons of saber-waving horsemen, dotted with garish bits of color where guidons fluttered above them, hurled headlong at the enemy encampment.

Stuart's "Invincibles" were paid a surprise visitation. "To horse!

123

to horse!" gray-clad officers yelped as the Union cavalry came charging down upon them.

Confederate troopers were in the saddle at moment of impact. Custer and Pleasonton struck them all of a heap, bowling Rebs down like ninepins. Brigades collided in a dust-driving cyclone of confusion. Sabers streaked and clattered, troopers rasped and bellowed, chargers reared and screamed. There was hacking and slashing right and left, fore and aft. Riderless horses, flecked with blood, bolted madly to the open country; while others, wild-eyed with befuddlement, darted aimlessly up and down the clashing lines.

Custer whacked his way through swarms of mounted artillery-men, driving them out of their batteries and into the woods. One of the "redleg" officers fired at him point-blank. The whisping bullet burned the edge of his ear. Gritting his teeth, Custer closed with the Rebel and gave him a slicing before he could again cock his revolver. A dark crimson jet squirted from his severed throat, speckling Custer's jacket and pants. The officer gurgled and plunged from his startled horse.

Custer laughed hysterically to think that one could kill so easily. But the sight repelled him, sickened him; he retched, and dashed away to slay another who would not surrender. For that was the war game, after all—surrender or die, kill or be killed—and one either found it fun, a challenge to play, however sickening and repulsive it seemed to romantic sensibilities, or one went out of his mind. Armstrong, flattering himself that he could not be killed, played the game in defiance of death, not in defense of life.

The bloody rough-and-tumble soon opened out into a running fight over stone walls and rail fences, through woods, into and out of ditches, up and down hills. When Colonel Davis was shot dead by a Confederate trooper, and the 8th New York broke and re-treated, Captain Custer assumed full command. His horse tumbled twice in the mad, murderous scramble of charges and counter-charges; but he (with Colonel Wesley Merritt of the 8th Illinois) held over half of the brigade together, and rounded up all the men and guns he could possibly handle, having personally snap shot a Rebel officer (in retaliation for Davis) while fighting on the run.

Pleasonton drove Stuart to the outskirts of Brandy Station,

endeavoring to thrash him in detail; but Old Jeb's rallying powers obliged Old Whiplash to fall back to the Rappahannock at noon. Wainwright considered the Battle of Brandy Station as "decidedly the largest cavalry fight this war has yet produced."

Captain Custer, whirling his hat on the tip of his blade, let loose a "Buckeye yell" as he frisked up to General Pleasonton with two batteries of captured horse artillery, a flock of prisoners, and a splendid gold-fringed Southern Cross battle flag superscribed above crossed cannon barrels on sleek silk: *From the Ladies of Charlottesville to Stuart's Horse Artillery, Our Brave Defenders.*

Back at G.H.Q., General Hooker actually shook Custer's hand and slapped him on the back. "Captain," he said, pouring a drink, "you and General Pleasonton are to be complimented on the successful execution of my orders; and needless to say, I'm sure I'll have a great deal more for you to do in days to come."

Captain G. A. Custer was again cited for "gallantry throughout the fight."

Pleasonton said little or nothing, as was his nature, but he was well satisfied that Custer could hold his own in any crisis. They had fallen upon, in scattered brigades, the whole of Jeb Stuart's cavalry corps; and they had driven it, in mad disorder, for several miles— past Brandy Station, toward Culpeper—before last-ditch rallies forced a reversal. In so doing, they disrupted and delayed Lee's northward advance long enough for Hooker to get his troops in marching order. A marathon race for Maryland and Pennsylvania was in the making, and the finish line would be Gettysburg.

★ 15 ★

ALDIE:
LITTLE KIL

GENERAL Hooker now desired to take Richmond by storm, thus clipping the wings of General Lee, but President Lincoln was prepared to reject such a plan: "If the head of Lee's Army is at Martinsburg, and the tail of it on the Plank-road between Fredericksburg & Chancellorsville, the animal must be very slim somewhere. Could you not break him?"

Fighting Joe brandished a champagne bottle in Old Whiplash's face. "Al," he blared, "we've got to break Lee's neck once and for all. The people in Washington are on tenterhooks, Baltimore is digging in for a siege, and all the bigwigs are clearing out of Harrisburg. They think the Rebs are about to overrun the North. Hell, our only worry is Jeb Stuart. He's like a bolt of lightning. Go after him, Al. Cripple him, chop him up. If you can't cut off large slices from Lee's hindquarters, then don't fail to take small ones."

Followed slowly by the 80,000 Federal infantry, Alfred Pleasonton and Armstrong Custer went chasing after Jeb Stuart. They caught up with him at Aldie, about forty miles northwest of Aquia Creek Landing, below the Bull Run Mountains. It was Wednesday, June 17, 1863.

Colonel Hugh Judson Kilpatrick, commander of the 1st Cavalry Brigade (2nd Division), sat his horse with proverbial *sang-froid*. "Little Kil," they called him; or (more apropos) "Kill-Cavalry," because of his unrelenting energy. He was an Irish bantam with bushy Dundrearies, hawkish nose, and a gashlike mouth. The so-called Kilpatrick hat was aslant on his sandy head. It was a black wide-awake with brim turned up on the left and down on the right. Like Custer, the "shoneen" colonel sported a richly engraved toledo blade. Three years older than "Pleasonton's pet," Kilpatrick had been valedictorian (*magna cum laude*) of the first West Point graduating class of '61. Consequently, he looked down his long nose at the "presumptuous popinjay" (Custer) who was stealing everyone's thunder. But none dared dispute with Old Whiplash, whose word was law. One only despised "that jackanapes" in silence, hoping a bullet would soon terminate his reckless pretensions.

Having driven Rebel vedettes through Aldie and skirmished with gray squadrons beyond the town, Kilpatrick's vanguard brigade was first to encounter Stuart's horse artillery ranged below Ashby's Gap. Little Kil held back before the guns, awaiting orders from Pleasonton and exchanging long-range carbine fire with the enemy.

Suddenly, in the breathless tension of a lull, Custer came galloping up to the front. He was slapping his ebony steed with a yellow-straw plantation hat, and long golden locks streamed over his shoulders. His blue denim blouse was flapping unbuttoned, his sweat-soaked red neckerchief fluttered in the breeze, and his battered black jack boots were a match for tattered white-duck trousers.

"Three cheers for Colonel Kilpatrick!" Captain Custer cried, fanning the air with his broad-brimmed benjy, as he whisked along the shouting column.

Pulling up beside the dundreary-bewhiskered colonel, this freckle-faced aide-de-camp whipped out his sword, bobbed it in a flashy salute, then waved it toward the enemy position a thousand yards ahead. He smiled as he spoke. "General Pleasonton sends you his regards, sir, and directs you to take that battery and every man behind it."

Kilpatrick grinned, answering in his sharp twang, "Give my regards to the General, and tell him the day is ours."

Custer colored slightly. "We can both tell him, Colonel—after the fight's over. I'm going with you."

Kilpatrick grimaced. My God, what cheek! "Mind you keep your place," he cracked.

127

Custer's lip curled. "I shall be seen, if not heard, sir."

According to Sergeant Joseph Fought, Pleasonton's chief orderly-bugler, "If Capt. Custer observed that it was important to make a movement or charge, he would tell the commander to do it; and the commander would have to do it—would not dare question—because he knew Capt. Custer was working under Gen'l Pleasonton, who would confirm every one of his instructions & movements. . . . Custer was always in the fight, no matter where it was. He was a conspicuous figure from the first, attracting attention wherever he went."

Kilpatrick sneered at this thunder-stealer, then pulled out his long slender toledo. "Ready, Cal?" he said, glancing at Colonel Calvin S. Douty of the 1st Maine Cavalry.

Douty nodded, saber in hand. His regiment led the assault column of three deployed outfits, the 1st Maine and the 2nd and 10th New York.

"Attention for the charge!" Kilpatrick rasped. Regimental officers repeated his signals. "Draw sabers! Column forward, trot *ho!*"

Wheeling around, Custer clapped heels to "Old Harry" and loped forward across the field. An electric shock seemed to silence the thousands behind him. He looked back and beckoned with his sword. His voice rang. "Come on, boys!" It was a grandstand play, and it worked. A progressive pace from the trot to the charge was passed through in that very instant. God damn him! the two colonels must have thought, but were caught up in the contagious fervor of the moment.

Kilpatrick flourished his blade, shrilling a nasal, "Come on!"

"Come on!" Douty echoed; and buglers brayed the "Charge."

Yelling and cheering burst on Custer's ears as a hurricane of horsemen rolled forward at full gallop. Hallelujah! This was it— the fiercest pleasure in life—a cavalry charge. It was better than having a woman, far better than a drinking bout. A dynamic sense of power possessed him. With glaring eyes and flaring nostrils, horse and rider were wild and wanton, conscious of only one mad desire: to trample, trample, trample down. Kearny's credo echoed in his memory: Charge! And when you hear the "Recall" blown, it's not meant for you!

In a few seconds, Kilpatrick and Douty were abreast of Custer, waving their weapons and hollering like demons. It was a furious race for the guns, and for a moment Custer feared he would lose the advantage of his headstart. But Old Harry, with thoroughbred spirit and frenzy, inched forward at a dead run, his rider raving-drunk with the orgastic rush of emotion.

The long blue lines, broken by their own breakneck speed into huge clusters, bounded over grassy acres strewn with dead and wounded men and horses. They were met by a raking fire. Custer saw sheets and spurts of scintillant-red flame ripping through the wispy-blue veil of smoke that hung over the field, blurring radiant sunlight. Slugs and shrapnel whined and shrieked in deadly chorus, riddling the ranks and mowing down horses and riders.

Unseen by Custer, Colonel Douty threw up his arms, swayed backward, then bounced to the ground with a bullet hole in his head. Before his foot jerked loose from the stirrup his frightened mount dragged him several yards, then veered off to the right.

Shot in the neck, Colonel Kilpatrick's charger tumbled to the ground with a piercing whinny. Captain Custer turned his head for a second, saw Little Kil take a flying spill.

With his two competitors out of the race, Armstrong eased back to a gallop—and imagined himself a brigadier, leading his hundreds alone. The pungent-hot stench of gunpowder pricked his nostrils and made him screw up his burning, watery eyes as he whirled his toledo and shouted the brigade on to victory or death. The boys in blue fixed their eyes on those blazing red-yellow ringlets like a guiding star, for their leader seemed to have a charmed life. The feathery hearts of a moment ago were now hardened, and every raw trooper was a fire-eater.

Captain Custer and the 1st Cavalry Brigade, 2nd Division, swept through the enemy position in a swirl of dust and smoke. Stuart's horse-artillerymen scattered like leaves in a storm, and the Blue troopers hewed them down right and left.

One of the mounted Confederate officers swerved in the saddle

129

and fired his revolver point-blank at Custer. He missed; and an instant later Custer fetched the man a blow that toppled him to the ground, his left arm hanging by a shred of flesh. A second Invincible challenged Custer on the run. The two swordsmen rode along side by side in a torrent of dust, swinging and parrying. This clanging duet of cold steel ended abruptly when Custer gag-checked Old Harry, forcing his opponent into a standing fight. With masterful strokes, Armstrong knocked the gray-clad cavalier off balance, then off his horse by splitting his head like a melon.

(Custer now found himself a lone Yankee in Rebel territory, perhaps a mile from his own lines. A chill of anxiety raced through his body. He looked around. Scattered masses of Jeb Stuart's "hossbackers" were jogging past, casting casual glances. Why didn't they attack him? The reason suddenly struck him. It was his hat! Old straw plantation "slouchers" were a pride and joy of the Southern Confederacy. The rest of his "uniform" was so irregular as not to be identifiable!)

Custer laughed to himself. But as he was trotting away, devil-may-care, one of the Invincibles recognized him by his golden ringlets. The man rushed at Curly with glittering saber. Custer blocked his blow and slashed him across the face, knocking him off his horse. Before the others could overtake him, Custer, flushed and shivering, dashed to safety with a sigh of relief.

Late that afternoon, battle artist A. R. (Al) Waud of *Harper's Weekly* sketched Captain Custer in and out of action. Autie sent one of the rough drawings home to Libbie. It depicted a dashingly slipshod youth, the Dixieland benjy aslope on his unkempt curls, leading a cavalry charge with uplifted saber. He wrote: "Everyone tells me I look more like a Rebel than [like] one of our own Army!"

That evening, General Pleasonton cited Captain Custer for valor and sent his name to President Lincoln for special promotion. Besides shattering General Stuart's horse-artillery, the "Custer Brigade" had taken a hundred prisoners and one flag. Joe Hooker again pumped a blushing hero's arm, slapped his shoulder, sounding off in praise to a hard-drinking and indifferent staff.

"Captain Custer has been strongly recommended to Governor Blair by Generals Hooker, Burnside, Stoneman, Humphreys, Copeland, Stahl, and Pleasonton." So stated the Michigan papers, proud of their adopted son. "Gen. Hooker asserts that we have not a more gallant man in the field, and that wherever there is a daring expedition or hard fighting to be done, he is always among the foremost."

Colonel Wainwright describes the Battle of Aldie as "not a large affair, nor did our men go clear thro' the gap [in order to cut Lee in half]." However, "The affair at Brandy Station certainly did a great deal to improve the morale of our cavalry, so that they are not now afraid to meet the 'Rebs' on equal terms." With a loss of over five hundred men, Stuart was compelled to join his chief in the Shenandoah Valley. Washington and Baltimore were now deemed secure, and only Pennsylvania lay in danger.

Around the campfire, Curly and his fellow staff officers raised their tin coffee cups in toast: "To promotion—or death!"

GETTYSBURG:
THE BOY GENERAL

FRIDAY evening, June 26, 1863, found Captain G. A. Custer and the U.S. Cavalry Corps at Camp Frederick in west-central Maryland. Driving rain beat a droning tattoo on ankle-deep mud as he lurched from the saddle after a long and wearisome ride, posting inlying and outlying pickets around the entire three-division corps. "He was very careful of our defences," Sergeant Joseph Fought (Custer's orderly) relates. "He made it a point not to depend on others in placing pickets, but saw to it himself. In consequence we were often out together at all hours of the night, and ran terrible risks." Fought, who tagged after Custer like man's best friend, observed that Pleasonton relied on his special aide in everything; hence his "Trusty" was "more valuable to him than his brigade commanders."

Sloshing into the headquarters tent with water beading down his slicker, Curly swished off his flop hat and was hailed by a volley of waggish how-de-do's: "Gentlemen, General Custer!" "Good evening, General!" "Halloo, Gen'l!" "How are you, General?" "Why, General Custer, I congratulate you!" "You're looking well, Gen'l!" The salty salutations came from all quarters of the marquee, where staff officers were seated in an atmosphere of cigar smoke and popping corks.

Custer reddened, drew rein on a hot and hasty temper, then slogged over to the field table to make out his report. Tight-lipped and lowering, he endured their laughter.

"All right—all right—all right." Custer waved his arm at them. "Go ahead and laugh," he muttered. "Laugh all you damn well please. I'll be a general yet, before this is over." A smile crept over his face. "Just you wait and see."

It was a standing joke at cavalry headquarters that Custer would never rise above the staff rank of captain so long as Old Whiplash or some other big gun could use him as an all-purpose slavey, a human dynamo for special detail. He was too valuable to lose, for such energy and versatility were precious-hard to come by in "West Point popinjays." Custer had answered his banterers with bravado, fearing there might be something in what they said: a constant, haunting torment that perhaps he was "too good" to be a general, since it appeared that behind every good superior was a better subordinate, his backbone.

Curly's grumbles stirred up a gale of guffaws. It seemed as if his fellow staff officers were bent on triggering him to tears. Well, he'd damn soon show 'em! Cheeks aflame, bright eyes ablaze, Custer slammed down his pen and jumped out of his seat. An open-mouthed stillness gripped the raucous gathering. Custer stared daggers through bluish-white wisps of tobacco smoke, seeking out a likely victim.

At that crucial moment, Lieutenant George W. Yates stood up and walked over to the table. He was one of Armstrong's old Monroe gang, and he knew just how far his friend could be pushed. Besides, it was Custer's influence that had got him an appointment as one of Pleasonton's aides.

"Look on the table, old fellow," he said with a wink and a grin. "We're not pulling your leg." Yates pointed to a large official envelope lying atop the scatter of maps and other documents on the big field table.

Custer darted a glance, then turned pale. He picked it up with a quivery hand. He could hardly believe his eyes! But there it was, penned across the front of the envelope in bold script: *Brig.-Gen'l George A. Custer, U.S. Vols.*

A second later all the fellows at cavalry headquarters were crowded around, shaking his hand and slapping him on the back. Custer was too carried away to utter a single word. Looking as if he had seen a ghost, the "shavetail general" forced a weak smile.

When the congratulations were over, Armstrong plopped down

133

in a chair, ripped open the envelope with jittery fingers, and read the special order from Washington. As his eyes passed over the precious paper, he felt as if he were going to make a damned fool of himself and cry. Only when the H.Q. boys asked him to read the "boost-script" aloud did "Old Curly" master his feelings and find words to thank them for their bouquets and apologize for his brickbats.

In a rush of emotion, Autie dashed off a note to Libbie: "Be the first at home to hear of my good fortune. Believe it or not, I have been promoted to a *Brigadier-General!* I certainly have great cause to rejoice. I am the youngest Gen'l in the U.S. Army by over two years—in itself something to be proud of. My appointment dates from the 20th of June. I owe it all to Gen'l Pleasonton. He has been more like a father to me than a Gen'l."

"How fortunate that Gov. Blair had nothing for you!" Judge Christiancy later wrote to his enterprising acquaintance. "Every step of your remarkable advancement has been due to your own merit, without favor—often in the face of opposing influences, often of political origin."

Mr. Lincoln had said to Mr. Bingham: "Phil Kearny was *my* brigadier. Now that he's gone, I look for someone to fill his boots."

"That someone is Captain Custer, Mr. President."

Lincoln shrugged. "Then he's my brigadier!"

"Nobody knew it was going to happen," says Sergeant Fought. "It was a great surprise."

And so it was! First Lieutenant of Regulars, Brevet Captain of Volunteers, now a full-fledged Brigadier General. Few men ever made such a jump. Surely none of his age!

On the following morning (June 27), Custer was issued a dark-blue tunic with a silver-embroidered star on each shoulder strap. At age twenty-three, he was the youngest "big boot" in the United States Army, again making military history. James Gordon Bennett of the New York *Herald* hailed him as "The Boy General with the Golden Locks." From that day on, "the Boy General with his flowing yellow curls" became darling of the war-gods. As Old Whiplash said to this observed of all observers, "An officer is like an actor on the stage, before a watchful audience. A good officer,

like a good actor, can hold attention at his command. He can make
his audience imagine themselves the hero of the play. He can make
'em feel what he himself feels, do what he himself does. Fear—
stage fright—he may have, but must never show it if he would
hold his audience and magnetize them to his command. Play your
part better than anybody else, and you'll carry the show with top
billing."

Well, Custer had already proven himself a good actor—a *grand
poseur*—the first characteristic of a good or popular officer. But
he previously fancied himself as having played a supporting role,
and the prospect of an independent part now filled him with
anxiety. Therefore, in his letter of acceptance to Secretary Stanton,
Armstrong made mention of the fact that he was "only twenty-three
years old": a precautionary excuse for possible blunders. The psychological adjustment from special favor to full responsibility
would have to come in action. And come it would, very easily; for
Custer must always be the boy hero, the glory-hunter, playing a
desperate game in defiance of death—just for the fun of fighting
and just for the hell of "every man for himself, the devil for all."

Fighting Joe Hooker was unable to break the "gray-bellied
mule," as Lincoln termed Lee's army. Beauty Stuart again rode
around the Union Army, and this time Hooker was out. "The
removal was done in the same dirty manner in which Stanton does
everything of the sort," Colonel Charles S. Wainwright declared.
"He seems to take special delight in being as offensive as possible."
On June 27, 1863, Major General George Gordon Meade was
appointed General-in-Chief of the Grand Army of the Potomac.
Slab-sided, hollow-eyed General Meade, with his scraggy barbed-
wire beard, looked and walked like an old circuit preacher, but
talked like a metropolitan pundit. The Boys in Blue called him "a
slow old plug." One even described him as "a damned goggle-eyed
old snapping-turtle." And Wainwright thought he had an "infernal
temper." Could he possibly win a cross-country marathon race to
the North? That man in the White House sure hoped so. What a
disenchantment if the tortoise-and-hare parable was just a jet
from the gasworks!

135

Brigadier General George Armstrong Custer was commissioned C.O. of the 2nd Brigade, 3rd Division, U.S. Cavalry Corps. In this stellar role he commanded the 1st, 5th, 6th, and 7th Michigan Volunteer Cavalry, along with Battery M of the 2nd U.S. Artillery. Judson Kilpatrick, Custer's divisional chief, was now a senior brigadier; yet poor Alex Pennington, who had graduated (Class of '60) ahead of both, was still a mere captain of artillery: Battery M. However, Armstrong would see to it his old pal got what he deserved (for meritorious services), what he had been denied for lack of political influence.

Governor Blair, Judge Bacon: sit up and take notice! . . . *Attention, Your Excellency! I had wanted the 7th Michigan, and I have got the Michigan Brigade! I had wanted colonelcy, but I have got generalship! . . . Attention, Your Honor! Am I not a worthy son of Monroe? I have earned recognition and respect, reputation and rank, as I said I would. And I have earned the right to your daughter's affections, which you cannot now deny me.*

General Custer cast aside his regulation tunic and rigged up a personalized uniform to fit his new identity. No more the ragtag-and-bobtail adventurer in straw sloucher, threadbare blouse, ragged trousers, and battered boots. No more the careless, unkempt, slipshod harum-scarum struggling to achieve realization and fulfillment, a place in the sun. That place was won; and the victor needed a unique identification with Glory, whose child he was.

Taking one of the dozen navy-blue flannel jumpers he had removed from a captured Confederate gunboat on the James River, Custer stitched a big gold-embroidered star on both tips of the broad triangular collar. Ripping the yellow silver-star "punkin rinds" from his castoff service coat, he sewed them on the shoulders of a gold-trimmed glossy black velveteen jacket embellished with a double row of gilt buttons. The swanky collar was worn outside the swagger coat, and around his neck went a bright-red-silk waterfall tie emblazoned with a silver pin. Custer seamed the sleeves of his jacket, from the gold-braided cuffs up to the elbows, with five golden figure-eight loops and silver bullion. His "lightning-rod pants," sleek black velveteens with gold-lace stripes, were tucked into top boots fitted with gilded gooseneck spurs. White gauntlets

136

and a low-crowned, broad-brimmed black felt slouch hat (gilt-corded and asterisked) completed the costume. With his tawny mustache and tuft, and saffron tresses fringing his shoulders, Old Curly looked as if he had just stepped out of a Vandyke. To General Meade and his staff, this image of a Cromwellian cavalier had all the earmarks of martial madness.

Brigadier Custer was now center of attraction in the big parade, and he was delighted. All his airy hopes and ambitions were at last a reality. But the Boy General appeared so foppish and effeminate that his jealous rivals called him the reincarnation of Prince Rupert ("The Mad Cavalier") or of Maréchal Murat *le Magnifique,* a "prancing peacock" who fought for the bloody fun of it. He had hopped over the heads of them all, and each would have gotten a great kick out of seeing his fine feathers plucked.

"The Boy General looked so pretty and so unlike the stern realities of war," wrote Captain Fred Whittaker of the 6th New York Cavalry, "that he was certain to be quizzed and ridiculed unmercifully unless he could compel the whole army to respect him. There was envy enough about his sudden elevation, as it was! . . . He assumed an abrupt and distant manner at first, was curt and decided in his orders, and made himself felt as master from the first hour. . . . He was compelled to be cold and distant at first, as Napoleon was, and for the same reason; otherwise 'I should soon have had them [his subordinates] clapping me on the back and giving me advice.' "

Artillery Lieutenant Tully McCrea, who had been a Custer roommate at the Point, was also amazed at what he saw. He had known Fanny as an inveterate "cribber" and "very dissipated." He was "too clever for his own good . . . always connected with all the mischief that is going on . . . never studies any more than he can possibly help," and "will always have cause to repent of his folly." However, "I admired & partly envied Custer's free & careless way, and the perfect indifference he had for everything." For all his folly, he was now a general! And "He is the same careless, reckless fellow that he was then." Custer, to McCrea, was "the most romantic of men. . . . Last summer, when he was in the Peninsula, he vowed that he would not cut his hair until he entered

137

Richmond. He has kept his vow, and now his hair is about a foot long & hangs over his shoulders in curls just like a girl. . . . You may think from this that he is a vain man, but he is not; it is nothing more than his penchant for oddity. He is a handsome fellow, and a very successful ladies' man. Nor does he care an iota how many of the fair ones break their hearts for him. What a monster! methinks I hear you say. Perhaps he is. But he is a gallant soldier, a whole-souled generous friend, and a mighty good fellow; and I like him & wish him every success in his new role."

"This officer is one of the funniest-looking beings you ever saw," wrote Colonel Theodore Lyman of Meade's staff, "and looks like a circus-rider gone mad!" But "His aspect, tho' highly amusing, is also pleasing; as he has a very merry blue eye & a devil-may-care style." Others thought him "a madcap harlequin." That he scented his hair was an incitant for fellow officers also to accuse him (in secret) of treating his locks with curlers and curlpaper, and of wearing stays—this in allusion to his new ramroddy posture, replacing his old slouchiness. Custer's ruddy complexion and explosive temper made him seem a clandestine boozer in the estimation of many who could not see the little boy ("My voice is for war!") in the big man.

However, the envy, jealousy, ridicule, and scorn of others made him all the more determined to justify the "freak" by extravagant deeds, not empty words. Like self-consciously audacious Citoyen-Général Napoléon Bonaparte, Custer freed his pent-up frustrations on the battlefield and made his pretentious appearance a challenge to all the world to sit up and take notice of him. And when certain martinets took unsuccessful exception to his bizarre and unauthorized dress, Custer answered rationally, "I want my men to recognize me on any part of the field."

Captain James H. Kidd of the 6th Michigan was both amazed and amused by Custer's appearance. It was at Hanover, Pennsylvania (June 30, 1863), that the Michigan Brigade first saw their new brigadier. "Tall, lithe, active, muscular, straight as an Indian and as quick in his movements, he had the fair complexion of a school-girl. Superbly mounted," he sat his charger "as if to the manner born." His extravagant dress gave him "a rakish air. His golden hair fell in graceful luxuriance to his shoulders. . . . A keen eye would have been slow to detect in that rider with the flowing locks and gaudy tie, in his dress of velvet and of gold, the master-spirit that he proved to be. That garb, fantastic as at first sight it appeared to be, was to be the distinguishing mark which . . . (like the white plume of Henry of Navarre) was to show us where, in the thickest of the fight, we were to seek our leader; for where danger was, where swords were to cross, . . . there he was—always. Brave, but not reckless; self-confident, yet modest; ambitious, but regulating his conduct at all times by a high sense of honor and duty; eager for laurels, but scorning to wear them unworthily; ready and willing to act, but regardful of human life; quick in emergencies, cool and self-possessed, his courage was of the highest moral type: his perceptions were intuitions." Portrait of an arche-typal hero—not without fantasy, not without fact.

In one week, with no time to spare, General Custer put his novice command through a "course of sprouts" that made them smart with *esprit de corps*. "They'll not shrink from their baptism of fire," he assured Kilpatrick. "I'll have 'em shaken down in good order." Raw recruits hated him at first for a "hell-driver," an "iron-arse." Custer, striving to live down an undisciplined past, adopted all the characteristics of a martinet, a dandified backbreaker. The spur of conscience rubbed him raw. But when he had made soldiers of his men, and demonstrated his own fortitude, they could not help but respect him. Older officers, "noncoms" and "shoulder-straps," at first resented his youthful authority. Some were political appointees, others veteran volunteers—all disdainful of Regular Army discipline and "new-fangled West Point notions." "All the other officers were exceedingly jealous of him," Joe Fought noted. "Not one of them but would have thrown a stone in his way to make him lose his prestige. He was way ahead of them as a soldier, and that made them angry." Strong-willed, self-sufficient, Armstrong exerted no effort to win their friendship or enlist their aid. He would command their co-operation and allegiance in action; though they scorned him now, they would respect him later.

139

"Tramp, tramp, tramp: the boys are marching!" But who really cared? It was a war of strange contrasts. In Virginia, heart of the rebellion, Southern hospitality was a sacred tradition that (though restrained) was rarely violated. The "damnyankees" met with cold and cautious kindness, but kindness just the same. As the army moved north again, a great change or contradiction in human values was apparent. "The people along the road sell everything," Wainwright noted, "and at very high prices. . . . Many of the inhabitants, tho', will not sell, but give all they can; and we are cheered thro' all the villages by good wishes & pleasant smiles." This in Maryland, the "buffer state." "The Pennsylvanians do not give us an over-warm welcome; they are much more greedy than the Marylanders. . . . They fully maintain their reputation for meanness."

Custer, for one, asked himself: "Are we fighting for the wrong people? What is our cause, that it alienates rather than unites?" These were the most vital, most haunting, questions that any soldier could then pose; for without satisfactory answers, they meant that the war must continue as a duel to the death, determining not who was "right" but who was "left." *C'est la guerre!* What, after all, does any armed conflict prove save the superiority of one fighting machine over another? And yet wars are waged for a cause, though it be pure power lust; and without a cause, whence comes the will to fight? But fight soldiers must—for principle, if not for people. And if not for principle, then for each other.

As fate would have it, Meade and Lee met quite by accident. The shock of meeting was momentous. It touched off the Battle of Gettysburg, turned the gray tide, tolled the death knell of the Confederacy.

The first day of fighting was eventful for "Black Jack" Buford's vanguard 1st Division of the Cavalry Corps, which encountered Heth's Confederates on the ridges west of Gettysburg. Old Pop Reynolds (1st Corps), whom Custer vividly recalled as Academy Commandant, was killed while coming to Buford's aid.

Far to the east, Gregg's (2nd) and Kilpatrick's (3rd) divisions were scouting and skirmishing. Their instructions were to hunt up Stuart, cut him off from Lee, prevent him from flanking the Federal infantry pushing up from the south. Stuart was like a phantom that first day, hitting and flitting, and Custer saw nothing of him.

Thursday, July 2, 1863. The afternoon air was hot and heavy, saturated with sulphurous fumes and ringing with earth-shaking roars.

Brigadier General G. A. Custer, resplendent in bedizened black velveteen, trotted gaily down Harrisburg Pike toward Gettysburg. The 2nd (Michigan) Brigade jogged in column of fours behind him. They spearheaded General Kilpatrick's 3rd Cavalry Division. Objective: destroy Jeb Stuart; turn the Southern tide from its deluge of the North.

"Good God!" Meade exclaimed to his chiefs of staff. "If Lee gets Gettysburg, we're lost!"

At four o'clock, Custer's brigade, feeling its way toward the right flank of the Army of the Potomac, advanced within sight of Hunterstown, five miles northeast of Gettysburg. Still no sight of Jeb Stuart. Where in hell was that gray ghost?

Raising his gloved hand for the column to halt, Old Curly pulled out his binoculars and scanned the southwest. He gazed at an eternity of rolling dark-green, purplescent hills wreathed with bluish-white smoke. Pillars of gunpowder reek, driven by a volcano's-breath breeze, drifted across lush emerald meadows and golden-yellow fields, hovering over orchards and woods, scudding around and through the crisscross of zigzag fences latticing the Pennsylvania farmlands. Now and then he caught a glimpse of Gettysburg, with its spires gleaming in the shimmery sunlight. On every side of this peaceful little town, the most desperate and decisive battle of the Civil War was raging.

Custer's verbal orders from Kilpatrick were to continue covering the Union right wing against a Confederate flank attack, and especially to be on the lookout for Stuart's Raiders, lest they cut off communications and supplies. Until this moment, these routine instructions had proved most wearisome and unproductive.

The "Murat of the American Army," as the Duc d'Orléans had styled him, aimed his field glasses straight down the turnpike. There, like a huge stumbling block stretched across the road and

141

into the fields outside Hunterstown, stood a massive cavalry blockade.

General Custer turned in the saddle, motioned to Captain Henry E. Thompson of the 6th Michigan. Thompson spurred up alongside his brigadier.

"We have only one way to go," Custer said with a wry smile, "and that's forward." He tossed his head jauntily. "Kil wants us to keep the route open. Are we going to let Old Jeb stand in our way?"

Thompson smiled nervously. "I hope not, sir!"

Custer slapped his thigh. "Well and good! Now, order out Company A for a mounted charge down the road. Instruct Colonel Gray to dismount two other companies as skirmish lines on either flank. The battery will support."

Thompson blinked. "But, General, there may be a whole division ahead!"

Custer scowled. "What d'you mean, *whole division?* A brigade at best. Now carry on, Captain."

"But——"

Custer reddened. "Don't argue with me! Just do as I say."

Thompson saluted blankly, swung his horse around, obeyed his brigadier's command. A squadron hurled against a brigade, or (God forbid!) perhaps a division. Heaven help us! he thought.

"Captain Pennington!" The boy general addressed his artillerist. "Bring up your guns! Place three on either side of the road, to cover the skirmishers. Fire only in the event of repulse. Shrapnel."

Custer stared down the highway. Stuart's Invincibles stood in massive extended order, carbines perched on their hips. They watched and waited, silent and cocksure. And defiant. The only movement Custer could see was the nervous flicking of their horses' tails.

Company A, 6th Michigan Cavalry, jangled forward. Two more companies dismounted and fanned out in skirmishing order across the wheat fields on either side of the pike. Pennington unlimbered and ranged his six howitzers, loading with canister to pepper the enemy's tail in event of repulse.

All was ready. Captain Thompson was about to signal the charge when (without warning) the boy general flashed his long toledo blade, motioned his staff to stay back, and dashed out in front of Company A, shouting, "I'll lead you this time, boys. Come on!"

His gold braid aglitter and gilt spurs twinkling, a silver-star pin turning up the right brim of his black hat, Old Curly charged down the road at a dead run. In a blinding surge of dust, whooping and yelling, Thompson's troopers sprinted after him.

Enemy carbines crackled like fireworks, and Custer met with a shock. He got a bitter taste of what Kilpatrick had swallowed at Aldie—a mouthful of dirt. Shot through the head, Custer's horse took a flying spill. Its rider, sprawling, had the wind knocked out of him for a few seconds.

Captain Thompson pitched from his mount, mortally wounded, and Stuart's men lurched forward with a wild Rebel yell.

Gasping and gagging, General Custer floundered to his feet amid a blinding swirl of dust and horsemen. One of the saber-swinging Butternuts swerved to cut him down. He may well have been killed were it not for a teenaged trooper named Norval Churchill, who shot the Confederate point-blank with his revolver.

"General!" the lad yelped, thrusting out his hand. Custer grabbed hold and made a flying mount, landing on the croup of Churchill's horse. The two Federals then galloped back to the brigade with remnants of Company A. Over the rolling carbine fire of skirmishers in the fields, Pennington's battery hurled a salvo into the Rebel roughriders, who were jolted back by the shattering blasts and went scuttering through Hunterstown in full retreat.

Custer's first indiscretion as a general set a pattern for his every move till the day he died. Having little concern for his own safety, he cared little for that of his men, whom he expected to be as fool-hardy as himself.

Custer detested in others what he never regretted in himself—presumption—and he presumed, correctly, that the 6th Michigan would be too astounded by his audacity to blame him for the loss of their favorite captain. Soldiers are awed by an officer who does not *send* but who *leads* them to their death. Such a leader has been touched by the gods of war, and is beyond all reproach. It was therefore hard to hate Custer, even for impetuousness and pre-sumption; for to hate him would be to hate raw courage, gallantry,

143

heroism—the ideals of manhood.) In Whittaker's words: "Hating him at Hanover, they began to respect him at Hunterstown; after Gettysburg they adored him."

⚹ With one squadron of horse, Custer had ventured to attack Wade Hampton's entire division of Stuart's Cavalry Corps, losing nearly every man of the headquarters troop (Captain Thompson and thirty-two troopers) and nigh his own life to boot. ("Pop, you & me can whip all the Whigs in Ohio!") Meade, in his official report, called the action "indecisive." But the fact remains that Hampton was routed by Pennington's battery, which "saved the day," and fell back beyond Hunterstown.

His fair face streaked with sweat and grime, his yellow hair tousled and dusty, his black velveteens powdery and bedraggled, that evening (in camp outside Hunterstown) General Custer appointed Private Churchill as one of his special orderlies, in grateful recognition of a life saved.

The striker's first assignment was a tough row of buttons to shine. Meanwhile, Armstrong sat in his underwear and thought of Libbie. And of the fact that Little Kil had cited him for gallantry. ("Gallantry!" the cynics fumed. "An act of folly. Kill-Cavalry must have fallen on his head at Aldie. He confounds bravery with stupidity.")

What a crackbrained tactician that upstart crow decked in peacock feathers had shown himself! "Suicide Custer," they called him, and "Crazy Curly"; "glory-grabber," "headline-hunter," "hellbending fool." Fifth from the foot of his class in Cavalry Tactics, third from the bottom in Strategy. But he had led the Corps in pure cussedness, daredevilry, bravado: characteristics he would never live down, try as he might. Blind to his own impetuosity, his own audacity, he saw only glory where sudden death lurked. "His food was glory"—poison to his mind, peril to his body—but he was without fear, he of a charmed life; he had stared death out of countenance, and he truly believed he could not be killed. Custer's Luck! A happy-go-lucky defiance of death, "kind Nature's signal of retreat."

144

★ 17 ★

CRESS RIDGE:
COME ON, WOLVERINES!

Friday, July 3, 1863, 3 P.M. Brigadier General G. A. Custer and the 2nd Michigan Cavalry Brigade stood in open order along Low Dutch Road, above Hanover Pike, about two miles west of Gettysburg and northeast of the Union right on Culp's Hill. They stood as lone sentinels; for the 3rd Division had been pulled back to support the endangered left flank on Little Round-Top, leaving Custer's vanguard brigade to await relief by General Gregg, whose 2nd Cavalry Division was on the move to replace Kilpatrick on the right rear flank. This sudden shift of units seemed to indicate that Meade, on Pleasonton's advice, considered Little Kil best able to handle the impending crisis on the left. But did he also consider that Stuart's demonstrations on the right, toward the Federal rear, were an equal threat? The 5th Michigan had been skirmishing all morning with hit-and-run hossbackers; and Pennington was keeping up a long-range duel with masked batteries on Cress Ridge, about 1,500 yards to the northwest.

The atmosphere was like a fiery furnace, scorching Armstrong's streaky face. He breathed a piercing, poisonous air. The stench and smudge of burnt sulphur and saltpeter stung his eyes, pricked his nostrils. A deafening roar shivered the ground beneath him.

Custer raised his binoculars, viewed horse batteries advancing and unlimbering on the ridge and pike ahead. Enemy vedettes annoyed his right, which soon drove the harassers back into the woods with repeating Spencers, while Pennington's rapid-fire three-inch guns held down Rebel artillery. Enemy horse were amassing

145

fast, from the north and west. Gregg had damned well better hurry, Custer thought, licking dry lips and glancing southward.

Though he faintly heard, he could not see the breath-taking spectacle being enacted beyond Rock Creek. Gushes of blue and gray, tipped with sprays of glimmering steel, roared on rugged sea-green slopes. Rolling volleys shattered and blazed, vomiting billowy drifts of bluish-white. A thunderstorm of shellbursts peppered hill-tops with puffs and plumes of smoke, as Union and Confederate artillery played a slaughterous game of give-and-take.

Far to the west, on Cemetery Hill, a sign admonished trigger-happy intruders: *All Persons Found Using Fire-Arms in These Grounds will be Prosecuted with the Utmost Rigor of the Law.* Irony of circumstance!

Where Custer stood, in an isolated fateful arena, the drama was similar—though on a lesser scale. Weaponry crackled and crashed, spurting in fields and blossoming on hills; and the shriek of shells and whistle of slugs, the jets of earth and showers of shrapnel, were as deadly real in this scene of action as several miles away. Stray bullets hissed and hummed overhead, and every minute a spent shot came bounding across the pastures like a bowling ball. Idle troopers amused themselves by ducking and dodging. One un-fortunate show-off, daring to stop such a deadly deceiver as he would a rolling baseball or hot grounder, suffered a smashed foot. The horror on nearby faces was a startling contrast to the expectant grins of a second before. Fun there was for the Grim Reaper. When men laughed, it was because they were afraid; and if they wept, it was because they could no longer laugh. When men neither laughed nor wept, they goddamned the ineffable absurdity of it all, the tragicomedy of "epidemic insanity."

At a few minutes after three, a haggard-looking youth came dusting up the road and checked his lather-flecked steed in front of the brigadier. "Gen'l Custer?" he saluted.

"Yes?" Custer snapped, at first not recognizing the grimy un-shaven scarecrow.

"Sir, I'm Lieutenant Yates of Gen'l Pleasonton's staff."

"George! I didn't recognize you! Enough of this ceremony. How goes it, you old son of a gun?"

146

They shook hands heartily, grinning like minstrels.

"Big thing, Aut! Pleasonton directs you to move your brigade southwest on the double."

Custer scowled. "What for?"

"In support of Hancock's corps on Cemetery Ridge. Pleasonton says you'll receive further orders from Kilpatrick when you rejoin your division."

"Hold on!" Custer said as Yates reined his horse around to bolt away. "What's up?"

"Hancock says, 'Send every man you've got!' The Johnnies are launching an all-out assault on our center."

When the A.D.C. was gone in a stream of dust, Old Curly raised his field glasses and peered westward. Jeb Stuart's Invincibles were still there. Ribbons of mounted raiders laced the groves below Cress Ridge, scouting and skirmishing. No telling how many hossbackers were concealed in the trees on and behind the hill. Hampton's whole division, he reckoned. Five thousand sabers, to say the least! And where was Fitzhugh Lee with *his* five thousand? Lying in wait also, to swoop down and around upon Meade's flank and rear while Longstreet attacked in front?

Why didn't Old Jeb advance? Did he deem Custer a mere blind, a bait to lure him into a trap that would be sprung by Old Whiplash? Time alone would tell.

General Custer ordered his brigade to mount, break by the right to march to the left by column of fours. Pleasonton had said come on the double; but Curly moved at a cautious pace down Low Dutch Road, keeping his sharp blue eyes cocked to the right.

The terrain was almost perfect for effective, full-force cavalry maneuvers. It pained Custer to leave his post. Kilpatrick had put him there, pending Gregg's arrival, to keep a check on Stuart and to cover communications. That "Gray Fox of the Confederacy" was making a play for time. The minute Custer was out of sight, he'd be in the open and up to something.

Oh, well. Orders were orders!

Just as Custer reached Hanover Pike, he spotted the chief of the 2nd Cavalry Division spanking up in a torrent of dust, far ahead of his troopers. He recognized Brigadier General David M. ("Old

Steady") Gregg and his staff by their huge red-and-white swallow-tailed D.H.Q. flag with its big gold-embroidered 2 and crossed sabers.

As General Gregg approached the column, General Custer swept off his hat. His streaming hair flamed in garish sunlight.

Squinty-eyed, spindle-shanked Gregg looked like a hillbilly with his beat-up service hat and bushy beavertail beard. "You're not running out on me, General?" the old campaigner drawled tongue in cheek, scratching his shaggy bib with a long-stemmed pipe.

Custer blushed, cracking a wry smile. "Not running out, General. Just walking in!"

Gregg snorted. "Pleasonton tells me Kilpatrick wants you back with him on the left, while Hancock needs you in support of the center. Longstreet is mounting an all-out attack on Cemetery Ridge. Well, I've got only three thousand sabers with which to hold this ground against Old Jeb, who reportedly has three times that number over there in the woods and along the ridge."

"Jesus!" Custer blurted. "If Stuart should break through this line, he'll play such havoc with our rear as must weaken our whole position. He'll cut off supplies, communications—expose us to a snagging crossfire. So reduced, our center must give way—our flanks roll up—and by Jesus, we'll be licked in detail! Unless, sir —*unless* we poke out 'the Eyes of Lee.' "

Custer pulled out an old order and showed it to Gregg:

4 P.M., July 2

Custer—

Ewell is knocking hell out of Howard on Culp's Hill. If H. cannot hold ground, we are flanked. Cut E.'s communications; harass his rear; at all hazards, relieve pressure on H.

Kilpatrick

"Has the situation changed any in twenty-four hours?" Custer asked.

Gregg shook his head. "Damned little! This order is as valid now as it was yesterday. Has it been expressly countermanded, in writing?"

148

"No, sir; it was merely superceded by a verbal request for me to rejoin my division. Without adequate support to dispose of Stuart, it was hardly feasible for me to cut Ewell's communications—much less harass his rear."

"Very well, General," Gregg said. "Disregard unwritten orders. You never received 'em. You misunderstood them. I want you to stick here with me. I'll take full responsibility. I need you to help even the odds. As far as I'm concerned, Hancock can hold his own with Buford. It's our job to stop Jeb Stuart. The situation is such that we may save a whole army from almost certain disaster. We must maintain this position to the last man of us. If Stuart closes the vise, our cause will be a desperate one indeed. We must keep it open, cost what it may."

Custer nodded smartly, flipping his sporty black turnup back on his head. "I understand, sir. And I agree perfectly." He recalled Hancock the Superb's justifiable disregard of orders at Williamsburg, and how it had decided a desperate clash. The present situation was very similar. Custer again had the honor to help save an army; and if he succeeded, as before, no one would dare hint at insubordination. "We hold the trumps of battle lost or battle won. I'll gladly share in the responsibility, General." He held out his hand.

Gregg screwed up his eyes and smiled. The two men shook warmly.

Gregg said: "Much obliged to you, General. May I suggest you deploy your brigade beyond those trees?" He turned and pointed to a belt of orchards. "I expect Stuart is just playing for time, looking for a smart chance to take the offensive. Seeing you withdraw, he'll likely make his move."

Custer nodded, grinning. "I think Jeb has been champing the bit for me to make myself scarce. By your leave, General, I'll draw him out for the kill!" He blindly welcomed the challenge to protect and save the Army of the Potomac.

While Custer withdrew his command out of enemy view, behind a veil of groves in the southeastward direction from which Old Steady had come, Gregg dismounted the 1st New Jersey and 3rd Pennsylvania Cavalry of McIntosh's 1st Brigade (joined by skir-

149

mishers of the 5th Michigan, already on foot) and sent them forward as feelers to draw out Stuart's horsemen with a baiting carbine fire.

Four o'clock. Dark fleece streaked the fiery heaven, causing an eerie glow.

"Looks like rain," Gregg remarked.

"Hallelujah!" Custer responded, darting a glance at the cloud-flecked northeast sky. "Let it pour blue blazes. 'Twill settle the infernal dust."

Suddenly, a gray-crested wave of cavalrymen rolled out of the groves skirting Cress Ridge. This was it! Three crack regiments of Fitzhugh Lee's division scattered the blue skirmishers, driving them back over rail fences and rock walls in a rattling blaze of revolver and carbine volleys.

Custer dashed in and out of the trees to where Pennington had masked his battery. "Captain," he shouted, waving his hat, "feed 'em your pills!"

"Pennington's pills" were a deadly dose of grapeshot and canister, administered at once. Caught in a cross fire, the gray brigade foundered and was forced back up the gentle slope of Cress Ridge.

Custer whistled and cheered, swinging his hat. "That's the stuff, boys—that's the stuff!" He darted back to his brigade.

Wade Hampton's division, amassed on the hillside a thousand yards away, formed column of squadrons and advanced to the attack.

General Gregg turned to his colleague. "General Custer," he drawled, "are you prepared to put Jeb Stuart's nose out of joint?"

Old Curly, who had been eager for action all afternoon, flashed a jaunty smile and answered, "My fists are up, General Gregg."

Gregg emptied his pipe, clawed his whiskers thoughtfully. "Wheel out the 1st Michigan in column of squadrons. Deploy the 5th and 7th as flankers on the left. I'll hold the 6th in reserve. General McIntosh will strike from those woods on the right with his brigade. It is your charge to smash Stuart's center, then let your flankers scatter the pieces."

Custer nodded and touched his hat. "A splendid plan of action, General. But may I add one thing?"

150

"Please do!"

"If it appears that Stuart is giving us any trouble, I beg leave you'll order Captain Pennington to double-charge his guns and pepper the Fox's tail with shrapnel. If that should not succeed, pray have him triple-shot 'em and blow Stuart's backside off."

"Very well, General! Now, put those people out of action—and good luck to you."

David Gregg spurred away to apprize Brigadier General John B. McIntosh of the projected counteroffensive.

Armstrong Custer darted forward, whisking out his burnished toledo, the blade tempered for moments of glory. "Colonel Town!" He saluted the 1st Michigan's commander with a bright flourish of steel, then pointed to the advancing foe. "General Gregg directs us to put those people out of action. Are you agreeable?"

Colonel Charles H. Town returned his salute with a hard smile. "By all means, General!"

Custer's high-pitched voice blared the formational commands; and the 1st Michigan Volunteer Cavalry wheeled (by column of squadrons at a trot) out of the trees, across Low Dutch Road, into the open fields. The 5th and 7th fanned out on the left flank, advancing at a walk across the shell-torn meadowland. General McIntosh, under woodland cover, inched forward on the far right.

"Keep to your sabers, boys!" Custer said, raising his sword. "Keep to your sabers! . . . Close order! Guide center!"

The long, rolling gray wave, peaked with fluttering pennants, headed down the slope and into the blue breaker at a jogging pace.

Custer, his ringlets waving beneath bright steel, rose to the gallop and shrilled, "Come on, you Wolverines!"

Bugles blasted the "Charge," guidons streamed. The 1st Michigan bounded forward in a burst of speed, thundering at the top of their voices. A forest of flashing sabers danced on churning billows of dust.

Old Curly, riding four lengths ahead of his Wolverines, plunged into the roaring sea of Invincibles. A second later the two columns of cavalrymen crashed together with the impact of an avalanche. The collision dashed whole squadrons to the ground in a writhing, shrieking tempest. As one eyewitness (Captain William E. Miller

151

of the 3rd Pennsylvania Cavalry) described it: "The meeting was as the crash of ocean waves breaking on a rock-bound coast, and men and horses rolled and tossed like foam upon the crest."

Custer was thrown from his horse, but immediately sprang to his feet. A pistol shot grazed his shoulder, clipping off one of his "punkin rinds" and singeing his skin.

Custer heaved into an empty saddle. Slashing right and left, he plunged through the fury. When a Federal trooper whacked down Hampton's standard-bearer, Custer hooked the general's gold-fringed Southern Cross on the tip of his toledo. At that moment a sweeping saber missed him by inches, but gashed his mount's left flank. The ear-splitting rasp and clang of cold steel jolted his nerves as he carved a crimson path. Bullets zipped and whistled by his head, sticky-warm blood speckled his face and spattered his clothes. Horses screamed, riders cursed, sparks flew from clashing hoofs. Men hit the dirt, dying hot and hard.

And then it was all over. All over but the wailing and moaning. Ripped to shreds, Jeb Stuart's Invincibles hobbled away. Over two hundred dead Federal cavalrymen was the heavy price paid for breaking the sword arm of Robert E. Lee.

But the Confederates paid a heavier price, and lost the prize. Not only below Cress Ridge, but on Cemetery Ridge. For while Custer and Stuart were fighting their duel to the death, General Pickett was leading his fifteen thousand Butternut Boys up the long gentle slope in a suicidal attempt to smash Meade's center. The gray tide was turned at the end of day, the cloud-curtained sunset of the Confederacy.

For three nightmarish days, the seething air had been alive with lead. Alive with the wheeze and drone of murderous hail, with the barking of cannon and the chatter of muskets. Alive with the rattle of drums and the blare of bugles and the roar of voices, as a myriad blue and gray ribbons and a myriad glittering steel hedges were laced with tissues of smoke and flame.

Now the simmering air was dead, and the raindrops' pitter-patter began to sprinkle a myriad mangled rotting corpses and to wash lichen-mottled rocks of the brains and bloodstains and the guts and bits of flesh sticking to them. "Now," writes Colonel Wainwright, "the reaction showed to what a tension every nerve had been drawn for three days. While the revulsion brought a most pleasant feeling, it was one almost of lassitude, like the removal of a fever from the system. A feeling of intense enjoyment, but not of activity." He would soon have cause to add: "Gettysburg may hereafter be classic ground, but its inhabitants have damned themselves with a disgrace that can never be washed out. . . . Nine-tenths of the men had cleared out, leaving the women behind them, and gone off to look after their own safety. Now the danger was over, they came back: great strong able-looking fellows most of them, but not one had courage enough to take a musket in hand for defence of his own home. Hundreds from the country around, too, came down in their waggons to . . . gaze & gape at the dead & wounded. But not one lifted a finger to help the tired soldiers remove the one or bury the other. . . . Instead of helping us, they were coming in shoals with their petty complaints of damages. . . . I think that Meade might & should have seized every able-bodied citizen he could get his hands on, and forced them to do all the burying. I would have armed cavalry with cowhides & driven them like slaves to the work."

Custer agreed. "These mean-minded, dastardly clods should be horse-whipped & their noses rubbed in the blood of those who gave their lives in defence of their miserable existence & property. By God in Heaven, I would hang every wretch for a traitor who refused to assist in removal of the wounded & burial of the dead. To suppose that Americans could display such selfishness & indifference, when their very destinies are at stake, would be unworthy if it were not true." But, as Wainwright opined, "Americans of both sides are not elated by success or depressed by defeat as most people are." And human nature being what it is—often immutably selfish and ignorant—who could expect more from cold or luke-warm patriots?

G. A. Custer, scraped and scratched and battered and bruised, flopped down in his tent and scrawled his first official report as a brigadier general. He was overspent and ached to the bone, and a humdrum "goose-drownder" pounded the canvas, but he grasped

153

the spirit to pen with boyish pride: "I cannot find language to express my high appreciation of the gallantry and daring displayed by the officers and men of the First Michigan Cavalry. They advanced to the charge of a vastly superior force with as much order and precision as if going upon parade, and I challenge the annals of warfare to produce a more brilliant or successful charge of cavalry."

Colonel Wainwright comments in defense of such vainglory: "Our Cavalry has done some very good service on this campaign, much more than ever before, and a man would hardly be a cavalry officer if he did not talk big. That seems to have been one of their characteristics in all ages & all armies."

General Kilpatrick, in his own official report, added: "To General Custer and his brigade, Lieutenant Pennington and his battery, . . . all praise is due." Neither he nor Pleasonton breathed a word about disregard of orders. It was "a mistake," not disobedience. The battle was won. Why make a fuss?

Custer had lost over 250 troopers during that three-day bloodfest at Gettysburg; but with the support of McIntosh and the guidance of Gregg (who lost about forty men) he succeeded in turning the tide cavalrywise, saving Meade from a disastrous rear attack by Stuart. If the slaughter south of that sleepy little Pennsylvania town was the most decisive battle of the Civil War, what then can be said for the fierce clash of cavalry that occurred to the east? To say that Custer saved (or even helped to save) the day may be exaggeration. But who can tell what might have been, had his electrifying energy and magnetizing valor not shattered Stuart's projected rendezvous with Pickett? A master strategist Custer was not, or even a great general in theory; yet he surpassed all others in a most enviable quality, absolute fearlessness, and in the ability to put into practice what others could only propose. Here was a tactical instrument, independently reckless and venturous. Here was Fortune's fair-haired darling, spreading a contagion of faith and fortitude. Here was a creature of Glory, tilting at windmills and breaking down the gates of hell. He rode through hell as if it were a fool's paradise, hotly pursuing that grim rider on a pale horse.

154

The day after Gettysburg was the most wildly jubilized Fourth of July since '76. Vicksburg had fallen to "Unconditional Surrender" Grant, Uncle Bob Lee was whipped by "Old Plug" Meade. The Union seemed secure, the Confederacy doomed.

The war might have been over that very day had it not been for Meade's standstillism. "We had them within our grasp," Mr. Lincoln lamented. "We had only to stretch forth our hands and they were ours. But nothing I could say or do could make the Army move." For the rest of the summer he kept repeating to one and all, as if haunted by an incubus of self-humiliation: "Our army held the war in the hollow of their hand, and they would not close it! I have no faith that Meade will attack Lee. Nothing looks like it to me. It's the same old story of the Army of the Potomac. Imbecility, inefficiency; don't want to *do*." The soubriquet "Tardy George" was now applied to McClellan's third successor.

Oh, well! The Grand Army of the Potomac had lost a quarter of its manpower. Bloody but unbowed, the Boys in Blue were in line for a long rest. Meanwhile, Marse Robert and the Boys in Gray limped back to "Ole Virginie," there to recuperate.

But there was no rest for the Union Cavalry. Through driving rain, mud, and darkness, they pursued Lee out of Pennsylvania into Maryland, harassing his rear. On July 5, Custer's brigade overtook and captured "Old Baldy" Ewell's field train of 300 supply wagons, 15 ambulances, and 1,300 rear guards. In the saddle for nearly twenty-four hours, spearheading a relentless chase through violent thunderstorms and deadly night, the boy general finally flopped in the mud for a two-hour nap. He wanted to, and perhaps would have, cut off Lee's retreat across the Potomac; but Meade ordered Pleasonton to order Kilpatrick to order Custer's withdrawal.

Custer and Kilpatrick were furious. "We had Lee in the palm of our hand," Armstrong raged, echoing Lincoln almost word for word, "yet we let him slip through our fingers. We could have ended this war on the banks of the Potomac, but a continuation seems to be to Meade's political advantage."

Pleasonton rasped, "Old Plug is afraid to risk another fight.

155

Says he needs more troops. A poor excuse. So does the enemy! He wants Bob Lee to escape."

Custer's orders were not to cross the Potomac; but he dogged Lee's rear guard to its very banks, taking fifteen hundred prisoners, two guns, and three flags on July 14. Kilpatrick reported to Meade: "In this campaign [June 28 to July 14, 1863] my Command has captured 4500 prisoners, 9 guns, and 11 battle-flags." He added, as usual, "To Gen'l Custer & his Brigade . . . all praise is due."

General Kil took sick leave the following day, giving Old Curly temporary command of the 3rd Division. On the seventeenth, with the approach of Meade's infantry vanguard, Pleasonton ordered Custer to ford the Potomac below Harpers Ferry. Bands crashing, troopers piping, the long blue snake slithered southward into Dixie:

> Carry me back to Old Virginny:
>   There's where the cotton and the corn an' 'tatoes grow;
> There's where the birds warble sweet in the springtime;
>   Carry me back where my heart am long to go.

Free at last, with a whole division to call his own! *Hallelujah!*

General Custer plunged fifty miles into enemy territory, down the verdant basin of the Blue Ridge and the Catoctin Range, skirmishing with Jeb Stuart at the west base of the Bull Run Mountains. Without orders, but with Pleasonton's blessings, he crossed the Rappahannock on July 23. It was Custer's forlorn hope to force Meade into aggressive action by thrusting his division between the Confederate corps of Longstreet and Hill, thus allowing Old Plug to beat Marse Robert in detail.

Not wishing to embarrass Kilpatrick by his audacity, Custer bivouacked the 1st (Devin's) and 3rd (Merritt's) brigades at Amissville. With his own twelve hundred, he immediately pushed fifteen miles south to Culpeper and forged on over the Rapidan River toward Orange Courthouse—nearly twenty miles more—to overtake A. P. Hill.

It was Old Curly's illusion that the Michigan Brigade could take on the entire Army of Northern Virginia, but a recoiling collision with Hill's rear guard convinced him that help was needed. Falling back to Amissville, he implored Pleasonton to dispatch the whole Cavalry Corps to his aid. "Lee is within our grasp," he wired. "Send support at once. Will flank him at the North Anna, cut him up to be whipped in detail."

But General Meade would not be spurred into offensive operations. "I will not be dragooned by that harebrained peacock!" he bellowed. "Order him back at once!"

Pleasonton telegraphed: "Can send no support. Retire to Warrenton Junction." He then wrote to his pet: "Meade is a pusillanimous procrastinator—a prototype of McClellan, who hesitated to fight for fear of getting licked. Expect nothing from him."

Custer (in fear of court-martial) was obliged to abandon his "harebrained scheme" and withdraw across the Rappahannock to Warrenton ("a wretched hole"), about ten miles northeast of Amissville, there to sweat and stew in profane damnation of "that pusillanimous procrastinator."

Meanwhile, Lincoln and Halleck were wiring Meade: "You are strong enough. . . . *Fight*. . . . Do not let the enemy escape. . . . Press Lee tenaciously. Destroy him if you can, and the war will end." Vain pleas! The President clenched his fists. "Oh, it's terrible—*terrible*—this weakness, this indifference!" General Wadsworth, applying in disgust for a transfer west, ascribed "an otherwise unaccountable slowness of attack" to his assumption that "there are a good many officers of the Regular Army who have not yet entirely lost the West Point ideas of Southern superiority." It is apparent that Custer did not labor under such a delusion, brainwashed though he was by "Southron chivalry," but saw in such cotton-belt bravado a challenge to Northern manhood. He respected the Old South, but did not stand in awe of it; nor was he of that U.S.M.A. generation trained and educated almost exclusively by Southern gentlemen. There had been a time when West Point belonged to Jeff Davis, but what psychological effect that may have had is purely speculative. The only certainty, in relation to Custer and others, was expressed by Sam Wainwright: "There is a curious jealousy in our army, a grasping after power . . . which must be owing to our new-fledged generals not knowing the exact

157

duties & powers of their position, and consequently being afraid that they will not get all they are entitled to."

Several weeks of agonizing inactivity followed. In answer to Libbie's weekly letters, Autie was finally able to scratch a note before the end of July: "I have been thro' many dangers since I last wrote you. . . . I had 3 horses shot under me. . . . The bullet has not yet been molded to kill me. Was I ever scared? Only once. Familiarity with death breeds contempt. I believe more than ever in Destiny. . . . Did Judge Bacon think my promotion deserved or not? Or did he maintain a dignified silence? The Gov't has been in the habit of laying on the shelf all the unfortunate Gen'ls who have failed to do 'just so.' When I was a mere Lieut. or Capt., I was safe. But now that I have changed the bars for a star, I might for some mismanagement be displaced; so that he (your Father) has every reason for wishing me to succeed. . . . Do not fear for me. You know me well. I may lose my position among men—I may lose *everything*—yet there is a strange, indescribable something in me that would enable me to shape my course through life, cheerful if not contented. If the time should ever come for me to give you up, I hope it will find me the same soldier I now try to be—capable of meeting the reverses of life as those of war."

★ 18 ★

HARTWOOD CHURCH:
ANNIE JONES

O_N August 4, 1863, Kill-
Cavalry returned from leave of absence to steal Old Curly's
thunder. For three eventful weeks the boy general had wielded the
3rd Division like a whirlwind, sweeping seventy-five miles into
the heart of Old Dominion, hot on the heels of Robert E. Lee.
Meade had snatched glory from Custer's grasp, refusing to follow
up his offensive strategy, and now Kilpatrick was back to reduce
him once more to a junior brigadier. But never one to brood, save
for a moment or two of explosive frustration discharged on the drill
field, Armstrong made every disappointment a spurlike challenge
to greater ambition and impetuosity. He became a desperate man,
playing a desperate game.

Turning slipshod volunteers into polished regulars was a tough
proposition, but Old Curly had time and determination. Equal to
the task, he made the Michigan Brigade second to none in fighting
spirit and *esprit de corps*. They demonstrated their pride by adopt-
ing as their "red badge of courage," their emblem of identity,
Custer's scarlet cravat. Over a thousand flaming neckties, and
many a shock of flowing hair, characterized "Old Curly's Bluedevils." Many a starry-eyed youth deserted his own unromantic
outfit just to ride with quixotic General Custer's fabulous brigade.
It was indeed the showpiece and prodigy of the Army of the
Potomac, the echoed expression of its prime mover, from its rory-
tory band to its swashbuckling staff. "I've won their respect," he
once told Pleasonton. "Their affection is where it belongs: for the
corps."

Also in August of '63, a bandannaed Negro woman (and runaway slave) by the name of Eliza Brown "jined up with the Gin'l to git me a passel of this hyar freedom business of the good Massa Linkum." Custer hired her as his personal "mess-moll." An orphaned hobbledehoy called Johnnie Cisco served as General Custer's tableboy, groom, and valet, and preferred sacking out with Custer's pack of prize hounds and horses rather than in a tent of his choice. The "boy brigadier" appointed two Monroe cronies, Captains Jacob L. Greene and George W. Yates, as his adjutant and aide-de-camp respectively.

Old Curly's headquarters (at Warrenton Junction) was a three-ring circus of bummers, drummers, carpetbaggers, and tail waggers. A "peacock" himself, he attracted rare birds.

Then trouble hit camp in the form of a teenage *femme fatale.* Autie was scrawling his latest note to Libbie: "We are living in magnificent style. The inhabitants have long been without sugar, coffee & salt; and for these they exchange butter, milk, eggs & vegetables. Ladies young & old whose husbands are in the Rebel Army come flocking to Hd.-Qrs., their little baskets of produce on the arm."

Suddenly, H. Judson Kilpatrick came tromping into Custer's private tent with a comely white wench. Though a married man, Little Kil maintained his old West Point reputation as a "dark-horseman" or one addicted to "notorious immoralities."

With his usual wolfish grin, Kilpatrick introduced the dark-eyed damsel as Miss Annie E. Jones, who aspired to be a "nurse." But how could he be certain she was not a spy? 'Twas common knowledge that Jeb Stuart kept a "left-hand wife" in the field. Could she not be that hussy?

Indeed not! Miss Jones was "sparerib" to *no* secesh. Her loyalties lay *completely* with the Union.

(Annie Jones had become Judson Kilpatrick's mistress. She did sack duty and horizontal drill with him for all of a week; and he presented his "morale-booster" with a horse, a major's jacket and cap, and a pass to sight-see the camp. Pity his poor wife, lonesome with child in Washington!)

The 3rd Division's honorary *mascotte* played havoc with inlying and outlying pickets, exposed herself to Rebel snipers, then high-tailed it over to the enemy lines for a two-night stand with romantic Major John Singleton Mosby, raider *extraordinaire* and son of a preacher.

That was the last straw. When Miss Jones dared return, General Kilpatrick sent her packing. Custer declared that he showed good sense in putting the extinguisher on a dangerous nuisance.

For the balance of summer, General Custer and his Michigan Brigade drilled recruits and rode hot on Mosby's trail: feinting, sparring, seeking to stop that elusive "Gray Ghost" from cutting communications, highjacking convoys, bushwhacking reinforce-ments. To counteract the hit-and-run tactics of Mosby's Rangers, Custer organized a 300-man *corps d'élite* of partisan raiders—but with trifling success. Guerrilla warfare is the forte of local folk, not outsiders, so Armstrong had two strikes against him from the start. Instead of acting, he found himself *re*acting, haunted by that Gray Ghost to wildest frustration. He had met his match—a formidable foe, shifty and unchivalrous—but he took that double dare with vengeful resolution: "I'll catch that fox if it's the last thing I ever do." Custer's personal vendetta with Mosby would reach its climax a year later in the Shenandoah.

By mid-August, 1863, the 3rd U.S. Cavalry Division (still spearheading and clearing a route for the slowly advancing Army of the Potomac) had shifted its base of raiding operations thirty miles southeastward to Hartwood Church, a sleepy crossroad sev-eral miles above the Rappahannock, northwest of Fredericksburg. On the thirteenth, General Custer opened communications with General Pleasonton at Rappahannock Station: "All quiet along my line to-day." Complaining about local citizens who were en-gaged in sniping and other deadly activity under protection and in violation of "paroles from the Hd.-Qrs. of the Army of the Po-tomac," he added pointedly, "I can suppress bushwhacking, and render every man within the limits of my Command practically loyal, if allowed to deal with them as I choose [by admonitory hangings]."

Four days later, a directive was issued by Army Chief of Staff

161

A. A. Humphreys to General Pleasonton, granting General Custer full authority "to arrest every one who disregards a parole or pledge." However, "the loose statements upon this subject contained in the letter of Gen'l Custer do not impress the Maj.-Gen'l Comdg. [Meade] with the suitableness of intrusting to that officer the discretion he suggests: of dealing with those within the limits of his Command as he might choose." Amen! Repeated arrests, but no decisive hangings. Secesshers were to be handled with kid gloves, not an iron fist. Custer laughed in disgust.

In the first week of September, 1863, the 3rd Cavalry Division was still bivouacked at Hartwood Church, still holding open communications with the slowly advancing G.A.P. All quiet, perfectly quiet, on the line of the Rappahannock.

One evening, at twilight, a wagon came rumbling up outside Brigadier Custer's canvas bungalow. Annie Jones had returned.

Custer ordered her out of camp. When she refused to leave, he threatened forcible expulsion. Ah, but dare he flout higher authority? She handed him several slips of paper—passes from the War Department, from Dr. Jonathan Letterman (Surgeon-in-Chief) and General Warren—giving her permission to visit the army as "a sister of mercy." Indeed, Miss Annie E. Jones had been officially placed as hospital nurse in the 3rd Cavalry Division. And under escort! Despite a general order that no females were to accompany troops in the field unless directly attached to the medical department and under direct supervision of Dr. Letterman. Kilpatrick's and others' outrageously amorous escapades and an alarming rate of venereal disease had helped change the moral climate.

Custer handed back the passes, again ordering her to leave and never come back. He stated that neither General Warren nor Dr. Letterman had any authority in the 3rd Cavalry Division, and that he did not see any specific mention of the Cavalry Corps in that War Department pass. Nothing but a direct order from Kilpatrick, approved by General Pleasonton, could allow her to remain with this division; and only Custer's approval could allow her to stay in his brigade. "You shall get none of these," he assured her. "Now

162

please to leave, else I shall be forced to turn you out like a common bummer."

Expostulating on his "ungallant conduct," Miss Jones declared that she had given herself the trouble of coming thirty miles just to see him; and that the ambulance and escort had been graciously assigned to her by none other than Major General Gouverneur Kemble Warren ("Old Topog" and "Hero of Little Round-Top"), Chief of Army Engineers and Custer's math instructor at the Point: ugly-tempered, cross-grained, "the darkest horseman of the freaks." "If they only think me a good general," he once remarked to Colonel Wainwright, "I don't care to be considered a gentleman." Wainwright found him subject to "awful fits of passion . . . a species of insanity over which he has no control," and was convinced "that he has a screw loose." So it would seem from his risky indulgence of Miss Jones!

As noted, "that damned crazy fool" Kilpatrick was not original in his "gallant" treatment of Miss Jones. The Confederacy also had its share of libertine cavaliers, foremost of whom was Jeb Stuart, whose wenching was as notorious as his favorite novel, *Fanny Hill: Memoirs of a Woman of Pleasure*. Custer recalled a cartoon in *Harper's Weekly* of April 4, 1863, captioned "General Stuart's New Aid" and depicting a frisky belle cantering through the enemy camp. "The rebel cavalry leader, *Stuart,* has appointed to a position on his staff, with the rank of Major, a young lady residing at Fairfax Court-House, who has been of great service to him in giving information, etc." Jeb's doxy and honorary A.D.C. was Miss Antonia Ford, a doctor's enterprising daughter. Mosby had employed her as gay deceiver in his spectacular capture of General Stoughton and staff behind Federal lines in March of '63, and there was little doubt in Custer's mind that he was using Annie Jones for the same purpose.

Curly called for his adjutant general, Jake Greene, and instructed him to see that Miss Jones went back to General Warren at Centerville first thing in the morning. Come morning: "I refuse to see her." So the boy general answered a last-ditch appeal delivered by his embarrassed adjutant. "Make her leave."

163

Annie had met her match and acknowledged defeat graciously. Exit Annie Jones—till the spring of '64.

Kilpatrick comments cynically: "To Custer, fighting and fornicating are incompatible. When he feels the need for a woman, he leads a wild cavalry charge and stampedes the Old Adam out of his system."

★ 19 ★

CULPEPER COURTHOUSE: THE WOUND

Sunday, September 13, 1863.
Objective: Jeb Stuart's headquarters at Culpeper Courthouse.

Major General Alfred Pleasonton and the entire 10,000-man U.S. Cavalry Corps swooped down from the northeast in a huge crescent, five miles long, the southern point held by Brigadier General George Armstrong Custer and his 2nd Michigan Brigade.

Gregg's and Buford's divisions, right and center, were first to strike Stuart's defensive position around Culpeper. Kilpatrick soon followed to complete the encircling movement—save for Custer, on the far left, who got temporarily bogged down in a swamp after he had forded the Rappahannock.

Captains Greene and Yates never heard him swear so vociferously as on that confounding occasion. *Goddamns* and *Jesus Christs* echoed in the marshland. Fussing and fuming, flushed with frustration, Custer waited only long enough for the 1st Michigan to disembarrass itself from the bog.

"Colonel Town!" he then snapped. "We advance at once!"

Yates spoke up: "Aren't we going to wait for——?"

"Damn 'em!" Custer flashed back. "Let 'em stick in the mud!"

How destiny bedeviled him! How glory played hard to get! But he would call their bluff. Damned if he'd be left in the lurch, losing his place in the sun to Tom Devin or Wes Merritt of the 1st and 3rd Brigades! He would finish in front, neck or nothing.

As soon as the 1st Michigan rolled out of the woods fringing Culpeper, Custer quickly sized up Stuart's position on Kilpatrick's side of the small town. The Old Gray Fox had unlimbered two

165

batteries of light artillery along Georgetown Pike, behind which were planted several squadrons of cavalry.

Old Curly pranced far ahead of his deployed regiment of blue-clad, red-cravatted troopers. The Invincibles watched him intently. So did his own Wolverines. Custer was swanked out in his famously unique hussar jacket, scarlet tie, and tight pants of faded black velvet trimmed with tarnished gold lace. A raider's gray fedora sat aslant on flaxen locks, and gilt spurs glinted at the heels of glossy Wellingtons.

The guns opened up on Kilpatrick's flank, checking his advance by terrorizing Merritt's brigade with a tempest of grape and canister. Merritt raced about, attempting to restore order and re-form the line for a charge.

Custer seized upon that crucial moment of confusion and panic. He dashed to the rear of Merritt's wavering column, commandeered the 1st Vermont Cavalry, and made himself a brigade. This audacious act aggravated the already strained relations between Custer and Merritt, a disharmony occasioned by Armstrong's high-handed assumption of divisional command back in July. Merritt dared not mention it to Pleasonton, for fear of rebuke; but he later complained to Kilpatrick, who merely shrugged and said, "Nothing venture, nothing win!"

General Custer whirled his toledo and cried, "For the guns! Charge, Wolverines!"

Sabers flashing, pennants flying, a thunder-gust of horsemen tore across the fields at full gallop. ("On every occasion I can make men follow me to hell!") Inspired by Custer's spirit, emboldened by the 1st Vermont's example, the rest of Brigadier General Wesley Merritt's outfit went charging after in one mad rush to achieve the éclat of Balaklava.

The Confederate gunners let loose a hailstorm of shrapnel. At this final salvo, a shell splinter ripped open the withers of Custer's horse and sent the General sprawling to the grass. He was too excited to notice his own injury. Springing to his feet, he made for a riderless mount and leaped into the saddle.

In short order, the 1st Michigan (followed by the 1st Vermont and the 2nd and 5th New York) had taken the batteries by storm, routed the supporting squadrons, captured Jeb Stuart's head-quarters and supply train. Forced to beat an inglorious retreat, Old Beauty abandoned a half-eaten chicken dinner and two of his mistresses, Antonia Ford and Laura Ratcliffe. Custer's men finished the meal, then took possession of Stuart's "spareribs."

After the charge, Curly came jogging up to Old Whiplash with a devil-may-care grin on his grimy face. Blue eyes sparkling, he saluted and said jauntily, "How are you, Fifteen-Days'-Leave-of-Absence? Look here!" He raised his left leg. "They've spoiled my boots, but they didn't gain much there. I stole 'em from a Reb!" (Pleasonton glanced from shrapnel-torn boot leather to ragged trousers, observing a bloody blotch on the inside of Custer's thigh.) "Damned near spiked my battery!"

"How bad is it?" Pleasonton cracked.

"Only a slight laceration. But——"

"Good! That handsome charge will get you your two weeks' leave, and that unworthy wound ten days to boot."

"I thank you, sir!"

"But just you mind now: that extended leave is granted only on condition you speak your piece to the father of that little filly in Monroe. I'll settle for just a formal engagement this time. But next time, if you come back foot-loose and fancy-free, I'll horsewhip you for dereliction of duty!"

The battle-scarred boy general, hero of a minor crisis reversed to a decisive moment, could now rest on his laurels. *Harper's Weekly* of October 3 would depict him storming the enemy batteries, and "Custer" would become a household word throughout the land.

"Have driven the enemy out of Culpepper," Pleasonton reported to Meade. "He is retreating to the Rapidan. . . . Gen'l Custer was wounded in the charge capturing the guns that were taken, and his horse was killed under him. His gallantry was distinguished."

Until the day of his death, Custer boasted but one battle wound: superficial, yet painful. "I cannot be killed!" he laughed. And destiny laughed with him, while others laughed at him.

167

★ 20 ★

MONROE: HAIL, THE CONQUERING HERO COMES!

Custer raced home just as fast as the iron horse could carry him.

> Hail, the conquering hero comes!
> Sound the trumpets, beat the drums!

Autie was lauded and lionized by the proud citizenry of Monroe, but all he cared for was seeing Libbie Bacon again.

The Judge was at Traverse City on legal business, so two young lovers were free to enjoy each other's company without restraint. Beneath a weeping willow in the Bacon garden, they plighted their troth "till death do us part." Armstrong sealed the pledge by slipping his good-luck class ring on the finger of his "little girl." (*Per angusta ad augusta!*)

Libbie said, "I didn't know how much I loved you till after you left last spring. If it weren't for your letters, I think I'd have died."

"I guess it was you that kept me fighting so hard. I had to get back to my little girl."

"I know you love me true."

"Libbie, marry me before I go back. It will make me the happiest man alive."

"Oh, you darling boy, I'd marry you this very minute if it weren't for Pa's unconquerable prejudice. I can never even *think* of marrying you till I somehow change his mind about the 'misery,' as he calls it, of being a soldier's wife."

"Well, I feel if the Judge *really* values your happiness, he won't

168

refuse if he learns from his own daughter's lips our true intentions towards one another. 'First be sure you're right, then go ahead!' I always ask myself, 'Is it right?' If I'm satisfied it is, I let *nothing* swerve me from my purpose."

"So be it, then."

As fate would have it, Judge Bacon did not return to Monroe until late Sunday evening, October 4. General Custer was obliged to go back to war early the next morning. No time now for that heart-to-heart talk. *C'est la guerre!*

But Libbie dared not wait any longer, lest she lose that golden-haired man of her dreams. So she broke the news of their betrothal a few minutes after the Judge stalked into the house.

Daniel Bacon hemmed, fidgeted, then turned to his better half: "Well, wifey, what do you think?"

"I think it's just grand!" Rhoda Pitts Bacon chirruped, and that settled it—for the time being.

The following rosy-fingered morn found the Judge and his daughter at the railroad station to bid the boy brigadier a fond farewell. In that precious little time before departure, Judge Bacon clasped General Custer's hand and rumbled most encouragingly of his prospective son-in-law's prospects in the military profession.

"I picture a bright future for you, m'lad," he said starchily, "and I shall be dashed disappointed if I don't hear great things of you soon."

Custer hadn't time to tell the Judge what lay nearest and dearest to his heart. The engine whistle shrieked, the conductor shouted " 'Board!'", and all Custer could say was, "I desired to speak to you, sir, but never got the opportunity! I shall write you as soon as I can."

"Very well," the Judge answered, smiling rigidly. He squeezed Armstrong's hand. "Goodbye."

"Goodbye, sir."

Libbie embraced her fiancé for a second. They touched their lips to each other's cheek. "God be with you, my darling Autie," she murmured.

The town band struck up a popular tune, and the send-off throng

169

burst into song: "When Johnny comes marching home again, hurrah! hurrah!"

Tears in his eyes, a heaviness in his throat, Custer waved his gray felt turnup as the cannon-ball express steamed him away.

Libbie watched, till teardrops blurred a vision of sadness; and she thought:

> Go where glory waits thee!
> But while fame elates thee,
> Oh, still remember me! . . .

The faces dimmed in Custer's eyes, and their voices faded in his ears: "The old churchbell will peal with joy . . . to welcome home our darling boy . . . and we'll all feel gay when . . ."

When . . . *when?*

★ 21 ★

RAPPAHANNOCK:
YANKEE DOODLE!

T HURSDAY, October 8, 1863.
Sundown. General Custer received a hearty reception at Camp
Culpeper from Johnnie Cisco, Aunt Eliza, and all the Wolverines
of his Michigan Brigade. Regimental bands thundered "Hail to the
Chief!," and every trooper erupted three rousing cheers.

Old Curly stood silhouetted against the golden lantern glow
flooding his headquarters tent. His voice quavered at first: "Thank
you, boys. I'm sure glad to be back. But I'm a bit sorry to see our
camp no nearer Richmond than when I left! Well, in the next day
or two I hope to remedy that. I'll see to it we all get some action!"

Sunday, October 11. Rumors became confirmed reports. Old
Spades Lee was executing a right-flank movement in order to force
Meade north of the Rappahannock and cut off his communications
with the Capital. Old Plug Meade and his Grand Army of the
Potomac abandoned Camp Culpeper and withdrew thirty miles
northeast to Centerville, their old stamping ground between Richmond and Washington. As far as Custer was concerned, the fall
campaign had fallen flat. Lee had proven too illusive, master of his
own dominion. There was no hope for it but to beat an orderly
retreat. In so doing, Meade could pick his own ground, choose his
own terms on which to fight.

Pleasonton's Cavalry Corps brought up the rear, covering blue-
clad infantry columns as they sloshed across the Rappahannock
and slogged up Warrenton Pike. It was a walking-running fight
most of the way. Stuart's Black-Horse Raiders harassed the flanks,

hitting and flitting, but no massive attack materialized until the Federal infantry were out of immediate danger.

Early afternoon. On the northern outskirts of Brandy Station, nearly ten thousand Confederate cavalrymen dared to cut off George Gordon Meade's mounted rear guard by thrusting themselves in between the Rappahannock and the 3,000-man trailing division of Judson Kilpatrick. Scattered gray squadrons also menaced, flank and rear.

An aide galloped back to the 2nd Brigade with this characteristic message:

> Custer—
> Jeb ahead, blocking the ford. Await orders from Gen'l P.
> > Kil

Custer turned to Old Whiplash, who was riding beside him in front of the 5th Michigan: "Something decisive must be done at once, sir. We're outnumbered—surrounded! We'll either have to cut our way out or surrender."

"Surrender?" Pleasonton exploded. "Never heard of the word!"

Custer beamed. "By heaven, sir, we'll die with our boots on before we lay down our sabers." His voice sharpened, spiritedly. "By your leave, General, I should like to take my brigade and cut an opening to the river."

Pleasonton snapped his whip, nodded grim-faced. "Do your best! Strike left, towards Beverly Ford. Devin will take the right, Merritt center."

Custer saluted, swung his horse around, ordered the 1st and 5th Michigan Cavalry into two solid columns of assault. The 6th and 7th deployed as flankers and support. As his troopers were sidling and shuttling into position, Old Curly addressed the nearest drum major: "Strike up 'Yankee Doodle!' "

Brassy rhythms rode the breeze. Armstrong quickly unclasped his locket and took what might have been his last look at "the girl I left behind me." Fired with enthusiasm, he tucked the locket back in his blouse and shouted, "Attention for the charge! Draw sabers!"

172

Snatching off his campaign cap, he tossed it to Captain Greene. His long hair fluttered in the brisk wind.

General Custer pranced front and center, stood up in his stirrups, then yelled out, "Boys of Michigan! There are some unfriendly people between us and home. They think they can stop us, though all we have to do is open a way with our sabers. Well, I'm going home! Who else goes?"

Old Curly's Wolverines raised their sabres, burst into a rousing cheer.

Stuart was seeking revenge for Gettysburg, and his well-timed maneuver at the Rappahannock seemed to be the showdown of a personal vendetta between himself and his nemesis. If Stuart could cut off and crush Custer, he would settle a score and rid himself of a most formidable foe. But he underestimated his objective.

Custer wheeled about, pulled out his long straight toledo. "Brigade forward, trot *ho!*" He swung the blade and rose to the trot, turning in the saddle to see a wave of cold steel glittering in gilded sunlight. Apart from Libbie, he had never seen a prettier sight, "one of the most inspiring as well as imposing scenes of martial grandeur ever witnessed upon a battle-field." Close behind him paced his color-bearer, flaunting a new battle flag that was about to pass through a baptism of blood; and the multitude of guidons and regimental banners emblazoned the brigade like varicolored blossoms in a meadow of blue.

"Gallop *ho!*" The jogging columns smoothed their pace to a rolling canter, a gathering run.

"Charge!"

Whooping and hollering, bugles ringing in their ears, Old Curly and his Wolverines hurled themselves furiously at Jeb Stuart's Invincibles. Halfway across the field, a sunken road piled them up like Napoleon's Cuirassiers at Waterloo; but Custer, master of every emergency, restored order and re-formed his men in a matter of moments. "We're surrounded," he cried, "but all we need do is open a way with our sabers! It's a mighty responsibility; but, boys, I'm confident you're more than equal to the task!" Their cheer of enthusiasm was his welcome reassurance.

With the 5th Michigan on the right and the 1st on the left in

173

column of squadrons, and with the 6th and 7th holding the enemy in check flank and rear, Old Curly and his Bluedevils again advanced for the break-through. At the same time, Brigadiers Thomas C. Devin and Wesley Merritt pitched into Stuart's right and center, striving to weaken his lines for a shattering final assault en masse.

It was 2 P.M., and from then until nightfall the raging blue breakers crashed against a seemingly unshaken wall of gray.

Captain Willard Glazier, 2nd New York Cavalry, witnessed the boy general's dynamically magnetic spirit: "Custer, the daring, terrible demon that he is in battle, . . . dashed madly forward in the charge, while his yellow locks floated like pennants on the breeze. . . . Fired to an almost divine potency, and with a majestic madness, this band of heroic troopers shook the air with their battle-cry." Between each assault, artillerists A. C. M. Pennington and S. S. Elder "handled their batteries with great agility and success, at times opening huge gaps in the serried lines of the enemy. . . . No one who looked upon that grand panorama can ever forget it. On the great field were riderless horses and dying men; clouds of dust from solid shot and bursting shell occasionally obscured the sky; . . . long lines of cavalry were pressing forward . . . , their drawn sabres glistening in the bright sunlight. . . . Charges and counter-charges followed in quick succession. . . . It was a scene of wild commotion and blood."

Custer had two horses shot from under him within fifteen minutes, but he led every charge. His ferocity made such an impact on Little Kil, himself "putting the very devil into" his men, that he hooted jokingly, "Custer, what ails you?"

"Oh, nothing," was the reply. "Only *we* want to cook *our* coffee on the Yank side of the Rappahannock, not at Libby or Andersonville [prisons]!"

And so they did. Custer inspired his men to keep driving. At sundown they finally slashed yawning gaps in Stuart's lines, compelling him to retire in sheer exhaustion, then dashed across the river to safety. By eight o'clock the boy general and his battle-scarred brigade gazed at a myriad campfires suggestive of a glowing, smoky fairyland of Chinese lanterns and fireflies. According to Whittaker, "The sight was a fair specimen of the pusillanimous

174

policy of General Meade in this celebrated retreat. It was a courting of disgrace"; for the infantry "had been compelled to lie idle all day, passive spectators of a fight which their presence could have determined."

Monday, October 12. While General Kilpatrick was citing his right-hand man for gallantry, Autie was penning a letter to Libbie: "Yesterday we passed thro' the greatest Cavalry battle ever witnessed on this continent. . . . Oh, could you but have seen some of the charges that were made! While thinking of them I cannot but exclaim, 'Glorious War!' "

Then, marching up to the cannon's mouth, General Custer wrote *pro forma* to Judge Bacon. "It is true that I have often committed errors of judgement," he defended his impulsiveness, "but as I grew older I learned the necessity of propriety. I am aware of your fear of intemperance, but surely my conduct for the past two years (during which I have not violated the solemn promise I made my sister, with God to witness) should dispel that fear. You may have thought my conduct trifling, yet it was not to make gossip. I left home when but sixteen, and have been surrounded with temptation, but I have always had a purpose in life."

Three days later, Autie sent a hasty pencil scrawl to Libbie: "We are now encamped on the Bull Run battle-field, where as 2nd Lieut. I heard my first battle-shot. I am at this moment sitting under a stately oak that bears many a battle-scar, surrounded by graves, many washed by rain so that skulls & skeletons are visible. . . . I dreamed of my little girl last night, and was so disappointed to wake & find it but a dream. How often I think of her! Even in the thickest of the fight I can always find time to think of her."

175

★ 22 ★

BUCKLAND MILLS:
BUCKLAND RACES

Monday morning, October 19. General Meade ordered the Cavalry Corps to fan out westward, to hunt up Jeb Stuart and head off his reported flank movement, a threat not only to the Army but to the Capital. Kilpatrick's 3rd Division was launched from Manassas (Bull Run) several miles northwest to Gainesville, then down Warrenton Pike, Custer's brigade in the lead.

Sighting Gray reconnaissance squadrons on the road ahead, Old Curly and his Wolverines whipped after them at full gallop. It was a running fight for several miles to Buckland Mills, where Hampton's division was bivouacked with Stuart's headquarters. Old Beauty abandoned his breakfast and all his H.Q. wagons, beating a hasty retreat, as the boy general and his Bluedevils thundered into view.

On first sight of Stuart, Custer had sent Captain Yates back to Kilpatrick, requesting full support; but Kilpatrick, not wanting to play second fiddle in Custer's show, ignored the request and held his pace.

Having located and dislodged at least half of the enemy cavalry, Custer was content to rest, water, and feed his horses and men before pressing on in pursuit. Not so Kill-Cavalry, who had trailed close behind, offering no support.

"Well done, Custer!" he cracked, glancing about with wild eyes and wild grin. "You've driven 'em from a very strong position. But no time to waste. Can't dally here, not even for the horses'

176

sake. Mount up straightway. We're pushing on to round up Old Jeb for the kill."

Seemingly unconcerned, Custer sipped his coffee. "Mind you don't run into a trap."

"Hah! You talk as if you're not coming."

"Oh, I'll be along directly. As soon as my men are fed and my horses watered and rested."

Kilpatrick reddened. "To hell with your goddamned men and horses! I'm off, and you'll either keep up or shift for yourself."

Custer gestured jauntily. "Good luck!"

Little Kil bolted away, waving on the 1st and 3rd Brigades, whose winded mounts would be no match for the fresh steeds ahead.

"Damned fool!" Custer muttered to his staff, seated around the campfire. "He'll kill half the horses and cripple the other half, just to be led into ambush. Stuart wouldn't run without a fight, except to wear down our horses and spring a trap."

A trap it was; for at that moment Fitzhugh Lee's division, swooping down from the right to strike Kilpatrick flank and rear, fell upon Custer's bivouacked command. What followed was soon to be called the "Buckland Races," in which the Michigan Brigade lost 150 troopers by capture. It was, for Custer, an orderly rout— thanks to his painstaking *sang-froid*—but all of Kilpatrick's studied coolness and presence of mind were put to flight by panic and chaos as Wade Hampton took him in flank and Fitzhugh Lee (with infantry and artillery) assailed his rear.

October 20. Gainesville, Virginia. In depths of discouragement, Armstrong communicated with Elizabeth: "Yesterday was the most disastrous this Division ever passed thro'. . . . My only consolation is that I am in no way responsible for the mishap, . . . and the only success gained by us was gained by me; tho' I cannot but regret the loss of so many brave men—all the more painful because it was not necessary."

Several days later he again took pen in hand: "We have occupied our present camp [at Gainesville] . . . to repair our losses of the past few weeks, give our horses rest & forage, and fit ourselves for

177

service. . . . I do not believe a father could love his son more than Gen'l Pleasonton loves me. He is as solicitous about me & my safety as a mother about her only child. You should see how gladly he welcomes me on my return from each battle! His usual greeting is: 'Well, boy, I'm glad to see you back. I was anxious about you.' He often tells me that if I risk my life so much he will place me in such a command that I shall never have the opportunity."

At last, the anxiously awaited letter from Judge Bacon arrived. Armstrong ripped open the envelope with jittery hands. He read: "I believe in the sincerity of your affection—in your energy, ability & force of character. I have always admired you, and am more than gratified at your well-earned reputation and high & exalted position. None the less, I will go no further than to promise to speak to Libbie on a matter which she is at full liberty to communicate to you. For my part, the subject broached calls for weeks—months, even—of deliberation."

Armstrong was flabbergasted. He didn't know what to make of it! That same hour of October 27 he sat down and dashed off a note to Elizabeth: "Of myself he spoke in terms both encouraging & flattering. But he owns that it may be weeks (perhaps even months!) before he can make up his mind to give a decided answer. . . . What does he mean?!"

What did he mean indeed! General Custer was under the impression that Judge Bacon and his daughter had come to an understanding on the night before he left Monroe. And to think that His Honor had charged *him* with caprice! So, the Judge was playing cat-and-mouse with him simply because he hadn't the heart to give up a good thing: his doting and devoted daughter. Well, Custer would damn soon see about that! Unlucky at war made him all the more determined upon being lucky at love. He could stand a reverse from General Stuart, but he would not bear another setback from Judge Bacon. Never taking even an implied "No" for an answer, in his immediate response Armstrong begged a definite decision one way or the other.

On November 1, 1863, he wrote to Libbie: "I mentioned that Mosby had captured 2 of my orderlies, out foraging. Yester-day, a party of my men (while scouting) came across the body of one,

Cadet George Armstrong Custer, Class of 1861.

Captain Custer and "Rose" (1862).

A Sharpshooter, dead at Fredericksburg.

A Sharpshooter, dead at Gettysburg.

Death on a misty morning: Gettysburg, July 5, 1863.

Sheridan and his generals, 1864. (L to R): Sheridan, Forsyth, Merritt, Devin, and Custer.

Their chances were small: romantic young Confederates, 1861.

Old Curly, the "boy general." 1865.

General George Armstrong Custer.

Autie, brother Tom, and Libbie, 1865.

Drill team, Army of the Potomac, 1862.

Parades end! The war is over!

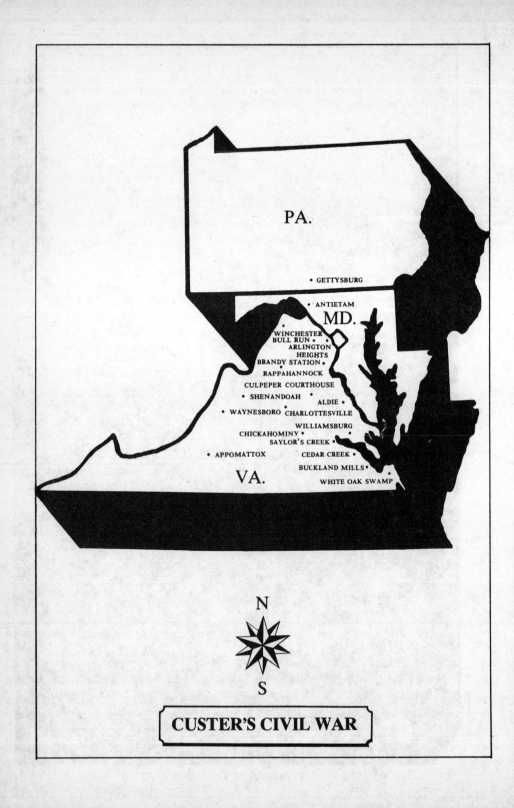

PA.

• GETTYSBURG

• ANTIETAM

MD.

WINCHESTER
BULL RUN •
ARLINGTON
HEIGHTS
BRANDY STATION •
• RAPPAHANNOCK
CULPEPER COURTHOUSE
• SHENANDOAH
• ALDIE
• WAYNESBORO   CHARLOTTESVILLE
WILLIAMSBURG
CHICKAHOMINY •
SAYLOR'S CREEK •
• APPOMATTOX   CEDAR CREEK •
BUCKLAND MILLS •
VA.   WHITE OAK SWAMP •

N

S

CUSTER'S CIVIL WAR

Pvt. Corser, pierced in the back by a rifle-bullet. The Rebels had emptied his pockets of everything but a miniature of his wife & child. This, the regular work of a 'Southern gentleman'—a minister's son [Mosby]. A young man of 25, shot down like a dog & stripped of all but his trousers. What can I write to his poor wife? How I pity her when she learns of her fate! She wrote to him 2 or 3 times a week. That is *love*. Habituated as I am to scenes of death & sorrow, I could not help but shed tears over his ignominious end. They even shot his horse. Well, I have sworn never to take another Mosby man alive; and if ever I should be so fortunate as to lay M. himself by the heels, I shall not hesitate to hang him like a common criminal. . . . I hear that Kilpatrick is to be made a Major-Gen'l & ordered West. I am pleased. . . . If he does not go West, I will! Since 'Buckland Races,' he & I are 'on the outs.' "

He added a postscript: "I wrote Friend Nettie [Annette Humphrey, Captain Greene's fiancée]: 'What makes you think *I* am going to take a young lady on my staff, and who do you think is The Young Lady?' " Playful Annette had sent him that sketch from *Harper's Weekly* depicting "Gen. Stuart's New Aide," changing "Stuart" to "Custer" and indicating the equestrienne as "A Young Lady in Monroe."

MONROE: GENERAL AND
MRS. G. A. CUSTER

WHEN the Army of Northern
Virginia withdrew below the Rapidan, the Grand Army of the
Potomac inched southward and encamped at Brandy Station for
the coming freeze. Custer begged leave to go home for a short
spell—say a week or two—on a promise that he would "get in
double harness" with Miss Bacon.

"If you go out and lay Jeb Stuart by the heels," Pleasonton replied, "I shall see to it you have as extended a leave as you'll need
to hitch yourself to that nice young lady in Monroe."

A ghost of a chance, collaring Jeb Stuart, and Old Whiplash
knew it!

No need now to husband his resources when he would be "batch-
ing it for God knows how long." "I could live on the money I
squander," he wrote to his sister. "I lost $10 to-day I bet on a
horse-race with Gen'l Kilpatrick." Finding a common interest and
emotional outlet—gambling—Old Curly and Little Kil had agreed
to let bygones be bygones, patching up their differences for the sake
of *esprit de corps*. Custer, who by nature found it burdensome to
nurse a viper in his bosom, was always the first to forgive and
forget.

Not all of Armstrong's princely pay was gambled away in worri-
ment over Judge Bacon's "pure cussedness" and Gen'l Pleasonton's
refusal to furnish a furlough. Some of it went to the folks in Monroe, for kid sister Maggie's education at Boyd's Seminary or for
Pop's other expenses in a big town. Generosity, even to extrava-

gance, was ever a Custer virture. Though selfish in his plucking of glory, he gave freely of its fruits.

Without wine and women, the troops turned to gambling. "This vice has been growing very rapidly in the Army," Wainwright noted, "both among officers & men." Custer became quite adept at it, and his reputation as a sharp at brag or poker was equaled only by his passion for horse racing. At the Point, "gambling in Qrs." had piled up demerits in the "skin book" under the name of Cadet Custer; and his unauthorized betting on Old Wellington had won him many a plebe's allowance from home.

The dull routine of camp life, of practice drill and basic training, was a strain on Custer's high-strung temperament. What he later wrote of his first idol, Fighting Phil Kearny, was a revelation of himself: "He constantly chafed under the restraint and inactivity of camp life, and was never so contented and happy as when moving to the attack."

In a fit of desperation, anxious to break the insufferable monotony, Custer put Pleasonton's jest into action. For nearly two months he raided across the Rapidan, endeavoring to waylay Old Jeb; but the Gray Fox, like the Gray Ghost, was just too cunning for capture. The boy general's only reward for his abortive attempts was a big reprimand from Old Whiplash for commandeering vedette patrols and outlying pickets.

On November 12, General Custer dispatched a characteristic complaint to the newly created Cavalry Bureau in Washington, declaring that the majority of the horses on which recruits arrived were "unserviceable, and are really a more indifferent lot than those sent to Washington as unserviceable"; that "numerous complaints" had come to him from regimental commanders concerning "the inferior quality of horses" supplied by Camp Arlington; and that his command suffered about as much from this outrage "as it does from the weapons of the enemy." General Pleasonton, in his endorsement, further declared that "there is in the present system of supplying the Cavalry of this Army with horses & equipments something so radically wrong that the interests of the Service im-

181

peratively demand an immediate . . . application of some very stringent remedy."

General Stoneman, chief of the Cavalry Bureau, replied testily: "All requisitions from the Army of the Potomac up to date have been filled with the best the Gov't has on hand. I have understood that Custer's brigade are great horse-killers."

It was Custer's contention that thieving bureaucrats were sending back, as "serviceable remounts," the same unserviceable mounts ("broken-down nags") retired to Camp Arlington. Requisition records indicated purchase and disposal of fresh horses when, in fact, government funds were being pocketed: the same old story as a year before, when the Quartermaster General's records showed that ten thousand horses had been sent to McClellan and only a thousand actually reached the army. Many were undoubtedly stolen, sold to the South or to Union officers at a premium, while others apparently sprouted wings and took flight to never-never land.

Profiteering and graft had a field day under General-in-Chief Halleck and Quartermaster General Meigs, red-tapers whose reports (according to Wainwright) were "prevarications if not downright lies." Tuft-hunter Kilpatrick, who had every political reason not to rankle the Administration, was officially satisfied with Rosinantes and rackabones—so long as they did not collapse under a trooper's weight. If Custer's brigade were "great horse-killers," the name Kill-Cavalry claimed the wrong man!

Resigned to his temporary fate, Custer contented himself with a love-letter relationship. After "My dearest Armstrong" and other modest greetings, Libbie soon expressed herself to "My Darling Boy": "Ah, dear man, if I am worth having am I not worth waiting for? The very thought of marriage makes me tremble; but am I not selfish to wish that *every* triumph might belong to the Flower of the Army!" Closing with "Your loving Girl," she added, "If you tease me, dear boy, I will go into a convent for a year."

In the same parcel that brought this note, General Custer found a reply from Judge Bacon. Quivering with anticipation, he ripped it open and read: "Pressed in this matter, and having learned from my Daughter how much her happiness is really interested in you, I yield at last. I consent to the Marriage, and would be proud to welcome you as my Son-in-law. . . ." Hallelujah!

Every line from his soul mate was torture to his anxious heart: "Oh, how I long to see you! The worst about loving a soldier is that he is as likely to die as to live, and how should I feel if my soldier should die before I have gratified his heart's desire? . . . My Dear Beloved Star, . . . I have often said because I love so many I could never greatly love one. Foolish girl I was! If loving with one's whole soul is insanity, I am ripe for an insane asylum. . . . My dearest, if you are not already repaid for your abstinence, my pride in you would repay you."

Returning from a Yuletide leave of absence, General Pleasonton promised General Custer a furlough in February, provided he joined "Miss Bacon's household brigade."

Armstrong sent the glad word to sister Lydia-Ann Reed: "I am coming home in Feb'y to be married to Libbie Bacon. The Judge has given us his blessings, and all is in arrangement. . . . Please have my shirts done up by the time I get home. . . . Tell Pop I forgot to get his consent. . . . Give my love to Mom & all, and *write soon.*"

Libbie called on the Custers and Reeds in early January, and the Custers and Reeds soon came to call on the Bacons, and for the first time in Monroe history the Methodists and Presbyterians buried the hatchet.

Libbie penned to her cousin-confidante, Rebecca Richmond: "You will not be more surprised than I am to know that I am going to be married in Feb. to Gen'l Custer. I did not expect it till next winter, but Armstrong pleaded so urgently. . . . I no longer walk in the shadows, but in bright sunshine. . . . My happiness is unspeakable! Oh, Rebecca, it is blissful beyond words to love & to be loved. . . . I do not say Armstrong is without faults. But he never touches liquor or tobacco, nor frequents the gaming-table [!], and tho' not a professing Christian yet respects religion."

Elizabeth continued communication with her "intended": "I hope we may be so happy, my love. I would rather live in a tent, outdoors with you, than in a palace with another. There is no place

I would not go to gladly, live in gladly, because—*because I love you.*"

While personal matters were being settled, military affairs seemed far from satisfactory. Congress had yet to confirm Custer's commission as brigadier general, and there was some indication that a filibuster was brewing:

Senate Chamber, Washington
Jan. 2nd, 1864

Brig.-Gen'l G. A. Custer
2nd Brig., 3rd Div. Cav. Corps, A. P.
Sir:
    Your appointment as Brigadier-General, U. S. Volunteers, has been sent to the Senate. Before I can vote for your confirmation, I desire to be informed whether you are what is termed "a McClellan man."

Yours respectfully,
Zach. Chandler
U.S.S., Michigan

Republican Senators Zachariah Chandler and Jacob M. Howard of Michigan called into question the boy general's alleged citizenship of the Wolverine State. As fiery Old Zach declared, "Why should we forfeit honor to a native son in favor of a transplanted hard-shell Buckeye?" But Congressman William Kellogg disagreed, contending that this was no time for petty partisanism: that General Custer represented the Union, not any one State. Mr. Bingham echoed that sentiment. But opposition was still strong, so General Pleasonton advised his protégé to apply decisive pressure.

Custer appealed by letter to Judge Christiancy and to his future father-in-law, moguls of Michigan politics, entreating them to influence Senators Chandler and Howard in his interest. Howard, a moderate, was soon swayed; but radical Chandler required subtle persuasion from War Secretary Stanton (an Ohio Democrat) and from President Lincoln himself, who now said of Custer, "He's my Brigadier," adding, "He's a fighter, and we can ill-afford to hold our fighters back."

184

Armstrong then scrawled to Judge Bacon: "The subject has caused me no little anxiety, but now my fears are at rest. I would have written you at once when I learned of the efforts made to injure me, but did not wish to trouble Libbie. You would be surprised at the pertinacity with which certain men labor to defame me. I have paid but little attention to them, trusting to time to vindicate me. And I do not fear the result. It was reported that I was a 'Copperhead' [a Southern-sympathizer], a charge completely refuted. Sen. Chandler has expressed himself warmly in my favor. So, too, Mr. Kellogg—that it is not possible for any clique to defeat me."

According to Wainwright, "The cry of 'Copperhead,' 'Rebel sympathiser,' has such a power now; and the name is so freely applied to every one who dares to have an opinion in the slightest degree at variance with those in power, that few have strength of mind enough to utter them."

Custer suspected—and rightly so—that mean-minded Kilpatrick was behind much of this smear campaign in Congress, where he entertained several powerful friends. Kilpatrick, ever jealous and contemptuous of Custer, had challenged (to the point of fisticuffs) his pro-Southern sentiments at West Point; hence, the "folly of youth" branded Old Curly a Copperhead. Already stigmatized as a McClellan man, a wild man or mossback independent, the controversial conservative strove to prove his patriotism with the sword rather than the word. In so doing, he had earned his star.

Confident now that it could not be taken from him, Armstrong raced home to Monroe, home to claim his bride. At last!

Tuesday evening, February 9, 1864.
"The most splendid Wedding ever seen in the State of Michigan," as Judge Daniel Stanton Bacon judged it, was about to begin. Mrs. Gadabout and Gobetween would talk of it for years to come. All of Monroe that could get inside the First Presbyterian Church crammed pews and jammed the aisles. The Monroe papers were full of the romance of "our distinguished townsman," and wellnigh the whole town turned out in freezing weather to see the ceremonies.

8 P.M. The organist piped up the wedding march; and two imposing processions converged at the pulpit, where the Reverend Mr. Erasmus J. Boyd (pastor and schoolmaster) waited to perform the ritual.

Brigadier General George Armstrong Custer was elegantly arrayed in his regulation full-dress uniform: gold-striped lightning-rod pants and dark-blue yellow-sashed frock coat embellished with epaulets, gilt buttons, and gold braid. His golden hair was shorn "quite short" for the occasion: a shock to everyone!

Accompanied by Mrs. Rhoda Pitts Bacon and by his best man, Captain Jacob L. Greene, the boy general beheld his approaching bride with a flush of self-esteem. Elizabeth Clift Bacon "won all hearts" as she swayed down the aisle on her father's arm, a serene smile setting her face aglow. The bride wore a billowy white silk gown looped with gold cavalry lace, and a misty green veil floated back from a tiara of orange blossoms crowning her chestnut-brown tresses. A bouquet of red roses tied with yellow ribbon tremored in her hands. Judge Bacon, his grand old Websterian head towering haughtily above the gaping congregation, struggled hard to choke down the desolate feeling that overcomes a possessive father giving up his only child to another man.

The *beau sabreur* joined hands with his *belle femme* in a perfect service, after which the enraptured newlyweds rushed to the Bacon residence for a lavish reception.

Cousin Rebecca was introduced to Armstrong, and pronounced: "He isn't one bit foppish or conceited. He is a simple, frank, manly fellow. And he fairly idolizes Libbie. I am sure he will make her a true, noble husband. As for Libbie, she is the same gay, irrepressible spirit—unaffected, natural, the old school-girl Libbie, tho' now the wife of a famous Brigadier-Gen'l. They cannot but be happy."

The Judge later wrote to his Grand Rapids relations: "Elizabeth has married entirely to her own satisfaction & to mine. No man could wish for a Son-in-law more highly thought of! Bennett in his N. Y. *Herald* had said so much about the 'Boy General with his flowing yellow curls' that at first all were disappointed in Armstrong's [shorn] appearance. But acquaintance with him changed

186

every body's views. Every where, without exception, he made a *most favorable* impression." (Fiery and flamboyant on the battle-field, where he acted out his inner self, America's Murat was mild-mannered and unassuming in the drawing room—unless involved in some practical joke, an old Custer vice.)

At midnight, Autie and Libbie were given a glorious send-off as they boarded the Cleveland-bound train. Final destination: Virginia. Honeymoon at Army Headquarters on the Rapidan River. What an adventure that would be for a simple-hearted girl!

Cinnamon returned first to his old haunts, there to reminisce about "the dear days beyond recall." When they got off the train across the Hudson from West Point, Autie and Libbie found the river ice-crusted and the ferry ice-locked. So they hired a hefty timberjack, who pulled Mrs. Custer over the frozen water on his sled while the General pushed from behind.

"I never dreamed there was so lovely a place in the United States," Elizabeth wrote to the folks in Monroe. "Everyone was delighted to see Autie. Even the dogs welcomed him!"

On the cannon-ball express to Washington, Libbie found herself "in trouble." She was flabbergasted to see her blithesome bridegroom turned into a human thundercloud. It was their first quarrel, the first time she saw him lose his temper.

"I'll be damned if any dark-horse professor can claim the privilege of kissing *my* wife without permission!"

"But he was a regular Methuselah," Libbie protested laughingly. "And those cadets who showed me Lovers' Walk were like school-boys with their shy ways and nice, clean, friendly faces."

"Hm! Well, I ought to send you back home to your people—like any other naughty little girl who can't stay away from bad boys."

"Well, you left me with them, Autie!"

"Hmm! So I did!"

The two simpered, then burst out laughing. The crisis ended in a hug and a kiss.

Soon a second bone of contention was tossed into the Custer love nest. Armstrong wanted Elizabeth to stay in Washington (where it was "safe") after a brief visit to the front, but Elizabeth insisted on following her husband (regulations permitting, like it or not!) right into the very jaws of death.

The General's lady had her way, and always would—"for Autie's sake." Custer found it easier to command a whole brigade than one woman. But he learned to like it, and adapted with grace, never regretting his step from single blessedness to marital bliss. He respected strength of purpose, especially in a female, and was obedient to it. General Custer never surrendered, save to his wife. And he would attempt a thousand glorious victories just to suffer Love's single vanquishment.

"Libbie has two wills of her own," he would often say. "I have lent her mine for safekeeping."

★ 24 ★

CHARLOTTESVILLE: CUSTER'S RAID

"ALL quiet, and mud-bound, along the Rapidan."—E. A. Paul, New York *Times*.

General and Mrs. G. A. Custer established their home and headquarters in an old farmhouse at Stevensburg, five miles southeast of Culpeper. There they lived in military style. No roughing it for the wife of a brigadier! "There are lots of women in the Army now," noted Colonel C. S. Wainwright—indeed, nearly a thousand wives and countless nurses—so Elizabeth Custer was no exception.

"Such style as we go in! Most army officers' wives have to ride in ambulances," Libbie informed her folks, "but my Gen'l has a carriage with silver harness that he captured last summer, and two magnificent matched horses. We have an escort of 4 or 6 soldiers riding behind."

While the doughboys and "mudmashers" in their log-and-canvas shebangs and dugouts griped, "Our grub is enough to make a mule desert and a hog wish he was never born," the big brass of the Grand Army of the Potomac enjoyed six-course spreads of fancy fixin's—everything from soup to nuts. "Drunken rascals," the lot of 'em—except for the likes of Old Curly, who refused even wine at these stylish feasts.

For all of a honeymoon month, the budding army wife slowly but surely accepted the idiosyncrasies of her boy general. And she did so in silent amusement, though at first she suffered the terrible temptation to ask Autie why he brushed his teeth with salt after every meal, why he scented his yellow mane with cinnamon oil, and why he always seemed to be washing his big bony hands with spicy toilet soap. (His fair, freckled skin reacted unfavorably to hard soap and water—especially in cold, dry weather.)

Sunday, February 28, 1864. It was a raw, wet, windy afternoon. Libbie, trembling with anxiety, watched tearfully as her husband rode out of Camp Stevensburg at the head of his 2nd Michigan Cavalry Brigade—the renowned Wolverines, Old Curly's Blue-devils—fifteen hundred strong.

Destination: Charlottesville, about forty miles southwest, in the heart of enemy territory.

Objectives: Circuit Lee's left flank, cut off rail communications with Richmond by destroying the Gordonsville & Lynchburg R.R. bridge over the Rivanna River, demolish the Confederate supply depot at Charlottesville, and divert Stuart long enough for Kilpatrick to carry out his "madbrained mission."

While in Washington, socializing "on sick leave," Kilpatrick had convinced the President that (if Custer could effect a diversionary movement) Kilpatrick could raid Richmond and release the 15,000 Union captives—many of whom were his own men, lost at "Buck-land Races"—in Belle Isle and Libby Prisons. It was a wanton but worthy play for glory, perhaps precipitated by a recent tragedy. "He has just lost [by death] his wife & only child," Colonel Wainwright reveals, "and they say he is gloomy & desperate—just in the state to try something wild."

With Custer as his pawn, to feint before Stuart, Kilpatrick delivered his bold stroke—and missed the mark. He got stuck in the proverbial Virginia mud just outside of Richmond, and was forced into a footrace down the Peninsula to Harrison's Landing by Texas Tom Rosser's 5000-man cavalry division, which was guarding the Queen City of the South. Three thousand abandoned horses and over three hundred troopers thus fell into enemy hands. A fanatic peace commissioner, delegated by Mr. Lincoln to offer amnesty to all secessionists willing to surrender their allegiance to the Confederacy, was also left in the mud. Peg-legged Colonel Ulric Dahlgren (son of the celebrated admiral and ordnance inventor) swore to hang Jeff Davis and Company on a sour-apple tree, should

Kill-Cavalry take and burn Richmond. He was sniped to death and mutilated by Mosby's men. As "Uncle John" Sedgwick put it, "The great raid was a great failure"; and what was left of Kilpatrick's command "must be carried back [to camp] in steamers, like a parcel of old women going to market."

But while Kilpatrick failed, and miserably, Custer came through with flying colors—"without having suffered the loss of a man." He and his troopers covered nearly a hundred miles in forty-eight hours, through ice and snow and freezing rain, with precious little sleep. They had burned the bridge, burned the depot, and barely escaped being trapped by Fitzhugh Lee, Marse Robert's rich-bearded nephew. Fifty prisoners, taken by surprise while patrolling the depot, was no mean haul!

On March 2, Pleasonton officially expressed to Custer his "entire satisfaction" at the result of the expedition, and "the gratification" he felt at the prompt manner in which the duties assigned to him had been performed.

"Mission accomplished—but for that damn fool Kilpatrick!" Autie said, almost breathless with exuberance, as he embraced Libbie. "By golly, I've outfoxed the Gray Fox!"

On March 19, 1864, the front page of *Harper's Weekly* depicted General G. A. Custer leading a cavalry charge; and on the twenty-sixth the front-page feature was "General Custer's Raid," a two-sheet spread of drawings by A. R. Waud. While Kilpatrick was cast in the shade ("They are down on Kilpatrick for his miserable failure before Richmond"), Custer basked in a blaze of glory.

191

25

STEVENSBURG:
ANNIE'S REVENGE

O<small>N</small> Tuesday, March 22, 1864, a stormy petrel dunged in the Custer love nest.

A thick packet was delivered early that morning to General Custer by one of General Kilpatrick's aides. Marked "Confidential," it contained "Report respecting a young lady calling herself *Annie E. Jones,* supposed to be a Rebel Spy" and "Statement in regard to her adventures in the camps of the *Middle Department* & the *Army of the Potomac,* and her connection with various officers since Aug., 1861." These documents being "respectfully referred" to General Pleasonton by General Meade, "he deems it due to Brigadier-Gen'ls Kilpatrick & Custer that they should have an opportunity to offer such explanations, if any, as they may desire to present respecting so much of this communication as relates to them." Pleasonton thereupon "resp'y ref'd" the matter to Kilpatrick, who "respectfully submitted" same to Custer "for compliance with the requirements" of a full explanation.

According to an unsigned letter dated "Falls Church, Jan. 18th" [1863] and sent to General Heintzelman (then commanding the defenses of Washington) at Alexandria, Miss Jones was to all appearances "a Rebel spy" who "has in her possession (and has shown it to a number of persons) a pass anywhere within the Confederate lines. . . . She boasts of being the friend of some of the most prominent officers of the Southern Army. . . . She makes no hesitation of avowing her feeling for the South, saying that they are right and must eventually triumph. Her acquaintances among

192

Union officers are numerous; and as she is very well educated and intelligent, she easily interests and engages their attention, and might obtain from them the most important information."

An investigation made by Lieutenant Charles H. Shepard (provost marshal, Fort Albany, Virginia) "could not find any person who supposed her to be a spy," but discovered that she had first come to camp with the 135th New York Volunteers as "Daughter of the Regt."; that she was an orphan, her guardian being the Reverend Phineas Stowe of Boston; that "She denies of ever having been South"; that she was arrested twice and accused of espionage, but had "proved her loyalty beyond question." Again stating that he "could not find any person who had ever heard her make any disloyal remarks," Shepard concluded: "The letter containing the charges was evidently written by a female who is jealous of her, as her former lover is paying some attention to this Miss Jones, and I found she was very anxious to have this Miss Jones out of the way. It was a very amusing investigation on the whole."

Notwithstanding, Miss Jones was re-arrested by order of General G. K. Warren (Centerville, September of '63) for acting as a spy, giving secret information to Rebel raiders, "harboring and concealing enemies of the U.S.," and breaking her parole by entering Virginia. Annie's second arrest found her in Old Capitol Prison, Washington, where she signed a statement setting forth her "intention of offering my services as a Hospital nurse. . . . While in the various camps, I was furnished by the commanding officers with a tent, and sometimes occupied quarters with the officers." After stating that she was the "guest" of Generals Sigel and Pope and their staff officers at Fairfax Courthouse and Centerville respectively, Miss Jones matter-of-factly relates that she remained with General Julius Stahl until he was relieved—"when I joined Gen. Kilpatrick's command, and went to the front, as the friend and companion of Gen. Custer. We made our head-quarters near Hartwood Church. While stopping at this point, Gen. Kilpatrick became very jealous of Gen. Custer's attentions to me, and went to Gen. Meade's head-quarters, and charged me with being a Rebel spy. I was then arrested and sent to Gen. Martindale, Military Governor

193

of Washington, who committed me to the Old Capitol Prison."

Annie's story is not consistent with the official records. Kilpatrick made no such charge, neither at G.H.Q. nor the Provost Marshal's Office, but merely ordered Miss Jones (after her reputed rendezvous with Mosby) out of his command. She was subsequently arrested by order of Warren, at Centerville, on charges of consorting with enemy raiders in that area.

"I have spent two years and a half in the Union Army," she owns, "and during this time have been the guest of different officers: they furnishing me with horses, orderlies, escorts, sentinels at my tent or quarters, rations, &c. . . . I invariably wore Major's straps. I have repeatedly passed . . . into the Rebel lines, and was once captured by Mosby and . . . detained one or two days." She concluded that "during no part of the time that I was with the Federal Army was I employed as . . . Hospital nurse, but as a companion to the various commanding officers—as a private friend or companion."

By her own admission, Annie's release from Old Capitol Prison was greatly influenced by her becoming "intimately acquainted" with the assistant superintendent (Mr. John S. Lockwood, who was subsequently discharged) and the chief jailer, a Captain Mix. She adds: "During the entire time since my leaving home in 1861, I have led a very roving and maybe questionable life. I am now very unwell, owing to my long confinement and other causes [perhaps an abortion or two], and desire to be released from custody in order that I may return to my home and friends."

Custer was infuriated. If anyone had taken Annie Jones as a "friend and companion," it was that lecher Kilpatrick. She had been his "weed-monkey" (a young girl who hangs around camp) for all of a week. Didn't the Bluedevils allude to her as "Gen'l Kil's Aide" and "Kill-Cavalry's Campfollower"? What a slanderously humiliating accusation, that "Gen. Kilpatrick became very jealous of Gen. Custer's attentions to me"! Perhaps a lame excuse to explain away her subsequent arrest for "monkeying" with Mosby's men. However, he would set the record straight:

194

Hd.-Qrs., 2nd Brig., 3rd Div.
Cav. Corps, Army of the Potomac
Mar. 22, '64

Statement of Brig.-Gen'l G. A. Custer in regard to Annie E. Jones
. . . she [Miss Jones] was at my Head-qrs. about one week,
during which time she was never allowed to go outside my lines
or even to visit the outer posts; although she frequently expressed
a desire to do so. Her whole object and purpose in being with
the Army seemed to be to distinguish herself by some deed of
daring. In this respect alone, she seemed to be insane. It was only
my disinclination to use force towards her that induced me to
permit her to stay the short time I have mentioned. So far as her
statement in relation to Gen'l Kilpatrick and myself goes, it is
simply untrue. I do not believe she is or ever was a spy. This
part of her reputation has been gained by her imprudence.

Respectfully Submitted.
G. A. Custer
Brig.-Gen'l*

Custer, not so rashly naïve as Kilpatrick, did well to cover up.
Already branded a Copperhead, he dreaded the stigma of "traitor"
—which the old slur "McClellan man" implied in radical circles.
The Annie Jones affair had him worried for some time, suspecting
it as a setup designed to blackmail him or compromise his position.
In any case, Custer had gallantly, and charitably, disembarrassed
Kilpatrick from a scandalous plight. And Kilpatrick, though he
said little and wrote nothing, was undoubtedly grateful, considering
the way he had "flummoxed," as Hancock expressed it, before
Richmond. Another *faux pas* would have been disastrous.

In February of '64, Colonel Lyman (like Wainwright) had observed: "There are perfect shoals of womenkind now in the Army,"
many living "a sort of Bedouin life. . . . Such a set of feminine
humans I have not seen often; it was Lowell factories broken loose
& gone mad." Now, a month later: "Until further orders," proclaimed General Meade anew, "the employment of Females as
officers' servants is prohibited." (Exception made for Aunt Eliza!)

* All documents relating to the Annie Jones affair are from the National
Archives, Washington, D.C.

26

WASHINGTON: OLD
BLOOD-AND-WHISKERS

MAJOR General Ulysses Simpson Grant, commander of the Grand Army of the Cumberland, was now appointed Lieutenant General in supreme command of the Armies of the United States by President Lincoln. Old Plug Meade retained his commission as G.I.C. of the Potomac forces, but under Grant's supervision.

A year before, Custer had heard scuttlebutt to the effect that certain Washington bigwigs wanted to sack "Old Blood-and-Whiskers," like Little Mac, for slowpokery. But Mr. Lincoln would near none of it. "I can't spare that man. He fights!" If nothing else, "Uncle Sam" Grant was a fighter. As the Boys in Blue and Gray said, "When that old cuss is around, there's sure to be a big fight somewhere!" When blatant hydropots raised a storm over the appointment of a "drunk" as General-in-Chief of the U.S. Army, Mr. Lincoln responded, "What brand does he drink? I'd like to send a barrel of it to the other generals."

General Custer first became conversant with the new G.I.C. on a special lightning express en route to the Capital from Camp Stevensburg. Grant was railing up the Orange & Alexandria Line to accept his commission from Mr. Lincoln in an official ceremony and social affair to be celebrated in his honor. Custer was on that train to enjoy a honeymoon jaunt with his lovely wife, whom he wished to show off to Washington society, but particularly for the purpose of finding a respectable boardinghouse. In another month or so, General Grant would be launching the Federal forces on their spring campaign; and a full-scale offensive against General Lee and the Queen City of the South was no theater for a woman to attend. Libbie must again be "the girl I left behind me." Her objections were overruled by a general order: "All ladies are hereby instructed to leave camp."

"Stumpy, unmilitary, slouchy & Western-looking—very ordinary, in fact." Thus Colonel Wainwright appraised General Grant. "It is hard to believe that he is a great man"—especially since he was "distinguished for the mediocrity of his mind, his great good nature & his insatiable love of whiskey." According to Richard Henry Dana, Jr., Grant was an "ordinary, scrubby-looking man with a slightly seedy look." And though he had the appearance of one who had once taken "a little too much to drink," he also revealed "a clear blue eye and a look of resolution, as if he could not be trifled with, and an entire indifference to the crowd about him."

The Custers found "Sam" Grant to be an unassuming maverick with twinkly sea-blue eyes, tight mouth, and a shock of reddish-brown hair. Short and slim, this hard-drinking cigar-smoking Buckeye was slouchy in form and slipshod by nature. Ruddy-complexioned, he wore an expression as if "determined to drive his head through a brick wall." Grant was forever stroking his rugged, rusty, close-clipped beard with his left hand; and when he talked—which to Libbie seemed all the time—the unconventional General had a habit of lifting and lowering his cupped right hand, letting it rest only at intervals on his knee.

Attired in the tarnished uniform of a major general, and dragging philosophically on one stogie after another, the shabby-genteel "Hero of Fort Donelson" amused Autie and Libbie with his self-effacing cracker-barrel humor.

"Y'know, Mrs. Custer," he said, "small army men invariably ride horses seventeen hands high. Take my favorite charger Cincinnati. He makes me look like a flea on a dog's back." To Armstrong he whispered, "Y'know, I don't remember a damn thing I learned at West Point."

Fearing his cigars might strangle the boy general's better half,

197

Unconditional Surrender did most of his smoking out on the car platform—until Custer begged him to return on a plea that the Mrs. didn't mind the stink so long as the distinguished tobacconalian didn't. Grant roared with laughter and returned to his seat across from the personable Mrs. Custer.

"Father, you have a modest son-in-law," Libbie penned proudly. "Instead of speaking with men who could do so much for him, Autie sat by me & only spoke when necessary." She then added, "Tho' disappointed in Grant's looks, I like him very much."

Sight-seeing Federal City with her hubby, the discerning Mrs. General Custer was impressed by that elegant edifice called the Capitol and anything but impressed by that "wrangling set" known as the House of Representatives assembled therein. "Such a want of order, of dignity!"

Their big moment finally arrived when Congressman William Kellogg of Michigan introduced them to President and Mrs. Abraham Lincoln. During the subsequent chat held by three great leaders of men, Custer heard Lincoln say to Grant, "All I ever wanted was someone who would take the responsibility and act. As we say out West, if a man can't skin he must hold a leg while somebody else does!"

To which Grant replied, "Whatever happens, Mr. President, there will be no turning back."

Lincoln smiled, clasping Grant's hand. "With a brave army and a just cause, may God sustain you."

Libbie informed her folks all about the Washington reception: "I can't tell you what a place Autie has here in public opinion. I thought that a Brigadier would not be anything, but I find that mine is someone to be envied. It astonishes me to see the attention with which he is treated everywhere. One day at the House he was invited to go on the floor, and the Members came flocking round to be presented to him. . . . One said, 'So you are the youngest General in the Army. Well, I wish there were more like you!" And when some old fogey objected to his confirmation as Brig-Gen'l on account of his youth, the rest said, 'Pity there aren't more like him!' . . . The President knew all about him when Autie was presented to him, and talked to him about his promotion. None of the other Gen'ls receive half the attention, and their arrivals are scarcely noticed in the papers. . . . I wonder his head is not turned! Tho' not disposed to put on airs, I find it very agreeable to be the wife of a man so generally known & respected."

★ 27 ★

BRANDY STATION: LITTLE PHIL

A<small>FTER</small> several weeks of being lionized by the Northern elite and glamorized by such publications as *Harper's Weekly* and the New York *Tribune,* George Armstrong Custer was obliged to leave his beloved Elizabeth and return to the theater of war.

The ride back to camp was fateful in that Ranger Mosby missed capturing, by an hour, Generals Custer and Grant and staff. A delayed train helped save the Union. "Autie never told me a word about it!" Libbie wrote home. Her long trial was just begun.

General Custer hopped off the train at Brandy Station on Friday, April 15, 1864. There he was surprised to learn of a sudden shake-up and reorganization in the Army of the Potomac. General Pleasonton was no longer Chief of the Cavalry Corps. Custer's "Dutch uncle" had been replaced by a fiery Irishman from the Western front, Major General Philip H. Sheridan, "Hero of Missionary Ridge."

Custer led his horses and dogs out of the stockcar and cantered over to Cavalry Headquarters. He was extremely eager to meet this man they called "Little Phil." According to Colonel Wainwright, a change in cavalry commanders had long been needed. "Neither Stoneman nor Pleasonton proved themselves equal to the position." The fact is, Old Whiplash had made himself a much-hated man in the eyes of Meade, whom he accused (before the inquisitional Joint Committee on the Conduct of the War) of incompetence and indifference during the Gettysburg campaign. Such testimony sealed Pleasonton's doom in the Eastern theater of military service.

Custer saw Sheridan as a broad-shouldered bantam with mossy black hair and piercing, almond-shaped eyes. A narrow-rimmed billycock hat sat squarely on his square head; and arched eyebrows, coupled with a trim fluffy beard and mustachios, accented his solid red face. In Wainwright's words, "he appeared exceedingly affable & pleasant . . . , but certainly would not impress one by his looks any more than Grant does. He is short, thick-set & common Irish-looking . . . with rather a jolly face, but not a great one. He dresses & wears his hair much in the Bowery soap-lock style, and could easily pass himself off for one of the 'b'hoys.' " Colonel Lyman described him as looking "very like a Piedmontese" and as making "everywhere a favorable impression."

Sheridan was forever smiling, in a frownish sort of way, like an East Side imp; and the lyric brogue of his boglander parents was traceable in his twang. Custer liked him. Unlike Little Kil, Little Phil was no shoneen—no ass wagging his ears. Sheridan seemed to be a good and game sport, a toughie who could take it as well as dish it out. He owned an ornery temper, and he cussed a blue streak, but there was nothing "highfalutin you-be-damned" about this hard-fighting featherweight. No, he was a capital fellow: a diamond in the rough.

Within a few minutes after they first shook hands, Custer and Sheridan were addressing each other as "Curly" and "Phil." Camaraderie radiated between them almost at once. Custer did not stand in awe of Sheridan as he had of Pleasonton, but viewed him in the role of an older brother, gruffly good-natured, jovially masterful. He would be ruled by him, and yet would rule; for Little Phil was an "old softy" under the skin. One had only to humor him to get one's own way.

The new cavalry chief invited his star brigadier to stay over-night at corps headquarters so they could get better acquainted. Custer accepted at once. This Sheridan was sure worth knowing, worth working for and liking.

Custer (brigaded with Tom Devin and Wes Merritt) also greeted his new division commander, an old acquaintance, Brigadier General Alfred T. A. Torbert. This tall, scowling, brown-Dundrearied cavalryman swanked about in a star-embroidered jumper, bell-

201

bottom trousers, and a star-studded fedora. Torbert was assigned the 1st Division; D. M. Gregg, the 2nd; and the 3rd went to one of Grant's pets, a promising young go-getter named James H. Wilson. Custer had known Wilson in the good old days of Little Mac, when both were "angelfaces" on Pleasonton's staff. He, and perhaps Wesley Merritt, felt put out by these sudden transfers for preferment; felt piqued by Grant's packing the G.A.P. with his own darlings, to the detriment of many who had given the grand old army its identity. "Replacements should come to subordinate positions," Custer contended. "We who have fought with the Army of the Potomac, since its very inception, should be its leaders." But Grant was now in control; and Grant favored his old standbys, like it or not. "With the possible exception of Gettysburg," he privately declared, "this army hasn't done a damn thing worthy of its spirit; and I mean to make it move with an infusion of Western blood: the blood that took Vicksburg and rolled Bragg in the dust."

In any event, Custer was glad to get rid of Kilpatrick, who was transferred to "Uncle Billy" Sherman's Grand Army of the West. Thus was the G.A.P. relieved of what Meade's Headquarters diagnosed as "a chronic pain in the fundament." Of course, Old Curly would miss Kill-Cavalry's horse races—both of them having matched the best thoroughbreds in the service—but gambling was one of the vices Libbie had cautioned her "darling boy" against, so self-abnegation was in order. Indeed, it would take a loving woman's touch to discipline the free-spirited darling of war-gods.

While he had the chance, Old Curly wangled a two-day leave from Little Phil for May 1 and 2. Another opportunity like this might never come for a week of Sundays. U.S. Grant had ordered an all-out advance of the Union Army for Wednesday, May 4.

"Oh, Autie," Libbie said, "I can't tell you how lonely I have been. It's a far worse trial then I thought it would be. And yet, darling, I'm prouder to be your little girl than if I was the wife of the President—or even a queen!"

Asked if she had seen Mr. Lincoln again she answered, "Yes; the Kelloggs took me. . . . Autie, I think he's the gloomiest, most painfully careworn-looking man I ever saw in my life. How I feel for poor Mrs. Lincoln! I think I know what she must suffer."

"Did he speak to you?"

"Oh yes! In spite of his careworn face, he's still the prince of jokers. He took my hand very cordially and said: 'So this is the young woman whose husband goes into a charge with a whoop and a shout. Well, I'm told he won't do so anymore!' I replied I hoped he would! He said: 'Oh, then you want to be a widow, I see!' He laughed, and so did I. Was I not honored, darling? I'm quite a Lincoln girl now! I even bade Mr. Hay tell Mrs. Lincoln he'd have gained a vote if soldiers' wives were allowed one."

"And me a McClellan man! By God, Mrs. Custer, you ought to be ashamed of yourself."

The conversation turned to General Pleasonton, about whom Libbie had plucked much from the local grapevine. "People are saying he was removed not on account of any hard feelings between him and General Meade, but because his two sisters—maiden ladies, both living here—have talked so badly about the President and the Secretary of War; and it was supposed these were his views they were repeating."

"Well, let that be a warning to my little girl to keep her darling nose out of military and political matters. I learned to hold my tongue long ago. General McClellan taught me the virtue of *that* lesson."

Custer had an image to protect, a pageant of agreeable independence, and none must now take it from him but at the greatest risk.

When he returned to camp, on the eve of the great spring campaign, Armstrong wrote: "My Brigade never looked better. I am more than proud of it. I wish my little girl might be present to enjoy the splendid sight. We are in readiness to advance. Weather & roads are favorable. This is probably the last letter you will get from me before the coming fight. The entire army moves to-night & begins crossing the Rapidan at Germanna Ford. Do not be over-anxious. Gen'l Sheridan (who has reviewed the entire Cav. Corps) and Gen'l Torbert say that I have the finest & best Brigade of Cavalry in the entire Army. I am laboring to make it still better. Communication with Washington will probably be abandoned for several days, but do not borrow trouble. Remember: No news is good news! . . . On the eve of every battle in which I have been engaged, I have never failed to commend myself to Destiny's keeping. After having done so, all anxiety for myself is dispelled. I feel that my destiny is 'in the hands' of a Higher Power. This belief, more than any other fact or reason, makes me brave & fearless as I am."

★ 28 ★

YELLOW TAVERN: JEB STUART GOES TO GLORY

At the first flush of May 5, 1864, over a Virginia countryside beaming with green buds and purple blooms, General Custer and his 1st Michigan Brigade clip-clopped across a pontoon bridge spanning the Rapidan at Ely's Ford and jogged southward into the swampy, entangled Wilderness where Robert E. Lee's veterans were waiting.

"Them Rebs'll pick us off like on a possum hunt!" one grizzled vet in blue remarked.

"Damnation," retorted another voice of experience, "don't you see Old Curly there? As long as he ain't scared, I ain't!"

Aunt Eliza ("a jewel of a servant"), driving her chuck wagon alongside the General, shook with glee and said, "Gin'l, the men-folks reckon you can do as much as the Awmighty!"

For several days the Blue and the Gray played a deadly game of hide-and-seek in dense pine jungles and snarled scrubland. The Battle of the Wilderness was bushwhacking on a grand and slaughterous scale. But neither side outgamed the other. It was a running standoff as both armies slid slowly southward, spilling blood all the way.

It was impossible for cavalry to maneuver effectively in that vast entanglement, so Sheridan threaded forward in a lacework formation. Gregg screened the advance; Wilson covered the flanks; Torbert brought up the rear with its crawling, sprawling leviathans of wagons and guns. Stuart's Black Horse Raiders played at hit-and-run, attempting to dismember the monsters and cripple Grant, but Torbert held the huge train together and fought them off in an indecisive two-day series of dismounted skirmishes.

With Torbert suddenly on the sick list, due to a spinal abscess, Merritt, as highest-ranking brigadier, assumed temporary command of the 1st Division. Custer now saw his chance to cut loose, and cut loose he did. Dull routine be damned! Let Merritt and Devin guard the artillery and supply train. He was pushing south—through dead of night, through fog-shrouded inferno, where flash and crash made forest primeval a chamber of horrors—down Brook Pike, into and out of the ghostly Wilderness, to where Sheridan and Gregg held Todd's Tavern in open country that stretched to Spotsylvania Courthouse.

Saturday, May 7. An ominously still day, finding Blue and Gray on the ragged edge of nervous breakdown. The "battle," a languishing chaos of guerrilla warfare, had played itself out to a restorative standstill. At Todd's Tavern, G.H.Q., General Meade was growling: "What in God's name do you mean, sir, to allow Stuart to draw you into his own ground? What's wrong with our horse, that you can't lick Stuart on *our* terms and in *our* time?"

Sheridan, "that bandy-legged little mick," glared in a controlled rage. His words erupted like spit, quick and sharp: "Beg pardon, General: the only thing *wrong* with our horse is a bad case of inactivity. I rather call it a mean and unmanly tarriance."

"How dare you, sir!" Meade exploded, then settled into sarcasm. "And what, pray tell, would you do?"

"By God, General, I'd go out and whip Jeb Stuart!"

"You think you can?" Grant idly interjected, gnawing his cigar.

"Goddamme if I don't!"

Meade flicked his hand. "Now, sir, be amenable to reason——"

"Reason be damned!" Sheridan thundered. "If you, sir, can do better, *you* command the cavalry. As I cannot have a free hand to act as I see fit, the job is completely yours." And out he stormed, all fire and fury.

When the atmosphere cooled, Grant cocked an eye at Meade and drawled dryly, "Says he can whip Stuart, eh? Then we'll let him go out and do it."

Meade, who had held Sheridan back in fear of a Confederate

flank movement and an imperiled supply line, was obliged to nod. Nothing venture, nothing win!

As gamy as Lee, Grant was hell-bent on hammering out a victory whatever the cost. "So help me," he exclaimed, "I propose to fight it out on this line if it takes all summer." He summoned Phil Sheridan, said, "Go out and whip Jeb Stuart once and for all. If he gives you any great trouble, keep pushing with all your might. That's the way to connect. Hammer, hammer, hammer away. Take all the prisoners you can. Only *get Jeb Stuart*."

Marse Robert's remark, "It's well war is so terrible, or we should get too fond of it," meant nothing to "Butcher" Grant. Mr. Lincoln had at last found a blood-and-guts general.

Old Curly was all ears as Little Phil briefed his division chiefs and brigadiers on a daring *coup de maître* in prospect: "We're going out to fight Stuart's cavalry. We'll be moving in one column around the right flank of Lee's army till we get to his rear. It's my intention to fight Stuart wherever he shows himself. We'll give him a fair, square fight. Our move will be a challenge to Stuart for a cavalry duel behind Lee's lines, in his own country. We're strong, and I know we can beat him. I'll expect nothing but success."

Wednesday, May 11, 1864, 3 P.M.

Inching southward in a column thirteen miles long, with wagons and pack mules, Sheridan's twelve thousand troopers and seven flying batteries were determined to beat the "Flower of the Confederacy" at his own old game—a long, sweeping raid around the enemy lines. Objectives: cut off Lee's communications with the Southern capital, plunder his supply lines, effect a diversionary movement in order to lure Stuart into an open fight and prevent his further harassment of Federal communications, scare the pants and pantalets off the people in Richmond, and—hopefully—decisively whip Old Jeb in the bargain.

So far, since May 9, General Custer and his advance-guard Wolverines had singlehandedly wrecked Beaver Dam Station, blown up three locomotives, highjacked nearly ten million dollars' worth of munitions and supplies, ripped up ten miles of (Virginia Central) railroad tracks, torn down ten miles of telegraph lines,

207

and freed nearly four hundred Federal captives en route to Libby
Prison—all on his own hook—while Sheridan, far behind with the
rest of the Corps, was fighting off Confederate raiders.

Now, only six miles north of Richmond, Sheridan's Raiders and
Stuart's Invincibles came face to face on the road to Yellow Tavern.

In extended order across Brook Pike and neighboring fields,
Beauty's crack troopers discharged a rolling carbine fire and
opened up on Little Phil's right wing with a battery of light guns.

The 1st U.S. Cavalry Division, holding the right of Sheridan's
battleline, was still under temporary command of Wes Merritt.
Custer sprinted over to this clean-cut, clean-shaven, boyish-looking
brigadier and said abruptly, "Merritt, I'm going to charge that
battery."

Merritt smiled agreeably, flicking his swagger stick. "Go in,
General. I'll give you all the support in my power."

Custer nodded with a brisk grin and spurred back to his brigade.

At that moment Sheridan pulled up alongside the trim, personable Merritt. "Say, what's Custer up to?"

"I expect he's going to charge for the guns, sir."

"Well, bully for him! I'll wait and see it."

Custer dashed down the line, drew rein in front of the 3rd
Division. "Wilson," he snapped, "I'm going to charge that battery.
Order out the 1st Vermont. I'll need 'em for the job."

Brigadier General James H. Wilson, a gaunt and nervous
sabreur, answered irritably, "What piece of highhandedness is this?
Does Sheridan know your intentions?"

"Never mind Sheridan. Merritt knows my intentions."

"Well, I'm sorry, General; but I cannot give you the 1st Vermont
without Sheridan's confirmation."

"All right—*all right,* goddammit—go to Sheridan, if you must."

Custer, a scowling heated crimson, watched Wilson spur away—
then commandeered the 1st Vermont Cavalry in almost the same
manner he had "borrowed" them from Merritt, at Culpeper, last
September.

"It seems he already has 'em!" Sheridan snorted, pointing to a
flamboyant figure leading the 1st Vermont to the right of the line.

"Why, the audacity—!" Wilson blurted, tense with anger.

Phil smiled fiercely. "Let him go, Jimmy. Fools rush in where angels fear to tread."

Old Curly dismounted the 5th and 6th Michigan, deployed them in skirmishing order as flankers. Back and forth he darted, wheeling and gag-checking his mount with breath-taking precision. "First Vermont!" he addressed Colonel Addison W. Preston, then accosted Colonels Stagg and Granger: "First and 7th Michigan! Form squadrons! First Michigan front, 1st Vermont and 7th Michigan in support!" Over two thousand troopers rolled and shuttled into position.

Brigadier Custer flipped off his black slouch hat and shouted, "By column of squadrons, forward at the walk! Drum Major, strike up 'Yankee Doodle!' Dress to the colors, boys! Hold your lines!" He darted a leftward glance. "The eyes of General Sheridan are upon you!"

Canister shot whistled and crashed high overhead, casting down scattered showers of lead, as the 1st Michigan Brigade paraded forward to the brassy swing of that doggerel air:

> Yankee Doodle is a tune
> Americans delight in:
> Good to fiddle, dance or sing,
> And just the thing for fightin'!

Custer drew out his toledo. He turned in the saddle, resting the blade against his shoulder. "Wolverines," he shrilled, "draw sabers! Trot *march!*"

Sheridan and Merritt looked and listened as distant bugles blared the "Trot" and solid blue squadrons jogged onward, sabers glinting and guidons aflutter. The rasping of cold steel from clattering scabbards was music to Armstrong's ears, and he tingled with anticipation. Horses snuffed and flounced, startled by bursting shells, but their discipline was superb. The advance was nerve-racking, and when the climax came, it came as a dreadful explosion.

Within direct carbine range of the enemy, Old Curly raised his sword. "At a gallop! . . . Buglers, sound the '*Charge!*'" A hot flash raced through him as he clapped spurs to his charger. "Come on, Wolverines!"

209

Custer bounded ahead like a thunderbolt, his hurricane of "bluedevil" horsemen rumbling and roaring at his heels. Flaring sabers, flaming neckties, flickering pennants: a massive streak of brute force, hurled forth like billows of the wild resounding sea. Sheridan and Merritt saw those onrushing breakers smash at full speed into Stuart's left flank, breaking and tearing it apart.

Through whirlgusts of horsemen colliding at a dead run, the boy general caught a fleeting glimpse of the dashing "Buckskin Cavalier" with his luxuriant dark-red beard and gray felt turnup festooned with a sweeping sable plume. Major General J. E. B. Stuart was making a desperate effort to rally his shattered ranks: "Go back! Go back and do your duty as I have done mine, and our country will be safe! Go back! go back! I'd rather die than be whipped!"

Jeb's destiny was fulfilled. Sergeant John A. Huff (Company A, 5th Michigan,) perched against a rail fence, drew a bead on General Stuart and shot him in the liver. Jeb, age thirty-one, died the following evening. "I can scarcely think of him without weeping," said General Lee.

Curly's Wolverines outflanked the Invincibles, put them to flight, seized the howitzer battery, and rounded up a hundred prisoners. One of them was Stuart's aide-de-camp, Captain Dorsey. Custer rode up to him and said; "How is General Stuart? Is he badly hit?"

"Yes, damn you," Dorsey lashed back; "and we ought to kill every one of you for it!"

Custer crimsoned, yanked his horse away.

At that moment, General Sheridan was turning to his fellow spectator: "Merritt, send a staff officer to Custer and give him my compliments. Tell him the charge was splendid, bully! The conduct of himself and his brigade deserves the most honorable mention."

General Merritt also sent his congratulations: "Headed by an intrepid commander, the Michigan Brigade is at the top of the ladder."

Sheridan scribbled a preliminary report: "Custer's charge was brilliantly executed. . . . The Confederate Cavalry was badly broken up. . . . The engagement ended by giving us complete control of the road to Richmond."

Least enthused was General Wilson, whose 1st Vermont had lent impetus to the onslaught. "All glory goes to Goldilocks and his Michigan Brigade—as usual," he remarked sardonically to Merritt. "I dare say that man would ride roughshod over us all in order to win this war singlehanded."

Merritt smiled. "You mustn't take Custer too seriously. He means well. An obstreperous little boy, struggling to grow up."

"At our expense!"

"Oh, I shouldn't think that. I trust his intentions. And I thank God we've got him on our side!"

Merritt, once resentful of Custer, had (by nature and necessity) adopted an attitude of philosophical indulgence. *Esprit de corps!*

Several days later, at Haxall's Landing on the James River, Autie penciled to Libbie: "We have passed thro' days of carnage & have lost heavily, but we have been successful. The Michigan Brigade has covered itself with undying glory. . . . I led the charge in which we mortally wounded Gen'l Stuart. . . . Suffice it to say that *our* Brigade has far surpassed all its previous exploits, and that your Boy was never before the object of such attention & has succeeded beyond his highest expectations."

Armstrong stopped writing for a minute to reflect on what had happened May 12, when they brushed past the Queen City of the South. A reception committee of Virginia Militia terrorized General Wilson and his vanguard 3rd Division, and Little Phil had to send Old Curly up to save them.

For some unaccountable reason, Wilson demonstrated incompetence and confusion when under fire. His highly excitable nature seemed to unnerve him at the critical moment, causing incredible clumsiness in an emergency. While Custer welcomed the challenge of crisis, which sharpened his martial sensibilities, Wilson stumbled over a mental block apparently fashioned by a temperament in defiance of sudden violence and the awesome responsibility of independent command. Here was an engineer, not a demon of battle.

In the evening of May 11, at Yellow Tavern, Sheridan had said

211

to his subordinates, "Stuart is whipped, Lee's communications with Richmond broken. The road is open to the James. *Listen!*" The gentle roar of spring rain could not drown out a frantic clanging of alarm bells in the Confederate capital. "They're in a blue funk down there. By God, we could capture Richmond if we wanted to; but we couldn't hold it. Seeing as how our mission is accomplished, we shall swing down the Peninsula to Butler's army at Haxall's Landing, camp and provision, then rejoin Grant and Meade."

After an eight-hour rest, at midnight the Union Cavalry Corps dragged southeastward through streaming dampness and heavy muck. The roads were laid with mines, but Sheridan the Bold was not to be dismayed. Like sheep to the slaughter, he sent Rebel prisoners ahead to spring them. Mist-enshrouded daybreak found the sodden column at Mechanicsville Bridge, on the south bank of a raging and swollen Chickahominy. Save for piles and stringpieces, the span was an untraversable wreck.

Flash! crash! A sharpshooting detachment of Virginia Militia (the Richmond Invincibles), lying in ambush on the north bank, let loose a volley that unhorsed several troopers and struck terror in the van. *Boom!* Half a mile to the rear, the outworks of Richmond erupted smoke and flame—a weird, hectic flush on the misty, opalescent face of dawn.

Instead of dismounting skirmishers and calling up a battery to answer the surprise attack effectively, James H. Wilson (whose 3rd Division stood fire) seemed to take leave of his senses and allowed his advance to shoot haphazardly across the river like a cockeyed crew of trigger-happy duck hunters.

"General, we're surrounded!" yelped one of Wilson's aides to the corps commander.

"*Surrounded!*" Sheridan bellowed. "Surrounded by a lot of department clerks! For Christ's sake, man, what is Wilson doing about it?"

"God help me, sir," the lad gulped. "He doesn't seem to be doing anything!"

Sheridan blazed red-hot, his face the very Devil's but for horns.

212

(Temperamentally, according to one observer, Sheridan was "a terribly ugly man. . . . When anything went wrong, he was perfectly savage.") "God damned imbecile!" He turned to Custer, who was fidgeting spiritedly beside him. "Go ahead, Curly. Drive those rascals out of our way."

Custer replied with a sharp salute, then rattled some orders that sent the 1st Michigan tearing after him to the riverside.

"Pull your men back!" he called to Wilson. "Michigan will open the way!" His eyes darted sharply. "Bring up a battery!"

Wilson responded dutifully, a man now in his element, executing workaday orders.

Custer lurched from his horse, tossed the reins to his orderly. "Colonel Stagg! Dismount and detach Company A. Cover our advance with line of fire. . . . Company A—in skirmishing order— follow me!"

Three howitzers shelled the opposite bank, and carbines crackled in rolling volleys, as Old Curly and his Wolverines charged onto the bridge with sabers and revolvers in hand. They bounded from girder to girder, shouting lustily, but the enemy fled before they could be reached.

"Yellow bastards, see 'em run!" a Michigan sergeant guffawed, slapping off his cap. "Funks, the lot of 'em!"

A couple of enterprising Richmond newsboys greeted Custer and his mud-soaked Bluedevils on the north bank, hustling the *Examiner* and *Times* and *Whig* at two bits a copy. "Is Old Jeb dead?" was the question in every mind and on every lip.

"Get this goddamned bridge in repair!" Sheridan trumpeted. "Be hanged if we'll cower like sitting ducks under the guns of Richmond! Get a move on, before Custer leaves us all behind!"

Custer (his velveteen uniform speckled with mire, a ruddy stubble fringing his florid bony features) greeted Sheridan with a boyish grin, and in Phil's fierce smile of approbation was read an affection aroused by mutual respect. Custer was Sheridan's spearhead, his *enfant perdu* and instrument of destiny. Their unspoken understanding was that each, for glory's sake, would benefit the other.

213

Wayworn and ragged, the U.S. Cavalry Corps shambled into Ben Butler's encampment (Army of the James), at Haxall's Landing, on May 14. There Autie continued his long letter to Libbie:

"Wilson proved himself an imbecile & nearly ruined the Corps by his blunders. Gen'l Sheridan sent for me to rescue him from these. . . . The 1st Vermont, now under Wilson, sent over to our Brigade & asked if they could not obtain 'a pair of Custer's old boots' to command them. Gen'l Merritt said 'Custer saved the Cavalry Corps,' and Gen'l Sheridan told Col. [Russell A.] Alger [of the 5th Michigan], 'Custer is the ablest man in the Cav. Corps.' . . . You are in my thoughts always, day & night. I am only sorry you may be caused anxiety on your Boy's account. Do not fear. I ride with Destiny."

★ 29 ★

TREVILIAN STATION: CUSTER'S FIRST STAND

U NABLE to yield to "the greatest temptation of my life," that of taking and holding Richmond, Phil Sheridan marched his rested and refitted troopers back to the Army of the Potomac along the North Anna River. It was May 24, 1864.

Relating running fights with Hampton's roughriders, in which he gladly bore the brunt, Armstrong penned to Elizabeth: "I have added fresh laurels to the Mich. Brig., and have received the most flattering compliments & congratulations almost daily, but you need have no fears regarding my vanity. Did you observe that in the headings of the N.Y. *Herald* no Cavalry General's name was mentioned besides that of Sheridan & your Boy? Some of the Richmond papers also speak highly of me. When I think how successful I have been of late, and how much has been said of my conduct & gallantry, I think, '*She* will hear of it, and will be proud of her Boy!' That is all the reward I ask."

"We expect Lieut.-Gen'l Grant will march right into Richmond," wrote one of Billy Sherman's boys. "If he fails, it will be because he has not his old troops with him. The Army of the Potomac never did anything."

After the horrors of the Wilderness and the bloodfest at Spotsylvania, Grant confessed, "I never knew what fighting was before." But the Grand Army of the Potomac stood its ground, despite tremendous losses, and would take Richmond whatever the cost. Both armies continued to sidle and battle southward, Lee keeping

215

between Grant and Richmond. "How long this game is to be played it's impossible to tell," said General Meade, "but in the long run we ought to succeed."

Between May 31 and June 3, Custer's Bluedevil Brigade was foremost in opening the road to and holding the line at Cold Harbor, ten miles northeast of Richmond. It was a stunning defeat for Meade's infantry. Sheridan's cavalry, blood but unbowed, saved the day from worse slaughter. Armstrong informed Elizabeth: "Our Brigade lost heavily, but was victorious. . . . The Mich. Brig. turned the tide (as usual) in our favor, but the Infantry under Gen'l Warren [whose 5th Corps Custer was protecting] was not so successful. Fighting is still going on. All is well."

Happy-go-lucky Curly, whose optimism was the madness of maintaining that everything was all right when it was all wrong, saw success in every failure and exaggerated each insignificancy with childlike simplicity. An apologist (Engineer Captain William Ludlow) explains that "He was apt to exaggerate in statement, not from any willful disregard of the truth, but because he saw things bigger than they really were." This ghastly war was a great game for him, and as Colonel Lyman aptly remarked, "Tho' fighting for fun is rare, men like Custer attack whenever they get a chance—and of their own accord."

Meade, in a quiet moment, commented on Grant's bravado ("I mean to fight it out on this line if it takes all summer"): "I'm afraid the Rebellion cannot be crushed this summer, and getting into Richmond will be like going to Hell."

In mid-June, Grant ferried his forces across the James and laid siege to Lee at Petersburg, southern key to the Queen City. The Blue and the Gray were determined to fight each other to death over Richmond. When Meade suggested that Billy Yank and Johnny Reb were becoming like the proverbial Kilkenny cats, who fought till nought was left but their tails, Grant answered grimly, "Our cat has the longer tail." Colonel Wainwright commented, "When the Comdg. Gen'l himself admits that his only dependence is on being able to furnish the most men to be killed, not much can be said for the science of the campaign—especially as the estimates now are that we lose two to one." Confederate newspapers called him the "Butcher from Galena" and "Butcher Grant," and even Federal Secretary of the Navy Gideon ("Grandmother") Welles admitted that "Grant has not a great regard for human life," but he would win this brutal war *coûte que coûte.*

Taking the seceshers at their own word—"The railroad is our backbone"—U. S. Grant called on Phil Sheridan to "put a kink in Bob Lee's back" by wrecking the Virginia Central Railway. Such a crippling *coup de main* might force him out of Petersburg and drive him to the Richmond wall.

Saturday, June 11, 1864, 6 A.M. Objective: Trevilian Station, strategic junction, fifty miles northwest of Richmond.

Launched several miles ahead of the main column on a mission to burn the depot, General Custer and his 1st Michigan Brigade ran into the rear guard of Wade Hampton's cavalry corps. Without troubling to survey the situation, Custer acted on characteristic impulse. He whipped out his saber. "Come on, Wolverines!"

Custer and his Bluedevils shot like a thunderbolt into the Gray column, rounding up wagons and remounts and several hundred prisoners, all of which were lost as quickly as won.

Suddenly the Michiganders found themselves fighting for their lives, surrounded and under attack by two mounted Rebel divisions: those of "Fitz" and "Rooney" Lee.

Old Curly dismounted his Wolverines, ordered them to form a defensive triangle. Throwing off his jacket, he rolled up his sleeves and pulled out his revolver to make a stand.

The Confederates charged in spurts, by troops rather than squadrons, for three smoking-hot hours. Was Hampton playing cat-and-mouse with Custer, or did he have a healthy fear of him? What matter! Lead was flying and men dying nonetheless.

At the height of this duel, tall, slim, smooth-shaven Captain Alex Pennington came running over to Custer and puffed, "They've taken one of our guns, sir, and I think they intend to keep it!"

"*Keep it!* I'll be damned if they do!" Custer spat dust from his mouth. "Come on! Help me round up some men to retake it."

In short order, Custer, Pennington, and thirty troopers snatched

217

the fieldpiece away from its captors before they could haul it very far.

As Custer was racing back to the triangle, he was struck on the arm by a spent slug. He was too excited to feel the pain. Suddenly a 5th Michigander fell face-down in front of him, shot through the heart. The trooper was still in the death struggle as Custer hefted him onto his shoulders and made tracks into the lines. The man was already dead when another spent ball hit Custer on the shoulder, stunning him for a few seconds.

At that moment Color Sergeant Mitchell Belvir (1st Michigan) trotted over, swaying in the saddle. "General, they've killed me," he gasped, clutching his chest where the bright blood dribbled out between his fingers. "Take the flag!"

"Don't worry, Sergeant," Custer said, helping the dying lad off his horse. "If they want it, they have to get me first!" He ripped the sacred brigade banner from its staff and stuffed it into his smudgy, sweat-soaked blouse.

At nine o'clock, Sheridan came to the rescue and chased Hampton away, taking five hundred prisoners. Trevilian Station was reduced to ashes, the tracks were torn up, and "Mission Accomplished" was again the glad word as Little Phil's crack cavalrymen retired to White House Landing on the Pamunkey River. There, on June 21, Autie scrawled to Libbie: "Never has the Brigade fought so long or so desperately. We lost over 400."

He paused for a reflective second, then went on in a heat of expressiveness: "Would you like to know what they have captured from me? *Every thing except my tooth-brush!* . . . But I regret the loss of your letters more than all else. I enjoyed every word you wrote, but do not relish the idea of others amusing themselves with them—particularly as some of the expressions employed were of a highly personal nature. *Somebody* must be more careful hereafter in the use of *double-entendre!*"

Libbie responded: "I suppose some Rebel is devouring my epistles, but I am too grateful to feel badly about that. . . . There can be nothing low between man & wife if they love each other. What I wrote was holy & sacred. Only cruel people would not understand the spirit in which I wrote it. . . . How I laughed

218

when I heard that the inevitable tooth-brush had not been taken! Whatever would you do without it? And, my dear, I have not cried for a week since learning that you came out of that Trevillian engagement alive! . . . I went . . . to Mt. Pleasant Hospital. . . . Most of the Cavalry wounded at Trevillian were there. Oh, Autie, if you could have seen how their faces lighted up when they learned who I was! I can feel it yet—their love for you. One little fellow said of the Michigan Brigade, 'Where *our Boy* goes, we will go!' Oh, how I wish they were my words! . . . Col. [George] Gray [7th Michigan] can't say enough in praise of you. He told Judge Christiancy you are the most perfect gentleman he ever met. He never heard you say a word against anyone."

Admirers of the late-lamented Jeb Stuart stirred up a startling rumor, and for one disquieting day Washington newsboys were yowling, "*Extra! extra!* Custer killed! Read all about it! *Custer killed!*"

"*Killed?*" thundered Secretary of War Edwin M. Stanton to a breathless gathering of follow-up reporters. "No! He was hemmed in on all sides by the enemy, cut his way through with his sword, and covered himself with glory."

While Sheridan was on his Trevilian Raid with Torbert's and Gregg's divisions, Wilson was sent south to wreck the Petersburg & Lynchburg Railroad. He wrecked it all right, and his entire division to boot! "The [Wilson] Cavalry Expedition finished off most disastrously & ingloriously," Wainwright noted in his journal. "They were caught by the enemy [at Reams Station, ten miles south of Petersburg] completely with their breeches down, attacked in front & flank, utterly stampeded & driven to the 4 winds." Wilson lost over fifteen hundred troopers and fifteen guns, and the sixty miles of track he managed to rip up were soon relaid owing to the fact that he failed to twist the rails out of shape. Considering Sheridan's "indecisive" expedition, Wainwright concludes: "As to these Cavalry Raids destroying the Railroads so as to starve them [the Confederates] out of this place [Petersburg] & Richmond, it is all stuff. . . . We are not only beaten, but disgracefully."

Custer also wrestled with pen and ink: "The papers have no

219

doubt informed you of the disgrace brought upon a *portion* of the
Cav. Corps by that upstart & imbecile Wilson. . . . It was Gen'l
Sheridan's intention to send the 1st Vermont to my Brigade on his
return, but I fear there will be but few of that gallant Regt. left.
All who knew Gen'l W. prophesied a disastrous outcome, but the
most charitable never imagined the half of it! Even Gen'l Grant in
his high & responsible position cannot fail to learn wisdom from
this disgrace. Grant obtained the confirmation of Wilson's appointment by the Senate; but it will require influence even more powerful
to satisfy the people (above all, the Army) that this was a judicious
measure, in view of his total ignorance & inexperience of Cavalry,
because he was a favorite staff-officer of Gen'l Grant. I hope the
authorities have learned from this unnecessary disaster that a man
may be a good Engineer but an indifferent Cavalry leader. One
might as well expect that a person with a good singing voice should
necessarily have a talent for painting. . . . You cannot imagine
what a blow this humiliation is to our esprit-de-corps, and to the
pride each member of the Cavalry feels in our organization. We
have labored long & arduously to establish an honorable record,
and our efforts have been successful; and now to have this imbecile, this court favorite, tarnish our fair fame is discouraging to
say the least. We of the 1st & 2nd Divisions have the consolation of
knowing that we were in no way connected with it. We also know—
the whole Army knows!—that it was not the fault of the brave
men who compose the 3rd Div., but that the sole blame rests on
Wilson & on those who, knowing his deficiencies, placed him in
such a position of responsibility."

He added, "And so 'Somebody' thought her Boy intended to
chide her a least little bit about her captured letters! Ha-ha, dear
one, you do not know him if you suppose he intended to 'chide'
his heart's idol. I only wished to impress on you the need of more
prudence in writing. But the effect was not lasting—for the very
next letter would afford equal amusement to my Southern acquaintances as those now in their hands."

Libbie answered, "I shall not again offend my dear Boy's sense
of nicety by departing from that delicate propriety which, I believe,
was born in me."

220

According to Captain William W. Blackford, Jeb Stuart's chief engineer, "Some of the letters to a fair but frail friend of Custer's were published in the Richmond papers, and afforded some spicy reading, though the most spicy parts did not appear." That "fair but frail friend" was none other than Libbie; and the letters, intercepted by Rebel raiders between the Pamunkey and the Potomac, were a packet composed during the Trevilian Raid. (The assumption that these *billets-doux* were addressed to a Washington mistress is characteristically Victorian, for it just wasn't seemly that husband and wife should indulge in literary love-making)

SHENANDOAH:
THE GRAY GHOST

GENERAL Grant gave the U.S. Cavalry Corps a much-needed and well-earned rest for the blistering-dry month of July, 1864. All excitement now seemed to be in Washington, which Little Mac had branded "a sink of iniquity" as well as a hotbed of Rebel intrigue. Like other army wives, Libbie Custer soon found herself fighting off the amorous advances of "gentlemen" (*e.g.,* skirt-chasing Congressman Kellogg and Senator Chandler) who assumed that lonely females were any male's fair game. Indeed, marital love was "a rare thing in this horrid city."

Libbie was offered an opportunity to leave Washington, and she took it—joyfully. Navy Secretary Welles had arranged for Senator Chandler and Mr. Kellogg, accompanied by a select number of ladies, to visit "the front" before Petersburg. The answer to all her prayers! How she had grown to deplore Federal City! "You don't know how barbarous the life is here. This city is a Sodom crowded with sin which the daylight sees as well as the night. . . . The longer I stay here, the more I am afraid to go out by myself. I walk in terror for fear of being taken for one of the 'ten thousand' [streetwalkers who haunted the Capital]." Hardly words of comfort to an anxious husband! There seemed to be only two exceptions to the rule of debauched bureaucrats and blackleg politicians: Speaker Colfax and Congressman Bingham.

On Friday, July 8, the plush Presidential yacht *River Queen* weighed anchor at City Point on the James, ten miles northeast of

Petersburg. Among the eager army wives on board was Mrs. General Custer, escorted by Congressman Bill Kellogg.

Autie raced up the gangplank into Libbie's open arms. He was the first husband on deck to welcome his better half with a kiss and a hug.

That evening, Little Phil brought his field band aboard for a topside hop. He instructed the "boiler-makers" to play as loud as they pleased, in order to drown out the humdrum rumble of siege guns endlessly echoing on the shellburst-studded horizon.

"You should have seen Gen'l Sheridan dance!" Libbie lettered her folks. "It was too funny. He had never danced until this summer, and he entered into it with his whole soul." Her opinion of "the blustery bantam"? "He is so bright, so agreeable! All West Pointers are so jolly & full of brotherly feeling."

On Saturday afternoon, the gleaming-white *River Queen* steamed up the Potomac with General and Mrs. Custer on deck. Phil had allowed Curly a weekend leave because Libbie was such a "damn good dancing teacher" and a "damn beautiful dancing partner."

The two lovers were lavishly happy, standing arm in arm at the rail. Aye, that old river looked like a silver snake slithering down to the sea. And listen! Don't you hear the Marine Band throbbing on Capitol Hill? Far, far from the blasty, bloody front.

Uncle Bob gave Uncle Sam a dose of his own medicine. When Sheridan had left the scene of his "dirty work," Lee sent his "bad-man," Lieutenant General Jubal A. ("Old Jubilee") Early, up the Shenandoah Valley on a raid to end all raids. For two hell-fired months, "Jube" and his graybacks terrorized and blackmailed Maryland and southern Pennsylvania, throwing a big scare into Washington. Mr. Lincoln sounded the distress signal, and Grant answered: "I want Sheridan put in command of all the troops in the field, with instructions to follow Early to the death." Stanton objected: "He's too young for so important a command!" (He was only thirty-three!) But Unconditional Surrender wouldn't take no for an answer. Nor would that man in the White House.

The crucial moment was at hand. Grant's Virginia campaign had

223

proven indecisive, almost a failure, and his spectacular attempt to storm Petersburg (July 30) resulted in "a most miserable fizzle," as Wainwright termed it. "Never has the Army of the Potomac been so demoralized as at this time." Said Lincoln's personal secretary, John Milton Hay: "Everything is darkness and doubt and discouragement." But there was one star of hope, rising in the dismal sky, and that star was Philip Henry Sheridan. "Damn Stuart!" the bantam had crowed. "I can thrash hell out of him any day!" And did he not? And could he not "thrash hell out of" Old Jube as he had Old Jeb? By God, he could! "Goddamme if I don't!"

On August 11, 1864, Sheridan got his orders from Grant: "Attack Early, drive him out of the Valley, and destroy that source of supplies for Lee's Army."

Appointed general-in-chief of the 30,000-man Army of the Shenandoah (Middle Military Division), comprising both infantry and cavalry, Sheridan boosted Torbert as Chief of Cavalry and spearheaded the new fighting machine with his "bright young men," Merritt and Custer. Merritt was assigned the 1st Division, Army of the Potomac Cavalry, and Custer retained command of the 1st (Michigan) Brigade. A silent, sullen man, Major Marcus A. Reno, was appointed Torbert's chief of staff, and was destined to leave his mark on Custer's page in the Book of Glory.

The anxious hours of August 10 caught Old Curly making another last-minute headlong dash to Washington, perhaps for a final farewell, whereupon another special telegram from that inevitable Irishman brought him racing back to his post after a night of stolen pleasures. "By Jesus, I've a mind to dress Libbie as an orderly and let her ride with Eliza!" he confessed to Colonel Russell A. Alger of the 5th Michigan. "God help me, I can't bear to leave her!" But bear he must—war before love.

Grant said, "Go in, Phil. Let your headquarters be in the saddle. Follow Early to the death."

Within a month, Sheridan had cleaned out the Shenandoah as far as Harpers Ferry. He burned, looted, and hanged. "Citizens of Virginia!" he placarded across the countryside. "You are hereby notified that for every Soldier of the Union wounded or assassinated

224

by Bushwhackers in any neighborhood within the reach of my Cavalry, the houses and other property of every Secession Sympathizer residing within a circuit of five (5) miles from the place of outrage shall be destroyed by fire, and that for all public property jayhawked or destroyed by these Marauders, an assessment of five (5) times the value of such property will be made upon the Secession Sympathizers residing within a circuit of ten (10) miles around the point at which the offence was committed."

The Shenandoah Valley, Granary of the Confederacy, swept southwestward like verdant trenches from the Potomac to the James. These rich farmlands, cradled and furrowed by three mountain ranges, were an Abundantia feeding the Rebellion—besides being a roost for Mosby's raiders, whose continual cutting of Grant's communications with Washington was a prime mover of Sheridan's task force.

The Gray Ghost, the Robin Hood of Virginia, the preacher's prodigal son and lawyer was wily and wiry John Singleton Mosby. "Attention is invited to the activity & skill of Col. Mosby," Lee penned to Richmond. "He has killed, wounded, and captured . . . about 1200 of the enemy, and taken more than 1600 horses & mules, 230 beef-cattle, and 85 waggons & ambulances, without counting many smaller operations." These "smaller operations," also "of great value" and "highly creditable to himself & his Command," included scouting and spying. A formidable foe was he, wizard of guerrilla warfare, but he finally met his match in George Armstrong Custer.

In Southern eyes, U. S. Grant truly earned his epithet "Bloody Butcher" when he wired Sheridan: "When any of Mosby's men are caught, hang them without trial." But Sheridan, more the romantic, did not regard them as common outlaws. In scattered bands, they were of little danger to his massive movement. "Leave 'em alone," he facetiously advised his subordinates. "They serve as a very good provost guard, preventing straggling and desertion in this man's army." Indeed, they clung to Little Phil like jackals to a lion, slinking along at a safe distance, eying him furtively. "Don't strike unless struck," he added. "Ignore 'em as outriding campfollowers. We can't afford to be chasing phantoms all over the Valley, the better to be whipped in detail by Old Jube—wherever he is.

Then came Grant's directive to "get" Mosby, at all risks. And Old Curly was the man to do it, with a vengeance. For the Gray Ghost had dared to ambush Sheridan's rear guard, burning a hundred wagons and making off with a herd of prisoners and pack animals. This was the last straw. The sacred honor of the Cavalry Corps had been violated, and flagrantly.

On August 16, seven Mosby partisans were rounded up. One (the leader) was hanged *in terrorem,* the others shot by firing squad. Mosby cried bloody murder, claimed that innocent citizens had been executed; but Sheridan reasoned that as "innocent citizens" were harboring guerrillas in their homes, "innocent citizens" were as guilty as self-professed mosstroopers and freebooters. And so it began, *guerre à mort:* affairs of honor enacted in dishonor, with an ingloriousness unworthy of two gallant cavaliers. Each perversely demanding satisfaction for fancied insults, each struggling to protect "the bubble Reputation"; each fighting to maintain his own pride, his own dignity, his own identity. Thus began the most virulent personal vendetta of the Civil War: a duel to the death between Custer and Mosby, a feud to end all feuds.

General Custer earned a notorious name by lynching or shooting every secesh bushwhacker and jayhawker he could lay his hands on. He held the all-time record for having gunned down and strung up the greatest number of Colonel Mosby's Rangers, pinning "Such is the Fate of All Mosby's Men" to their swinging corpses. Needless to say, Mosby wanted Custer dead or alive. Hence, Old Curly became one of the select few Union officers with a Confederate price on their heads. Besides, diehard seceshers were haunted by a vengeful hate because it was Custer and his men who had killed their beloved Jeb Stuart.

August saw sporadic, indecisive clashes during Sheridan's drive (or demonstration) to Harpers Ferry. On the sixteenth, at Cedar Creek, Gibbs' Reserve (rear guard) Brigade of Merritt's Division was pinched off by a division of "Fighting Dick" Anderson's corps. Custer wheeled about, charged to the rescue. Dismounting the 1st Michigan on a hillock commanding the north bank of the stream, he hurled his Bluedevils into Anderson's flank. The gray column shattered and scattered on the south bank, with heavy losses, leaving three hundred prisoners and two stand of colors in Custer's hands. "Great credit is due Gen'l Custer for the masterly manner in which he handled his Command," Merritt reported to Sheridan; and news dispatches read, "Sheridan is taking good care of Early."

Then the tide began to turn. On the following day, measure for measure, Wilson's 3rd Division was cut off and cut up at Winchester by Fitzhugh Lee's 1st Division. On the eighteenth, at Berryville, Mosby launched retaliatory attacks on Custer's pickets and foraging parties. Several troopers were killed, wounded, or captured.

"Colonel Alger," Custer cried, "I mean to return evil for evil until these scoundrels cease their depredations. Order out your men. I want every barn and farmhouse in this immediate area burned to the ground. Confiscate all livestock and free any slaves you find. These secesh shall pay dearly for their disloyalty."

Alger's 5th Michigan did its dirty work, but not without reprisal. Nearly two dozen Wolverines were sniped to death or wounded by Mosby sharpshooters. Dispatch riders and vedettes were picked off, scouts and patrols potted.

In the Shenandoah, glamour was fast going out of war; and the glory of battle was buried, like the phoenix, in ashes of destruction. Custer could feel the bitter change of atmosphere, sense the all-consuming element of relentlessness. It was frightening, at first. Here was a valley of death, an abode of the damned, where once had been "a land flowing with milk and honey." For men at war had cursed it, and blighted it, by their hatred and their cruelty.

August 25. Major General J. C. Breckinridge, Early's chief of staff, attempted to take Sheridan in flank with his corps. Merritt met the assault head on—with his suicidal shock troops, the 1st Brigade. Custer and his Michiganders plowed into four infantry divisions, were swallowed in chaotic rough-and tumble, then

227

emerged to suffer a blast of musketry that blew them hell-for-leather across the Shenandoah River. Were it not for Devin's 2nd Brigade, pushing Breckinridge in flank, Old Curly might have been captured with his entire command.

"A close shave, that!" he cried, his normally pink complexion paled to a sickly tinge of fright.

By the end of the month, Sheridan's Army of the Shenandoah was peacefully encamped in the vicinity of Harper's Ferry, resting and preparing for the big push southward to "get" Early.

Autie hinted to Libbie of the rare sensation which had chilled him on the twenty-fifth, when he endured "a severe & very trying engagement." All the fire was frozen out of his rattling-high voice, and "This is the first time I have not been remarkably profane during the heat of battle." Indeed, "during the whole time I never used a single oath!" And what frightened Custer? Occasions when the enemy didn't break and run before the tempest of his on-slaughts. "Well-disciplined infantry can, and will, receive a cavalry charge without breaking," he declared. "They let us ride clean through 'em, which exposed our rear to their fire. It's an old *ruse de guerre*. I refuse ever again to fight infantry!"

Armstrong informed Elizabeth of one bright ripple in a dark sea of troubles. At a colonnaded plantation mansion embellished with pearl-white galleries, an old Negro butler begged Gen'l Custer to wait upon the mistress of the house before setting a torch to it. Abashed by such hospitality, then suspecting treachery, Custer was reassured when he swept off his hat and bowed before the gracious Mrs. Colonel Lewis W. Washington, mother of Cinnamon's West Point crony.

"God bless you, General," she said, holding his hand. "I swore I should never speak to a Yankee, but James told me I must make an exception of Custer should he ever come this way; and now, sir, I want very much to thank you for your uncommon kindness to my son."

"'Twas nothing, ma'am," Custer fumbled, red-faced, then gushed nervously, "How is Jim? Where is he now?"

At last word, Colonel James B. Washington was fine, one of the proud defenders of Petersburg, on Marse Robert's general staff. Armstrong also learned, with mixed emotion, that John W. Lea was with Jubal Early as colonel of the 5th North Carolina Infantry. Well, Old Gimlet and I may soon meet again! It later comforted Custer to think that had he been captured on the twenty-fifth, Lea's recommendation and presence would have guaranteed a speedy exchange. Or would it? G. A. Custer was now the most "wanted" man in the G.A.P. "If the Rebs should ever lay you by the heels," Sheridan chortled, "they'll string you up directly. A caution not to get caught!"

Before taking leave of Mrs. Washington, whose property was left undevastated, General Custer was obliged to accept a precious family heirloom: one of a set of large, eagle-engraved buttons from a dress coat made for and worn by George Washington. Armstrong later had the handsomely carved conch-shell button with silver shank set as a brooch for Elizabeth's birthday.

"Now, sir, hurry away!" said the woman whose hospitable and motherly instincts yearned to detain Custer a while longer. "Catch up with your command, lest our own boys should get you. And God be with you."

On Saturday, September 10, driven by loneliness to love's desperation, Elizabeth Custer steamboated up the Chesapeake & Ohio Canal to meet her husband at Harpers Ferry. Armstrong ran a twenty-mile gantlet of Rebel snipers and freebooters just to be with her for a few hours. Libbie insisted on staying in town as long as Autie was encamped at Berryville, so he straightway scouted up a respectable-looking lodginghouse. All that Libbie had carried with her from Washington was two weeks' worth of clothes. "If I need anything else," she told him, "I'll go back for it! But I expect you're all I'll ever need."

On the following day, from camp, Autie dashed off a note to "My dear little Army Crow—following me around everywhere": "Not even the supposed proximity of Mosby's gang could drive away my happy thoughts of you. During the ride back I spoke but once; and I fear the two officers with me deemed me unsociable, or wrapt in my own importance."

229

As often as he could, Armstrong defied Mosby's mosstroopers and streaked up the highway to Harpers Ferry. When he couldn't come to his "sweet Rosebud," he wrote. And it was all he could do to keep her from riding right out to camp in one of the government wagons that came rolling in with daily forage and rations.

★ 31 ★

WINCHESTER: THE
REBELS WHIRLING

MONDAY, September 19, 1864. Two A.M. Phil Sheridan's Army of the Shenandoah pulled up stakes at Camp Berryville and made a beeline westward to Opequon Creek, five miles east of their target: Winchester, Queen City of the Shenandoah. Jubal Early and his 20,000-man guerrilla army had thrown up earthworks along the west bank of the shallow stream, where they were determined to make a last-ditch stand.

There was a bracing nip in the morning air, and tall trees fringing the Opequon were ablaze with autumn foliage, as General Custer cheered his vanguard 1st Brigade across the creek, stampeding half of Steven Ramseur's division (Old Jubilee's left wing) out of its emplacement to a defensive position on higher ground. The two remaining brigades of the 1st Cavalry Division, striking at points close to Custer, cleared out the remaining rifle pits and rolled up Early's left flank toward Winchester Heights.

Having flanked the enemy, Custer turned to Merritt and said, "I'm riding to Sheridan. Will report directly."

Merritt nodded. "I'll hold ground."

Custer dashed back over the Opequon, to the Federal center, where he found Wilson's 3rd Cavalry Division (screening the 6th and 19th Infantry Corps) dismounted and wavering before a raking fire. The "upstart imbecile," as Curly called him, had ordered his troopers to halt, unhorse, and lie down—when one death-defying charge could have smashed the gray stumbling block in short order.

231

And Livingston's Horse Artillery Brigade, attached to Wilson's command, stood disengaged at the rear. What stupidity!

Suddenly, up bolted a red-faced rampageous Irishman. "For Christ's sake," Sheridan roared, "help me get these Goddamned funks across before they're shot to pieces!"

Custer flipped off his hat. "Just give the word, and I'll move 'em!"

"How's the right? I see you're across."

"We've got 'em flanked, driven from their outer defenses. Merritt is holding fast, awaiting orders to advance."

"Bully! I'm taking the left across to bottle 'em up. I want you to push from the center. Early will break if we clamp a vise on him. We can then whip him in detail, by God!" Sheridan jerked his black steed about, shouted a final word: "Once across, keep pushing! Don't stop for the life of you—*don't stop!* Drive 'em to hell!" And away he spanked.

9 A.M. General Custer drew his sword and dashed to the front of the 3rd Division, right past a staggered General Wilson. Captain LaRhett L. Livingston began unlimbering, ranging, and loading a couple of batteries to cover the proceedings. "Fire when ready!" Custer trotted to the fore of J. B. McIntosh's 1st Brigade. "Bugler," he said, "sound 'Boots and Saddles'! Drum Major, strike up 'Yankee Doodle'! . . . By column of squadrons, dress to the center! . . . Steady, boys! Not too fast. Let 'em fire away! We'll charge before they can reload."

Leaden hail peppered the water, and grapeshot hissed along the banks, as Custer pranced forward and pointed his toledo at the enemy position. "Attention for the charge! *Draw sabers!*"

"Three cheers for Gen'l Custer!" someone bellowed.

"By God, Custer's a brick!" another responded.

An outburst of approbation shook the 1st Connecticut Cavalry into fighting fury: "Custer's the man for us!" . . . "A tiger for Curly!" . . . "Hurrah for Old Curly!"

Armstrong waved his blade, and a long surge of blue heaved ahead with glittering crest and a thunderous yell. Splattering full-speed across the creek, through a howling gale of Minié balls that lasted only an instant, Wilson's cavalry swept over the earthworks

232

and chased Early (in a running fight) to the rugged outskirts of Winchester. There, Old Jube again determined to make his last stand—embittered by the death of General Bob Rodes, cut down in Custer's second assault on the Opequon. But Little Phil kept pushing, pushing—on all sides, at all hazards—till Early crumbled and shattered and beat a disorderly retreat before the crashing hoofs of Old Curly's Bluedevils. "Come on, Wolverines! Hallelujah!"

"The confusion, disorder, and actual rout produced by the successive charges of Merritt's First Cavalry Division would appear incredible did not the writer actually witness them." So testified Lieutenant William H. Harrison, 2nd U.S. Cavalry. "We have just sent the Rebels whirling thro' Winchester," Sheridan ("bathed in the golden glory of the setting sun") reported to Stanton, "and are after them to-morrow."

A week later the stampede was complete. Early was run out of Winchester, Strasburg, and Front Royal, then limped down to Port Republic to await reinforcements. Meanwhile, Sheridan was master of the Valley. He had taken over three thousand prisoners, nine battle flags, and five pieces of artillery. Of these, Custer could claim seven hundred captives, seven colors, and all the guns. And though Merritt (in Torbert's report) took the credit, Custer was satisfied when breveted Colonel of Regulars—a spectacular jump from 1st Lieutenant!

Mr. Lincoln immediately telegraphed General Sheridan and the Army of the Shenandoah: "Have just heard of your great victory. God bless you all, officers & men. Strongly inclined to come up & see you." Stanton, Grant, Sherman, and Meade also wired their congratulations "for your great battle & brilliant victory"; and the General-in-Chief "ordered each of the Armies here [before Petersburg] to fire a salute of 100 guns in honor of it. . . . If practicable," he added, "push your success & make all you can of it." Which Sheridan did, but replied, "I claim nothing for myself. My boys Merritt & Custer did it all."

Libbie, back at her boardinghouse on Capitol Hill, looked out at cheering parades and listened joyfully as a battery at the War Department fired a hundred-gun salute. Her darling Autie scrawled

233

excitedly: "Your Boy has been brevetted Col. in the Reg. Army, and pending official confirmation, *Major-Gen'l* of Volunteers! . . . Imagine my surprise, as I watched the retreating enemy, to see every man—every officer—take off cap & give 'Three Cheers for Gen'l Custer!' It is the first time I ever knew of such a demonstration except in the case of Gen'l McClellan. . . . Gen'l Merritt was present during part of my engagement, but never gave me an order or suggestion, even. The battle was called by many 'the handsomest fight of the war.' "

On Friday, September 30, the "Hero of the Shenandoah" (Fighting Phil Sheridan) caused a shake-up in his victorious army. Grant's unpopular protégé, James H. Wilson, went the way of Kill-Cavalry and other flashes in the pan. He was given an "Irish promotion": kicked downstairs, to Sherman's Army of the West, for having "made an ass of himself" at Opequon Creek. The 3rd U.S. Cavalry Division was given to the cavalier who had led it to victory, Brevet Major General George Armstrong Custer.

Autie scribbled the glad tidings to "My Rosebud": "Your Boy Gen'l has been assigned to permanent command of a Division! It is the largest & best in the Army of the Shenandoah. Am I not fortunate? I had to leave my old Brigade & Staff, but Gen'l Sheridan has promised I shall trade one Brig. for the old as soon as practicable. You would be surprised at the feeling shown. Some of the officers said they would resign if the exchange were not made. Some actually cried! Axtell, the Band-master, wept. Some of the Band threatened to break their instruments. . . . I now have a Hd.-Qrs. Tent almost as large as a circus-tent! When I get back my old Brigade, I shall have almost every wish in regard to a Command gratified."

★ 32 ★

SHENANDOAH: FIRE AND SWORD

GRANT'S orders to Phil Sheridan for the first week of October, 1864, were as follows: "In pushing up the Shenandoah Valley, it is desirable that nothing should be left to invite the enemy to return. Take all provisions, forage & stock wanted for the use of your Command. Such as cannot be consumed, destroy. Do all the damage to railroads & crops you can. Carry off stock of all descriptions & negroes, so as to prevent further planting. If the war is to last another year, we want the Shenandoah Valley to remain a barren waste."

"When I'm finished, by God," Sheridan gasconaded, "a crow won't be able to fly through the Shenandoah without carrying his own rations." For the ravagement Early had perpetrated on Maryland and southern Pennsylvania, Sheridan would wreak havoc in the Valley of Virginia, destined a "vale of sorrows."

As usual, General Custer (with Merritt in support) was elected to do the dirty work. And he did it, for five devastating days. For eighty-five miles, from Winchester to Waynesboro, a broom of fire swept the Shenandoah. Barns and granaries and supply depots were burned down, bridges and arsenals blown up, over ten miles of the Virginia Central Railroad ripped apart, droves of livestock and scores of Negroes confiscated, and hundreds of homesteads plundered and ruined.

"Sheridan's Robbers," they were called, and Custer "Attila the Hun." Vandal Custer, Scourge of the North! "I mean to put the fear of Hell in these people," he said to Merritt, "and God help them if they welcome Early's return."

235

"Welcome him or not," Merritt answered dryly, "they'll have but ashes to offer."

From horizon to horizon, the stagnant Indian-summer atmosphere reeked with the smoke of countless conflagrations. As one war correspondent put it, "The completeness of the desolation is awful." It was too lurid to contemplate "the wailing of women and children mingling with the crackling of flames. . . . Relentless, merciless, the torch has done its terrible business in the Valley."

Sheridan reported to Grant: "The whole country from the Blue Ridge to North Mt. has been made untenable for a Rebel Army. I have destroyed over 2000 barns & over 70 mills, have driven in over 4000 head of stock, and have killed & issued to the troops over 3000 sheep. . . . The Valley, from Winchester up to Staunton (92 miles), will have but little in it for man or beast."

"Keep on," Grant replied, "and your good work will cause the fall of Richmond."

★ 33 ★

THE VALLEY:
WOODSTOCK RACES

Daybreak, Sunday, October 9, 1864.

For the past couple of days, Phil Sheridan's flying column was badgered flank and rear by Rebel cavalry spoiling for a fight. When he learned they weren't merely potshot raiders, but a large unit of mounted reinforcements from Lee to Early, Sheridan said to Torbert in no uncertain terms, "Stop, and either whip 'em or get whipped."

Brawny, brawling Brigadier General Thomas Lafayette ("Texas Tom") Rosser, hopefully dubbed "Savior of the Valley," was Old Curly's challenger this day. A few years before he had been Cinnamon's fellow cadet and bosom buddy, a swarthy *caballero* whose favorite piece of literature was Prescott's *Philip II*. Now, a formidable foe, he was out to kill or be killed. Sheridan said to Custer, "I want you to crucify this so-called Savior of the Valley."

T. L. Rosser and his celebrated Laurel Division, so named from the laurel sprigs in their slouch hats, had been rushed north to brace up the crippled divisions of L. L. Lomax and B. T. Johnson; hence their claim to fame as "Jubilee's Saviors."

While Lomax and Johnson tried Merritt's patience, Rosser dared to pinch Custer's rear. "For God's sake, sir, are we to suffer such indignities?" Old Curly addressed Little Phil. "Are we in retreat, or are we equal to slapping these fleas? I demand satisfaction!"

"You'll get it," Sheridan snapped, then called for Al Torbert. "We'll teach that nuisance a lesson he'll never forget. . . . Al, I want Rosser cleaned out; and if you can't do it, by God I'll take

237

the cavalry and do it myself. I shall wait right here till the job is done, and done directly."

On this fateful day, as Frederick Whittaker expressed it, Custer would begin to transform Wilson's lackluster command (joined by the Michigan Brigade) into "the most brilliant single division in the whole Army of the Potomac, with more trophies to show than any, and so much impressed with the stamp of his [Custer's] individuality that every officer in the command was soon to be aping his eccentricities of dress, ready to adore his every motion and word."

A flamboyant staff of cavaliers, headed by the debonair darling of the United States Cavalry, accompanied the 3rd Division skirmish line across smooth rolling fields bounding Strasburg Pike. A brilliant and brassy "jimbang" of bandsmen rode close behind, playing "Yankee Doodle." A billowy D.H.Q. banner, superscribed with past victories, overtopped the advancing lines.

The bright-haired warrior with a flaming scarlet necktie trotted leisurely along, whistling that macaronic tune and tapping his boots with a riding whip, his flashy blue eyes darting sharply about and his wanton red-gold ringlets flung from side to side as he jerked his head in that peculiar nervous manner.

General Custer's "dashing" division swept slowly over the turfy surface of the graceful Valley, ablaze with autumn grandeur. It was a magnificent arena for a cavalry fight, he thought. A far cry from the scrublands of the Wilderness, where all fighting had to be done on foot! Here there was plenty of room to deploy—well-nigh thirty miles wide of it!—and the ground was like a smooth green velvet carpet, not haggled with fences or studded with the cavalry-crippling stones of eastern Virginia.

They rolled gallantly on by brigade front, regiments in parallel columns of squadrons deployed in double rank, again "one of the most inspiring as well as imposing scenes of martial grandeur I ever witnessed upon a battle-field"; and patiently waiting for them were the daredevil divisions of Thomas L. Rosser and Lunsford L. Lomax, gritty *sabreurs* burning to avenge the wholesale destruction of their homelands. This was to be a severe and decisive battle, both knew. Aye, a grudge fight—a fight to the death.

"Attention!" Custer shrilled, swinging his spirited horse about to face the walking column. "By squadrons, double rank: front into line, *ho!*"

Bands blasted "Rally Round the Flag, Boys!" and "Glory, Glory, Hallelujah!" as Curly's Bluedevils deployed into tactical units. Far to the left, Merritt's 1st Division aligned itself against Lomax and Johnson. The odds there were nearly equal. But Rosser, with thirty-five hundred sabers, boasted a thousand more than Custer. Three brigades against two. What of it? the boy general thought. That's my edge! The greater the danger, the greater the glory!

The Blue and the Gray fanned out face to face, and skirmishers opened up at each other with their carbines. Custer watched the long thin lines go jogging on, waving to and fro as each trooper loaded and fired at will.

Custer signaled with a flick of the arm, bugles flared, and Pennington's horse artillery galloped up and unlimbered on the crest of a gentle knoll. The salvos of his batteries mixed a crashing report of howitzers with a sharp crack of carbines in the crisp clear air of a bright and garish autumn morning. A strong breeze whisked away the curling wisps and little puffs of bluish-white smoke before they could drape the field and blur the view. It was exciting, romantic, intoxicating! A shiver of glorious delight flashed through Armstrong's wiry form as he gazed back at a dark-blue sea of horsemen shimmering with the burnished steel of their drawn sabers and radiantly flecked with streaming guidons.

Out loped General Custer from his personal staff, far ahead of the three-mile line, his glittering figure in full sight of both challenging forces. Sweeping off his broad sombrero, he flourished it down to his knee in a gallant salute to his former friend and honorable foe. The chivalry of a knight in the lists! A fair fight, sir, and no malice!

General Rosser, having witnessed Old Curly's "gallus" gesture through his field glasses, turned to his own personal staff of resplendent *chevaliers* and said, pointing with a smile: "You-all see that long-haired officer down there bowing? Well, that's 'Fanny'

A person given to vain displays & empty chatter.

Custer—him the Yanks are so damn proud of—and I'm going to give him the licking of his life today. See if I don't!"

Brigadier General W. C. Wickham slapped his gloves against his thigh, rasping, "Damned popinjay, we're going to bust him up! Boys, give out with 'Bonnie Blue Flag' and drown those damnyankees in song!"

Custer clapped the black sloucher back on his gleaming curls, and a second later the 3rd Division was skimming on at a trot. "Let's have a fair fight, boys!" he called (as at West Point), hearing the Laurel Division burst out in competitive singing. "No malice! . . . 'Yankee Doodle, keep it up: Yankee Doodle dandy!' . . ."

The pace slowly quickened. Rosser's and Lomax's batteries discharged a ricochet fire, and the rattling of carbine volleys rolled along the Confederate line. A storm of bullets sizzed and zinged overhead, pitter-pattering all around and kicking up the turf, winging or cutting down a few horses and men. Despite this wonted distress, "the union of the line was perfect."

The trot rose to a gallop; and a savage yell burst from every throat as that long, wild wave of bluecoat cavalry charged for the grayback wall at breakneck speed. Lines and formations were lost in confused clumps of saber-swinging troopers whose battle-crazed steeds nearly leaped out of their skins in a mad race for the Rebel guns and horsemen.

Nothing short of an earthquake could stop them now. Phil Kearny's words still rang in Custer's ears: "On every occasion I can make men follow me to hell!" Custer inspired his men to the frenzy of demons. They rejoiced in him, flung orders to the winds for him. He was like a thunderbolt, striking fitfully, frantically, without counting the cost. His brilliant daredevilry blasted the forces of precaution and discretion. The thought of possible repulse never gave him pause. To him of a charmed life, to him who could not be killed in battle, such a thought would have been self-defeating and delusive.

Like a curling blue streak, Custer's two brigades raged around Rosser's flanks in a huge semicircle; and Texas Tom was hit by a hurricane of charging horse that blew him clean off his feet. Taken in flank by Merritt, Lomax (and Johnson, by chain reaction) broke and ran. Rosser's division was driven back ramble-scramble for nearly two miles. Then, shamed by the frantic squalling of their leader, they made a desperate stand only to be stampeded again by Custer's troopers.

Through skeins and drifts of dust and smoke, horsemen Blue and Gray ran the so-called Woodstock Races: a ten-mile chase down the Shenandoah Valley from Strasburg to Woodstock. The running fight, ending in panicky flight, finally pushed the Confederates twenty-five miles south to Mount Jackson. The so-called Buckland Races, of a year ago, had finally been avenged—and outrivaled. As Sheridan put it, "It was a regular frolic for our boys," which lusty expressiveness (*e.g.*, "I directed Torbert to finish this 'Saviour of the Valley' ") Colonel Wainwright found "even more buncombe-ish than usual" and "undignified, unsoldierly, . . . disgusting." Be that as it may, the job was done; and Sheridan could Barnumize however he pleased.

In his personal report to General Grant, General Phil called the work of October 9 "a general smash-up," a "wild stampede," a "complete rout . . . the like of which was never before seen." In his official report as Chief of Cavalry, whose responsibility it was to whip or be whipped, General Torbert wrote: "There could hardly have been a more complete victory & rout. The Cavalry totally covered themselves with glory, and added to their long list of victories the most brilliant one of them all & the most decisive the country has ever witnessed. Brig.-Gen'ls Merritt & Custer . . . particularly distinguished themselves."

General Custer, in his own dispatch as the "Winner of Woodstock Races," was proud to proclaim: "Never since the opening of this War has there been witnessed such a complete & decisive overthrow of the enemy's Cavalry," which had shown itself "deficient in confidence, courage, and a just cause."

✶The unhostile rivalry between Armstrong Custer and Wesley Merritt began growing bitter after Woodstock Races, or the Battle

241

of Tom's Run. Officially, Custer had taken six guns and Merritt five; but unofficially, Custer complained to Sheridan that Merritt had claimed those five fieldpieces in default of the 3rd Division's ability to hang on to them during the long chase down the Valley. "Merritt followed on my heels," he declared, "picking up everything I had taken and was compelled to leave behind, and then claiming it for himself."

Sheridan listened, nodded, said nothing—until he saw Merritt. "Wes," he smiled, gripping his shoulder, "let Custer have his guns if it makes him happy. No cause to get him riled. I'll bide no breach of *esprit de corps.*"

Sheridan's word was law: obey or be damned.

Custer got his guns—all but one, the only one Rosser and Lomax escaped with. Therefore, in a bedeviled spirit of bravado, the boy general sent this notice to the newspapers of Washington and Richmond:

> Hd.-Qrs., 3rd Cav. Div.
> Army of the Shenandoah
> Oct. 10th, 1864
>
> *Attention*
> Having captured all but one of the guns of Stuart's Horse Artillery in the Woodstock Races of the 9th inst., I am offering a reward of One Thousand U.S. Dollars ($1,000.) to the person (or persons) who brings me that gun or who enables me to take it.
>
> G. A. Custer
> Bvt. Maj.-Gen'l., U.S.A.

The entire 3rd Division subscribed to this jackpot, which was never claimed. Instead, a note from Rosser:

> Dear Fanny,
> You may have made me take a few steps back to-day, but I'll be even with you to-morrow. Please accept my good-wishes & this little gift—a pair of your drawers captured at Trevillian St.
>
> Tex

And another, after reading the reward notice:

Dear Fanny,

Please to know that the gun you so urgently seek will be sent to Richmond, there to be bronzed & inscribed: "This rare & unobtainable piece, worth $1000 to Gen'l Custer (gun-collector of the Federal Army), was a prize unwon by the Yankees at Woodstock Races, Oct. 9th, 1864."

Tex

Finding Rosser's gold-laced gray dress coat too big for him, Custer sent it as a souvenir to Libbie and then wrote Tom a characteristic note in recognition of having captured the Texan's headquarters wagon:

Dear Friend,

Thanks for setting me up in so many new things, but would you please direct your tailor to make the coat-tails of your next uniform a trifle shorter.

Best Regards,
G.A.C.

P.S.—How do you expect me to keep you from getting killed if you insist on exposing yourself the way you do!

★ 34 ★

CEDAR CREEK:
SHERIDAN'S RIDE

WEDNESDAY, October 19, 1864.
The 3rd Cavalry Division lay bivouacked outside Middletown, on the left flank of the Army of the Shenandoah. At crack of dawn, General Custer was shaken out of his sleep by a vibrant thunder-clap. He lurched up from his cot and listened. That thunder was the booming of guns. The thought struck him like lightning: They were under attack! With Phil Sheridan and his staff a dozen miles away to the north, at Winchester, Jube Early was launching a full-scale surprise attack on his encampment along the north bank of Cedar Creek.

Custer jumped into his pants and boots, yanked on his jacket, grabbed his sword. At that moment Captain George Yates entered the tent, breathless and taut-faced in his long woolen underwear.

"The Rebs have hit us on the left!" he panted. "God knows how many of 'em! They say Crook's Corps is all knocked to pieces, on the jump. The 6th and 19th are giving way. God Almighty, they've got us flanked!"

"Flanked hell!" Armstrong answered, flushed and scowling. "I'll be damned if they're going to make mincemeat of *us!* Sound 'Boots and Saddles'! Order the men out in their drawers! Sabers, pistols, carbines! Tell [Bandmaster] Axtell to strike up 'Yankee Doodle.' We're getting the division under arms, and the Rebs be damned!"

Custer charged out of the tent, his aide-de-camp close behind. The smog-shrouded woods all around that huge bivouac (for five miles along the creek) echoed and re-echoed with crash of cannon,

244

crackle of musketry, and the unearthly howling of Confederates.

While two-thirds of the panic-stricken Army of the Shenandoah were scattering in every direction, General Custer and the 3rd Cavalry Division stood their ground. His troopers turned out in their long underwear, formed a defensive line around their own camp, and held off the enemy all morning.

From gray blur of dawn till hazy splendor of midday, Old Curly trotted to and fro, listening to the tune of lead and talking to his men: "Steady, boys! Let's make a stand. General Sheridan will be along directly, and he'll damn soon see *we* didn't run!"

Shortly after twelve, General Custer heard a roar of voices erupt from the north line of defense. Spurring up to the position, he saw General Sheridan galloping down Valley Pike on his big black charger Rienzi. Custer let out a holler with his wildly cheering troopers, then hurtled forward to welcome Little Phil.

"Hang on, boys!" the ruddy-faced Irishman thundered, waving his cap and cantering through the cavalry lines in a billow of dust. "We're going to get the Goddamndest twist on those graybacks! We're going to lick 'em clean out of their boots!"

General Torbert was first to greet the fiery-eyed chief as he checked his grimy-wet steed: "My God, I'm glad you've come!"

"So am I!" Sheridan barked, shaking Torbert's hand and grinning fiercely. He mopped his sweat-streaked brow on the arm of his dusty tunic. "This never would have happened if I'd been here. I tell you it never should have happened. But seeing as how it has, we're going to get a twist on 'em: the Goddamndest twist you ever saw!"

Custer reined up alongside, clapped both hands on Sheridan's shoulders, and kissed him on the cheeks. "Your presence here saves the day, Phil!" he said, blushing.

Sheridan mussed Curly's hair affectionately. "The devil take us, man, if we don't give 'em the Goddamndest beating they ever got in their bloody lives!"

4 P.M. Sheridan's shattered forces were now rallied for a comeback. "The whole line will advance!" he bawled. "General Emory, the 19th Corps will move in connection with the 6th. The right of

the 19th will swing towards the left. Custer, take the right. Merritt, the left. Crook, hold the rear. . . . Forward!"

Nearly half of Early's troops were grubstruck, drunk with plunder, in riotous disarray after their walkover victory. But they hastily reorganized to strike Sheridan in flank when he returned to retake his abandoned camp.

Sheridan, riding with Custer and Emory on the right, noticed this sudden change of front to outflank his own flank movement. "Look!" he said, pointing forward-right with his field glasses. "Early is extending his line, making a right-oblique. Custer, I want you to charge into the angle, cut Early in half. By God, we'll whip him in detail!"

Custer nodded, saluted with a smile, spurred over to his command. Sabers were drawn: the trotting division in brigade echelon, close columns of assault. "Gallop *ho!*"

"Go in, Custer!" Sheridan roared. "Emory, swing your 1st Division head-on into the enemy; your 2nd into their right flank. . . . Go on, boys: give 'em hell, God damn 'em! We'll make coffee out of Cedar Creek tonight!"

"Charge! charge!" Custer shrilled, leading his Bluedevils into the angle, through the masses, of Old Jubilee's army. At the first onslaught, Early was chopped in half. Then regiment after regiment, brigade after brigade, was smashed to fragments; and like hard clods of clay under a driving rain, whole divisions crumbled to bits and melted away.

"By Jesus, Phil," Custer exclaimed, vaulting out of the saddle, "we've cleaned 'em out and got their guns!"

"Goddamned if we haven't!" Philip the Bold guffawed. Sixteen hundred prisoners, twenty-four guns, and ten flags! Hallelujah!

Custer and Sheridan flung their arms around each other's neck, slapped and hugged, then cavorted laughingly about the campfire. Curly swung off to embrace Al Torbert and pull him into the fling, but "Old Muttonchops" (as he was called) held the frolicker at arm's length with a frowning smile. "There, there, old fellow. Don't capture me!"

E. A. Paul, special correspondent for the New York *Times,*

246

wrote Armstrong up as the "Hero of Cedar Creek": "Custer, young as he is, displayed the judgment of a Napoleon."

On the following day, a dispute arose over who captured the two dozen enemy cannon and who *re*captured the two dozen guns taken by the enemy in their predawn surprise attack. Custer claimed he did, but Merritt cried foul play. So when Sheridan was making out his official report, Torbert leaned over the field table and said, "Beg pardon, sir, but hadn't some of the guns better be credited to Merritt?"

"*No*," the chief retorted. "I saw Custer take 'em."

And that was that! But not at Headquarters, 1st Cavalry Division, where Brevet Major General Wesley Merritt later scratched an angry letter to Major William Russell, Assistant Adjutant General of the Cavalry Corps: "My attention has been called to a congratulatory order which appears in the newspapers over the signature of Brig. Gen'l G. A. Custer, Comdg. 3rd Cav. Div., in which he claims that 45 of the 48 guns captured . . . were taken by the 3rd Division. I had before heard from different sources that such claims were made by officers of the 3rd Div., but took no notice of them; as I did not think it possible, from what I knew of the pursuit of the enemy on the south side of Cedar Creek, that such unfounded assertions as were current could receive the support or indorsement of Gen'l Custer. But since this official recognition of over-weening greed of some of the 3rd Div. for the rightful captures of my Command, I think it my duty to my officers & men to declare the statement alluded to above as without foundation in truth. . . . I have no personal ambition to gratify in this matter. . . . This Division lost almost as many in killed & wounded on the south side of Cedar Creek as the 3rd Div. lost during the entire day. Forty-five out of 48 guns are scarcely captured usually without loss, while the remaining 3 are productive of more bloodshed than that experienced by an entire Division of Cavalry in a pitched battle. I make this statement in justice to the living as well as to the dead heroes of the 1st Cav. Div. True, as some friends urge, the Division has enough glory for any one Command, but not enough not to feel such wholesale robbery as is attempted to be practiced on it in this instance. I would remark, in conclusion, that it is possible Gen'l Custer did not write the order attributed to him in the newspapers."

Alas, he did—and it reads as follows:

Head-Quarters, Third Cavalry Division
October 21st, 1864

Soldiers of the Third Cavalry Division:

With pride and gratification your Commanding General congratulates you upon your brilliant and glorious achievements of the past few days. On the 9th of the present month you attacked a vastly superior force of the enemy's Cavalry, strongly posted with Artillery in position and commanded by that famous "Saviour of the Valley," Rosser. Notwithstanding the enemy's superiority in numbers and position, you drove him twenty miles from the battle-field, capturing his Artillery—six pieces in all; also his entire train of waggons and ambulances, and a large number of prisoners. Again, during the memorable engagement of the 19th instant, your conduct throughout was sublimely heroic and without a parallel in the annals of warfare. In the early part of the day, when disaster and defeat seemed to threaten our noble Army on all sides, your calm and determined bravery while exposed to a terrible fire from the enemy's guns added not a little to restore confidence to that part of our Army already broken and driven back on the right. Afterward, rapidly transferred from the right flank to the extreme left, you materially and successfully assisted in defeating the enemy in his attempt to turn the left flank of our Army. Again, ordered upon the right flank, you attacked and defeated a Division [Rosser's] of the enemy's Cavalry, driving him in confusion across Cedar Creek. Then, changing your front to the left at a gallop, you charged and turned the left flank of the enemy's line of battle and pursued his broken and demoralized Army a distance of five miles. Night alone put an end to your pursuit. Among the substantial fruits of this great victory you can boast of having captured five battle-flags, a large number of prisoners (including Major-General Ramseur), and forty-five of the forty-eight pieces of Artillery taken from the enemy on that day, thus making fifty-one pieces of Artillery captured within the short space of

ten days. This is a record of which you may well be proud—a
record won and established by your gallantry and perseverance.
You have surrounded the name of the Third Cavalry Division
with a halo of glory as enduring as time. The history of this War,
when truthfully written, will contain no brighter page than that
upon which is recorded the chivalrous deeds, the glorious triumphs, of the soldiers of this Division.

> G. A. Custer
> Brevet Major-General
> Commanding Division

This stylish grandiloquence, designed to inspire *esprit de corps,*
stirred up a storm of controversy characterized by Merritt's remark: "Custer would have it believed that he alone saved the day
with his so-called 'Bluedevils.' I rather fear the poor fellow is possessed by blue devils!"

Custer answered Merritt's protest in a letter to Major Russell,
stating flatly that "this [the 3rd] Division captured from the enemy
45 pieces of Artillery, a large number of prisoners, &c." and "Since
other Commands have seen fit to contend the just claims of this
Division to the honor of having captured the 45 pieces of Artillery
. . . , I respectfully but most earnestly request that the Chief of
Cavalry [Torbert] will give . . . an official decision. . . . If there
exists any doubt in his [Torbert's] mind in relation to the facts
concerning the captures, I would suggest the appointment of a
Board composed of officers who are wholly disinterested regarding
the question to be decided."

Well, there existed no *expressed* doubt in Torbert's mind—at
least not after Sheridan settled the issue once and for all, arbitrarily
informing Merritt: "As far as I'm concerned, this question of the
captured guns is a decided one. It's dead—you understand? *Dead.*
See that it remains so, or suffer the consequences. I'll bide no contradiction, *nor* dissension."

Sheridan, indeed, was absolute dictator. And Custer was above
reproach. However, Torbert's official report gives Custer and Merritt an equal number of guns for the entire campaign. The issue
died hard.

Mr. Lincoln telegraphed General Sheridan on October 22: "With great pleasure I tender to you & your brave Army the thanks of the Nation, and my own personal admiration & gratitude, for the month's operations in the Shenandoah Valley & especially for the splendid work of Oct. 19, 1864."

Sheridan, just commissioned a full-rank Major General of Regulars, addressed Grant: "General, I want my brave boys, Merritt & Custer, promoted by brevet to Maj.-Gen'ls, U.S. Regs." His wish was granted.

Colonel C. S. Wainwright penned prophetically: "I cannot help thinking that these victories [at the Opequon and Cedar Creek] are the beginning of the end, the death-blows to the Rebellion. . . . I have never seen the time when the Army thought the War so near its close as now."

The upset at Cedar Creek marked the beginning of the end for the defiant defenders of Petersburg. They were battling on borrowed time, till ammunition and supplies ran out. "Hold on with a bull-dog grip," the President advised his Lieutenant General, "and chew & choke as much as possible." Grant replied, "I have had many hard experiences in my life, but I never saw the moment when I was not confident that I should win in the end."

The whole Confederacy was dying rapidly. While slaughter and stalemate raged around Petersburg, General Sherman made Georgia and South Carolina "howl." Sherman's Bummers, like Sheridan's Robbers, pursued a ruthless scorched-earth policy. The cotton belt's goddess of plenty was raped to death. "My aim is to whip the Rebels, to humble their pride," Sherman declared. "They have sowed the wind and must reap the whirlwind. . . . You can't qualify war in harsher terms than I will. War is cruel, and you can't refine it; and those who brought war into our country deserve all the curses and maledictions a people can pour out." When "Mad Old Billy the Vandal Chief" had left the cotton belt a howling waste, he became worthy of his middle name: Tecumseh. But that "red-bearded beast" and "damyankee brute," who fondly referred to the Grand Army of the West as his "whiplash," was sadly disenchanted: "War is hell. I am sick and tired of war. Its glory is all moonshine. It is only those who have neither fired a shot nor heard

250

the shrieks and groans of the wounded who cry aloud for blood, more vengeance, more desolation."

Far to the north, Phil Sheridan continued to ravage the Shenandoah with fire and sword. He slashed the jugular vein that fed life to the Confederacy, and he bled the Rebellion white. "The people here are getting sick of the War," he scratched to Grant. "Heretofore they have had no reason to complain, because they have been living in great abundance. When I get thro', the Valley will have nothing in it for man or beast. A crow will have to carry its rations if it flies across the Shenandoah."

Unable to survive without communication with Richmond, the scattered remnants of Jubal Early's army limped southward in ignominious retreat. With his supply lines to Baltimore and Washington open, Sheridan could afford to live in a wasteland. Over three million dollars' worth of damage was perpetrated by Federal troops in the Shenandoah.

Over twenty years later, when the bitterness of other men had been sweetened by Christian charity, Thomas L. Rosser would wave the bloody shirt: "I have seen it reported recently in the newspapers that Gen'l P. H. Sheridan, U. S. Army, contemplates . . . another ride up the Shenandoah Valley. I had hoped that our beautiful valley would never again be desecrated by his foot-prints. Cold, cruel & brutal must be the character of this soldier who fondly cherishes memories of the wild, wanton waste & desolation which his barbarous torch spread thro' the Valley, laying in ashes the beautiful & happy homes of innocent women, young & helpless children, and aged men, and who over these ruins boasted that 'now a crow cannot fly over this valley without carrying its rations.' . . . I have forgiven the brave men of the Union armies whom I met in honorable battle, and who finally triumphed over us in the great struggle. Among them I can now name many of my warmest & truest & most-prized friends. . . . Sheridan is not one of this kind. . . . I now say to . . . our gallant comrades who are now in the Valley, that I hope you will allow this man to make his triumphant ride up the Valley in peace, but have him go like the miserable crow, carrying his rations with him."

While leading newspapers North and South denounced General

251

Rosser's letter, General Sheridan had only this to say: "Rosser hasn't forgot the whaling I gave him in the Valley, and I'm not surprised that he loses his temper when he recalls it."

Among Rosser's "warmest & truest & most-prized friends" was Custer. Wondrous strange that Old Tom should have forgiven Fanny his vandalism in the Valley, save that a subordinate was not officially held accountable for the instructions of his superior! Custer only obeyed orders, did his unpleasant duty—with apparent pleasure.

WASHINGTON: OLD EVIL-EYE

E LIZABETH Custer wrote home: "Armstrong is now a *Major-Gen'l*. His taking 51 guns in 10 days is said to be without a parallel in history."

On Sunday, October 23, Libbie was in Newark, New Jersey, visiting her stepmother's relations. While she was seated at the breakfast table, one of the family came rushing in with the New York *Times* and read that General G. A. Custer had arrived in Washington with a carload of captured battle flags to be presented to the Secretary of War.

Libbie turned pale; her heart froze. She would miss him! By the time she returned to the Capital, Autie would have gone back to the army. Oh, if she had only known! If he had only told her he was coming, she would have been there to greet him—as always. But again, and ever again, she must suffer heartache.

Libbie ran upstairs. She cried as never before, knowing that she might not see him again, for she lived with a gnawing fear that each fleeting moment together would be their last. And because these rare intimacies with Autie were so precious to her, it pained her twice as much that such a moment was missed.

She wept for nearly ten minutes, and the womenfolk lamented with her, when suddenly the little folk of the house began to scream, "He's come! he's come!"

And come he did indeed, bounding up the stairs.

"Oh, Autie!" She sighed in his arms. "I never dreamed——!"

"I know," he said, kissing her. "It seems the Hon'ble Mr.

Stanton was taken ill, so the flag presentation has been postponed till tomorrow. That's why I've come to take you back with me."

Husband and wife hopped aboard the afternoon cannon-ball express and raced forty miles an hour to Federal City, where the following day found them climbing into a chartered omnibus enroute to Capitol Hill. With a Rebel flag flying from every window of the bus, General and Mrs. Custer and company breezed up Pennsylvania Avenue amid a storm of cheers, waving hats, and fluttering handkerchiefs.

"Washington has not had many such sensations," the *Star* reported. "The soldiers in the city were jubilant, and when they met Custer in the street, would give him a hug; and some of the old soldiers would kiss Custer's hand."

A colorful parade of standard-bearers marched into the War Department, where starchy old Edwin M. Stanton welcomed them in one of his uncommon moods of good cheer.

Center of attraction at the presentation of trophies was gallant Major General Stephen D. Ramseur's famous battle flag, superscribed "On to Victory," captured by two teenage troopers named Sweeny and Lyons. Having ripped the splendid souvenir from its staff during the Battle of Cedar Creek, the proud lads now presented it to the Secretary of War tacked to a bamboo fishing rod reminiscent of Tom Sawyer and Huck Finn.

Steve Ramseur and Aut Custer had chummed together at West Point. The dark-eyed scowler was one of Fanny's hazing plutes: "*Mistah* Ramseur to you, animule!" Shot through both lungs, he had been taken prisoner at Cedar Creek. At sundown, the ambulance bearing him to safety was stopped on Strasburg Pike by Old Curly and his staff. "Who have you got there?" the frightened driver was asked. "Do not tell them," said a weak voice from within. Custer started. "Is that you, Ramseur?" No answer. "By golly, I'd know that voice anywhere! Boys, conduct this wagon at once to Sheridan's Headquarters—and guard it well. It contains an old acquaintance." Custer, with Merritt and Pennington, saw him before he died. Ramseur begged Fanny to snip off a lock of his dark hair and send it to his beloved wife, who had just given birth to their first child. With it Custer sent the white rose Steve

254

had worn into battle in honor of the daughter he was never to see. These were his last words: "Armstrong, I knew if I fell into your hands, you would treat me kindly."

When all the trophies were presented by their captors, Secretary Stanton cleared his throat and rasped, "On behalf of the President of the United States, I thank you all, brave gentlemen, for your tokens of victory and valor. Now each member of this delegation will receive a medal from the Government in appreciation of his services to the country."

General Custer then spoke up: "By your leave, sir! While my boys are here in Washington waiting for their medals, should they not receive their pay as if on duty? And should they not have their way paid to their homes and back to camp?"

Stanton knit his brow, fingering a forked and scraggly white-streaked beard, then nodded abstractly, "As you wish, General." He cracked a slight smile, leering at the blue-clad band through his round-rimmed spectacles. "To show you how good generals and good men work together, I have appointed your commander Major General." Taking Custer by the hand, Mr. Secretary added, "General, a gallant officer always makes gallant soldiers."

This surprising announcement of official confirmation met with a burst of cheers from the honored troopers. Custer, flushed with pride, was at a loss for words; so Private Sweeny piped out, "The 3rd Division wouldn't be worth a red cent if it wasn't for Old Curly!" The room rang with laughter, and "Old Evil-Eye" Stanton patted the lad on the head. Noted the Washington *Star:* "The embarrassed looks of Genl. Custer, as he bowed his thanks, showed that his modesty was equal to his courage."

After the presentation, Secretary Stanton and General Custer engaged in a brief tête-à-tête:

"Aren't you a son of Emanuel Custer, the one from Ohio?"

"Yes; that I am!"

"Ah! Well, he was once a client of mine—and a damn good Democrat, too! I'm a Buckeye myself, y'know. So, why have you never been to see me?"

"Because I never had any business to bring me to your office, sir!"

255

"Well, I'll be——!"

"No offense, Mr. Secretary. Every time I see my father—which isn't often—he always says, 'Go see Stanton. He'd be glad to see you.' But I never would, for fear you might think I was seeking something."

"Well, like it or not, you've found it! You've got your commission, Major General Custer. Now go out and win this cussed war!"

Custer left Mr. Stanton's office with the feeling that the Secretary wasn't such a bad sort after all. Why did Pleasonton, for one, call him a "Machiavellian Radical"? And why did most generals hate him? "I do not like his looks," Wainwright declared, portraying Stanton as "a long-haired, fat, oily, politician-looking man." McClellan recalled that Stanton "never spoke of the President in any other way than as 'the original gorilla.'"

The fact is, Secretary Stanton didn't bear liking. His energies were not devoted to winning popularity contests, nor would his perverse temper allow such indulgence. Stanton was, to be sure, "the pestiferous, bull-headed potentate of the War Office." Custer would patronize him to advantage, but in so doing would concur with Sheridan's estimation: "Intimate association convinced me that the cold and cruel characteristics popularly ascribed to him were more mythical than real."

Back at the boardinghouse, Custer wrote Stanton a long and eloquent letter, revealing his impassioned sentiments as a War Democrat and as an ardent backer of McClellan's Union Party in the upcoming Presidential election: "The Peace Commissioners I am in favor of sending to Richmond are from the cannon's mouth. Let the people of this country support the soldiers. We are fighting for human rights, liberty, and the preservation of a free people. We entered this struggle determined to restore the Union & re-establish the Government. I have risked all that I have, and my life itself has been perilled on scores of battle-fields, for this noble cause. Shall the blood of those patriot heroes which has been poured out upon the altar of our country, as a sacrifice to freedom & independence, be shed in vain?"

★ 36 ★

WINCHESTER: BROTHER TOM

ARMSTRONG railed back to the Army of the Shenandoah's winter quarters at Winchester, where he penned to Elizabeth on October 28, 1864: "I am sending for you to visit camp! You must make up your mind to fewer comforts than you now enjoy. You will lead a real soldier's life! . . . Bring riding-habit & one small trunk. You will not need any nice dresses this time."

In early November, Libbie left the political front and wrote to her folks from Camp Winchester: "Pa used to show up the horrors of Army Life for a lady: 'Gypsying! No better than riding on the Plains in a covered waggon!' But, Father, I assure you, in this age of delicate females none is better adapted to Army Life than your daughter. It seemed so strange at first to sleep in a tent, completely out of doors—almost no furniture, the free winds of Heaven playing with the canvas walls. But Oh, so exciting! . . . A soldier's life is glorious! For Hd.-Qrs. Autie now has a large, roomy Virginia mansion. . . . We have such gay times. I have never felt so much at home. . . . Aut's brother Tom has received a commission in a Michigan Regt. & is with us. Such an open-hearted boy, he adds much to our family circle—for as such I consider the Staff. In fact, dear Father & Mother, no happier woman lives than your devoted daughter."

Mrs. Major-Gen'l G. A. Custer, decked out in a brass-buttoned dark-green riding habit with bright-red hunting cap, became queen of the camp and social lioness for the frosty months of 1864–65. The new swanker and practical joker in winter quarters was

257

"Brother Tom": nineteen-year-old Second Lieutenant Thomas Ward Custer, second youngest of Armstrong's three kid brothers. This blue-eyed, flaxen-haired bean pole idolized and emulated "big bub Aut" with ambitious devotion. When not twanging away on a jew's-harp, sowing his wild oats with camp tramps, or sneaking a swig or a fag behind the strict teetotaler's back, Brother Tom was "helling about" in horseplay with his pace-settingly prankish beau ideal. Libbie cocked an indulgent eye at the shining example. Boys will be boys!

On November 8, 1864, Aut appointed Tom his adjutant general in the absence of Jake Greene, who was held captive by the Rebels. (Seeing that Phil Sheridan had similarly assigned his own kid brother Mike, no one could accuse Custer of setting a nepotic example.) "And if anyone thinks it's a soft thing to be a commanding officer's brother," Lieutenant Tom asserted, "he misses his guess!"

When off duty, General and Lieutenant were frolicking brothers. At all other times, the contrast was startling. No familiarity, no favoritism. Tom knew his place, and kept it—or suffered severely for breach of discipline.

On the same rainy day that Armstrong appointed Thomas his personal aide and adjutant, Mr. Lincoln was re-elected President of the United States by a narrow margin over General McClellan. The Railsplitter's comment: "For such an awkward fellow, I'm pretty surefooted! It's a slip, not a fall."

Libbie had written from Washington at the height of the hoopla: "Autie, it is treasonable & unwomanly, but way down in my heart I want peace on any terms; for much as I love my country, I love you more. . . . I am for Abraham. It is generally tho't now that Lincoln will be elected. But I never say so, for fear people will think I am repeating your sentiments—and I don't even know them."

Autie replied simply: "My doctrine has ever been that a soldier should not meddle in politics." At least not directly!

After Christmas, Judge and Mrs. Daniel Stanton Bacon journeyed to Winchester to visit their daughter and son-in-law and to attend the January Inauguration ceremonies in Washington. Armstrong was unable to escort them to the Capital, so Elizabeth had to let him on the inside track by letter: "Andy Johnson was drunk, unfortunately. Mr. Lincoln appeared with great dignity. . . . I attended the Inaugural Ball with Sen. Chandler. . . . The ladies' costumes were superb. Velvets, silks, diamonds dazzled my eyes."

Now that she was back in Washington, "lonesome & anxious," Elizabeth recalled with what excitement she had written her parents from Winchester (December 4, 1864): "I am the only lady in the Army. The wives of officers have been ordered out. Gen'l Sheridan thought women interfered with soldiers' duties." But not that "dark-eyed loveliness"! She added: "Tom is a fine boy. He has improved so much." Libbie had all but adopted Brother Tom, but her gentle attempts at reform were a private joke with the imp and his older brother. "Has the Old Lady taught you to say your prayers yet, angelface?"

★ 37 ★

FRONT ROYAL:
IN TERROREM

Wₕₗₑ Sherman's Bummers made Georgia howl, presenting Savannah to Mr. Lincoln as a Christmas gift, Sheridan's Robbers rode herd on Mosby's Raiders. Acting under Grant's and Sheridan's orders to execute all guerrillas without trial, Custer had begun his relentless campaign against Mosby on September 23, 1864, at Front Royal, Virginia.

That morning, a raiding party of Confederate Rangers had attacked a Union ambulance train and killed its escort leader, Lieutenant Charles McMaster (2nd U.S. Cavalry). When Custer's brigade came to the rescue, a half dozen of the enemy were rounded up. Aggravated by McMaster's death, and by the fact that Mosby held several captive Michiganders to ransom, Custer ordered four of the Rebels shot and the other two hanged. The whole town turned out for the spectacle, which was perpetrated to the sombrous rhythms of the "Dead March" and the jeers of enraged secessionists. Others stood dumb-struck, in morbid curiosity, as the executions were enacted with military precision. "Such is the Fate of All Mosby's Gang" was pinned, *in terrorem,* to the dangling body of Ranger Overby. The swinging corpse of Ranger Carter bore this notice: "Hung in Retaliation for the Death of Lieut. McMaster, 2nd U.S. Cav."

On October 3, Lieutenant John R. Meigs (Sheridan's chief engineer) was ambushed and slain by Rebel snipers inside the Union lines. "For this atrocious act"—Sheridan addressed Custer with cold deliberation—"I want all houses within an area of five miles

260

burned to the ground. We'll teach these murdering secesh a lesson they'll never forget."

Custer obeyed without question. Vengeance was sweet to his boyish taste. He was indeed "Sheridan's Firebrand."

On the twenty-ninth, Colonel Mosby reported to General Lee: "The enemy captured 6 of my men near Front Royal; these were immediately hung by order & in the presence of Gen'l Custer. It is my purpose to hang an equal number of Custer's men whenever I capture them."

Lee endorsed Mosby's purpose in a note to Secretary of War James A. Seddon: "I have directed Col. Mosby . . . to hang an equal number of Custer's men in retaliation for those executed by him." Seddon responded: "Gen'l Lee's instructions are cordially approved."

At Rectortown, on November 6, the twenty-seven prisoners from Custer's Michigan Brigade drew lots to determine their fate. Five of them were lynched that black, rainy night. The sixth, Captain Charles Brewster (one of Custer's aides), escaped at the connivance of his guard, a fellow Mason. Mosby attached a manifesto to one of the victims: "These men have been hung in retaliation for an equal number of Col. Mosby's men, hung by order of Gen'l Custer at Front Royal. Measure for measure."

While Sheridan was boasting to Grant, "We have disposed of quite a number of Mosby's men," Mosby was scrawling to Sheridan: "Some time in the month of Sept. six of my men, who had been captured by your forces, were hung & shot in the streets of Front Royal by the order & in the immediate presence of Brig.-Gen'l Custer. A label affixed to the coat of one of the murdered men declared that such punishment would be the fate of Mosby & all his men. Since the murder of my men, not less than 700 prisoners (including many officers of high rank) captured from your Army by this Command have been forwarded to Richmond; but the execution of my purpose of retaliation was deferred in order, as far as possible, to confine its operation to the men of Custer. Accordingly, on the 6th inst., six of your men were by my order executed on the Valley Turnpike, your highway of travel. Hereafter, any prisoners falling into my hands will be treated with the kindness due to their condition—unless some new act of barbarity shall compel me reluctantly to adopt a line of policy repugnant to humanity."

States Mosby's *Memoirs:* "No further 'acts of barbarity' were committed on my men." Indeed, Sheridan ordered his subordinates: "Leave Mosby's men alone, so long as they leave us alone. Live and let live. Besides, they keep coffee-boilers [stragglers] in line." ("Sheridan's Provost Guard" became proverbial, a standing joke.)

★ 38 ★

WAYNESBORO:
FLAGS FOR TAD

Executive Mansion, Washington
March 1st, 1865

Maj.-Gen'l G. A. Custer
Tad wants some flags. Can he be accommodated?

A. Lincoln

Thursday, March 2, 1865. Warm afternoon rain came roaring down, melting the Shenandoah Valley into a vast mudhole. General Custer sat in the courthouse at Waynesboro, in the shadow of the Blue Ridge Mountains, eighty-five miles southwest of Winchester. He was dashing off a dispatch to General Sheridan, a dozen miles northwest at Staunton:

Gen'l—
Have just whipped Early! Captured 11 guns, 16 battle-flags, 1600 prisoners, 200 waggons & ambulances, &c. Am in hopes of catching Early. Pursuing him thro' Rockfish Gap. My loss is slight.
(3 p.m.)   Custer
P.S.—Another handsome battle-flag was just captured!

New York *Times* correspondent E. A. Paul reported, "Gen'l Custer deserves the credit for planning & executing one of the most brilliant & successful fights in this or any other war. . . . When Custer got back into camp, after chasing Early into the mountains, the Rebel prisoners waved hats & cheered him."

Impetuously, with only fifteen hundred troopers of his mud-

263

delayed division, Old Curly had surrounded Waynesboro and sprung the trap in a blinding downpour. Of twenty-five hundred Butternuts, the remains of Early's army, only nine hundred escaped.

For gallantly leading the last charge that chased Old Jube into the mountains, Tom Custer was boosted to Brevet Captain by his acclamatory brother.

Early was "busted up" decisively, at last. He who had ballyhooed, "I'll clean Phil Sheridan up!" He who had been the "Commissary Guard of the Confederacy." A million dollars in military stores, the productive region around Waynesboro, were put to the torch. And one of the guns taken was, much to Custer's delight, the very piece for which he had offered a bounty of $1000. Some wag—perhaps Rosser—had painted this inscription on the barrel: "For Gen'l Phil Sheridan, U.S.A., Care of Gen'l Jubal Early, C.S.A."

If the golden-maned boy general now got full coverage in the Northern press, much to the dismay of jealous rivals, it was because all reporters stuck close to the greatest and most glamorous wartime newsmaker ever to court their favors.

On the following day, through mizzly "Tuckahoe" country, an unrelenting General Custer and his 3rd Cavalry Division splish-sploshed twenty miles eastward to Charlottesville, Virginia, where the obsequious mayor and an official delegation handed him the keys to the city (and to "Thomas Jefferson's own University of Virginia") in token of surrender. "But this little scene [Sheridan notes] did not delay Custer long enough to prevent his capturing, just beyond the village, a small body of cavalry and three pieces of artillery."

Old Jubilee had lost everything except his life, and was now on the run to Richmond. Custer chased him as far as the South Anna River, which Early and an orderly swam like two terrified houn'-dogs—then scampered over the piedmont—while Custer and his boys crowed, whistling and waving their hats. (Jube would remain an "Unreconstructed Reb" for the rest of his days, and his unforgettable moment of infamy was when he escaped like a soaked rat from a sunken ship.)

264

After detailing a squad to protect Monticello from blue-clad looters, Custer set up headquarters for the day (March 3) at an elegant old colonial mansion outside Charlottesville. While he, Tom, and the rest of his personal staff were seated on the porch waiting for their dinner, a pair of troopers came trotting up with a young civilian between them.

"What's this?" said Custer, lurching out of his seat and striding over to the steps. "They seem to have a prisoner."

The troopers halted in front of the gallery; and one of them, a sergeant of the guard, saluted. "General, I have a prisoner. He says his name is Farish—Captain Farish—and that he lives here."

"Is that so, Captain?" Custer said to the dark-haired Virginian.

"Yes, Gen'l," was the immediate answer.

"Then how do you account for the civilian clothes?"

"Well, Gen'l, these togs belong to a miller twelve miles down the road."

"Indeed! And how did you come by them? Why aren't you in uniform? To what outfit do you belong?"

"Sir, I'm on the personal staff of Gen'l John G. Walker, and am on leave to see my kinfolk."

"D'you know I could very well hang you for a spy?"

"I'm surely no spy, Gen'l! Only a soldier come to see his kin."

"Well, Captain, in that case you won't be needing a guard. You can go to your folks." Custer dismissed the two troopers.

Captain Thomas Farish jumped from his horse, beaming. "Do you mean I shan't be treated as a spy, sir?"

"No. Only as a prisoner on parole. I can't promise you anything, but I'll do my best to get you exchanged."

"Oh, thank you, sir! You're surely most kind, Gen'l."

"Well, I'll send you over to Monticello with a note to General Sheridan. Seeing that he served at the Point with 'Old Mud' Walker, I'm certain he shall do all in his power to get you exchanged on my recommendation."

Captain Farish embraced the Yankee, tears streaming down his cheeks. "Gen'l Custer," he declared, "as an enemy I hate you. But I love you as a brother!"

Custer blushed, patting Farish on the back.

As Farish was about to enter the house, Custer noticed that he was in his stocking feet. "Captain, you can't go to your folks— much less before General Sheridan—that way!"

"But Gen'l," he said, shrugging, "I have nothing else!"

"Well, your feet look about the same size as mine. Here—take mine!" So saying, General Custer pulled off his boots and handed them to a flabbergasted Captain Farish.

On Custer's recommendation, Sheridan released Farish; and according to Colonel Alex Pennington, whom Custer esteemed "my able & gallant time-honored associate," the Farish family cherished "the pleasantest remembrances of Custer & spoke warmly of his kindness to them."

With Jubal Early out of the war, Phil Sheridan made a dash for City Point on the James River to rejoin Grant and the siege of Petersburg. On the way, in accordance with orders, Custer and Devin (ably assisted by over two thousand freed Negro slaves) wrecked three-quarters of the Virginia Central Railroad and completely cut the James River Canal: two main supply lines between Richmond and Lynchburg. The deathblow had been delivered, but the victim would be long in dying.

"The hardships of this march far exceeded those of any previous campaigns by the cavalry," Sheridan would write of his "Mud March of '65." "Almost incessant rains had drenched us for sixteen days and nights, and the swollen streams and wellnigh bottomless roads east of Staunton presented grave difficulties on every hand; but surmounting them all, we destroyed the enemy's means of subsistence, in quantities beyond computation."

In sixteen days and nights, through driving rain and knee-deep mud, (Custer and his command had covered nearly three hundred miles of enemy territory and had destroyed forty-six canal locks, five aqueducts, forty canal and road bridges, twenty-three railroad bridges, over a hundred miles of track, fourteen mills, two factories, twenty-seven warehouses, and immense quantities of munitions and supplies) All in all, a colossal accomplishment! In so doing, however, he and "Old Tommy" Devin (now in command of the 1st Division) ruined nigh three thousand horses; and their week's rest

266

at White House Landing on the Pamunkey necessitated remounting as well as provisioning for the twenty-five-mile march southwestward to City Point on the James.

On March 20, 1865, Armstrong wrote to Elizabeth: "Oh, how lonely I feel for my little one! . . . I long for the return of peace. . . . Destiny has been more than kind to me, and I humbly trust I may ever have a grateful spirit."

General Custer sent his battery of captured Confederate battle flags to Washington, where Mrs. Custer presented them to Secretary of War Stanton "for Tad Lincoln." "Oh, what a happy day that was!" she wrote her husband. "The proudest of my life. Mr. Stanton introduced me as 'the wife of the gallant Gen'l.' . . . Before leaving, I told the Sec'y I was waiting for a letter from you; and Mr. Stanton replied, 'Gen'l Custer is writing lasting letters on the pages of his country's history.' "

★ 39 ★

FIVE FORKS:
A HAPPY OMEN

MAJOR General P. H. Sheridan and his Army of the Shenandoah paraded into City Point on March 26, 1865. Colonel Wainwright comments: "They looked as if they had had a hard march of it: the officers very seedy. . . . I do not know when I have seen such a dirty-looking lot of men."

Major General W. T. Sherman and a detachment from his equally grubby-looking Grand Army of the West came marching in the following day, to concert plans of action for a final full-scale offensive strategy. The stage would now be set for the last act in this long and deplorable drama.

"Phil," Lieutenant General U. S. Grant said as they walked through the woods behind the siege lines at Petersburg, "Sherman urged me to wait till he could bring his army up from North Carolina; but I couldn't agree to this, any delay would give Lee time to reopen his communications north of the James. No, now is the time to strike—now that he's crippled. I'm determined to move at once. I mean to end this business right here and now, and you're the man to do it—with my full support."

"That's the stuff!" fiery-tongued Phil replied. "Let's end this Goddamned business once and for all."

Mr. Lincoln regarded Unconditional Surrender as "a very determined little fellow." He had therefore advised Grant to force an immediate surrender out of Lee. "I want submission, no more bloodshed. Let them once surrender, and they won't take up arms again."

General Robert E. Lee gazed sad and weary-eyed at the Sunset

268

of the Confederacy. "I shall endeavor to do my duty and fight to the last," he said to those tattered remnants slowly starving in the wormy, lousy, ratty trenches around Richmond and Petersburg. "But you must not be surprised if calamity befalls us."

"I see no escape for Lee," Sheridan said to Grant. "I think, if things are pushed, Lee will surrender."

Grant replied, "Then push things!"

And so he did. Sheridan started the big push on March 29, 1865. Destination: Burkesville Junction, about forty-five miles west of Petersburg. Objective: wreck the Southside and the Richmond & Danville Railroads, thus slitting Lee's last two arteries of supply and setting him up for the kill. He would then have to come out and fight, and surrender or die, or starve to death where he was now embattled. Either way, a hopeless choice!

Sheridan to Grant: "I can drive in the Rebel cavalry with one hand, with the other strike Lee's right so damned hard he'll bounce out of Petersburg. By God, we've got 'em just where we want 'em. I tell you I'm ready to strike out and go to smashing things!"

A glint in the eye, a quick puff on his cigar, a flick of the hand: "Go on, Phil—and good luck."

With twelve thousand troopers and Major General G. K. Warren's 5th Army Corps, Sheridan the Bold pushed southwestward in an encircling, diversionary movement—for the kill.

"Big thing ahead," muttered a Michigan cavalryman. "Look at Old Curly."

"Drunk?" ventured a raw recruit.

"Drunk!" the veteran snorted. "Who, *him?* Not on your life, sonny! He smells a battle. And when Old Curly smells a battle, his face turns red as a raspberry."

Indeed, Custer's countenance was a barometer of emotion: flushed with excitement, twitching with impatience, taut with anticipation.

Sheridan's mud-march to Dinwiddie Courthouse, a shabby crossroad in pine barrens fifteen miles southwest of Petersburg, was one of the most exasperating the Cavalry Corps ever experienced. Horses and mules sank belly-deep in boggy muck, and many a mud-bound wagon had to be abandoned. Only the buoyant hope of an imminent end to strife raised weary and depressed troopers from sloughs of deep-sucking despair) Sinking hearts were also lifted by Old Curly's cracks: "Boys, if the folks at home ever ask if you've been through Virginia, you can answer 'Yes—in a number of places!' "

General Lee telegraphed President Davis, on tenterhooks at Richmond: ⁄¹The movement of Gen'l Grant to Dinwiddie C.H. seriously threatens our position, and diminishes our ability to maintain our present lines in front of Richmond & Petersburg. . . . I fear he can readily cut both the Southside & Danville RRs., being far superior to us in Cavalry.ʰ

Immediate solution? Send George Pickett's and Bushrod Johnson's divisions to head Sheridan off at Five Forks, five miles north of Dinwiddie and two-and-a-half south of the strategic Southside Line.

Saturday, April 1, 1865, 4 P.M. General Sheridan dashed off a dispatch to General Grant: "I am holding in front of Dinwiddie C.H., on the road leading to Five Forks, with Gen'l Custer's Division. The enemy are in his immediate front. Will attack directly Warren is up & in position."

The pungent-wet pine woods echoed with regimental bands blasting "Nellie Bly" and "When Johnny Comes Marching Home," with the crackle of twelve-shot Spencers, with the blare of bugles.

Grant's aide-de-camp, dark-bearded Colonel Horace Porter, had ridden in from Army Headquarters as an official observer of Sheridan's grand maneuver. "General Grant sends his compliments, sir; says this movement is entirely in your hands: that you must be responsible for its execution. The General says he has every confidence in you."

"Well, bully! The enemy is falling back steadily. We've had several brushes, but nothing decisive yet. Been obliged to dismount half the cavalry as skirmishers, driving 'em into their defenses. I'm damn tired of the delays in getting the infantry up against 'em. Mud or no mud, I tell you we've got to act fast and furious. This battle must be fought and won before the sun goes down. I'm going to strike 'em with all we've got, as soon as I can get Warren

270

into line. I think Pickett will make a last-ditch stand at Five Forks, but by God we'll carry his works or be blasted to hell!"

According to Porter, Sheridan "fretted like a caged tiger." When the 5th Corps finally arrived on the right, it was led by 2nd-Division Commander Romeyn B. Ayres.

"Where's Warren?" Sheridan thundered.

"In the rear, sir, making dispositions."

"God damn him, I'll have his rank for this delay! . . . Well, Ayres, it seems you must save the honor of the 5th Corps. Take the left, Crawford the center, Griffin the right. Advance in echelon on the enemy's left and rear, and storm those works at any risk. Don't stop till they're ours. The cavalry will strike center, blowing 'em open like a barn door in a windstorm. Go in, Ayres, and give 'em hell!"

Little Phil clapped spurs to big black Rienzi and charged up the spongy road to where Old Curly's 3rd Cavalry Division stood in line of columns facing the enemy earthworks. Bands blasted "Hail to the Chief!" and "Hail Columbia!", and thousands of voices roared, as the brandy-faced Irishman came galloping down the lines through a storm of spent bullets, waving his billycock hat and bellowing: "We're going to give 'em the Goddamndest whipping they ever got!"

"Merritt"—Sheridan addressed his new Chief of Cavalry—"I want you to send Devin's division forward on foot. Let him take Pennington's brigade of Custer's division, as skirmishers, and storm those works in front. Custer will strike left and rear with two mounted brigades. Go ahead!" He then addressed Brigadier General Thomas C. Devin's dismounted 1st Division: "I want you men to know we've got a record to make before sundown that will make all Hell tremble! Now up and at 'em!"

Sheridan reined in alongside Custer. The two men grinned at each other. Sheridan whisked a sleeve across his sweaty brow and jerked a thumb at the mile-long line of mud-and-log fieldworks blockading the vital intersection of Ford and White Oak Roads, at Five Forks, two thousand yards ahead. "George Pickett has every intention of stopping us here," he puffed. "I have every intention of pushing through. Let's go!"

271

Custer unsheathed his sword, perched his cavalier hat on the point, then flaunted it and signaled the "boiler-makers" to strike up "Yankee Doodle." His voice rang out: "Left oblique, forward *ho!*"

Custer held his head high as he jogged along next to Sheridan. His old blue blouse was now decorated with two gold stars, and over it he wore a major general's dark-blue jacket with two silver-embroidered stars embellishing each shoulder strap. His trousers were now of the regulation sky-blue, with broad yellow stripes, but his boots (like his slouch hat) were Confederate Army issue. The long golden curls and scarlet necktie were still as conspicuous as ever. In fact, every mud-spattered trooper in the Bluedevil Division had adopted something of the slipshod elegance of Old Curly. There were more shocks of shaggy hair, more red chokestraps, more bizarre blouses in the 3rd Cavalry Division than anywhere else in the U.S. Army!

Custer looked haggard and overwrought. He had eaten little and slept less in the past few days. The feverish excitement of the grand finale was so sensational, so soul-stirring, that he forged ahead on unrelenting nervous energy.

"Squadrons: right into line, *wheel!* Gallop *ho!*"

Wells's 2nd and Capehart's 3rd Brigade rolled like smooth blue breakers in the roaring sea.

"*Charge! charge!*"

Bugles blaring, guidons flaring, a torrent of Federal horsemen hurled itself at the Confederate earthworks. A mile-long tempest of smoke and flame burst before them, spewing a hell-fire of grapeshot and musket balls. But not even the Devil himself could stop them now.

As his wildly racing steed was gathering to hurdle over the works, Armstrong grabbed his new battle flag from the wounded color-bearer. It was "the handsomest flag in the Army"—"a happy omen"—a huge red-and-blue silk banner with white crossed sabers and the number 3 embroidered on both sides, the handiwork of Elizabeth Custer.

Sheridan followed Custer's example. He snatched his own H.Q. flag from the standard-bearer and vaulted over the embankment

272

with his companion, scattering Rebel gunners like chaff before the wind. Shooting and slashing, trampling and stampeding, Sheridan and Custer worked and witnessed the "Waterloo of the Confederacy."

"Go for 'em!" Sheridan bellowed. "Round 'em up!"

"Bullets were like a bee-swarm," Colonel Porter recalls. "Sheridan dashed about from one part of the line to the other—shaking his fist, waving the flag, yelling, swearing, praying."

"Have a care, sir," Custer gaily shouted. "You'll get yourself killed!"

"By God, sir," Sheridan snapped back, "I've never taken any command into battle with the slightest desire to come out of it alive unless I won." He grabbed Custer's arm, ranting in a rush of emotion, "Go after 'em! Smash 'em! You understand? Goddammit, I want you to give it to 'em!"

"All right—all right!" Custer rattled, mad with impatience. "I'll give it to 'em!"

And away he flew, waving his hat, his yellow mane and scarlet tie fluttering in the breeze.

Sheridan bolted off to the right, to God-damn the 5th Corps over the breastworks. "Come on, men! Move at 'em on the jump, or you'll not catch a one! At 'em—*at 'em!* They're on the run! Christ Almighty, get a move on!"

Pickett (like Early) escaped by the skin of his teeth, leaving behind a major general's gray-and-gold dress coat and a beautifully engraved shotgun. Five thousand Johnnies threw down their weapons and began waving handkerchiefs, drawers, shirts, towels—anything white—in token of surrender. The rest ran, or were killed. Custer, riding like a Valkyrie, shattered Rooney Lee's rear-guard cavalry and drove in a thousand more fugitives. Lee's right wing was broken off and smashed. This was the beginning of the end of the Army of Northern Virginia, Marse Robert's pride and joy.

"The most momentous day of the War . . . a glorious day; a day of real victory." So Charles Wainwright esteemed the engagement at Five Forks.

"Everybody was riotous over the victory," recorded Horace

273

Porter. "It meant the beginning of the end, the reaching of the 'last ditch.' It pointed to peace and home."

Sheridan reported to Grant: "I have overthrown Pickett, taken 6 guns, 13 battle-flags & nearly 6000 prisoners."

Grant wired the President, anxiously waiting at City Point: "I have just heard from Sheridan. He has carried everything before him . . . and is now pushing his success. I have ordered an immediate assault along the lines."

On Sunday, April 2, Petersburg was taken by storm (Parke's 9th Corps) and abandoned by the enemy. Early that same day, Richmond surrendered to Weitzel's 25th Corps (Army of the James) and was evacuated by President Davis and his Cabinet, who fled to Danville and ultimate captivity.

"Thank God I have lived to see this!" Lincoln exclaimed. "It seems to me that I've been dreaming a horrid dream for four years, and now the nightmare is gone."

"To all intents," Wainwright entered in his journal, "the Rebellion may be said now to be over. Certainly it is on its last legs. If those legs are long enough to enable Lee to get around us & join [Gen'l Joe] Johnston in N. Carolina, they may be strong enough to give us one more big fight. All the heart & spirit being gone, tho', strength of leg is not likely to amount to much." He added, perhaps with wounded pride: "So, after 3 years of fighting, it is not the Army of the Potomac which enters Richmond as victors."

Only one dark incident scarred brilliant victory: the arbitrary removal of Gouverneur Kemble Warren from high command. Warren, who (like another engineer, Wilson) had apparently cracked under the strain of responsibility and strife, did not lead his corps into action—but lolled in the rear, sending aides to the front *pro forma*. Sheridan, whose terrible temper had been demonstrated at West Point when he pursued an imperious superior with fixed bayonet (for which he suffered a year's suspension), replaced Warren with "bluff & bellicose" Brigadier General Charles Griffin, Custer's rawboned tactics prof at the Point. "Won't you reconsider this, General?" Warren had asked in anger, and the answer was even uglier: "Reconsider *hell!* I don't reconsider my decisions. Obey the order!" And that was that!

274

In the evening of April 1, New York *World* correspondent G. A. Townsend nearly stumbled over G. A. Custer in his haste to interview General Sheridan. Old Curly lay fast asleep—his head on a log, his curls covering his face—sprawled in the flickering glow of the pine-barren bivouac.

> ... innocent sleep,
> Sleep that knits up the ravell'd sleave of care,
> The death of each day's life, sore labour's bath ...

⋆ 40 ⋆

SAYLOR'S CREEK: TOM'S
RED BADGE OF COURAGE

FORCED out of Petersburg by the smashup at Five Forks, General Lee abandoned Richmond and headed westward along the north bank of the Appomattox River in a desperate effort to reach Lynchburg or Danville and join forces with Joe Johnston, who was staggering up from North Carolina after his defeat by "Cump" Sherman.

Mr. Lincoln told General Grant, "Let the thing be pushed," and the Great Hammerer answered at once: "Pursuit will be immediately made."

Sheridan the Inevitable and Custer the Incredible led the mad cross-country chase. Their orders were quite simple: Hunt Lee down, head him off, hack him to pieces. As Phil said to Curly, "We'll pursue Old Spades till he finds that last ditch to die in!" With Early and Pickett out of the running, there were but Ewell and Longstreet to go.

"I feel confident of capturing the Army of N. Va., *if we exert ourselves*," Sheridan notified Grant. "I see no escape for Lee."

Grant agreed: "All we want is to capture or beat the enemy." Meade, "black with bile," added, "Intercept & destroy Lee's Army."

It was determination pitted against desperation, a hundred thousand against forty thousand. "We are pelting after Old Lee as hard as the poor doughboys' legs can go," penned Colonel Ted Lyman, Meade's adjutant; and a Confederate officer wrote: "Tired & hungry, we push on. It is now a race for life or death."

On Thursday afternoon, April 6, 1865, General Custer and his

3rd Cavalry Division ripped into Lee's rear guard at Saylor's
Creek, helping to cut off the corps of Old Baldy Ewell and capture
some eight thousand Confederates.

Captain Tom Custer with his older brother led the mounted
assault on Ewell's wagon train. He was first to leap his horse over
the barricades, on top of the enemy, who were pouring out a torrent of lead. Tom grabbed the 2nd Virginia Reserve Battalion
colors and shouted "Surrender!" In that instant the color-bearer
jerked up his pistol, shot him point-blank in the face.

The bullet tore through Tom's left cheek and broke out the
back of his neck. Burnt powder speckled his face like a burst of
fine pepper. Clutching the flag in one hand, Tom drew his revolver
with the other and shot the color sergeant dead.

As General Custer cleared the barricade, his charger was popped
from under him by fleeing graybacks. He jumped up to see Brother
Tom with blood streaming down his blackened face, gasping, "Aut!
The damn Rebs shot me, but I got their flag!"

Tom yanked the reins to dash on, but Armstrong laid hold of
the halter. "Where d'you think you're going?"

"After Ewell!"

"You damn fool, can't you see you're bleeding like a stuck pig?
Get to the rear and find a surgeon before you drop dead!"

"Is that an order?"

"That's an order!"

Armstrong then turned to Orderly-Lieutenant James Christiancy,
son of the celebrated Judge: "Jim, conduct Captain Custer in
arrest to the nearest ambulance. If he tries to get away, shoot him!"

Tom obeyed with stricken looks, but he was well rewarded for
his gallantry and obedience. Armstrong appointed him Brevet
Lieutenant Colonel and wangled a Congressional Medal of Honor
for his kid brother.

This was the second Medal of Honor that Tom was awarded,
and the second Confederate battle flag he had seized singlehanded,
in one week. A Civil War precedent! The first token of valor had
been earned on April 3, during the cavalry skirmishing at Namo-
zine Church, where Tom captured the enemy colors and fourteen
prisoners, three of them officers. To make the feat even more diffi-

cult, his horse was shot from under him, the second in three days. Tom thought it strange that no one had ever bothered to confer at least a half-dozen Congressional Medals on "big bub Aut" for his sundry exploits, inasmuch as the decoration was authorized in '62 and bestowed like gimcracks ever since, but older brother answered in jest, "I never asked for it, so nobody ever gave it to me!" He then added, characteristically: "To prove to you how much I value and admire my brother as a soldier, I think that *he* should be the general and I the captain."

Armstrong wrote to Elizabeth: "When Tom first joined me, I was anxious concerning his conduct. But now I am as proud of him as can be, as soldier & brother. He has quit the use of tobacco, is moderate in drink, is respected & admired by officers & all who come in contact with him."

April 6, 5 P.M.

"My name is Kershaw—Gen'l Kershaw, sir. I desire to surrender my sword to you, Gen'l Custer."

"Why, General!" Custer beamed, taking his hand. "I'm glad to meet you. I feel I ought to know you."

"True, Gen'l. We've often met, but not under circumstances favorable to cultivating an acquaintance."

Custer chuckled. "Well, I assure you, sir, I always had great respect for you and your command when you confronted us in the Valley."

Kershaw bowed. "Well, sir, and I look upon you as one of the best cavalry officers this or any other country ever produced. I shall, indeed, consider it an honor to surrender my sword to you."

"General, you flatter me to blushing: my one great weakness. But it's an honor, coming from one of the best generals commanding the finest division in the Confederate Army. I'd accept your sword with gratitude, sir, but I beg you to keep it."

"God bless you, sir! Ever since the battle at Cedar Creek, when you and Gen'l Sheridan embraced each other after the fight, I've had a most perfect admiration for you, Gen'l. I read a full account of it in the New York *Herald* some days after the engagement. All through today's battle I directed my men to concentrate their fire

278

upon your headquarters flag, knowing you were there always at the front. While I should have deprecated the idea of killing a man so brave, good and efficient as yourself, sir, yet I knew it was my only hope!"

Custer laughed. "General, I'm afraid you merely succeeded in killing my best horse!"

Distinguished-looking, white-mustached Major General Joseph B. Kershaw, sword in hand, admired his victor: lithe, tall, sinewy figure in tight-fitting olive-green corduroy ranger's outfit and scarlet neckerchief; bright, quick-moving blue eyes; sharp nose, high cheekbones; florid, freckled complexion; luxuriant reddish-gold ringlets; a snappy, nervous manner and a cocksure, jaunty air radiating the habit of command. Here was "the redoubtable Custer, whose name was as familiar to his foes as to his friends." In Whittaker's words: "His name and figure, when only a division commander, were better known all through the Union, and attracted more compliments from Confederates, than those of any corps commander then in the Army of the Potomac."

A moment later, Lieutenant General Richard S. Ewell (Old Baldy or "Pegleg Dick," as he was affectionately called) came jouncing up on a flea-bitten bag-o'-bones nag, Rifle, and sourly tendered his sword to General Custer in token of surrender. Old Curly accepted the weapon with pleasure when the one-legged, bald-pated, popeyed "old buzzard" loudly squawked that "some Goddamn bluebellied Yankee trooper" had stolen his wallet and pocket watch. Embarrassed beside him, on a thoroughbred mare, sat another prime prisoner: Major General George Washington Custis Lee, the bearded image of father Robert E. Lee. On the other side of the "cantankerous old coot" stood his faithful crutch-carrying "striker," an Apache boy named "Friday," memento of duty in the Southwest. Ewell was indeed a "nervous wreck," as one staff officer described him: twitching, trembling, stridulating and gesticulating. No wonder they called him "Old Woodcock"! Poor devil, Custer thought. Should be put out to pasture.

Kershaw records: "With soldierly hospitality our host made us feel welcome; and, despite our misfortunes, we enjoyed not a little the camp luxuries—coffee, sugar, condensed milk, hard-tack,

279

broiled ham—spread on a tent-fly converted into table-cloth, around which we sat on the ground, Custer & his Rebel Guests. After supper we smoked & talked of subjects of common interest, dwelling on the past. Our host, with true delicacy, avoided the future, which to us was not an inviting topic. We slept beneath the stars, Custer sharing his blankets with me. As the last bugle-call sounded 'Tattoo' & 'Taps,' silence reigned, broken only by the neighing or snorting of a horse, the cough of some wakeful soldier. Custer was soon asleep. As I lay there, watching the glittering hosts of Heaven, I buried my dreams of Southern independence. The God of Battles had deserted our banners. I bowed my spirit in submission. Mine, thenceforth, the task to help bind my bleeding country's wounds."

Old Dick Ewell, seated dejectedly by the fire, muttered to Phil Sheridan, "Our cause is gone. Lee should surrender now, before more lives are wasted."

Sheridan, stretched out on a blanket, was composing his report to Grant: "Up to the present time we have captured Gen'ls Ewell, Kershaw, Barton, Corse, Hunton, Dubose & Custis Lee, 7 or 8000 prisoners, 16 pieces of Artillery, 37 flags, and 3 or 400 waggons. Most of these fell into the hands of the Cavalry. If we keep pressing, I don't doubt but Lee will surrender."

Custer was in high spirits on the morning of April 7, giving Kershaw a cheery greeting and attending to routine military affairs with the breeziness of a frisky colt. Colonel Frank Huger, whose South Carolina Artillery Battalion had been captured by Old Curly, was reminded of his plutonic hazing of plebe Fanny at the U.S.M.A. when Custer rolled dice with him for possession of his handsome gold "gooseneck" Spanish spurs, purportedly those worn by Presidente-General Antonio López de Santa Anna when taken prisoner in 1836. Huger (like Santa Anna) decried the loss ever after, declaring that Custer had robbed him with loaded dice.

Custer's fond farewell to Kershaw was climaxed with all the pomp and circumstance of glorious war: "He [Custer] shook my hand, mounted a magnificent charger & rode proudly away, followed at a round gallop by his splendid escort bearing 'the fallen flags' "—all thirty-one of them taken by his division. "As he neared his conquering legions, cheer after cheer greeted his approach.

Bugles sounded; sabres flashed as they saluted; and the proud cavalcade filed thro' the open ranks & moved to the front, leading that magnificent column in splendid array. Methought no Roman victor had ever a more noble triumph."

Suddenly, General Custer's headquarters band (mounted on blooded grays) struck up "The Bonnie Blue Flag" as the blue procession passed in review. Curly waved his hat, and Federal troopers tossed hardtack-loaded haversacks to the dazed multitude of half-starved Confederate captives.

General Kershaw lifted his hat, shouted, "There goes a chivalrous fellow! Let's give him three cheers!"

Rebel yells rose at once, like the loud-resounding sea. And as the 3rd Division rumbled away, in pursuit of Lee, the soul-stirring rhythms of "Dixie" throbbed from afar.

281

★ 41 ★

APPOMATTOX:
THE WHITE FLAG

Sheridan again wired Grant: "If the thing is pressed, Lee will surrender." Old Three-Stars relayed the message to City Point, where President Lincoln wired back: "Let the *thing* be pressed."

"Keep pressing!" Grant flashed to Sheridan. He then communicated with Lee: "The results of the last week must convince you of the hopelessness of further resistance on the part of the Army of Northern Va. in this struggle. I feel that it is so, and regard it as my duty to shift from myself the responsibility of any further effusion of blood by asking of you the surrender of that portion of the C. S. Army known as the Army of Northern Va."

Lee replied: "Tho' not entertaining the opinion you express of the hopelessness of further resistance on the part of the Army of No. Va., I reciprocate your desire to avoid useless effusion of blood & therefore, before considering your proposition, ask the terms you will offer on condition of surrender."

"He's stalling for time," exploded Brigadier General John A. Rawlins, Grant's quick-tempered chief of staff and alter ego.

Unconditional Surrender smiled suggestively. "We have none to spare."

Cadaverous-looking Henry A. Wise, defender of Petersburg, reasoned heatedly with a hopeful-beyond-hope Robert E. Lee: "Nothing remains, Gen'l Lee, but to put your poor men on your poor mules and send them home in time for spring plowing. This army is hopelessly whipped."

Lee advised Wise to heed a campfire ballad:

> The race is not to them that's got
>   The longest legs to run,
> Nor the battle to that people
>   That shoots the biggest gun.

"Nil desperandum," Lee said. "Hope is cheap as despair."

Saturday, April 8, 1865. It was late afternoon when a staff officer from Chief of Cavalry Wesley Merritt instructed Major General George Armstrong Custer to halt and rest his command, which was still spearheading the hunt for Lee.

"Send my compliments to General Merritt," Custer said to the waiting aide, "and tell him I've just learned from an enemy prisoner that the Rebels are unloading four trains of supplies at Appomattox Station. Tell him that unless I get further orders from General Sheridan, I'll continue my march and capture those trains."

The 3rd Cavalry Division now stood on the sandy Southside Road, watering their horses at South Fork Creek, only two miles southeast of Appomattox Station. Custer swept off his hat, shouted, "Forward, fast trot!"

A mile up the road, Old Curly and his Bluedevils came in sight of an elegantly huge plantation mansion. As the jogging, jingling, far-flung thread of horsemen approached the homestead, two young ladies came running down the lane leading to the highway.

"They're robbing us!" one of them shrieked, her dress hanging in shreds from her naked body.

"They're trying to murder us!" the other shrilled, waving her arms frantically.

Without saying a word, General Custer drew rein and jumped from his horse. He raced up the walk, the two Southern ladies close on his heels, ringing in his ears: "We've been outraged! Oh, God in Heaven, help us!"

Custer bounded up the gallery steps just as a blue-clad infantry-man came barreling out the front door, his arms loaded with loot. Custer smashed him in the face with a solid right fist, and the scalawag measured his length on the porch.

Charging through the house, Armstrong collared another bluecoat varmint making tracks out the back door. Losing his grip on the man, Custer grabbed an axe that was standing by the stove and heaved it out the entranceway, hitting the rascal on the back of the head and knocking him over cold.)

A moment later the boy general was in the saddle again, blushing at the tearful thanks of two distraught belles and ordering his provost marshal to place a guard on the premises, then hang the two marauders as a deterrent example.

Shredded smoke draped the treetops ahead, tarnished gold in the sunset, and locomotives brawled in the ominous calm that made the deathbed of day. Provisions had at last arrived from Lynchburg, twenty miles to the west, and were being detrained and loaded in commissary wagons for delivery to Lee's distressed army. These wretched remains of a once-mighty fighting machine were now but a day's march from salvation: Lynchburg, City of Hills. As Custer approached Appomattox Station, the Confederate vanguard was staggering into the sprawling whistle stop called Appomattox Courthouse, only three miles away.

General Custer turned to Colonel Pennington, commander of the 1st Brigade: ("Alex, I want you to take your men and circle those woods to the left. Detach a regiment to tear up the tracks and pull down any telegraph lines towards Lynchburg. Hold the pike at all hazards, until Devin and Crook come up. Lee *must not* escape. D'you understand?"

"Perfectly." Pennington saluted, reined away.)

Custer signaled to Colonels Wells and Capehart, who addressed their brigades: "Squadrons, front into line! Attention for the charge!"

Bugles blaring the "Charge," Custer and his men thundered down on Appomattox Station, routed the Confederate vedettes, and captured the four trains of supplies hitherto destined to save Lee's army from disaster.

But if Lee couldn't have those munitions, damned if Grant could either! Masked batteries suddenly opened fire from the woods north of the railroad tracks, pitching dozens of shells into the engines and boxcars and wagons.

It was now dusk, and a hazy atmosphere made all movement

hazardous, but Custer dismounted his division and went in after the guns. Wells and Capehart entreated him not to make any such move till day light, but Custer grabbed his headquarters flag and responded dramatically, "I go! Who will follow?" For all he knew, Lee's whole army lay in ambush. Yet, in the words of Colonel F. C. Newhall (Sheridan's adjutant general), "Custer might not well conduct a siege of regular approaches, but for a sudden dash—Custer against the world!" What lay in and beyond those black-jack oaks was R. L. Walker's sixty-gun Reserve Artillery Battalion, supported by M. W. Gary's South Carolina Cavalry Brigade.

A clatter of carbine fire to the far left suggested that Pennington had struck the enemy in flank. Custer slammed forward like an avalanche, right and center: long dark lines, howling and cheering. Flashing and roaring burst from black shadows of the forest, and Custer's bluecoats charged into what seemed the infernal regions: a pandemonium of blazing echoes. Through the trees they thrashed, winnowing all before them, and emerged to mount for a master stroke that would smash Lee's convoy.

Artillery Lieutenant W. F. Robinson "could plainly see Gen'l Custer sitting on a white horse in the centre of a long line of Cavalry; and he was heard urging his men to charge, telling them that there was only a handful of Confederates opposing them. I urged my men to take good aim & shoot at Gen'l Custer, and I shot at him a number of times myself"—but without success, for "I bear a charmed life" was written on his forehead by the hand of Fortune. However, "We loaded & fired so fast . . . that Custer couldn't get his Cavalry to charge us."

Walker's grape-and-canister barrage was so raking as to defy all daring, until Devin and Crook came up in support of Custer's wavering column. Then, hit-and-run maneuvers slowly drove Walker and Gary back upon Lee's bivouac in a mad scramble of men and horses, wagons and guns. The dead of night found Custer counting thirty-five fieldpieces, a thousand prisoners, seven flags, and two hundred supply wagons.

With Appomattox Road and Lynchburg Pike held by Sheridan's horsemen, Lee was completely cut off from all escape. Humphreys' and Wright's corps were swinging down from the northeast to close

285

the vise, while Griffin and Ord crawled up in support of Sheridan. Time had run out on the Army of Northern Virginia.

In a cottage near the depot, a delighted warrior scribbled this dispatch to Grant:

> Cavalry Hd.-Qrs.
> April 8th, 9:20 P.M.
>
> Gen'l—
> . . . Custer is still pushing on. If Gen'l Griffin & the 5th Corps can get up to-night, *we will perhaps finish the job in the morning.* I do not think Lee means to surrender until compelled to do so.
> P. H. Sheridan
> Maj.-Gen'l

"We must keep Lee pinned down at Appomattox Courthouse," Sheridan said to Custer late that sleepless night, "and by God we'll finish the job in the morning. Give him no rest. I want skirmishing kept up all night. Old Spades won't surrender till he's forced to do so, but Christ knows he's reached the last ditch. If our Goddamned infantry can get to the front, the Rebellion will be crushed tomorrow." Sheridan's face reddened, and his dark eyes flashed fiercely, as he opened and snapped shut his hand. "We've got 'em, God damn 'em—we've got 'em like *that.* Now smash 'em, I tell you," he roared, slamming his right fist into his left palm again and again. "*Smash 'em, smash 'em, smash 'em!*"

Custer nodded, a wry smile on his lips. He'd smash 'em all right, come morning.

Palm Sunday, April 9, 1865.

It was an uncanny morning, charged with the presence of Destiny. The rolling countryside glowed with a misty green and yellow of blossoming springtime, and mating birds twittered in nearby woods. All was quiet now, after a restless night of terror—sniping, skirmishing—and after a fog-blinded sunrise of musketry and cannonade, sparring and clashing, in a forlorn Confederate hope to break through the Federal cavalry barricade that blocked the way to freedom. Lee nearly succeeded, until Grant's infantry loomed large in support of Sheridan. Then, a fleecy haze veiled the crystal heavens; and it began to rain.

Charles Carleton Coffin of the Boston *Journal* observed that "With that Sunday's sun the hopes of the Rebels set, never to rise again. The C.S.A.—The Confederate Slave Argosy, freighted with blood & groans & tears, the death-heads & cross-bones at her mast-head—was a shattered, lifeless wreck."

11 A.M. A warm, gentle breeze stirred General Custer's head-quarters flag as he sat his horse and watched the approach of two mounted officers in full-dress gray. There was a tense, ominous stillness at Appomattox.

The foremost rider held up a white linen towel—flag of truce—on the tip of his saber. He addressed Colonel George G. Briggs of the 7th Michigan, who rode forward to receive him: "I'm Cap'n Simms, from Gen'l Gordon. Where's your commanding officer: Sheridan? I have a message for him."

"He's not here, but General Custer is. You'd better see him."

"Can you take me to him?"

Briggs nodded, reined about.

Custer scowled as the parleyers pulled up and saluted. He lifted his hand in respectful response. "Who are you," he snapped, "and what do you want?"

"I'm Cap'n Simms of Gen'l Longstreet's staff," answered the young officer holding the white flag. He swallowed hard, then added stiffly, "Sir, I'm the bearer of a message from Gen'l Gordon to Gen'l Sheridan, asking for a suspension of hostilities till Gen'l Lee can be heard from. He has gone down the road to meet Gen'l Grant, to have a conference as to the proposed surrender."

Custer nodded sharply. "Yes; well, tell General Gordon we'll listen to no terms but that of unconditional surrender. We're behind your army now, and it's at our mercy."

Captain Simms screwed up his face: "Will you allow me to carry that message back?"

General Custer colored slightly. "Yes—certainly! Go on."

"Do you wish to send an officer with me?"

Custer hesitated, then said "Yes. . . . Colonel Briggs, please to accompany the captain back to the enemy lines." He then turned to his chief of staff, Colonel Edward W. Whitaker, and said in a stage whisper, "Ed, carry my message to Longstreet. Immediate and unconditional surrender."

Whitaker nodded, saluted, spurred off with Briggs and the two parleyers.

Custer then addressed one of his aides: "Ride to General Sheridan, fast as you can. Tell him Lee has surrendered, don't charge, the white flag is up. Got that? *Lee has surrendered; do not charge; the white flag is up.* Now ride like hell!"

Whitaker and Briggs soon returned from Longstreet and Gordon, accompanied by a Confederate staff officer. "I'm from Gordon and Longstreet," the Rebel announced heatedly, "and Gordon says for God's sake cease hostilities or hell will be to pay."

"I'm not in sole command upon this field," Custer flashed back. "I'll report the request to General Sheridan, but I can only cease hostilities upon an announcement of unconditional surrender."

Whitaker spoke up: "These people must take us for damned fools. Insults from Longstreet, and one 'Southern gentleman' [General Gary] shouted in my face: 'We're South Carolinians, sir, and we don't surrender. I'll be damned if I surrender!' Besides which, many of Gordon's troops are still firing on our own people—even those under flags of truce—such being the shots we now hear."

Custer responded angrily, "Whitaker, return with this officer and tell Longstreet that I cannot and will not suspend hostilities without his assurance that Lee's army is here and now to be unconditionally surrendered. Get me his answer as soon as possible."

At that moment another young staff officer in gold-laced gray came galloping up, waving a pair of white underdrawers on the end of a stick. "Sir," he panted, saluting Custer, "I'm Colonel Peyton from Gen'l Gordon, who has just received notice from Gen'l Lee of an official truce. Gen'l Lee desires a cessation of hostilities until he can hear from Gen'l Grant as to the proposed surrender."

Custer flicked his hand, replied, "Tell General Gordon that Lee has surrendered. Tell him to lay down his arms at once. The war is over."

"But——!"

"*But* nothing! Tell him!"

"Well, beg pardon, sir, but perhaps you'd best tell him that yourself!"

"Well, lead the way, Colonel, and I damn soon will!"

After an all-night vigil, on the ragged edge of impatience and anticipation, high-spirited Armstrong suddenly broke loose like a wild stallion long fretting and champing in harness. There was no stopping him now. Or so he thought!

General Custer and Colonel Peyton sprinted across the slick wet fields, into the coldly glaring Confederate lines. Lieutenant General John B. Gordon, a rawboned young scowler with lavish imperial and a foppish mop of jet-black hair, cocked an icy-blue eye at the notorious Curly as he came pounding up far ahead of Green Peyton. Gordon was attracted by Custer's long tawny locks and slender grace. The boy general was swanked out in a dark-blue sack coat with the largest shoulder straps of a two-star officer that Gordon had ever seen, and around his neck flapped a gorgeous red waterfall scarf fastened by a big gold pin boldly inscribed *G. A. Custer, Maj.-Gen.* The Confederate later described the Federal as "of strikingly picturesque appearance . . . and a superb rider." Another noted that he "bore himself in the manner of a conqueror."

Custer saluted Gordon with a flourish of his toledo, then instantly resheathed the blade and said briskly, "I'm General Custer, and bear a message to you from General Sheridan. The General desires me to present you his compliments, and to demand the immediate and unconditional surrender of all the troops under your command."

Gordon, Longstreet's chief of staff, glowered and answered respectfully, "You will please, Gen'l Custer, return my compliments to Gen'l Sheridan and say to him that I shall not surrender my command."

"Well, in that case," Custer replied dryly, slowly reddening, "General Sheridan directs me to say, General Gordon—if there's any hesitation about your surrender—that he has you surrounded and can annihilate your command in an hour."

Gordon's scarred face tightened, and his eyes blazed fierce and cruel. "It'd put fight into a whipped chicken just to look at him!"

someone observed. But Gordon answered evenly, "I'm not easily
shaken by threats, Gen'l Custer. Like as not, I'm as well aware of
my particular situation as Gen'l Sheridan is. Moreover, I have
nothing to add to the simple message that Gen'l Lee has asked for
a truce. If Gen'l Sheridan continues the fighting in the face of a flag
of truce, the responsibility for the resultant bloodshed will be Gen'l
Sheridan's, not mine—and hell will be to pay!"

Custer frowned, flushed with disconcertion. "All right—all right,
then," he growled, "take me to General Longstreet."

Gordon bared his teeth for a second, then drew a sigh of disgust
and turned to his aide-de-camp. "Major Hunter," he grated, "you
will please conduct Gen'l Custer to Gen'l Longstreet."

As Custer and Hunter cantered down the Confederate lines,
Custer called out to the gaping Boys in Gray, "This is unconditional surrender! This is the end!"

"Glory be to God!" responded a Rebel officer.

"Aye," said another; "and on earth peace, goodwill toward
men."

Having arrived at his destination, General Custer sprang from his
horse, fluttering a white handkerchief. "Where can I find General
Lee?" he snapped.

A staff officer shrugged. "With Gen'l Grant, I reckon."

"Then where's General Longstreet?"

The officer pointed, frowning at this apparent "peacock."

Custer swaggered up to Lieutenant General James Longstreet,
Lee's "Old Warhorse," who was standing with his personal staff on
the main road to Appomattox Courthouse.

"I've come to demand your instant surrender!" Custer blurted
as he stalked past Longstreet's openmouthed aides. "We're in a
position to crush you, and unless you surrender at once we'll
destroy you."

Old Pete Longstreet lurched forward: a beefy, lordly gentleman
sporting a grizzled Vandyke and dressed in a faded, threadbare,
buttonless uniform. "By what authority do you come in our lines?"
he bellowed.

"General Longstreet," Custer said in a sharp and excited voice, "in the name of General Sheridan and myself I demand the unconditional surrender of this army. I am General Custer."

"I'm not in command of this army!" Old Pete rasped. "Gen'l Lee is, and he's gone back to meet Gen'l Grant in regard to our surrender."

Custer smirked. "Well, no matter about Grant! Sheridan and I are independent of Grant today, and we demand the surrender be made to us. If you don't do so at once, we shall renew hostilities; and any bloodshed will be on *your* head, not ours."

Longstreet was burning with rage. "Goddammit, sirrah, who in hell do you think you are? I tell you Gen'l Lee is in communication with Gen'l Grant. We certainly won't recognize any subordinate!"

Custer turned a heated crimson. "By Jesus, we'll destroy you if you don't surrender at once!"

Longstreet exploded: "Again be reminded, sirrah, that I am *not* the commander of this army—and that you are within our lines without proper authority, addressing a superior officer as an inferior. Your flagrant and outrageous actions are a disgrace and a disrespect to both Gen'l Grant and myself; and if I *were* in command of this army, I would not receive such a message even from Gen'l Sheridan! But I suppose you know no better, and have violated the decencies of military procedure because you know no better, but it won't save you if you do so again! Now, go and act as you and Sheridan damn well choose; and I'll teach you a lesson you won't forget!" He raised both hand and voice. "Now go, Goddammit—*go!*"

Custer sneered. "I'll be back. You can stake your life on it!"

"Oh well," Longstreet snarled. "If you do that, I'll do my best to meet you."

Old Pete turned away gruffly—and so did Old Curly, swearing under his breath. Lee's Warhorse then said: "Colonel Manning, please order Gen'l Johnson to move his division to the front, to the right of Gen'l Gordon. Colonel Latrobe, please order Gen'l Pickett forward, to Gen'l Gordon's left. Do it at once!"

Custer's bluff had been called. "Well, General," he said sardonically, "it *would* be a pity to have more blood upon the field. Perhaps we'd better wait till we hear from Grant and Lee. I'll speak to General Sheridan about it. Don't move your troops yet."

"Very well, sir," Longstreet answered calmly. "Then I suggest the truce be respected. And as you are now more reasonable, I will say that it is for Gen'l Lee and Gen'l Grant to determine the future of our armies. Good-day, sir."

Noticeably cooled off, Custer touched his hat and swung into the saddle. As he passed out of earshot, Old Pete burst out "*Ha!* That young man has never learned to play 'brag' [bluff poker]."

The staff joined him in laughter; for all knew that Johnson's and Pickett's divisions were a mere myth, scattered to Aeolus at Five Forks and Saylor's Creek.

1:30 P.M. General Custer raced back to the Federal lines, waving a white handkerchief over his head and shouting to his Blue-devils, "It's all right, boys! Lee has surrendered!" Volleys of cheers pelted him as he rode from one end of the U.S. Cavalry Corps to the other, looking for his chief. "Where the hell's Sheridan?" he finally said, breathless, to Colonel Whitaker.

"He and Merritt have gone up to Appomattox for a parley with Lee."

"Where in Appomattox?"

"I think they said the McLean house, sir, just up the road." (The village only had a half-dozen houses, and that one wouldn't be hard to find. It was the biggest in town!)

"All right—all right—lead out the whole division. We're marching to Appomattox!"

With regimental bands throbbing "The Girl I Left Behind Me," General Custer and his 3rd Cavalry Division paraded past the Confederate lines along the rain-sodden road to Appomattox.

> Then to the South we bore away
> To win a name in story,
> And there where dawns the sun of day
> There dawn'd our sun of glory:
>
> Both blazed at noon on Freedom's height,
> Where in the post assign'd me
> I shared the glory of that fight,
> Sweet girl I left behind me.

"Custer's Command on this occasion presented a most striking & beautiful effect," wrote Colonel Frank A. Burr of the 2nd Michigan Cavalry. "Following the Gen'l & his Staff floated not less than 25 Rebel battle-flags; and these, with Division, Brigade & Regimental Colors of the Command, the red neckties of the men, and the blue & yellow of their uniforms, made a picture (as with flashing sabres they moved into view) at once thrilling & beautiful."

And their leader? Colonel Newhall has sketched him: "Custer of the golden locks, his broad sombrero turned up from his hard-bronzed face, the ends of his crimson cravat floating over his shoulders, gold galore spangling his jacket-sleeves, a pistol in his boot, jangling spurs on his heels, and a ponderous claymore swinging at his side—a wild daredevil of a General, and a prince of advance-guards, quick to see and act."

> Full many a name our banners bore
>   Of former deeds of daring,
> But they were of the days of yore
>   In which we had no sharing:
>
> But now our laurels freshly won
>   With the old ones shall entwined be,
> Still worthy of our sires each son,
>   Sweet girl I left behind me.

By Custer's orders, thousands of blue-clad troopers tossed their hardtack kits to thousands of hungry graycoats. "Three cheers for Gen'l Custer!" the ragged and grubstruck Johnny Rebs yelled, swinging their hats. "*Hooray* for Billy Yank! *Hoorah* for Ole Curly!"

Custer bobbed his sloucher in salute.

As they neared the village, blurred by misty drizzle, the boy general instructed his band to strike up "Battle Hymn of the Republic." By far-flung column of fours, Curly's Bluedevils marched slowly into Appomattox to a heart-swelling crash of music: "He has sounded forth the trumpet that shall never call retreat . . . Glory, glory, hallelujah!"

Standing off to the right of the road, surrounded by a sagging

293

fence and blossoming locusts, the McLean house was a large, two-story, red-brick structure with whitewashed wooden verandah, sun porch, and wide seven-step stoop. Staff officers lolled about the lawn, the gallery, the steps: silent, expectant, expressionless.

"Column, *halt!* Right *turn!* Prepare to dismount! *Dismount!*"

4 P.M. Just as General Custer was about to lurch out of the saddle, his eyes and ears were attracted by a clumping of booted feet on the porch twenty feet in front of him. He glanced up and eased back in the saddle, at once recognizing the majestic figure of General Robert Edward Lee.

"Column, *attention!* Prepare to mount! *Mount!* . . . Draw sabers! Present sabers!"

Lee, radiating a solemn grandeur with his trim silver-white beard and noble stature, was immaculately garbed in an untrimmed gray full-dress uniform buttoned to the throat. His ornaments were a beautifully embroidered red-and-yellow sash, gold spurs, and a gold-sheathed ceremonial sword. His hands were encased in glowing white gauntlets.

With his usual quiet dignity, General Lee signaled his orderly to bring up his horse. While the handsome gray steed was being bridled, Marse Robert stood on the lowest step and gazed sadly in the direction of the valley beyond. There lay his beloved Army of Northern Virginia, now a dream of the past. Mingled emotions of relief and regret must have gripped his heart at the end of this epic tragedy. Custer saw the great man slowly strike the palm of his left hand with his right fist in an absent sort of way, apparently oblivious of all around him. He did this three times, then was recalled from his reverie by the approach of his orderly and horse. Lee mounted immediately.

At that moment, Custer observed Lieutenant General Ulysses Simpson Grant stepping out the front door. What a contrast! Old Three-Stars, stroking his short shaggy beard and puffing away at a stubby cigar, looked careworn and bedraggled. He was wearing an unbuttoned, dusty dark-blue fatigue jacket; and his rumpled, powdery trousers were tucked into old mud-spattered boots.

General Grant clumped down the stoop, glanced up at General Lee, and saluted him by tipping a shabby black fedora. Lee raised his handsome gray soft brim respectfully, then started off at a slow trot on his spirited Traveller. Grant now climbed onto his big bay charger, Cincinnati, and reined away. The crowd of staff officers soon followed.

It was at that dramatic instant that General Custer turned to his bandmaster, Major Axtell, and murmured that one electrifying word: "*Dixie*." The bandmaster nodded with a smile, and seconds later it thundered across the peaceful countryside:

> *. . . I wish I was in Dixie:*
> *Hooray! hooray!*
> *In Dixieland I'll take my stand,*
> *To live and die in Dixie! . . .*

Tears welled in Marse Robert's eyes as he turned in the saddle and touched his hat to Old Curly, who returned the salute by sweeping off his own hat with a gallant bow.

George Armstrong Custer's unofficial assumption was now a reality. Lee had surrendered. The war was over.

★ 42 ★

McLEAN HOUSE:
THE TABLE

GENERAL Custer hopped from his horse and hurried into the McLean house, where he found General Sheridan handing the owner his good-luck charms (two ten-dollar gold pieces) for a small, oval-topped, varnished pine table.

"What's that?" Curly said.

"The Surrender Table!" Phil replied, grinning. "The terms of agreement were written and signed on this only a short while ago. Some trophy, eh? Take it!"

Custer gaped.

"Go on, take it! It's yours!"

Sheridan thrust the table into Custer's arms. "Goddamme, sir! Nobody deserves this more than you. This was a cavalry victory; and by God, Custer, you did most in making it so. Give this table to Libbie as a token of her husband's great achievements. I'll scratch out a formal presentation. She might appreciate it."

Little Phil sat at Major Wilmer McLean's marble-topped console table and dashed off the following note to "Mrs. Gen'l Custer" in Washington:

Appomattox Court-House, Va.
April 9th, 1865

My Dear Madam,

I respectfully present to you the small writing-table on which the conditions for the surrender of the Confederate Army of Northern Virginia was written by Lt.-Gen'l Grant; and permit

296

me to say, Madam, that there is scarcely an individual in our Service who has contributed more to bring about this desirable result than your very gallant husband.

Very respectfully,
Phil H. Sheridan \
Maj.-Gen'l

Sheridan handed Custer the note, slapped him on the shoulder, said, "Take the memento of victory with my compliments to Mrs. Custer."

Custer blushed, faltering, "How can I thank you, Phil?"

"Not at all! I said it once, and by God I'll say it again: you're the most deserving of this relic. Besides, you're the only one of my officers who hasn't been spoiled by marriage!"

Sheridan chortled as he watched Custer bound down the stoop with the surrender table on his shoulder, swing up into the saddle, then prance away like a happy-go-lucky boy, balancing the well-won trophy on his golden head and (observed Horace Porter) "looking like Atlas carrying the world."

Brigadier General Joshua L. Chamberlain (1st Division, 5th Corps) chuckled and pointed: "Sheridan's Robber!"

There was much frolic and fraternizing that fateful afternoon and evening between the Blue and the Gray.

"Hullo, you damned redheaded Rebel!" Custer called laughingly to Major Andrew Cowan (3rd Division Artillery Brigade, 6th U.S. Army Corps), garbed in tattered gray. "When the hell are you coming back?"

"Directly!" Cowan replied, hurdling his horse over North Branch Creek. He had been in enemy hands for several days.

"That Goddamn Fitzhugh Lee," as he was known to the Boys in Gray, came looking for Custer, his great Nemesis. Fitz, as a cadet staff lieutenant, had been Assistant Instructor of Cavalry Tactics at the Point in Fanny's day; and now, a towering hulk with long silky beard, he embraced the boy general with a hearty roar and went rolling to the ground with him in schoolyard rollick.

Among others, Colonels James B. (Jim) Washington and John

297

W. (Gimlet) Lea were reunited with their old buddy in blue. All but Tom Rosser. Now where the devil was that damned Texan? Well, it seems he had made a clean getaway—to his wife's home near Hanover Courthouse, eighty-five miles northeast of Appomattox. Curly finally caught him, in early May. En route from Richmond to Washington, he launched a special raid on Rosser's refuge. Lieutenant Christiancy delivered an ultimatum at the front door:

Dear Friend,
    The house is surrounded. You can't get away. Come on out & surrender yourself.

Regards
G.A.C.

He did, vociferating, "Thunderation, man! Wasn't it enough that you broke up my shad-bake at Five Forks, you needs must disrupt my domestic tranquility as well?"

Custer later wired Grant, *pro forma:* "Gen'l Rosser voluntarily came within our lines & surrendered himself."

Yes, the War—the grand and glorious game of gentlemen warriors—was over.

Armstrong spent the late hours of April 9 compiling his official report and composing a farewell order to his beloved Bluedevils. As he was thus occupied, Colonel Ed Whitaker stepped into the H.Q. tent holding a relic that Custer had sent him to find. It was the now-famous flag of truce, a white towel tied to an oak branch. He who had taken more trophies than any man in the Union Army prized this one above all others except the little pine table.

HEAD-QUARTERS, THIRD CAVALRY DIVISION
Appomattox Court-House, Va.
April 9th, 1865

Soldiers of the Third Cavalry Division:
    With profound gratitude to the God of Battles, by whose blessings our enemies have been humbled and our arms rendered triumphant, your Commanding General avails himself of this his first opportunity to express to you his admiration of the heroic

manner in which you have passed through the series of battles which to-day resulted in the surrender of the enemy's entire army.

The record established by your indomitable courage is unparalleled in the annals of war. Your prowess has won for you even the respect and admiration of your enemies. During the past six months, although in most instances confronted by superior numbers, you have captured from the enemy, in open battle, 111 pieces of field-artillery, 65 battle-flags, and upwards of 10,000 prisoners of war, including 7 general officers. Within the past ten days, and included in the above, you have captured 46 pieces of field-artillery and 37 battle-flags. You have never lost a gun, never lost a color, and have never been defeated; and notwithstanding the numerous engagements in which you have borne a prominent part, including those memorable battles of the Shenandoah, you have captured every piece of artillery which the enemy has dared to open upon you. . . .

Let us hope that our work is done and that, blessed with the comforts of peace, we may be permitted to enjoy the pleasures of home and friends. For our comrades who have fallen, let us ever cherish a grateful remembrance. To the wounded, and to those who languish in Southern prisons, let our heart-felt sympathy be tendered.

And now, speaking for myself alone, when the war is ended and the task of the historian begins; when those deeds of daring which have rendered the name and fame of the Third Cavalry Division imperishable are inscribed upon the bright pages of our country's history, I only ask that my name may be written as that of the Commander of the Third Cavalry Division.

G. A. Custer
Brevet Major-General Commanding

Late that night, by a lone campfire, Colonel Whitaker came upon General Custer sitting upright on a log, a cup of coffee in his hand, sound asleep. Ed was bringing his chief a copy of General Sheridan's personal report to General Grant. In it the "Inevitable Irishman" had paid a familiar tribute: "I know of no one whose efforts have contributed more to this happy result than those of Custer."

On Monday morning, as the rain came roaring down on his canvas roof, Armstrong sat at his field table and dashed off a letter to Elizabeth. He trembled with enthusiasm, and his hand darted across the paper as never before:

> Prospect St. (Lynchburg & Petersburg
> RR.), Va., April 10th, '65

My Darling,

Only time to write a word. Heart too full for utterance. Thank God *PEACE* is at hand! And thank God the 3rd Div. has performed the most important duty of this campaign! The 3rd Div. has always been in the advance. Oh, I have so much to tell you—but no time. The Army is now moving back to Brandy St. I hope the last shot has been fired in this war—that we shall soon be enjoying the rich blessings of peace. "Hurrah" for Peace & my Little Durl!!

> Your loving Boy,
> Armstrong

P.S.—I never needed rest so much as now. However, I feel more than repaid for risk & labor.

P.P.S.—and very urgent!—Can you consent to come down & be a Captain's wife?

> Autie

Custer, a Major General by brevet only, must still officially have been a Captain in the Regular Army! Although the record remains mysteriously unclear.

"All praise to the U.S. Army," a jubilant Judge Bacon wrote his daughter from Monroe; "for, under God, the most formidable Rebellion that ever was has been crushed. It makes a Great Man of Sheridan, and has added new Laurels to *the greatest young General of this or of any other Age*." He then added: "Your Marriage brings a corresponding happiness to me, being Father-in-law to a man whose reputation is Second-to-none any where."

Shortly after Armstrong handed the outgoing mail to his orderly, a dispatch rider came rushing in with an important telegram. It was sent from City Point, and signed by Rear-Admiral David D. Porter. General Custer read: "Mrs. Custer will be in Richmond to-morrow."

Hallelujah!

★ PART II ★

★ INTRODUCTION ★

Colonel W. A. Graham, esteemed student of Custer, wrote that "but for the 'blaze of glory' that formed the setting for his dramatically tragic departure at the hands of yelling savages, he would probably be just another name of a long list of names in our histories of the Civil War, in which as 'The Boy General' he made an outstanding record as a leader of cavalry." But the Civil War hero and the demigod of the Wild West are brothers under the skin, and each is equally responsible for the transcendence of man into myth.

Those who brand Custer a "glory-hunter," in the worst sense of that word, unwittingly perpetuate the myth: a myth bred by notoriety and fed by controversy. Many would label Custer an exhibitionistic crackpot and suggest psychiatric treatment were he alive today. He escaped the age of scientized soul-searching, but nonetheless had to contend with the do-gooders of the "plush period."

"Pity the warrior who is content to crawl about in the beggardom of rules! What genius does must be the best of rules." Thus wrote Clausewitz, and thus acted Custer. The boy general won his spurs by breaking all the so-called rules. He was the great exception, and Destiny was his champion-apologist.

Much of Custer's character and personality is buried in the legend and controversy that enshroud him. The Chicago *Tribune*, in its 1876 obituary, appraised him as "a brave, brilliant soldier, handsome and dashing; but he was reckless, hasty and impulsive, preferring to make a dare-devil rush and take risks rather than to move slower and with more certainty; and it was his own mad-cap haste, rashness, and love of fame that cost him his own life."

Major Marcus A. Reno lamented that "so brilliant an officer as Custer" should have suffered from "great personal ambition," and Major General James H. Wilson commented: "The truth about Custer is that he was a pet soldier who had risen not above his merit, but higher than men of equal merit. He fought with Phil Sheridan, and through the patronage of Sheridan he rose; but while Sheridan liked his valor and his dash, he never trusted his judgment. . . . Custer was always aflame. He was like a thermom-eter. He had a touch of romance about him; and when the War broke out he used to go about dressed like one of Byron's pirates in the Archipelago, with waving shining locks and broad flapping sombrero. Rising to high command early in life, he lost the repose necessary to success in high command. . . . But we all liked Custer, and did not mind his little freaks any more than we would have minded temper in a woman. . . . Custer's glorious death and the valor of his men will become a legend in our history. . . . We all think, much as we lament Custer, that he sacrificed the 7th Cavalry to ambition and wounded vanity."

Colonel Samuel D. Sturgis, grieved at the loss of his son Jack (who died on Custer Hill), lashed out at the man and the myth: "What I especially deprecate is the manner in which some papers have sought to make a demigod out of Custer, and to erect a monument to Custer. . . . Custer was a brave man, but he was also a very selfish man. He was insanely ambitious for glory, and the phrase 'Custer's Luck' affords a good clue to his ruling pas-sion."

Perhaps the most venomous of Custer's detractors was Captain Fred Benteen, who expressed himself thus: "I am not ready to subscribe to any effort of the public's opinion to convince me that Custer was a great man or great warrior. . . . I'm only too proud to say that I despised him." He added, however: "Cadets for ages to come will bow in humility at the Custer shrine at West Point;

and if it makes better soldiers & men of them, why the necessity of knocking the paste eye out of their idol?"

General McClellan regarded Custer as "a warm, unselfish & devoted friend"; as "one of the most brilliant ornaments of the Service & the Nation—a most able & gallant soldier, a pure & noble gentleman"; and felt that "his death was as he would have had it, with his face to the foe, encouraging his men to the last." Lawrence Barrett, the celebrated actor, also assures us that he "died as he would have wished to die," and Frederick Whittaker agrees that he "found the one thing needed to complete his character as an ideal hero of romance—a glorious and terrible death on the battle-field."

Therefore, although by virtue of virulent debate we are often led to believe it, tactics alone did not cause the disaster at the Little Bighorn. Perchance, tactics were merely a means to an end in the designs of individual destiny. Custer had reached the zenith of his glory in 1876. It was a suitable fate for a child of fortune: a fate that insured him immortality. As the tide of events would probably have turned had he been militarily successful, Custer could only have pined away like a caged animal; and it is hard to imagine the golden-haired hotspur as a pensioner, much less a featherbed politician. Besides, he was under a suicidal cloud: a cloud of "redemption or death."

In this century, the Custer Controversy was much inflamed by Van de Water's *Glory-Hunter,* a superb piece of debunkery, and by Errol Flynn's unexcelled portrayal in "They Died With Their Boots On," an equally superb piece of glamorization. Of course, Custer has always remained one of our greatest myths—a cliché oft repeated in jest—but periodically he is revived in earnest.

The recent official whitewash of Major Reno, a typical "anti-hero," has been part of the revitalized "discredit Custer" campaign —as were those puerile Indian-baby fables circulated so avidly by the late Mari Sandoz and others who, however, cannot produce "documentary evidence" to support them. And well-meaning Indian associations and others have vigorously protested the airing of WABC-TV's series suggestively titled "The Legend of Custer,"

305

and any projected movie spectacular not traditionally anti-Custer or pro-Indian, on the premise that "glamorizing Custer is like glamorizing Billy the Kid." So Custer continues to excite and obsess the popular imagination, and the great controversy rages on! But when all is said and done, it will remain the contention of this author that the tragedy of Custer is that he died at the hands of those he most admired. He died, in the best sense, a poetic death.

What Colonel Graham aptly called "the greatest battle ever waged between the red man and the white, between a receding and an advancing race," has caused more ink to be spilled than the Battle of Gettysburg; and so it is no wonder that the bibliography is monumental. However, only those works of major importance are listed at the end of this book.

D. A. KINSLEY

306

⋆From Far Dakota's Canyons⋆

(A Death-Sonnet for Custer)

From far Dakota's canyons,
Lands of the wild ravine, the dusky Sioux, the lonesome
stretch, the silence,
Haply to-day a mournful wail, haply a trumpet-note for
heroes.

The battle-bulletin,
The Indian ambuscade, the craft, the fatal environment,
The cavalry companies fighting to the last in sternest
heroism,
In the midst of their little circle, with their slaughter'd
horses for breast-works,
The fall of Custer and all his officers and men.

Continues yet the old, old legend of our race,
The loftiest of life upheld by death,
The ancient banner perfectly maintain'd,
O lesson opportune, O how I welcome thee!

As sitting in dark days,
Lone, sulky, through the time's thick murk looking in
vain for light, for hope,
From unsuspected parts a fierce and momentary proof,
(The sun there at the centre though conceal'd,
Electric life forever at the centre,)
Breaks forth a lightning-flash.

Thou of the tawny flowing hair in battle,
I erewhile saw, with erect head, pressing ever in front,
bearing a bright sword in thy hand,
Now ending well in death the splendid fever of thy deeds,
(I bring no dirge for it or thee, I bring a glad triumphal
sonnet,)
Desperate and glorious, aye in defeat most desperate,
most glorious,
After thy many battles in which never yielding up a gun
or a color,
Leaving behind thee a memory sweet to soldiers,
Thou yieldest up thyself.

WALT WHITMAN

307

★1★

WASHINGTON:
THE GRAND REVIEW

E
SCORTED by Senator Zacha-
riah Chandler and members of the Joint Committee on the
Conduct of the War, Elizabeth Custer arrived at the Queen City
of the South on board President Lincoln's personal gunboat, the
Baltimore, in the evening of April 10, 1865.

Tuesday morning, April 11. George Armstrong Custer came
bursting into the Executive Mansion at Richmond, bolted up the
grand staircase, darted into President and Mrs. Jefferson Davis'
private bedchamber. Quietly he approached the bed, leaned over,
and planted a kiss on Libbie's cheek.

Libbie sat up. "Autie!" She flung her arms around his neck and
hugged him. "Autie, what a delightful shock! I never expected . . ." And when he had dried her eyes she said, "Oh,
Autie, when you heard of Lee's surrender, didn't you cry?"

He smiled. "With pleasure!"

They ran their fingers through each other's hair, gazing into
each other's eyes. Autie broke the spell with a boyish grin. "By
Jesus, I've been fighting four years to get into this place—and my
little girl beat me to it!"

Saturday, April 15, 1865. President Abraham Lincoln was
dead. ("Now he belongs to the ages," Secretary of War Stanton
remarked.

"Daughter! Daughter!" wrote Judge Bacon. "What is to become
of us as a Nation & as Individuals? This is the most gloomy day

309

in the History of the Continent. The thought that a man such as Andy Johnson—lunatic, drunkard—is to be at the Head of the Gov't at this, the most critical period of our National Existence, is *awful* beyond words. I may be one of those who will ask Gen'l Grant to take the Gov't in his own hands."

Meanwhile, Senator Chandler was saying to Secretary Stanton, "Don't you think Custer has done enough to have a full commission?"

"My God," Old Evil-Eye exclaimed, "what hasn't he done!"

The long march from Richmond to Washington delighted Autie and Libbie: "Libbie riding in a spring-waggon at the head of the column with me," Armstrong informed his father-in-law. "She endured the fatigue well, and enjoyed the novelty." In her own behalf Elizabeth added: "Father dear, remember how you used to try to frighten me out of marrying a soldier—'No better than gypsying in a covered-waggon on the Plains'? Well, I think it grand fun! Gen'l Sheridan says I make no trouble, and he is always willing I should come."

Yellow Tavern, Trevilian Station, Culpeper Courthouse, Brandy Station, Warrenton Junction, Catlett Station, Bull Run (Manassas Junction). These they passed, and many others. Familiar places, full of haunting memories: full of happiness and heartbreak, terror and valor, infamy and glory, hatred and love. Many a tale could be told of each, and was—by an eager knight to an attentive damsel.

> Farewell the tranquil mind; farewell content;
> Farewell the plumed troops, and the big wars,
> That makes ambition virtue. O, farewell.

Tuesday, May 23, 1865. 9 A.M. It was a sparkling-clear springtime morning, and the thunder of a thousand drums shivered the air, as a hundred thousand battle-scarred veterans of Mr. Lincoln's Army swung past the Capitol and swept straight up Pennsylvania Avenue.

310

From her seat in the Presidential reviewing stand, Elizabeth Custer watched with excitement and anticipation as the long broad ribbon of blue rolled slowly toward her from the glowing white dome on Capitol Hill.

Sabers drawn and trumpets sounding, Sheridan's ten thousand cavalry spearheaded the great parade; for they were the final cause of victory. Little Phil, on special duty in the Southwest, wasn't there to lead them; but he chose the next best man to take his place. And that man was the most glamorous hero of the Civil War. Merritt was Chief of the Cavalry Corps, but Sheridan had said, "You, Curly, will ride in my honor."

General Custer pranced up Pennsylvania Avenue on Don Juan, a magnificent, high-spirited, thoroughbred bay. Long golden curls, gleaming in the sunlight, danced on the star-studded collar of the boy general's dark-blue blouse. His bright-red necktie blazed like a crimson cascade, and his buckskin breeches were tucked into glossy-black jack boots flashing the same gold spurs worn by Santa Anna during the siege of the Alamo. White gauntlets and a broad-brimmed, star-emblazoned black turnup touched off the characteristic regalia of America's daredevil dandy.

Sabers glittered, guidons fluttered, and bands crashed from one end of Capitol Hill to the other. Thousands upon thousands of cheering, whistling, singing spectators were jam-packed along the tree-lined avenue. Mobs crammed the housetops and jammed the windows, and individuals half crazed with joy cluttered the trees. "Here comes Custer!" they shrilled. "Hurrah for Old Curly!" People went wild, pressing halfway into the broad thoroughfare to lionize him.

Armstrong stared straight ahead, now and then cutting an eye at the roaring, tossing waves of his fans. Billows of soft-colored parasols, bobbing hats, and dazzling-white handkerchiefs made Don Juan snort and shake his head, pitching his rump from side to side in a kind of caracole. It was all Custer could do to keep the stallion under control and at the same time retain his own dignified composure.

The far-flung cavalcade, assembled by column of platoons, was

311

now approaching the White House and the flag-festooned reviewing stand. Custer knew Libbie would be there watching, with
General Grant and President Johnson and such government dignitaries as Secretary Stanton.

Arrayed in a white taffeta skirt, blue satin wrap, and black
velvet riding cap garnished with a scarlet feather, Elizabeth Custer
rose to her feet and waved the fringed linen towel that had helped
make her husband the center of attraction at Appomattox. She
had already sent her father the "surrender table," cautioning him
to take good care of it and adding, "Don't give away even a
splinter. They tell me I might sell it for a million dollars!" But
she confessed to liking Sheridan's note of presentation more than
the souvenir itself.

When General Custer was within two hundred yards of the reviewing stand, a shrieking flock of some three hundred white-clad
schoolgirls began waving penny flags and bursting into song: "Hail
to the Chief who in triumph advances!" It was the first big surprise of that stupendous day. It was also the most fateful. Suddenly, unexpectedly, Old Curly was pelted by a fragrant shower
of wreaths and bouquets. Instead of dodging the floral missiles, he
tried to catch a few of them; and that's when Don Juan took
the bit in his teeth.

Before Custer could gather up the reins, the startled charger
bolted forward like a bay-colored tornado. As horse and rider
flew past the Presidential grandstand, Custer jerked up his sword
to salute "Uncle Sam" and "King Andy." The impulsive attempt
knocked off his hat, but before he could lose his balance as well,
Custer dropped his blade and gag-checked his horse. Then, with
his cinnamon-scented hair streaming in the sunshine, he wheeled
around and dashed back to the head of the parade "by one of
the most magnificent exhibitions of horsemanship."

"See him ride!" the crowd roared. "That's Custer!"

Meantime, Grant's eldest son and aide, Lieutenant Fred Dent
Grant, who fairly idolized Old Curly, had darted out and picked
up Custer's hat and sword. He ran down and handed them to the
haggard-looking cavalier, whose ghostly face was now deeply

312

flushed. Custer yanked the dusty turnup low over his eyes, then jogged on past the reviewing stand with head erect and saber at rest.

Disabled veterans of Antietam, Gettysburg, and the Wilderness staggered to their feet and hailed the boy general with cheer after cheer. Custer brightened when he heard them shout, "A tiger for Old Curly!"

He snatched off his hat in gallant salute and beamed at the multitudes screaming with delight. For a second he caught a glimpse of his "little girl," waving to him from the official grandstand almost directly behind white-bewhiskered Secretary Welles. He flicked his sword chivalrously, then flipped back his hat.

"Will those of us who saw that last grand review," wrote one eyewitness, "ever forget those two pictures—Custer conquering his runaway horse, and Custer at the head . . . of the most gallant cavalry division of the age, as with the hot flush of victory yet visible on their bronzed faces he led it through the Capital at a gallop march? It was but a momentary vision, but one that has fixed itself upon at least one memory in indelible lines."

This special reporter for the Detroit *Evening News* was joined in his "One Glimpse of Custer" enthusiasm by the New York *World* correspondent, who echoed the sentiments of a myriad onlookers. General Custer's dash was "like the charge of a Sioux chieftain" and "attracted more attention, admiration & cheering to him than anything else could have done."

But there were those—perhaps disenchanted—who suspected that the Murat of the American Army had made a desperate play to the gallery. Major Henry E. Tremain, General Crook's A.D.C., was ambivalently impressed by "that notorious incident" which swept Custer "past the reviewing officer—the President of the United States—his Cabinet, the military, civil and diplomatic functionaries of this and many other countries, not in the stately and sedate manner of a warrior chief on his prancing charger, but shooting like the wind." He asked shrewdly, "Was this a disappointment, or was the sensation agreeable? Who among the

313

spectators or performers at this state occasion will forget 'how Custer's horse ran away with him'?"

> Farewell the neighing steed, and the shrill trump,
> The spirit-stirring drum, the ear-piercing fife,
> The royal banner, and all quality,
> Pride, pomp, and circumstance of glorious war.
> And o you mortal engines, whose rude throats
> The immortal Jove's dread clamours counterfeit,
> Farewell. Othello's occupation's gone!

TEXAS: THE AUGEAN TASK

LATE afternoon, May 23, 1865. Shadows were fading in the outpost of advancing darkness. For an uncanny moment, Camp Arlington was hushed in tribute. Then: "Three cheers and a tiger for Old Curly!" Voices roared like cannon fire, and caps rocketed into the air like windrows of waterfowl. The end had truly come. This was farewell—forever. Libbie later wrote: "I began to realize, as I watched this sad parting, the truth of what Autie had been telling me—that no friendship was like that cemented by mutual danger on the battle-field."

He fought back the onslaughts of emotion which strove to unnerve him; and when he could fight no more, the tears streaked down his cheeks, his tightened lips trembled, and he quivered like one overcome with fright. When Libbie saw the suffering on her husband's face, and heard the ovation to him, she wept as well—in joy and in sorrow.

> I have touched the highest point of all my greatness;
> And from that full meridian of my glory,
> I haste now to my setting: I shall fall
> Like a bright exhalation in the evening,
> And no man see me more.

There seemed to be no honor too great for a grateful nation to bestow upon its beloved hero—a seat in Congress, a staff appointment in Washington, the governorship of Michigan, the Presidency of the United States.

Libbie was elated, but Autie was less enthusiastic. He respectfully refused to wear any laurels but those won in battle to save the Union. The "blushing honors" of public office were not his ambition, nor was he a "featherbed soldier." George Armstrong Custer was by nature and aspiration a knight-adventurer, a paladin somehow strayed from the age of chivalry, and as such he sought his destiny and glory.

Elizabeth was disappointed at first that her husband didn't accept one of the several political jobs so lavishly offered him as meal tickets to the White House. But she soon changed her attitude when Judge Daniel Stanton Bacon stepped in and admonished her thus: "My Child, put no obstacles in the way to the fulfillment of his Destiny. He chose his profession; he is a born Soldier; there he must abide."

More understanding now of Autie's spiritual happiness, the hunger of his soul that must be satisfied if he was to live at peace with himself, Libbie replied to her father appreciatively: "I am married to an independent, high-minded man. I have nothing more to ask for, as I believe the best of everything on earth has already been given to me. I am prouder far to be his wife than I would be to be Mrs. President or a Queen."

"Daughter," the Judge answered, "continue to do as you have always done. Follow Armstrong every where."

And so, when Custer followed Sheridan into the wild and wanton Southwest, Libbie went with him. She had roughed it before, and she would rough it again—all for her Autie.

Custer hastened to Texas at the beck and call of Little Phil, who desperately needed a man of mettle to help him clean out the hornet's nests of bounty jumpers, jayhawkers, mosstroopers, bushwhackers, and scalawag carpetbaggers, who were flagrantly riding roughshod over the lawless yucca country.

General Grant agreed with General Sheridan that General Custer was equal to the Augean task. "I mean to endorse Gen'l Custer in a high degree," Grant wrote to Mr. Stanton. Sheridan's sentiments were a matter of public record. "Custer," he had said openly, "you're the only man that never failed me."

Phil had been appointed Military Commander of the 5th Reconstruction District (Military Division of the Southwest and Gulf, comprising Louisiana and Texas, with headquarters at New Orleans) and his orders were explicit to protect this hotbed of rebellion from the imperialistic ambitions of Louis Napoleon's puppet, Maximilian, who, in defiance of the Monroe Doctrine, had raped Mexico while Uncle Sam was embroiled in a schizophrenic disorder; and (in Grant's words) "to restore Texas & that part of Louisiana held by the enemy to the Union in the shortest practicable time, in a way most effectual for securing permanent peace." In this full-scale peace offensive, General Custer was appointed Chief of Cavalry, Military Department of Texas.

The long trip south—by train to Louisville, by steamer to New Orleans and Alexandria—was a refreshing *divertissement* to a warworn and anxiety-wasted couple, and Eliza's agreeable chatter enlivened the otherwise uneventful evenings: "Well, Miss Libbie, I set in to see the war—beginnin' and end. There was many niggers that cut into cities and huddled up thar, and laid around and saw hard times; but I didn't set down to wait and have 'em all free *me*. I helped to free myself!"

In early July of '65, Armstrong wrote to Father Bacon from "Aleck" (Alexandria, Louisiana), a Godforsaken pesthole crawling with vermin and varmints: "When the waggons are loaded, we will start for Texas. . . . This country is wholly unlike Virginia. It is more like notions formed from 'Uncle Tom's Cabin.' Slavery was not as mild as in States whose proximity to Free States made kindness desirable to prevent the enslaved from seeking freedom across the border. The knowledge that runaways would have to traverse hundreds of miles of slave or hostile country placed slaves at the mercy of their owners, in the Red River country, and every plantation had its Simon Legree & humble Uncle Tom. In the mansion where I now write is a young negro woman whose back bears the scars of 500 lashes given at one time, for going beyond the limits of her master's plantation. If

317

the War has attained nothing else, it has placed America under a debt of gratitude for all time—for removal of this evil."

Having seen the inhuman horrors of Deep South slavery, Custer (influenced by the relatively civilized status of slaves in Maryland and Virginia) altered his old view that "It is the Union we are fighting for, not the abolition of slavery." Ignorance of politics and economics had blinded him to the fact that disunion was the direct result of a social-political states-rights controversy over slavery and North-South economic rivalry.

Advising the Judge to invest in rich soil which was now ("owing to the absence of slave-labor & current money") two thirds cheaper than before the war, Armstrong prophesied rampant squatterism and carpetbaggery: "Immigration from the Free States to the Southern & South-western country is likely to come soon. . . . A wealthy planter informed me that land bought at $150 per acre paid for itself in 2 yrs. . . . P.S.—Libbie bids me tell you my hair is cut short. She cut it for me. I find it more comfortable in this climate."

While at the Alexandria cavalry depot, organizing and provisioning the 2nd Volunteer Cavalry Division, Old Curly was challenged by forces that swore he would never reach Texas alive. The buckoes with whom he had to contend were rawhide, rough-riding veterans of the Western armies, seasoned to loose discipline and freebooting action. Exiled to "hell's kitchen" and dull routine, after four years of fighting and foraging, these men were tired and homesick. Besides, they wanted no part of a possible war with imperial Mexico. Smoldering dissatisfaction flared in outbursts of insubordination and desertion—to such an alarming extent that an all-out mutiny of Sheridan's occupation forces seemed imminent, until Custer nipped the evil in the bud.

He acted with the same dispatch that prompted him to cane a sneering restaurant proprietor who had refused to serve Eliza because she was a "dirty nigger." Deterrent examples were made of a troublemaking sergeant and a bounty-jumping private of the 3rd Michigan Cavalry. They were arrested, court-martialed, sentenced to be shot. The regiment reacted with a threat: "If they die, Custer dies."

Armstrong smiled at his frightened wife. "A barking dog rarely bites. I'll call their bluff."

"Oh, Autie, don't——!"

"Don't *what?* Don't execute my sworn duty as an officer? I have no choice. A question of who is in command here needs to be settled, once and for all. It's either me or them. God help this country if it's *them!* They'll cut loose and run riot from here to the Lakes."

The day of decision dawned, the prisoners paraded into the town square. It was to be a public spectacle, as it had been at Front Royal in the Shenandoah. Staff officers appealed to Custer not to be present, implored him to pack a revolver. He laughed. "I've weathered four years of war with only a scratch. Am I now to die like a dog in this Godforsaken hole?" He ordered them to appear unarmed, like himself. "Give 'em no cause to doubt our purpose, most of all our resolution. If we must die, it will be in cold blood. But never fear, gentlemen. I have faith in human nature."

And with this faith, he rode forth with his trembling staff to stare death out of countenance. The assembled troopers—fully armed! —followed his glare as he faced them down, man by man, slow-pacing along the lines while a firing squad prepared the culprits for execution. Though muscles tightened, expressions contorted, no one moved and none spoke a word. This was the test. Back at headquarters, a tearful wife buried her head in a pillow—awaiting the worst.

Custer's voice rattled: "If any man of you has a mind to take my life, let him do so now." No response. "Very well, Major"— he addressed the provost marshal—"carry out the execution."

"Ready!" the P.M. said; at which Custer spurred forward, grabbing the blindfolded sergeant's arm and pulling him aside. "Aim! *Fire!*" The marauding deserter dropped into his grave. The insubordinate mischiefmaker, spared at the last second by Custer's design, lived to swear eternal loyalty to Old Curly.

319

There was no more trouble with the 3rd Michigan. But there were forty-five hundred men in that division, and not all of them believed this story, nor were they impressed by examples. For this reason, Sheridan gave Custer a free hand to "Use such summary measures as you deem proper to overcome the mutinous disposition of the individuals in your Command." He used them, with success!

August found the 2nd Cavalry Division on a grueling 150-mile westward march—through reeking pine barrens, over dust-gagging flats and hog-wallow prairie—to Hempstead, Texas, their base camp on the Brenham & Galveston Railroad. There, in late summer and fall, General Custer began to plunderproof the Lone Star State by issuing the following general order to all volunteer occupation troops under his command:

"Numerous complaints having reached these Head-Quarters of depredations having been committed by persons belonging to this Command, all Officers & Soldiers are hereby urged to use every exertion to prevent the committal of acts of lawlessness which, if permitted to pass unpunished, will bring discredit upon the Command. Now that the War is virtually ended, the Rebellion put down, and peace about to be restored to our entire Country, let not the lustre of the past 4 years be dimmed by a single act of misconduct toward the persons or property of those with whom we may be brought in contact. . . . All Officers & Soldiers of this Command are earnestly reminded to treat the inhabitants of this Department with conciliation and kindness, and particularly is this injunction necessary when we are brought in contact with those who lately were in arms against us. You can well afford to be generous and magnanimous. It is expected, and it will be required, that those who were once our enemies, but are now to be treated as friends, will in return refrain from idle boasts which can only result in harm to themselves. If there still be any who, blind to the events of the past 4 years, continue to indulge in seditious harangues, all such disturbers of the peace will be arrested and brought to these Head-Quarters. Every Enlisted Man committing depredations on the persons or property of Citizens will have his head shaved and, in addition, will receive twenty-five (25) lashes in his back—well laid on."

The relentless and successful execution of these measures to restore law and order soon aroused a storm of self-righteous indignation and protest from a swarm of Reconstruction Radicals, carpetbaggers and scalawags, and uninformed (or misinformed) do-gooders. Custer was blacklisted for "wanton brutality," for "flogging and degrading men who had fought for their country, while favoring those who had turned traitor to it." He was even accused of violating the so-called Reconstruction Laws, which provided that "no cruel or unjust punishment shall be inflicted" on "disturbers of the public peace and criminals."

Custer answered these charges immediately, in a detailed report to District Adjutant General A. L. Lee: "Regarding the report that Gen'l Custer issued orders to flog any soldier who shall forage, altho' the troops under his command complain that they are not properly subsisted & have no money wherewith to purchase supplies; that they are in a rebellious district, surrounded by Rebels who have plenty, &c., &c., I respectfully submit: . . . Unauthorized foraging by soldiers not under legitimate organized control, or absent without leave, is highway robbery & housebreaking—often murder. Indiscriminate foraging was of daily occurrence when I assumed command late in June, 1865. Citizens were assailed, knocked down & robbed in open day. Houses were broken into & ransacked, women insulted & maltreated. Yet no steps were taken by Regimental Officers to check these outrages. My instructions from Maj.-Gen'l Sheridan were 'to treat the inhabitants of the country in a conciliatory manner, and to establish a rigid discipline among the troops, and to prevent outrages on private persons & property.' Since my order—head-shaving & lashes—discipline has been restored. Complaints of outrages have ceased. In my opinion, conditions were such that nothing less severe would have had any effect."

A New York *Times* correspondent reported in March of 1866: "Gen'l Custer, knowing that the trial for desertion was a farce, tried every humane way to save his army from going to pieces, but failed. He then tried a new way, and flogged several men & shaved their heads. This had the desired effect, but brought down the friends of these soldiers upon him, who charge him with being disloyal, inhuman, and everything that is bad. Now, I leave it to every one if Custer didn't do right."

Following Lincoln's assassination, with anarchy imminent, Judge Bacon had prophesied: "Oh! the worst of this calamity will not be confined to war. Our Land, even after peace is restored, will be filled with cut-throats & villains."

Not all those "cut-throats & villains" were a "lost generation" of Confederate veterans, discharged or reactivated Federals, and freed Negroes. Many were vengeful planters, deprived of free labor; political opportunists, waving the bloody shirt; prideful citizens, resenting Yankee intrusion on their "sacred soil." Addressing himself to the problem of "political banditti," Sheridan had wired Grant and Custer: "Texas has not yet suffered from the War, and will require some intimidation." Southern scalawags and spoilsmongers were rooted out only to be replaced by Northern carpetbaggers and five-percenters.

But Texans were soon reconciled to "foreign" occupation, so long as the "damnyankees" protected their lives and property from boodlers and freebooters both Northern and Southern. Libbie was then able to declare, perhaps with her usual "noble temptation to see too much in everything": "You would hardly believe in the short time we have been here what a favorite Autie has become. He could be elected to Congress! There seems no honor too high for them to bestow on him. The soldiers are now in an excellent state of discipline, and the planters live undisturbed. . . . Our own relatives (aside from the home ones) would not do so much for us as some of these Texans who were prominent & active Rebels. We shall never forget their kindness to us. No country in the world can equal the South for hospitality."

She added proudly, "Autie has fine opportunities every day for making a fortune in land, or cotton, or horses, or in buying Gov't claims; but he feels that so long as the Gov't needs his active services, he should not invest."

Although Armstrong kept a loaded revolver under his pillow at night, he penned to Judge and Mrs. Bacon from Camp Hempstead: "We are leading a quiet, contented, normal life. Horsebackriding is one of our chief pleasures. Libbie (I never saw her in better health) is now an expert horse-woman, so fearless she thinks nothing of mounting a girthless saddle on a strange horse. You should see her ride across these Texas prairies at such a gait that even some of the staff-officers are left behind!" And then to matters of moment: "I am in favor of elevating the negro to the extent of his capacity & intelligence, and of our doing everything in our power to advance the race morally & mentally as well as physically—also socially. But I am opposed to making this advance by correspondingly debasing any portion of the white race. . . . I regard the solution of the negro problem as involving difficulty & requiring greater statesmanship than any political matter that has arisen for years."

In order to gauge Southern sentiment toward the Negro—with a view to solving the explosive problems of social resentment and racial hostility, removing the state of martial law, and eventually evacuating all forces of occupation—Custer assigned his adjutant general (Captain Jacob L. Greene) the unenviable task of acting as intelligence agent for the Department of Texas. Greene reported in January, 1866: "Self-interest no longer demands consideration for the negro. As Freedman he is disliked, despised. Murders of negroes are frequent, and actual slavery exists in regions remote from the troops. A war of races, indiscriminate murder & destruction of property—every outrage would result were Gov't protection now withdrawn."

Thus was Custer faced not only with insubordination and desertion and marauding, but with sedition and corruption and intrigue. Equal to the task, he restored a semblance of civilized law and order to what had been a savage wilderness of terrorism and mob rule. King Chaos answered to King Custer, and bowed to a just *argumentum baculinum*.

Old Pop Custer, itching with wanderlust, came to the Lone Star State as forage agent for Old Curly's division of occupation. "Little to do & fine pay" was a splendid inducement, besides satisfying the pioneer spirit. With him came Nettie Humphrey—now Mrs. Jake Greene—a welcome companion for Libbie.

Agent Emanuel, Aide Tom, and General Aut rode to the hunt with raucous packs: the dog-loving knight's beloved squires. Afflicted with buck fever, Tom accidentally shot one of his brother's dogs—and was never allowed to forget it. "Oh, Tom's a good shot, a sure aim. He's sure to hit something!" And pertinent newspaper clippings were "carelessly" dropped on Tom's dresser. For example: "An editor went hunting the other day, for the first time in 22 years, and he was lucky enough to bring down an old farmer by a shot in the leg. The distance was 66 yards."

Libbie disliked hunting, and it pained her to see dead game, but she philosophically reconciled herself to the distasteful traits in Autie's character.

Dogs! They and horses were ever Libbie's rivals for Autie's exclusive attention. But the conflict thus aroused was harmless and humorous, and Libbie delighted in Eliza's good-natured wigging: "You keer more for those *pesky, sassy* old hounds than you does for Miss Libbie. Gin'l, I'd be 'shamed if I was you. What would your Mother Custer think of you now?"

Wintertime found the 2nd Cavalry Division again on the move, through mesquite barrens and over prairies the color of dry blood, trekking 125 miles westward to Austin, King City of Texas. There, the chase gave place to the race; and Armstrong was again in his element. "Now, Father," Elizabeth penned monitorily, "don't wrinkle up your brows when I tell you that we race horses. . . . Autie is considered the best judge of a horse here. The Texans supposed no one in the world could ride as well as themselves—and they do ride splendidly—but those who saw Armstrong keep his place in the saddle when 'Don Juan' ran away with him at the Grand Review in Washington concede that he *does* know how to ride, however mistaken his views on patriotism may be. We now have 3 running-horses & a fast pony, none of which has been beaten. . . . We are running out to the stables half our time."

Armstrong was having the time of his life, even while performing the unpleasant and unrewarding task of taming Texas. His uncommon energy and enterprise were inexhaustible, galvanic, almost superhuman. He met every challenge, every emergency, and triumphed.

The Honorable Alexander J. Hamilton, Provisional Governor of Texas, testified to General Custer's "wise and efficient conduct of an affair as much administrative as military." General Sheridan also praised him for successfully handling a tough job, recommending (with Mr. Bingham) that he be commissioned a full Major General in the Regular Army. But to no avail. The jackleg politicians and spoilsmongers stuck at nothing to comb Custer out of their hair; and they finally made a connection, publicly branding him a "Copperhead Democrat" while they privately characterized him as a "nigger-loving Radical."

The bureaucratic, self-interested "powers that be" quickly disposed of Custer when his period of enlistment was up. He was mustered out of the Volunteer Army on January 31, 1866 (without pension or praise) and "kicked downstairs" to his old Regular Army rank of Captain, 5th U.S. Cavalry. His "compo" of $8,000 a year was accordingly reduced to $2,000, and he was ordered to report to Washington pending further instructions. At twenty-six, Custer considered himself a busted man, stripped of all the dignity and honor he had ever rated as a warrior-patriot.

(Sick at heart, he chased trains back East—alone. He couldn't afford to take his wife, so Elizabeth journeyed up to Monroe (on the last of their savings) to stay with her folks.)

April found Armstrong on a fortune-hunting junket in New York City, still waiting for something to turn up at Washington concerning his future in Uncle Sam's Army. Social, political, and economic contacts came easy to him; for he was a big name, a

325

rara avis, a commercial advantage. Society lionized him; the worlds of business and politics began to revolve around him, and he was offered executive positions and government posts. But Custer could not fancy himself a jack-in-office, a swivel-chair man, a featherbed civvy. He felt conspicuously uncomfortable in toppers and swallowtails, and longed for slouchers and buckskins. These were anxious, uncertain days of readjustment, of drifting and groping. These were days without blazing glory, made bearable only by retreat into shadowy glamour: the fool's paradise of would-bes and has-beens.

General Custer was wined and dined by such bigwigs as George Bancroft, William Cullen Bryant, and Charles O'Conor. But the solicitations of every celebrity in New York City made him none the richer, save in sophistication. He was obviously out of his element, yearning for the hard but simple life.

Friday, May 18, 1866. Judge Daniel Stanton Bacon died of heart disease. Armstrong rushed out to Monroe for the funeral. The whole town mourned its most venerable citizen, pioneer, and enterpriser. A hero's bright homecoming was overshadowed by gloom.

Elizabeth penciled in her diary: "I should be far more miserable but for Armstrong's care. He keeps me out-of-doors as much as he can. I do not wear deep mourning. He is opposed to it. . . . Armstrong is thinking of going to Mexico. The [Juárez] Gov't there offered him handsome inducements. I am opposed to it. I do not want him ever to go into battle again. But if he goes, I shall go with him."

326

★3★

MIDWEST:
SWING AROUND THE CIRCLE

B ENITO JUÁREZ and Porfirio
Díaz were determined to rid their homeland of Emperor Maximilian. They offered Custer a commission as Major General of
Caballeros, adjutant general of the Mexican revolutionary forces,
and a yearly pay of $16,000 in gold—on condition that Custer
supply at least a thousand mounted mercenaries, the expense of
which would be incurred by Juárez & Co.)

Sheridan and Grant were highly "enthused." "If you conclude
to go," Phil scrawled from New Orleans, "you would have my
warmest support."

U. S. Grant, now General of the Army, sent a letter of recommendation to the Mexican ambassador in Washington, Don Matías
Romero: "This will introduce to your acquaintance Gen'l Custer,
who rendered such distinguished service as a Cavalry Officer during the War. There was no officer in that branch of the Service
who had the confidence of Gen'l Sheridan to a greater degree than
Gen'l C., and there is no officer in whose judgment I have greater
faith than in Sheridan's. Please understand, then, that I mean by
this to endorse Gen'l Custer in a high degree."

Captain G. A. Custer, 5th U.S. Cavalry, applied to the War
Department for a year's leave of absence. Object: special duty in
Mexico as military attaché (soldier of fortune) to the army of
independence and deputy-defender of the Monroe Doctrine. Permission denied by Executive Order, despite Mr. Stanton's begging
and abuse. With the nation's wounds sorely in need of binding,

327

President Johnson sought to pursue a foreign policy of noninter-
ference. (Besides, he dared not entrust such an unprecedented
enterprise to a twenty-six-year-old prodigy, the reckless boy wonder of a gentleman's war.)

Captain Custer was again kicking and cooling his heels, "awaiting orders." As of April 28, he was granted leave of absence "till
further orders"—but was forbidden to leave the country under
penalty of losing his commission.

In mid-March of '66, a bill had passed through Congress
increasing the standing army by ten new Regular cavalry regiments, to be raised for special duty in the South and West. Stanton offered one of these virgin outfits to Custer—full colonelcy
of the 9th Cavalry, a Negro regiment—but on July 6, Custer
applied for appointment to a more influentially active post: that
of Inspector General, U.S. Cavalry. Now, with all the political
support he deemed necessary, Custer flattered himself that Fortune would again smile upon him; that the job would be his,
merely for the asking. But certain bigwigs in Washington—many
of them pretended friends—were reluctant, even afraid, to entrust
such freehanded authority and executive responsibility to a potential, if not proven, "wild man." Kept in a subordinate (and
therefore politically "safe") role, the ambitious maverick could
do precious little damage to bureaucratic machinery, well greased
with oil of palms.

(The fates had frowned once more—despite the fact that Old
Curly was bombarded with bribes to run for political office, as
Congressman or even Governor of Michigan or Ohio) "But I'm no
speechmaker," he protested. Besides, he was leery of politics.
Perhaps he was aiming for the virtually unattainable: generalship
of the Army. Would that satisfy him? Hardly. It was just another
desk job. Meantime, he must wait—and hope.

 July 28, 1866. Through the persuasion of General Grant, and
the special favor of Secretary Stanton, George Armstrong Custer
was commissioned Lieutenant Colonel of the newly raised 7th

328

U.S. Cavalry, destined to become the most glorious and notorious outfit in the American army.

Custer was now a top-rate Regular with a virgin regiment. His assignment: Fort Riley, Kansas, Lieutenant General William Tecumseh Sherman's Military Division of the Missouri. The Western Frontier! The Great Plains! Active duty! A brave new world to conquer! Libbie's prayers, and Custer's Luck, had prevailed.

Before heading out to the tall-grass country, General and Mrs. Custer joined President Andrew Johnson's National Union Party and accompanied him by special invitation on his sensational "Swing Around the Circle," a grand junket organized to sell King Andy's liberal Reconstruction Policy. As a glamorously popular figure, Custer was (hopefully) bound to improve Johnson's unenviable image; among radical Republicans and mossback Democrats, the President was considered a sottish Southern sympathizer who played kid-glove politics. Besides, "His Accidency" felt he owed the boy general this *beau geste,* since Custer had politely refused the pretentious offer of colonelcy of the 9th (all-Negro) Cavalry.

"Andy is as firm & upright as a tomb-stone," Armstrong had written in admiration. "I believe in acts, not words. Unlike some public characters, he does not swallow his own words." And so Custer served as Johnson's personal bodyguard and image-builder. He occupied the adjoining room in every hotel suite, with loaded revolvers at his bedside, because Mr. President had been threatened with assassination. And while Autie slept like a log, Libbie suffered many a restless night. With good reason! Flames of fury had been whipped by such winds as Chandler and Wade and Congressman Bingham, crackling and roaring that the former Confederate States of America must be treated as a conquered nation deprived of ante-bellum autonomy. In a self-righteous play for power, they demanded the so-called slave vote: the unqualified enfranchisement and naturalization of the Negro.

General Custer was one of four delegates at the National Union Convention in Philadelphia on August 14, 1866; he could not in good conscience endorse a pseudo-liberal program (or "abolitionist plot") designed by rival forces to reopen the nation's wounds for partisan advantage by political, economic, and social subjugation of Dixie. (He had seen the Deep South's dangerously precarious position, wavering on the brink of mobocracy; and he was certain that an absolute reign of terror, enforced by lynch law, would sweep the former slave states were whites virtually disenfranchised and blacks unconditionally licensed) As he had often written and said, "I am *opposed* to elevating the negro by correspondingly debasing the white-man. This, to me, is a travesty tantamount to National suicide." So he supported Johnson, who stood on a platform of Lincolnian sincerity and common sense. And he signed a manifesto that "We who fought and gave our blood to perpetuate this Union will not permit it to be severed by Chas. Sumner, Thad. Stevens, and other [Radical-Abolitionist] co-conspirators." For Custer, the political die was cast.

At Buffalo, wild cheers of "Speech! speech!" obliged Armstrong to respond blushfully, then forcefully, "I'm no speechmaker, but I fought four years to defend the Constitution and to save the Union. Now, come election, I only hope that you good people will vote for the Constitution as it is and the Union as it was. Thank you!"

Cleveland; Detroit. Jeering mobs greeted the Presidential party. "Hang him!" agitators hooted at King Andy. The Illinois *State Register* advised all "loyal citizens" to avoid Johnson "as they would any other convicted criminal." The Illinois *State Journal* accused "Gen. Custer and his associates" of consorting with "subjugated traitors": the old copperhead smear.

When the Presidential party rode the rails into Michigan, it was the first week in September, 1866. The lightning express had to be backed up the track from Detroit to Monroe for a whistle stop rally in the Custers' home town. Trumpet-tongued crowds of flag-waving "Wolverines" welcomed their boy hero and the cluster of government dignitaries.

Fiery old Secretary of State William H. Seward stepped out on the rear platform of the flag-festooned caboose, held up his hands for silence, then shouted to the expectant throng, "I find that

330

General Custer has a difference in the way he enters towns. When he enters an enemy town, he goes in straight forward and the enemy backs out. When he brings us into his own town, he backs us in!" The welcoming crowd rumbled with laughter. "I give you the two great cities of ancient and modern times—Nineveh and Monroe—both distinguished for light-horsemen before the Lord: Nimrod and Custer!"

Wild, whistling cheers and three rip-roaring tiger yells greeted the home-coming hero.

In St. Louis, extremist bands played "The Rogue's March." Grant got drunk, Seward got violent—as usual. And Johnson, in a fit of pot-valor, lost his dignity by shouting, "Stevens, Sumner, and [Wendell] Phillips liken themselves to Jesus Christ and call everybody else Judas. *Hah!* Well, if we must hang, thank God they shall be crucified!"

When the crowds grew uglier, drew too close for comfort, General Custer took the Chief Executive by the arm and urged him to beat a dignified retreat.

The Terre Haute lunatic fringe failed to derail the Presidential express; but a prearranged riot came off splendidly at Indianapolis, where pistol-packing rowdies cried, "Shoot the damned traitor!" and plugged some poor devil who happened to object.

General Grant, in one of his rarest rages, endeavored to silence the mob by appealing to their lost sense of honor: "For the credit of your city, hear us all speak!"

A heckler guffawed and answered, "For the sake of our city, go to hell!"

"God damn 'em!" Custer grated, itching to do what the permissive police seemed content to leave undone: read the riot act with bats and bullets. Libbie shuddered in horror, hearing the uproar and fearing the worst, hidden in a hotel with other terrified ladies of the grand but inglorious "Swing Around the Circle."

When billies swung and brawlers scattered, Armstrong commented sharply to Admiral David G. Farragut, "Wait till October [and the nominations of Congressional candidates], and more groans than these will be heard."

331

O tempora! O mores! In almost every city, at nearly every whistle stop, the campaigners were confronted with organized hostility incited by local bosses masquerading as respectable citizens. In vain, Secretary Seward introduced President Johnson as "an absolutely honest man" who "gave up fortune—everything—for the preservation of principles that patriots hold sacred." In the public mind, His Accidency was an unregenerate Rebel, an ass in lion's skin. The North wanted the South to pay dearly for its folly, for the bloodshed and sorrow of four dreadful years; and when King Andy refused to hang Jeff Davis & Co., pleading that passion and prejudice be laid aside for the common good, the Age of Hate came into its own.

At New Market (Scio), Ohio, Johnson was booed and Custer hurrahed by placard-bearing crowds at the railroad station. Custer turned to Johnson in apologetic embarrassment, saying, "This is my native town, but I'm ashamed of it."

"Down with King Andy!" agitators chanted. "A rope for His Accidency! Hang Sir Veto!"

Red-faced and wild-eyed, Custer leaned over the platform rail and shrilled, "I was born only a few miles from here, and I'm ashamed of you! Your insults to the President are an insult to me." He then swung aside. "Conductor, signal the engineer. We're leaving this damned place at once." He darted into the coach, rattling to Libbie, "By Jesus, I'll never visit this place again. We're not welcome."

Spotting another swarm of rabble-rousers at Steubenville, Custer advised Johnson to move on to Cadiz without stopping. As they rolled through the station, Armstrong poked his golden head out a window and accosted the mob in language that made Elizabeth shudder.

The reception at Cadiz was cool but polite, prompting Custer to remark, "As a Harrison County man, I'm glad for the President's sake to meet some respectable citizens of the district—having hitherto encountered some of the worst."

"Not worse than the Rebels!" someone retorted.

"Oh, worse by far!" said Custer. "For the Rebels have repented."

In private he said to Elizabeth, "I've had enough of this madness," and she agreed.

They sped to Monroe, for a final farewell before departure to St. Louis and the Great Plains. The Presidential Reconstruction Tour had been a smashing failure, and Custer was in no mood to remain and help pick up the pieces. Politics and politicians be damned! He had been used, injured in the public eye, for a noble purpose doomed to ignominy. Never more! It was army life for him, the elements he understood and loved.

"Nothing hurt Custer's political and military future like the movements of this summer," Whittaker concludes, "all of which were owing to his generous impulsive way of doing things. Honest to the backbone himself, he could not imagine that others could be less so; and he fell, bound hand and foot, into the midst of a den of hungry political wolves who would have picked his bones clean had he staid much longer. Like Juvenal refusing to go to Rome, he could reply when he was asked the cause of his non-success in politics, 'Nescio mentire' [I know not how to lie]. It tells the whole story."

4

KANSAS: THE GREAT PLAINS

OCTOBER 7, 1866. In Libbie's words, "exuberance of spirits" and "wild demonstrations of joy" attended the last moments of packing. Autie pranced about like an imp. The West would perchance prove the greatest, most glorious challenge of his life. Vast, majestic, untamed virgin lands peopled by free-spirited savages and noble beasts. The siren song of the wild had captured his fancy, intoxicated his senses.

With four horses, a pack of dogs, a small menagerie, and Aunt Eliza, General and Mrs. Custer set forth by train on their great adventure into the Garden of the West.

At St. Louis, en route to Fort Riley, the Custers struck up a lifelong friendship with Lawrence Barrett. Custer was something of a frustrated footlighter, and Barrett had served as an infantry captain in the Civil War, so both social lions had a lot in common. Whenever they met backstage, or in a hotel room, the great tragedian would hail the boy general with "Well, old fellow, hard at work making history, are you?" Each having a flair for the dramatic, even in private life, where they continued to act out their public roles, the two would then engage in some Shakespearean swordplay—to the indulgent amusement of Libbie.

Libbie again clipped Autie's hair rather short before they left St. Louis. He asked her to do it, because long curls would make the stifling heat of the Plains even less agreeable.

About 110 miles west of Kansas City, nestled in the fork of the Republican and Smoky Hill rivers, Fort Riley stood as a lone

334

sentinel in the trackless, treeless expanse of rippling reddish-yellow buffalo grass: the Great Plains. It was November 3, but that quadrangular adobe outpost still baked beneath a blazing clear-blue sky heaped with pillars of cloud and steeped in a soft haze on the far horizon. It was a gorgeous spectacle of Nature's primitive simplicity. Now, as never before, Old Curly's reckless and restless spirit could wander free as the air over the Great Spirit's "happy hunting-grounds."

"Old Cump" Sherman (G.O.C., Military Division of the Missouri) was one of the first to welcome the Custers to their new home. He was a lean, slouchy "spitfire" with wrinkled red face, thatchy grizzled-red hair, a close-clipped rusty beard, and sharp beady eyes. He acted and spoke on the spur of the moment, chewing and puffing on one cigar after another.

"General Sherman," Custer said, "I want you to know my wife. She slept four months in a wagon and twice that in a tent."

"How d'you do, ma'am?" Sherman snapped, bobbing his head cordially. Seconds later he remarked, "Child, you'll find the air of the Plains is like champagne!"

He laughed at Old Curly's quip: "It's easier to command a whole division of cavalry than one woman!" Old Billy was a married man, too, and a trifle henpecked.

The first few weeks in a strange new land were full of wonder, excitement, and discovery. Libbie penciled in her diary: "Autie scarcely leaves the garrison behind him, where he is bound by chains of form & ceremony, when he becomes the wildest & most frolicsome of light-hearted boys. His horse & he are one."

Husband and wife would tease each other in dashes across the prairie; but Autie, flying far ahead of Libbie, was always the greatest wag. "Come on, Old Lady! Hurry up that old plug of yours! I have one orderly—don't want another!"

Once, when their mounts were galloping neck and neck, Armstrong gave Elizabeth the shock of her life by snatching her out of the saddle "with one powerful arm" and holding her poised for a moment in mid-air: a stunt made memorable by the genius

335

of artist Frederic Remington. Sir Galahad never wearied of demonstrating his prowess and playfulness.

The dead winter months in a frontier fort were enlivened by the buffalo-hunting visits of such "great guns" as James Gordon Bennett and P. T. Barnum. When not "on the grind," training raw troopers or entertaining distinguished guests with hunting excursions, Custer was hard at work writing his war memoirs for *Galaxy Magazine.* With his wife sitting beside him in the study, reading or sewing, he would sometimes look up and say, "Aren't we happy, Libbie?"

★5★

SMOKY HILL:
THE HANCOCK EXPEDITION

WEDNESDAY, March 27, 1867. The 7th U.S. Cavalry, Colonel Andrew Jackson Smith and Lieutenant Colonel George Armstrong Custer commanding, rolled westward out of Fort Riley over a wind-swept prairie plateau and across the Republican River. The regimental band played "The Girl I Left Behind Me" till the long blue ribbon of horsemen had faded into the purple haze of the horizon.

There was breathless silence as the column left the garrison. No expedition was launched with shout and song when loving, tearful women were left behind. The barrack rooms and Officers' Row were as still as if death had set its seal upon the doors. There was no sound but the sobbing of wives and sweethearts.

The hours of those first wakeful nights seemed endless to Elizabeth.

"Miss Libbie, is you awake?" Eliza would whisper anxiously, sitting in a rocker by the bed.

"Oh, yes—and have been for ever so long."

"What's you doin', child?"

"Counting, saying over hymns, snatches of poetry, the Lord's Prayer backward—anything to try and put myself to sleep."

"Oh, in mercy's name, child, say some rhyme to me; for I's past all hope of sleep while I's so unhappy now the Gin'l's gone!"

Libbie recited to a humming and rocking Eliza:

"There's something in the parting hour
  Will chill the warmest heart;
Yet kindred, comrades, lovers, friends
  Are fated all to part.
But this I've seen, and many a pang
  Has pressed it on my mind—
The one who goes is happier
  Than those he leaves behind."

Major General Winfield Scott Hancock, "Thunderbolt of the Grand Army of the Potomac," was in the saddle, masterminding this full-scale spring campaign against hostile Indians—mostly "Dog-Soldiers" (*Hotâmitânyo*) or berserkers—who had been raiding construction crews of the Union and Kansas Pacific Railroads and making a deadly nuisance of themselves at white settlements along the Republican and Smoky Hill rivers.

Centers of attraction on the grand punitive expedition included special correspondent Henry M. Stanley of Bennett's *New York Herald,* artist-reporter T. R. Davis of *Harper's Weekly,* and chief scout James Butler ("Wild Bill") Hickok: a strapping, golden-haired, long-mustachioed gunslinger pranked out in a ten-gallon hat, buckskin pants, and a jazzy Zouave jacket of scarlet, black, and gold.

The biggest military force ever seen on the Plains—fourteen hundred horse and foot, light artillery, and pontoon train—had hit the glory trail at a cost to Eastern taxpayers of approximately $1,500,000. Colonel Andy ("Old Rawhide") Smith, on detached service with Hancock's headquarters, turned all eight companies of the 7th over to his indispensable and indefatigable "hell-driver."

"Old Eagle-Eye" Hancock—"Hancock the Superb" of the gilded era of glorious war—was Old Tecumseh's subordinate as C.O., Department of the Missouri (Military Division of the Missouri), and his much-publicized Kansas Expedition would be the last glory-grab of a fading soldier who had seen better days as "Thunderbolt of the G.A.P."

"Sherman the Crazy," as he was jocosely called early in the

338

Civil War, progressed by leaps and bounds to "Sherman the Terrible": a (to him) flattering title that still applied, but now to the Plains Indian in lieu of the Southern Secessionist. He had wired General Grant with characteristically practical decisiveness: "We must proceed with vindictive earnestness against the hostile Indians—even to their extermination—men, women & children. Nothing less will reach the root of the case." And to Hancock he declared: "By Hell, sir, we must take these wild Indians in hand and give 'em a devil of a thrashing!" And with good reason, echoed the Montana *Post*. "It is high time the sickly sentimentalism about humane treatment and conciliatory measures should be consigned to novel-writers, and if the Indians continue their barbarities, wipe them out."

The *Hotâmitânyo,* or Sioux-Cheyenne dog-warrior society, was so called because of its roving, predatory ferocity and foulness. It was (in Custer's words) "the most mischievous, blood-thirsty & barbarous band of Indians that infest the Plains." Like rabid curs, these perverse bucks preyed upon red man and white with equal violence and virulence. The fact that they were outcasts and outlaws, hated and feared by their own people, points up the most significant underlying tragedy of the Indian Wars: the difficult distinction rarely made between "hostiles" and "friendlies," between the vicious pariah dogs and the pedigreed hunters. All Indians apparently looked alike—or so the excuse was—and to make distinctions seemed relatively unimportant; there was no place for "savages" in the sun of "civilization." To the Army, goaded by settlers and guided by Indian agents, went the task of distinguishing—and extinguishing.

In his *Galaxy* memoirs, General Custer stated: "The clique generally known as the Indian Ring [pseudo-humanitarian bureaucrats of the Department of the Interior] were particularly malevolent and bitter in their denunciations of General Hancock for precipitating, as they expressed it, an Indian war. . . . It may be asked, what had the Indians done to make this incursion necessary. They had been guilty of numerous thefts and murders during the preceding summer and fall, for none of which had they been called to account. They had attacked the stations of the overland-mail route, killed the employees, burned the stations, and captured the stock. Citizens had been murdered in their homes on the frontier of Kansas; murders had been committed on the Arkansas route. The principal perpetrators of these acts were the Cheyennes and Sioux. The agent of the former [Colonel Edward W. Wynkoop, Fort Larned], if not a party to the murder on the Arkansas, knew who the guilty persons were, yet took no steps to bring the murderers to punishment. Such a course would have interfered with his trade and profits. It was not to punish for these sins of the past that the expedition was set on foot, but rather by its imposing appearance and its early presence in the Indian country to check or intimidate the Indians from a repetition of their late conduct."

Turning off the Smoky Hill Stage Road at Fort Harker, a log-and-mud stockade seventy-five miles southwest of Fort Riley, Hancock's column crossed Smoky Hill River and followed the snowswept Santa Fe Trail another seventy-five miles southwestward to Fort Larned on the Arkansas River. There, for the first time in his life, Custer came into close contact with someone other than the "noble savage" of James Fenimore Cooper.

He was quick to note that "each one was supplied with either a breech-loading rifle or revolver—sometimes with both—the latter obtained thro' the wise foresight & strong love of fair play which prevails in the Indian Dept., which (seeing that its wards are determined to fight) is equally determined that there shall be no advantage taken, but that the two sides shall be armed alike; proving, too, in this manner the wonderful liberality of our Gov't, which not only is able to furnish its soldiers with the latest improved style of breech-loaders to defend it & themselves, but is equally able & willing to give the same pattern of arms to their common foe. The only difference is that the soldier, if he loses his weapon, is charged double-price for it; while to avoid making any such charge against the Indian, his weapons are given him without conditions attached."

General Hancock had instructed Agent Wynkoop to call a peace

340

council of all tribes then amassed in the snow-blown Arkansas-Smoky Hill river basin. When only a token handful of chiefs and braves showed themselves for the grand powwow, Old Eagle-Eye smelled a rat and ordered Custer out to hunt up the wild bands —reputedly encamped in the area of Pawnee Fork, about forty miles west of Larned.

Warm, thawing winds whisked the valley bare of its white mantle of winter. Custer and the 7th Cavalry dashed away in dead of night, April 15, followed at daybreak by Hancock's slow-moving infantry and artillery. A couple of hours' hard riding brought the hunters to their quarry, a large and apparently sleeping village.

Enacting simple strategy, Custer dismounted his troopers and surrounded the swarm of tepees—only to find them abandoned, lifeless, but for a few dogs and invalids.

Disappointment flared to indignation when Armstrong entered a chief's lodge and discovered, wrapped in a buffalo robe, "a little Indian girl—probably 10 yrs. old—not a full-blood, but a half-breed." At first an object of curiosity, she soon proved an object of pity; for "The Indians—an unusual thing for them to do toward their own blood—had wilfully deserted her. But this, alas! was the least of their injuries to her. After being shamefully abandoned by the entire village, a few of the young men of the tribe returned to the deserted lodge & upon the person of this little girl committed outrages the details of which are too sickening for me to describe."

At twenty minutes to three in the morning, Autie penciled to Libbie: "I do not anticipate war, or even difficulty, as the Indians are frightened to death & only ran away from fear."

As Custer himself styled it, a futile pursuit followed. The Indians seemed to vanish in that mysterious purple haze. Frustrated, infuriated, dispirited, he shut himself up in his tent to brood and sulk. He had at last met his match, an elusive challenge, and it maddened him to be outwitted. But heartening thoughts of Elizabeth soon imposed upon this boyish abandon, luring him back to his usual airiness and deterministic self-assurance. He then scribbled: "In years long-numbered with the past, when I was verging upon manhood, my every thought was ambitious—not to be wealthy, not to be learned, but to be great. I desired to link my name with acts & men, and in such a manner as to be a mark of honor—not only to the present, but to future generations. Now, my ambition has been turned into an entirely new channel. Where I was once eager to acquire worldly honors & distinctions, I am content to try & modestly wear what I have —and feel grateful for them when they come—but also my desire now is to make myself a man worthy of the blessings heaped upon me.

While Hancock marched south to Fort Dodge on the Arkansas, there to parley with the Kiowas and Arapahoes, Custer continued his northward pursuit of the marauding Sioux-Cheyenne dog-warriors across Smoky Hill River.

Scout Hickok, patrolling the Smoky Hill Stage Road west of Fort Hays, "obtained intelligence which confirmed our worst fears as to the extent of the Indian outbreak. Stage-stations at various points along the route had been attacked & burned, and the in-mates driven off or murdered. All travel across the Plains was suspended, and an Indian war with all its barbarities had been forced upon the people of the Frontier." At Lookout Station, fifteen miles west of Hays, Custer found smoldering ruins and three stationkeepers—"so mangled & burned as to be scarcely recognizable as human beings. The Indians had evidently tortured them before putting an end to their sufferings. They were scalped & horribly disfigured. Their bodies were badly burned, but whether before or after death could not be determined."

Custer immediately reported these atrocities to Hancock, who later notified Grant, in response to a trumped-up charge that he had precipitated hostilities by pursuing a punitive policy: "When I learned from Gen'l Custer (who investigated these matters on the spot) that . . . they [the hostile Indians] attacked & burned a mail-station on the Smoky Hill, killed the white-men at it, dis-embowelled & burned them, fired into another station, endeavored

342

to gain admittance to a third, fired on my express-men both on the Smoky Hill & on their way to Larned, I concluded that this must be war, and therefore deemed it my duty to take the first opportunity which presented itself to resent these hostilities & outrages."

Custer pointedly remarks in his memoirs: "This . . . was the signal for an extensive pen-and-ink war, directed against him [Hancock] & his forces. This was to be expected. The pecuniary loss and deprivation of opportunities to speculate in Indian commodities, as practised by most Indian-agents, were too great to be submitted to without a murmur." Pointing a finger of guilt at Colonels Jesse W. Leavenworth and E. W. Wynkoop, Custer records that both these agents "admitted to Gen'l Hancock in conversation that Indians had been guilty of all the outrages charged against them; but each asserted the innocence of the particular tribes under his charge & endeavored to lay their crimes at the door of their neighbors." He concludes: "Here was positive evidence from the Agents themselves that the Indians against whom we were operating were guilty & deserving of severe punishment. The only conflicting portion of the testimony was as to which tribe was most guilty. Subsequent events proved, however, that all . . . had combined for a general war throughout the Plains & along our Frontier."

Wynkoop's Cheyennes, particularly the *Hotâmitânyo,* had already demonstrated their hostility; and Leavenworth's Kiowas, soon after the Fort Dodge powwow, were found to have butchered several white families on the Texas border. The "Box Massacre" was typical. This family of seven was assaulted in their wagon by Chief Satanta and his "braves," whose salutatory volley killed the father and one of the children. These two were scalped and otherwise mutilated. The youngest child, a babe of a few months, was snatched from its mother's arms and dashed against a tree. The four survivors were later sold to the highest bidders, for use as vehicles of lust.

On May 1, 1867, Armstrong wrote to Elizabeth from Fort Hays, one hundred twenty-five miles southwest of Fort Riley:

343

"Nothing heard of Indians for days. 'All quiet on the Smoky Hill. . . .' Tell Eliza I am in search of an Indian husband for her —one who won't bother her to sew buttons on his shirts & pants. Nor would his washing be heavy! And one dish at a meal would satisfy him."

He wrote the following day: "When we surrounded the Indian camp [at Pawnee Fork], I mentioned having found a little half-breed girl, almost insensible, covered with blood. When able to talk she said, 'Those Indian men did me bad.' God knows how many times they had violated her. Woe to them if I overtake them! . . . I wrote a very strong letter recently (to Gen'l Sherman) *against* an Indian war, depicting as strongly as I could the serious results that would follow—putting a stop to trains on the Overland Route, interfering with the work on the U. Pacific RR., &c.—all of which would be a National calamity. I regard the recent outrages as the work of small groups of irresponsible young bucks, eager for war. The Indian stampede, I said, I consider caused by fear of our forces. I ended my letter with the hope that my opinion would be received as intended; that should a war be waged, none would be more determined than I to make it a war of extermination. But I consider we are not yet justified in declaring such a war. . . . How I wish you were here! You would enjoy a buffalo-hunt. There is nothing so nearly resembling a cavalry charge as a buffalo chase. You would be carried away with excitement!"

While scouting for hostiles beyond a flying detachment, Armstrong himself was carried away with excitement, a bad case of "buffalo fever" that nearly cost him his life.

Scanning the misty-green ocean of grassland with his field glass, Custer spotted a huge bison grazing alone about a mile ahead. A nearby arroyo would enable him to approach the animal unseen till almost within pistol range.

Calling his half-dozen staghounds to follow him, Custer nudged his thoroughbred steed forward at a jog trot into the gully. They sprang up on the range several hundred yards from the buffalo, who jerked up his short-horned and shaggy-maned head, stared for a few seconds, then swung around and went lumbering away as fast as his beefy legs could carry him.

Custer whipped out his revolver, clapped heels to his horse, and gave chase after the bull, the lean white staghounds barking at its hoofs. Moments later, Custer was galloping neck and neck with the biggest bison he had ever seen.

Any number of times he could have pressed the muzzle of his six-shooter against the shaggy body of the huge humped beast, close by whose side he yelled in delight, but each time he withdrew the weapon, as if to prolong the excitement.

Mile after mile they sped over the prairie, till a drooping tongue and husky breathing made clear the buffalo's struggle. Determined to end the chase and bring down his game, Custer pressed the muzzle of his revolver against the animal's shoulder. In that split second the bison swerved to gore the horse, which veered aside to avoid the attack. Custer raised his pistol hand to keep control of the reins. As he did so, his finger accidentally yanked the trigger.

A bullet penetrated the horse's brain. Running at full speed, the charger fell dead in a flying tumble. Catapulted out of the stirrups, Custer vaulted into the air and sprawled on the plain. Leaping to his feet, he stood like a statue. The buffalo stared at him, and he stared at the buffalo. Then, with a defiant snort, the brute lurched aside and loped away. Custer's never-forgotten sensation of "staring down a buffalo," was immortalized by Remington.

"What a fine fix we're in!" Custer said to his staghounds, who were sniffing at the carcass and whining ominously.

Alone and lost, in the heart of hostile country, with a dead horse and buzzards circling high overhead, he looked all around, wondering which way to go. The dogs kept peering in one particular direction, anxious to leave this deathly spot. They yapped and howled at his heels. He decided to oblige them.

With one parting glance at his dead steed, and clutching a Colt in each hand, Armstrong set out on an uncertain journey. As long as the buzzard-clustered carcass was visible, he kept gazing back

345

at it as his guiding point, thus holding a steady course as he limped along across the shimmering flats, under a boiling sun. When he lost sight of the carcass, he had to direct his steps by means of weed tufts or buffalo skulls. He constantly scanned the horizon, each moment expecting to find himself pounced upon by Indians.

Custer had slogged three or four miles when far ahead he saw a slowly rising column of dust being kicked up by one of three things: white men, red men, or the humpbacks of the Plains. He crawled into a gully, calling his dogs to huddle around him, keep still, and hold their tongues. The cause of his anxiety was still several miles away; but whoever or whatever it was, it was certainly approaching.

Custer leveled his field glass on the edge of the arroyo. Through an almost blinding glare and clouds of dust, he could barely make out the forms of mounted men. *Indians!*

Never during the War had Old Curly peeled an eye at a masked battery or an oncoming column with half the apprehension he now suffered, watching till his eyes burned. Then—*hallelujah!* He spotted a cavalry guidon fluttering above the onrushing riders, who were veiled in drifts of dust. Never had the display of stars and stripes been more gloriously welcome than now!

Custer scrambled over the top and waved his hat. The dogs were surely in for a splendid meal that carefree evening!

★6★

FORT HAYS:
GROWING PAINS OF THE 7th

ARMY life at Fort Hays, a desolate hell of sandblast wind and blistering heat, was described by Autie to Libbie in glowing terms of a resort of unlimited sport. The harsh, rugged realities of nature in the raw thrilled him and filled him with a sense of power: a reckless romance that blinded him to eyesores, deadened him to heartaches. He took to this wild, wanton land, and he made himself a part of it, body and soul.

But others could not adapt, and would not—with good reason. As one old soldier expressed it: "In a life of monotony, away from home, what was there for a man to do—but desert or get drunk?" *Forty miles a day on beans and hay!*

Ravening ghouls of the desert drove raw recruits to desperation, madness. Wayworn horses, broken down by extreme heat and cold, dropped dead because there was no feed at Hays. It had all been bartered or sold to the Indians, by black marketeers masquerading as government agents. And so had the fresh army rations, leaving Hancock's troops to sicken or starve on Civil War surplus: moldy bacon, maggoty hardtack, wormy beans.

According to Custer, "desertions from the ranks became so frequent & extensive as to cause no little anxiety." Citing "the insufficiency & inferior quality of the rations furnished the men," who were made "the victims of fraud" by profiteers in the Quartermaster's Department at Fort Leavenworth, Custer elaborated:

"Unbroken packages of provisions shipped from the main depôt

347

of supplies [Fort Leavenworth] . . . were, when opened, discovered to contain huge stones for which the Gov't had paid so
much per pound according to contract price. Boxes of bread were
shipped & issued to the soldiers of my Command, the contents
of which had been baked in 1861—yet this was in 1867! . . . Bad
provisions were a fruitful cause of bad health. Inactivity led to
restlessness & dissatisfaction. Scurvy made its appearance, and
cholera attacked neighboring stations. For all these evils, desertion
became the most popular antidote. To such an extent was this the
case, that in one year one regiment lost by desertion alone more
than half of its effective force."

Custer was here referring to the 7th Iowa Volunteer Cavalry,
then garrisoned with the 7th U.S. Regular Cavalry at Fort Hays.
His methods of putting down mutiny, insubordination, drunkenness, and desertion were no more popular in Kansas than in
Louisiana and Texas; for they were the methods of a man who
would shake other men into discipline with an exemplary vengeance.

Mutineers were shaved bald, stripped naked, paraded through
camp in the broiling noonday sun—to the degrading rhythms
of *"The Rogue's March."* Insubordinates were dumped into the
hoosegow: a hole in the ground, fifteen feet deep by thirty feet
square, boarded over and labeled *Guard-House*. Drunkards were
treated to a ducking-stool douse in the river. And deserters were
horsewhipped and "skinned" by the regimental barber. To prevent
desertion and drunkenness, a cordon of sentries was strung around
the 7th bivouac, with orders to shoot prowlers and that "No enlisted man shall be permitted to visit the Post ["a perfect sink of
iniquity," says Whittaker] without a written order signed by the
Adjutant." To prevent insubordination and mutiny, the following
admonition was issued: "Insurgents and deserters shall be hanged
or shot without benefit of trial."

For "outrageous and relentless brutalization" of the 7th Iowa,
it was proposed in the legislature of that state that Colonel Custer
"should be brought to trial and subjected to condign punishment."
The proposition never materialized, but its cautionary repercus-

348

sions served to change Custer's methods from retaliatory to re-habilitative. As he informed Libbie: "I have notified the Companies that on the 4th [of May] we will have a foot-race—distance, 300 yds.—the Co. producing the winner to be excused from guard & fatigue duty for one week, the winner from same duties for 20 days. I hear much excitement about it. I want to give the men exercise, innocent amusement, something to do. It is also proposed that the officers of the 7th Cav. match those of the Post-master's Division, the party that kills the smallest number of buffalo to pay for a champagne-supper for the entire group."

Shipping the moldy bacon and maggoty bread back to Leavenworth, with a note advising the Commissary Department to investigate its crooked contractors, Custer organized hunting parties and scoured the country in quest of fresh meat: bison, elk, antelope, and other big game. These hunts also served a functional and monotony-breaking purpose, as Armstrong noted to Libbie: "I know of no better drill for perfecting men in the use of fire-arms on horseback, and thoro'ly accustoming them to the saddle, than buffalo-hunting over a moderately rough country. No amount of riding under the best of drill-masters will give that confidence & security in the saddle which will result from a few spirited charges into a buffalo-herd."

May 4, '67: "I have just returned from Gen'l Hancock's tent. He leaves at 6 for Ft. Leavenworth. Col. Smith will go with him as far as Ft. Harker, perhaps to Riley. If so, you could come back with him. . . . Should he go no farther than Harker, I will start for you on his return here. So look for Col. S. or me within 7 days, and commence packing. . . . We have a most beautiful camp. You will be delighted with the country. . . . Oh, we will be so, *so* happy!"

May 6: "You remember how eager I was to have you for my little wife? Well, I was not as impatient then as now! I almost feel tempted to desert & fly to you!! I would come if the cars were running, this far. [The railhead was then at Fort Harker.] We will probably go on another scout shortly, and I don't want to lose a day with you."

349

May 7: "Your Boy went buffalo-hunting! Seven officers in our party. Maj. Cooper was sent back to camp, drunk—so beastly drunk he could scarcely sit on his horse. His friends desired him to be placed in one of the ambulances taken along to carry the meat. But I told them this would not be permitted; that if he chose to act in a disgraceful manner & could not ride his horse, he must be left behind. His friends then placed him in charge of a Cavalry Pvt. & sent him back to camp. Had I been on duty I should have placed him under arrest, but it was a social occasion. He became drunk before we were 3 miles from camp—to the surprise of the other officers, none of whom had been drinking. Our party killed 12 buffalo. The tongues were exhibited as evidence!"

"My danger in connection with the Indians was twofold," Elizabeth wrote later, recalling her ambivalent feelings about joining Armstrong. "I was in peril from death or capture by the savages, and liable to be killed by my own friends to prevent my capture. . . . I had been a subject of conversation among the officers—being the only woman who, as a rule, followed the regiment—and without discussing it much in my presence, the universal understanding was that anyone having me in charge in an emergency (where there was imminent danger of my capture) should shoot me instantly."

By force of passion, Custer's prudent sense of danger at times assumed an infantile state. Never doubting his own apparent indestructibility, he flattered himself that his wife enjoyed the same guardian angel.

On Saturday, May 18, Libbie and Eliza rolled into the Fort Hays cavalry encampment in a hospital wagon. Autie swept Libbie into his arms, hustled her into his log-and-canvas shebang.

"It seemed to me the end of all the troubles that would ever enter my life had come when I was lifted out of the ambulance into my husband's tent."

Despite desertions and discontent, fun and frolic fared well at Fort Hays. As was his wont, Colonel Custer turned Cavalry Headquarters into a zoo tenanted by wolves, coyotes, prairie dogs, jack rabbits, raccoons, porcupines, wildcats, badgers, rattlesnakes, owls, eagles, hawks, young antelopes, deer, buffalo calves—even a pelican—and an inevitable slew of hounds and horses. Eliza, saucily indulgent of Custer's idiosyncrasies, remarked: "Mercy sakes, Miss Libbie, one o' them pesky pets is as precious as if it was a goldmine!"

PLATTE RIVER:
THE CUSTER EXPEDITION

WHEN Hancock and Smith left Hays for Department Headquarters at Leavenworth, there to receive further orders from Sherman, Custer was assigned temporary command of the District of the Upper Arkansas. It became apparent that Old Eagle-Eye's demonstration was a *brutum fulmen* when Cheyenne and Sioux dog-warriors resumed their unrelenting raids in the Smoky Hill-Platte River country, burning settlements and stage depots, attacking coaches and construction camps of the Union-Kansas Pacific.

Governor Samuel J. Crawford, urged by two railroad presidents and furious settlers, appealed to General Sherman for military protection. Prior to planning and executing a decisive campaign, Sherman ordered Custer to launch an expedition against the hostile bands: to track them down, round them up, hold them for the kill.

Custer's official instructions, soon to prove of great consequence and controversy, were as follows:

The Brev. Maj.-Gen'l Comdg. [Smith] directs that you proceed with your Command . . . to Ft. McPherson, at which point you will find a large supply of rations & forage. . . . From Ft. McPherson you will proceed up the South Fork of the Platte to Ft. Sedgwick. . . . If every thing is found to be quiet & your presence not required . . . you may come South to Ft. Wallace, at which point you will find further instructions. The object of the Expedition is to hunt out & chastise the Cheyennes, and that portion of the Sioux who are their allies, between the Smoky Hill & the Platte. It is reported that all friendly Sioux have gone South of the Platte, and may be in the vicinity of Fts. McPherson or Sedgwick. You will (as soon as possible) inform yourself as to the whereabouts of these friendly bands, and avoid a collision with them."

Saturday, June 1, 1867. Colonel Custer and a 350-man squadron of the 7th Cavalry set out on their momentous scout to Fort McPherson, 175 miles northwest on the South Platte River, Nebraska Territory.

On June 8, thirty miles from the Platte, Armstrong penciled to Elizabeth: "The officers of the 7th—the entire camp—is wrapped in deep gloom by the suicide of Maj. Cooper while in a fit of delirium-tremens. . . . Another of Rum's victims! But for intemperance Maj. Cooper would have been a useful & accomplished officer, a brilliant & most companionable gentleman. He leaves a young wife, shortly to become a mother. One by one, all came to gaze on him who but a few minutes before had been the companion of our march. Actuated by what I deemed my duty to the living, I warned the other officers of the fate of him who lay there dead. I told them this was not the death of a soldier. All felt deeply—particularly his intimates, who shared his habits. May the example be not lost on them! I thank God my darling wife will never know anxiety thro' intemperance on my part. Would I could fly to her now! But a wise Providence decrees all."

The suicide of Major Wyckliffe Cooper, Custer's second-in-command, was only the first in a series of tragic episodes that would haunt the glory hunter till his dying day. Cooper, a Kentuckian who had served with distinction in the Federal cavalry, had been a manic-depressive and had drunk himself into a fool's paradise. That dreamworld was shattered when Custer confiscated his whiskey supply, threatening to have him court-martialed for dereliction of duty unless he straightened out. In a fit of desperation, Cooper took the downward path.

Certain officers of the 7th never forgave Custer for (as they judged it) having "killed" Major Cooper. And the teetotaler's stagy *verbum sapienti,* over Cooper's corpse, was rather distasteful to a hard-drinking lot: "Gentlemen, this is not the death of a soldier. It is unnecessary, standing as we do in the presence of such an example, that I should say more." Custer's field book reveals why the Cooper family later accused him of indirect homicide: "Funeral [at Fort McPherson] as quiet as possible, suicide not being entitled to military honors." From that fateful evening, Armstrong's peace of mind was ravaged by a war of nerves.

Custer and the 7th had reached Fort McPherson, on the Platte, during the afternoon of June 10. Cooper was buried on the eleventh. "Rec'd telegram from Gen'l Sherman, at Ft. Sedgwick, in regard to Indians & a movement against them. The Command is to move at 6 a.m. to-morrow [June 12]."

Enraged by reports of continued depredations by dog-warriors, Sherman the Terrible had wired General Grant on the tenth: "The only course is for us to destroy the Hostile, and to segregate the peaceful & maintain them. Grant agreed, though reluctantly. The wartime stigma of "Butcher" still haunted him. Sherman had a flexible conscience, a ruthlessly realistic understanding of "the inevitable," and instructed Custer to await marching orders. No mention was made of appeasement, compromise, conciliatory powwows with the "red devils." By their own actions, war to the death seemed predestined.

But not in Custer's mind. On his own initiative, the yellow-haired chief called a peace council with Pawnee-Killer's band of Sioux warriors, then in the vicinity. Custer had cause to regret his good will. "While protesting strongly in favor of preserving peaceful relations with us, the subsequent conduct of the chiefs only confirmed the suspicion that they had arranged the council not to perfect a friendly agreement with us but to spy out & discover, if possible, our future plans & movements. In this they were disappointed."

Sherman railed into McPherson from Sedgwick, 125 miles due west, on the following day. "Indian promises aren't worth a damn," he growled to Custer. "The redman must be taught a lasting lesson. All who refuse to obey the whiteman's law must be killed." Observing Custer's frown, Sherman waxed philosophical: "It's an inevitable conflict of races, one that must occur when a stronger is gradually displacing a weaker."

Sherman's verbal orders to Custer were peremptory: "I want you to clean out that Augean stable of hostiles along the Republican River. Capture or kill all you can. Written instructions will follow."

In Pawnee, the Republican was *Kîrârûtâ* (Shit Creek) because it was polluted by herds of buffalo. The stream spread over four hundred miles eastward out of Colorado Territory to join the Smoky Hill at Fort Riley. It cut a swath through rugged country, canyon-cleft and bluff-barricaded. Hunting Indians in such tablelands would be like trying to fetch water in a sieve. But Custer was game.

Southwestward the 7th pushed, heat-dazed and dust-crazed, driven to uncertain desperation by "Old Iron-Ass." Yet their awe of him transcended the severity of a Godforsaken region, and they followed him unflinchingly.

On June 24, 1867, the column lay bivouacked on North Fork of the Republican. In an unguarded moment between darkness and daylight, Colonel Custer was brought to his feet by the sharp crack of a carbine. Lieutenant Tom, officer of the day, poked his blond head through the tent flaps and shouted, "They're here!"

Seconds later, the still air was shattered by wild war whoops and brisk gunfire. Libbie learned from her waggish spouse that "Gen'l Custer on this occasion appeared in a beautiful crimson robe (red flannel robe-de-nuit) very becoming to his complexion. His hair was worn *au naturel,* and permitted to fall carelessly over his shoulders. In his hand he carried gracefully a handsome Spencer Rifle. It is unnecessary to add that he became the observed of all observers."

Custer had grabbed his carbine and burst out of the tent, dashing shoeless as well as hatless to the point where attack seemed to be concentrated. The first flush of daylight revealed several hundred mounted warriors intent on stampeding his *remuda* at the rear of the camp. Alertness saved the occasion; for every trooper was armed and out of his tent in short order, forcing the Indians back with carbine blasts.

When the attackers withdrew across North Fork, Custer sent forward one of his interpreters to arrange a parley, as "It was desirable that we should learn, if possible, to what tribe our enemies belonged." The hostiles agreed to meet the yellow-haired chief and six of his officers, on the riverbank. "To guard against treachery, I placed most of my Command under arms & arranged with Tom that a blast from the bugle should bring assistance to me if required."

Seven "long knives," accompanied by bugler and interpreter, dismounted on the grassy bank and gazed across the shallow stream at a savage procession threading through tall weeds and willows. Custer signaled his escort to unholster revolvers and tuck them in their belts. The bugler, who held their horses, was admonished: "Watch every move they make. Upon the first appearance of violence or treachery, sound the *Advance*."

"*Pawnee-Killer!*" Custer breathed, recognizing the head chief who waded on foot.

"That treacherous dog!" another muttered, fingering his revolver.

Custer said, "Hold your tempers. Let him speak his piece."

Pawnee-Killer, he thought, *who had overwhelmed us with the earnestness of his professions of peace; and who, after partaking of our hospitality under the guise of friendship, and leaving our camp laden with provisions and presents, returned to attack and murder us within a fortnight.*

Extended hands and the familiar salute of "*Hâo!*" greeted the scowling soldiers. According to Custer, "Pawnee-Killer & his chiefs met us as if they were quite willing to forgive us for interfering with the success of their intended surprise of our camp in the morning." Not mentioning the duel at dawn, the white chief attempted unsuccessfully to learn by verbal strategy the locality of

356

the Indians' village and their future movements. Equally unsuccessful were the red chief's subtle endeavors to penetrate Custer's plans. Indeed: "Suspicious of their intentions, I kept one hand on my revolver during the continuance of our interview."

The conference was about to end indecisively when a young brave, armed to the teeth, lunged out of the willows on the opposite bank and came splashing over with a throaty "*Hâo!*" He was soon followed by another, then another, until four bucks had swelled the red delegation to eleven.

"Do you forget the conditions under which we meet?" Custer snapped, indicating the newcomers. "You are violating your part of the agreement."

Pawnee-Killer smiled coldly, motioning with his leathery hand. "My young men feel well disposed toward you, Longhair. They came over only to shake hands and say 'Hello.' "

Custer raised his head in a half-nod, scowling. "No more of your men must come."

Pawnee-Killer shrugged, expressionless. The conversation was picked up, carried warily until another bunch of braves decided to cross the stream and pay their respects to *Pêhîhonskâ:* "Longhair" Custer. That was the limit of patience. "We all felt convinced that the coming-over of these warriors, one by one, was but the execution of a preconceived plan whereof we were to become the victims as soon as their advantage in numbers should justify them in attacking us."

Custer said pointedly, "Remember our agreement. We have observed *our* part of the bargain faithfully. *You* have not. So long as our talk continues, not another warrior of yours must cross the river." He called the chief's attention to his bugler. "If any more of your braves dare to cross over, I shall tell that man to sound the signal that will bring my entire command to my side in a few moments." He stared Pawnee-Killer straight in the eye.

The Indian's lips loosened in a cryptic smile. Eyes pantherlike, he at once waved to his braves on the other side to stay put.

The interview ended with a request for sugar, coffee, and ammunition—which Custer curtly refused, without explanation.

357

A standoff had been tacitly agreed upon, by virtue of Custerian bluff. An attempt to follow Pawnee-Killer failed. The Indian pony outdistanced the cavalry mount. Custer fretted. "God damn 'em, we'll track 'em to the ends of the earth!" That he would. It was the run-ragged 7th's greatest fear.

Reaching the North Republican riverhead, near the South Platte in Colorado, Custer telegraphed Sherman for further instructions. Fort Sedgwick lay about fifty miles northeast of Riverside Station, into which flashed a reply that dispatches were on the way. A temporary halt, and rest, was therefore in order.

Armstrong characteristically described his forced march up North Fork as "the painful journey, under a burning July sun, of 65 miles without a drop of water for our horses or draft-animals. This march was necessarily effected in one day, and produced untold suffering among the poor dumb brutes. Many of the dogs accompanying the Command died from thirst & exhaustion." No mention of *human* suffering! Not that "Old Hard-Arse" didn't care about his men. He cared they should follow him to Hell and then sleep. "Those unfortunate persons who have always been accustomed to the easy comforts of civilization, and who have never known what real fatigue or hunger is, cannot realize or appreciate the blissful luxury of a sleep which follows a day's ride in the saddle of half a hundred miles or more."

Receiving no written orders from Sherman, Custer again wired the fort and was surprised to learn that the Division Commander had long since dispatched Lieutenant Lyman S. Kidder and ten troopers of the 2nd Cavalry with letters of instruction. Colonel Custer immediately replied that nothing had been seen or heard of Lieutenant Kidder's detachment, and therefore requested telegraphic copies of the important dispatches:

"The instructions of Gen'l Sherman were for me to march my Command [southward] across the country from the Platte to the Smoky Hill River, striking the latter at Ft. Wallace. Owing to the low state of my supplies, I determined to set out for Ft. Wallace at daylight next morning."

Move he must. Yet one thing haunted him, made him hesitate.

"Great anxiety prevailed throughout the Command concerning Lt. Kidder & his party. . . . Knowing that the Indians would in all probability maintain a strict watch over the trail, to surprise any small party which might venture over it, I felt in the highest degree solicitous for the safety of Lt. K."

After careful consideration, Custer decided to put Kidder out of his mind and move as ordered. Nothing must stop him now. Not even mass desertion, which erupted in the predawn hours of July 7.

The causes of dissatisfaction and demoralization among the troopers were many, yet those for which Custer may have been responsible were few. Foremost was his indefatigability, and his assumption that others were (or rather should be) equal to such hard driving. An average of twenty-five miles a day, in rough terrain and raging heat, was torture to horse and man; but "If I can stand it, they can!" was the hell-driver's boast. "Iron-Ass Curly," they called him, and "Horse-Killer Custer."

"He was a dare-devil," one veteran writes, "but most of the men didn't like him. He was too hard on the men & horses. He changed his mind too often. He was always right. He never conferred enough with his officers. When he got a notion, we had to go. He wouldn't listen to the other officers."

Custer lays the blame for desertion upon "inferior & insufficient rations," and upon the golden lure of "our most valuable & lately discovered mining-regions [in Colorado]. The opportunity to obtain marvellous wages as miners, and the prospect of amassing sudden wealth, proved a temptation sufficiently strong to make many of the men forget their sworn obligations to their Gov't & their duty as soldiers. The legal penalty for desertion in time of war was death, but the desperate were not deterred by such knowledge in their attempts at escape to the mines.

Between thirty and forty desperadoes bolted to "freedom" during the night. "Let 'em go, God damn 'em!" Custer responded to the reporting provost marshal. "They won't get far in *this* country." The regiment marched at daybreak, as planned. Kidder and

359

deserters be damned! No one, nothing, must stop the unrelenting pursuit of redskins.

"In the vicinity of the Platte River," Armstrong informed Elizabeth, "35 of my men deserted in 24 hrs. Was apprehensive for the whole Command, as we had (and still have) before us a long march thro' hostile country. When breaking camp, about 5 a.m. on the 7th [July], 13 of my men deliberately shouldered their arms & started off for the Platte—in the presence of the entire Command, in open day. Not knowing but that the remainder of the Command (or a considerable portion of it) might leave as well, I felt that severe & summary measures must be taken. I therefore directed Tom, Maj. Elliot, and Lts. Cooke & Jackson, with a few of the guard, to pursue the deserters & bring them back to camp—dead or alive. Seven of the deserters, being mounted on our best horses, made their escape. Six were brought back to camp. Three were shot down while resisting arrest; these only wounded. The remaining 3, by throwing themselves on the ground & feigning death, escaped being shot. Wounds were treated, but did not prove serious. Anticipate no further trouble."

Though Colonel Custer had been plagued by drunkenness and desertion ever since he took subordinate command of the 7th Cavalry, this incident was the last straw. Scurvy-haunted, gold-hungry troopers had been slipping away at an average of fifty a month; but the July 7 loss was the largest yet for a twenty-four-hour period.

Phil Sheridan, acting as Provost Marshal of the Division of the Missouri, had instructed Custer to shoot down all bounty jumpers without benefit of court-martial. Custer had not been so cold-blooded, preferring to pardon those who surrendered without a fight, but now he had lost all patience and pity.

When the three wounded runaways came jolting back to camp, tied belly-down across their saddles, they were yelling bloody murder. Custer was first to welcome them back. Pulling his revolver, he cocked and pointed it at each of them. "If you don't stop that Goddamn racket, I'll blow your brains out!"

That shut them up at once.

Custer then ordered the other three turntails to be shaved bald, stripped bare, and paraded through camp with bugles blaring "The Rogue's March":

> Poor old soldier, poor old soldier:
> He'll be tarred and feathered and sent to Hell,
> Because he would not soldier well!

All but two of Custer's "skinners," or herd-teamsters, had been arrested for mutiny or insubordination. According to his degree of individual guilt, each was horsewhipped or spread-eagled stark naked in the roasting sun (the prey of ants and flies and other plagues) till he cried "*Peccavi.*" And several troopers, seized for mutinous conspiracy, were repeatedly doused in the Platte by being horse-dragged across a ford with lariats tied to their legs.

"The effect was all that could be desired," Custer soon assured his wife. "There has not been another desertion."

Custer pushed on toward Fort Wallace, about a hundred miles to the south, there to provision and await further orders. "The march to Wallace from the Platte was a forced one." So reads Custer's field book for July, 1867. However, he still blamed wholesale desertion on "the gross neglect & mismanagement of the Commissary Dept.," which "subjected both officers & men to needless privations." Hardtack and bacon boxes, marked *1860,* were sources of scurvy and dysentery. Coffee and sugar were long-lost luxuries. "That desertions will occur under the most stringent & prohibitory laws I have no doubt," Custer reported to Head-quarters, "and I am equally certain that many that have taken place can be attributed to the mismanagement of the Commissary Dept." This indictment did not endear him to military bureaucrats, who bitterly awaited the opportunity to discredit "Sir Brag."

July 12. The sun was high in the heavens, burning the very soul out of a heartless land, when Colonel Custer spotted the bloated carcass of a white horse lying spectral and ominous on the shimmering plateau. He and his escort spurred forward, dis-

361

mounted to examine their disquieting find. The animal had apparently been shot within the past few days; and though it was stripped of trappings, the brand *U.S.* indicated "government property."

A shudder of recognition, and each was convinced that here lay one of the mounts belonging to Lieutenant Kidder's detail—apparently ahead of them on the trail to Fort Wallace.

The column pressed on at a slow trot. Two miles had melted away, into a blinding glare that rimmed the horizon with molten fire, when they came upon another dead cavalry horse, blistered and bursting in the Kansas furnace. Unshod pony tracks were everywhere, as were the prints of shod saddlers. The suspense, the anxiety, was almost maddening.

The pace quickened. Custer's imagination worked feverishly. *A running fight!* he thought, fretting. *A race for life!* He later fancied: "How painfully, almost despairingly exciting must have been this ride for life! A mere handful of brave men struggling to escape the bloody clutches of the hundreds of red-visaged demons who, mounted on their well-trained war-ponies, were straining every nerve and muscle to reek their hands in the life-blood of their victims. It was not death alone that threatened this little band. They were not riding simply to preserve life. They rode, and doubtless prayed as they rode, that they might escape the savage tortures, the worse-than-death which threatened them. Would that their prayer had been granted!"

Arrowing into a valley where tall grass shivered in a hot breeze, Custer and the 7th saw several large buzzards gliding lazily in circles to the forward-left of the trail. A familiar reek, sickening sweet, glutted an atmosphere already heavy with heat-stench and alkali dust. It reminded Armstrong of "the horrible sensations experienced upon a battle-field when passing among the decaying bodies of the dead."

Frantic curiosity spurred them on, through rushes and willows, until "a sight met our gaze which made my very blood curdle. Lying in irregular order, and within a very limited circle, were the mangled bodies of poor Kidder and his party—yet so brutally hacked and disfigured as to be beyond recognition save as human beings. Every individual of the party had been scalped and his skull broken—the latter done by some weapon, probably a toma-hawk—except the Sioux chief Red-Bead [Kidder's guide], whose scalp had simply been removed from his head and then thrown down by his side. This, [Will] Comstock [Custer's scout] informed us, was in accordance with a custom which prohibits an Indian from bearing off the scalp of one of his own tribe. This circum-stance, then, told us who the perpetrators of this deed were. They could be none other than the Sioux, led in all probability by Pawnee-Killer. Red-Bead, being less disfigured and mutilated than the others, was the only individual capable of being recog-nized. Even the clothes of all the party had been carried away. Some of the bodies were lying in beds of ashes, with partly burned fragments of wood near them, showing that the savages had put them to death by the terrible tortures of fire. The sinews of the arms and legs had been cut away, the nose of every man hacked off, and the features otherwise defaced so that it would have been scarcely possible for even a relative to recognize a single one of the unfortunate victims. We could not even distinguish the officer from his men. Each body was pierced by from twenty to fifty arrows, and the arrows were found as the savage demons had left them—bristling in the bodies. While the details of that fearful struggle will probably never be known—telling how long and gallantly this ill-fated little band contended for their lives—yet the surrounding circumstances of ground, empty cartridge-shells and distance from where the attack began, satisfied us that Kidder and his men fought as only brave men fight when the watch-word is victory or death."

Colonel Custer wrote to Lieutenant Kidder's father, "No historian will ever chronicle the heroism which was probably here displayed. We can picture what determination, what bravery, what heroism must have inspired this devoted little band of martyrs when surrounded & assailed by a vastly overwhelming force of blood-thirsty, merciless & unrestrained barbarians—and that they manfully struggled to the last, equally devoid of hope or fear."

Silently, sadly, men of the 7th dug a common grave for their fellow soldiers of the 2nd Cavalry. *Esprit de corps,* burnt out of the regiment by a terrible land and a tireless leader, was suddenly rekindled by sparks of indignation and vengeance. Custer exploited this new burst of energy, driving his men ever harder. On, on to Fort Wallace and fresh supplies and relentless campaigning —until every hostile was humbled in the dust.

★8★

FORT RILEY: ARREST

Sundown, July 14, 1867. Jogging dog-tired into Fort Wallace, a hodgepodge of dilapidated dugouts and tumble-down shebangs, Old Curly and his flying detachment found the garrison (Captain Albert Barnitz and two companies of the 7th) half dead from starvation and disease and repeated attacks. Marauding Cheyennes had cut off the stage lines and supply trains from Kansas City to Denver.

(Custer also learned that a flash flood had washed out Fort Hays, causing a mass evacuation to Fort Harker. No news of Libbie! Only two postriders and no stagecoaches for weeks. No word from General Sherman, or even General Hancock! No telegraphic communication for weeks.)

Famine, fever. Stage lines broken, telegraph wires cut. Washout, emergency evacuation. Hostiles, dog-warriors. Libbie . . . *Libbie!*

Armstrong turned to his aide and adjutant, Lieutenants Thomas W. Custer and William W. Cooke, and said excitedly, "Order out a 75-man detail on the best mounts we've got. All our empty wagons as well. We're riding to Harker for rations and medicine."

Monday, July 15. A blood-red sun sank into the purple sea of the Great Plains as Colonel Custer and his special detail—many called it a "forlorn hope"—cantered eastward out of Fort Wallace.

Custer forced-marched 150 grueling miles over the Smoky Hill Stage Road to Fort Hays. He made it in fifty-five hours, at 3 A.M.

365

of the eighteenth, stopping only long enough to water the horses and gulp down black coffee. Burnt-out stage and telegraph stations glared at him along the roadside. Stripped, scalped, mangled, and scorched corpses—some bloated and bursting, others torn apart by carrion birds and coyotes, all riddled with arrows—littered the blistered, cactus-studded flats with skeletons.

Only two of the seventy-five troopers had been lost, picked off by Cheyenne snipers. Custer later avowed: "Frequent halts & brief rests were made along our line of march," and "occasionally we would halt long enough to indulge in a few [*i.e.*, six] hours' sleep." Those who accompanied him swore otherwise: that he drove them like the devil, until the rear became a desperate confusion of slackers who fell prey to Indian ambush and they lost two of their number. Custer merely states that they had, without authority, "halted some distance behind"—but does not say why. The fact is, after a hundred miles of relentless riding, they were too stunned to go on.

Old Hard-Arse justified his doggedness by admitting, "It was far above the usual rate of a leisurely-made march, but during the same season & with a larger Command I marched 60 miles in 15 hours. This was officially reported, but occasioned no remark." He added, after citing a ninety-miles-in-twenty-four-hours forced march made during the War, that, in 1866, "I marched a small detachment 80 miles in 17 hours—every horse accompanying the detachment completing the march in as fresh condition, apparently, as when the march began." However, still no mention of the *human* condition! At any rate, 156 deserters from the 7th Cavalry between April 18 and July 13 was a fair record compared with other regiments on the frontier, whose scurvied and demoralized members were bolting by fifties and hundreds a month.

July 18, 3 P.M. Custer caught an hour of sleep, then pushed onward. Stragglers at flood-ravaged Fort Hays told him of an explosive outbreak of cholera at Harker. All those not on the sick list had been evacuated to Fort Riley. For all he knew, Elizabeth lay dying of cholera at Fort Harker!

Custer turned to his second-in-command, Captain Louis

McLane Hamilton, and muttered sharply, "Rest the men till day-break, then move out. I'm going ahead to Harker. Supplies will be ready to load when you arrive. If any of the men give you trouble, don't hesitate to shoot. Shoot to kill!" (Twenty of the escort had already deserted.)

Armstrong, Brother Tom, Adjutant Cooke, and two volunteer troopers swung into the saddle and galloped off to Fort Harker. They made it in less than twelve hours, a distance of sixty miles, by 2 A.M. of the nineteenth.

The post was deserted except for cholera patients, doctors and nurses, and a few bummers. At last word, Libbie was all right, had left with Eliza in an ambulance, under escort, to Fort Riley. *Thank God!* Armstrong heaved a sigh of relief; yet he was still apprehensive, fretting under the least delay. Nothing would satisfy him but to see his beloved wife alive and well.

Letters awaited him, full of anguish and anxiety that made him frantic.

It was the dead of night. Custer flashed telegrams to Forts Sedgwick and Leavenworth (Sherman and Hancock), announcing the fate of Kidder and his detachment. Then he dashed into head-quarters, rousing Colonel A. J. Smith from a troubled sleep.

After Custer had rattled off a brief report, bleary-eyed Smith pointed to his absent adjutant's bunk and drawled, "Well, here is Weir's bed. Lie down and take some sleep."

"No, General!" Custer blurted, addressing his superior by Civil War rank. "I'd like to go up to Riley and see my wife. How long can you give me?"

Smith knit his brow, motioning absently. "I can't spare you. You must remain."

Custer exploded: "God damn it, sir, I *shan't* remain. The train leaves at three, and I'll be on it."

"You damned fool. How dare you?"

Custer was cut down by Smith's retort. "But, General, I see no occasion for my presence until the supply train and escort are ready to return to Wallace. I beg of you: give me a day with

Libbie. It's been two months since I last saw her, and she may be dying—even dead!—of cholera."

Smith softened, moved by the desperation in Custer's eyes and voice. "Very well. But hurry back—hurry back. We shall want you directly."

Custer nodded, darted out the doorway.

"Wait a minute! I'll go on and get Weir. He'll show you over to the depot."

Custer glanced at his watch. "It's close to three now!"

"Have no fear. You'll make it."

When Colonel Smith had fetched Adjutant-Lieutenant Thomas B. Weir, on special duty at the telegraph office, a train whistle shrilled ominously.

Custer fussed. "We must get off at once in order to catch the train."

Weir handed him an official envelope. "Orders from G.H.Q., sir."

"Damn 'em!" Custer muttered, thrusting the dispatch in his jacket and striding forward. "To the depot!"

"Remember me to Mrs. Custer, and give my respects to the ladies!" Smith called after him, smiling to think that Custer had missed the train. But that didn't stop Old Curly.

Instructing Tom and Cooke to await Hamilton and the wagons, then load them with the needed supplies for Fort Wallace, he grabbed a fresh relay horse by the halter, dashed out of Harker, and spanked seventy-five miles across the desolate prairie to Riley. One thought, one hope and vision, spurred him on: Libbie.

It was just before noon, Friday, July 19, 1867. Elizabeth Custer was heartsick, in a daze, pacing the floor of her quarters on Officers' Row. Suddenly her heart lightened at a familiar sound: the clank of a saber, and with it those brisk, bounding steps she knew so well. The door flew open.

Autie and Libbie flung themselves into each other's arms. She wept with joy, and hugged him desperately; and he, tears in his eyes, caressed her with trembling hands. Eliza, half-crying, half-scolding, flitted about like a headless hen between the kitchen and the parlor, then finally settled down to fixing a meal.

It was one, long, perfect summer day; and it would be theirs for a lifetime.

"Certainly, General Custer is a good cavalry officer: brave, energetic, intelligent. He served brilliantly during the War, and accomplished a good deal against the Confederate cavalry. What has he done against the Indians? Nothing. Vainly he exhausted men & horses, pursuing the Indians without making contact with them, and his best reports amount to four or five men killed to one of the enemy."

So reads the journal of Colonel Philippe Régis de Trobriand, French military attaché in Dakota Territory and a colorful member of McClellan's staff during the Rebellion.

Custer's summer campaign was a failure, putting a lame and impotent conclusion to Hancock's punitive spring expedition. Phantom dog-warriors had scattered and vanished, melting into the fluid fire and abysmal shadows of the prairie. They had driven the yellow-haired chief to desperation, infecting his spirit with fury and fear. Completely elusive, they hit and ran through a phantasmagoria of depredations: raiding and wrecking the railroads, robbing and raping the settlements, enraging Sherman and Hancock with murders and mutilations at a cost to themselves of only six braves killed between March and September of '67. Surely no one was to blame, for the Army had much to learn about Indian fighting and psychology, but a scapegoat was straightaway and conveniently set upon to atone for the apparent sins of omission and commission.

After Custer's diplomatic encounters with Pawnee-Killer, in which the *beau sabreur* acted on his own hook, Sherman took a dim view of him whom he had described as "very brave even to rashness—a good trait for a Cavalry officer."

". . . He has not too much sense," the General decided, adding that Old Curly had "no excuses to offer for his attempt to act a political part."

369

Although "I can't well do without him," Colonel Smith merely regarded Custer as a "dandified young buck." General Hancock seemed to concur—still envisioning Armstrong as the slipshod, curly-pated, pink-cheeked, devil-be-damned maverick at Williamsburg who "was glad to aid Gen'l Hancock on that day" and who "captured a Captain & 5 men without any assistance, and a large Rebel flag!"

No sooner had Lieutenant Colonel Custer reached Fort Riley than he was handed a telegram from Colonel Smith, ordering him to return to Harker at once. It was as if Custer had left without permission! Accompanying the curt directive was a copy of Hancock's special orders of July 13, stating: "The Cavalry should be kept constantly employed."

Armstrong raced back to Harker by rail, demanding an explanation from Old Rawhide.

"Take your troubles to Hancock," Smith answered angrily. "You read the S.O. He wants you constantly employed, and I regret having let you go without his knowledge."

Custer, obedient to duty, acquiesced without an argument. What need? He had seen Libbie and comforted her. Yes, "There was in that summer of 1867 one long, perfect day." She worshiped him for it: his noble sacrifice, his *beau geste*. "It was mine, and—blessed be our memory, which preserves to us the joys as well as the sadness of life!—it is still mine, for time and for eternity." To a devoted wife this was sufficient justification for one of the biggest mistakes of her husband's life.

Sunday, July 28. Lieutenant Colonel George Armstrong Custer was placed under arrest, pending court-martial proceedings, by order of Major General Winfield Scott Hancock. Charges were preferred by Colonel Andrew Jackson Smith and Captain Robert M. West.

Yes, Colonel Smith had once said of Custer, "God damn that dandified young buck, I can't well do without him!" But when reprimanded by General Hancock for allowing Custer to abandon his command in savage territory, and at a dangerous and desperate time, Smith changed his mind and washed his hands of the whole

The Frontier Custer, 1868.

Custer, The Indian Fighter, 1868.

Custer and a "King of the Forest."

A Photo Studio Expedition: Custer and Grand Duke Alexis, 1872.

Colonel Custer, 1872.

Custer: Evening Dress, 1874.

Lieutenant Colonel G. A. Custer, 1876.

Captain Thomas W. Custer, 1876.

Custer and Indian Scouts, Dakota Territory, 1876.

Staff and their wives. Dakota Territory, 1874. Custer is standing, third from left.

The Lone Survivor. "Comanche," 1887.

BROWN BROTHERS   BROWN BROTHERS
Custer's Last Stand by V. Mercaldo.   Battlefield Cemetery. Little Big Horn, Montana.

affair. Why should he be held responsible for Custer's caprices? So he preferred charges to save his own skin.)

And what of Captain West? How did he fit into this controversy? By now, all the officers of the 7th Cavalry were about equally divided for and against Old Curly. West happened to head the clique *against*.

"But why notice it?" Armstrong reasoned with an indignant Elizabeth. "Don't I know what *I've* been through to gain *my* victory! That fellow, you must remember, has fought and lost— and knows in his soul he'll go to the dogs if he doesn't hold up— and Libbie, he can't do it, and I'm sorry for him."

West had indeed lost! A brigadier general during the War, cited for valor at Five Forks, he had been "kicked downstairs" to captain. For Robert West, the record read: "Arrest for intoxication while on duty" and "Drunk & disorderly when on duty." Custer, who had precious little patience with boozers, was therefore hard on him, assigning him menial tasks worthy of a shave-tail, in hopes of "straightening him out." West reveled in his revenge.

★9★

FORT LEAVENWORTH:
THE TRIAL

THE accused was escorted a hundred miles east to Fort Leavenworth, there to stand trial. The accused's wife went with him on the train. Sheridan, then in Washinton, offered them his rent-free quarters. On military parole, Custer was not obliged to sit in jail.

From September through November, 1867, Custer kept up a steady correspondence with an old acquaintance, the noted lawyer-statesman Robert J. Walker, former Secretary of the Treasury and Governor of Kansas Territory. On September 30, Armstrong wrote: "I have obtained evidence that last spring, when desertions were so numerous, Gen'l Hancock telegraphed Gen'l Sheridan to shoot deserters down. Gen'l Sheridan has been summoned to testify that he ordered me to shoot without trial for the same offence. He himself called my attention to this, and urged me to introduce it in evidence. He assured me that in any & all circumstances I could count on him as my friend, and that the authorities in Washington regard my trial as an attempt by Hancock to cover up the failure of the Indian expedition. Capt. West is drinking himself to death—has delirium-tremens, to such an extent the Prosecution will not put him on the witness-stand!"

Libbie wrote to her anxious father-in-law: "How little the trial troubles us! It is progressing finely for Aut. . . . Autie took a leave himself, knowing none would be granted him, and Gen'l Hancock ordered his arrest. It sounds quite solemn to unaccustomed ears, but officers look on it as an ordinary occurrence—

especially when one has done so little worthy of punishment as Aut has. When he ran the risk of a court-martial in leaving Ft. Wallace, he did it expecting the consequences. But he did it for *me,* above all else; and we are quite determined not to live apart again, even if it means he must leave the Army otherwise so delightful to us."

Captain West, leading witness for the prosecution, eventually testified he heard Colonel Custer issue the following orders to Major Elliot on the day three deserters were shot down: "Stop those men! Shoot them where you find them. Don't bring in any alive."

Captain Frederick W. Benteen, another anti-Custerite, gave evidence he heard his commanding officer shout to Lieutenants Custer, Cooke, and Jackson, "Bring back none of those men alive." He then elaborated: "It was like a buffalo hunt. The dismounted deserters were shot down, while begging for their lives, by General Custer's executioners: Major Elliot, Lieutenant Tom Custer, and the executioner-in-chief, Lieutenant Cooke. . . . Three of the deserters were brought in badly wounded, and screaming in extreme agony. General Custer rode up to them, pistol in hand, and told them if they didn't stop making so much fuss he would shoot them to death."

Both West and Benteen said that when the regimental surgeon dared to approach the three wounded runaways, Custer stopped him and said, "Doctor, don't go near those men. I have no sympathy for them."

Dr. I. T. Coates, a personal friend of his commanding officer, later testified that Custer gave such an order only as a threat to potential deserters—that none, if wounded in flight, would receive medical treatment—for soon thereafter, Coates added, Custer whispered to him, "My sympathies are not with those men, but I want you to give them all necessary attention. I'll have them placed in a wagon, out of sight. You may attend them after a while."

The prisoners were subsequently treated in full at Fort Wallace, where pure water could be had for dressing wounds. One of them died there on July 17, allegedly of "bad treatment."

Hard-drinking Fred Benteen had a studied contempt for Custer that dated back to their first meeting at Fort Riley, in the winter of '66. Benteen, like West, had been a distinguished brigadier of volunteer cavalry during the War; and he had shared his fellow officer's fate of having been reduced to captaincy and subordinated to "the most self-appointed general in this man's army." A staunch cynic-realist, disenchanted and embittered by personal tragedies, Benteen could stand no "romantic nonsense" in the dirty game of war. For this reason, Old Curly was, in his jaundiced eyes, a detestable farce)

Benteen, with sardonic deliberation, bore witness to Custer's brutalization of his troops: "The gang of prisoners were marched through company streets, preceded by trumpets sounding *The Rogue's March*. Their heads were then shaved, and the poor devils were spread-eagled on the plain until they cried 'peccavi.' I reported this to Department Headquarters. . . . On arrival at Fort McPherson, the same orders issued at Hays were carried out. Men of the command arrested were soused in the Platte River—a lariat having been tied to their legs—and this repeated till they were nearly drowned. This also I reported to D.H.Q." In conclusion, Benteen accused Custer of evicting sick and footsore troopers from the hospital wagons to make room for his sick and footsore dogs. The courtroom rumbled with laughter.

Charges of "excessive cruelty" and "illegal conduct" were challenged when Sherman's, Sheridan's, and Hancock's official orders to shoot or otherwise punish all bounty jumpers and mutineers were placed in evidence.

Custer explained away the forced-marching charge to the amusement of all but the accusers. He said: "Forced marching is one of the necessary evils of war. Sinful? Yes. But scarcely unorthodox!"

The charge of lost government mounts was laughed out of court when Custer offered to pay for them out of his own pocket. No one seemed to know exactly how many were lost! "Only seven, so

far as I know," Custer testified. "Surely I can't be held accountable for them! I should first have to find the seven deserters who
took them, and even that is no guarantee they are all still in un-
lawful possession of seven United States horses!"

The two troopers whom Custer allegedly "allowed to be killed"
were sniped by Indians at Downer's Station, about fifty miles west
of Fort Hays. "These men had halted without authority some
distance behind the command, when they were jumped by twenty-
five or thirty Indians. Had they kept in the ranks, or even offered
any defense, this would not have occurred. Instead, they put
spurs to their horses and attempted to escape by flight. Two of
them were killed in the running. Lost in the line of duty? I should
think not! If desertion was their game, they paid dearly for it."

But Custer was also accused of abandoning their bodies without
burial, of not pursuing the attackers or even halting long enough
to investigate the incident. He answered that the station patrol
buried them, and that time and circumstances did not allow chasing a few snipers like will-o'-the-wisps. But Custer was still a
murderer in Benteen's eyes.

The most serious accusation, that of being A.W.O.L. from
Fort Wallace, wasn't so easily rationalized. But Custer forged
ahead regardless.

"As to my leaving Fort Wallace without permission: I had to
leave Fort Wallace and get to Fort Harker—the nearest point of
open communications—in order to obtain permission to leave Fort
Wallace, where I vainly expected to find General Hancock or due
instructions from General Sherman. Finding neither, I was obliged
to place myself in a position of discovery." He then added emphatically: "Without fear of contradiction, I assert that had I
failed to report at Harker or the nearest point of direct communication—and had General Hancock been there awaiting me,
as I then supposed he was, and had any misfortunate result in
the campaign ensued—had this been the case, I assert without
fear of contradiction that I would have been court-martialed for
disobedience of orders. And yet, for obeying those orders—

which, it seems to me, could not be mistaken—I am being court-martialed today."

Custer stated that on June 14, while he was at Fort McPherson, General Sherman arrived from Fort Sedgwick, giving him a free hand to hunt hostiles along the Republican River. "Don't confine yourself to orders if your better judgment leads you elsewhere. Go to Denver City, if you wish. You can even go to Hell, if you want to." These were Old Tecumseh's characteristic words as Custer recalled them.

Custer's defense counsel, one-time fellow cadet at the Point, Major Charles C. Parsons, produced in evidence General Hancock's dispatch of July 13, 1867: "To Gen'l Smith, Comdg. Dist. of Upper Arkansas: The Maj.-Gen'l Comdg. desires you to give instructions to Gen'l Custer's Command, which it is understood will arrive at Ft. Wallace about the 17th inst., that until further orders it will operate thro' Ft. Wallace as a base & between the Arkansas & the Platte. He will habitually draw his supplies from Ft. Wallace, but a sufficient quantity of supplies has been placed at Fts. Hays, Dodge, Larned & Lyons, in order that if he should find it necessary to visit these forts he will be able to obtain ample supplies. . . . The Cavalry should be kept constantly employed."

Parsons rightly contended that the defendant had obeyed these orders to the letter; that he had reached Fort Wallace only to find it in a state of siege and privation, and that in order to keep his command "constantly employed," he found it necessary to visit Fort Hays for "ample supplies." His trips to Forts Harker and Riley were justified by General Sherman's wire of June 27: "I don't understand about Gen'l Custer being on the Republican, awaiting supplies from Ft. Wallace. If this be so, and he finds that all the Indians have gone south, convey to him my orders that he proceed with all his Command in search of the Indians towards Ft. Wallace & report to Gen'l Hancock, who will leave Denver for same place to-day."

When Custer arrived at Wallace, expecting to find "further orders," he found that Hancock had passed on toward Leavenworth (Dept. Hd.-Qrs.) without a word to anyone. Duty therefore obliged Custer to "report to Gen'l Hancock," wherever he may have been! And that duty took him all the way to Riley—and Libbie.

Sherman's directing Custer to report at once to Fort Wallace and await further orders had been supplemented by a communiqué from Hancock, signed by Smith's adjutant. When Weir testified for the defense, Custer presented it as evidence:

> Hd.-Qrs., Dist. Upper Ark.
> In the Field, Ft. Harker, Kas.
> July 16th, 1867
>
> *Bvt. Maj.-Gen'l G. A. Custer, Comdg. 7th U.S. Cavalry*
> General:
> The Bvt. Maj.-Gen'l Comdg. [Smith] directs me to forward to you the accompanying communication from Dept. Hd.-Qrs. [Hancock] for your information & guidance, and to say that he expects you to keep your Command as actively employed as the condition of the animals will permit. You will see by the communication referred to that you are not restricted in your movements to the vicinity of Ft. Wallace, but are to operate wherever the presence or movements of Indians may lead you.
> I am, very resp't'y, y'r obed't Serv't,
> *T. B. Weir*
> 1st Lieut. 7th Cav., A.A.A.Gen.

The official catch, however, lay in those last words: "wherever the presence or movements of Indians may lead you." No such presence or movements led Custer all the way to Fort Harker. But he had a damned good excuse, he thought. With all communications cut off, the garrison at Fort Wallace was on its last legs for want of food and medicine. Such a critical state of affairs made this "last, lone outpost" vulnerable to Indian attack. He therefore determined to save the garrison from certain death by disease, starvation, and massacre by running the gantlet for relief supplies. And that he did, without leaving the fort unprotected in his temporary absence!

377

But what justified his making that lone, hard ride to Fort Riley—and Libbie? Oh, he was looking for General Hancock! Not finding him at Harker, Custer reckoned he must be at Riley. He wished to report to him in person for detailed instructions concerning the perilous situation at Wallace. Unfortunately, the General wasn't to be found at Riley. He was in Leavenworth at the time. (And even more unfortunate—for no sound, logical reason whatsoever!—Colonel Smith then preferred charges, Captain West ardently supported them, and General Hancock ordered Colonel Custer's immediate arrest.)

Major Joel H. Elliot, followed by other members of the so-called Custer Gang, substantiated their commanding officer's testimony: "Not finding General Hancock at Fort Wallace, General Custer said that he was ordered by General Sherman to report to Hancock and was disappointed at not finding him there. In the absence of further instructions, General Custer told me he felt it his duty to follow General Hancock to Fort Harker, report to him, and ascertain what orders—if any—were awaiting him. . . . When General Custer left Fort Wallace, it was my opinion—and, so far as I can testify, that of all the other officers—that the command would not be engaged, or in condition to be actively engaged, for at least three or four weeks. The horses were nearly all barefoot, and required shoeing; and the first horseshoes in sufficient quantities for issuing to the command reached Wallace about the fourth or fifth of August, by a train escorted by Captain Hamilton. My energies were therefore fully employed, for nearly a month, in recuperating the command and preparing it for the field. Without supplies, and without shoes, the cavalry could hardly have been kept constantly engaged as ordered by General Hancock, who was nowhere to be consulted."

Enough said!

On Sunday, October 13, Libbie wrote to Pop Custer: "The Court closed yesterday. The final decision may not be heard for some time, from Washington, but Autie will hear by telegram from Gov't friends. The trial has developed into nothing but a plan of persecution for Autie. I can't write much! In two days

378

this (last) week I copied about 50 pages of foolscap for the defence—a labor of love, of course."

Custer remarked to Parsons: "The court is packed against me. That's easy to see!"

Captain Robert Chandler, Hancock's aide-de-camp, acted as judge advocate. The tribunal numbered Smith's and Hancock's friends. The die was cast.

On November 8, the Washington Bureau of Military Justice issued a "Review of the Trial of Gen'l G. A. Custer" to War Secretary Lorenzo Thomas:

Bvt. Maj.-Gen'l G. A. Custer, Lt.-Col. 7th U.S. Cavalry, was tried in Sept. & Oct. last by Gen'l Court-Martial convened at Ft. Leavenworth, Kansas, by order of the General-in-Chief, under the following Charges:

I. Absent without leave from his Command
   Finding: *Guilty*

   In that Accused did, at or near Ft. Wallace, Kans., on or about July 15th last, absent himself from his Command without proper authority & proceed to Ft. Harker, Kans., a distance of about 275 miles: this at a time when his Command was expected to be actively engaged against the Indians.

II. Conduct to the prejudice of good order & military discipline
    Finding: *Guilty*

    1. Finding: *Guilty*. In that Accused, immediately after his Command had completed a long & exhausting march, and when the horses belonging thereto had not been rested & were unfit for service, did select a portion of said Command (namely 3 Comdg. Officers & about 75 men, with their horses) and did execute a rapid march from Ft. Wallace to Ft. Hays: the said march being upon private business & without authority, and damaging the horses of the detachment.

    2. Finding: *Guilty,* but attach no criminality. In that Accused, while executing an unauthorized journey on private business from Ft. Wallace to Ft. Riley, did procure certain

379

mules belonging to the U. S. for the conveyance of himself & part of his escort: this July 17th, 1867.

3. Finding: *Guilty.* In that Accused, when near Downer's Station, Kans., July 16th, 1867, after receiving information that a party of Indians had attacked a small party detached from his escort near said station, did fail to take proper measures for the repulse of said Indians, or the defence or relief of said detachment; and further, after the return of such detached party with report that 2 of their number had been killed, did neglect to take any measures to pursue such Indians or recover or bury the bodies of those killed.

Addit'l Charges (Conduct prejudicial to good order & military discipline)

Finding: *Guilty*

1. Finding: *Guilty.* In that Accused, while en route commanding & marching a column of his Regt. (6 Companies strong) from the Valley of the Platte River to the Valley of the Smoky Hill River, did, when ordering a party of 3 Officers & others of his Command in pursuit of supposed deserters who were then in sight leaving camp, also order the said party to shoot the supposed deserters dead & to bring none in alive: this on "Custer's Cavalry Column Trail," 15 miles south of Platte River, 50 miles S.W. of Ft. Sedgwick, Col. Terr., July 7th, 1867.

2. Finding: *Guilty.* In that Accused did order enlisted men of his Command to be shot down as deserters, but without trial, and did thus cause 3 men to be severely wounded: this July 7th, 1867.

3. Finding: *Guilty,* but attach no criminality. In that Accused, after 3 of his Command had been shot down & wounded by his order, did order said men to be placed in a Gov't wagon & hauled 18 miles, neglecting & refusing to permit them to receive medical treatment: this July 7th, 1867.

4. Finding: *Guilty.* In that Accused did order & cause the summary shooting as a deserter, but without trial, of one Priv. Chas. Johnson, Co. E, 7th Cav.; whereby said Johnson was so severely wounded that he soon after (to wit, on

the 17th July, 1867, at or near Ft. Wallace, Kans.) did die: this July 7th, 1867.

The Accused pleaded "Not Guilty" under all the Charges & Specifications.

The conclusion unavoidably reached . . . is that Gen'l Custer's anxiety to see his family at Ft. Riley overcame his appreciation of the paramount necessity to obey orders which is incumbent on every military officer, and that the excuses he offers for his act of insubordination are after-thoughts.

The Court find the Accused as indicated in the margin of each Specification, . . . and sentence him:

Sentence: To be suspended from rank & command for one (1) year, and forfeit his pay proper for the same time.

Wednesday, November 20. Libbie broke the news to Pop Custer: "Father, the sentence is unjust as possible. Autie merits acquittal. . . . It does not disturb us, tho', for now we can be together. . . . Autie & I are the wonder of the garrison, we are in such spirits!"

"Custer was the most convenient scapegoat [for the "ridiculous failure" of Hancock's campaign]," says Whittaker; "so they degraded him, on a flimsy pretence," because it seemed "necessary to punish some one to silence public sneers." However, convicted of being absent without leave from Fort Wallace, Custer received a commuted sentence of temporary rather than permanent suspension. President Johnson, Secretary Thomas, and General Sheridan each had a hand in saving him from a "bobtail" or dishonorable discharge by the Judge Advocate General's Office.

General Grant noted in his official endorsement: "The reviewing officer, in examining the testimony in the case, is convinced that the Court, in awarding so lenient a sentence for the offences of which the Accused is found guilty, must have taken into consideration his previous services."

Colonel Custer dropped a line to his friend and adviser, Mr. Walker: "All with whom I have conversed deem the verdict not sustained by the evidence, as I have been adjudged guilty on some specification on which the Judge-Advocate declined to take testimony; viz., my journey to Ft. Riley 'on private business.' However, I have written Gen'l Sheridan to make no effort to obtain a remission of any portion of my sentence. I would not accept it. . . . I am like Micawber, 'waiting for something to turn up.' "

╳Something turned up soon enough. The ghost of Major Wyckliff Cooper, kingpin of the anti-Custer ring before his suicide. Smarting at not having succeeded in busting Custer to an inglorious civvy, Captain West and his coterie ("a crew of drunken pickpockets," as Old Curly called them) received the vociferous and venomous support of Cooper's friends and family in blaming Custer for his disgraceful death, officially listed as "from excessive drinking." They besieged the War Department for satisfaction; and when that failed, they hinted the "yellow peacock" had paid Brother Tom (who first found the body) to shoot the Major.

(Captain Benteen openly asserted: "Major Cooper was out of whisky when he shot himself because that damned fool Dr. Coates, acting under orders from Custer, wouldn't even give him a drink to straighten out on." But he was the only anti-Custerite prudent enough not to accuse "*le grand poseur*" of staging a suicide)

The Bureau of Military Justice, prodded by certain pressure groups, suggested that Custer be tried for murder—the "murder" of Trooper Johnson—but deigned to leave such a decision to President Johnson and General Grant. Not wishing to be embroiled in further controversy, the unpopular Chief Executive washed his hands of the whole affair. And the General-in-Chief merely commented (*pro forma*) that "the leniency of that sentence, considering the nature of the offences of which Gen'l Custer is found guilty, is to be remarked on."

On January 3, 1868, the tree of vengeance bore fruit. Colonel Custer and Lieutenant Cooke were arrested on a civil charge of murder. Accused of having caused the death of a teamster, by flogging and exposure, they were arraigned on the eighth by Judge Adams of Leavenworth. When it could not be proven that the skinner died of a sunstroke induced by brutalization, the defendants were discharged. Thus, a last-ditch effort at "nailing"

Custer "before a court of competent jurisdiction" failed miserably.

According to anti-Custerites, the so-called Custer Clan ("those damned cormorants" to Captain Benteen) was a gang of murderers, thieves, liars, and "arrant, rascally, beggarly, lousy knaves." And "there were many officers in the 7th who wouldn't have believed Gen. Custer on oath!" Worst of all, the great stickler was himself an insubordinate. "From Hancock, Custer performed his first 'cutting loose' act. Hancock didn't relish it, and rounded him up."

Armstrong didn't trouble himself to answer his accusers in kind. Though even General Hancock had turned against him to save face, which seemed more justifiable than grinding an ax, Custer had no regrets. Not as long as he had Libbie. And his brilliant war record. These they could never take from him.

★10★

INDIAN TERRITORY: BATTLE OF THE WASHITA

MONROE, Michigan. Thursday evening, September 24, 1868. Armstrong and Elizabeth had just sat down to dinner at the Emanuel H. Custer residence when the doorbell jingled. A moment later, kid-brother Boston rushed into the dining room waving a telegram. Armstrong ripped it open and read:

> Hd.-Qrs., Dept. of the Mo.
> In the Field, Ft. Hays, Kans.
> Sept. 24th, 1868
>
> *Gen'l G. A. Custer*
> Monroe, Mich.
>   Gen'ls Sherman, Sully & myself, and nearly all the Officers of your Regt., have asked for you; and I hope the application will be successful. Can you come at once? 11 Cos. of your Regt. will move about the 1st of Oct. against hostile Indians, from Medicine-Lodge Creek toward the Wichita Mts.
>   *P. H. Sheridan*
>   Maj.-Gen'l Comdg. Mil. Dept. Mo.

Could he come at once! Too excited to eat, Armstrong kissed his wonder-stricken wife and dashed down to the telegraph office. An answer flashed over the wires to Sheridan, Hancock's successor, at Fort Hays: "Will start to join you by next train."

Even before official confirmation of his reinstatement, Custer was racing southwestward to the Great Plains, just as fast as the iron horse could carry him. Libbie would follow, as soon as she finished packing, bearing with her that document.

Custer later wrote that he did not regard his arrest and trial "in a fault-finding spirit. I have no fault to find. It is said that blessings sometimes come in disguise. Such proved to be true in this instance."

A fellow officer regarded Custer as "a natural optimist. He took rose-colored views of everything." More aptly fatalistic, *Beau Sabreur* flattered himself: "It is a happy disposition that can content itself in all phases of fortune by saying that 'that which cannot be cured must be endured.' I had frequent recourse to this and similar consoling expressions in the endeavor to reconcile myself to the separation from my Command."

If the disgrace of "rustication" had no profound effect upon him, inactivity certainly had rankled Custer's restless spirit. A man who could rationalize his chastisement as a blessing in disguise—as an "unintentional favor" on the part of those "who, whether intentionally or not, had been a party to my retirement"— must have pretended that he was "living in involuntary but unregretful retirement from active service."

In any case, according to Sherman, Custer was "ready & willing now to fight the Indians, instead of visiting his wife & ruining his Regt."

"We ask only to be let alone," proclaimed Black-Kettle (*Mô-katâvatâ*), Chief of the Cheyenne Nation. "All we want is that you yellowfaces keep out of our country. We don't want to fight you. This is *our* country. The Great Spirit gave it to us. Keep out, and we will be friends."

White America was trekking west, but Black-Kettle shut his eyes to the handwriting on the wall. And the proudest of his people, with blood in their eyes, vowed to hold the white wolf by the ears.

War parties of Cheyenne, Arapaho, Kiowa, Comanche, Plains Apache, and Sioux continued to terrorize white settlements in

Kansas, Colorado, and Texas. In less than two months at one period, 124 homesteaders were burned out and killed.

On August 17, 1868, Governor Crawford wired President Johnson: "I have just returned from N.W. Kansas, the scene of a terrible Indian massacre. On the 13th & 14th inst., 40 of our citizens were killed & wounded by hostile Indians. Men, women & children were murdered indiscriminately. Many of them were scalped, and their bodies mutilated. Women, after receiving mortal wounds, were outraged & otherwise inhumanly treated in the presence of their dying husbands & children."

Crawford demanded immediate government action; and his appeals, piling up with those of railroad officials and army officers, resulted in "Executive Clemency" for Colonel Custer.

Black-Kettle, though understandably malcontent, was no troublemaker; and his token efforts for peace with the white intruders did not endear him to his old associates, headed by Kiowa Chief Satanta (White-Bear). Though not directly responsible for the evil elements in his midst, Black-Kettle encouraged them by his appeasement and double talk. But with Indian law so loose, and each tribe a stratocracy of independent powers, the old Cheyenne was obliged to ignore, if not to indulge, the worst of his people.

A firm believer in "our manifest destiny," Sherman declared: "Either the Indians must give way or we must abandon all west of the Missouri River & confess that 40,000,000 whites are cowed by a few thousand savages. . . . I have stretched my power & authority to help them; but when they laugh at our cordiality, rape our women, murder our men, burn whole trains with their drivers to cinders & send word they never intended to keep their treaties, then we must fight them." He added pointedly: "When we come to fight Indians, I will take my code from soldiers & not from civilians." A loud-resounding slap at what Custer called "well-meaning but mistaken philanthropists" and "pretended but not disinterested friends of the Indians"!

Colonel Wynkoop, Agent for the Cheyennes and Arapahoes, was foremost among the profiteers who insisted that arming the Indians was tantamount to befriending them. Indian Affairs Com-

386

missioner N. G. Taylor replied: "If you are satisfied that the issue of arms & ammunition is necessary to preserve the peace, and that no evil will result from their delivery, let the Indians have them."

The Colonel did—about 240 pistols and rifles, with ample powder and lead—and the result was one of the most bloody outbursts of red savagery ever experienced in the Missouri Division. In August of '68, a war party of 260 "braves" abandoned Wynkoop's Fort Larned Reservation and perpetrated a series of murders, rapes, plunders, and burnings that caused Governors Crawford and Hall to declare Kansas and Colorado a disaster area.

Indian Affairs Superintendent Thomas Murphy notified Commissioner Taylor of unprovoked depredations, adding, "I earnestly recommend that the Indians who have committed these gross outrages be turned over to the Military, and that they be severely punished. When I reflect that at the very time these Indians were making such loud professions of friendship at Larned, receiving their annuities, &c., they were then contemplating & planning this campaign, I can no longer have confidence in what they say or promise. War is surely upon us."

General Sherman, in a communiqué to Secretary of War John M. Schofield, supported Murphy's recommendation and disposition: "All the Cheyennes & Arapahoes are now at war. Admitting that some of them have not done acts of murder, rape, &c., still they have not restrained those who have; nor have they on demand given up the criminals as they agreed to do. The treaty made at Medicine-Lodge [in 1867] is, therefore, already broken by them. . . . No better time could be possibly chosen than the present for destroying or humiliating those bands that have so outrageously violated their treaties & begun a devastating war without one particle of provocation; and after a reasonable time given for the innocent to withdraw, I will solicit an order from the President declaring all Indians who remain outside of their lawful reservations to be outlaws, and commanding all people—soldiers & citizens—to proceed against them as such."

But the innocent would not withdraw, and so they would suffer with the guilty. Sherman's policy was approved by General Grant: "Our settlements, &c., must be protected—even if the extermination of every Indian tribe is necessary to secure such a result." Even General C. C. Augur, liberal member of the Indian Peace Commission ("The Olive-Branchers" or "Quakers"), admitted that "the Indians must be terribly whipped before they can appreciate kindness."

In September and October, 1868, Sherman advised and apprized Grant and Schofield: "No better time could possibly be chosen than the present for destroying or humbling those bands that have so outrageously violated their treaties. I hope he [Sheridan] may get hold of them & obliterate them. . . . I will urge Gen'l Sheridan to push his measures for the utter destruction & subjugation of all who are outside [the Reservation] in a hostile attitude. I propose that he shall prosecute the war with vindictive earnestness against all hostile Indians, till they are obliterated or beg for mercy."

Red-faced General Sheridan slammed his fist down on the field table. "The only good Indians I ever saw were dead!"

Red-faced General Sherman nodded. "Yes; and the more we can kill this year, the less we'll have to kill next year. For the more I see of these Goddamn red devils, the more convinced I am that they all have to be killed or be maintained as a species of paupers. Their attempts at civilization are simply ridiculous. We have tried kindness, till it is construed as weakness. Now we must deal with 'em on their own terms."

Custer listened in patient silence. He did not hate "redskins," but it wasn't his job to love them. He understood the Indian—even sympathized with him—but it wasn't his duty to tolerate. He was obliged to return evil for evil, and no flexible conscience was needed in the light of Indian atrocities.

Lieutenant Colonel Custer rode out of Fort Hays for Fort Dodge, seventy-five miles southwest on the Arkansas River, there to join his command. It was Sunday, October 4, 1868. Before he left, he breakfasted with Little Phil and received his first instructions.

"Custer, I rely on you in everything. You're the only man that never failed me. That's why I'm sending you on this expedition without special orders, leaving you to act entirely on your own judgment. Since nothing positive is known as to the exact whereabouts of Black-Kettle's lodges, any instructions I might give would have to be general in terms. Just scout out the winter hidingplaces of hostiles, and settle the score wherever you find 'em."

Custer reached Fort Dodge in a couple of days—"rather good for some one out of practice!"—and found Brigadier General Alfred Sully (commanding the Upper Arkansas District) with a punitive force consisting of the 3rd U.S. Infantry (five companies), the 19th Kansas Volunteer Cavalry (Ex-Governor and Colonel S. J. Crawford commanding), and eleven troops of the notorious 7th U.S. Regular Cavalry.

Custer's estimation of Sully as a soldier was anything but favorable, for Sully was one of those "featherbed generals" whose habits placed him "comfortably stowed away in his ambulance" while on campaign. Custer, the inexhaustible man of action, had little patience for or understanding of age-induced infirmities. So a clash was inevitable.

Sully's column, with Custer and the 7th spearheading it, pulled out of Fort Dodge on November 12. Their destination was Indian Territory, that unrevealed mystery south of the Arkansas. A week later found them establishing a base of operations on North Fork of the Canadian River, seventy-five miles south of Dodge. This was Camp Supply. Sheridan, commanding the Missouri Military Department "in the field," arrived soon thereafter with last-minute instructions for Sully and Custer.

Armstrong noticed that Phil, with advancing age, had taken on the aspect of "a low-comedy man"—to borrow the expression of one reporter—and that his squatty hulk and careless attire, close-cut iron-gray hair and ruddy weatherworn face composed a "grotesque figure," a true "guy." But he was still the fire-eater of the

389

Shenandoah, Sheridan the Bold, and his orders were explicit: "You will proceed south in the direction of the Antelope Hills, then toward the Washita River, the supposed winter seat of the hostile tribes. You will destroy their villages and ponies, kill or hang all warriors, and bring back all women and children alive."

Jim Bridger, celebrated pioneer-scout, spoke up: "Ginral, you cain't hunt Injuns on the Plains in winter; for blizzards don't respect man or beast."

"All the better for us!" Custer answered. "We can move; the Indians can't. If we attempted to fight 'em in a warmer season, as was our old mistake, we should yield to them the advantages of climate and supplies, of bountiful forage for their ponies, immense herds of game for their war parties, allowing them to move freely from point to point. We should then be meeting them on ground of their own selection. Winter will hold 'em down for the kill."

Custer then persuaded Sheridan to leave the infantry behind, and with them General Sully. "They'll only hamper our progress in tracking the hostiles, and I'm firmly confident the 7th Cavalry is equal to any band of Indians on the Plains."

Indeed, Old Iron-Arse had licked his eight hundred troopers into perfect shape, and had introduced inspiriting competition by organizing a company of sharpshooters under the command of crack-shot Lieutenant Cooke. He even instituted a "coloring of the horses," whereby each company was distinguished for its breed of mount, the better to promote *esprit de corps*. "There is no need of fluttering guidons & stirring trumpet-calls to identify them," noted one observer. "Something in the snap & style of the whole regiment stamps them at once. I know the 7th Cavalry at a glance."

What need of "Old Featherbed" Sully and his footsloggers? What need, indeed, for Colonel Crawford and his omnium-gatherum of ill-mounted and ill-trained volunteers? Leave 'em all behind! "The 7th can handle anything it meets."

Sheridan nodded. "I believe it can. The field is entirely yours."

Custer was ecstatic. That night, the 7th Cavalry's band serenaded General Sheridan. Sully retired to Fort Dodge in disgust. Phil's pet, "like Balaam's ass," had stolen his thunder.

On Sunday evening, November 22, Armstrong dashed off a letter to "My Sweet Little Army Crow" at Fort Leavenworth: "Some of the officers think this may be a campaign on paper, but I know Gen'l Sheridan better. We are going into the heart of Indian country, where white troops have never been before. . . . My official actions shall not be tarnished by a single unjust or partial act. I do not long for glory or fame; I only long for my little girl. My reward is centered on ending this trying separation as soon as possible."

Daybreak, November 23, 1868. Bundled in buffalo robe and fur cap, full-bearded Colonel Custer made a last-minute inspection of his wagon train, and rode up to General Sheridan's tent for the usual farewell.

"So long, old boy," Phil said with a hearty handshake. "Take care of yourself. Keep me informed if anything turns up. And good luck!"

Custer saluted. "If this white stuff stays on the ground a week, I promise you—we'll get our Indians." His sharp voice shattered the brittle air. "Trumpeter, sound *To Horse!* . . . Seventh Cavalry, prepare to mount! *Mount!* . . . Seventh Cavalry, by column of twos, forward *ho!*" The "Advance" blared, instantly muffled by the gray-horsed band booming *The Girl I Left Behind Me*:

> Then to the West we bore away
>   To win a name in story,
> And there where sets the sun of day
>   There dawn'd our sun of glory . . .

Compass in hand, Old Curly pranced far out in front—beyond the scouts and guides, into the blinding storm, his horse knee-deep in frosty flakes. He was again in his element.

Thursday, November 26, 1868. 10 P.M. The sharp crunching of hoofs on the hard crust of frozen snow blanketing the Washita

River valley, Indian (Oklahoma) Territory, was a ghostly sound in the vast sepulchral stillness. A long ribbon of wraithlike forms snaked steadily southward by moonlight. Camp Supply, about sixty miles away to the north, now seemed like part of a lost world. Custer and his 7th Cavalry were piercing the heart of Redman's Land. Looming up on either hand were the majestic and forbidding Antelope Hills, "those boundless solitudes—so silent that their silence alone increases their grandeur."

Chief Little-Beaver, head of the Osage scouts, stalked along on foot beside the yellow-haired chief. Suddenly he stopped, sniffing the cold air.

Custer checked his mount, raised his hand for a halt. "What's the matter?" he whispered, glancing at the shadowy terrain ahead.

"Me don't know," Little-Beaver gestured with frosty breath, "but me smell fire."

Yellowhair perked up his foxlike nose. "I don't smell anything." He looked back and swung his arm. "Let's keep moving."

A half-mile later, Little-Beaver pointed to the black belt of timber on their left. "Look," he muttered. "Me told you so."

Custer saw a handful of glowing ashes on the edge of the woods. He grinned. "Redman has better nose than whiteman. That fire must have been set by ponyboys. A sure sign we're near our game." Yellowhair slipped off his horse. "Little-Beaver, you and Hard-Rope follow me. We'll go up on that rise and have a look."

The two Osages nodded, gliding after him like panthers. Just before they reached the crest of the ridge, Little-Beaver motioned for Custer and Hard-Rope to hang back while he took a cautionary look.

Custer watched intently as the gray-haired chief crept forward to the top of the pine-clustered hill and gazed out into the valley beyond. Little-Beaver instantly flicked his hand up above his eyes—a sign that he saw something—then crouched down and came creeping back.

"What is it?" Custer asked with bated breath.

Little-Beaver pointed. "Heaps Injuns down there."

Custer crept up to the crest, the two Osages at his heels. Keep-

392

ing low, so as not to be seen in the moonlight, he peered over the brow of the hill and sighted a huge dark mass on the flats below—about a half-mile away.

Custer looked long and hard, then whispered to Little-Beaver: "What makes you think that's Black-Kettle down there? Could be a herd of buffalo, or even wild horses."

Little-Beaver grunted. "Me heard dog bark." Seconds later he mumbled, "Injun pony herd," as if to convince himself.

Custer waited quietly, breathlessly, to be convinced. Moments seemed like hours, but he was soon rewarded for his patience. All three of them heard the barking of a dog in the heavy timber off to the right of the mysterious herd. Then the tinkling of a pony bell echoed faintly, and Custer was now convinced that this was an Indian *remuda*. Black-Kettle's village must lie a short distance beyond the herd, along the Washita River. *Hallelujah!*

Just as Custer turned to retrace his steps back to the anxiously waiting troopers, another sound (vibrant in the crisp atmosphere of the valley) caught his ears. It was the cry of an infant.

Yellowhair glanced at Little-Beaver. "We attack at dawn."

Leaving the two Osages to keep a sharp lookout, Custer made tracks back to his command and called a council of war. It was now close to midnight. When all the senior officers were huddled in a small circle, Custer told them in a low tone what he had seen and heard. Then he detailed his plan of action:

"We're going to employ the hours between now and daylight to completely surround the village. Needless to say, I want complete silence to be observed when this movement is taking place. At daybreak, or as soon as it's barely light enough for the purpose, we'll attack the Indians from all sides. Since we number about eight hundred, I'm dividing the regiment into four battalions of equal strength. By this disposition it's hoped we'll prevent the escape of every Indian in the village. Major Elliot, I want you to take Companies G, H, and M, move downstream to the left, and circle behind the village. Captain Thompson, take B and F, and strike the village from the right-rear in connection with Major Elliot. Captain Myers, you shall take E and I and strike from the

393

timber on the right. Captains Hamilton and West and I will go in from here with two squadrons of the remaining four companies. I shall expect every detachment to be in position, ready for the attack, by daylight. Elliot and Thompson will therefore move out immediately, as they have the longest route to cover. There's plenty of time, so we needn't rush. And remember: everything hinges on the element of surprise. We've got to catch 'em napping. That necessitates a concerted assault. The signal to close in will come from the band. When you hear 'em strike up *Garry Owen*, sound the *Charge* and do your job. All I can say now is good going and good luck."

The night grew stinging-cold, but no fires were allowed. The troopers were even ordered not to stamp their feet or pace back and forth to keep warm. The crunch-crunch of solid snow might sound the alarm to Black-Kettle's braves. So the men had to be satisfied with swinging their arms, shaking their legs, and swaying to and fro; many gently slapped their horses with gloved hands to keep them from freezing.

Pulling the cape of his fur-lined greatcoat over his head, Custer huddled on warm buffalo robes with his pack of staghounds and drifted off to sleep for about an hour. When he awoke, he reached for his pocket watch. It was two hours before dawn. The moon had vanished; they were now shrouded in blackness.

Custer stretched to his feet and stalked slowly about the bivouac. He found the troopers hunched together in squads of three and four at the feet of their horses. Soon he spotted the ten Osage warriors, with their chiefs Little-Beaver and Hard-Rope. They were sitting cross-legged in a circle, wrapped in their shaggy buffalo blankets, dragging languidly on long white clay pipes. Close by crouched Joseph E. ("Californie Joe") Milner, Custer's chief of scouts. "Half-man, half-horse, half-alligator," this giant ridge-runner sported magnificent red whiskers, a flaming curly mane, and a huge black sombrero. He rode a mule named Maud, looking like a pair of tongs on a chairback, and a stubby old brierwood pipe was always sticking out the corner of his mouth.

Milner, who despised all discipline, nonetheless respected Custer as a "hoss man" instead of an "ambulance man." His first question on meeting Old Hard-Butt, "D'you b'lieve in cotchin' Injuns in ambulances er on hossback?", was an obvious slap at old General Sully, who campaigned against Indians "on wheels, jist as ef he war goin' to a town fun'ral in the States, an' stood 'bout as much chance o' cotchin' redskins as a six-mule team would o' cotchin' a pack of thievin' ki-o-tees!"

Custer's attention was suddenly attracted by a remarkable sight in the paling sky. For a second he felt a thrill of apprehension. Above the black etching of the ridge ahead, in bold relief against the purplescent canopy of heaven, a small ball of golden fire slowly ascended. Everyone stared in blank astonishment. And the higher it rose the bigger it swelled in brilliance, radiating the most gorgeous blend of colors.

"Bejaisus." Californie Joe gaped, scratching his ginger mop. "How long it hangs fire! Why don't it explode?"

"What is it, anyhow?" asked another white scout.

Custer breathed more freely. "No mystery, gentlemen," he said, gazing at the phenomenal sparkle in the frosty sky. "You are now looking at the brightest and most beautiful of morningstars." ✳ *Son of morningstar"*

The "Star of the Washita," like Napoleon's "Sun of Austerlitz," became proverbial; and Old Curly would henceforth be immortalized in Cheyenne legend as "Son-of-Morningstar."

A white, still dawn was breaking over the dark crest ahead as Colonel Custer led his 7th Cavalry slowly up the pine-dotted slope. It was freezing cold, but the troopers were obliged to leave behind their overcoats and haversacks so as to have free play for fast action. The sharp crunching of hoofs on crusted snow might have alerted the Indians were it not for their huge pony herd, which was now stomping and blowing for fodder.

The cayuses began to scud off nervously into the timber as a long cavalcade of bluecoats came inching down into the icy valley. Birch-bark lodges stood like tall white sentinels among the bare trees skirting the icebound Washita. Custer saw whiffs of smoke

395

curling up from their conical peaks. The entire village was steeped in silence.

Armstrong shivered, as much from nerves as from the cold. This was his lucky break, his chance to regain past glory. All other considerations bowed before this ruling passion. It was now or never, neck or nothing, triumph or disgrace. He would stand the test at any cost to anyone.

Colonel Custer was about to turn in the saddle and signal the attack when a rifleshot cracked on the far side of the village. Dogs began to bark, and there was a rustle of life in the tepees. Major Elliot had been spotted, but it was too late now for Black-Kettle and his tribe.

"Let 'er rip!" Old Curly cried; and at once the brass band burst out with its raucous regimental air, "Garry Owen":

> We'll break windows, we'll break doors,
> The watch knock down by threes and fours,
> Then let the doctors work their cures
> And tinker up our bruises!

The famed Irish quickstep, soon to legendize the 7th as "The Garryowens," blasted across snow-blown flats till saliva froze in the instruments. "Platoons, front into line! Gallop *ho!*" Cheers echoed in a continuous roar, and bugles blared the "Charge," as all four cavalry units plowed hell-for-leather into the village.

Half-naked braves popped out of their tepees, sounding the war whoop. Grabbing their rifles, bows and arrows, they sprang behind frosted trees or bounded over the frozen banks and into snow-choked gullies. Armstrong and Tom Custer picked them off with their revolvers as they weaved in and out of the trees and pounded around the lodges, scattering mud and slush, shouting like buffalo hunters riding down game.

Blood splashed and splattered over trampled snow, and bodies leaped and sprawled. Squaws screamed, ponies squealed, troopers swore, arrows whirred, and carbines crackled. It was a hell of sound and slaughter.

The first victims were Black-Kettle and his wife, shot dead in front of their tepee at the initial volley. Sub-chief Little-Rock died too, defending his family against the inevitable. Nude Indians, male and female, plunged into numbing water—to be slashed by broken ice. Children were trampled under raging horses, and pockets of braves were killed in gullies by Cooke's sharpshooters. One squaw, attempting to escape with a captive white boy, was surrounded by several troopers. When she pulled a knife and ripped open the little lad's stomach, "retributive justice reached her in the shape of a well-directed bullet."

Not until the sun was high and hot did the last shot ring out over the valley. Dozens of dead and dying Indians cluttered the ground. The rest had fled to tall timber downstream, abandoning their small band of women and children to the longknives.

Colonel Custer rode over to the field hospital, where Dr. Morris J. Asch and his assistant surgeon were treating a dozen wounded troopers. Brother Tom had been winged in the hand. Captain Louis McLane Hamilton lay stone-dead, shot in the back, some said by Lieutenant Cooke. Hamilton, grandson of the great Alexander, had been a Custer man. After the court-martial, he had become a loner, associating with neither faction. "When my time comes," he had said, "I hope I'll be shot through the heart in battle." His hope was almost fulfilled.

Custer spied a little bugler boy sitting on a pile of buffalo robes near where Dr. Asch was bandaging Tom's hand. The lad's face was smeared with blood, which was trickling down his cheek from a wound in his forehead. At first glance, Custer thought a bullet had pierced the boy's skull.

"What happened to you, sonny?" he said.

"Oh, an Injun shot me in the head with a steel-pointed arrow, sir!" the bugler answered matter-of-factly.

"Well, that's sure an odd-looking arrow wound!"

"The arrow struck me just above the eye here; and when it hit the skull it glanced under the skin and came out here near my ear, making it look like it went right through my head!"

"Well, who pulled it out? *You?*"

397

"Oh, no, sir! I was afraid to. It just stuck there till I got here. The arrow was barbed, and it couldn't be pulled out all at once, so Doc had to cut off the steel point first. He's letting the bad blood drain out and the skin stretch back in place before he dresses it."

"Well now, young fellow, you certainly bear your suffering manfully! By the way, did you see the Indian who pegged you?"

The bugler boy shoved a hand deep down in his trousers pocket and fished up the fresh scalp of a Cheyenne. "If anybody thinks I didn't see him, sir," he said nonchalantly, "I want 'em to take a look at that!"

The death chant rose in full chorus, unnerving in its horror, as women and children were rounded up and placed under protective guard. "This was quite a delicate mission," Custer noted later, "as it was difficult to convince the squaws & children that they had anything but death to expect at our hands."

On Sunday morning, November 29, Californie Joe burst into Phil Sheridan's tent at Camp Supply.

"Well, Joe"—the General cracked a frowning smile—"what brings you back so soon? *Running away?*"

The frontiersman snorted. "By Jeese, I've jest made that thar ole critter o' mine out thar git up an' dust fer the last thirty-six hours! I tell yer it's a big thing, an' we jest made them red devils git."

Sheridan's ruddy face glowed. "So you've had a fight!"

"Weel," Joe drawled, scratching his beard with the stem of his pipe, "we've had suthin'! *You* may call it fightin', but *I* calls it wipin' out the varmints. Yass, an' sech a one as they won't have agin, I tell ye!"

Sheridan glanced at Custer's semi-official report and dashed off an immediate personal reply: "The Battle of the Washita River is the most complete & successful of all our private battles, and was fought in such unfavorable weather & circumstances as to reflect the highest credit on Yourself & Regt."

When Californie Joe came back to camp on the Washita, after

carrying the good news to Little Phil, Adjutant W. W. Cooke proudly read the following document to officers and men of the Fighting 7th:

> Hd.-Qrs., Dept. of the Mo.
> In the Field, Depôt on N. Canadian
> At Junction of Beaver Creek
> Ind. Terr., Nov. 29th, 1868

Gen'l Field Orders No. 6:

The Maj.-Gen'l Comdg. announces to this Command the defeat, by the 7th Regt. of Cavalry, of a large force of Cheyenne Indians under the celebrated Chief Black-Kettle, re-enforced by the Arapahoes under Little-Raven & the Kiowas under Satanta, on the morning of the 27th inst., on the Washita River, near the Antelope Hills, Indian Territory, resulting in a loss to the savages of 103 warriors killed (including Black-Kettle), . . . the complete destruction of their village & almost total annihilation of this Indian band. . . .

The energy & rapidity shown during one of the heaviest snow-storms that has visited this section of the country, with the temperature below freezing-point, and the gallantry & bravery displayed, resulting in such signal success, reflect the highest credit upon both the officers & men of the 7th Cavalry; and the Maj.-Gen'l Comdg. . . . desires to express his thanks to the officers & men engaged in the Battle of the Washita, and his special congratulations are tendered to their distinguished commander, Brev. Maj.-Gen'l G. A. Custer, for the efficient & gallant services rendered, which have characterized the opening of the campaign against hostile Indians south of the Arkansas.

By Command of

Maj.-Gen'l P. H. Sheridan

Major Joel H. Elliot and nineteen troopers were missing. Custer was told they had charged off in pursuit of runaway Indians, with Elliot shouting, "Here goes for a brevet or a coffin!" There was now little chance of their ever being found alive. Elliot was a glory hunter, and such men spun the thread of their own fates. Custer styled him "a young officer of great courage & enterprise." According to Benteen: "Elliot, like myself, was 'pirating' on his own hook. . . . Elliot . . . had, in underhand ways, been 'peppering' Custer, thinking he was not aware of it—but he was."

The ghost of Joel Elliot would haunt Armstrong Custer as malignantly as that of Wyckliff Cooper, for the Hero of the Washita was soon accused (by Benteen and West) of having abandoned the Major to his fate.

Over eight hundred cayuses were corraled by Captain Benteen and his troop. Custer ordered them all to be slaughtered. They were of no use to the cavalry, but the Indians must never get hold of them again. "If we retained them, they [the Indians] might conclude that one object of our Expedition against them was to secure plunder—an object thoroughly consistent with the Red-man's idea of war. Instead, it was our desire to impress upon his uncultured mind that our every act and purpose had been simply to inflict deserved punishment upon him for the many murders and other depredations committed by him."

While 875 ponies were being slaughtered, the village of seventy-five lodges was burned to the ground. Retribution was complete.

11

WASHITA: MEYOTZI

FIFTY-THREE squaws and papooses were brought before "Strong-Arm" and "Buffalo-Calf," as Armstrong and Thomas were called by the Plains Indians. Californie Joe acted as interpreter.

Having assured them that they would be treated with all due respect, and that he was no fork-tongued butcher of women and children, Big Chief Yellowhair (*Hâyotzi*) was immediately surrounded by grateful squaws clamoring to shake his hand.

After the adulation, a queenly middle-aged woman spoke up in her native tongue: "I am Mawissa, sister of Chief Black-Kettle. You claim to be a chief. This man [she pointed to Californie Joe] says you are the big chief of longknives. If this is true, and you are what he claims, show that you can act like a great chief and secure for us that treatment which the helpless are entitled to."

Joe translated to Custer; and Mawissa's petition met with the hearty approval of her female companions, who grunted their assent.

Before Custer could ask what was her pleasure, Mawissa stepped into the gathering of squaws, took a timid young Cheyenne girl by the hand, and led her over to him.

"This is Princess Meyotzi," she said, "daughter of Chief Little-Rock. He too was killed by your longknives; but when he lived, Little-Rock was second in rank to my dead brother Black-Kettle. Meyotzi is seventeen summers. She is now without father and

401

mother; but the fruit is ripe for a great warrior to pluck and eat, so she will no longer need a father or mother."

(Mawissa then placed the young girl's hand in that of Yellow-hair, shut her eyes, and began to mumble a singsong of Cheyenne formulas. Custer was flabbergasted. He stood in respectful indulgence, holding Meyotzi's hand, while the gray-haired matron cast up her eyes in trancelike reverence and moved her hands slowly down over his and the girl's face, moaning, "*Mânito! Mânito!*"

Knowing that Manito was the Great Spirit of Magic Potency, Custer's curiosity got the better of his silence. He turned to an old squaw-man and whispered, "What's this woman doing, Joe?"

With a broad grin on his face, Milner replied, "Why, she's marryin' you to that thar young squaw!")

Custer blanched, then reddened. "You damned fool," he muttered. "You know damn well I'm already married. If this is your idea of a joke . . . !"

Still flushed with anger and embarrassment, Custer blurted at Milner: "Tell this woman I appreciate her kindness, but according to the whiteman's laws I can't marry her young friend. Now tell her!"

Joe shrugged and relit his pipe. "No use in that now, Ginral. You an' her is already hitched!"

"Is that so?" Custer snapped. "Well, since you seem so damned pleased, perhaps you'd like to explain this woman's motives."

"That thar's easy enough t'onnerstand, Ginral. Married—as *they* call it, mind ye—to that thar squaw, she'll tell ye all the rest of 'em is her kinfolks; an' as a nateral sort o' thing, you'll be 'spected to kinda provide an' take keer o' yer wife's relations. That thar's jist as I told ya, fer don't I know! Didn't I go an' marry a young Cheyenne squaw, an' give her ole pa two o' me best ponies fer 'er, an' twarn't a week till every tarnal Injun in the village—young an' old—come to my lodge! An' didn't me squaw try to mek me b'lieve they was all relations o' her'n, an' that I oughta give 'em some grub; but I didn't do nothin' o' the sort."

"Well, then, how did you get out of it?"

"Git out of it! Why, I jist took all me ponies an' traps, an' the fust good chanct I lit out. That thar's how I got out of it! An' lemme tell ya; I was satisfied to marry one er two of 'em, but when it come to marryin' a whole dern tribe"—he shook his shaggy head—" 'scuse me!"

Mêyotzi: "Yellow-Sprout," or "Young-Grass-that-Shoots-in-Spring." Like so many Indian names, enchantingly poetic. And Meyotzi was a vision of lyric beauty. Custer described her as "an exceedingly comely squaw possessing a bright cheery face, a countenance beaming with intelligence, and a disposition more inclined to be merry than one usually finds among the Indians. . . . Added to bright laughing eyes, a set of pearly teeth and a rich complexion, her well-shaped head was crowned with a luxuriant growth of the most beautiful silken tresses rivalling in color the blackness of the raven and extending, when allowed to fall loosely over her shoulders, to below her waist."

Did he taste the forbidden fruit of the wilds? And in so tasting, did he dream of Libbie? How simple and pure was his husbandly love? If in the least sophisticated, the least egocentric, did it make Meyotzi the fanciful fulfillment of a lonely soldier's yearning for the girl he left behind him? Because Yellowhair was so kind and respectful, Meyotzi loved him. Her love was Indian—the duty-bound dedication of squaw to buck—but it was also free, from the heart.

To Tom Custer, Buffalo-Calf, Meyotzi was "Sally-Ann"—just another convenient and compliant wench. She submitted to him because he was Yellowhair's brother, and that was the proper thing to do. But Tom abused his fraternal rights, and everyone knew it. It was a standing joke among the senior officers. As Fred Benteen put it, "Custer winks at being cuckolded by his kid-brother. That relieves him of his own blanket duty!"

There is much speculation as to whether Custer consummated his "marriage" to Meyotzi, known also as "Mo-nah-see-tah." The Indians, with a kind of halfhearted pride, claim he did; but the question to be considered is whether they confused Armstrong with

403

Tom, who dressed and looked somewhat like his older brother. Meyotzi seems to have kept silence concerning the whole affair, perhaps in deference to her own dignity "as belonging to the cream of the [Cheyenne] aristocracy, if not to royalty itself."

Custer said: "Although never claimed as an exponent of the peace policy about which so much has been said and written, yet I entertained the most peaceable sentiments toward all Indians who were in a condition to do no harm nor violate any law. And while cherishing these friendly feelings, and desiring to do all in my power to render our captives comfortable and free from anxiety regarding their future treatment at our hands, I think even the most strenuous and ardent advocate of that peace policy (which teaches that the Indian should be left free and unmolested in the gratification of his simple tastes and habits) will at least not wholly condemn me when they learn that this touching and unmistakable proof of confidence and esteem offered by Mah-wis-sa, and gracefully if not blushingly acquiesced in by the Indian maiden, was firmly but respectfully declined."

12

FORT COBB: THE GLORY
OF THE WASHITA

December 2, 1868. With band crashing ("Ain't I Glad to Git Out o' the Wilderness") and colors flying, Old Curly and his Fighting 7th paraded into base camp on the North Canadian River. Custer saluted Sheridan with a saber flourish, and Phil, with an Irish grin, waved his battered old billycock hat.

"In speaking of the review afterwards," Autie wrote Libbie: "Gen'l Sheridan said the appearance of the troops, with the bright rays of the sun reflected from their burnished arms & equipments as they advanced in beautiful order & precision down the slope, the Band playing & the blue of the soldiers' uniforms slightly relieved by the gaudy colors of the Indians (both captives & Osages), the strangely fantastic part played by the Osage guides—their shouts, chanting their war-songs & firing their guns in air—all combined to render the scene one of the most beautiful & highly interesting he remembered ever having witnessed."

"Bully for you, my boy!" Sheridan roared in the G.H.Q. tent, slapping Custer on the back. "You've wiped out the disgrace of two futile years of campaigning. Christ knows, I was damned worried about the safety of your command in this cold and snow! But I kept in mind that the immediate effect of a signal victory would be to demoralize the hostiles and expedite our ultimate success."

On December 1, Sheridan informed Sherman that Custer had "wiped out old Black-Kettle & his murderers & rapers of helpless

405

women." Sherman wired his congratulations from St. Louis, following this communiqué from the War Department and Secretary Schofield: "I congratulate you, Sheridan, and Custer on the splendid success with which your campaign is begun."

Sherman esteemed the Washita affair a "great success which I regard as decisive & conclusive," and Sheridan assured him: "One month more will let us out of this country with a fair settlement of the Indian troubles on the condition that punishment should always follow crime."

The same spirit who, in the Shenandoah Valley campaign of 1864, had so successfully inaugurated the 'whirling' movement, was now . . . determined that . . . re-enforced by the biting frosts of winter we should continue to 'press things' until our savage enemies should not only be completely humbled, but be forced by the combined perils of war and winter to beg for peace and settle quietly down within the limits of their reservation. So Custer stated in his memoirs.

Accordingly, on December 7, General Sheridan and Colonel Custer marched southward with eleven companies of the 7th U.S. Regular Cavalry and ten of the 19th Kansas Volunteer Cavalry. Destination was Fort Cobb on the Washita, over a hundred miles southeast of Camp Supply, and objective was to round up all "strays" (hostiles) not dealt with on November 27. Accompanying the expedition as guides and interpreters were Mawissa (Black-Kettle's sister), Meyotzi (Little-Rock's daughter and Yellowhair's "left-hand wife"), and a Sioux squaw whose identity is unknown. The inevitable Californie Joe went along too)

Friday, December 11, 1868. While scouting the Washita battleground, Colonel Custer and a hundred-man patrol found the bodies of Major Elliot and sixteen troopers. They were stripped and frozen stiff, savagely mutilated and bristling with arrows. It was a saddening, sickening spectacle.

In the words of *Herald* correspondent D. R. Keim, a scene was witnessed sufficient to call forth the rebuke of every benevolent

& enlightened mind against the darkened intellects of the so-called philanthropists.

"No words were needed to tell how desperate had been the struggle before they were finally over-powered," Custer recorded. "Seeing the hopelessness of breaking thro' the line which surrounded them—and which undoubtedly numbered more than 100 to 1—Elliot dismounted his men, tied their horses together & prepared to sell their lives as dearly as possible."

The official report of Dr. Henry Lippincott (Assistant Surgeon, 7th Cavalry), who examined the corpses, is illustrative of the "good medicine" practiced by dog-warriors. As a grim testimony to "the Red-man's blood-thirsty & insatiable vengeance," we read that Major Joel H. Elliot suffered "2 bullet-holes in head, 1 in left cheek; right hand cut off, little finger of left hand cut off, left foot almost cut off, private parts cut off; deep gash in right groin, deep gashes in calves of both legs; throat cut." The body of Sergeant-Major Walter Kennedy, whose head was partly cut off, revealed twenty-one bullet wounds. Others were scalped, completely decapitated; "right ear cut off," "skull fractured," "penis cut off," *ad infinitum, ad nauseam.*

"In addition to the wounds & barbarities reported by Dr. Lippincott," Custer informed Sheridan, "in the deserted camp lately occupied by Satanta with the Kiowas, my men discovered the bodies of a young white woman & child—the former apparently about 23 yrs. of age, the latter probably 18 mos. old. . . . Upon our attacking & routing Black-Kettle's camp, her captors (fearing she might be re-captured by us & her testimony used against them) had deliberately murdered her & her child in cold blood. The woman had received a shot in the forehead; her entire scalp had been removed & her skull horribly crushed. The child also bore numerous marks of violence."

When word of these atrocities reached the settlements, frontier newspapers began printing such solutions to the Indian problem as: "Offer a reward of $500. for each Indian's scalp brought in, and in less than six months we will have an end of the Indian war and will have peace with the red devils on a permanent basis."

Fortunately for the advancement of American civilization, the Army did not subscribe to this so-called solution. The New York *Times* suggested: "We must come back to the old army policy of reservations—peace for the Indian on the reservation, war for his hostilities outside the reservation." The Chicago *Tribune* agreed, adding: "The first thing that the savages need is so much war and of such kind as shall result in their settlement on reservations. . . . When the War Dept. has done this, . . . then philanthropy can have its turn."

Sheridan wrote to Sherman from Fort Cobb: "I do not care one cent, as far as I am concerned myself, whether they [the hostile Indians] come in or stay out. If they stay out, I will make war on them winter & summer as long as I live, or until they are wiped out. They cannot come in here & make peace with me now, and then commence killing white people again in the spring. If I make peace with them, I want it to be a peace which will last; and if they commit robberies & murders afterwards, they must be punished."

"You must all come in," Custer warned them. "Not only the chiefs and squaws, but braves as well. This reservation is now the only ground left for the Indians. All other ground is bad."

Sheridan added: "I am not a bad chief, nor is my friend Yellowhair. We are not bad men. If you come in here and do as we say, I will not be a bad chief to you."

December 19. Late that night, Armstrong wrote to Elizabeth: "The Cheyennes, Kiowas & Arapahoes are hastening in to give themselves up. They are sick of war since the Battle of the Washita. So am I. I am as impatient as a crazed animal to have them come in, so that I can start on my homeward journey rejoicing." Two weeks later she got the glad word:

Ft. Cobb, Ind. Terr.
Jan. 2nd, '69

My Darling Girl,
The last remaining tribes of hostile Indians—Apaches & Comanches—have sent in their head chiefs to beg pity from us.

Yesterday (what a Happy New Year!) a grand council was held near my tent. All the head chiefs of the Apaches, Kiowas, Comanches, Cheyennes & Arapahoes were assembled. I was alone with them except for one officer, who took stenographic notes of the speeches. (I now understand sign-language!) . . . The arrogance & pride is whipped out of the Indians. They no longer presume to make demands of us; on the contrary, they have surrendered themselves into our keeping. As in the case of the tribes here now, no promise or inducement has been held out. I have made no pretense to be friendlily disposed. Whatever I have asked the tribes to do, or accede to, has been in the form of a demand. They have, from the commencement of this campaign, been treated not as independent nations but as refractory subjects of a common gov't. . . .

✗Almost at once, there arose a scandalous uproar back East about what was fondly called "Custer's Washita Massacre." Gunrunners and dollar do-gooders in the Indian Bureau (Department of the Interior) stood behind the swarms of "sobbyists" that stormed Washington, ballyhooing the Vanishing American's inalienable rights. None of these seemed concerned with Indian atrocities, or with a realistic means of preventing them. Apparently, only white men were on the warpath, wantonly wiping out their red brethren, who were nobly defending their sacred land with shiny new Winchester carbines generously supplied by Indian agents "for hunting purposes only."

The imputation of having deliberately slaughtered innocent Indians—men, women, and children—was all a part of the "get Custer" campaign. But when his faithful friends in the War Department threatened to expose a few confidential records—"Arrest for intoxication while on duty," "Arrest for disorderly conduct & excessive drinking," etc.—chronic bellyachers and troublemakers like Captain West kept their mouths shut.

All of them, that is, except one. And he, for a while, would remain anonymous.

"Before setting out on the last Expedition," Custer explains in his memoirs, "I had stated to the officers in a casual manner that

409

all parties engaged in the conduct of the contemplated campaign against the Indians must reconcile themselves in advance, no matter how the Expedition might result, to becoming the recipients of censure and unbounded criticism; that if we failed to engage and whip the Indians, labor as we might to accomplish this, the people in the West (particularly along and near the Frontier, those who had been victims of the assaults made by Indians) would denounce us in unmeasured terms as being inefficient or luke-warm in the performance of our duty; whereas if we should find and punish the Indians as they deserved, a wail would rise up from the horrified humanitarians throughout the country, and we would be accused of attacking and killing friendly and defenceless Indians.

"My predictions proved true. No sooner was the intelligence of the Battle of the Washita flashed over the country than the anticipated cry was raised. In many instances it emanated from a class of persons truly good in themselves and in their intentions, but who were familiar to only a very limited degree with the dark side of the Indian question, and whose ideas were of the sentimental order. There was another class, however, equally loud in their utterances of pretended horror; who were actuated by pecuniary motives alone, and who (from their supposed or real intimate knowledge of Indian character and of the true merits of the contest between the Indians and the Government) were able to give some weight to their expressed opinions and assertions of alleged facts. Some of these last described actually went so far as to assert not only that the village we had attacked and destroyed was that of Indians who had always been friendly and peaceable toward the whites, but that many of the warriors and chiefs were partially civilized and had actually borne arms in the Union Army during the War of the Rebellion. The most astonishing fact connected with these assertions was not that they were uttered, but that many well-informed people believed them."

He adds that despite all outcries of indignation, honestly or otherwise evoked, the U.S. Government "was in earnest in its determination to administer proper and deserved punishment to

410

the guilty." Indeed, the Government had no choice. Its duty was to protect United States citizens, whose votes were very important to those in office.

The "Glory of the Washita" was assailed on many fronts. One of the most vociferous assailants was crusader Wendell Phillips, so-called Prophet of Liberty, who delivered the following diatribe to an enraptured audience of self-righteous indignationists:

"I blush today at the swords of the Republic, crimsoned and disgraced by blood better than theirs. Sheridan—*Sheridan*—sends Custer out, with his sword ready-drawn against the Indians; and Custer sends a letter to Sheridan, 'I have had a glorious victory,' and Sheridan heads a dispatch: 'A brilliant victory.' You read on, and Custer says: 'I came on a Cheyenne village—silent as night, careless as children, unheeding danger. I descended on the sleeping group, and slew men and women; and when the sun rose, I found myself in possession of 875 head of horses; and as I could not carry them, I shot them.' Oh, the American soldier descended on a peaceful village, filled with agriculture and industry and property, sleeping in peace under the flag of the Republic; and like a ruthless savage, he trod it out in blood. (*Shame! shame!*) You send your generals, fresh from the great war that taught the nation that we had no eye to see race, to herald that victory to Washington as a brilliant success. Oh, it was a coldblooded butchery!"

The cry went up that Custer had wantonly slaughtered women and children. Cheyenne fugitives (who certainly weren't there to see for themselves) informed Indian agents that a rumored twenty-five innocents had been slain on that terrible morning, but did not comment on how or why.

Custer stated his case thus: "Savages though they were, and justly outlawed by the number and atrocity of their recent murders and depredations on the helpless settlers of the Frontier, I could not but regret that in a war such as we were forced to engage in the mode and circumstances of battle would possibly prevent discrimination. . . . Before engaging in the fight, orders had been given to prevent the killing of any but the fighting strength of the

411

village; but in a struggle of this character it is impossible at all times to discriminate—particularly when, in a hand-to-hand conflict such as the one the troops were then engaged in, the squaws are as dangerous adversaries as the warriors; while Indian boys between ten and fifteen years of age were found as expert and determined in the use of the pistol and bow and arrow as the older warriors."

Sherman and Sheridan defended Custer on grounds that the death of any women and children, after the precautionary issuance of such a prohibitive order, was purely accidental or due to individual acts of cruelty for which Custer could not be held accountable. "Did we cease to throw shells into Vicksburg or Atlanta because women & children were there?" Sherman reasoned. "War is cruel, and you cannot refine it."

The charge that Custer had attacked a friendly village, massacring innocent Indians in their beds, was also dismissed by the Division Commander in a letter to Sheridan (December 23, 1868): "This you know is a free country, and people have the lawful right to misrepresent as much as they please—and to print them—but the great mass of our people cannot be humbugged into the belief that Black-Kettle's camp was friendly with its captive women & children, its herds of stolen horses & its stolen mail, arms, powder, &c.—trophies of war. I am well-satisfied with Custer's attack, and would not have wept if he had served Satanta & Bull-Bear's band in the same style. I want you all to go ahead—kill & punish the Hostile, rescue the captive white women & children, capture & destroy the ponies, lances, carbines, &c. &c. of the Cheyennes, Arapahoes & Kiowas. Mark out the spots where they must stay, and then systematize the whole (friendly & hostile) into camps with a view to economical support until we can try to get them to be self-supporting like the Cherokees & Choctaws."

But allusions to "the murdered Black-Kettle" persisted. According to Yale ethnologist George Bird Grinnell, who lived with the Cheyennes, "Black-Kettle was a striking example of a consistently friendly Indian who, because he was friendly and so be-

412

cause his whereabouts were usually known, was punished for the acts of people whom it was supposed he could control."

"I have worn the uniform of my country 55 years," wrote Major General William S. Harney, member of the Indian Peace Commission, "and I know that Black-Kettle was as good a friend of the U.S. as I am."

Sherman and Sheridan laughed at such assertions. Accusations that they were carrying on a war of extermination were also dismissed with patient scorn. "As to 'extermination,'" Sherman wrote, "it is for the Indians themselves to determine. We don't want to exterminate or even to fight them. At best it is an inglorious war, not apt to add much to our fame or our personal comfort; and for our soldiers, to whom we owe our first thoughts, it is all danger & extreme labor—without a single compensating advantage. To accuse us of inaugurating or wishing such a war is to accuse us of a want of common sense, and of that regard for order & peace which has ever characterized our Regular Army. The injustice & frauds heretofore practised on the Indians, as charged, are not of our making; and I know the present war did not result from any acts of ours." Reiterating that "Indian wars never bring honors or reward" ["War is hell; its glory is all moonshine"], Old Tecumseh declared: "I will say nothing & do nothing to restrain our troops from doing what they deem proper on the spot, and will allow no more vague charges of cruelty or inhumanity to tie their hands. . . . I feel certain that the great mass of our people sustain us fully, but we cannot silence those who have an interest in keeping up an eternal war on the Plains; for 'None are so blind as those who will not see.'"

> Ft. Cobb, Ind. Terr.
> Feb. 9th, '69

Dear Little Durl,

To-day is our wedding anniversary! I am sorry we cannot spend it together, but I shall celebrate it in my heart.

None of us feel that we could or ought to leave here until the Indian question is settled. Without delicate handling by persons of experience in Indian affairs, we are liable to lose all the benefits of the winter campaign & be plunged into another war with the southern tribes. . . .

I have been very strict with the officers. Have no favorites where duty is concerned! I have had Tom in arrest, also Yates, for drunkenness & disorderly conduct. George is "huffy," but I hope will soon get over it. Tom is cuter than ever, but he is becoming a little wild. A few more nights in the guard-house should tame him down. Nevertheless, his conduct grieves me. . . .

Custer spent a couple of months settling the "Indian question" by co-signing peace treaties, relocating tribes on special reservations, and running down renegades who refused to bury the hatchet. Sherman ordered him to "*kill* all hostiles," but Custer was not now desirous of shedding blood arbitrarily; so he wielded the weapons of diplomacy whenever possible.

He performed a Herculean task, despite the well-meaning interference of Major General William B. Hazen, Superintendent of the Southern Indian District and special Peace Commissioner for the Indian Bureau. Custer vividly remembered him as "Old Hazer" Hazen, who had arrested him at the Point in '61 for "conduct unbecoming an officer and a gentleman" and for "inciting to riot." After distinguishing himself in the Civil War, Hazen was appointed to the unenviable post of protecting poor Indians from bloodthirsty cavalrymen. When his mission of peace and charity came to nought, the Indian Bureau and the War Department called a temporary truce—so long as the shady interests of neither could be served by further competition.

The trouble began with Sheridan's telegram to Sherman (December 2, 1868): "Something should be done to stop this anomaly. I am ordered to fight these Indians & Gen'l Hazen is permitted to feed them."

Five months before, Major General John Pope had written General Sherman: "I know no task more hopeless than the attempt to keep the peace in Indian country under the operations of the organized system of fraud & rascality known as the 'Indian System' & administered by the Indian Bureau.

On October 1, 1868, the New York *Herald* ascribed the Indian embarrassment "to the bad management of the Interior Department, and to the correlative fact that the Government is the ally of the Indian and furnishes him the means to murder our soldiers."

"If Gen. Sherman shall succeed in crushing out the Indian contract and Interior Dept. thieves who swarm on our Indian frontier," the *Tribune* proclaimed, "he will perform a service no less glorious than he has heretofore rendered the country."

Proposed transference of the Indian Bureau (Department of the Interior) to the War Department was one of the most hotly contested issues of Manifest Destiny. Secretary of War or Secretary of the Interior: who could best be trusted to control this vital and controversial bureau?

Custer wrote: "The Army as a unit, and from motives of peace & justice, favors giving this control to the Sec'y of War. Opposed to this view is a large, powerful & at times unscrupulous party, many of whose strongest adherents are dependent upon the fraudulent practices & profits of which the Indian is the victim . . . practices & profits which only exist so long as the Indian Bureau is under the supervision of the Interior Dept. . . . It seems almost incredible that a policy which is claimed & represented to be based on sympathy for the Red-man, and a desire to secure to him his rights, is shaped in reality & manipulated behind the scenes with the distinct & sole object of reaping a rich harvest by plundering both the Govt. & the Indians."

He shrewdly concluded: "To do away with the vast army of agents, traders & civilian employees (which is a necessary appendage of the civilian policy) would be to deprive many members of Congress of a vast deal of patronage which they now enjoy." Then he asked: "Who ever heard of a retired Indian-agent or trader in limited circumstances? How do they realize fortunes upon so small a salary?" The answer was that both agent and trader worked hand in glove to defraud both the Government and its wards; that between agent and Indian "there is no system of accountability"; that "the agent, instead of distributing to the Indians all of the goods intended for them by the Govt., only distributes one-half & retains the other half"; and that the dishonest agent then providently transferred "the unissued portion of the annuities from his Govt. store-house to the trading-establishment of his friend the trader," thereby reaping a harvest of kickbacks from illegal sales.

And Custer added pointedly, "Is it to be wondered at that Army Officers (who are often made aware of the injustice done the Indian yet are powerless to prevent it, and who trace many of our difficulties with the Indians to these causes) should urge the abolishment of a system which has proven itself so fruitful in fraud & dishonest dealing toward those whose interest it should be their duty to protect?"

In *Report of the Joint Special Committee on the Condition of the Indian Tribes* (January, 1867) there is a statement: "While it is true many agents, teachers, and employees of the Government are inefficient, faithless, and even guilty of peculations and fraudulent practices upon the Government and upon the Indians, it is equally true that military posts among the Indians have frequently become centers of demoralization and destruction to the Indian tribes; while the blunders and want of discretion of inexperienced officers in command have brought on long and expensive wars the cost of which, being included in the expenditures of the Army, are never seen and realized by the people of the country."

When Sheridan and Custer reached the Washita twenty miles above Fort Cobb on December 16, 1868, General Hazen insisted by special courier "that all the camps this side of the point reported to have been reached [by Sheridan and Custer] are friendly, and have not been on the war-path this season."

These "friendly" camps belonged to Satanta and Lone-Wolf, two of the bloodthirstiest Kiowas ever to terrorize the Plains. Custer and Sheridan contended, from Indian-captive reports, that Kiowa hostiles had been encamped below Black-Kettle on the

416

Washita that fateful morning of November 27. Hazen disagreed, producing evidence to the contrary.

Custer's contention was based on the testimonies of Mawissa, and other Indians present during the battle. Hazen relied on his own knowledge and that of his subordinates, both civil and military, who stated that very few if any Kiowas were encamped on the Washita with Black-Kettle; that they had, as a tribe, come to the Fort Cobb reservation a week before the fight; and that all the chiefs were asleep in Hazen's tent on the night of the twenty-sixth.

Hazen would write that Custer "erred greatly in his statement that the Kiowa Indians (as a tribe) were in the Battle of Washita, and that I was wrong in not permitting his Command (20 days after) to fall upon them—men, women, and children—and destroy them, when gathered together in promised security under my charge. . . . That the Kiowas have at all times richly deserved the severest punishment, I have constantly maintained; but punishment under such circumstances as it was desired to inflict it on the 17th day of December, 1868, while they were resting under the most sacred promise of protection, I could never assent to."

However, Hazen had written Sherman on December 7: "I have never had faith in Satanta [chief of the hostile Kiowas]; and if he finally gets a drubbing with the rest, it will be better for everybody. I think by large presents of coffee & sugar he might have been bought for peace, but not for a valuable & lasting one. . . . The prevailing sentiment reported of the people [i.e., half of the Kiowas under Satanta] who have gone out to the hostile camp [of Arapahoes, Cheyennes, and Comanches] is no doubt war-like, and altho' professing peace, will likely be found in the next fight. I am more strongly of the opinion than ever that Gen'l Sheridan should do his work thoro'ly this winter, and that it will then be lasting. . . . To suppose the late battle decisive, and cease offensive operations, would be very unfortunate."

On Hazen's urging, Satanta and Lone-Wolf rode out of Fort Cobb on December 16 to parley with Custer and Sheridan under a white flag supplied by the Superintendent. Custer, true to form, spurred far beyond the column to meet them with a small escort of officers and scouts. Such demonstrations of daring were sure to awe "savages" into discretion. He confronted the Kiowa chieftains, acutely aware that "Large parties of their warriors could be seen posted in the neighboring ravines & upon the surrounding hill-tops. All were painted & plumed for war; and nearly all were armed with one rifle, two revolvers, bow & arrow—some of their bows being strung—and their whole appearance & conduct plainly indicating that they had come for war."

"Our hearts are good; our tongues are straight," Satanta asserted, but Yellowhair nonetheless refused to take his outstretched hand. The chief thereupon jerked it back, pounded his chest, roared, "Me Kiowa!"

Custer was not impressed—least of all when Lone-Wolf caressed his buckskinned arm and rumbled, "Heap big nice son-a-bitch! Heap son-a-bitch!"

Learning that the rest of the tribe had fled southward at his approach, Custer threatened to hang Satanta and Lone-Wolf unless they returned—which they did directly. Meanwhile, Custer amused Satanta by engaging in a series of shooting matches with his twenty-year-old son, purportedly the tribe's greatest marksman. Custer's luck and skill won out; and indeed, "I attached no little importance to these frequent & friendly meetings between Satanta's son & myself. Any superiority in the handling or use of weapons, in horseback exercises, or in any of the recognized manly sports, is a sure stepping-stone in obtaining for the possessor the highest regard of the Red-man."

Custer boasted that regard.

★13★

WICHITA MOUNTAINS:
THE ROUNDUP

"THE Indian question, so far as the Kiowas are concerned, is regarded as settled—at least for the time being—and it becomes our next study how to effect a similar settlement with the Cheyennes & Arapahoes, who fled after the Battle of the Washita & are supposed to be somewhere between the Wichita Mts. & the western border of Texas." So Armstrong wrote to Elizabeth on February 16, 1869. Shortly thereafter, he devised a plan whereby war might be averted and the renegades persuaded into peaceful return to their reservations. "There are those who would have the public believe that the Army is at all times clamorous for an Indian war," and that General Custer was a glory-hunting Indian hater, but he would make them eat their words at a time when successfully drastic measures could have won him considerable *éclat*.

Custer laid his plan before General Sheridan: "We have some fifteen hundred troops, a force ample to cope with all the Indians on the Plains. But since the Washita campaign, it would be extremely difficult if not impracticable to move so large a body of troops near their villages and expect 'em not to scatter like grouse. It would also be impracticable to move upon them stealthily, as they're more than ever on the alert. If we must intimidate them into a state of reason, it should be by moral rather than military power. I believe, Phil, that if I can see the leading chiefs of the two hostile tribes and convince them of the friendly desire of the

419

Government, they might be induced to return to their reservation.

Sheridan scowled, rubbed his grizzled mustache. Was this Custer talking? Sounded like a Quaker! Lost in wonder, he muttered, "You don't mean to go alone?"

"Certainly not! I fear I'm not sufficiently orthodox as a peace commissioner to believe what so many of that order preach but fail to practice: that I could take an olive branch in one hand, the plan of a schoolhouse in the other, and unaccompanied by force, visit the Indian villages in safety. No; with your approval, Phil, I should like to select forty men, two officers, and a medic from the 7th, with Chiefs Little-Robe [Cheyenne] and Yellow-Bear [Arapaho] as guides, and set out in search of the hostile camp."

"Well," Sheridan ventured with uneasiness, "the nature of your proposition is such that I won't order you to execute it; but if you volunteer to go, I'll give you the full sanction of my authority and every possible assistance to make this mission a successful one. However, let me order you to exercise the greatest caution against the treachery of these red devils, who might be only too glad to massacre your party in revenge for their smashup on the Washita."

Custer providently chose Lieutenant Cooke's sharpshooters as his escort, accompanied by Captain Tom Custer, Captain Sam Robbins, and Dr. Renick. Neva, a trusty Blackfoot who had been one of Frémont's scouts and was Kit Carson's son-in-law, served as interpreter. "I need not say that in the opinion of many of our comrades our mission was regarded as closely bordering on the imprudent, to qualify it by no stronger term."

Indeed, none other than Captain Benteen ("one of the most prudent officers of my Command") was so convinced of Custer's folly that he contrived to slip a loaded derringer into his hand on departure, remarking dryly, "You'd better take it, General. It may prove useful to you."

Custer later confessed: "It was given me under the firm conviction that the Indians would overwhelm & massacre my entire party; and to prevent my being captured, disarmed & reserved for

420

torture, that little pistol was given me in order that at the last moment I might become my own executioner—an office I was not seeking, nor did I share in my friend's opinion." Benteen was always good for a grim joke, at which Custer was never amused.

Southwestward they rode, toward the Wichita Mountains.

On January 24, 1869, a fretful Phil Sheridan cautioned his "pet": "My dear Custer, . . . Keep close watch to prevent Cheyennes & Arapahoes from getting the advantage of you."

Phantoms of worry were dispelled when Sheridan received glad word from Custer that Little-Raven's Arapaho village had been entered without incident, and that a friendly council produced the promise (immediately fulfilled) that all Arapahoes would return to their reservation without fear of intimidation or punishment by the bigknives.

When informed that the Cheyennes were nowhere to be found, Sheridan replied (January 31): "If the Cheyennes do not come in at once, I will move out against them. I hope this will not be necessary, but if so let me know. I will make them feel lightning."

Raw weather and scant supplies forced Custer back to base camp without locating the Cheyennes. It was a hunger-haunted march of eighty miles in sixteen hours, during which the forlorn detachment devoured horseflesh *faute de mieux.*

"I did not tell you of my intentions," Autie informed Libbie on February 8, "fearing that you might be anxious; but I am now back safe & well. We have been to try & bring in the Indian villages, and have had what some people would term a rough time. . . . But I enjoyed it all, and often thought of the song:

> The bold dragoon he has no care
> As he rides along with his uncombed hair.

He added, recalling the powwow with Little-Raven: "I wish you could see with what awe I am held by the Indians. A sound drubbing, you know, always produces this. They have given me a name, 'Mon-to-e-te,' which means 'Strong-Arm. . . .' Tell Eliza I am tired of living on roast horse & parched corn, and will soon be

421

at home & want soup every day. . . . Gen'l Sheridan . . . said
again, for the 50th time, that I could go East at the earliest possible moment; but I tell him, as I always have, that I would not
go till the work was all done."

> Camp Wichita, Medicine-Bluff Creek, I.T.
> Mar. 1st, '69
> . . . I am going to march over a portion of the country to
> which everyone is a stranger & the distance unknown. . . . I
> shall be glad to get on the move again. I have remained in camp
> until I am tired of it. I seldom care to stay in one camp over
> 2 or 3 days. I am almost as nomadic in my proclivities as the
> Indians themselves! . . .

Tuesday, March 2, 1869. Lieutenant Colonel G. A. Custer,
with fifteen hundred men of the 7th U.S. Cavalry and the 19th
Kansas Cavalry, moved westward "in quest of the recalcitrant
Cheyennes"—to "administer to them such treatment as their past
conduct might merit & existing circumstances demanded." Another object of this punitive expedition was to secure the release
of two white girls held captive by the hostiles since before the
Washita campaign.

Sheridan had refused to ransom a Mrs. Clara Blynn and her
little son Willie, later brutally murdered by Arapahoes (Custer
claimed the Kiowas, on Mawissa's authority) during the Washita
rout. "After having her husband & friends murdered, and her own
person subjected to the fearful bestiality of perhaps the whole
tribe, it is mock humanity to secure what is left of her for the
consideration of 5 ponies." So Sheridan reasoned, assuring Sherman that "the red fiends, one after another, ravish the [captive
white] women until they become insensible." He makes no mention of children, though it is to be assumed that repeated abuse
would also render them unworthy of civilized consideration.

Custer thought far differently from his superior, and one of his
greatest hopes was to rescue white prisoners—particularly women
and children—at any cost.

422

When, after a long and exhausting hunt, he and his Osage trackers finally located the hostiles, Custer's first thoughts were for the safety of the captives. "I knew that the first shot fired on either side would be the signal for the murder of the two white girls. While knowing the Cheyennes to be deserving of castigation, and feeling assured that they were almost in our power, I did not dare to imperil the lives of the two white captives by making an attack on the village—altho' never before or since have we seen so favorable an opportunity for administering well-merited punishment to one of the strongest & most troublesome of the hostile tribes."

With the head of the column over a mile behind him, Yellowhair sought a truce. Advancing toward the village in a zigzag manner, he guided his horse in a series of circles betokening a desire to powwow. Now and then he glanced furtively to the rear, measuring the column's approach with as much concern as he observed the enemy's disposition before him.

A dozen warriors spurred forward to honor his intentions, but drew rein a short distance away. They shook their lances menacingly, affecting fierce scowls and spitting freely. With revolver in left hand and right hand held aloft, Custer signaled for the spokesman to meet him midway.

Pro forma, white man and red exchanged monosyllabic greetings and clasped hands. In the course of the conversation that followed, Custer learned to his unrevealed satisfaction "that the village of the entire Cheyenne tribe was located on the stream in front of us, and that Medicine-Arrow (the head chief of the Cheyennes) was in the group of Indians then in view."

"Send for Medicine-Arrow," Yellowhair motioned. "I wish to talk with the head chief."

The spokesman grunted, turned aside, hailed one of his companions, who dashed back for Medicine-Arrow. The big chief soon came galloping up with his lieutenant, Little-Robe, and about twenty braves in paint and feathers.

"*Hâo!*"—"*Hâo!*" and handshakes opened the confrontation, during which Medicine-Arrow was advised that Yellowhair had

423

come with enough longknives to avenge any contemplated act of treachery.

"The women and children of our people will be much excited and alarmed by the presence of so many bigknives," the chief rattled. "To put them at ease, I urge you to accompany me into the village at once and show them that no attack will be made."

Custer nodded, signing for them to go on.

"At a gallop!" Medicine-Arrow invited, to which Yellowhair responded favorably by digging his heels into his horse.

"Some may regard this movement on my part as having been anything but prudent, and I will admit that viewed in the ordinary light it might seem to partake somewhat of a foolhardy errand. But I can assure them that no one could be more thoroughly convinced of the treachery and blood-thirsty disposition of the Indian than I am, nor would I ever trust life in their hands except it was to their interest to preserve that life; for no class of beings act so much from self-interest as the Indian, and on this occasion I knew (before accepting the proposal of the Chief to enter his village) that he and every member of his band felt it to be to their interest not only to protect me from harm but to treat me with every consideration."

The great conclave in Medicine-Arrow's tepee is enriched by legend. Seated cross-legged on a buffalo robe to the right of the chief ("the post of honor") (and to the left of the Cheyenne medicineman, full-bearded Yellowhair in fringed buckskins received the pipe of peace from the weirdly incanting Keeper of the Sacred Medicine Arrows, who clasped Custer's right hand to his heart: ". . . by which, no doubt, it was intended to neutralize any power or proclivity for harm I may have been supposed to possess.)"

For a moment, Armstrong puffed away "with as great a degree of nonchalance as a man unaccustomed to smoking could well assume." But when the medicineman solemnly insisted on his retaining the pipe till the end of invocation, Custer grew anxious at making "a miniature volcano" of himself. "I pictured to myself the commander of an important expedition seated in solemn council with a score & a half of dusky chieftains, the pipe of peace being passed, and before it had left the hands of the aforesaid commander, he becoming deathly sick—owing to lack of familiarity with the noxious weed or its substitutes. I imagined the sudden termination of the council, the absurdity of the figure cut, and the contempt of the chiefs for one who must, under the circumstances, appear so deficient in manly accomplishments."

Fortunately for Custer's peace of body and mind, "divine tobacco" worked no devilish mischief. Not so the shaman, who was (unbeknownst to his victim) putting a curse on the yellow-haired chief.

While he mumbled and grumbled the appropriate formulas, Medicine-Arrow addressed Custer in the Cheyenne tongue: "You are a treacherous one, O Creeping-Panther; but if you come with a bad purpose, to do harm to my people, you will one day be killed with all your men."

"Then [according to G. B. Grinnell] the arrow-keeper with a pipe-stick loosened the ashes in the pipe and poured them out on the toes of Custer's boots, to give him bad luck." The curse was complete.

Late that evening of March 15, during a powwow held at Custer's headquarters, it was learned that the Cheyennes planned to steal away while the yellow-haired chief was thus diverted. Custer, equal to any emergency, had skillfully seized four of the sub-chiefs and held them as hostages pending unconditional surrender of the two white girls and an immediate return to the reservation near Camp Supply.

Several days passed, during which Medicine-Arrow made a play for time while slowly moving his tribe away. He promised to give up the white captives, but only after Custer had given up his own prisoners; to which Custer replied that unless the girls were released by the following sunset, the four chiefs would be hanged and hostilities opened—"cost what it might."

The ruse worked. The two girls were released at sunset. "Men whom I have seen face death without quailing found their eyes filled with tears, unable to restrain the deep emotion produced by this joyful event."

In a letter dated March 24, Armstrong told Elizabeth the story of the two girls. "It is that of hundreds of other women & girls whose husbands, fathers, or brothers take their lives in their hands & seek homes on the Frontier. They had been traded repeatedly from the hands of one chief to those of another; and they had suffered daily outrages at the hands of the young men, who deem it a test of manhood to forcibly abuse a captive female in gangs, to the exhaustion & insensibility of all—the last warrior to survive the assault being considered the most manly. Besides indignities & insults far more terrible than death itself, the physical suffering to which the two girls were submitted was too great almost to be believed. They were required to transport huge burdens on their backs, large enough to have made a load for a beast of burden. They were limited to barely enough food to sustain life; sometimes a small morsel of mule-meat, not more than an inch square, was their allowance of food for 24 hrs. The squaws beat them unmercifully with clubs whenever the men were not present. Upon one occasion, one of the girls was felled to the ground by a blow from a club in the hands of one of the squaws. Their joy therefore at regaining their freedom after a captivity of nearly a year can be better imagined than described."

Writing from the Washita battleground, Autie had proclaimed in the same letter: "I have been successful in my campaign against the Cheyennes. I out-marched them, out-witted them at their own game, proved to them they were in my power, and could & would have annihilated the entire village of over 200 lodges but for 2 reasons. 1st.—I desired to obtain the release of the two white women held captive by them, which I could not have done had I attacked. 2nd.—If I had attacked them, those who escaped (and absent portions of the tribe also) would have been on the warpath all summer; and we would have obtained no rest. These reasons alone influenced me to pursue the course I have; and now, when I can review the whole matter coolly, my better judgment & my humanity tell me I have acted wisely. You cannot appreciate how delicately I was situated. I counselled with no one; but when we overtook the Cheyenne village, and saw it in our power to annihilate them, my Command (from highest to lowest) desired bloodshed. They were eager for revenge, and could not comprehend my conduct. They disapproved & criticized it. I paid no heed, but followed the dictates of my own judgment—the judgment upon which Gen'l Sheridan said he relied for the attainment of the best results. He had authorized me to do as I pleased, fight or not. And now my most bitter enemies cannot say that I am either blood-thirsty or possessed of an unworthy ambition. Had I given the signal to attack, officers & men would have hailed it with a shout of gratification. I braved their opinion & acted in opposition to their wishes; but to-day not one but says I was right, and any other course would have been disastrous. Many have come to me & confessed their error." As for the Cheyennes, "I think we have rendered them sick & tired of war."

Lieutenant Colonel Horace L. Moore, who had replaced Governor Crawford in command of the 19th Kansas, styled Custer's order not to attack the village "a wet blanket saturated with ice-water." His volunteer troopers, many of whom had lost loved ones by Indian atrocities, branded Old Curly "a coward and a traitor." But Custer did what Sheridan probably would never have done: substituted diplomacy for force of arms, in favor of two miserable creatures "unworthy of rescue."

On March 6, Sheridan scratched a note to Custer from Camp Supply: "Just rec'd wires from Gen'ls Sherman & Grant, requiring me to report at Washington without delay. I start to-morrow. . . . I will push your claims on the subject of promotion as soon as I get to Washington; and if anything can be done, *you may rely on me* to look out for your interests. . . . *P.S.*—I feel very anxious to hear from you."

Sheridan heard from Custer: good news, but also bad. According to a Kansas cavalryman, "Custer fed us on one hard-tack a day & *The Arkansaw Traveller*." On March 1 of '69, Autie informed Libbie that "My Command has been living on quarter-rations of bread for 10 days. Gen'l Sheridan has been worried almost to distraction. I wish some of those responsible for this state of affairs, who themselves are living in comfort & luxury, could be made to share the discomforts & privations of troops serving in the field."

Now, the situation was no better: "Have I told you how shame-

427

fully the Commissary Dept. has treated the Command? Gen'l Sheridan is terribly enraged at Gen'l Van Vleit [Chief Quartermaster, Department of the Missouri] & curses him not a little. . . . We feel that troops undergoing the severities & unusual hardships of a winter campaign, such as ours, should receive every comfort the Gov't can give. . . . If Gen'l V. could only hear the execrations heaped on his head!"

Custer and his column marched back to base camp on a diet, as usual, of mule and horse and parched grain. *God damn all government drones and profiteers!*

Two footnotes to the campaign are of controversial interest. While at Fort Sill, below the Washita and at the foot of the Wichita Mountains sixty miles south of Fort Cobb, Captain Tom and several other officers of the 7th Cavalry "Custer Gang" took the mercurial cure for venereal disease. Fort Sill medical records (January–February, 1869) listed as treated those who had entertained sexual contact with infected squaws. Apparently, Armstrong's observation that Tom "is becoming more profane & a little vulgar" was more meaningful than meets the eye. And his careless remark that Meyotzi (Sally-Ann) "had become a great favorite with the entire Command" would justify Benteen's sneer that Yellowhair, symbolically married to Meyotzi, had been cuckolded not only by Brother Tom but by any number of the Custer Clan. It is alleged that these same medical records (now missing) bore G. A. Custer's name, by virtue of the curse of Venus, which poses several possibilities.

Camp Wichita, Fort Sill. Friday evening, February 19, 1869. "Officers' Call" had been sounded from regimental headquarters, and all but one of Colonel Custer's staff hurried into his big Sibley tent. There they saw him sitting cross-legged on the bench of his field table, tapping the sole of his boot with the handle of a rawhide riding whip. He motioned for them to squat around the inside walls, then stood up straight. His face was slightly flushed in the flickering glow of lanternlight, and it was easy to see that he was smoldering.

Custer paced back and forth, switching his buckskinned legs with the "hide-tickler." "It has been reported to me," he announced, "that some one of you has been belittling the Washita campaign, and therefore making a fool of the regiment. Now if I hear any more of this dangerous nonsense, and find out who has been disgracing his regiment, I'll horsewhip him!" Custer cracked his quirt, then snatched up a newspaper from the table.

At that moment Captain Fred Benteen came sauntering up to the entranceway. He was a short and slim "Dutchie" with a ruddy clean-shaven face, bright blue eyes, and a shock of wavy gray hair. He was puffing on a meerschaum.

Custer darted a glance at Benteen, then looked at the newspaper and said, "This letter I am going to read first appeared in the St. Louis *Democrat* of February ninth. Here it is now in the New York *Times* of February fourteenth." Custer read aloud with bitter sarcasm:

"Fort Cobb, I.T., Dec. 22, 1868

". . . On the 11th we camped within a few miles of our 'battle of the Washita'; and Gens. Sheridan and Custer, with a detail of one hundred men mounted as escort, went out with the view of searching for the bodies of our nineteen missing comrades, including Maj. Elliot.

"The bodies were found in a small circle, stripped as naked as when born, and frozen stiff. Their heads had been battered in, and some of them had been entirely chopped off; some of them had had the Adam's apple cut out of their throats; some had their hands and feet cut off, and nearly all had been horribly mangled in a way delicacy forbids me to mention. They lay scarcely two miles from the scene of the fight. . . .

"Who can describe the feeling of that brave band as, with anxious beating hearts, they strained their yearning eyes in the direction whence help should come? What must have been the despair that, when all hopes of succor died out, nerved their stout arms to do and die? . . .

"And now, to learn why the anxiously looked-for succor did not come, let us view the scene in the captured village scarce two short miles away. . . . Does no one think of the welfare of

429

Maj. Elliot and party? It seems not. . . . Officers and soldiers are watching, resting, eating, and sleeping. . . . The commander occupies himself in taking an inventory of the captured property. . . . That which cannot be taken away must be destroyed.

"Eight hundred ponies are to be put to death. Our Chief exhibits his close sharp-shooting and terrifies the crowd of frighted, captured squaws and papooses by dropping the straggling ponies in death near them. Ah! he is a clever marksman. Not even do the poor dogs of the Indians escape his eye and aim as they drop dead or limp howling away. . . . The work progresses! The plunder, having been culled over, is hastily piled; the wigwams are pulled down and thrown on it, and soon the whole is one blazing mass. . . . Surely some search will be made for our missing comrades. No, they are forgotten. Over them and the poor ponies the wolves will hold high carnival, and their howlings will be their only requiem. . . .

"Two weeks elapse; a larger force returns that way. A search is made and the bodies are found strewn round that little circle, frozen stiff and hard. Who shall write their eulogy? . . ."

Colonel Custer slammed the paper down on the table. His reddened face was taut with rage. "That's the Goddamndest thing I ever read in my life," he sputtered, "and it could only have been written by an officer of the 7th." He snapped his rawhide. "By Jesus, that man deserves to be horsewhipped; and if he's here now, I want him to step forward."

Custer glared about the tent. No one moved or dared utter a sound.

No one, that is, but Captain Benteen. He shifted his revolver to a handy position on his belt, unsnapped the holster flap, strode forward into the tent. "All right, General, I guess I'm the man you're after. You can start your horsewhipping here and now. I wrote that letter."

Custer smirked. "How noble of you, Captain. Sorry, but I want the saddle to go just where it fits."

"Well, here's your horse, General. While I can't back all the blame, still I'm ready for the whipping you promised."

430

"*Ha!* Calling my bluff, eh? Stand where you are, Captain. The rest of you are dismissed."

When the other officers had left the tent, Custer and Benteen stood alone face to face. Custer flicked his whip against his leg, and Benteen patted his holster. They stared at each other with wry smiles, then Custer said dryly: "I'll see you again on this matter, Captain. You're dismissed."

Benteen nodded and swung out of the tent. Those were the last words ever said by either man to the other on the subject of that notorious letter. Benteen ran and told reporter Keim (who then informed Sheridan) of Custer's horsewhipping threat, and Sheridan hastened to advise Custer to drop the whole scandalous matter. By that time, Custer had cooled off and was in a better mood to forgive and forget.

Benteen later wrote: "I wasn't ashamed of it [the letter], didn't care a damn for Custer, and owned straight up that I was the miscreant who had given it to the world. . . . Sheridan gave Custer a piece of his mind about the matter. . . . Everybody—I mean most of the captains & all of the subalterns in the 7th—seemed to be positively afraid of Custer. . . . I never fought Custer in any but the most open-handed manner, always going face-to-face for it . . . and showed him thro' all the history of the 7th Cav. that I was amply capable of taking care of myself. . . . Being in a Regt. like that, I had far too much pride to permit Custer's outfit driving me from it."

The character of Frederick William Benteen, who was not in the Army "for glory-going purposes" and who remained Custer's staunchest enemy, is worthy of note.

"He was rather a singular character, proud & a little vain perhaps," commented General E. A. Garlington, then a lieutenant in the 7th. "He was not an habitual drinker, but once or twice a year he would begin & keep it up for days. . . . It was during such periods that he became abusive & insulting to those whom he disliked or disapproved of. He was much liked by most of the officers in the regiment, and they took care of him in such periods." (These annual drunken fits were apparently brought on

431

by his wife's misfortunes: "I lost 4 children in following that brazen trumpet around." With a weak constitution that subjected her to constant illness, Trabbie Benteen was hard pressed by frontier living.)

According to Colonel (then Lieutenant) C. A. Varnum, "Benteen drank & played poker, and when under the influence of liquor would utter sneering remarks. He was a law unto himself, and a soldier of undoubted courage."

It was inevitable that two rugged individualists, the one a romantic and the other a cynic, should clash as if the cherished identity of one depended upon the elimination of the other.

Captain Robert M. West resigned his commission on March 1, 1869. Reason: ill health. He lived seven months, then dropped dead, a victim of alcoholism. Colonel Andrew J. Smith was pensioned off the Army Register on May 6. Custer was glad to be rid of them. But a fresh thorn was thrust in his side when Major Marcus A. Reno arrived to replace Captain West. Custer knew Reno to be an old acquaintance of General Hazen. He smelled a rat. Was his regiment being infiltrated with Indian Ring agitators or informers?

The reason for Sheridan's sudden recall to Washington is found in Sherman's telegram to him of March 6, 1869: "Grant has been inaugurated [President of the United States]. He has just nominated me for General & you for Lieutenant-Gen'l." Custer was thrilled, for Phil's promotion and heightened influence would surely add feathers to his own nest. The beloved chief's promise echoed in his mind: "I will push your claims on the subject of promotion as soon as I get to Washington; and if anything can be done, *you may rely on me* to look out for your interests."

Though "damned with faint praise," Custer (in Whittaker's words) "had done what no other officer in the American Army had yet succeeded in doing. . . . In seven months he had closed the campaign which commenced in 1867, when Hancock let the Cheyennes slip from between his fingers. . . . Custer had ended the whole war and placed the frontier in peace, alone and unassisted, *just because he was given his own way. . . .*"

432

★14★

NEW YORK:
FORTUNE HUNTING

★M<small>ID-SPRING</small>, 1869. All quiet on the Western Frontier. Colonel Custer and his 7th Cavalry marched 250 miles northward, out of Indian Territory and into Kansas, back to the Union Pacific railhead at Fort Hays. Meyotzi, her womb swollen with child, accompanied the column in an ambulance requisitioned for her by the yellow-haired chief.

When Custer reached Hays on April 7, he read with delight a wire from Sheridan in Chicago: "I am very much rejoiced at the success of your expedition, and feel very proud of our winter operations & of the officers & men who bore privations so manfully. I presume you will want a leave, and so spoke to Gen'l Schofield; and if you desire such, you can have as long as you please."

Armstrong hopped a lightning express to Fort Leavenworth, where he raced into Libbie's arms.

With Colonel Smith on the retired list, Major General Samuel D. ("Old Buckskin") Sturgis was assigned commanding officer of the 7th Cavalry. Custer considered this a slap in the face, "the unkindest cut of all." His exploits and accomplishments had won him a public reputation of being the best Indian fighter on the Plains, but self-interested officialdom dared not act upon its reluctant recognition of the fact. Instead of rewarding him with what he had earned by virtue of sagacious enterprise, "the powers that boodle" advised the "wild man" to rest on his laurels as field chief

433

of the famed Garryowens. Sheridan, apparently, could do nothing. His hands were tied by bureaucratic red tape.

Sam Sturgis, finding himself the innocent pawn of this controversy, filed a strong bid to bow out as nominal head of the Fighting 7th:

> Hd.-Qrs., 7th Cavalry
> Camp near Ft. Hays, Kas.
> August 13th, 1869
>
> *To the Adjutant-Gen'l, U. S. Army*:
> . . . In forwarding this communication, I respectfully ask for favorable consideration of Gen'l Custer's worth & former services; of the arduous and important services rendered by him against the Indians of this Dept., while in command of the 7th Cavalry. There is, perhaps, no other officer of equal rank on this line who has worked more faithfully against the Indians, or who has acquired the same degree of knowledge of the country & of the Indian character. If, however, it should be deemed impracticable to give him the command he desires, I would respectfully recommend that he be permitted to accompany the Hd.-Qrs. of the Regt.
>
> > *S. D. Sturgis*
> > Col., 7th Cav.
> > Bvt. Maj.-Gen. U.S.A. Comdg. Regt.

Application unsuccessful. "We deem it impracticable. . . ."

Late August, 1869. According to medical records, a fair-haired boy was born to Meyotzi in the stockade at Fort Hays. She named him Yellow-Bird. It has been assumed, by many Cheyennes and anti-Custerites, that the child was sired by Yellowhair; but the weight of evidence seems to rest on Brother Tom. Autie and Libbie certainly wanted a child, and their disappointment in this desire raises a significant question.

Indian testimony, though generally revealing, is particularly apocryphal. "When my mind darkened with thoughts of Meyotzi's disgrace, I spilled dead ashes from the peacepipe on Yellowhair's

434

boots, thus cursing him unto eternity." So spoke Brave-Bear, Cheyenne war chief, when in fact it was Medicine-Arrow's shaman who enacted this devilish deed. His comments on Meyotzi are interesting if not reliable: "She was a proud woman; she kept silence as the child of the soldier-chief grew in her womb. Finally, when the soldier-chief was talking peace with us, Meyotzi told him she was happy to bear his child. After that, he shunned her like a plague."

(Yellow-Bird was therefore ignored and abused—as was his mother, who later left the tribe with Mawissa to join the Sioux, some said in an attempt to be near her "Son-of-Morningstar," others to be with a people not so prejudiced in their pride. Whatever the truth, such is the stuff of which legends are made.)

"The Indian war has ended." This was Keim's final report from Fort Hays in the spring of '69. "There is not a hostile Indian within the limits of the Missouri Dept. The refractory tribes have been entirely subdued." Several years later, Custer informed the American public: "From and after the Washita campaign the frontiers of Kansas have enjoyed comparative peace and immunity from Indian depredations. No general Indian war has prevailed in that part of the country."

As Lieutenant General, Philip H. Sheridan was assigned command of the Military Division of the Missouri, with headquarters in Chicago. Arriving at Hays City en route to the depot, Colonel Custer dispatched a message to Sheridan in which he repeated what he had written his wife during the winter powwows: "Without delicate handling of the Indian question by persons of experience in Indian affairs, we are liable to lose all benefit of our last winter's campaign & be plunged into another general war with the southern tribes. I think this can be avoided."

President Grant, in his Inaugural Address of March 4, declared: "The proper treatment of the original occupants of this land—the Indians—is one deserving of careful study. I will favor any course toward them which tends to their civilization and ultimate citizenship."

435

Sherman left St. Louis for Washington, there to assume general-ship, with a dark outlook: "If I was an Indian, I'd behave worse than the Indians do. The whiteman has no business in this God-forsaken country."

The summer of '69 found Armstrong and Elizabeth at Fort Hays, enjoying the hospitality of Colonel and Mrs. Nelson A. Miles. Miles, whom the Indians called "Buffalo-Soldier," was a first-rate officer and hunting companion: a broad-shouldered six-footer with steel-blue eyes and Prussian mustachios, who had been awarded the Congressional Medal of Honor for valor during the Civil War. Libbie Custer and Mary Miles were purportedly the first (and perhaps the last) white women to hunt buffalo with their husbands. Miles appraised Custer as "ambitious and enter-prising," one of the most fearless cavalry leaders the Civil War produced.

Though enterprise could be enacted on the Great Plains, it was ambition (and boredom of routine) that prompted Custer to write General of the Army W. T. Sherman on June 29, requesting the position of Commandant at West Point. Application was denied. The Army apparently had better use for its golden-haired hero—or, more likely, dared not entrust a post of high executive re-sponsibility to one so wild and unpredictable. In any case, Custer accepted the disappointment with philosophical indifference. If he were meant for the job, destiny would have ruled in his favor. Custer's Luck worked in strange and fitful ways.

In late autumn, 1869, Custer abandoned his wild life on the Plains and began to enjoy an extended leave of unlimited term back East. Dropping Libbie off in Monroe, he railed over to Chicago for a get-together with Sheridan. His old gang went with him. He wrote "the Old Lady" on December 2: "Tom & the rest of the staff are enjoying what they think a good joke—at my expence. We had seen a performance of Lydia Thompson's 'Blondes' at the Opera House, and the *Times*—a bitter, Copper-head sheet—informed the public that I was pursuing blondes now instead of the dusky maidens of the Plains."

Three days later, on Sunday, George Armstrong Custer encountered his thirtieth birthday. "To-day added another year to my calendar," he penned wistfully. "I hope I may profit by the experience it carries with it." Some twinge of conscience now prompted him to form a resolution that "From the 1st of Jan., and for ever, I cease (so long as I am a married man) to play cards or any other game of chance for money or its equivalent." In so resolving, "I experience a new-found joy. I breathe free'er, and I am not loath to say I respect my manhood more." Apparently, the cardsharps of Chicago had had a field day with the impulsive cavalier.

The year 1870 was an uneventful one for the Custers, with routine duty at Fort Hays. The summer of 1871 found Armstrong fortune hunting in New York City, Elizabeth visiting the folks in Monroe. Virtual inactivity had driven Custer to a desperation burdened with fears of oblivion and anxiety as to his financial future. He seemed to be going nowhere, doing nothing of note. All prospects now seemed to lie in the East. He sought the phantom of sudden wealth—and was led a merry chase.

"Few wealthy people seem to enjoy their married life," he informed "Dear Old Stand-by." "I have yet to find husband & wife here who enjoy life as we do." Several days later, "Darling Stand-by" learned that banker August Belmont and wife "speak very highly of me—Mr. B. most encouragingly of my business prospects. Is it not strange to think of your Bo meeting to confer with such men as Belmont, Astor, Morton & Bliss?"

Some sense of satisfaction must have prompted Custer to add that "Capt. [Robert] Chandler (formerly of Gen'l Hancock's staff), who was Judge-Advocate at my trial, is now in an insane asylum in Washington."

All-night conferences with stockbrokers and financiers, eager to use Custer to advantage, aroused linen-closet gossip in the Metropolitan Hotel. "The old Irish servant who takes care of my room looks at me with suspicion when I return—sometimes not till morning, the bed not having been touched. I think she believes I do not pass my nights in the most reputable manner. In fact, circumstances (as she sees them) are against me."

437

Having served as official observer in the Franco-Prussian War, General Sheridan arrived in New York to say, "Custer, I wish you had been with me!" and "Custer, you with that 3rd Division could have captured King William six times over!" Generals Merritt and Torbert joined the reunion at the Fifth Avenue Hotel, where Torbert insisted that Custer pay him a visit in Delaware.

Among other escapades, financiers Larry and Leonard Jerome escorted Custer to Belmont Park at Saratoga, where he watched the races ("in the midst of enjoyment") but refrained from betting. Larry Jerome, through daughter Jennie, was destined to become Sir Winston Churchill's grandfather.

Between sporting with Colonel Jerome Napoleon Bonaparte and James Gordon Bennett II, Custer attended the lavish dinner parties of such "talented & distinguished men" as Horace Greeley ("whom I once threatened to horse-whip!") of the New York *Tribune,* writer-adventurer Bayard Taylor, journalist Whitelaw Reid, poet-stockbroker E. C. Stedman, and Charles A. Dana of the New York *Sun.* Stedman, for one, "told me that during & since the War [in which he had served as correspondent for the *World*] I had been to him—and, he believed, to most people, the beau ideal of a Chevalier Bayard, 'knight *sans peur et sans reproche*'; and that I stood unrivalled as the 'young American hero. . . .' I was so complimented & extolled that, had I not had some experience, I should have been overwhelmed!"

While dining at Delmonico's with *arbiter elegantiae* and "King of the Lobby," Uncle Sam Ward, Custer was seriously advised "that our natures partake of the characteristics of whatever fish, flesh, or fowl we eat." In other words, "You are what you eat!"

Custer's eyes twinkled. "Well now, Mr. Sam, what effect would the rattlesnake have on a fellow? I've enjoyed that dish for the past six years." Ward suddenly lost his appetite.

Like his friendship with the great dramatic actress Clara Morris, and even his intimacy with Lawrence Barrett, Custer's platonic relationship with the attractive and celebrated dramatic soprano, Clara Louise Kellogg, is characteristically Victorian. "Miss Kellogg cannot endure affectation in man or woman," Libbie learned.

438

And "Miss Kellogg is very dainty in regard to gentlemen." Walks on Broadway, evenings at the theater or opera, lunch at Delmonico's; such were the simple pleasures.

"Ghosts will always rise up in my recollection of Custer—the 'Golden-Haired Laddie,' as his friends called him." So Clara Louise Kellogg says in her memoirs. "He was a good friend of mine; and after the war was over he used to come frequently to see me and tell me the most wonderful, thrilling stories about it, and of his earliest fights with the Indians. He was a most vivid creature; one felt a sense of vigour and energy and eagerness about him; and he was so brave and zealous as to make one know that he would always come up to the mark. I never saw more magnificent enthusiasm. . . . When on horseback, riding hard, with his long yellow hair blowing back in the wind, he was a marvellously striking figure."

Renowned Washington sculptress, Vinnie Ream, a child prodigy who enobled Lincoln in marble, begged Custer to come to the Capital and sit for a marble bust. The boy general begged off:

> My Dear Vinnie,
> . . . You are young, and have obtained a foot-hold upon the ladder of fame far in advance of your years—to attain which others in your profession of acknowledged genius have been compelled to devote a lifetime. Go on, dear friend, conquering —and to conquer. Your victories are lasting and, unlike mine, are not purchased at the expence of the life-blood of fellow creatures—leaving sorrow, suffering, and desolation on their track.
> > Faithfully yours,
> > *G. A. Custer*

★15★

KENTUCKY: SPECIAL DUTY

AFTER a financially unfruitful season of *divertissement* in New York, Custer was ordered back to active service in Kentucky, where the 7th Cavalry had been sent by President Grant to smash up the Ku Klux Klan and moonshining rackets.

It was now September, 1871. Custer was stationed at Elizabethtown—"Betsy," he dubbed it—and Libbie sped down from Monroe by rail to join him. Without his wife to brighten the dullness, special duty in the Bluegrass State would have been an insufferably humdrum existence for the world-famous Indian fighter.

"Autie would like to be on the Frontier," Libbie wrote to Pop Custer, "but spends his leisure reading & writing." Custer's literary labor of love was a series of articles for *Galaxy,* entitled "My Life on the Plains, or Personal Experiences with Indians."

Detailed in Louisville to purchase remounts for the regiment, Gen'l Custer soon fell in with all the slick "hoss-traders" of this horsy state. But lucky in love and war didn't necessarily mean lucky in the racing racket, and a run of sour luck caused Old Curly to swear off the sport of kings for the rest of his married life. Word has it that he lost $10,000 in racing three thoroughbreds (his own) that were drugged or overweighted.

Another reason for leaving "L'ville" was Colonel Blanton Duncan, an "Unreconstructed Reb" who (during a political debate) alluded to Colonel Custer as "a lackey of nigger-loving carpetbaggers." Custer jumped to the platform and slapped

Duncan's face, demanding immediate satisfaction; but friends separated them before a duel could be arranged. (A similar incident had occurred at Austin in '66, where a newspaper editor who had referred to forage agent Emanuel H. Custer as "a remnant of Sherman's Bummers" was nearly horsewhipped by Old Iron-Butt. And to make matters worse, Armstrong's ferocious staghounds slaughtered a slew of domesticated dogs and pigs in the Louisville area—which resulted in a petition for his removal.)

"Personally I should have preferred the Plains, but for your sake," husband informed wife. "Duty in the South has somewhat of a political aspect, which I always seek to avoid."

Custer was perhaps even more out of place as a teetotaler. "When the gentlemen ask him what he will take—Everybody in Kentucky drinks!—he says 'A glass of Alderney [milk]' & toasts in that while they take whiskey, brandy, wine." But "How grateful I am Autie does not drink."

Custer worked feverishly on his *Galaxy* articles, hoping they might in some measure reclaim his old glory, fearing to remain merely "one long-haired cavalryman in serviceable condition." *My Life on the Plains; or, Personal Experiences With Indians* began serialization in May of '72 and saw book form in 1874. Its success was immediate, making G. A. Custer as much a literary lion as a national hero, but its repercussions were far-reaching.

One to react was W. B. Hazen, who composed a pamphlet entitled *Some Corrections to "My Life on the Plains,"* wherein he took exception to Custer's criticism of his conduct at Fort Cobb. Hazen wrote: "His exceptionally brilliant record, his fame, which was so justly and splendidly earned, and the long and admiring acquaintance which I have had with him, makes it impossible for me to believe that he could intentionally write or speak otherwise than with perfect regard for truth and justice." Benteen, however, always referred to his superior's effort as "My Lie on the Plains."

January, 1872. Generals Custer and Sheridan, with 5th Cavalry scout Colonel William F. ("Buffalo Bill") Cody, played host to

441

Czar Alexander II's third son, twenty-one-year-old Grand Duke Alexis (Aleksei Aleksandrovich) Romanov, on a grand buffalo hunt in southern Nebraska.

The excursion was a spectacular success, and sharpshooters Armstrong and Alexis were duly photographed together in their respective sporting outfits. Custer impressed the prince with his fluent profanity, and Cody advised him to gargle with whiskey every morning instead of brushing his teeth.

Lawrence Barrett observed that Custer's "truly American characteristics gained him a friend whose quick eye discerned the depths of that genuine nature and valued it. The friendship which arose between the Russian Grand Duke and General Custer . . . was very honorable to both. The polished courtier discerned in the young Democrat those sterling qualities of manhood which maintained their individuality in the midst of ceremonies and flatteries, and the correspondence which passed between them upon the return of the Grand Duke to Russia was highly gratifying to Custer."

Custer continued to feel the agony of inactivity, of exile, in Elizabethtown. It was unlike him to be moody, to lack interest in his reading and writing, to speak of his lot as that of an outcast. He had failed in New York, failed as a civilian; but what hope did the life of a soldier yet hold for him? Fortune hunting had gone the way of glory hunting, and there seemed to be little left but to follow the beaten path to oblivion. The glory trail had vanished. *Where*? It agonized his sense of enterprise that he could not find it, that it would not reveal itself, that it had been a mocking illusion all these years of ecstasy and anguish.

Libbie saw the curtain of despair ringing down about him, and she was powerless to prevent its darkening envelopment. Only force of circumstance could lift the pall, would guide the clouded luminary into a blaze of glory.

In the spring of '72, Custer welcomed a new brother-in-law and staff officer, Lieutenant James Calhoun: a handsome, golden-haired, six-foot Buckeye. It was hard to believe that sandy-haired,

442

freckle-faced kid sister Maggie (Margaret Emma) was married—and to the "Adonis of the Fighting 7th"! Aye, the so-called Custer Gang (or Clan) was steadily growing into one big happy family—the better to protect itself from Benteen & Co.!

February, 1873. Armstrong burst into the house, hoisted Elizabeth onto the dinner table, tossed a chair into the kitchen. Aunt Eliza poked her head through the doorway and squealed, "Land sakes alive, Gin'l! Chairs don't grow on trees in these here parts!"

"Bid good-riddance to these here parts, 'Liza gal!" Custer said gleefully, swinging a screaking Libbie off the table and around the room. "We're heading West: lock, stock, and barrel!"

"But where——?"

"Dakota Territory! The Yellowstone country! The Northern Pacific Railroad wants to push through the Badlands; and it shall be our job to escort surveyors through country seen by only a handful of whites, and to protect construction crews against Indian resistance. Y'know, Bunkie, the Sioux don't want any iron horses racing across their happy hunting-grounds—and I can't say I blame 'em!—but who can stand in the way of progress and civilization? They'll have their own way, whether I and those poor savages like it or not. So if all adventurous Americans are bent on and destined to head West, tame the wild frontier, and extend the States to the Pacific Coast, I can't see but why I shouldn't be one of the first to lead the way and cut the Gordian knot."

Except for her husband's discontent, Elizabeth Custer had been happy and secure in the domestic tranquility of Kentucky. But happiness and security were not all hers to claim, and she yielded to the beckoning of Manifest Destiny. Her diary reads: "This removal to Dakota means to Autie a reunion with his Regt. & summer campaigns against Indians; to me it means months of loneliness, anxiety & terror. But I shall honor my Father's dying words: 'Follow him everywhere. It is your Destiny to make him happy.'"

443

16

DAKOTA TERRITORY:
THE BLIZZARD

Y ANKTON, on the Missouri, capital of Dakota Territory. The Custers detrained on the open plain skirting the James River, about a mile east of town. While Camp Sturgis was being erected by the 7th Cavalry, Old Curly unloaded his litter of dogs, his thoroughbreds, cages of mockingbirds and canaries, and other traveling companions of the Custer Menagerie. When Autie suggested that Libbie should follow the officers' wives into Yankton, where a comfortable hotel awaited them, she chose to remain with her husband in a tent—"and fortunately for what followed I did so."

It was mid-April, but what the Custers never realized is that Yankton suffered "eight months of winter and four of very-late-fall." A blizzard fell upon them unawares, driving them into a deserted cabin that seemed little better than those ramshackle dugouts or shebangs endured by the Army of the Potomac. Exhausted from overexertion and the excitement and anticipation that impelled him like a human dynamo, Custer became deathly ill—and was forced to bed by weakness and his wife's urgings. Snowblasts penetrated every crack and cranny in the shack, creating a suffocating illusion of being buried alive.

When Adjutant Cooke reported for evening orders, Custer instructed him to break camp and direct the troopers into Yankton: there to be sheltered in houses, sheds, stables, and any other available room.

"And you, General?"

444

"I shall remain here."

"But Mrs. Custer——"

"I shall stay with my husband," she replied, administering a strong dose of medicine to her patient.

Cooke saluted and fought his way out the door, through torrents of wind-driven flakes; and "In a short time the camp was nearly deserted. . . . The townspeople, true to the unvarying Western hospitality, gave everything they could to the use of the Regt. . . . The sounds of the hoofs of hurrying horses flying by our cabin on their way to town had hardly died out before the black night closed in & left us alone on that wide, deserted plain."

Those thirty-six hours of storm-wrought imprisonment were one long nightmare for Elizabeth Custer. The wind shrieked like a thousand demons released from hell, rocking and shaking the little house with their frozen claws and blowing fury. Armstrong was too ill even to speak, so she found no comfort in his reassuring voice—only horror in his wild rambling fits. She administered medicine with benumbed fingers, constantly shaking encrusted snow from blankets and clothes as it sifted in like Kansas sand sprays.

A dull crash jolted her out of a delirium, and she saw a half-dozen bewildered troopers pry open the snow-banked door and in dazed motions indicate that two of their number were badly frozen. "Their sufferings were intense, and I could not forgive myself for not having something with which to revive them. Autie & I were both so well always that we did not even keep liquor for use in case of sickness."

(Libbie looked in terror at that deadly stupor which betokens hopelessness, when suddenly she recalled a bottle of alcohol that was kept to fill the lamps. The victims revived, but "Poor fellows! they afterwards lost their feet, and some of their fingers had also to be amputated.")

Morning came like evening, dimmed by drifts and swirling gusts; and "I grew more & more terrified at our utterly desolate condition. . . . When night came again & the cold increased, I believed that our hours were numbered." Unearthly sounds rose

445

above the roar of Nature. A drove of fear-crazed mules dashed against the cabin, seeking shelter and warmth, and their brays were fraught with sepulchral horror. They kicked and pushed and huddled, then rushed madly away in desperation—"and were soon lost in the white wall of snow beyond. All night long the neigh of a distressed horse, almost human in its appeal, came to us at intervals. I pried the door open once, thinking it might be some suffering fellow-creature in distress. The strange, wild eyes of a horse—peering in for help—haunted me long afterwards. Occasionally a lost dog lifted up a howl of distress under our window, but before the door could be opened to admit him he had disappeared in the darkness. When the night was nearly spent, I sprang again to the window with a new horror; for no one, until he hears it for himself, can realize what varied sounds animals make in the excitement of peril. A drove of hogs, squealing & grunting, were pushing against the house; and the door which had withstood so much had to be held to keep it from being broken in."

Were it not that she was kept so busy, Libbie may well have lost her senses. Sleep came in refreshing fits, disturbed by dreadful noises and the need to attend her delirious husband and the distressed soldiers. "To be in the midst of such suffering, and yet have no way of ameliorating it—to have shelter, and yet to be surrounded by dumb beasts appealing to us for help—was simply terrible. Every minute seemed a day—every hour a year."

Armstrong was able to eat at daybreak, for the breaking of his fever so revived him that he began to make light of the danger in order to quiet Elizabeth. "The snow had ceased to fall; but for all that it still seemed that we were castaways & forgotten, hidden under the drifts that nearly surrounded us. Help was really near at hand, however, at even this darkest hour. A knock at the door, and the cheery voices of men came to our ears. Some citizens of Yankton had at last found their way to our relief."

Libbie collapsed, although "I tried to smother the sobs that had been suppressed during the terrors of our desolation." Autie comforted her "by tender words," but "reminded me that he would not like any one to know I had lost my pluck when all the danger I had passed thro' was really ended."

With Colonel Sam Sturgis recalled to St. Paul for staff duty at Headquarters, Department of Dakota, Lieutenant Colonel G. A. Custer assumed full command of the 7th Cavalry during its 250-mile mud-trek up the Missouri River to Fort Rice, below the Northern Pacific railhead at Bismarck.

Strikingly attired in green riding habits, Libbie Custer and Maggie Calhoun rode at the head of the regiment with their husbands. Frolic-dashes over the plains, potshots at game on the run, and the usual Custer Clan banter filled those toilsome hours of marching.

Libbie penciled in her diary: "It often happens that my travelling-waggon is the hospital for an ill or foot-sore dog. Autie has to stop very often to attend to wounded paws, but experience is teaching the dogs to make their way very skillfully where the cactus grows. . . . It is of no use trying to keep the dogs out of my tent. They stand around & eye me with such reproachful looks if I attempt to tie up the entrance & leave them out. If it is very cold when I return from the dining-tent, I find dogs under & on the camp-bed—and so thickly scattered over the floor that I have to step carefully over them to avoid hurting feet or tails. If I secure a place in bed, I am fortunate! Sometimes, when it has rained & all of them are wet, I rebel. The steam from their shaggy coats is stifling; but Autie begs so hard for them that I teach myself to endure the air at last. . . . Fortunately, in pleasant weather, I am let off with only the ill or injured ones for perpetual companions."

The column paraded into Fort Rice on June 10, band blasting "Garry Owen":

> We are the boys that take delight in
> Smashing the Limerick lights when lightin',
> Through the streets like sporters fightin',
>   And clearing all before us!

447

Elizabeth and Margaret soon proceeded to Bismarck under escort, and from there they railed to Monroe. There was no place for women on a dangerous mission. Besides, Rice was not conceived to accommodate army wives. There was barely enough room and sustenance for officers and men, who were obliged to share common quarters: a rather degrading necessity in those days of sharply drawn lines of martial caste.

So it was separation again, made painful by compulsion. Separation scarcely bearable but by the grace of letters and prayerful expectation.

★17★

MONTANA TERRITORY: THE YELLOWSTONE EXPEDITION

F RIDAY, June 20, 1873. Dressed in a flaming-red blouse, buckskin breeches, and a white felt hat, Colonel Custer led his 7th Cavalry out of Fort Rice and westward into the forbidden Yellowstone country.

Major General David S. Stanley commanded the two-thousand-man expedition. Custer knew him to be an incompetent sot, a featherbed infantry officer who liked "being comfortably stowed away in his ambulance." Well, the teetotaler had had enough of drunkards in uniform; and he favored no intentions of letting Stanley ruin the enterprise.

Nor had Stanley any inclination to let Custer run the show. He knew the man by rumor and report, and this unfavorable information was confirmed in his mind by a characteristic incident that took place on the tenth. The 7th Cavalry had reached the river point opposite Fort Rice, where Captain Joseph Lafarge met them with his transport steamer.

"Gen'l Stanley has directed me to ferry yer troops across, Colonel," the old salt said.

Custer nodded. "Very well. Repair to the wheelhouse. I shall take charge of the proceedings."

Thus began a heated dispute between sailor and soldier, the one insisting on his right to stevedore the regiment onto his own boat, and the other challenging that right on the opinion: "That damned washtub couldn't hold but two companies without sinking!"

449

Insulted, Lafarge stalked back to his boat and steamed across without Custer, hooting, "For all I care, youse can start swimmin'!"

Seeing the 7th stranded, Stanley demanded an explanation from Lafarge, who cursed Custer roundly as an arrogative imbecile.

"Take me across," the General said. "*I* shall supervise the proceedings."

And so he did, much to Custer's and Lafarge's mutual dissatisfaction.

Accompanying the expedition as official observer was Captain Frederick Dent Grant, the President's oldest son and Sheridan's new aide-de-camp. He had been offered to Sherman for a goldbrick's desk at the War Department, but Old Cump wouldn't have him. "Grant has fallen into the hands of the Indian Ring, and I'll be Goddamned if I admit a spy to Army Headquarters!" So Sheridan took him, without choice, then appointed the youth as Stanley's A.D.C. and recalled Sturgis to fill the vacancy. All in all, a neat shuffle!

Camp on Heart River, D.T.
June 26th, '73

My Darling Sunbeam,

. . . Our march has been perfectly delightful. I never saw such fine hunting! We have encountered no Indians. . . .

The day we arrived here I was lying half-asleep on a buffalo-robe in my tent when I heard "Orderly, which is Gen'l Custer's tent?" I sprang up. . . . It was my old friend Gen'l Tom Rosser, now Chief Engineer for N. Pacific R.R. I spread the buffalo-robe under the fly of the tent; and stretched out in the moon-light, we listened to one another's accounts of the battles in which we had been opposed. It seemed like the time when we were cadets together, huddled under one blanket, discussing our dreams of the future. Rosser said the worst whipping he ever had was the one I gave him at "Woodstock Races" (well I remember it!), when I captured everything he had—including that uniform of his now in Monroe. Rosser (I call him "Tex") asked if you did not accompany me almost everywhere; so you

450

see what an extensive reputation for campaigning you have! And, do you know, he tells me he thinks I am anxious to get back to you. But I did not tell him I was already counting the days! . . .

The officers (Tom & Mr. Calhoun included) have been sitting night & day, playing cards, since we left Ft. Rice. . . . I congratulate myself daily—as often as the subject enters my mind—that I have told Satan to get behind me so far as poker is concerned. You often said I could never give it up. But I have always said I could give up anything—except you. . . .

> Yellowstone River, Montana Terr.
> July 19th

My sweet Rosebud,

Well, here we are at last—encamped on the banks of the far-famed & to you far-distant Yellowstone! How I have longed for you during our march into what seems a new world, a wonder-land! . . . No artist—not even a Church or a Bierstadt—could fairly represent the wonderful country we passed over; while each step of our progress was like each successive shifting of the kaleidoscope, presenting to our wondering gaze views which almost appalled us by their sublimity. . . . What would you think to pass thro' thousands of acres of petrified trees, some of which are 12 ft. in diametre, with trunks & branches perfect! No country equals this region in the number & character of its petrifactions. . . . I am making a rare collection of the fossils that the country is rich in—animal, vegetable & mineral specimens. I intend to give them to the college [Michigan University] at Ann Arbor. . . .

How I wish that some of our home-boys who possess talent & education, but lack means & opportunity, would cut loose & try their fortunes in this great enterprising Western country, where the virile virtues come out in full-fledged manhood. It is such a pleasure when I can help young men who evince a disposition to help themselves. I never forget those who gave me my first encouragement in life. It is such a comfort to me to feel independent. In this country, no man need fail in life if determined to succeed. . . .

Custer now told of official troubles, beginning June 27. On that day he and the 7th rode through thirty miles of badlands to where the Little Missouri crosses Heart River, there to aid the railway engineers and their cavalry escort in constructing a pontoon bridge of wagon frames and water barrels over a stream 30 feet wide and 10 feet deep. "I superintended & planned it, and about 180 men worked to complete it . . . in about 2 hrs.—over which the whole Command & waggon-train passed [on July 1]." Custer added: "The Engineers have been escorted daily by the Cavalry, so find themselves progressing far more rapidly than when dragging along with the 'Web-Feet' [infantry] as heretofore. Gen'l Rosser cannot speak too highly of the 7th."

It seems, however, that Old Curly "cut loose" without consulting Stanley—and left infantry and supply train fifteen miles in the rear: "stuck in the mud, they say—but probably thro' lack of energy; for Capt. Smith took our waggons back to the main line for supplies, and returned with them loaded. . . . Gen'l Rosser considers this Expedition too unwieldy to perform the work well, and I agree with him." In their opinion, Stanley and his "webfeet" need never have come—were quite unnecessary and a drag on Northern Pacific wheels. Besides, from all appearances, "Rosser & I do not think we are going to have any serious Indian troubles." Were it not for Custer's cavalry, Rosser declared openly, the job of surveying would never get done according to schedule. And so the Custer-Stanley controversy began.

"Gen'l Stanley is acting very badly—drinking, as usual—and I anticipate official trouble with him. I should greatly regret this, but fear it cannot be avoided. Rosser has told me how badly Gen'l S. behaved last year, some days being so overcome that the [first and unsuccessful] expedition could not go on. [This initial enterprise failed because of Stanley's incapacitation, thus necessitating a second survey with teetotaler and taskmaster Custer along.] One morning, the Engineers started at the appointed hour; but Rosser, looking back from a high bluff, saw that the Infantry camp was still standing. On going back, he found the officers searching for the Gen'l—but in vain. Finally Maj. Worth

452

told Rosser confidentially that, having found Gen'l S. dead-drunk on the ground outside the camp, he had carried him into his own tent (tho' he & the Gen'l were not on good terms) for the honor of the Service. He was then lying there in a drunken stupor.

"Rosser said he told Gen'l Stanley in St. Paul (before starting) that he would have a different man to deal with this year, in command of the 7th Cav.; one who would not hesitate, as Second-in-Command, to put a guard over him (Stanley) if incapacitated. Gen'l S., Rosser said, acknowledged that he knew this & would try to do better. But whiskey has too strong a hold on him.

"Our officers are terribly down on him. One day when intoxicated, after leaving Rice, he abused Mr. Balarian [the 7th's Own Sutler] in such coarse terms—calling him foul names like 'dirty Jew bastard' & 'damned thieving foreigner'—and threatened to hang him should he seek to come into camp at any time. Why? Because Balarian (who ignores Gen'l S.) sells whiskey cheap only to those who can hold it! Now Mr. B., who is a great favorite with our officers, asked me what he should do. I bade him come into camp with me, whiskey & all, and no one has been hanged as yet! Gen'l Stanley, in one of his fits of ill-humor, ordered Capt. Grant to go to the 7th Cav. & inspect Mr. Balarian's waggons & stores, and if he found any spirituous liquors there, to take an axe & spill the contents of barrels. This would have injured Mr. B. financially, as he had thousands of dollars' worth on hand. Capt. Grant was greatly mortified (being fond of whiskey himself), but fortunately Mr. B.'s waggons were so far in the rear it was hours before they arrived. So, after chatting with me on pleasant topics, Capt. G. said, 'Well, my tent leaked last night; so I guess I'll go back & take a nap. By that time the waggons may be in. And I hope the Sutler will have anything of the kind hidden before I come to inspect.' Our officers regarded Gen'l S.'s order as persecution, and were eager to help. So Mr. B. loaded his drinkables into one waggon & made the rounds of our temperate officers—leaving with each a keg of brandy, case of rum, or barrel of Bourbon, for temporary keeping. Never were temperate officers so well provided with intoxicants! Then Gen'l S.

453

re-considered (fearing he might be cutting his own throat, I suppose) and cancelled his order to Capt. G. to inspect. But fearing this might be a trap, the officers retained their keep for a few days till the excitement was over."

Benteen summarized: "Stanley got drunk, so the game was thrown into Custer's hand, and thus he 'got away with Stanley.' "

Autie's letter continued lightheartedly: "I am prouder & prouder of the 7th, Libbie. Not an officer or man of my Command has been seen intoxicated since the Expedition left Ft. Rice."

In the meantime, pot-valiant General Stanley was writing to his wife (June 28): "I have seen enough of Custer to convince me that he is a cold-blooded, untruthful & unprincipled man. He is universally despised by all the officers of his Regiment, excepting his relatives & one or two sycophants. He brought a trader [Balarian] in the field without permission, carries an old negro woman & a cast-iron cooking-stove, and delays the march often by his extensive packing-up in the morning. As I said, I will try, but am not sure I can avoid trouble with him."

And July 1: "I had a little flurry with Custer, as I told you I probably would. . . . Without consulting me, he marched off 15 miles, coolly sending me a note to send him forage & rations. I sent after him, ordered him to halt where he was, to unload his waggons & send for his own rations & forage, and never presume to make another movement without orders. . . . He was just gradually assuming command, and now he knows he has a Commanding Officer who will not tolerate his arrogance."

On August 15, Stanley reported that Custer "behaves very well since he agreed to do so." For all of a week, the 7th Cavalry had brought up the rear of the column and its commander held in nominal arrest. "You are the most insubordinate and troublesome officer I have ever dealt with," Stanley had sputtered on July 1. "You may consider yourself under arrest, and take your station in the rear." Now, on Rosser's insistence, Custer was back in the lead with his troopers, riding far ahead like the great pathfinder he was, guiding that massive mission through canyons and coulees like deep livid scars on the green and yellow hide of nature.

Yellowstone River, above Powder River
July 31st, 4 P.M.

Good-Morning, my Sunbeam!

Soon you will be counting our separation by weeks instead of months, and will be on your way to a Post on the frontier of Dakota. . . . The mail brought many newspapers with allusions to the Expedition & references to your "Boy General." I send you an extract from the *Chicago Post* calling him the "Glorious Boy." . . . The officers & men of the 7th are behaving admirably, while scarcely a day passes without one seeing an Infantry officer too intoxicated to be fit for duty. . . . You have no idea how whiskey alone has delayed the Expedition & added to Gov't expenses. Gen'l Rosser says it's a disgrace to the Service, and I (needless to say!) agree. . . .

P.S.—Tell Maggie Mr. Calhoun makes a splendid Adjutant.

Monday, August 4, 1873; 11 A.M. Colonel Custer and a ninety-man scouting party were bivouacked in a cottonwood grove on the banks of the swift-flowing Yellowstone, near the mouth of the Tongue River.

It was a breathless, cloudless day—hot enough to roast a mule. Old Curly sat in the sweltering shade of his tent, stripped down to his long white underwear, scrawling a letter to Libbie.

Suddenly there was heard the cracking of carbines and a frantic outburst: "Indians! Indians!"

Adjutant Calhoun darted into the headquarters tent. "Indians are galloping this way, sir!"

Custer jumped to his feet. "How many of 'em?"

"About a dozen, sir! From the way they're yelling and waving blankets, I reckon they mean to stampede the horses."

Custer grabbed his Remington sporting rifle and dashed out of the tent. "Bring in your horses, men!" he yelled to his troopers. "Bring in your horses!"

455

Instantly a swarm of cavalrymen raced over to the picketlines and led their mounts into the bivouac.

Custer turned to the bugler. "Sound *Boots and Saddles!*" Then to Captain Myles Moylan, Calhoun's brother-in-law: "Mount the squadron and move out in pursuit!" Custer lurched into the saddle, brandishing his rifle. "Jim, Tom, Bloody-Knife—follow me!"

Custer clapped heels to his horse and charged off after the swirling cluster of hostiles. Sprinting far ahead of Moylan's skirmish lines, he chased yelping Sioux across the yellow plain to within several hundred yards of another cottonwood grove upriver. He then checked his steed and raised his rifle for the horsemen behind him to halt where they were.

Custer signed to Bloody-Knife, his fierce-looking young Arikara scout, who loped up alongside. "We're being decoyed into a trap."

The Arikara grunted gravely. Each eyed the timber with nervous intensity.

Custer turned in the saddle and waved his Remington. "Dismount! *dismount!* Prepare to fight on foot!"

A torrent of screaming braves gushed from the trees, their breechloaders barking. Custer's horse reared and tumbled to the ground. He leaped clear, shouting to Bloody-Knife, "Pick off the chief!"

Custer jerked up his rifle, drew a bead on the head buck. Bloody-Knife leveled at the same warrior, a half-naked savage with painted physique, fluttering war bonnet, and feathered lance. Both fired at once. Man and pony collapsed in a flying spill. Struck with alarm, his several hundred whooping followers swung off to attack Moylan, were met with a murderous volley, and bolted away.

Leaping into the saddle behind Bloody-Knife, Custer "rode as only a man rides whose life is the prize"—back to the dismounted triangle of troopers.

Setting fire to sun-scorched grass, the Indians charged behind a flaming veil, whirling in fitful spurts, shrieking and shooting.

"*Now,*" Custer said to Moylan, "let's mount and drive 'em off!"

456

Taking advantage of their own curtain of smoke, Custer countercharged the Indians and scattered them like sheep. "Had they been willing (as white-men would have been) to assume greater risks, their success would have been assured." Outnumbered three to one, and almost completely surrounded, Custer and his detachment would have been wiped out but for a presence of mind that enacted the dictum: "Attack is the best defense."

Rosser, in a letter to Elizabeth, declared that "I thought him then one of the finest specimens of a soldier I had ever seen."

Custer says: "The only satisfaction we had [from the fight] was to drive at full speed for several miles a force out-numbering us 5 to 1." The Indians, however, were satisfied in having slain Veterinary Surgeon Holzinger and Sutler Balarian, who had wandered off (unarmed) ahead of the main column in search of fossils. Flattering themselves for being safe between Stanley and Custer, they were surprised by several warriors fleeing Moylan's first volley. Holzinger's bald head was smashed by a tomahawk, his stout body riddled with arrows. Balarian, whose hair was clipped close, escaped scalping; but his genitals were mutilated, his thighs gashed. Both had been stripped and robbed. The Fighting 7th vowed terrible vengeance, for the jolly old men had been "great favorites."

"So far as the troops attacked were concerned," Custer adds in his report to Stanley, "the Indians (to offset their own heavy losses) had been able to do us no damage except to wound one man & two horses."

For the next several days, Custer shadowed red phantoms over rock-ribbed hills, down dark-timbered dells, across sage-and-cactus flats, exchanging long-range volleys with bunches of Sioux on the opposite bank of a raging river.

When hundreds of hostiles amassed in his front on August 11, he threw forward a two-company skirmish line and the regimental band blasting "Garry Owen"—which had the anticipated effect of forcing "a disorderly flight."

Custer informed Stanley that "The Indians were made up of . . . principally Uncpapas, the whole under command of Sitting-Bull,

457

. . . who for once has been taught a lesson he will not soon forget." Alluding to "a sentimental Gov't manipulated & directed by corrupt combinations," Custer emphasized the fact that "The arms with which they fought us (several of which were captured in the fight) were of the latest improved patterns of breech-loading repeating rifles; and their supply of metallic rifle-cartridges seemed unlimited, as they were anything but sparing in their use. So amply have they been supplied with breech-loading rifles & ammunition that neither bows nor arrows were employed against us." His conclusion is pointed: "I only regret that it was impossible for my Command to effect a crossing of the river before our presence was discovered, and while the hostile village was located near at hand, as I am confident that we could have largely reduced the necessity for appropriation for Indian supplies the coming winter."

On Friday, August 15, Custer and his command sighted Pompey's Pillar, a lone-sentinel bluff rising sheer from the Yellowstone to a craggy height of 150 feet. Here, nearly 380 miles west of Fort Rice, the Northern Pacific survey ended and the expedition prepared to return—without incident. Custer's last flurry with Indians occurred at Pompey's Pillar, where bathing big-knives were briefly fired upon by red strays, "causing a great scattering of naked men."

Custer spearheaded the return march, keeping (as usual) as much distance between himself and Stanley as he dared. He doubled back by way of the Musselshell River, penetrating unmapped virgin territory teeming with big game. In his glory now, nothing could stop him!

"The country was entirely unknown; no guides knew anything of the route before us. Gen'l S. did not think it wise to venture into the unknown & uninviting region with his Command, but I did not feel inclined to yield to obstacles. . . . At Hd.-Qrs. it was not believed that I would get thro'. So strong was this impression, that S. authorized me to burn or abandon all my waggons or other public property if (in my opinion) such steps were necessary to preserve life. I could not help but smile to myself, as I

458

had no idea of burning or abandoning a waggon. After we had separated from the main column, Rosser (who accompanied us with the Engineers) remarked to the officers, 'How positively sanguine the Gen'l is that he will make this trip successfully!' And so I was! I assured him from the first, and from day to day, that the 7th Cav. would bring them thro' all right. What was the result? We had the good 'Custer luck' to strike across & encounter, instead of serious obstacles, the most favorable country yet met by us for marching!"

While on this dangerous lark, Custer the sharpshooter brought down an enormous elk (dubbed "King of the Forest") at 250 yards with his Remington. This and other animals he carefully prepared for preservation, having become an ardent pupil (amateur zoologist and taxidermist) of the expedition's scientific corps. As he informed Libbie, "You should see how very devoted I am to this! I can now preserve animals for all practical purposes. Often, after marching all day, a light may be seen in my tent long after the entire camp is asleep; and a looker-on might see me, with sleeves rolled above the elbow, busily engaged preparing the head of some animal killed in the chase."

The Audubon Society and Smithsonian Institution, as well as friends and family, were the recipients of Custer's rare specimens and splendid trophies. Libbie, when confronted with the visceral details of Autie's new-found joy, did not care for "a fine buffalo-head"—much less "the head & skin with claws of a big grizzly-bear."

> Camp in Montana Terr.
> Sept. 12th

Good-Morning, my Sunbeam!
. . . Mr. Eccleston [Rosser's assistant chief engineer] told me he has been writing the N. Pacific authorities as to whom the success of the Expedition is due: "When others saw obstacles & turned back, you went forward & led the way. As an act of justice, I want our people to know this." My Girl never saw people more "enthused" over her Bo than these R.R. representatives! . . .

459

Contrasting radically with Stanley's comments, Custer then proceeded to answer his wife's solicitude concerning an old scandal: "In regard to my arrest [by General Stanley] & its attendant circumstances, I am sorry it ever reached your ears. . . . Suffice it to say that I was placed in arrest for acting in strict conscientious discharge of what I knew to be my duty—a duty laid down expressly in 'Army Regulations.' Never was I more confident of the rectitude of my course, and of the official propriety of my position, knowing that I would be vindicated in the end. Gen'l Stanley was incapacitated by intoxication, so I assumed temporary command. Within 48 hrs., when sober again, Gen'l S. came to me & apologized in the most ample manner—acknowledging that he had been in the wrong, hoping I would forget it, and promising to turn over a new leaf. Twice did he repeat: 'I humbly beg your pardon, sir. I not only make this apology to you, but if you desire it, will gladly do so in the presence of all your officers.' With his subsequent faithful observance of his promise to begin anew in his official relations with me, I banished the affair from my mind. Nor do I cherish any but the kindliest sentiments towards him; for Gen'l Stanley, when not possessed by the fiend of intemperance, is one of the kindest, most agreeable & considerate officers I ever served under. Looking back I regard it, as do other officers, as a necessity; that an issue was forced on us, and that by my opposing instead of yielding, the interests of the Service were advanced. On one occasion, whiskey was destroyed by friends of Gen'l S. as the only means of getting him sober. This was publicly avowed. It had no connection with my difficulty with him, altho' the papers have coupled the two incidents together. Since my arrest, complete harmony exists between Gen'l Stanley & myself. He frequently drops in at my Hd.-Qrs., and adopts every suggestion I make."

Ft. Abe Lincoln, Dakota Terr.
Sept. 23rd

My Darling Bunkey,
    Well, here we are at last—not only "as good as new," but (if anything) heartier, healthier, more robust than ever! I have not

drawn a single sickly breath since we started on the Expedition; and if ever a lot of hale, hardy, athletic young fellows were assembled in one bunch, it is to be found in the officers of the 7th Cav. What a history & reputation this 7th Cavalry has achieved for itself! Altho' a new & young Regt., it has left all the older fellows in the lurch—until to-day it is the best & most widely known of any in the Service. . . .

The Expedition is now considered over, and I am relieved from further duty with it. . . . You may rely upon it that no grass grew under our feet on that return march! I knew that my family—consisting of One—was in advance somewhere; and, as the saying goes, I just "lit out."

Ft. Lincoln, D.T.
Sept. 28th

Darling,

. . . When you find that your dear Bo has just sent the 7th Cav. Band to serenade Gen'l Stanley on his departure for Ft. Sully, you will perhaps say to yourself, "He has been too forgiving again." Well, perhaps I have. [Libbie notes that Stanley "had been a persistent and exasperating enemy of my husband during the summer; and I could not forget or forgive, even after apologies were offered, especially as they were not offered in the presence of others."] I suppose you think I am of a very forgiving disposition. Well, perhaps I am. But I often think of the beautiful expression uttered by President Lincoln, and feel how nearly it expresses my belief: "With malice toward none, with charity for all." And I hope this will ever be mine to say.

Your devoted Boy,
Autie

Libbie packed up all her belongings and rode the rails to Toledo. Relieved at last of anxiety and suspense, but lost in a flurry of excitement and anticipation, she could hardly wait to meet her husband. Not finding him at the station, as planned, Libbie left her luggage and hurried downtown to the nearest hotel. As she went swishing along, glancing into shop windows at the latest fashions, she was suddenly swept off her feet. It was Autie, on his way to the railroad station!

Libbie almost fainted. Armstrong's sunburnt face was flushed even redder, but she could still spot where he had shaved off a summer's growth of fiery whiskers.

"I was ribbed by some officers on the way out here. They said no man would dare shave in a railroad car going forty miles an hour unless he was getting ready to meet his mistress!"

★18★

BLACK HILLS: GOLD!

Fort Abraham Lincoln was the new home of the 7th Cavalry in Dakota Territory; and its commandant was Colonel Custer, "guardian and gatekeeper of the Northwest." Finished in the fall of '73, it stood like a lone sprawling log sentinel on barren flats along the west bank of the Missouri ("Big Muddy") River, a bowshot across from the rowdy frontier railhead of Bismarck. It was hell's waterhole, a no man's land blasted by whirlwinds of murky-yellow alkali dust, but it was all theirs: the Garryowens' own outpost.

"His sanguine temperament made it seem little short of an earthly paradise," Libbie later wrote of her husband's reactions to virtual banishment. "He did not seem to realize that the prosaic and plain Government buildings were placed on a treeless and barren plain."

"Libbie," he said, "I believe I'm the happiest man on earth!"

The Custers made their headquarters in a large frame house above Barrackroom Row. Over the door of Armstrong's sanctum sanctorum, emblazoned with trophies and mementos, hung a triply-underlined word to the wise: "*MY ROOM. Lasciate Ogni Speranza, Voi Ch'entrate* [All hope abandon, ye who enter here]. *Cave Canem* [Beware the dog]." It was in this den of dens that the "Hero of the Plains" wrote "Battling with the Sioux on the Yellowstone" and began his "War Memoirs" for *Galaxy*.

Though seemingly exiled, there was more to occupy Custer's idle hours than reading and writing. Libbie noted in her diary: "It

463

is no light social care to be the wife of the Commanding Officer of so large a Post, and I find my time fully taken up with entertaining. . . . Autie is very busy with his official duties, for there are over 800 troops here, but he hunts a great deal & is delighted with the climate."

Spring, 1874. Gold fever struck the Northwest Frontier. It arrowed out of *Pâsâpâ*, the sacred Black Hills: the Himalayas of America, home of the gods, forbidden Abode of the Spirit of Death.

On May 15, 1874, Lieutenant General Sheridan wired Lieutenant Colonel Custer from Chicago: "Prepare at once to outfit an Expedition to the Black Hills to investigate rumors of large gold deposits & survey area for possible establishment of Military Posts."

Rich in animal, vegetable, and mineral wealth—embraced by the Belle Fourche and Cheyenne Rivers, rising from a 6000-square-mile nest of plenty amid the gaunt and scarified badlands of Wyoming and Dakota Territories—the Black Hills took their name from the rough mantle of dark pines covering their pallid heights, and from the darkness of their very mystery and grandeur. Since the Fort Laramie Treaty of 1868, *Pâsâpâ* were respected as a Sioux-Cheyenne reserve: "set apart for the absolute and undisturbed use and occupation of the Indians." But the relentless march of industrial civilization would trample such treaties in the dust. Now, in the name of Manifest Destiny, that sanctuary of the Great Sioux Reservation was to be arbitrarily violated.

Thursday, July 2, 1874; 8 A.M. With the regimental band grinding out "Garry Owen" and "The Girl I Left Behind Me," Custer led his thousand-man expedition out of Fort Lincoln and southwestward into a wilderness of sage and cactus. On a mule behind him plodded his new orderly, kid brother Bos: an angel-faced roughneck in buckskins and porkpie hat, sporting long carroty sideburns and an impish smile. Aunt Marie, Custer's new cook, drove a chuck wagon far in the rear. Eliza had long since run off with a black mule skinner. Guiding the column was dead-eyed, rowdy-dowdy pony-express rider Martha Jane Canary: ✗ᵢ "Calamity Jane."

Sheridan's special aides, Major George A. ("Sandy") Forsyth and Captain Fred Dent Grant, complemented Custer's staff as official observers. Captain William Ludlow, chief of engineers whose duties including mapping and mining the Black Hills, was joined by such distinguished guests (the "scientific corps") as Yale paleontologist-zoologist George B. Grinnell, Minnesota geology-archeology professor Newton H. Winchell (brother of Michigan geologist Alexander Winchell), and stereoscopic photographer William H. Illingworth of St. Paul.

It promised to be "a romantic and mysterious expedition," "a regular picnic," and its fate was entirely in Custer's hands. He never felt happier, never more free. Not so Libbie. For "the black hour" had come again, "and with it the terrible parting which seemed a foreshadowing of the most intense anguish that our Heavenly Father can send to His children. When I resumed my life, and tried to portion off the day with occupations in order that the time should fly faster, I found that the one silver thread running through the dark woof of the dragging hours was the hope of the letters we were promised."

> Prospect Valley, D.T.
> 12 m. from Montana Line
> July 15th, '74

My Darling Sunbeam,
. . . Every one—officers, men & civilians—are in the best of health & spirits. We are now encamped in the most beautiful & interesting country we have seen thus far—so beautiful that I directed Capt. Ludlow, who is making a map of the country, to call it Prospect Valley. . . .

No signs of Indians till the day before yesterday, when about 20 were seen near the column. They scampered off as soon as observed. Signal-smokes were sent up all around us yesterday afternoon, but no hostile demonstrations have been made. Our Indian guides say the signals are intended to let the villages

know where we are, so that they may keep out of our way. . . .
We expect to reach the base of the Black Hills in about 3
days. . . .

Y'r devoted Boy,
Autie

P.S.—The Indians have a new name for me, but I will not
commit it to paper.

(That new name was *Wâmânûnâchâ,* "Thief-Chief" or "Prince
of Thieves" [gold-hunters]. It complemented "Squaw-Killer.")

Over 150 miles southwest to the Little Missouri, eighty miles
to the Belle Fourche, another 80 miles to Harney Peak and the
heart of the hills.

Camp near Harney's Peak
Floral Valley, D.T.
Aug. 2nd

My darling Girl,

. . . Well, little one, the Expedition has surpassed my most
sanguine expectations. We have discovered a rich & beautiful
country. We have had no Indian fights, and will have none.
We have found gold (no doubt about it!), and probably other
valuable metals. All are well, and have been the entire trip. . . .

This valley in one respect presented the most wonderful
as well as beautiful aspect. Its equal I have never seen; and
such, too, was the testimony of all who beheld it. In no public
or private park have I ever seen such a profuse display of
flowers. Every step of our march was amidst flowers of the
most exquisite colors & perfume. So luxuriant in growth are
they that men plucked them without dismounting from the
saddle! (Some belonged to new or unclassified species.) It was
a strange sight to glance back at the advancing column of
Cavalry & behold the men with beautiful bouquets in their
hands, while the head-gear of their horses was decorated with
wreathes of flowers fit to crown a queen of May. Deeming it
a most fitting appellation, I named this Floral Valley. . . .

Good-Night, my sweet Rosebud.

Y'r loving Boy,
Autie

466

Custer's official reports to Sheridan stated //that gold has been found at several places, and it is the belief of those who are giving their attention to this subject that it will be found in paying quantities. . . . Veins of lead & strong indications of the existence of silver have been found. . . . Veins of what the geologists term gold-bearing quartz crop out on almost every hillside. . . . Iron & plumbago have been found, and beds of gypsum of apparent inexhaustible extent. . . . On some of the water-courses, almost every panful of earth produced gold in small (yet paying) quantities. . . . The miners report that they found gold among the roots of the grass; and, from that point to the lowest point reached, gold was found in paying quantities. It has not required an expert to find gold in the Black Hills, as even men without former experience in mining have discovered it at an expense of but little time or labor.)*

When this news reached "civilization," the Great Sioux Reservation was doomed to extinction.

On August 27, 1874, Sheridan read on the front page of the Chicago *Inter-Ocean:*

GOLD!

The Land of Promise—Stirring
News From the Black Hills

The Glittering Treasure
Found at Last—A Belt of
Gold Territory Thirty Miles Wide

The Precious Dust
Found in the Grass Under the
Horses' Feet—Excitement
Among the Troops

The following day's headlines read:

THE GOLD FEVER

Intense Excitement in the City Yesterday
Over the News from the Black Hills

The Mining Offices and Bullion Dealers
Invaded by Anxious Inquirers

General Sheridan Warns Miners and
Prospectors to Keep Away from the Scene,
As by Treaty that Section is Exempt from
Settlement by the Whites

Some Doubts as to Whether All the
Gold Region is Within the Reservation

Sitting-Bull (*Tâtonkâyotâkâ*), spiritual chief of the Sioux Nation, was angered and saddened: "We have been deceived by the white people. The Black Hills country was set aside for us by the Government. It was ours by solemn agreement, and we made the country our home. Our homes in the Black Hills were invaded when gold was discovered there. Now, the Indian must raise his arm to protect his women, his children, his home; and if the Government lets loose an army upon us to kill without mercy, we shall fight as brave men fight. We shall meet our enemies and honorably defeat them, or we shall all of us die in disgrace."

Yellowhair's comment: "I can't say I blame the poor savages; but apparently there is no stopping progress and civilization, undesirable though they may be to the romantic spirit."

Sunday, August 30, 1874; 4:30 P.M. Colonel Custer and the Black Hills Expedition trotted triumphantly into Fort Abraham Lincoln, the "boiler-makers" again thundering "Garry Owen":

We'll beat the bailiffs out of fun,
We'll make the mayors and sheriffs run,
We are the boys no man dares dun
If he regards a whole skin!

468

Libbie went wild with joy when she heard that raucous, rory-tory tune. She hid behind the front door as Old Curly and his Garryowens came parading by, ashamed to be seen laughing and crying all at the same time. But when Autie dismounted in front of the stoop, Libbie lost self-control and rushed out onto the porch.

The troopers cheered and tipped their hats as they jogged past. Mrs. Custer turned as red as her bearded husband. But from "the clouds and gloom" of those long summer days, she again walked in "the broad blaze of sunshine" which her husband's happy-go-lucky spirit radiated.

"Miss Libbie," Aunt Marie remarked merrily, "you sho' has the Gin'l; and I declare, you don't mind whar you is so long as you has him!"

"Marie," Armstrong said, hugging his wife, "you're looking at the happiest twosome on earth! Our cook is the best, our horses are the best, our dogs are the best, our regiment is the best, our post is the best. Why, I declare, I wouldn't exchange places with anyone—not even the President!"

"He often said that his duties on the Plains were the happiest events of his life—not that he loved war for war's sake, but that he loved to feel that he was 'on duty.' The freedom of the Plains . . . amply replaced the allurements of civil life," wrote Lawrence Barrett.

Custer returned to Fort Lincoln—now "home" to him—to encounter official troubles that would have their shattering repercussions in days to come.

While Custer was on his "Black Hills picnic," certain citizens of Bismarck (including the Mayor) had organized a racket whereby grain and other stores en route from Fargo to Fort Lincoln were intercepted at the Missouri ferry and purloined to Bismarck warehouses. Setting spies at work, Custer learned all he needed to know in order to march his entire command into Bismarck, declare martial law, arrest the guilty parties, and confiscate the contents of their storehouses. A storm of protest burst, in which Custer was showered with such epithets as "dictator" and "tyrant," but justice in most cases was served—though the heavens fell.

An attendant aggravation was Custer's festering relationship with Robert C. Seip, civil sutler or post trader at Lincoln. When Seip (who was doubtless in league with the Bismarck gang) decided arbitrarily to raise his prices after "Custer's Bismarck Raid," and when no end of argumentation could induce him to lower them, the post commandant instructed his captains to purchase all supplies in Bismarck and resell them at cost to their troopers. Seip's violent reaction involved a letter to his patron and protector, Secretary of War William W. Belknap, who immediately ordered Custer to cease and desist from "unnecessary and illegal conduct." Custer acquiesced without choice, but accused Belknap of favoritism and jobbery in what he termed "the post-tradership racket" whereby (as of 1870) appointments of sutlers were taken out of the hands of army officers and placed in those of a spoilsmongering bureaucrat.

Custer was not alone in such accusations, for Hazen had also charged Belknap with political patronage—and suffered for it by being banished to desolate Fort Buford, on the Missouri north of the Yellowstone country.

Incidental to this dispute, in late summer of '75, Belknap stopped at Fort Lincoln on his special tour of inspection. Custer snubbed him, returned the basket of champagne sent by Seip for his reception, then savored the sweetness of revenge. Apparently he liked the taste, for he never forgave Belknap. In Barrett's words, "Custer believed the Secretary to be his enemy."

Then came another embroilment with the very man who supported him in many of his contentions about governmental corruption. Hazen had not endeared himself to Custer by his "Some Corrections to 'My Life on the Plains,'" nor were feelings more favorable with the publication of a pamphlet entitled *Our Barren Lands*. In it Hazen took Custer to task for his Yellowstone and Black Hills reports, in which "my esteemed colleague" praised the Great Northwest as "the very garden of America, only needing cultivation to develop into a Paradise." In Hazen's opinion,

470

this "Great Northwest" was nothing but a continuation of the "Great American Desert": "a barren waste utterly unfit for human habitation and incapable of permanent amelioration." Therefore, to encourage emigration to "Hazen's Barren Belt" would be "wicked beyond expression." The controversy raged to a mutual standstill.

★ WASHINGTON:
BELKNAP'S ANACONDA

On the Indian Ring

"**I** EXPECT to be in the field this summer with the 7th, and think there will be lively work before us. I think the 7th Cav. may have its greatest campaign ahead."

Wednesday, March 15, 1876. The Custers had no sooner arrived back at Fort Lincoln from a winter vacation in New York than Armstrong was handed an urgent communiqué from Washington. He was summoned to appear at once before the House Committee on Expenditures in the War Department, then investigating certain alleged "irregularities" and "abuses," and to give testimony that might help turn the Tanner President's "carpetbag government" inside out.

While in New York, the Custers had spent a good deal of time hobnobbing with their old and influential friend—the great gun of the *Herald* whose fiery father had glamorized "The Boy General With the Golden Locks"—Mr. James Gordon Bennett, Jr. In private conversation, Custer told Bennett that the Indian Bureau was a den of thieves run by "Useless" Grant's younger brother, Orvil. He also said that drummers, gunrunners, and carpetbaggers were tickling Orvil's palm with thousand-dollar bills for big-paying appointments to post traderships.

But that wasn't the worst of it. Custer also informed Bennett that Secretary of War William W. Belknap was raking in graft from frontier sutlers, quartermasters, and Indian agents, who were profiteering by smuggling rifles and liquor to reservation Indians and making soldiers pay through the nose (to cover their kick-backs to Belknap & Co.) for goods sold cheaper off limits. Custer then added jokingly: "The plea to the War Department by an honorable quartermaster, pestered by civilian grafters, is now proverbial: 'In the name of all the gods, relieve me from this position! They've almost got up to my price!' "

Custer's allegations corroborated those of Hazen, who had stirred up the hornet's nest by charging Belknap with bribery: the sale of a post tradership at Fort Sill to a sutler named Marsh. Custer could mention the same of Fort Lincoln, regarding Seip. The noose tightened around Belknap's neck.

On February 10, after the Custers had left for Fort Lincoln, a New York *Herald* editorial called for a Congressional investigation of the War Department and Indian Bureau. It branded William Belknap and Orvil Grant as boodlers and spoilsmongers, and invited the President to ask his kid brother how much of a haul he had made in the Sioux country by starving squaws and papooses whose government rations were stolen and sold at black-market prices, and whose fired-up braves were "jumping" the reservations with Army breechloaders and patent ammunition.

Fired by his conversations with Custer, Frederick Whittaker of Sheldon & Company (publishers of *Galaxy*) wrote: "The people of America will not fail to remark that Sitting-Bull's truest and most persistent allies are the Indian Department and the Indian-traders, who supply him with Winchester rifles and patent ammunition, so that his men are better armed than the troops of the War Department. . . . The corruption fund of this department is so great that public opinion has not yet succeeded in killing the abuse. Politicians of both parties are interested in the money, and nothing else holds the Indian Department together. The cost of the Indians to the Government has risen in ten years from less than a million to twenty millions annually, and Indian-agents and traders grow rich on the stealings of supplies used by Indians to kill soldiers, while the residue of the stealings goes into election funds."

In an interview with a Chicago *Times* reporter, Captain Benteen laid the blame for Indian outbreaks where he felt it belonged: "I think the Indian Bureau has been entirely responsible, and the cause has been the enormous pilfering and stealing from the Indians. . . . It is this constant robbery which goads them to outbreaks."

And Brigadier General George Crook, an old Indian fighter: "Greed and avarice on the part of the whites—in other words, the almighty dollar—is at the bottom of nine-tenths of all our Indian troubles."

"I would have more faith in the Great White Father if he had not so many bald-headed thieves working for him." These are the words of Sitting-Bull, and they explain much of what was to occur in the following months.

On December 1, 1875, Secretary of the Interior Zachariah Chandler had written War Secretary Belknap: "I have the honor to inform you that I have this day directed the Commissioner of Indian Affairs [Edward P. Smith] to notify . . . Sitting-Bull, and the others outside their reservations, that they must return to their reservations before January 31st, 1876; and that if they neglect or refuse so to move, they will be reported to the War Dep't as hostile Indians, and that a military force will be sent to compel them to obey the order of the Indian Dep't."

On the sixth, Commissioner Smith issued orders to Indian agents that all Sioux and Cheyennes found off reservations after January 31 were to be treated as hostiles (*i.e.*, to be refused shelter and supplies); that all reservation Indians were to be disarmed immediately, and that no further sale of arms and ammunition to Indians was to be enacted—under penalty of prosecution.

It is believed that many of those Indians (besides hot-blooded bucks and dog-warriors) who left reservations did so under threat or compulsion of starvation; that their defiance of the white government was a mere bid to hunt food, to provide for their victimized families. If so, then those directives from Washington were nothing less than death warrants; for without the means to hunt, the question of survival was left to chance. And that "chance" was a poor one indeed, in the dead of winter!

Having no good reason to trust the white man, Sitting-Bull determined not to suffer further degradation by surrendering himself into the deadly care of what Custer termed "a combination of rascals dedicated to enriching themselves at the Red-man's expense." In so determining, the spiritual leader of the great Sioux-Cheyenne Confederacy flung down the gauntlet before his tormentors, who contemptuously dismissed him as "Slightly Recumbent Gentleman Cow."

Grant's "Quaker Policy" was assailed unmercifully in the press, both East and West. His statement, "Our superiority of strength and advantage of civilization should make us lenient toward the Indian," was met with this rebuke in the Chicago *Tribune:* "Give us Phil Sheridan, and send Phil-anthropy to the Devil."

With Belknap's resignation on March 2, Sherman (once a figurehead) finally took control of what had been arbitrarily usurped: his full authority as General of the Army. Returning to Washington from "exile" in St. Louis, he immediately telegraphed Sheridan and Brigadier General Alfred H. Terry (commanding the Department of Dakota) that Colonel Custer had been instructed to repair at once to Fort Lincoln and prepare with equal dispatch for a spring campaign against the hostiles.

The Cheyenne *Daily Leader* rejoiced: "It is safe to say that the West now has one friend in high official position. . . . We have some confidence that the naturally perverse head of Gen. Sherman will lead him to persist that there is no peace; and after while, humanity may be beaten into the heads of the Indian-agents, ring-speculators, and pseudo-philanthropists of the East."

Custer, overjoyed by thoughts of active service and an independent command, did not welcome that inopportune communication from the House Sergeant-at-Arms, summoning him to appear before Representative Heister Clymer's investigating committee. He wired Clymer from Fort Lincoln on March 16:

"While I hold myself in readiness to obey the summons of your Committee, I telegraph to state that I am engaged upon an important Expedition intended to operate against the hostile Indians; and I expect to take the field early in April. My presence here is deemed very necessary. In view of this, would it not be satisfactory for you to forward to me such questions as may be necessary, allowing me to return my replies by mail?"

No, it was not satisfactory so to oblige an outraged Democratic Congress. Custer must testify in person.

"I am sorry to have you go," General Terry wired from St. Paul, "for I fear it will delay our movements. . . . Your services are indispensable."

Custer left Lincoln at once, alone, and so started a train of circumstances which was to end in the untimely death of the best cavalry chief on the American continent. But he did not leave in utter reluctance; for in his pocket was a letter just received from Colonel Miles at Fort Leavenworth, containing this provocative encouragement: "You have an opportunity now of clearing Washington of your enemies & that corps of lobbyists that have controlled legislation for years."

Already charged with neglect and incompetence, Columbus Delano had resigned as Secretary of the Interior and been replaced by Zach Chandler. The Bureau of Indian Affairs, as a self-defensive gesture, then issued its fateful order to "Sitting-Bull's band and other wild & lawless Indians residing without the bounds of their reservation." Unfortunately, even if Sitting-Bull wished to obey it, this order was issued and received too late to make any difference; and it was not until spring thaw that outlying tribes heard as much as a hint of it. The die was then cast, and every "hostile" prepared for the worst.

On March 2, 1876—the very day he tendered his resignation to President Grant—the House of Representatives resolved "That William W. Belknap, late Secretary of War, be impeached of high crimes and misdemeanors while in office." The Democrats in Congress, out to "get" the Republican Administration, thus began an inquisition of "the gigantic system of fraud by which the Indian Ring played into the hands of Army contractors."

Belknap was arrested on the fifth, before he could flee the country, and later gave testimony that laid the entire blame for illegal money transactions on his former wives: two sisters who had made

476

a consecutive killing on their husband's influence since '69. The all-male tribunal believed him, and he was subsequently acquitted, but scandal and shame continued to haunt Grant and hound his bureaucratic coterie.

Though Custer concurred with Sherman in his assertion that the Capital was "corrupt as Hell," he did not heed his warning to avoid it like "a pest-house."

Wednesday, March 29, 1876. Custer strode into the Capitol, was sworn in before the Clymer Committee, and answered questions put to him by the chairman (who, by a quirk of fate, had been Belknap's roommate at Princeton) and his associate, Mr. Robbins.

When asked (by Clymer) what effect the President's proclamation of January 11, 1875, had upon the value of post traderships along the Missouri, by its extension of the Great Sioux Reservation across the east bank of that river, Custer replied: "It greatly enhanced their value by making them a more perfect monopoly, by removing all opposition and rivalry." He then expressed his belief that the proclamation had dispossessed people who claimed (by virtue of the Homestead Act) that they had a title to such land, and that such arbitrary annexation also entailed the driving out of private (honest) traders in favor of government (dishonest) sutlers. The new law, in supporting a combination in restraint of trade, sealed the doom of free enterprise: "If any man shall introduce goods on an Indian reservation, they shall be confiscated."

In citing Seip for a profiteer, Custer stated that "the prices that were charged the officers and soldiers became so exorbitant that as many as could, purchased what they desired elsewhere. They did so until Mr. Seip made a written complaint and forwarded it to the Secretary of War, claiming that under the privilege which he held as trader, nobody—no officer even—had a right to buy anything elsewhere or bring it there, but must buy everything through him."

Custer then testified as to the alleged kickbacks involved in the Indian Ring, declaring that he had threatened Seip into a confession: that government traders "estimated their yearly profits at $15,000"; that "about one-third of it" was paid to J. M. Hedrick, Belknap's brother-in-law and inspector of internal revenue in Iowa; that another portion of it was paid to E. W. Rice, a Washington claim agent and "an intimate friend of the Secretary of War"; and that "the division of those profits was such that the trader was finally left with but about $2500 or $3000 out of the $15,000. I asked him then if he knew of any other person to whom this money was paid. He said that he knew positively only that he paid to Rice and Hedrick, but he was always under the impression that a portion of it went to the Secretary of War."

Custer's testimony now turned to Orvil L. Grant, the President's kid brother and a kingpin in the Indian Ring; that he and one A. L. Bonnafon had procured the sutlership monopoly of Standing Rock Agency and Forts Belknap, Peck (which General Stanley branded "the centre of all the villainy of the Indian Dep't"), and Berthold; and that it had come to Custer's knowledge that trader J. W. Raymond claimed to several people in Bismarck that he had paid Grant $1,000 for getting him the appointment as sutler at Fort Berthold from ex-Secretary of the Interior Columbus Delano. The absolutism of the Grant-Bonnafon combine was such, Custer later attested, that "An application came to me from the Indian agency at Standing Rock for troops to close up and remove the store kept by Mrs. Galpin, a full-blood Sioux squaw, who was engaged in trading with the Indians; and I declined to grant the request."

When asked what he believed to have been the effect (upon his troops) of Belknap's law of 1870, placing the appointments of post traders in the hands of the Secretary of War, Custer answered, "The effect has been to greatly embarrass them and add to the inconveniences of frontier life, which even under the most favorable circumstances are very great; as the troops and officers are required to pay what would be considered in the States exorbitant prices for everything, owing to the immense distances that goods have to be transported. That is the case always; but this law placing the appointment in the hands of the

Secretary of War, and then being used in the manner that he has used it—by putting these appointments at the disposal of a certain ring, and taxing the profits in this way by these exactions, all of which had to come out of the pockets of the soldiers and officers—has, as I said before, greatly increased the inconveniences and expense of living on the frontier."

After expressing his belief that Hedrick was raking in kickbacks from Fort Buford as well as Fort Lincoln, Custer made the pointed remark: "I always regarded the Secretary of War as a silent partner in all these transactions."

Samuel A. Dickey and Robert Wilson were trading partners at Fort Lincoln until the appointment of R. C. Seip; and according to Custer, Dickey and Wilson were removed "because they did not divide [their profits with Hedrick and Rice]." When a rumor reached Lincoln of their imminent removal, Dickey informed Custer: "I don't know whether you know it or not, but there isn't a post on this river that doesn't pay a tax except ours; and we don't pay simply because my brother is chairman of the Military Committee." But as soon as Dickey's brother "went out of Congress," Dickey "went out of the sutlership."

When asked if Seip was "a man of good moral character," Custer hesitated and smiled: "Well, sir, I would hate to testify to the moral character of any post trader in these times."

Returning to the controversial extension of the Great Sioux Reservation, Clymer requested Custer's opinion as to the President's "real object" in issuing that order. The rationalization was that he had issued it "out of care for the welfare of the Indians there, so as to prevent them from having unlimited supplies of rum." Custer said, "I don't believe that the Indians got one drink less by the extension of the reservation. . . . I think the profits of the traders left the morals of the Indians a long way behind. That was the general impression along the river, that the order was for the benefit of the traders."

Custer then testified that when Orvil Grant and Bonnafon attempted to remove a private trader named Thum from Fort Peck, Thum "obtained some affidavits showing that there were

479

some frauds in the Indian Department" in which Grant and others were "mixed up"; and that when Grant saw these affidavits, he allowed Thum to continue his trade. The "alleged frauds" involved the criminal selling to army posts of corn intended for reservation Indians: one of the prime causes of discontent, and starvation, among the Northern Cheyennes and Sioux. In this manner, "that corn was paid for twice by the Government." Custer added, "Speaking of Indian supplies, I have known boats passing up the river to trade off Indian flour to citizens along the river."

When prompted, Custer got another dig at Belknap by declaring that a contractor named Smith had informed him: "There is a great deal of smuggling, particularly in the whisky trade, across the British border"; and "one of the objects of the Secretary of War's visit [to the frontier] . . . was to effect some arrangement . . . by which facilities should be provided for getting whisky across the border at some reduced rate. . . . It was some arrangement by which the traders at those posts along the frontier would have increased advantages."

Custer later cited a letter he had received from Mr. Wilson, wherein he called attention to the sale of traderships on the Missouri River, and said that he expected to be able to prove that Belknap made these posts articles of traffic, and that he was the most corrupt official who ever occupied high position."

Clymer posed a loaded question: "Had the Secretary of War been a man of purity of character and integrity of purpose, could these frauds have continued going on?"

Answer: "They could not possibly."

"And it was because they were protected and shielded by him that they occurred?"

"They could not possibly have been carried on to anything like the extent they were without his connivance and approval; and when you ask me how the morale or character of the Army is affected, I—although belonging to the Army—think it is one of the highest commendations that could be made of the service to say that it has not been demoralized when the head has shown himself to be so unworthy."

Custer was re-examined on April 4. The investigating committee then learned how Belknap had "sealed the mouths and tied the hands" of Army officers by the issuance of an order (1873) forbidding them to "solicit, suggest, or recommend action to any member of Congress upon any military subject. . . . There has been no voice from the Army since that order was issued. . . . It is regarded by the Army as a step to place the control of all information that officers might be in possession of in the hands of the Secretary of War, so that nothing should get beyond him except that which he chose to transmit. And in connection with the recent developments, it was about the most effectual safeguard that he could have thrown around his conduct to prevent exposure."

During his jaunt in New York, Custer was foremost of those who persuaded *Herald* reporter Ralph Meeker (who had spent six months in Dakota Territory) to write an exposé of the Indian Bureau. On March 31, 1876, the *Herald* featured an extra (anonymous) article entitled "Belknap's Anaconda." Bennett allegedly sent Custer a check for $150. Seip, in his testimony, stated "that he understood General Custer had written an article for the New York *Herald* entitled 'Belknap's Anaconda'; that he cashed a draft on James Gordon Bennett for General Custer; that he knows nothing more about the matter."

Meeker, cross-examined on April 13, backed Custer's testimony by asserting that "the general opinion among the people out there [in Dakota] was that the Indian traders had to pay large sums to Orvil Grant, and that the post traders had to pay large sums to General Belknap and others in Washington; and when General Belknap came down through there, it was called a blackmailing tour on his part." He also confirmed the allegation that Belknap's "real object" in touring the Northwest was to establish a "whisky ring" on the Canadian border. "I understood that Secretary Delano and General Belknap and Commissioner Smith, I think, were going to have one grand divvy and a pool."

481

When questioned as to his assistance by General Custer, who had endorsed or cashed checks and telegraphically transmitted "scoops" for him in Dakota, Meeker responded: "He said that he was a Government officer, and it was his duty to see that the Government was protected, whether the officers above him were in favor of it or not. I told him I was astonished at his boldness. . . . He would generally say that he thought he was doing the right thing; that the Government, to his certain knowledge, was being defrauded; that he knew something about these Indian frauds, and that he thought they ought to be exposed. I told him I liked to hear him talk in that way, it was so different from the way many of the other officers talked. . . . I was convinced that General Belknap was a kind of a second ["Boss"] Tweed, and therefore I thought he was a man that would bear watching. . . . It was thought that the best thing I could do was to keep out of his way. So General Custer told me; and I thought that if a man like General Custer, so brave and with so good a record, would advise a newspaper correspondent to keep out of the way of the Secretary of War, he had a pretty good idea that the charges were true, and that the Secretary might lay for me. . . . It was the common talk that General Custer served him right [by snubbing him]. . . . The majority of the best people said that as the Secretary of War was the great national chief, they were glad to see there was one man who had the courage to treat him as he deserved."

Though regarding him as "one of the most splendid soldiers that ever lived," Colonel "Sandy" Forsyth (Sheridan's personal aide) thought that Custer's evidence "was all hearsay and not worth a tinker's damn"; that it was apparent "he did not know anything." The "radical [Republican] press" branded him a "retailer of gossip." However, the outcome of this explosive scandal was that many of the most flagrant abuses were abolished. Orvil Grant confessed matter-of-factly, acknowledging no regrets except that his share of the graft left much to be desired.

On March 30, 1876, the New York *World* broke a scoop, datelined Washington: "General Custer was the hero of a severe caning affair in which E. W. Rice, a claim-agent here, was the worsted party. Rice has long been an intimate friend of General Belknap's, and is believed by a good many to have been the medium through whom a large part of the post tradership money passed from the buyers to General Belknap. General Custer's testimony tended to prove this, the General testifying among other things that he had been told that in a certain instance a post-tradership was secured through the payment of $5000 to Rice. He (Rice) replied by a newspaper card, in which he said that if General Custer did say that any money was ever paid to him (Rice) for a post-tradership he was a liar. To-night Custer met Rice on G Street and gave him a very severe caning."

483

★20★

WHITE HOUSE:
THE UNKIND CUT

Oɴ April 1, Armstrong dashed off a note to Elizabeth, fretting back at Fort Lincoln. He had made his "Darling Sunbeam" stay put this time, because the Plains were blizzard-blown. "He took my breath away by telling me he could not endure the anxiety of having me go through such peril again. In vain I pleaded." No longer daring to press his proverbial luck where Libbie was concerned, he left her with a few comforting words: "Be sure it's all for the best, little one. You know we always find it so in the end." But "Life seemed insupportable until I received a despatch saying that my husband had again passed safely over that two hundred and fifty miles of country where every hour life is in jeopardy."

Washington, 4–8–76

My precious Darling,
   I cannot tell you how overwhelmed I am with engagements, but I cannot let my little girl's birthday pass without a word from her dear Bo! . . . I have been recipient of kindest attentions from all papers except a few radical. I am surprised if a morning passes without *some* abuse of myself! But leading papers thruout the country commend my courage. . . .
   "Sunset" Cox made an elaborate speech on the Indian question—citing the Battle of the Washita, "Garry-Owen," &c. After it he came up to me where I was standing & said, "Well, Custer, I guess I've taken your scalp." To which I replied, "Wait till I get you on the Plains! Then I'll turn you over to those gentle friends of yours. . . ."

Washington, 4–12–76

My Darling,

I calculate on one week more here. Should I be detained longer, I should give up all thought of a summer campaign & send for my Bunkey. . . .

The Cincinnati *Enquirer* & St. Louis *Republican* & other papers of that stamp commend me in highest degree, while the two radical papers controlled by the Belknap Clique vie with one another in abusing me. I do not let this disturb me. . . . The Belknap Clique leave no stone unturned to injure me. Mr. [Larry] Cobright, Agent for the Associated Press, said they had given him a lot of defamatory stuff about me that he had refused to use. . . . I know you are anxious, but I believe I have done nothing rashly. And all honest, straight-forward men commend my course. . . .

Washington, 4–17–76

My darling Sunbeam,

. . . To-day I appear before the Military Committee, to-morrow the Belknap Impeachment Committee, and hope to conclude my errand here. I have urged both Committees to release me; . . . for, as I have informed them, nearly all my evidence is hearsay. The Radical papers continue to serve me up regularly. Neither has said one word against Belknap. . . .

The lines you sent me are lovely. I showed them to a lady at this hotel. She said, "Your sweetheart sent them. Never your wife!" I told her "Both are one." "What? How long have you been married?" "Twelve years." "And haven't got over that?" "No. And never shall! . . ."

Your Devoted
Autie

Custer was growing desperate. Investigating committees and social engagements kept him on the run day and night. Would they never cease? Time was a-wasting. In another month, the 7th Cavalry would be marching off on its summer campaign against hostiles and renegades in the Yellowstone country. Come hell or high water, he just *had* to get back to Fort Lincoln—

485

before it was too late. Before General Terry perforce appointed Major Reno to take command, to leave without him, to steal his thunder and reap the glory.

The New York *Herald* editorialized: "Custer's statement that one regiment of cavalry—with pardonable pride he mentions his own Seventh—could handle the Sioux in one campaign as effectively as ten years of treaty-making and treaty-breaking, must be seriously regarded. In any such campaign, who else has the skill, the matchless daring, to equal his leadership? The Boy General of 1864 is now the mature Indian-fighter, the darling of his troops, and in the full prime of his great powers."

Custer was at philosophical cross purposes. His romantic spirit had sided with the South, yet reason obliged him to fight for the North; and though that same spirit was in sympathy with the Indian, making his delay in Washington less dreadful than others imagined, Custer was still an instrument of Manifest Destiny.

However, in taking issue with men like Sherman and Sheridan (who advocated an assimilation-or-extermination policy), Custer wrote that a rose-colored view "is equally erroneous with that which regards the Indian as a creature possessing the human form but divested of all other attributes of humanity. . . . In him we will find the representative of a race . . . incapable of being judged by the rules or laws applicable to any other known race of men. . . . In studying the Indian character, while shocked & disgusted by many of his traits & customs, I find much to be admired and still more of deep & unvarying interest. . . . Study him, fight him, civilize him if you can, he remains still the object of your curiosity—a type of man peculiar & undefined, subjecting himself to no known law of civilization, contending determinedly against all efforts to win him from his chosen mode of life. He stands in the group of nations solitary & reserved, seeking alliance with none, mistrusting & opposing the advances of all. Civilization may & should do much for him, but it can never civilize him. . . . He cannot be himself & be civilized; he fades away & dies. Cultivation such as the white-man would give him deprives him of his identity."

486

Custer comes to a remarkable conclusion—remarkable in that it absolves him of the epithet of "Indian-hater," and enhances the tragic glory of his fate, at the mercy of those he most respected and admired:

"If I were an Indian, I often think I would greatly prefer to cast my lot among those of my people adhered to the free open plains rather than submit to the confined limits of a reservation —there to be the recipient of the blessed benefits of civilization, with its vices thrown in without stint or measure."

In his attempt to return to the land of his predilections, Custer fell upon the biggest stumbling block of his career: President Grant. It wasn't enough that he had arrested Grant's son Fred for drunkenness during the Black Hills Expedition of '74. It wasn't enough that the great Indian fighter had, in his *Galaxy* articles and before the Clymer Committee, attacked or questioned the Tanner President's "carpetbag-Quaker policy." Now he had helped ruin brother Orvil and Unconditional Surrender's old comrade-at-arms, General Belknap. This was the last straw!

In a vengeful fit, President Grant ordered Secretary of War Alphonso Taft not to let Colonel Custer leave Washington under any circumstances. "He'll sit here and rot, if I have my way. Let Sherman appoint Terry to command the expedition out of Fort Lincoln. I'll tame that wild man if it's the last thing I ever do."

Saturday, April 29, 1876. The Belknap Impeachment Committee told Custer he was now free to leave the Capital—so far as *they* were concerned. Relieved of this responsibility, Custer flashed telegrams to Sheridan in Chicago and Terry at St. Paul: "Am on my way!" Or so he thought. Neither Sheridan nor Terry dared "okay" any unauthorized move, so no replies came from St. Paul or Chicago. Instead, Sheridan wired Terry that unless otherwise instructed he was to lead the punitive expedition against the Sioux: official War Department orders.

George Armstrong Custer called on Alphonso Taft, who said, "My hands are tied." Then he dropped in on his last resort,

487

William Tecumseh Sherman, General-in-Chief of the United States Army.

"I'd be damn glad to let you go," Uncle Billy said heartily. "You're just the man to bring Sitting-Bull to his knees. Go on to Fort Lincoln. Go on to Hell! Only get Sam's 'okay' before you do so."

Custer telegraphed Terry: "I will leave Washington at earliest moment practicable. My absence from my Command is wholly against my desire."

Monday, May 1, 1876; 10 A.M. Custer sat in the White House anteroom. He was fidgeting and sweating; again and again he rose to pace the carpeted floor.

2 P.M. Still sweating it out, still no word from the President. Custer finally lost patience. He lunged out of the White House and strode up to the War Department, where he burst unbidden into General Sherman's office.

Adjutant General Edward D. Townsend informed him that Sherman was out of town, but was expected back from New York before evening. Custer then informed Townsend: "Well, I'm leaving at seven to join my command. Will you give me written authority?"

"I don't see why not!" Townsend answered, snatching paper and pen. "Sherman and Taft have both said that your getting out of here as soon as possible is the best thing you could do under the circumstances. By the way," he added with a suggestive smile, "do you have Grant's permission?"

Custer answered abstractedly: "Oh, I shall get it before I go."

Townsend nodded. "This scrap of paper won't be worth a Confederate blueback if you don't! Stop off on your way out and get Marcy's endorsement."

With Inspector General Randolph B. Marcy's written authorization tucked into his tunic pocket ("It is my understanding that Gen'l Sherman desires you to proceed directly to your station, as Gen'l Terry requested; therefore, in the absence of the Gen'l, you have my consent."), Custer hastened back to the White House.

At 3 P.M., chief Presidential aide Rufus Ingalls stepped into the anteroom and said sheepishly, "I'm sorry, Custer." He shook his bald head and shrugged. "I asked the President if he knew you were waiting outside. He said he did. I had given him your card this morning. He says he doesn't want to see you. 'Tell Colonel Custer I refuse to see him,' he says. All this time—I tell you, Custer, *all this time*—I kept urging him: 'At least spare Custer the indignity of waiting outside. Send him a message to save his time. So much is due to his past services *at least*.' So *now,* after all this time, he says: 'I don't want to see him.' Custer, I'm sorry. Truly I am."

Custer smiled weakly, laying his hand on Ingalls' shoulder. "It's all right, old fellow. You want to wait just a minute till I write a note to that man in there?"

Ingalls nodded.

Custer sat down, pulled pencil and pad out of his jacket, scribbled the following message:

5–1–76

To His Exc'y the President:—

To-day, for the third time, I have sought an interview with the President—not to solicit a favor, except to be granted a brief hearing, but to remove from his mind certain unjust impressions concerning myself which I have reason to believe are entertained against me. I desire this opportunity simply as a matter of justice; and I regret that the President has declined to give me an opportunity to submit to him a brief statement which justice to him, as well as to me, demanded.

Resp'y submitted:

G. A. Custer
Lt.-Col. 7th Cav.
Bvt. Maj.-Gen. U.S.A.

"Here. Take this in to the President."
"But aren't you going to wait for a reply?"
"It's useless. He refuses to see me!"

489

Poor Grant, Custer thought as he walked out of the White House. *He's dying of rum and cancer, and jackleg politics.*

Custer packed some of his duds and headed over to Sherman's hotel. It was 4 P.M. The desk clerk told him that the General wasn't back yet from New York, but was expected before dark. Custer went and wolfed down an early dinner. He popped into Sherman's hotel again at six o'clock. No; sorry, not in yet. No telling when he would show up!

Armstrong hustled back to his own hotel, finished packing, and checked out. At 7 P.M. he was off to New York aboard the evening express. *Good riddance to Washington!* Foot-loose and fancy-free at last! A wild man at large, as yet untamed by the President of the United States.

Clouds gathered on the horizon of glory, and the thunder of doom rumbled in the West.

> My race of glory run, and race of shame,
> And I shall shortly be with them that rest.

490

21

ST. PAUL:
"LAME-HIP" TERRY

"GENERAL Custer blew into the *Herald* office like a fresh April breeze," wrote editor Joseph Clarke. "There was something so fine and broad and free in his carriage and his air, in the ruddy bronze of his face, in the laughing blue of his eyes, in the curl of his yellow hair, that one's heart went out to him. . . . Self-confidence shone in his open brow. Presently he was gone, and his absence left a painful void; the thought, 'he will risk everything rather than fail,' persisted. I do not recall another single meeting in my life that made the same impression of uplift and fatality combined."

Custer dined with Mr. and Mrs. Lawrence Barrett. "He predicted a severe campaign," the great tragedian later wrote, "but was not doubtful of the result. He was so associated with success, had escaped from so many dangers, . . . that he seemed invincible."

Charles Osborn, broker to the notorious financier and speculator Jay Gould, gave a luncheon in Custer's honor. Present was Major General Grenville M. Dodge, builder of the Union Pacific Railroad and Gould's associate in westward extension of rail travel. "Custer, in his conversation & in his assertion of what his regiment could do, said that his regiment could whip & defeat all the Indians on the Plains, and was very rash in his statements. . . . I said to him that . . . if he was going out to fight the Indians with any idea that they were to be easily whipped, he was greatly mistaken."

491

Dodge may have reminded Custer of Captain William J. Fetterman, who had boasted in '66: "Give me eighty men and I'll ride through the whole Sioux nation!" Fetterman was given his eighty men—was ambushed and annihilated, near Fort Phil Kearny, by a dozen Indians under Crazyhorse. He and Captain Fred Brown committed suicide, each shooting the other in preference to a slow death by torture. The so-called "Fetterman Massacre" thus became proverbial on the frontier for reckless daring and stupidity. Custer chuckled, said Fetterman was a fool; that the 7th Cavalry numbered far more than eighty men, and knew their enemy well enough not to get caught in such a ridiculous trap.

Armstrong spent only a few memorable hours in the Empire City, bidding hello and good-by to his many cultured and influential acquaintances, those who had encouraged and stood by him for the past decade. He wrote Elizabeth:

> My precious Sunbeam,
> . . . I have gotten more requests for articles from periodicals & dailies than 10 writers could satisfy. I am over-run with invitations! . . . Have seen hosts of friends. I hope to leave for Chicago to-night. . . . Do not be anxious. I seek to follow a moderate & prudent course, avoiding prominence. Nevertheless, everything I do (however simple & unimportant) is noticed & commented on. This only makes me more careful. And never mind about "U.S." The President is mistaken; but it will all come right at last, if I do my duty. If a consciousness of virtue establishes a claim to happiness, then I am happy! And I have no regrets. It is better to be Right than to be President!
> I have heard by telegraph from Gen'l Terry. I believe a mutual good-feeling subsists between us. He is anxious for me to return. . . .
> P.S.—I hope (before this reaches you) to telegraph, "I'm a-comin'!"

Fred Whittaker of *Galaxy* was one of the last in the East to bid Custer farewell. In his words: "Custer looked worn and thin, and somewhat worried, . . . a great change from the debonair cavalier.

492

... His manner conveyed the impression of a nervous man with his nerves all on edge, in a state of constant repressed impatience."

Early Tuesday morning, May 2, the following telegram from Sherman opened Sheridan's eyes: "I am this moment advised that Gen'l Custer started last night for St. Paul & Ft. Ab. Lincoln. He was not justified in starting without seeing the President or myself. Please intercept him at Chicago or St. Paul, and order him to halt & await further orders. Meantime, let the Expedition from Ft. Lincoln proceed without him."

Thursday morning, May 4, 1876. Custer stepped off the train at Chicago, where he was greeted by Colonel Forsyth of Sheridan's personal staff: "General, I'm obliged to inform you that you're under arrest by order of General Sherman." He added stiffly, "Here is my authorization," and thrust forward an official envelope.

"And here is mine, Sandy." Custer scowled, pulling out his clearance papers signed by Generals Townsend and Marcy.

"I'm sorry, Custer, but I cannot accept them. They've been countermanded by these orders."

Custer ripped open the envelope and snatched out four folded slips of paper. He skimmed over the first one, from Sheridan's adjutant: "Agreeably to instructions contained in the enclosed copy of a telegraphic despatch from the General of the Army, of the 2nd inst., the Lieut.-Gen'l Comdg. the Division directs you to remain in Chicago until the receipt of further orders from superior authority, to be furnished you thro' these Hd.-Qrs."

Custer then read Sherman's official wire. Sheridan's telegram to Terry, dated April 28, was also there for Custer to scan: "The Gen'l of the Army telegraphs me that instructions have been rec'd thro' the Sec'y of War, coming from the President, to send some one other than Custer in charge of the Expedition from Ft. Lincoln. . . . After a careful consideration of the situation, I think the best way to meet it (and that promising the most satisfaction & the greatest success) would be for you to go yourself."

493

Terry's reply to Sheridan, April 29: "I will go myself."

When Custer handed the slips back to their bearer, Forsyth said, "General Sheridan expressed a desire to see you at once."

"Well, I should think so!" Custer snapped, his face mantled with humiliation.

The two officers, coldly courteous to each other, hopped into a waiting hack and rode downtown to Division Headquarters.

Sheridan welcomed Custer as ardently as ever, but the boy general was in no mood for good cheer. "What's the meaning of all this, Phil?"

"Custer, I swear to Christ, I don't know any more about the cause of that order than you do. But consider yourself my honored guest while you're here."

"Thanks, but I'm not staying. Would you have any objection to my telegraphing Sherman for an explanation?"

"No. Go right ahead! And good luck!"

Moments later, a message flashed over the wires: "I have seen your despatch to Gen'l Sheridan directing me to await orders here, and am at a loss to understand that portion referring to my departure from Washington without seeing you or the President. . . . At my last interview with you, I informed you that I would leave Washington Monday night to join my Command; and you in conversation replied that it was the best thing I could do. Besides, you frequently during my stay in Washington called my attention to the necessity of my leaving as soon as possible."

Custer sweated it out all morning. When no response came, he wired another message to Sherman at 2:30 P.M.: "In leaving Washington, I had every reason to believe I was acting in strict accordance with your suggestions & wishes. I ask you, as General of the Army, to do me justice in this matter."

No answer. Custer knew why, and had hoped beyond hope. It wasn't Sherman who was putting him to the torture. Grant was working that rack from both ends, dead set on pulling his victim to pieces. Sherman had assured Custer that the President had no charges to make against him; but now, as Sherman remarked to

494

the President's secretary (U. S. Grant, Jr.), "Custer is now subject to any measure of discipline which the President may require."

Still kicking his heels, Custer made a last-ditch effort to arouse some response out of Sherman. That evening, for the third time, he telegraphed: "After you read my despatch of to-day, I would be glad if my detention could be authorized at Ft. Lincoln, where my family is, instead of at this point."

Not a word flashed back. "Grant's Revenge" was almost complete. *Almost.* Suddenly, a legion of fighting-mad Democrats rallied round their golden-haired hero. Editorials lamented that Custer was obliged, "as it were, upon bended knees, to beg of his inferior [Grant]." Barrett defended him as "the target of political rancor," adding, "How easily could he have trimmed his sail to the popular breeze, and floated into the smooth waters of political favor. The promotion which his valor had earned—which was due to his merit, which had been bestowed upon his inferiors—lay within his grasp; but the sacrifice was one from which his proud soul revolted."

The New York *World* blasted President Grant for "the most high-handed abuse of his official power which he has perpetrated yet. . . . There has never been a President of the United States before who was capable of braving the decent opinion of the country so openly and shamefully as this, for the sake of wreaking such a miserable vengeance."

The *Herald* asserted that Custer was being persecuted "simply because he did not 'crook the pregnant hinges of the knee' to this modern Caesar." It then branded Grant as an "irresponsible despot" with "absolute power to decapitate anybody offending His Highness or his favorites."

The Los Angeles *Herald* joined its allies in proclaiming: "The honest man [Custer] will live in history; the brute [Grant] will be consigned to historic oblivion and disgrace."

However, a few "radical rags" had their say against the Cavalier of the Plains. The St. Paul *Pioneer-Press,* for one, analyzed Custer as "an extra-ordinary compound of presumptuous egotism

495

and presumptuous mendacity which makes him the reckless and lawless being he is."

Custer recoiled at that jab: "I am not impetuous or impulsive. I resent that. Everything that I have ever done has been the result of the study I have made of imaginary military situations that might arise. When I become engaged in a campaign or battle, and a great emergency arises, everything that I ever heard or studied focuses in my mind as if the situation were under a magnifying-glass & my decision was the instantaneous result. My mind works instantaneously, but always as the result of everything I have ever studied being brought to bear on the situation. . . . I have done nothing but my duty—nothing that I have any apologies to make for doing, and nothing I would not do again under the same circumstances."

Sheridan wired a confidential message to Terry: "Custer followed Sherman's advice & one of the first things that happened was, figuratively speaking, a slap in the face when he tried to see the President. Custer seems to have taken this in his stride, as it were. But the next thing that came his way was a real 'haymaker.' Arrest & detention!"

On Friday morning, May 5, Sheridan handed Custer the following telegram from Sherman: "Have just come from the President, who orders that Gen'l Custer be allowed to rejoin his post, to remain there on duty, but not to accompany the Expedition (supposed to be on the point of starting against the hostile Indians) under Gen'l Terry."

Moments later another communiqué buzzed into General Headquarters, Military Division of the Missouri:

Washington, May 5th, 1876

Gen'l G. A. Custer, Chicago, Ill.

. . . Sent orders to Gen'l Sheridan to permit you to go to Abe Lincoln on duty, but the President adheres to his conclusion that you are not to go on the Expedition.

W. T. Sherman
General

496

Sheridan was in part responsible for this. In his guarded endorsement of Custer, whereby he besought Sherman's trust, Phil boasted: "I am the only officer who can control Custer. He is the only man that never failed me."

On Saturday morning, May 6, Custer arrived by rail in St. Paul, Gateway to the Northwest. He was fearful, hurt, desperate.

Swinging into Dakota Department Headquarters, Custer clasped the hand of Brigadier General Alfred H. Terry with both of his own. He smiled, but tears glimmered in his bright blue eyes. Seconds later the smile faded, became sickly, and Armstrong broke down and wept. All his iron nerve melted in convulsive sobbing.

"I beg of you, sir—you've got to help me. Damned if I'll be torn apart this way! I'd as soon a bullet in my brain. Terry, I beg of you—for God's sake, you've got to help me."

Terry stood in somber silence, his hands clasped behind him, gazing out the window. He was deeply moved, but dared not show it. He kept his back to Custer for several tense seconds, struggling to settle his mind, then turned slowly to face the man who had come to him in despair.

Alfred Howe Terry ("Hero of Fort Fisher") was full-bearded and tall, with wistful eyes and reflective bearing. The Indians called him "Lame-Hip," because he limped from a Civil War wound. Terry was soft-spoken and graceful, and he looked and acted more like a preacher than a soldier. He was an intellectual and a scholar, a Yale law graduate, and (in the estimation of his A.D.C. and brother-in-law, Captain Robert P. Hughes) "the kindest and noblest-hearted man I have ever known."

"I'll help you." He sighed, turning with a look of compassion rather than ambivalence. "I shall do whatever I can."

He later wrote: "Custer came to me, and with tears in his eyes, begged my aid. How could I resist it?"

Custer lunged forward and embraced Terry as a brother. Within a half-hour, the following dispatch flashed over the wires to the Windy City:

497

Hd.-Qrs., Dept. of Dakota
St. Paul, Minn.
May 6th, 1876

Adj't-Gen'l, Div. of Mo., Chicago

I forward the following:

"*To His Exc'y the President* (Thro' Military Channels):—

"I have seen your order, transmitted thro' the General of the Army, directing that I be not permitted to accompany the Expedition about to move against hostile Indians. As my entire Regt. forms a part of the proposed Expedition, and as I am the Senior Officer of the Regt. on duty in this Dept., I respectfully but most earnestly request that while not allowed to go in command of the Expedition I may be permitted to serve with my Regt. in the field. I appeal to you as a soldier to spare me the humiliation of seeing my Regt. march to meet the enemy & I not to share its dangers.

"*G. A. Custer*
Bvt. Maj.-Gen'l, U.S.A."

In forwarding the above, I wish to say expressly that I have no desire whatever to question the orders of the President or of my military superiors. Whether Lieut.-Col. Custer shall be permitted to accompany my column or not, I shall go in command of it. I do not know the reasons upon which the orders already given rest; but if those reasons do not forbid it, Lieut.-Col. Custer's services would be very valuable with his Regt.

A. H. Terry
Comdg. Dept.

Drawing a deep breath, Custer sauntered out for a cup of coffee. Returning to Headquarters, he overheard General Terry and another officer bandying heated words in the telegraph office.

"Look here, Bob," Terry was saying, "this is a scandalous shame. Custer has done nothing wrong. He has only obeyed the law and told the truth as he sees it. I say the President is taking a mean and cowardly advantage of his power to punish Custer indirectly because he daresn't do it directly."

The other voice was that of Captain Robert P. Hughes, Terry's aide-de-camp and brother-in-law. "Al, you're still a lawyer. You make no enemies. Why even after Fort Fisher, when you jumped over the heads of all those old West Pointers, they couldn't find it in their hearts to hate you. You're too damned goodhearted, and I just hope Custer isn't playing you for a fool."

Sheridan endorsed Terry's dispatch and forwarded it to Army Headquarters, on May 7, with these comments: "I am sorry Lieut.-Col. Custer did not manifest as much interest, by staying at his post, to organize & get ready his Regt. & the Expedition as he does now to accompany it. On a previous occasion, in 1868, I asked Executive Clemency for Col. Custer to enable him to accompany his Regt. against the Indians; and I sincerely hope, if granted this time, it will have sufficient effect to prevent him from again attempting to throw discredit on his profession & his brother officers."

Articles and editorials headlined "Grant's Tyranny—Custer's Degradation" and "Grant's Revenge—Custer's Banishment," to say nothing of "Grant's Hatred" and "Custer's Humiliation," drove Old Unconditional Surrender to the wall. A buzzer flashed from East to West:

> Head-Quarters of the Army
> Washington, May 8th, 1876
>
> *Gen'l A. H. Terry,* St. Paul, Minn.
>
> Gen'l Sheridan's enclosing (yours of yesterday) touching Gen'l Custer's urgent request to go under your command with his Regt. has been submitted to the President, who sent me word that if you want Gen'l Custer along he withdraws his objections. Advise Custer to be prudent, not to take along any newspaper-men (who always make mischief), and to abstain from personalities in the future. . . .
>
> *W. T. Sherman*
> General

George Armstrong Custer swanked out of Department Headquarters. It was Monday morning, May 8, and the past week now seemed like a dreadful nightmare from which he had just awakened in a joyous sweat. It was now "the boyhood of the

499

year, the time of the singing of birds." A couple of blocks to the Metropolitan Hotel, pack his bags, then full speed ahead to Fort Lincoln—and Libbie, and a summer campaign that promised undying glory. A fighting chance for redemption, to rewin his spurs and wipe out the shame that haunted his pride.

As he neared the hotel, Custer ran into Colonel William Ludlow, Chief Engineer of the Department of Dakota.

"By God, Custer, good to see you again! How goes it, eh?"

"You needn't look so foolish, old fellow. I'm gay as a lark!"

"By God, and aren't you now!"

"I've been restored to active duty. By Executive Order, no less! Terry and I plan to light out this evening for the Wild Mizzoo."

"Oh, then he'll be in command of the expedition?"

"It's all the same! The 7th Cavalry will have the lion's share of this campaign, just as it had back in '73. And I expect I shall be in the scouting saddle, spearheading the column as usual. First chance I get, I'll cut loose from Terry and make a killing. With my Garryowens behind me, I can whip all the Indians in the Northwest!"

"Custer's Luck, eh?"

"Well, perhaps. I got away with Stanley, poor sot, so I suppose I'll be able to swing clear of Terry."

The old soldiers shook hands and patted shoulders in parting; and when Ludlow wished Custer good luck, he got this reply: "I'm going to clear my name or leave my bones on the prairie."

500

★22★

FORT LINCOLN: GARRY OWEN IN GLORY

Generals Custer and Terry took a special express to Bismarck, whirling into Fort Abraham Lincoln by Wells-Fargo stagecoach on the night of May 9, 1876.

Tuesday afternoon, May 16. Terry had lunched with the Custers, and the three of them were now alone in the parlor. Libbie was plying a pair of horse clippers, cropping her husband's reddish-gold ringlets as close as she dared.

"My precious scalp won't be worth a continental damn when the Old Lady gets done!" he cackled.

Terry stirred in his seat, then said pensively, "Do you recall that editorial in the Boston *Post?* 'The history of relations between white man and red has been an unbroken story of rapacity, cruelty, and a complete lack of feeling on the part of the white.' Be that as it may, it bothers me to think the editor never took into account the history of relations between red man and red, which is scarcely more creditable than the annals of the white race."

Custer responded: "Those charitable busybodies back East have satisfied themselves that we're bent on punishing the redman solely for depredations against the white. What these angels of mercy care to ignore is that the Sioux have been invading and stealing land from the Crows and Shoshones for the past couple of years. Sitting-Bull refuses to make peace with the whiteman, and harasses every red cousin of his who does. He's an outlaw, a bully, and the desperadoes under his influence are a far cry from

501

those tribes that want to live in peace with the whites. The Crows, for one, were always a peace-loving nation. They appealed to us for help, and we intend to protect them. What could be more charitable than that! Are we to defend cutthroats and criminals, whatever their race? The Sioux have long been troublemakers, proud to be called 'Scourge of the Plains,' tyrannizing their neighbors at every turn. And as a warlike nation, they enslave their victims and live off the spoils of conquest. The Sioux want war, and they shall damn soon get it: a war to the death."

Terry pursed his lips and nodded gravely.

Custer continued: "Back in '73, Chief Blackfoot of the Crow Nation told a delegation of Indian-agents 'You ought not to give the Sioux guns and ammunition. You should wipe them all out. . . .' Here's a letter I got from Jack Smith, agent upriver. He says 'About half the warriors remaining at agencies have repeating rifles—Winchesters—and all others have breechloaders. Fully half the young men have pistols—one or more. I have known Indians to have three thousand rounds of ammunition for a single gun.' Comforting facts, are they not? Especially when one considers that my troopers are obliged to limp along with single-shot Springfields, none of which are worth a damn!"

Terry nodded, sad-eyed.

"They say 'Glory, on the frontier, means being shot by an Indian from behind a rock and having your name spelled wrong in the papers.' Well, I'm damned if I'll suffer such a fate!" Custer then leaned forward and said firmly, "Terry, a man usually means what he says when he lets his wife listen to his statements. Reports are circulating that I don't want to go out on the campaign under you. Well, I want you to know I *do* want to go and serve under you—not only because I value you as a soldier, but as a friend and a man."

"God bless you, sir," Terry breathed.

That night, while reading Mrs. Alexander's three-volume *Her Dearest Foe* (the latest English novel), Armstrong marked the sentence: "I have faith in my own fortunes, and believe I shall conquer in the end."

Wednesday, May 17, 1876; 5 A.M. Chief Trumpeter Henry Voss licked his lips and sounded the "General." Its brassiness blasted across the spongy drillfield outside the stockade of Fort Lincoln.

Old Curly's Garryowens, the Fighting 7th, tumbled out of their tents and loaded the supply wagons with dew-laden white canvas. The "Assembly" blared at six o'clock, and over seven hundred crack troopers of twelve companies scuttled into rank and file for roll call. With bugles blowing "Mount," then "Forward," officers and men of the 7th U.S. Regular Cavalry swung into the saddle, wheeled away from the picket lines, and jogged by column of fours into the fort.

A raw wind was whipping out of the east, and a mist hung ominously over the "Big Muddy," but greasy weather could not dampen the spirits of alkalied cavalrymen rarin' to hit the glory trail.

With guidons streaming and horses prancing and bandsmen crashing the 7th's own battle tune, "Garry Owen," Custer's famous regiment fanned out in column of platoons and marched around the parade ground.

> Our hearts so stout have got us fame,
> For soon 'tis known from whence we came;
> Where'er we go they dread the name
>   Of Garry Owen in glory!

Astride his blaze-faced, stocking-legged, snappy thoroughbred sorrel, Old Vic, Custer led the cavalcade. He was clad in fringed buckskins, bright red neckerchief, and a white broad-brimmed Western hat. He had a pearl-handled bulldog revolver on either hip, a Remington sporting rifle slung over his shoulder, and a big Indian scalping knife in his belt.

Florid-faced Custer, with his white sombrero and close-cropped golden-red hair, struck quite a contrast as he rode beside dark-bearded, fair-faced Terry with his sable campaign hat and dark-blue uniform.

503

On Armstrong's right trotted Elizabeth, dressed in a buckskin riding habit and scarlet hunting cap. Close behind paced Captain Tom Custer, senior officer of the five-company Custer Battalion, decked out in buckskins and a white slouch hat. He cut a dashing figure with trim sideburns and a tawny imperial that accented his bony cheeks. Beside him rode sprite-faced Boston and a new-comer to the family of personal aides, Henry Armstrong ("Harry" or "Autie") Reed: Custer's handsome, husky[5] teen-aged nephew.

Women and children lined the boardwalks of Officers' and Soapsuds Rows as the 7th Cavalry swirled slowly around the vast paradeground. With tears streaking down their cheeks, mothers held their little ones out at arm's length for a last look as proud fathers went rolling by; and toddlers, waving handkerchiefs tied to sticks and beating on old tin pans, stomped alongside the column in lusty chorus. When regiment and commander swept past the Indian quarters, a cluster of gaily colored tepees, the squaws and papooses of Yellowhair's red-skinned scouts wept and wailed while their braves thumped on tomtoms and hooted the war whoop. It was a chilling, bloodcurdling clamor; and Libbie breathed easier when it was over. "The most despairing hour seemed to have come."

The curveting hoofs of Custer's cavalry and the tramping feet of Terry's infantry chopped up the rain-soaked ground, and the slithering wheels of supply wagons and Gatling guns forged deep ruts across the gleamy flats, as the entire thousand-man expedition rolled out of Fort Abraham Lincoln to a pulsing lilt:

> The hour was sad I left the maid,
>   A ling'ring farewell taking;
> Her sighs and tears my steps delay'd—
>   I thought her heart was breaking.

> In hurried words her name I bless'd;
>   I breathed the vows that bind me,
> And to my heart in anguish press'd
>   The girl I left behind me.

504

A chilling breeze snapped at the cavalry's red-and-blue swallow-tailed headquarters pennant, emblazoned with white crossed sabers and a large gold 7. It lashed the swallow-tailed guidons with their stars and stripes, and it whipped out the gorgeous gold-fringed regimental standard with its golden eagle on a crimson field and the superscription: *7th U.S. Cavalry.* The blue-clad troopers pulled down their black campaign hats and hunched in the saddle, picturesquely slanted against the whistling wind, as they marched westward into the forbidden Yellowstone country, into a labyrinth of ravines, a land of deadly echoes.

It was 7 A.M., and cool gusts began to lighten and whisk away the heavy frost smoke hovering over the Missouri bottom lands. A warm sun slowly melted the haze, sucking veils of steam out of the sodden earth. Sunbeams burst like a shower of molten gold across the horizon, and the ribbonlike column of cavalry was mirrored in a radiant mist.

> The hope of final victory,
>   Within my bosom burning,
> Is mingling with sweet thoughts of thee
>   And of my fond returning.
>   But should I ne'er return again,
>   Still worth thy love thou'lt find me;
>   Dishonor's breath shall never stain
>   The name I'll leave behind me. . . .

Libbie Custer and Maggie Calhoun accompanied their husbands that first day out of Fort Lincoln. As the two-mile column snaked its way slowly through gently sloping hills, Armstrong often turned in the saddle and glanced back to admire his men. "Just look at 'em, Libbie!" he said excitedly. "Did you ever see a grander sight in all your life?"

In Libbie's words: "The soldiers, inured to many years of hardship, were the perfection of physical manhood. Their brawny limbs and lithe, well-poised bodies gave proof of the training their outdoor life had given. Their resolute faces, brave and confident,

505

inspired one with a feeling that they were going out aware of the momentous hours awaiting them, but inwardly assured of their capability to meet them."

Captain Tom laughed and waved his hand. "Take it from us, Old Lady. A single company of Garryowens can lick the whole damn Sioux Nation!"

Libbie smiled hopefully, indulgently, but there was a gnawing fear in her heart.

The next morning, after a tearful farewell, Armstrong lifted Elizabeth onto her horse. "So long, Maggie," he said, winking at his sister. "Rest assured I shall keep Jimmy in line for you." He then nodded to the escort sergeant and lightly slapped Libbie's mount. The small party rode away to the east.

Custer stood watching for a moment, tears still in his eyes. Then he turned sharply, and his freckled face was ghostly white. Looking at his brother-in-law, he smiled shyly and cracked: "Jim, a good soldier has two mistresses. While he's loyal to one, the other must suffer." He slapped Lieutenant Calhoun on the back and swaggered off.

> 46 m. from Ft. Lincoln
> May 20th, 9:15 P.M.

My Darling Girl,
. . . It is raining now, and has been ever since we started. Everybody is more or less disgusted—except me. The elements seem against us, but a wet season & bad roads can be looked for always in this region in the months of May & June. We have not seen any signs of Indians thus far, and hardly look for any for a few days yet. I have been extremely prudent—sufficiently so to satisfy my Little Durl. I go nowhere without taking an escort with me. I act as if Indians were near all the time! . . .

> On Little Missouri, D.T.
> May 30th, 10 P.M.

. . . Have had a tremendous day's work. I breakfasted at 4 o'clock, was in the saddle at 5, and between that hour & 6 P.M. I rode 50 miles over a rough country unknown to everybody—

and only myself for a guide. . . . Bloody-Knife looks on in wonder at me because I never get tired, and says no other man could ride all night & never sleep. I know I shall sleep soundly when I do lie down, but actually I feel no more fatigued now than I did before mounting my horse this morning! . . .

> Powder River (about 20 m. above
> its Mouth), Montana Terr.
> June 9th

. . . We are now in a country hitherto unvisited by white-men. Charley Reynolds, who had been guiding the Command, lost his way the other day; and Gen'l Terry did not know what to do. I told him I tho't I could guide the column. He assented; so I brought the Command to this point, over what seems to be the only practicable route for miles on either side, thro' the worst kind of Bad-lands. The Gen'l did not believe it possible to find a road thro'! When, after a hard day's work, we arrived at this river—making 32 miles in one day—he was delighted & came to congratulate me: "Nobody but Gen'l Custer could have brought us thro' such a country! He's the best guide I ever saw. . . ."

> On Yellowstone (at Mouth of
> Powder River), M.T.
> June 11th, 10:30 P.M.

. . . I am again acting as guide! And thro' Unknown Bad-lands!! Gen'l Terry came to my tent before daylight & asked me if I would try to find a road. He seems to think I have a gift in that way. Well, sure enough I found one, after passing thro' some perfectly terrible country; and we arrived here safely—waggons & all! . . . As I was up at 3 this morning & have had a hard day's march, and as it is now going on to 12, I must hie to bed & catch a little rest.

> Y'r devoted Boy,
> *Autie*

P.S.—We are living delightfully. I don't know what we (Tom & I) would do without Bos to tease. *You* might just as well be here as not!

507

Libbie answered:

Ft. Lincoln, June 21st

My darling Autie,

. . . I cannot but feel the greatest possible apprehension for your safety on this dangerous scout. Oh, Autie, I feel as if it was almost impossible for me to wait your return with patience. I cannot describe my feelings. I have felt so badly for the last few days, I have been perfectly unendurable to every one. Most of the time I have spent in my room, feeling myself no addition to any one's society. . . . Please look after yourself, my darling—not for me alone, but for the country we love & honor. With your bright future, and the knowledge that you are of positive use to your day & generation, do you not see that your life is precious on that account—and not only because an idolizing wife could not live without you?

And now I shall go to bed & dream of my dear Bo. God be with you, my darling. I love you always.

Your devoted Girl,
Libbie

This letter, and the ones that followed, never reached her husband. They were all returned unopened on that day of anguish yet to come.

Libbie would write: "With my husband's departure, my last happy days in garrison were ended; as a premonition of disaster that I had never known before weighed me down. I could not shake off the baleful influence of depressing thoughts. This presentiment and suspense, such as I had never known, made me selfish; and I shut into my heart the most uncontrollable anxiety, and could lighten no one else's burden. The occupations of other summers could not even give temporary interest."

★23★

YELLOWSTONE:
THE "FAR WEST"

W EDNESDAY, June 21, 1876; 3
P.M. General Terry, Colonel Custer, Colonel John Gibbon, and
Major James S. Brisbin were in council of war.

Terry spread his huge campaign map on a table in the cabin of
the supply steamer *Far West*, then moored on the Yellowstone
River at the mouth of Rosebud Creek, about 275 miles west of
Fort Lincoln. He marked out a route with his blue pencil, then
said to Custer:

"As soon as your regiment can be made ready for the march, I
want you to proceed up the Rosebud in pursuit of the Indians
whose trail was discovered by Major Reno a few days ago. Of
course, it's impossible for me to give you any definite instructions
in regard to this movement. Even if I could, I place too much
confidence in your energy and ability to wish to impose any
precise orders on you which might hamper your action when
nearly in contact with the enemy. However, these are my own
views of what your action should be. I should like you to con-
form to them unless you see sufficient reason for departing from
them."

Terry bent over the map, following the penciled line with his
finger.

"I think you should proceed up the Rosebud till you definitely
ascertain the direction in which the Indian trail leads. Should it
be found to turn towards the Littlehorn [*i.e.,* Little Bighorn], I
think you should avoid following it directly to the river. Keep

509

moving southward, perhaps as far as the headwaters of the Tongue, and then turn towards the Littlehorn—feeling constantly to your left—so as to prevent the Indians from escaping to the south or southeast. At the same time, Colonel Gibbon's column will proceed to the mouth of the Bighorn. As soon as it reaches that point it will cross the Yellowstone and move up at least as far as the forks of the Bighorn and Littlehorn. In this way, allowing for good timing and favorable circumstances, the Indians may be so nearly enclosed by the two columns that their escape will be impossible."

Terry eased back in his seat, eying the ceiling reflectively.

"Now I have calculated, averaging from ten to fifteen miles a day, the two columns should converge at rendezvous in approximately five days. That would set the date for concerted attack on the twenty-sixth. Now this plan of mine is founded on the belief that at some point on the Littlehorn a body of hostile Sioux will be found; and though it's impossible to make movements in perfect concert, yet by the use of guides and scouts the two columns may be brought within co-operating distance of each other. Needless to say, the success of this operation hinges on continual communication between the two columns. Now then, gentlemen. Though it's my expectation we shall arrive in the neighborhood of the Sioux village about the same time, and assist each other in the attack: if you, General Custer, arrive first, you are at liberty to attack *if* you deem prudent. Use your own good judgment, and do what you think best. It's reported that Sitting-Bull has fifteen hundred lodges, is confident, and intends making a stand."

According to the diary (6/21/76) of Lieutenant James H. Bradley, Gibbon's chief of scouts, "It is understood that if Custer arrives first, he is at liberty to attack at once if he deems prudent. We have little hope of being in at the death, as Custer will undoubtedly exert himself to the utmost to get there first & win all the laurels for himself & his Regt."

These statements, written "on the spot," refute the charge that Custer disobeyed Terry's orders by attacking the Indians on his own hook. That Terry virtually gave Custer a free hand is also confirmed by *Herald* correspondent Mark Kellogg (the newspaperman Sherman warned Custer "not to take along"), who reported: "It was announced by Gen'l Terry that Gen'l Custer's column would strike the blow."

"I wonder if we haven't already lost the element of surprise," Custer said dryly. "Reno's failure to follow up the trails has imperiled our plans by giving the Indians an intimation of our presence. Few officers have ever had such a fine opportunity to make a successful and telling strike, and few ever failed so completely to improve their opportunity. Reno made the mistake of his life in not pushing on and smashing up the village while he had the chance."

Terry shifted uneasily in his seat. "Well, General, if you find the Indians first, don't do as Reno did—run away—but if you think you can whip them, do so."

(Major Reno, detailed with a squadron to hunt up the Indian trail, searched the Tongue and Powder rivers and found nothing. His orders were not to go beyond the Tongue; but on his return march, in striking the headwaters of the Rosebud, he discovered a large Indian trail. Custer, in a *Herald* article entitled "Reno's Contempt of Orders," wrote: "Gen'l Terry, in framing the orders which were to govern Maj. Reno's movements, explicitly & positively directed that officer . . . not to move in the direction of Rosebud River; as it was feared that such a movement, if prematurely made, might 'flush the covey.' " Custer adds that Reno struck the Indian trail and followed it about twenty miles; "but faint heart never won fair lady, neither did it ever pursue & overtake an Indian village. Had Reno, after first violating his orders, pursued & overtaken the Indians, his original disobedience of orders would have been overlooked. But his determination forsook him at this point; and instead of continuing the pursuit & at least bringing the Indians to bay, he gave the order to counter-march." In referring to Reno's conduct as a "gross & inexcusable blunder," Custer boldly concludes: "A court-martial is strongly hinted at, and if one is not ordered it will not be because it is not richly

511

deserved." Nothing came of the matter, which must have rankled Custer into a recklessness justified by Terry's complaisance. If Reno could throw caution to the winds, and get away with it, Custer apparently saw no more reason for the new self-discipline that harnessed his spirit.)

The glory hunter said to Terry, "Well, as I see it now, this maneuver of ours will result in either a fight or a footrace; and the only real question is whether Sitting-Bull will sit long enough to allow us to close the trap around him!"

Terry asked, "How long will your marches be?"

Custer replied, "At first, I reckon, about thirty miles a day. That will later allow for plenty of reconnaissance time when in the vicinity of the enemy."

A moment later, Terry said to Custer with a worried look, "In consideration of the fact that you will be taking the most dangerous route, perhaps it would be well for me to take Gibbon's squadron of horse and go with you."

Custer shook his head. "That won't be necessary, General. The 7th can handle anything it meets. Besides, an extra squadron would be of no account."

"Well, then, would you like Major Brisbin's battery of Gatling guns?"

"No. They might embarrass me. I'm strong enough without 'em."

"You're sure of that," James S. Brisbin said sardonically.

"Absolutely," Custer answered. "I don't want them. I'm afraid they'll impede my march. Besides, as I said before, the 7th Cavalry can whip every hostile in the Northwest."

The council of war broke up at sundown. As the four officers were about to leave the *Far West,* Terry turned to Custer and said earnestly, hands clasped behind his back, "Custer, I don't know what to say for the last."

"Say whatever you want to say," Custer replied offhandedly.

"Well," Terry ventured, "use your own judgment and do what you think best if you strike the trail. And whatever you do, Custer, hold onto your wounded. Rather than remain here, I shall go with Gibbon. In any event, I only hope one of the columns finds the Indians." He added, barely audible: "I'll give you written instructions tomorrow, before departure."

When Custer was out of earshot, Major Brisbin muttered hotly to General Terry, "Begging your pardon, sir, but do you think it's such a worthwhile idea turning that wild man loose to go up the Rosebud after Lord knows how many redskins?"

Terry reflected, pursing his lips. "You don't seem to have any confidence in Custer."

"None in the world," Brisbin snarled. "I have no use for him— insufferable ass."

"Don't you think Custer's regiment can handle itself?" Terry added in a troubled voice.

"No. There's enough Indians for all of us. Possibly Custer can whip 'em with the 7th; but what's the use in taking any chances?"

"Well, I've had but little experience in Indian-fighting; and Custer has had much, and is sure he can whip anything he meets."

"General," Brisbin leered, "you underrate your own ability and overrate Custer's."

Big-bodied Brisbin, known to his troops as "Old Blatherskite" and "Grasshopper Jim," was so crippled with rheumatism that he had to hop around on crutches. "Lame-Hip" Terry pitied him. White-whiskered Colonel John Gibbon, who had been Custer's artillery instructor at the Point, was in slightly better shape than his second-in-command. The Indians called him "No-Hip" because, like his superior, a Civil War wound had given him a limp. Such was the condition of army officers sent to serve on the frontier! Custer and Miles were rare exceptions.

Terry turned to Gibbon and said, "Well, John, what do *you* think?"

"My lips are sealed," Gibbon rasped. "Hear no evil, see no evil, speak no evil."

Brisbin said, "In spite of his refusal, why not put my cavalry with Custer's and go yourself in command?"

Terry frowned. "Custer is smarting under the rebuke of the

513

President, and wants an independent command, and I wish to give him a chance to do something."

Meeting Brother Tom, Armstrong informed him of the conference and added arrogantly, "That was very clever of Brisbin to offer to go with me. But you know, this is to be a 7th Cavalry battle; and I want all the glory for the 7th there is in it."

Eerie darkness had fallen over the Yellowstone country when "Officers' Call" brought the 7th brass hustling into a lanternlit H.Q. tent. Colonel Custer was pacing back and forth, flicking his quirt against his thigh.

"We move up the Rosebud tomorrow noon," he said sharply. "Light marching order. No wagons, no tents. And *no* sabers. Twelve packmules per company. Fifteen days' rations of hardtack, coffee, and sugar. Twelve days' rations of bacon. Twelve pounds of oats per trooper. Each man will carry one hundred rounds of carbine and twenty rounds of revolver ammunition. Two thousand rounds extra per company, to be loaded on the mules. I suggest extra forage as well. Any questions?" Custer's keen blue eyes darted to and fro.

Captain Myles Moylan spoke up: "With only twelve mules a company, General, that extra forage will break 'em down for sure."

"Well, gentlemen," Custer rasped, snapping his whip, "you may carry what supplies you damn well please. You will be held responsible for your companies. The extra forage was only a suggestion, but bear this fact in mind: we'll follow the trail no matter how far it takes us, and we may never see the supply steamer again. In that case," he added cynically, "you'd better carry along an extra supply of salt. We may have to live on horsemeat before we get through."

He was taken at his word!

514

★24★

BADLANDS: INTO THE
VALLEY OF DEATH

AT twelve noon, Thursday, June 22, 1876, bugles sounded "Boots and Saddles." Troopers of the 7th Cavalry swung into their saddles, formed column of fours, and paraded southward up the Rosebud. It was a cloud-wrapped, wind-swept day, and nerves were raw.

Custer had spared no pains to make his Fighting 7th second to none in the service. As a Garryowen expressed it, "He was one damn son-of-a-bitch; but the 7th was Custer, and Custer was the 7th." And, in Libbie's words, "His buoyant spirits at the prospect of the activity and field-life that he so loved made him like a boy."

Lieutenant Winfield Scott Edgerly (Troop D) regarded his commander as "the incarnation of energy . . . like the thoroughbred he rode, champing the bit & chafing to be off, longing for action."

Herald correspondent Mark Kellogg observed Custer "flitting to & fro in his quick eager way, . . . the keen incisive manner for which he is so well known." Here was "the most peculiar genius in the Army; a man of strong impulses, of great-hearted friendships & bitter enmities, of quick nervous temperament, undaunted courage, will & determination; a man possessing electrical mental capacity, and of iron frame & constitution; . . . the hardest rider, the greatest pusher, with the most untiring vigilance, . . . and with an ambition to succeed in all things he undertakes." Kellogg concludes: "The Gen'l is full of perfect readiness for the fray with the hostile red devils, and woe to the body of scalp-hunters that

515

comes within reach of himself & brave companions-in-arms! . . . I go with Custer, and will be in at the death."

"The regiment's in splendid condition, General," Terry said to Custer as they reviewed the passing cavalcade. "It's the best-looking outfit I've ever seen."

"Thank you, General," Custer responded proudly. "I've done my best to make it so—second to none. Well, I must be off." Custer shook hands with Terry, Gibbon, and Brisbin. "So long, gentlemen," he said briskly.

"Goodbye," Terry murmured. "God bless you, and Godspeed. Do what you think best if you strike the trail."

"So long," Gibbon rasped. "Remember now, there are enough Indians for all of us!"

"Good luck," Brisbin said begrudgingly.

As Custer reined his horse around, Gibbon cracked: "Now Custer, don't be greedy. Wait for us!"

Custer rose to the trot, flipping off his hat in a jaunty salute. "I won't!" he called back laughingly, then charged to the head of his command in a swirl of dust.

"Now what the hell did he mean by that?" said Brisbin.

Terry chuckled into his beard. "Custer's happy now, off with a roving command and a free hand to whip every hostile in the Northwest. I hope he finds them; for if he does, I've no doubt he'll whip them as well."

Brisbin grunted. He had his doubts. "Just hope he doesn't bite off more than he can chew."

"Well, if he should," Gibbon said, "we'll be close enough to see he doesn't choke to death."

Twilight found the 7th Cavalry bivouacked on the west bank of the Rosebud, twelve miles below the Yellowstone. With his officers gathered around him by the headquarters campfire, Colonel Custer said nervously, "It has come to my knowledge that my official actions have been criticized by certain officers of this regiment at Department Headquarters. Now I'm willing to accept recommendations from any one of you at any time, but I want them to be made in a proper manner—not over my head or be-hind my back. In calling your attention to that paragraph of *Army Regulations* referring to the criticism of actions of commanding officers by subordinates, let me advise you that I shall take all necessary steps to punish the offenders should there be a recur-rence of the offense."

Captain Fred Benteen spoke up in his sneeringly respectful manner: "It seems to me, General, you're lashing the shoulders of *all* to get at *some*. Now as we're all present, would it not do to specify the officers you accuse?"

"Captain Benteen," Custer said dryly, "I'm not here to be cate-chized by you. For your own information, I want the saddle to go just where it fits. We're now starting on a scout we all hope will be successful, and I intend doing everything I can to make it both successful and pleasant for everybody. I'm certain that if any regiment in the service can do what's required of it, we can. I'll be only too glad to listen to suggestions from any officer of this command, if made in the proper manner. But I want it distinctly understood that I'll allow no grumbling, and shall exact the strictest compliance with orders from everybody—not only with mine, but with any order given by an officer to his subordi-nate. I don't want it said of this regiment, as one department commander said of another cavalry regiment, that 'It would be a good one if the colonel could get rid of his old captains and let the young lieutenants command the companies.' "

"Beg pardon, General," Benteen cut in, "but just who did you have in mind by that remark about grumbling?"

Custer stood with arms folded, legs firmly apart. "As I said before, I want the saddle to go just where it fits." His words were aggressive.

Benteen smirked, glancing around at his fellow officers. "Did the General ever know of any criticism or grumbling from me?"

"No, I never have." Custer smirked too. "But methinks you doth protest too much."

There had been "a lot of grumbling" since May 17, for the regiment wasn't paid till it was fourteen miles from Lincoln—and

517

the saloons of Bismarck. Sergeant Windolph commented: "I suppose it saved many a bad head, and the trouble of rounding up some of the worst drunks, but the men resented the fact they didn't get to go on their regular spree."

Custer continued: "Until further orders, no bugle calls except in an emergency. Marches will begin at five A.M. *sharp*. Only two things will be regulated from my headquarters: when to move out and when and where to go into camp. All other details on the march will be left to your judgment and discretion. Do what's necessary for your men. This responsibility entails company commanders to keep within supporting distance of each other, not to get ahead of the scouts or very far to the rear of the column." He then said in earnest, "I want to impress upon you the extent to which I now rely on your judgment, your discretion, your loyalty. Judging from the number of lodges reported by our scouts, we'll meet at least a thousand if not fifteen hundred hostiles. But I feel proudly confident that the 7th Cavalry can whip any number of savages thrown against it. If it can't, no other regiment in the service can. But to win, we need complete harmony in our ranks; and I'm sure we have it." Custer paused, staring wistfully at the fire, and his shaggy mustachios twitched. "Nothing more, gentlemen," he muttered with a brief sigh, "except that marches will be from twenty-five to thirty miles a day. That means husband your rations, for I intend to follow the trail and hunt 'em down even if it takes us into Nebraska."

As the council was breaking up, debonair Lieutenant Winfield Scott Edgerly of Benteen's Battalion addressed Custer: "General, won't we be stepping high when we get those Injuns!"

"Won't we!" Custer said spiritedly, adding with a frown: "But we can't get 'Injuns' without hard riding, and plenty of it! That's why I'm depending on you young officers. The worst that could happen is for Sitting-Bull to slip away from us just when we've got him roped."

While strolling over to his bivouac, Edgerly heard Lieutenant George D. Wallace remark to Lieutenant Edward S. Godfrey: "Y'know, God, I think Custer's going to be killed."

"Why? What makes you think so?"

"Because. I never heard him talk that way before."

Godfrey later wrote: "This 'talk' of his, as we called it, was considered at the time as something extraordinary for General Custer; for it was not his habit to unbosom himself to his officers. In it he showed concessions and a reliance on others; there was an indefinable something that was *not* Custer. His manner and tone, usually brusque and aggressive or somewhat curt, was on this occasion conciliating and subdued. There was something akin to an appeal, as if depressed, that made a deep impression on all present."

If Custer seemed "abstracted," if he "showed a lack of self-confidence," it was simply because there was no hope for him but to burn out his official disgrace in a blaze of glory. The responsibility for his own redemption in the eyes of Grant was almost too great for him to bear. He was going to run a terrible risk, with the lives of over six hundred men at stake; and if he failed, there was no hope for him—but death. And now, for the first time since Bull Run, death frightened him. "Custer's Luck" had lost its meaning, and fear of the final summons unnerved a spirit that had scorned "the king of terrors." Afraid to live in failure, afraid to die in defeat, Custer was agonized by suicidal anxiety until he presumed to know his enemy and flattered himself with contempt therefor. By egocentric fancy, he saved himself for an immortal tragedy.

Late that night, coyotes howled in chorus with "I'll Take You Home Again, Kathleen"; and Fred Benteen, wrapped in his buffalo blanket, growled, "For Christ's sake, dry up!"

Custer drove his 7th Cavalry thirty-three miles on the second day, twenty-eight miles on the third. They were now in the heart of the Montana Badlands, where sage-tufted, cactus-studded desert was gouged with gullies and baked a powdery gray. Patches of parched brown grass rippled in a hot breeze, and the raw dews of foredawn hung in a spectral haze over the horizon.

On the twenty-fourth, scout George B. Herendeen paced alongside Custer, pointed to the right and said, "Gen'ral, that thar's

519

Tullock's Creek; and here's whar I'm to leave you an' go down it to the other command."

Custer glanced at Herendeen, but said nothing. When the scout realized that his mission was not to be accomplished, he fell back again.

As Brisbin put it: "Custer . . . knew Herendeen was there to go down the Tullock & communicate with us, by Terry's orders, and in this Custer disobeyed distinctly the Dept. Commander's wishes & orders. He did not wish us to know where he was or what he was doing, for fear we would get some of the credit of the campaign."

After Herendeen had dropped back, Custer remarked to scout Lieutenant Charles A. Varnum: "Here's where Reno made the mistake of his life. He had six companies, and rations enough for a week. He'd have made a name for himself if he had pushed on after 'em."

Custer's mile-long column of dusty troopers was a dark ribbon rolling over the reft and broken flats—shrouded by choking alkali clouds that burned their eyes and blistered their lips, tortured by the wavering monotony of mirages.

Captain Benteen grumbled and growled to Major Reno: "Forced-marching us, God damn him. At this rate we'll kill the mules, cripple half the horses, frazzle the men—just to beat Terry and Gibbon to the punch. That cuss is out for glory, and he doesn't give a Goddamn for any of us."

Reno nodded glumly, and said nothing.

★25★

LITTLE BIGHORN: CUSTER'S LAST STAND

SUNDAY, June 25, 1876; 7 A.M. It promised to be a smoldering day in the valleys of the Rosebud and the Little Bighorn. Custer gulped down a bittersweet cup of alkali-flavored coffee, then threw off his buckskin jacket to appreciate the cooling effect of perspiration. He yanked off his blood-red neckerchief, rolled up the sleeves of his blue flannel blouse, opened two buttons at the neck. He could feel the heat oozing out of the dust, simmering on the rocks. Without a shave since he left Fort Lincoln, his beard and face were streaked with dust. This hawkish redneck of the wild frontier was a far cry from that popinjay boy general of the Civil War. No bugles, no sabers, no flashy uniforms. No cinnamon-scented ringlets. Here was the new image of an old nature.

Chief scout Minton ("Mitch") Bouyer came dusting into camp with several Arikaras. He pitched off his unsaddled cayuse and ambled over to Custer. Bouyer was a beefy, bull-faced half-breed with barbed-wire whiskers. Known to the Indians as "Two-Bodies" (*Wîchânûpâ*), he was the protégé of famed frontiersman and trail blazer, Jim Bridger.

"Gin'ral," Bouyer drawled, spurting a stream of tobacco juice, "we discovered the village. Down thar on the Littlehorn. It's a big-un!"

"How big?" Custer said.

Bouyer gnawed his tobacco, spat again. "Too big fer you to

521

tackle," he said. "Why, they's thousands and thousands o' Sioux and Cheyenne down thar."

Custer glared at Bouyer for a few seconds, then snapped: "I'll attack 'em! If you're afraid, Bouyer . . ." he added with a leer.

Bouyer spat. "I guess I can go wherever you do."

At that moment, Charles A. ("Lonesome Charley") Reynolds came riding up and eased out of the saddle. With him were several Crows. Reynolds was a civilian scout of long standing. Frontier folk called him "Lonesome Charley" because he never said much and liked to be by himself. Short, shy-looking, white-mustached, Reynolds was "Lucky-Man" to the Indians because of his bright blue eyes and seemingly charmed life.

"Biggest bunch of Indians I ever seen over there," Reynolds said matter-of-factly.

"Didn't I tell ya?" Bouyer interjected. "That's the biggest village ever seen in the Plains, and I bin around hyar over thirty years."

"The whole valley ahead for ten, twelve miles is scratched up by their trailing lodgepoles," Reynolds said.

"Yup," Bouyer chawed. "Biggest village I ever seen."

"A heap of 'em," Reynolds sighed.

Custer frowned. "We can whip 'em."

Reynolds said, "It'll take six hours' hard fighting to whip them."

"They's too many Injuns ahead fer us to handle," Bouyer drawled.

Custer lashed out: "There aren't too many Indians on the whole North American continent for the 7th Cavalry to handle."

"Well," said Bouyer, "I can tell ya we're gonna have a God-damn big fight."

Reynolds nodded sadly. "If we go in there, we'll never come out."

Bloody-Knife, who was squatting close by, rumbled some remark to one of his comrades.

Custer jerked aside, glowering. "What's that he says?"

Grizzled civilian interpreter Fred F. Girard answered, "He says we'll find enough Sioux to keep us fighting two or three days."

Custer snorted. "Oh, I guess we'll get through with 'em in one day." He then crouched beside Bloody-Knife and muttered, "What do you think of these reports? They say there are large camps of the Sioux and Cheyenne."

Bloody-Knife nodded gravely, dragging on his long clay pipe. He gestured sharply as he spoke: "This gathering of enemy tribes too many for us. All nations. Heap big roundup. Them waiting for us. Sitting-Bull and Crazyhorse, them not men-without-sense. Them have eyes on us. Spirits give me warning. Bloody-Knife no see the set of tomorrow's sun."

"What do you reckon will be the outcome of it all?"

"*Death!*"

Custer turned to Stabbed, another Arikara scout. "And you?"

Stabbed responded in sign language: "I feel as my brother feels."

Custer smiled wryly. "I don't doubt you, Bloody-Knife. What you say seems reasonable. I know you people. You're tricky like the coyote. You know how to hide, to bait, to creep up and take by surprise. But Yellowhair is no jackrabbit."

Custer stood up straight and stepped over to Bouyer. "Describe the village to me. Exactly where and how far is it from here?"

Bouyer pointed. "Twelve, fifteen mile mebbe. Beyond them hills, on t'other side o' the Littlehorn. It's all o' three miles long. Made up of hundreds and hundreds o' lodges. Above it and below and west of it are thousands and thousands of cayuses bein' close-herded."

"Take me to your lookout. I want to see for myself."

Throwing a leg over his barebacked sorrel, Old Curly rode slick-heeled to the Custer Battalion bivouac. "Hey, Tom!" he said. "Move 'em out at eight o'clock sharp. I'm heading up the divide to have a look. Follow my trail at a fast walk. We'll meet yonder and cross over the ridge before noon."

Custer, Bouyer, Reynolds, Girard, and Bloody-Knife galloped westward up the "hogback" to a lookout known as the Crow's-Nest. Lieutenant Charles A. ("Knifeface") Varnum and several Indian scouts were there watching and waiting.

Morning mist veiled the valley.

523

"I don't see anything," Custer said.

Varnum said, "Look for worms wiggling along the ground."

Reynolds said, "There's more Indians over there, General, than you ever seen in one place before."

"How d'you know?"

"I smell 'em."

The Crow and Cree scouts nodded, mumbling ominously.

Reynolds said, "That's the biggest pony herd any man ever seen."

"Biggest village," Bouyer added. "A heap *too* big."

Custer said irritably, "I've been on the Plains a good many years, and my eyesight is as good as yours. I can't see anything that looks like Indian ponies."

Bouyer blurted, "Ef ya don't find more Injuns in that valley than ya ever seen before, you can hang me!"

"All right—all right—all right! It would do a damned lot of good to hang you, wouldn't it?"

The sun climbed, the haze lifted.

Custer adjusted his binoculars and scanned the unveiled basin far below and beyond. There were Indian ponies grazing in that sea of grass. Hundreds of them, skirting the chalky buttes that rimmed the glistening Little Bighorn and its girdle of cottonwoods.

"I don't see any village," Custer said. "And that's not much of a herd for fifteen hundred lodges."

Reynolds said, "The village is on the other side of the bluffs, across the river."

"That's whar we seen it afore daybreak," Bouyer said.

Bloody-Knife grunted.

Suddenly two bare-skinned, blanket-waving boys came sprinting across the yellow-green flat and herded the cayuses into a winding ravine, out of sight.

"D'you think they spotted us?" Custer said, lowering his field glass.

"Not likely," Bouyer replied, chewing on his tobacco. "Jest drivin' 'em down to the river fer their mornin' drink." He spat, then added, " 'Tain't half the herd. They got 'em grassin' all over."

"Take our word for it, General," Reynolds added, lighting a cigarette.

10:30 A.M. A hollow rumble in the gorge signaled the approach of the regiment. Custer scrambled down from the Crow's-Nest and called for a halt. The 7th Cavalry had marched ten twisting, rugged miles up the divide since eight o'clock.

"Jesus Christ!" Captain Tom Custer shouted, bounding out of the saddle. "We've been spotted!"

"What d'you mean?" Armstrong knit his brow.

"One of Yates's packmules dropped a box of hardtack some ways back!" Tom swallowed to catch his breath, then wiped a sleeve across his streaked face. "A trooper reported it missing, so Yates sent a detail back on the trail to find it. They found it all right, and three hungry bucks to boot! They vamoosed as soon as they saw the detail. Our men were afraid to shoot, thinking they might only be drifters or neutrals, but [Captain] Keogh says he saw Indians scouting us along the ridges since early this morning. They must've seen our dust—at least that's what Keogh thinks."

"Where's Keogh now?"

"He's been scouting the rear with some of the Crows. He ought to be up pretty soon."

"Tell him to report to me at once. Have Reno dismount the men. Bring up my flag, and order 'Officers' Call.' "

"On the bugle?"

"Yes, on the bugle. What the hell does it matter any more how much noise we make? Now get a move on!"

Custer was all nerves, stalking to and fro, snapping his cowhide lash. "My intentions were to surround the village and attack before daylight tomorrow," he told his group of edgy, seedy officers in his hair-triggered tone. "We'd have taken 'em by surprise, like we did at the Washita. But that's of no account now. Our discovery makes it imperative for us to act at once. Delay would allow the

525

village to scatter and escape. I said this would turn out to be a fight or a footrace. If they won't make a stand, they'll have to out-run us; and we'll hunt 'em down to the last ditch. All right, gentle-men, we move at once to the attack!"

Custer flicked his whip. "The regiment will advance in three squadrons of assault. Major Reno, you will take Companies A, G, and M. Follow this trail straight down to the Littlehorn. Captain Benteen, you will take Companies D, H, and K. Follow the line of bluffs to Reno's left, scouting the ridges while he tracks the ravines. I will take Companies C, E, F, I, and L. We'll move to the right. Captain McDougall, you will take Company B to guard the packtrain. By this disposition we must cut off Sitting-Bull's escape to the south, east, or north. Gibbon and Terry will keep him from slipping away to the west. A three-mile interval between my battalion and Benteen's should be sufficient to clamp the hostiles up in a vise. If the scouts' reports are true, I have no doubt we're about to go into the fight of our lives. But I'm confident we shall be more than equal to anything we encounter. All I can say now is keep communications open and pitch into the enemy wherever you find him. Whatever you do, don't let him get away!"

"Hadn't we better keep the regiment together, General?" Ben-teen put in. "If this is as big a village as they say, we'll need every man we have for one massive strike."

"You have your orders," Custer muttered. Then he raised his voice again: "The respective squadrons will separate at the foot of the divide. The first company commander who notifies me that his men have paid strict obedience to my order against grumbling, that officer and company shall have the post of honor."

Captain Benteen strutted forward at once. "Your order has been strictly obeyed, General."

"Very well, then, Captain Benteen—*your* company has the ad-vance. Lead out your entire battalion!"

As the group was breaking up, a gust of wind struck Custer's headquarters flag and knocked it down. Lieutenant Godfrey picked it up and stuck it in the ground again, but it fell a second time.

Lieutenant Wallace regarded this as "a bad omen." And Reno noticed that Custer "did not wear his usual confident & cheerful air, but seemed rather depressed, as with some premonition of coming horror."

"God damn him," Benteen growled to Reno as they trudged back to the waiting column. "Sending us off on a wild-goose chase for glory. Rendezvous with Terry and Gibbon was set for tomorrow. Has Custer sent riders through to 'em? *No!* They don't know where in the hell we are. They'll be beating about the headwaters for days trying to find us. Custer doesn't give a Goddamn for Terry."

Reno, a swarthy man with trim mustachios, answered him abruptly, "We don't know *what* Terry's orders were. There's only one man here who does, and he's the one we have to obey—live or die."

"Well, all I can say is we're going to have a big fight on our hands. A hell of a big fight!"

According to Lieutenant George D. Wallace's daybook (6/24/76), "Gen'l Custer determined to cross the divide that night [June 24–5], conceal the Command, the next day [June 25] find out the locality of the village & attack the following morning [June 26] at daylight." In so doing, he would have been acting in near-concert with Terry and Gibbon.

Lieutenant Edward S. Godfrey concurs: "The General said . . . that he had not intended to make the attack until the next morning, the 26th, but our discovery made it imperative to act at once; as delay would allow the village to scatter and escape." Now, by quirk of fate, Custer's doom was sealed.

"Move well to the left, and sweep everything before you!" Custer called to Benteen as they were about to separate. "Pitch into anything you find, and report at once!"

"I thought it was rather a senseless order," Benteen later testified. "I did not know what I was expected to find. I supposed I was to hunt up some Indians! . . . There was no plan at all."

"Let us keep together!" Reno called over to Custer as Benteen was making his left-oblique. Custer lifted his hat jauntily, as much to say, "I hear you." He and Reno were now riding parallel, Custer's squadron on the right.

At approximately two o'clock, Custer waved to Reno to bear left and cross the Little Bighorn. Varnum rode up and reported having seen a large body of Indians in the valley ahead. "Warn Reno," Custer responded; and Varnum spurred away. He passed Girard, who was dashing back from the river with the same report.

2:15 P.M. Colonel Custer and his 280-man detachment had ridden several miles across the rugged, rolling basin of the Little Bighorn. A towering dust cloud dragged over the hills ahead, slowly trailing down to the river.

Fred Girard turned in the saddle, let out a whoop, and waved his hat to Custer from the top of a bluff. "Thar goes yer Injuns, runnin' like hell!"

Custer jerked his head aside and blurted to Adjutant Cooke: "Take a message to Reno. Tell him the hostiles are a couple of miles ahead, on the jump. Tell him to go in as fast as he can, cross the river, charge the hostiles wherever he finds 'em. Tell him he'll be supported by the whole outfit. Have him send word then at once. And have him relay an immediate message to Benteen to cross the river and move up from the south, drive everything before him, and notify me at once."

Lieutenant William W. Cooke snapped a salute and bolted away. "Cookey" was a strapping Canadian with a clipped accent and Dundrearies; Custer had nicknamed him "The Queen's Own."

Custer looked back at his command, motioned to the north, shouted, "Column of twos! Right-oblique! Forward at the gallop —ho!"

The troopers swung northward and to the right, weaving their way swiftly along gullies that ran like deep gashes through stubbled humps and chalky hogbacks bounding the Little Bighorn.

3 P.M. Colonel Custer, Captain Tom, aide Autie Reed, Lieutenant Cooke (who had just returned from Reno's command with

a report that the Indians were amassing to meet them), and orderly-bugler Giovanni Martini rode up a ravine to the crest of a ridge overlooking the ashy bluffs that rimmed a stream known to the red man as "Greasy-Grass," to the white man as "Littlehorn."

Custer pulled out his field glass and gazed intently at the western panorama. There it lay at last, the hostile Indian encampment. Huge circles of hundreds of buffalo-hide tepees shimmered in the sunlight, while smoke from a myriad campfires veiled the horizon. And as far as the eye could see, a grazing pony herd spread across the grassy flats.

Custer strained his eyes, adjusting the binoculars to penetrate the hazy atmosphere. Dogs, old men, and squaws shuffled around the lodges. He could also spot children romping naked. But where were all the warriors?

Custer snorted. "Well, I'll be damned!" he cracked, handing the glass to Brother Tom. "*Look*—we've caught 'em napping." He slapped his thigh, rasping a dry laugh. "Custer's Luck!"

Wheeling Old Vic around, Custer whipped off his shabby gray sloucher and waved it wildly to the five companies of cavalry down in the gulch. "Come on, boys! Hey, boys, we've got 'em! We've caught 'em napping! We'll finish 'em up and head for home!"

With Vic chomping at the bit, Custer turned to Martini and said excitedly but carefully, "I want you to take a message to Captain Benteen. Ride as fast as you can, and tell him to hurry. Tell him it's a big village, and I want him to be quick, and to bring the ammuntion packs."

"*Yessir!*" Martini saluted, reining away.

"Wait, orderly!" Adjutant Cooke said, spurring forward. Martini pulled up. "I'll give you a message." Cooke took out his pencil and pad, scribbled a note, then tore off the slip and handed it to the jumpy young Italian. "Now, ride as fast as you can to Captain Benteen. Take the same trail we came down. If you have time, and there's no danger, come back. But otherwise stay with your company."

Martini nodded, saluted, dashed off. The note read:

Benteen:
Come on. Big village. Be quick. Bring packs.
W. W. Cooke
P.S. Bring packs

("The Queen's Own" feared that Garibaldi's drummerboy-mascot might muddle the order with his "dago English.")

Tom Custer galloped back to his orderly, Sergeant Daniel A. Kanipe, and rattled: "Go to Cap'n McDougall. Tell him to bring packtrain straightaway. Tell him to come on quick—big Indian village. If you see Cap'n Benteen, tell him to come quick—a big Indian village."

Kanipe saluted and lurched his horse around, spanking after Martini. If one didn't get through, the other might! (They both did, but to no avail.)

Boston Custer, ambling up from the rear, passed Martini and Kanipe dusting down the trail. Armstrong yelled to his brother as he came plunging into the ravine, "Hey, Bos! You're about to go into a real fight—the greatest fight of your life! The biggest Indian camp on the North American continent is ahead, and we're going to attack it!"

Boston winced.

Armstrong was grinning like a wolf; and there was a savage sparkle in his eyes. He slapped his kid brother affectionately on the shoulder. "I reckon there'll be plenty of Indians for us all!"

Bos' voice quavered: "Mitch Bouyer says we'll find more redskins than all of us have bullets!"

Custer turned to his Crow scouts and said forcefully, by words and signs: "We're going to attack the village. We're going to have a terrible fight. You should all take heart, fight hard, make your every shot a killer. These people the Sioux are cutthroats and troublemakers. They prey upon the Crows and the palefaces. I'm going to teach them a lesson today they'll never forget. I'm going to whip every last one of them. When I finish the Sioux trouble, I'll build a fort where the Littlehorn flows into the Bighorn. Then you Crows may live in peace with us palefaces." He paused a second, then added: "I'm a great chief, but I may die in this battle. The Great Spirit look after you then! But if I live, my brother Bloody-Knife and I will take you all to Washington—to the medicine lodge of the Great White Father. Now this is the way I want it. When we attack the village, I want you to run off all the ponies you can. If any man of you isn't brave, and is afraid to take a scalp in order to stampede the herd, I'll take away his weapons and make a woman of him. If nothing happens to me, and you do as I say, I'll look after you in the future. Yellowhair is a man of his word. Help me whip the Sioux, and I'll become the Great White Father. Then we'll all live in peace and plenty."

One of the Crows gazed at the sun and moaned: "I shall not see you sink behind the Shining Mountains tonight." Then he cast his penetrating eyes on Yellowhair, saying, "You and I are going home today, by a trail we do not know."

Custer smiled wryly, pointing to Bos. "Your white brother there. His heart flutters with fear. His eyes roll in fright. When we've whipped the Sioux, he'll be a man."

Pulling off his blue fatigue blouse, Custer slipped on his fringed buckskin jacket and tied the crimson kerchief around his neck. With a flourish of his hat, he let out a whoop and led his Garry-owens at a canter up the ravine.

3:30 P.M. Colonel Custer and five companies of the 7th Cavalry swung westward to the left, jogging down Medicine-Tail Coulee toward the Little Bighorn. A vibrant crackle of carbines shattered the stillness. It burst from the cottonwood belt skirting the west bank of the river, echoing to the forward-left of Custer's command, beyond the embracing ridges.

Custer jerked his head at Cooke. "That must be Reno, giving 'em hell!"

Cooke nodded.

Custer shot a backward glance, whisked off his hat and hooted "Come on, boys!" He darted ahead at as swift a pace as the rough floor of the ravine allowed. With guidons streaming and bugles blaring, a couple of hundred cheering, bellowing horsemen thundered down the coulee behind him. Custer laughed. "Hold your horses, boys! There are plenty of 'em down there for all of us!"

The steep draw slowly opened out into a rolling river basin. Several hundred yards from the ford, a torrent of cavalrymen surged into an ambush of several Indians from Two-Moon's band of Cheyennes. Scouting Custer's advance, they determined to hold him off long enough for their fellow warriors to amass in self-defense. They fired down from the banks ahead, shot up from the mouth of the coulee, making much movement and noise. Their ruse worked.

Custer threw up his hand and drew rein in dust and gravel. The column ground to a halt behind him. He sat paralyzed for a few seconds, then realized the ruse and counterfeinted by thrusting forward with Yates' gray-horse troop, driving the snipers before him like flushed quail.

According to Gall, war chief of the Hunkpapa Sioux, "Longhair did not reach the river." Hundreds of howling Indians swept like a whirlblast down to the ford, their ponies stretching at a dead run over the shallow stream, gorging the mouth of the gully like bees aswarm in the hive. Most of Yellowhair's red scouts ran for their lives, and the last words heard from him were: "Courage, boys! We'll get 'em; and as soon as we do, we'll go home to glory!"

Custer waved and shouted. He pitched off to the right, scrambling madly up the escarpment, drawing his command over the ridge. The diversion was desperate. If his battalion were to remain effectively mounted, he needed level ground on which to maneuver. That ground lay across the river, where the villages sprawled. If he could endure broken terrain long enough to find another ford and draw the Indians onto his own ground, all would be well. If not, there was little hope but to hold a defensive position until Reno or Benteen came up.

Custer yanked the reins, dug in his heels. His leather-slapping troopers swung northward behind him, tailed by a hurricane of Indians who were dropping them out of their saddles like game on the run.

There was another ford, farther upriver, but Custer would

never reach it. Trapped between two slowly converging hordes of Sioux and Cheyennes, he was forced higher into the maze of hills that offered no escape but death. As one Teton war chief put it, "It looked like a stampede of buffalo."

4:15 P.M. Myles W. Keogh's and James Calhoun's companies, dismounted in skirmish lines, were chewed up in a matter of minutes. Tearing to the crest of a hummock topping the hogback ridge, Custer reined Old Vic around. *"Dismount your men! Dismount your men! Prepare to fight on foot!"* Bugles sounded "Dismount." Custer turned to his adjutant, ordered Captains George W. Yates and Algernon E. Smith to deploy their men at the foot of the knoll, facing the river, there to hold their ground to the last man. He and Tom would take their stand on the brow.

4:30 P.M. Inch by inch, Yates' and Smith's companies were whittled away by showers of arrows and lead. Thousands of Indians leaped from their ponies at the base of the ridge, where Keogh and Calhoun lay slaughtered in detail, and started swarming up the gullies.

4:45 P.M. Yates and Smith had stood their ground, and were wiped out to the last man.

Those fifty men on the ridge watched the hostiles coming, inch by inch, closer and closer. Fear gnawed at their stomachs; this was the end.

That ragged band of fifty troopers and civilians huddled around Custer's headquarters flag, which was firmly planted in the ashy soil. Their sweat-soaked togs were caked with alkali dust, so that they looked like a cluster of phantoms on the hilltop.

The valley of the Little Bighorn was a furnace. Smoke and dust hung in the glowing sky. Itching and burning, gagging in the stillborn atmosphere, they rubbed stinging, watery eyes and leveled their Springfields. Feathered heads popped up from gullies, then disappeared. But for every one that vanished, a dozen more appeared. Hundreds upon hundreds of feathered heads—bobbing up from arroyos that gouged the long, long slope, snaking in and out of sagebrush clumps and tall tufts of reddish-brown grass. Grass

533

and sage the color of dry blood, soil the consistency of powdered bones.

Carbines barked, revolvers cracked. Hacking, cursing soldiers stood or knelt or lay in a tight circle, picking off the surrounding enemy as they came up the hillside. Several fear-crazed troopers lunged out of the circle and ran screaming down the slope. Death alone stopped them.

While thousands massed around the foot of the hill, launching arrows in a curved fire to the crest, a few hundred braves scrambled up the slope. Custer and his band dropped them as they came. The Indians hung back in shallow notches, fired their breechloaders, then crawled on in spurts.

Shoot the horses! Shoot 'em before they're stampeded! Pile 'em round for breastworks! Dozens of dead horses were heaped in a circle around that desperate band. The smell was sickening, but that breastwork of carcasses was their only protection.

The erratic clatter of firearms on the brow of the hill clashed weirdly with the endless drone of arrows that came showering down to a maddening chorus of shrieks and war whoops. The barricade of carcasses was no shelter against this murderous storm. When a spray of bullets from below caused troopers to duck while reloading, a spatter of shafts from above quilled their shoulders and backs. Sobbing hysterically, they sagged to the dust.

"Once I saw Yellowhair," said Left-Hand, an Arapaho mercenary. "He was dressed in buckskin. It was almost at the end of the fight. He was standing up and had pistols in his hands, shooting into the Indians."

The romantic image emerges in glory. Custer grips his pearl-handled bulldogs with stiff, aching hands. He glares into the smoldering haze, blasting at every form that springs up before him. Streaks of gunfire split through smoky drifts, and at every burst he expects to hear the cheers of Benteen's battalion. What hope was there in Reno?

Hi-yi! hi-yi! That fiendish, maniacal yell is all he hears. It falls on his ringing ears like a death knell, ripping the molten air like howls from the depths of hell.

A handful of troopers huddle around the shredded headquarters flag. They feed and fire their red-hot Springfields with numbed fingers and stiffening hands. They fumble with dirt-crusted cartridges that jam in the overheated chambers. They pry out empty shells with their penknives, because breechblock ejectors bite clean through the soft copper rims. Then they run out of carbine ammunition—a piddling hundred rounds per man—and unholster their revolvers. Twenty rounds apiece. Soon, they will be turning their rifles into clubs.

Hi-yi! hi-yi! The copper-skinned foe worms ever closer, their serpentine bodies blazed with red and yellow and blue warpaint. These are the naked bucks who have braved the trials and tortures of the medicine dance. With scalping knives clenched between their bared teeth, with tomahawks clutched in their fists, they are gathering for the kill.

5 P.M. Nearly all have bled to death. Perhaps Custer, in a daze, glares into the creeping masses of warriors. Horror and woe paralyze his senses.

"It was not more than half an hour after the long-haired chief attacked us before he and all his men were dead," said Crow-King, Chief of the Hunkpapas.

"When I reached the top of the hill I saw Yellowhair," said Waterman, an Arapaho mercenary. "He was dressed in buckskin, coat and pants, and was on his hands and knees. He had been shot through the side, and there was blood coming from his mouth. He seemed to be watching the Indians moving around him. Four soldiers were sitting up around him, but they were all badly wounded. All the other soldiers were down. Then the Indians closed in around him, and I did not see any more."

"I have talked with my people," Sitting-Bull said. "I cannot find one who saw Longhair until just before he died. He did not wear his long hair as he used to wear it. It was short, and it was of the color of the grass when the frost comes. Longhair stood like a sheaf of corn with all the ears fallen around him. He killed a man when he fell. He laughed. He had fired his last shot. He rose up on his hands and tried another shot, but his pistol would not go off. I did not see it. It was told to me. But it is true."

535

The romantic image begins to fade. Custer is on his knees, grasping a soggy hole in the left side of his buckskin jacket. He laughs. The charm has fled his spirit. The luck has run out at last.

Custer lifts his head, and the earth and the sky reel before his glazed eyes. Dark blood dribbles out of his mouth and ears. Tears stream down his cheeks. The spirit is fleeing.

Indians are stalking toward him. Shadows, looming all around him. They come to take his soul.

Some of the Indians shrink from him, in awe. They are certain that Yellowhair has come back from the spirit world, back from the dead, to curse them. Others are not so superstitious, and dart forward.

Did his nerveless hand point the muzzle, pull the trigger? Or was the weapon wrenched from his grasp, the *coup de grâce* delivered by a Sioux hand?

The blast blackens his face, convulsing and contorting his features.

George Armstrong Custer is gone to glory.

The blood-red sun was dipping into a sea of flame when Meyotzi and Mawissa hastened up the long, sloping knoll to view the corpse of Yellowhair. A six-year-old boy named Yellow-Bird, presumably Custer's only child, tagged after them. He frowned at his reputed father's naked white body, untouched by mutilating hands.

"He was the greatest and handsomest white chief of them all," Mawissa said. "But here he now lies, food for worms."

Meyotzi knelt beside the body, saying nothing. Mawissa took a bone sewing-awl out of her buckskin pouch. Stooping, she jabbed the point deep into each ear of the corpse. "This is so Yellowhair will hear better in the happy hunting-grounds," Mawissa murmured. "He must not have heard our chiefs when they warned him that if he ever again rode the wartrail against our people, the Great Everywhere Spirit would then cause him to be killed."

Gazing in silence, Meyotzi composed the twisted features with loving fingers. The glory and romance of an age had passed.

EPILOGUE

"There he is, God damn him! He'll never fight any more." Thus Frederick W. Benteen identified the livid, swollen corpse of George Armstrong Custer on Tuesday morning, June 27, 1876. He said to Reno: "You know enough of me to know I'd have gone through to him if it was possible to do so. But anyhow, I'm only too proud to say I hated him."

Custer's naked body was found in a sitting position between and leaning against the nude bodies of two of his troopers, who were lying one across the other. His upper right arm was resting on the topmost body, and his right forearm and hand supported his head in a peaceful pose. Lieutenant James H. Bradley noted: "Probably never did hero who had fallen upon the field of battle appear so much to have died a natural death. His expression was rather that of a man who had fallen asleep & enjoyed peaceful dreams, than of one who had met his death amid such fearful scenes as that field had witnessed—the features being wholly without ghastliness or any impress of fear, horror, or despair." Lieutenant Godfrey observed that "he had been shot in the left temple and the left breast. There were no powder-marks or signs of mutilation." Meyotzi had apparently cleaned and closed Yellow-hair's wounds. As Dr. Charles Kuhlman so aptly commented, "It was not the fairies who laid him here all 'clean and bright' as a mortician might have done. Only someone with some kind of sentimental interest in him would have done that."

Marcus A. Reno scratched in his journal: "As a tribute to his

537

bravery, the Indians had not mutilated Gen'l Custer & he lay as if asleep; but all the other men had been most brutally mangled & had been stripped of their clothing." Low-Dog, Chief of the Oglala Sioux, stated: "The wise men and chiefs of our nation gave out to our people not to mutilate the dead white chief; for he was a brave warrior and died a brave man, and his remains should be respected." (As Sitting-Bull himself said, "My people did not want his scalp. He was a great chief. None of my people ever boasted to me that they had killed Custer." The passing of Yellowhair was enshrouded with that hallowed mystery worthy of a saint.)

This raises the question of suicide. The code of frontiersmen advised: "When fighting Indians, save the last bullet for yourself"; a notable example of its application was Captain Fetterman, who preferred death to torture.

Many of the Crow scouts were insistent that "Son-of-Morning-star shot self," that "Longhair shoot himself at end." One of the Sioux warriors stated: "When Longhair realized he alone was alive, he put his gun against his body and pulled the trigger." And Colonel Richard I. Dodge, one of the most authoritative students of the American Indian, wrote:

Suicide, though not common among Indians, is 'big medicine' —a high religious act. Through it the man rises superior to his gods. . . . I have never yet known a single case where the scalp of a suicide was stripped off, and in many cases the superstition is so strong as to prevent the Indians even from touching the body. If an unscalped body is found with many terrible wounds, gashed and mutilated, it was the deliberate purpose of the Indians to torment the soul; if it be found unmutilated with but one mortal wound, it is a case of suicide. . . . It is said that Custer's body was found unscalped and unmutilated. If so, my knowledge of Indians convinces me that he died by his own hand.

Many frontiersmen and Indians agreed. And as to the claim that Custer, by his very nature, could not have taken his own life, the circumstances of his fate made it most likely that he did so.

Thomas and Boston Custer, Henry Armstrong Reed, and William W. Cooke lay a few feet away from the General. According to Benteen, "There was an arc of a circle of dead horses around them." Boston and Reed were naked except for their white cotton socks. They had been butchered in the usual manner. So had Cooke, except that his magnificent Dundrearies were "scalped." Tom's body was a hideous sight. It was mangled beyond recognition. The only identification was a goddess of liberty and flag, and the initials T.W.C., tattooed above the elbow of his right arm. He had been scalped, and arrows quilled his crushed skull. His eyes and tongue had been torn out. His belly was slashed, and the entrails protruded. His heart and liver had been carved out, his thighs gashed, his genitals cut off. The Cheyennes hated him for his abuse of Meyotzi. The score was now settled.

Reno scratched in his journal: "The harrowing sight of those mutilated & decomposing bodies crowning the heights on which poor Custer fell will linger in my memory till death."

What happened to Reno, and to Benteen, on that fateful day which shocked and horrified the civilized world?

Major Reno and his battalion crossed the Little Bighorn, hung back in the cottonwoods when assailed by mounted warriors, and were soon stampeded across the river and into the hills, where Captain Benteen and his battalion came to their support. Though Benteen received Custer's urgent message, he followed Reno's trail to the river. Thus, with Reno and Benteen "holed up" in the hills—neither knowing nor, it is said, caring what had happened to Custer—hard and even desperate fighting kept up through June 26. Terry and Gibbon arrived to the rescue on the following morning, whereupon Sitting-Bull fled to suffer a later fate.

The Battle of the Little Bighorn is not ended. Controversy still rages. But the opinions of participants yet remain the last words. Captain Benteen and Lieutenant Godfrey branded Reno's retreat "a rout, a panic," and intimated that he had lost his nerve. Sitting-Bull asserted that "squaws and papooses could have dealt with Reno." Captain Moylan concluded that "Reno ought to have been shot." And so a scapegoat was found.

General Terry called Custer's action "a sad and terrible

539

blunder." A confidential dispatch to Sheridan comments: "For whatever errors he may have committed, he has paid the penalty; and you cannot regret his loss more than I do."

General Sheridan then made his official comment: "I do not attribute Colonel Custer's action to either recklessness or want of judgment, but to a misapprehension of the situation and to a superabundance of courage: the latter being extraordinarily developed in Custer."

General Sherman, though owning he had made "a terrible mistake," defended Custer's decision by stating flatly: "When Custer found himself in the presence of the Indians he could do nothing but attack." However, the New York *Times* quoted both Sherman and Sheridan as agreeing that Custer was "rashly imprudent to attack such a large number of Indians."

Major Reno made known the following: "Without attempting to communicate with either Terry or Gibbon, and without taking the trouble to ascertain the strength or position of the Indians, he divided his regiment into three separate battalions—an act which nothing can justify—and dashed against the Indians, thus recklessly driving his own and my commands into an ambuscade of 5000 Sioux."

Captain Benteen wrote: "Custer disobeyed orders from the fact of not wanting any other Command—or body—to have a finger in the pie, and thereby lost his life."

The Chicago *Tribune* editorialized: "He preferred to make a reckless dash and take the consequences . . . rather than . . . share the glory with others. He took the risk, and he lost." Captain Hughes added that the fiasco was caused by Custer's "foolish pride."

Sergeant Windolph philosophized: "Custer may have made a mistake to divide his command that Sunday afternoon of June 25, but the gods themselves were against him. . . . There were simply too many Indians for him." And Lieutenant Edgerly concluded: "Even if the blame for the disaster was due to General Custer, the fact remains that he and his five companies died heroic and glorious deaths."

A New York *Herald* correspondent interviewed Ulysses S. Grant: "Mr. President, was not Custer's massacre a disgraceful defeat of our troops?" Grant replied: "I regard Custer's massacre as a sacrifice of troops, brought on by Custer himself, that was wholly unnecessary—wholly unnecessary." However, the *Herald* noted, "The five massacred companies of Custer attest the inhumanity and imbecility of the Republican Administration."

"Who slew Custer?" asked James Gordon Bennett. "The celebrated peace policy of General Grant, . . . that nest of thieves, the Indian Bureau, . . . its mock humanity and pretense of piety— that is what killed Custer." The Yankton *Dakotaian* of July 7 headlined: "Custer and His Entire Command Swept Out of Existence by the Wards of the Nation and Special Pets of Eastern Orators."

In the early morning of July 6, 1876, the steamer *Far West* anchored off Fort Abraham Lincoln. On board were the wounded, and the bearers of sad tidings. A knock fell on the door of the Custer house, and Libbie and Maggie answered in their night-gowns. "At that very hour," Elizabeth later wrote, "the fears that our tortured minds had portrayed in imagination were realities. . . . The sun rose on a beautiful world, but with its earliest beams came the first knell of disaster. . . . This battle wrecked the lives of twenty-six women at Fort Lincoln, and orphaned children of officers and soldiers joined the cry to that of their bereaved mothers. From that time the life went out of the hearts of the 'women who weep,' and God asked them to walk on alone and in the shadow."

"Yellowhair has not returned," the Indians sang. "His woman is crying, crying. Looking this way, she weeps."

George Armstrong Custer, dead at the age of thirty-six, was laid in his final resting place at the United States Military Academy on Wednesday, October 10, 1877. After raising literary monuments to his memory, Elizabeth joined him on Thursday, April 6, 1933 —"into that realm where 'the war-drum throbs no longer and the battle-flags are furled.'"

SELECTED BIBLIOGRAPHY

ATHEARN, ROBERT G. *William Tecumseh Sherman and the Settlement of the West*. Norman, Okla.: University of Oklahoma Press, 1956.

BATES, CHARLES FRANCIS. *Custer's Indian Battles*. Bronxville, N.Y.: published by the author, 1936.

BRILL, CHARLES J. *Conquest of the Southern Plains*. Oklahoma City: Golden Saga Publishers, 1938.

BRININSTOOL, E.A. *Troopers with Custer*. Harrisburg, PA: Stackpole Co., 1952.

BURR, FRANK A., AND HINTON, RICHARD J. *"Little Phil" and his Troopers*. Providence, RI: J.A. and R.A. Reid, 1888.

CHANDLER, MELBOURNE C. *Of Garry Owen in Glory*. New York: Exposition Press, 1960.

CUSTER, ELIZABETH BACON. *Boots and Saddles*. Norman, Okla.: University of Oklahoma Press, 1966.

———. *Following the Guidon*. Norman, Okla.: University of Oklahoma Press, 1966.

CUSTER, GEORGE ARMSTRONG. *My Life on the Plains*. Norma, Okla.: University of University of Oklahoma Press.

———. "War Memoirs," *The Galaxy: An Illustrated Magazine of Entertaining Reading*, XXI–XXII, no. 5 (January–November, 1876).

DAVIS, BURKE. *To Appomattox: Nine April Days, 1865*. New York: Holt, Rinehart and Winston, Inc., 1959.

DAVIS, THEODORE R. *A Summer on the Plains*.

DELLENBAUGH, FREDERICK S. *George Armstrong Custer*. New York: Macmillan, 1917.

543

DENISON, FREDERICK. *Sabres and Spurs.* Central Falls, RI: The First Rhode Island Cavalry Veteran Association, 1876.

DODGE, COL. RICHARD I. *Thirty-Three Years among Our Wild Indians.* New York: Herman & Stevens, Inc., 1959.

DUNN, J.P. *Massacres of the Mountains.* New York: Archer House, Inc., 1958.

DUSTIN, FRED. *The Custer Fight.* Hollywood, CA: E.A. Brininstool, 1936.

———. *The Custer Tragedy.* Saginaw, MI: published privately by the author, 1939.

FOUGERA, KATHERINE GIBSON. *With Custer's Cavalry.* Caldwell, Ida.: Caxton Printers, 1940.

FREEMAN, DOUGLAS S. *Lee's Lieutenants.* 3 vols. New York: Scribner, 1942–44.

FROST, LAWRENCE A. *The Custer Album.* Seattle: Superior Publishing Co., 1964.

GLAZIER, WILLARD. *Three Years in the Federal Cavalry.* New York: R.H. Ferguson & Co., 1870.

GRAHAM, COL. W.A. *The Story of the Little Big Horn.* Harrisburg, PA: Stackpole Co., 1952.

———. *The Custer Myth.* Harrisburg, PA: Stackpole Co., 1954.

———. (ed.). *The Reno Court of Inquiry.* Harrisburg, PA: The Stackpole Co., 1954.

GRINNEL, GEORGE BIRD. *The Fighting Cheyennes.* Norman, Okla.: University of Oklahoma Press, 1956.

HANSON, JOSEPH MILLS. *The Conquest of the Missouri.* New York: Rinehart, 1946.

HAYCOX, ERNEST. *Bugles in the Afternoon* (the best "Custer novel"). Boston: Little, Brown & Co., 1944.

HUNT, FRAZIER. *Custer, The Last of the Cavaliers.* New York: Cosmopolitan Book Corp., 1928.

KIDD, JAMES HARVEY. *Personal Recollections of a Cavalryman With Custer's Michigan Cavalry Brigade in the Civil War.* Ionia, MI: Sentinel Printing Co., 1908.

KUHLMAN, DR. CHARLES. *Legend into History: The Custer Mystery.* Harrisburg, PA: Stackpole Co., 1951.

————. *Did Custer Disobey Orders at the Battle of the Little Big Horn?* Harrisburg, PA: Stackpole, Co., 1957.

LYMAN, THEODORE. *Meade's Headquarters 1863–1865: Letters of Colonel Theodore Lyman from the Wilderness to Appomattox,* ed. George R. Agassiz. Boston: The Atlantic Monthly Press, 1922.

McCLELLAN, GEORGE B. *McClellan's Own Story: The War for the Union.* New York: C.L. Webster & Co., 1887.

McCLELLAN, HENRY B. *I Rode with Jeb Stuart,* ed. Burke Davis. Bloomington, Ind.: Indiana University Press, 1958.

McCREA, TULLY. *Dear Belle: Letters from a Cadet and Officer to His Sweetheart, 1858–1865,* ed. Catherine S. Crary. Middletown, CT: Wesleyan University Press, 1965

MERINGTON, MARGUERITE (ed.), *The Custer Story.* New York: Devin-Adair Co., 1950.

MILHOLLEN, HIRST DILLON, *et al. Horsemen, Blue and Gray: A Pictorial History.* New York: Oxford University Press, 1960.

MILLER, DAVID HUMPHREYS. *Custer's Fall.* Des Moines, Ia.: Duell, Sloan & Pearce, Inc. (Meredith Press), 1957.

MONAGHAN, JAY. *Custer: The Life of George Armstrong Custer.* Boston: Little, Brown, 1959.

MOORE, JAMES. *Kilpatrick and Our Cavalry.* New York: W.J. Widdleton, 1865.

MOSBY, JOHN S. *Memoirs,* ed. Charles W. Russell. Bloomington, Ind.: Indiana University Press, 1959.

NICHOLS, ROY F. (ed.) *Battles and Leaders of the Civil War.* 4 vols. New York: Thomas Yoseloff, Inc., 1956.

PORTER, HORACE. *Campaigning with Grant,* ed. Wayne C. Temple. Bloomington, Ind.: Indiana University Press, 1961.

Review of the Trial of General G.A. Custer (National Archives).

RICKEY, DON. *Forty Miles a Day on Beans and Hay.* Norman, Okla.: University of Oklahoma Press, 1963.

RISTER, CARL COKE. *Border Command.* Norman, Okla.: University of Oklahoma Press, 1944.

RONSHEIM, MILTON. *The Life of General Custer.* Cadiz, O.: printed privately, 1929.

545

SCHAFF, MORRIS. *The Spirit of Old West Point.* Boston: Houghton Mifflin, 1907.

————. *The Sunset of the Confederacy.* Boston: J.W. Luce & Co., 1912.

SCOTT, R.N., et al. (eds.) *The War of the Rebelliion: A Compilation of the Official Records of the Union and Confederate Armies.* 130 vols. Published under the direction of the Secretary of War. Washington: Govt. Printing Office, 1880–1901.

SHERIDAN, PHILIP H. *Personal Memoirs.* 2 vols. New York: 1888.

SPOTTS, DAVID L.: *Campaigning with Custer.* Cadiz, O.: printed privately, 1929.

STECKMESSER, KENT LADD. *The Western Hero in History and Legend.* Norman, Okla.: University of Oklahoma Press, 1965.

STEWART, EDGAR I. *Custer's Luck.* Norman, Okla.: University of Oklahoma Press, 1955.

TREMAIN, HENRY E. *Last Hours of Sheridan's Cavalry.* New York: Bonnell, Silver & Bowers, 1904.

UTLEY, ROBERT M. *Custer and the Great Controversy.* Los Angeles: Western lore.

VAN DE WATER, FREDERIC F. *Glory-Hunter: A Life of General Custer.* New York: Bobbs-Merrill, 1934.

VESTAL, STANLEY D. *Sitting Bull, Champion of the Sioux.* Norman, Okla.: University of Oklahoma Press, 1957.

WAINWRIGHT, CHARLES S. *A Diary of Battle,* ed. Allan Nevins. New York: Harcourt, Brace & World, 1962.

WHITTAKER, FREDERICK. *A Complete Life of Gen. George A. Custer.* New York: Sheldon & Co., 1876.

WINDOLPH, C.A., as told to Frazier and Robert Hunt. *I Fought With Custer.* New York: Charles Scribner's Sons, 1947.

★INDEX★

Lee, General A. L., 321
Lee, Maj. General Fitzhugh, 77, 147, 149, 177, 191, 217, 227, 297
Lee, Maj. General George Washington Custis, 279, 280
Lee, General Robert E., 56, 73, 75, 88, 89, 91, 92, 94, 97, 98, 111, 116, 117, 120, 126, 135, 140, 152, 155, 156, 157, 159, 171, 190, 197, 207, 210, 212, 215, 216, 223, 225, 237, 261, 268–69, 270, 274, 277, 280, 281, 282–83, 284, 285, 286, 288, 290, 291, 294–95
Left-Hand (Arapaho mercenary), 534
Letterman, Dr. Jonathan, 162
Libby Prison, 174, 190, 208
Lincoln, Abraham, 12, 47, 54, 63, 75, 76, 82, 88, 89, 93–95, 96, 97, 99, 100, 112, 113, 120, 126, 134, 155, 157, 184, 190, 196, 198, 202, 207, 233, 250, 258, 259, 263, 268, 274, 277, 282, 309, 461
Lincoln, Mary Todd, 202, 203
Lincoln, Tad, 263, 267
Lippincott, Dr. Henry, 407
Little-Beaver, Chief, 392–93, 394
Little Bighorn River, 509, 510, 511, 539; battle of, 521–36, 539
Little Missouri River, 452, 506
Little-Raven, Chief, 399, 421
Little-Robe, Chief, 420, 423
Little-Rock, Sub-chief, 397, 401
Livingston, Capt. LaRhett L., 232
Lockwood, John S., 194
Lomax, Lunsford L., 237, 238, 239, 240
Lone-Wolf, Chief, 416, 417–18
Longstreet, Lieut. General James, 57, 58, 60, 90, 148, 156, 277, 288, 290–92
Los Angeles *Herald*, 495
Louis Philippe, King, 63
Louisville, Kentucky, 440
Low-Dog, Chief, 538
Ludlow, Captain William, 216, 465, 500
Lyman, Colonel Theodore, 138, 195, 201, 216, 277
Lynchburg, Virginia, 266, 277, 284
Lyons, Private, 254

Malvern Hill, Virginia, 78
Manassas, Virginia, *see* Bull Run
Mansfield, General, 21
Marcy, General Randolph B., 488
Marie, Aunt (Custer's cook), 464, 469
Marsh, Sutler, 473
Martindale, General, 193
Martini, Giovanni, 529, 530
Martinsburg, West Virginia, 126
Maryland, invasion of, 88, 93, 120, 125, 140, 155, 223, 235

Mawissa (Black-Kettle's sister), 401–02, 404, 406, 417, 422, 435, 536
Maximilian, Emperor, 317, 327
McClellan, Maj. General George B., 44, 47, 48, 49, 53, 56, 58, 63, 66, 67, 69–71, 73–74, 75–77, 82, 83, 84, 87, 88–90, 91, 92, 93–96, 97–99, 100–02, 104, 111, 112, 113, 114, 115, 116, 117, 119, 182, 203, 222, 234, 256, 258, 305
McCrea, Lieut. Tully, 137
McDougall, Captain, 526
McDowell, Maj. General Irvin, 21, 22, 23, 26, 27, 31, 36, 38, 52
McIntosh, Brig. General John B., 149, 150, 151, 154, 232
McLean, Major Wilmer, 296
McLean House, Appomattox Courthouse, Virginia, 292, 293, 296
McMaster, Lieut. Charles, 260
McNeely Normal School, Hopedale, Ohio, 4, 6
Meade, Maj. General George Gordon, 135, 137, 140, 144, 145, 152, 154, 155, 157, 159, 162, 167, 172, 176, 192, 193, 195, 196, 200, 206–07, 212, 216, 233, 277
Meagher, Brig. General Thomas F., 78
Mechanicsville, Virginia, 75, 212
Medicine-Arrow, Chief, 423–25
Medicine-Lodge treaty (1867), 387
Meeker, Ralph, 481, 482
Meigs, Lieut. John R., 260
Merritt, Brig. General Wesley, 14–15, 124, 165, 166, 172, 174, 201, 202, 206, 208, 209, 210, 211, 214, 226, 227, 231, 232, 234, 235, 236, 237, 239, 241–42, 247, 249, 254, 271, 283, 292, 311, 438
Meyotzi, Princess, 401–04, 406, 428, 433, 434–35, 536, 537, 539
Middletown, Virginia, 244
Miles, Mary (Mrs. Nelson), 436
Miles, Lieut. General Nelson A., 29, 32; later as Colonel, 436, 476, 513
Miller, Capt. William E., 151–52
Milner, Joseph E. ("California Joe"), 394–95, 398, 401
Missouri River, 444, 447, 463, 480
Mix, Captain, 194
Monroe, Michigan, 3, 46–47, 72, 104–14, 168–70, 180, 185, 325, 326, 330, 384, 436, 437, 448
Montana Badlands, 519–20
Montana *Post*, 339
Montana Territory, 449–61
Monticello, Charlottesville, Virginia, 265
Moore, Lieut. Colonel Horace L., 427
Morris, Clara, 438